W9-CFF-954

מסורה

ArtScroll Mesorah Series®

Rabbi Nosson Scherman / Rabbi Meir Zlotowit
General Editor

in the torah

The Chumash with translation and the complete
assic commentary of the master Rav and Maggid,

Rabbi Zalman Sorotzkin זצ״ל

Translated by
Rabbi Yaakov Lavon

Edited by
Mrs. Ethel Gottlieb

INSIGHTS

Published by
Mesorah Publications, ltd

FIRST EDITION
First Impression . . . July, 1994
Second Impression . . . January 2001

Published and Distributed by
MESORAH PUBLICATIONS, Ltd.
4401 Second Avenue
Brooklyn, New York 11232

Distributed in Europe by
LEHMANNS
Unit E, Viking Industrial Park
Rolling Mill Road
Jarrow, Tyne & Wear NE32 3DP
England

Distributed in Australia & Zew Zealand by
GOLDS WORLD OF JUDAICA
3-13 William Street
Balaclava, Melbourne 3183
Victoria Australia

Distributed in Israel by
SIFRIATI / A. GITLER — BOOKS
6 Hayarkon Street
Bnei Brak 51127

Distributed in South Africa by
KOLLEL BOOKSHOP
Shop 8A Norwood Hypermarket
Norwood 2196, Johannesburg, South Africa

ARTSCROLL MESORAH SERIES®
OZNAYIM LATORAH — INSIGHTS IN THE TORAH
Vol V: Devarim

4401 Second Avenue / Brooklyn, N.Y. 11232 / (718) 921-9000 / www.artscroll.com

---

ISBN:
0-89906-532-5 (hard cover)
0-89906-533-3 (paperback)

Typography by CompuScribe at ArtScroll Studios, Ltd.
4401 Second Avenue / Brooklyn, N.Y. 11232 / (718) 921-9000

Printed in the United States of America by Noble Book Press Corp.
Bound by Sefercraft, Quality Bookbinders, Ltd. Brooklyn, N.Y.

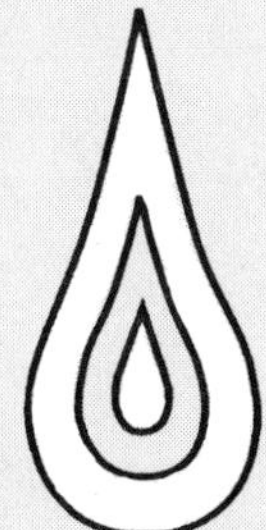

,,הנאהבים והנעימים בחייהם ובמותם לא נפרדו״
(שמואל ב׳ א׳ כג׳)

,,פירושו, לא נפרדו זה מזה, כי כאחד מתו, כמו שהיו בחייהם נאהבים זה לזה.״
(רד״ק שם)

,,בחייהם – עודם בחיים היו נאהבים ונעימים לכל בני אדם, ר״ל מאד היו מקובלים על הבריות וחביבים בעיני כולם. ובמותם לא נפרדו – אף אחר מותם לא נפרדו מן האהבה והנעימה כי עד עולם לא תשכח כי רבה היא.״
(מצודת דוד שם)

ספר זה הוקדש לעי״נ הנאהבים והנעימים

הר״ר נח ב״ר משה חיים ז״ל

וזוגתו

מרת שרה לאה בת ר׳ יוסף דוד ע״ה

למשפחת ליפינס

נלב״ע כ״ו שבט תשי״ג

ולעי״נ

ר׳ חיים זאב ב״ר יצחק ז״ל

נלב״ע ד׳ כסלו תשל״ד

וזוגתו

מרת מרים בת ר׳ מיכאל ע״ה

נלב״ע ל׳ חשון תשנ״ד

למשפחת העכטענטהאל

ע״י בנם וחתנם הרבני הנכבד
ראש וראשונה לכל דבר שבקדושה רודף צדקה וחסד
הר״ר **דוד ליפינס** הי״ו ובני משפחתו שיחיו
מעמודי התווך של הקהלה החרדית בקליבלנד, אוהייא, ארה״ב

This Sefer is dedicated in the memory of

Reb Noach and Mrs. Sorah Leah Lipins ע״ה

Reb Chaim Zev and Mrs. Miriam Hechtenthal ע״ה

by their distinguished son & family,

Mr. and Mrs. Dovid Lipins & family

Cleveland Heights, Ohio,
who are unique in their chessed
and whose lives are entirely dedicated to worthy causes.

This Sefer is dedicated in loving memory of

Mr. Harry Leo Stillman ע״ה

by his daughter

Mrs. Shulamit Selma Rothschild
and Family

New York — Jerusalem

לזכר עולם ולעילוי נשמת

רב צבי אריה בן הרב אליעזר יצחק ז״ל

נלב״ע ג׳ כסלו תשל״ד

הוקדש ע״י בתו

מרת שולמית רוטשילד ומשפחתה

ספר זה הוקדש לעי״נ
איש תם וישר אהוב על הבריות

הר״ר אברהם יחזקאל ב״ר ישראל שמעון הלוי ז״ל
למשפחת שווארץ

נלב״ע ב„יום גבר האויב ותבקע העיר״ י״ז בתמוז תשנ״ב

הוקדש ע״י בנו הרבני הנכבד

הר״ר פייטל פייבוש הלוי שווארץ הי״ו
קליבלאנד, אוהייא

This Sefer is dedicated
in the memory of

Irving C. Schwartz ז״ל

by his wife
Penny
and his children
Joanne Osinoff and Family, L.A. California
Fred Schwartz and Family, Cleveland Heights, Ohio

נר ה׳ נשמת אדם

,,כל שרוח הבריות נוחה הימנו רוח המקום
נוחה הימנו״ (אבות פ״ג מ׳ י״ג)

ספר זה הוקדש לע״נ

היקר באדם

שליח צבור נאמן

איש תם וישר

הר״ר בנימין ביניש ב״ר גרשון בארנשטיין ז״ל

נלב״ע כ״ה סיון תשמ״א

,,ארבעה מידות בהולכי בית המדרש;
הולך ועושה, חסיד״ (אבות פ״ה מ׳ י״ז)

ולע״נ

אחד שעסק בצרכי ציבור באמונה

ושזכה לעמוד לעזר ואחיסמך

בגופו ובנפשו בבתי כנסיות ומדרשות

ה״ה דוד ב״ר זאב פארסאף ז״ל

נלב״ע י״ט אייר תשמ״ט

הונצח על ידי הר״ר ישראל גרשון בארנשטיין ומשפחתו

סקוקי, איל.

❦ ❦ ❦

This Sefer is dedicated in the memory of

Mr. Beinish Bornstein ע״ה

Mr. Dave Parsoff ע״ה

By their family members

A family with a unique sense of

Chessed and Maasim Tovim

George and Rozzi Bornstein and Family

Skokie, IL, U.S.A.

◌ Preface

Ever since the first volume (*Bereishis*), of *Oznaim LaTorah,* appeared, the series has been accorded a warm and enthusiastic welcome. The public, recognizing the unique outlook on Torah wisdom offered in these volumes, has impatiently awaited the completion of the series. That long-anticipated day has now arrived: the final volume of *Oznaim LaTorah* on the Chumash is now making its appearance in English.

"The last is always best beloved" say *Chazal,* and here too, all the care and skill that went into the entire series has been lavished on this final volume.

My thanks go to the translators and editors who put their talents and energy into the sacred task of presenting the content and style of the original work in English, in all its unique quality and freshness of approach. At their head stands Rabbi Yaakov Lavon, the talented and energetic translator who spared no effort to bring this work to the English-speaking public; and to Mrs. Ethel Gottlieb and Rabbi Asher Margaliot, whose meticulous and skillful editing put the final polish on this volume.

No praise is too great for ArtScroll, the great house of Torah, and for its inspired directors, Rabbi Meir Zlotowitz and Rabbi Nosson Scherman. Special thanks also to Shmuel Blitz, director of Artscroll Jerusalem. Their expert touch guided the entire project unerringly from start to finish.

As this project now reaches its conclusion, I ask Hashem's blessing for the Lipins family of Cleveland, Ohio, whose support has made possible the publication of this series; and in particular for my dear and honored friend David Lipins, whose never-failing encouragement was invaluable to me. Without his enthusiasm the dream would never have been realized. May Hashem bless him and all his family in all their endeavors.

Last but no less precious, the families who have given their support to the appearance of this volume in print: Mrs. Selma Rothschild and her family (New York and Jerusalem), Mr. George Bornstein and his family (Skokie), Mrs. Penny Schwartz, and her son, a dear friend, Mr. Fred Schwartz and family (Cleveland Heights), and Mrs. Joanne Osinoff and family (Los Angeles), who have given generously in memory of their loved ones, so as to give them an everlasting memorial amidst the Torah of Israel.

This volume is especially dedicated by the Bornstein family to the speedy recovery of their friend, Yosef Shlomo Refael ben Sarah שיחי'.

May my grandfather's merit be their aid, and may Hashem grant them full reward for their publication.

Rabbi Michoel Sorotzkin
grandson of the author

Av 5754, Jerusalem

☙ From the Author's Preface

This book [of *Devarim*] is unique and different in its style and content from those that preceded it . . . it seems as if a Torah all by itself . . . it also has a unique name for itself: *Mishneh Torah,* "a repetition of the Torah," . . . and besides that name, which befits its content, it has another name too: *Sefer HaYashar*, "the book of the Just" (*Avodah Zarah* 25a), which needs explanation.

. . . But why is it called "the Book of the Just"? "R' Eliezer says, 'Because in it is said, *You shall do what is just and good in* HASHEM'S *eyes'* " (*Avodah Zarah, loc, cit.*). But in *Shemos,* too (ch. 15), it says "*You shall do what is just in His eyes*"!

A simple explanation would be that in the book of *Mishneh Torah* this injunction is repeated several times, whereas in *Shmos* it appears only once. One occurrence does not lend a name to a whole book.

The *Maharsha* suggests that this book teaches us to look beyond the minimal requirements of the *halachah* and act with kindness and forebearing, which is called "*what is just and good in Hashem's" eyes . . .*

In *Bereishis Rabbah* (ch. 6). I found a wonderful thing, that "the book of the Torah which must not be removed from [the king's mouth" refers especially to the book of *Mishneh Torah.* But why this book above all others? . . .

It would seem that this is because the king must put his fear upon the people, so that they will obey him; and he may exercise the death penalty according to his discretion, without the *beis din* procedure .... So he is in danger of becoming cruel and haughty, and may cease to treat his people kindly and generously. Therefore it is a *mizvah* for him, more than any other Jew, to do good and kindly deeds to one and all, the *halachah's* strict requirement. Since he must sometimes act more "cruelly" than the law's decree (for the good of the kingdom), he must offset that with more mercy and kindness towards the poor than what the law requires ... This temperament he is to learn from "the Book of the Just," which is full of commandments "to do what is just and good in Hashem's eyes" — that is, to go beyond the mere requirement of the Law ...

As I stand now, with the help of my Rock and Redeemer, at the completion of *Sefer Devarim*, I kneel and prostrate myself with thanks and praise to Hashem for all the good and the kindness beyond measure that He has done for me throughout the days of my life ... and for my wife and children ... And when G-d destroyed the cities of Europe, He saved us from the maelstrom and brought us to His holy mountain Jerusalem — may it be rebuilt soon, in our days — and gave me respite all around to be busy with His holy Torah ... He granted me grace to see the fifth volume of my book *Oznaim LaTorah* coming off the printing presses in all its beauty, and even to see my books loved by the Jewish people ... For all this I give praise and thanks to Him Who has done all this good for me, such kindness and miracles — through the merit of my hallowed forefathers — and for all Israel. And after giving thanks for the past I pray to God On High for the future, that He may not remove His kindness and His truth from me nor from my family forever, and that this Torah may not depart from my mouth nor from my descendant's mouths forever. Amen, may it be His will.

פרשת דברים

Parashas Devarim

א א אֵלֶּה הַדְּבָרִים אֲשֶׁר דִּבֶּר מֹשֶׁה אֶל־כָּל־יִשְׂרָאֵל
א

1.

1. אֵלֶּה הַדְּבָרִים — *These are the words.* The second, third, and fourth Books of the Torah are connected to *Bereishis* and to each other by the conjunctive *vav:* וְאֵלֶּה שְׁמוֹת, וַיִּקְרָא, וַיְדַבֵּר. The fifth book, however, begins differently, with the word אֵלֶּה alone, as if to say that it is separate from the others. This is because its content is so different from the other Books. It is replete with reproof and admonition. Moreover, in *Devarim* (*Deuteronomy*), Moses clarifies many *mitzvos* which have already been stated in the previous Books of the Torah. This is why the Book of *Devarim* is called *Mishneh Torah*, "a review of the Torah."

Nonetheless every word in it was spoken by Hashem, as verse 3 tells us: "...when Moses spoke to the Children of Israel, according to everything that Hashem commanded him to them." This Book preserves a connection with the rest of the Torah, as a later verse tells us: "So it was that when Moses finished writing the words of this Torah onto a book, until their conclusion" (31:24).

הַדְּבָרִים אֲשֶׁר דִּבֶּר מֹשֶׁה — *The words that Moses spoke.* "This was Moses, the man who had said, 'I am not a man of words' (*Shemos* 4:10). His speech disorder was healed when he began to study the Torah" (*Devarim Rabbah*, 1).

There is another way of understanding this phrase. People will listen to a speech for one of two reasons: either because the speaker is a silver-tongued orator who knows how to eloquently reach the heart of his audience, or because he is speaking on behalf of some illustrious personage, in which case he would command attention even if he were a ponderous speaker.

While still in Egypt, the Children of Israel did not know the God of their fathers, as we see from Moses' protest when Hashem first appointed him to redeem the Jews: "They say to me, 'What is His name?'" (*Shemos* 3:13). Nor did they yet recognize Moses as God's messenger: "but they will not believe me" (ibid. 4:1). Therefore Moses argued, "I am not a man of words," implying that only skilled oratory, which he lacked, would influence a people who knew neither God nor His messenger. But once they began to "believe in Hashem and in His servant Moses" and received the Torah from Hashem through Moses, they were ready to accept the reproofs of *Devarim* no matter how they were presented. For now they realized that Moses was speaking in Hashem's name.

The order of the verses in *Shemos*, Chapter 4, supports this interpretation. After all, one might assume that Moses would present his strongest argument — "I am not a man of words" and thus incapable of carrying out the task — before all other arguments. However, Moses realized that it was more logical to present the other arguments first, because once the people "believed in Hashem and in His servant Moses," there would be no need for a "man of words." Thus after the parting of the Sea of Reeds, when the people achieved "belief in

1

1 [1] *These are the words that Moses spoke to all Israel, on*

Hashem and Moses His servant," (ibid. 14:31), Hashem said to him, "These are the words which you shall speak to the Children of Israel" (ibid. 19:6), and at that time Moses did not answer, "I am not a man of words."

אֵלֶּה הַדְּבָרִים אֲשֶׁר דִּבֶּר מֹשֶׁה — *These are the words that Moses spoke.* Here the Torah hints that Moses did not indulge in idle words, as the Sages explain the phrase וְדִבַּרְתָּ בָּם: "You shall speak of *them,* not of idle things." A persons main topic of conversation should be the Torah and related subjects. The *Ohr HaChaim* interprets this phrase in a similar manner.

For Moses, the man of God, this was merely a minor accomplishment. Yet in our own times we merited the example of the *Chafetz Chaim*, זצוק״ל, who used his tendency to be talkative as a tool to keep away from sin. In order to avoid speaking or hearing idle words, he would talk endlessly to both students and visitors about Torah subjects and Jewish ethics. The great *tzaddik* R' Chaim Ozer Grodzinski, זצוק״ל, bore witness that the author of *Shemiras HaLashon* guarded his own tongue in a most original way: not by keeping silent, but by always fulfilling וְדִבַּרְתָּ בָּם, so that there was never a moment for idle talk.

אֶל־כָּל־יִשְׂרָאֵל — *To all Israel.* "If Moses had rebuked only some of the people, then the man in the street would have said, 'If I had been there, I would have answered him ... ' Therefore Moses brought the entire people together, from the greatest to the smallest, and said to them, 'Whoever has an answer, let him come forward and give it' " (*Sifre*).

It is impossible through conventional means for six hundred thousand men, not to mention all the women and children, to hear one man speak to all of them at once. Clearly, this was a miraculous phenomenon. Why was a miracle necessary for this particular occasion? After all, Torah can be learned from the teacher or from his student. If a person was not present when Moses was giving a lesson, or couldn't hear properly, he would learn it from Aaron, from one of his sons, or from the heads of the tribes (*Eruvin* 52). *Rambam* adds: "And afterwards everyone would go teach his brother what he had heard from Moses" (Introduction to the *Commentary on the Mishnah*).

However, there was no such arrangement when it came to rebuking the people. The difference is emphasized in this verse, "These are the words that Moses spoke to all Israel." All the people heard these words directly from Moses, so that no one could argue against the Torah which Moses gave them in Hashem's name, especially after they said to him at Mount Sinai, "You should approach and hear . . . and you should speak to us . . . then we shall hear and we shall do" (*Devarim* 5:24). But that is not the case with words of rebuke, which are likely to be rejected. Such words are always hated by scoffers. Moreover, the scoffers of that time held various grudges against Moses, who was giving the rebuke. Under these circumstances, if the reproof had been disseminated by

א בְּעֵבֶר הַיַּרְדֵּן בַּמִּדְבָּר בָּעֲרָבָה מוֹל סוּף בֵּין־פָּארָן וּבֵין־
ב־ג תֹּפֶל וְלָבָן וַחֲצֵרֹת וְדִי זָהָב׃ ב אַחַד עָשָׂר יוֹם מֵחֹרֵב דֶּרֶךְ
הַר־שֵׂעִיר עַד קָדֵשׁ בַּרְנֵעַ׃ ג וַיְהִי בְּאַרְבָּעִים שָׁנָה בְּעַשְׁתֵּי־
עָשָׂר חֹדֶשׁ בְּאֶחָד לַחֹדֶשׁ דִּבֶּר מֹשֶׁה אֶל־בְּנֵי יִשְׂרָאֵל

---

word of mouth, some people would have certainly claimed that had they been there, they would have argued against the reproof. Therefore Hashem performed a miracle and made sure that every person heard with clarity and had the immediate opportunity to speak up. In this way, no one would be able to discount the admonishment at a later time.

Furthermore, it was necessary for all the people to hear the rebuke expressly from Moses because for admonishment to have maximum effect it must be heard directly. He has witnessed their wrongdoings and become so upset, that his words burn like fire and his sighs break the listeners' hearts. When these same words are presented in writing, they cannot have the same effect, and a second-hand report from others who heard them is even less powerful.

A story is told about a *gaon* who was famous for his moving discourses. Everyone would run to hear him speak and listen to his words of rebuke. After his death, his discourses were collected and published, but for some reason they did not have a profound effect on their readers. People commented that although these were the very same speeches they remembered hearing from the great man himself, something was missing — the sigh that would escape his lips when he paused. That sigh, which rose from the depths of his heart, broke their hearts when they heard it. For only words that come from the heart can enter the heart.

2. אַחַד עָשָׂר יוֹם — *Eleven days.* "The distance from Horeb to Kadesh-barnea is an eleven day walk, but you accomplished it in three days in order to reach the Land faster. Yet because you became degenerate, God led you in circles around Mount Seir for forty years" (*Rashi;* see his computation). What wrong did they do? They craved meat and spoke disparagingly of the manna. If not for that, the Children of Israel would have immediately inherited Mount Seir (i.e., the lands across the Jordan), and would have entered the Land of Israel the next day, where they could eat meat and ordinary bread to their hearts' content. Why, then, did they cry out for meat and disparage the manna on the eve of their expected entry into the Land, when they had been eating it for over a year and had never complained about it previously?

The people apparently thought that the conquest of the Land was to come about by natural means, and accordingly they wanted to "build up their strength" for a month with actual bread and meat, not just the *taste* of bread and meat (or any other food they desired) offered by the manna. They hoped this would prepare them physically to wage war with the Canaanites. As long as they were sitting peacefully at Horeb, they were satisfied with manna. But, ironically, had they not sinned, they would not have needed physical strength or weapons in their war with the Canaanites.

1 the other side of the Jordan, concerning the Wilderness, con-
2-3 cerning the Arabah, opposite the Sea of Reeds, between Paran
and Tophel, and Laban, and Hazeroth, and Di-zahab; 2 eleven
days from Horeb, by way of Mount Seir to Kadesh-barnea.
3 It was in the fortieth year, in the eleventh month, on the first
of the month, when Moses spoke to the Children of Israel,

---

3. וַיְהִי בְּאַרְבָּעִים שָׁנָה . . . דִּבֶּר מֹשֶׁה אֶל־בְּנֵי יִשְׂרָאֵל — *It was in the fortieth year... when Moses spoke to the Children of Israel.* The Jewish people reached the border to the Holy Land thirty-nine days after they set out from Horeb. Now the time had come to explain the Torah fully and clearly to the Children of Israel. According to the original plan, the day they crossed the border they were to set up huge stones and inscribe upon them "all the words of this Torah, well clarified," as they were commanded much later, on the day they crossed the Jordan (*Devarim* 27:8). Originally, Moses was to have brought them into the Land and make the inscriptions on the stones himself, so that the nations of world would not be able to claim that they did not know what was written in the Torah. However, the people's sins interfered with the plan, and the original arrangement was delayed for forty years. Only then did Moses "speak to the Children of Israel, according to everything that Hashem commanded him to them" — admonitions and reproofs, blessings and curses — so that they should understand that they were entering the Land for the sole purpose of fulfilling the entire Torah. As for the inscription of the stones for all the world to see, that task was given to Joshua and the Elders of Israel because Moses never crossed the Jordan.

☙ בְּעַשְׁתֵּי־עָשָׂר חֹדֶשׁ בְּאֶחָד לַחֹדֶשׁ — *In the eleventh month, on the first of the month.* Moses passed away on the seventh of Adar. Therefore, he reviewed the Torah with the people for thirty-six days, the numerical value of this Book's opening word, אֵלֶּה. The *Gemara* teaches us that Rabbi Chanina bar Papa told the Angel of Death, "Let me be for thirty days, until I have reviewed my Talmud" (*Kesubos* 77). This is less time than it took Moshe Rabbeinu! But this should not be surprising, for Rabbi Chanina's intention was to study alone. Moses, on the other hand, had to explain the Torah to the entire people of Israel, answering every question, in addition to rebuking them for their sins. Therefore he needed more than thirty days.

☙ בְּאֶחָד לַחֹדֶשׁ — *On the first of the month.* "This teaches us that he rebuked the people only shortly before his death, just as Jacob had done with his sons. We find that Joshua, Samuel, and David followed the same practice" (*Rashi*). One of the reasons given for this is that one should not have to repeat his rebuke again and again (ibid.). But how does this look in light of *Chazal's* teaching? For the Torah says, "You shall reprove your fellow" (*Vayikra* 19:17), and the Sages comment, "Even a hundred times" (*Bava Metzia* 31).

We can explain *Rashi's* intent by saying that the verse in *Vayikra* applies only to one's "fellow," not to a father-and-son or rabbi-and-student relationship.

כְּכֹל אֲשֶׁר צִוָּה יְהוָה אֹתוֹ אֲלֵהֶם׃ ד אַחֲרֵי הַכֹּתוֹ אֵת א
סִיחֹן מֶלֶךְ הָאֱמֹרִי אֲשֶׁר יוֹשֵׁב בְּחֶשְׁבּוֹן וְאֵת עוֹג מֶלֶךְ ד־ה
הַבָּשָׁן אֲשֶׁר־יוֹשֵׁב בְּעַשְׁתָּרֹת בְּאֶדְרֶעִי׃ ה בְּעֵבֶר הַיַּרְדֵּן
בְּאֶרֶץ מוֹאָב הוֹאִיל מֹשֶׁה בֵּאֵר אֶת־הַתּוֹרָה הַזֹּאת לֵאמֹר׃

The son and the disciple are obligated to honor their father and their teacher; the father is obligated to discipline his son, and, to a certain extent, the rabbi must discipline his student. When a son or student habitually disobeys his elders, he becomes categorized as one who has "repeatedly transgressed." Then it becomes virtually impossible for him to correct himself. Thus, it is better not to bring up past events, unless the parent or teacher actually notices in the young person a desire to repeat past transgressions. Yet before one's death, it is good to remind the young of their sins and rebuke them. For at this time, the elder's words will have the force of a last will and testament, leaving a much deeper impression than ordinary rebuke.

ככל אֲשֶׁר צִוָּה ה׳ אתו אֲלֵהֶם — *According to everything that Hashem commanded him to them.* This phrase demonstrates that the reproofs were included among the items Moses had been commanded by God to say to the people in this "review of the Torah."

Later in his rebuke, Moses tells the people, "מַמְרִים הֱיִיתֶם עִם ה׳, you have been rebels against Hashem" (9:7). Yet Moses was punished for using very similar words at Meribah: "שִׁמְעוּ נָא הַמֹּרִים, Listen now, O rebels" (*Bamidbar* 20:10). What is the difference between these two occasions? And why did Hashem command Moses to use the same expression here, to which He had taken such exception previously?

The difference is that at Meribah the people were tormented by thirst, and Moses should have taken this into consideration and spoken to them gently. *Chazal* interpret Jacob's answer to Rachel similarly. When she said to Jacob, "Give me children!" it was improper for him to retort, "Am I instead of God, Who has withheld from you fruit of the womb?" (*Bereishis* 30:2). God rebuked him for speaking in this manner: "Is this the way to answer the tormented?" (*Bereishis Rabbah* 71). Yet now that the Jewish people were in a proper encampment and lacked nothing, they could be rebuked as necessary. In any case, Moses was speaking to a new generation, which had not sinned and which would not be especially pained by his choice of words in describing their fathers' deeds.

4. אַחֲרֵי הַכֹּתוֹ — *After he had smitten.* Before he defeated the kings, Moses was afraid that the people would not accept his rebuke and that the followers of Dathan and Abiram would answer him: "You did not bring us to a land flowing with milk and honey nor give us a heritage of field and vineyard . . ." (*Bamidbar* 16:14). But "after he had smitten Sihon . . . and Og," he opened the gates of the entire Land to the Children of Israel, since all the Canaanite kings had been paying tribute to these two great kings for their protection against pillaging soldiers. (See *Rashi* to *Bamidbar* 21:23.)

1 4-5

according to everything that HASHEM commanded him to them, [4] *after he had smitten Sihon, king of the Amorites, who dwelt in Heshbon, and Og, king of Bashan, who dwelt in Ashtaroth, in Edrei.* [5] *On the other side of the Jordan in the land of Moab, Moses began explaining this Torah, saying:*

Not only had Moses defeated these great kings, he had also divided their land and given "a heritage of field and vineyard" to the two-and-a-half tribes, and chiefly to the tribe of Reuben, whose scions, Dathan and Abiram, had demanded this inheritance. Moses was now confident that the people would listen to him.

5. בֵּאֵר אֶת־הַתּוֹרָה הַזֹּאת — *Explaining this Torah. Rashi*, based on the *Midrash*, explains that Moses interpreted the Torah for the people in all seventy languages (לְשׁוֹנוֹת). This is difficult to understand: why would Moses speak to them in languages they had never before heard? Certainly it made sense to inscribe the Torah on the stones in all seventy languages, so that every nation could come and copy it in its own language and script (*Sotah* 35), but there would be no practical purpose in explaining the Torah orally to the Jewish people in foreign languages. Other commentators say that לָשׁוֹן means "idiom", and *Rashi* is referring to the "seventy facets of the Torah." This explanation is correct.

⸎ The word "Torah" does not always mean the 613 *mitzvos*. In a number of places, we find the expression "the Torah *and* the *mitzvos*." In other words, the Torah encompasses much more than a set of commandments. Thus Joshua exhorts the people, "Only be very careful to do the *mitzvah* and the Torah that Moses, Hashem's servant, commanded you: to love Hashem your God and to walk in all His ways, and to keep His commandments and to cling to Him, and to serve Him with all your heart and with all your soul" (*Yehoshua* 22:5). From here it is evident that "the Torah" also includes walking in Hashem's ways (both according to the letter of the law and beyond it), clinging to Him, and serving Him with all one's heart and soul — in addition to fulfilling the formal *mitzvos*.

The Torah encompasses the fundamental concepts of our faith, as well: the history of heaven and earth, the deeds of our holy Patriarchs and the Chosen People, the day we stood at Mount Sinai, our ethical teachings, and more.

When the verse tells us that "Moses began explaining this Torah," the broader meaning is intended. Now Moses elaborates on some of the *mitzvos* which had previously only been briefly mentioned. He also reveals the *mitzvos* which he had privately received on Mount Sinai and reserved until the time of his death. Yet Moses also addresses the larger Torah. He rebukes the people, explaining in depth the ethical teachings of the Torah, in order to lead them to the ways of God and awaken their love and desire to cling to Him. These precepts are also an integral part of the Torah. In fact, Moses began his explanation with ethical admonitions and rebukes, for these have precedence over the *mitzvos*; as it is said, "Fear of Hashem is the beginning of knowledge" (*Mishlei* 1:7). Thus, Moses began (v. 6), "Hashem, our God, spoke to us in Horeb, saying, 'Enough of your dwelling by this mountain,' " and continued rebuking them until "This is the

א ו יְהוָה אֱלֹהֵינוּ דִּבֶּר אֵלֵינוּ בְּחֹרֵב לֵאמֹר רַב־לָכֶם שֶׁבֶת
ו־י בָּהָר הַזֶּה: ז פְּנוּ | וּסְעוּ לָכֶם וּבֹאוּ הַר הָאֱמֹרִי וְאֶל־כָּל־
שְׁכֵנָיו בָּעֲרָבָה בָהָר וּבַשְּׁפֵלָה וּבַנֶּגֶב וּבְחוֹף הַיָּם אֶרֶץ
הַכְּנַעֲנִי וְהַלְּבָנוֹן עַד־הַנָּהָר הַגָּדֹל נְהַר־פְּרָת: ח רְאֵה נָתַתִּי
לִפְנֵיכֶם אֶת־הָאָרֶץ בֹּאוּ וּרְשׁוּ אֶת־הָאָרֶץ אֲשֶׁר נִשְׁבַּע
יְהוָה לַאֲבֹתֵיכֶם לְאַבְרָהָם לְיִצְחָק וּלְיַעֲקֹב לָתֵת לָהֶם
וּלְזַרְעָם אַחֲרֵיהֶם: ט וָאֹמַר אֲלֵכֶם בָּעֵת הַהִוא לֵאמֹר לֹא־
אוּכַל לְבַדִּי שְׂאֵת אֶתְכֶם: י יְהוָה אֱלֹהֵיכֶם הִרְבָּה אֶתְכֶם

---

teaching that Moses placed before the Children of Israel" (*Devarim* 4:44). Only then did he begin: "These are the testimonies, the decrees, and the ordinances that Moses spoke . . ." (ibid. 4:45).

6. ה׳ אֱלֹהֵינוּ דִּבֶּר אֵלֵינוּ בְּחֹרֵב — *Hashem, our God, spoke to us in Horeb. Sifre* explains that Moses told the people, "I am not saying this to you on my own, but it is from Hashem's mouth." As previously noted, the Jewish people were unwilling to go on until they knew that God's "face of anger" had passed and that He Himself would go before them. Therefore, Moses assured them that he was not speaking for himself when he told them "turn and go," but for Hashem, Who would indeed go before them.

☙ רַב־לָכֶם שֶׁבֶת בָּהָר הַזֶּה — *Enough of your dwelling by this mountain.* After the episode of the Golden Calf, God no longer wanted to accompany the Jewish people through the Wilderness. He was going to send an angel to bring us to the Land He had promised to our fathers. But Moses could not accept this. He wanted Hashem to take us there Himself. Hashem therefore promised him, "My Presence will go, and provide you rest" (*Shemos* 33:14). *Chazal* explain the intent of this brief phrase: "Wait upon Me until the face of anger has passed, and then I will grant you peace." Moses insisted on this: "If Your Presence is not to go, do not take us from this place." And so the Children of Israel stayed there, waiting to hear from God that His "face of anger" had passed (*Berachos* 7b).

Moses now refers to this, as he explains that they did not leave Horeb until God said to him, "Enough of your dwelling by this mountain." Once they had made the *Mishkan* and its utensils to atone for having made the Golden Calf, Hashem was appeased and once again was willing to accompany them. This clarifies the *Midrash* in the *Sifre* which explains that "you have tarried at this mountain long enough: you have received the Torah and made the *Mishkan* and its utensils. This is enough to atone for you."

8. לַאֲבֹתֵיכֶם — *To your forefathers.* "After saying, 'forefathers,' why does Moses mention Abraham, Isaac, and Jacob again by name? To inform us that Abraham's merit alone would suffice; Isaac also had enough merit by himself, and Jacob's merit would also suffice" (*Rashi*). But when the Patriarchs are mentioned in the passage of rebuke in *Bechukosai*, it is to tell us that even after

1 [6] *HASHEM, our God, spoke to us in Horeb, saying: Enough of*
6-10 *your dwelling by this mountain.* [7] *Turn yourselves around*
and journey, and come to the Amorite mountain and all
its neighbors, in the Arabah, on the mountain, and in the
lowland, and in the south, and at the seacoast; the land of the
Canaanite and the Lebanon, until the great river, the
Euphrates River. [8] *See! I have given the Land before you;*
come and possess the Land that HASHEM swore to your
forefathers, to Abraham, to Isaac, and to Jacob, to give
them and their children after them.
[9] *I said to you at that time, saying, "I cannot carry*
you alone. [10] *HASHEM, your God, has multiplied you and*

---

the people repent, the merit of all the Patriarchs together will still be necessary to shift the balance in Israel's favor: "I will remember My covenant with Jacob, and also My covenant with Isaac, and also My covenant with Abraham will I remember" (*Vayikra* 26:42).

9. וָאֹמַר אֲלֵכֶם בָּעֵת הַהִוא — *I said to you at that time.* Why at that time in particular? When they were encamped at Horeb, every man had a good location for his tent; everyone was eating manna and drinking from Miriam's well; everyone was studying the Torah, and primarily living in peace; and there was scarcely a point of contention among them. The people would come to Moses chiefly to seek the word of God, and only if "they have a matter . . . I judge between a man and his fellow" (*Shemos* 18:16).

However, now that they were commanded to move and go directly to inherit the Promised Land, Moses could already see quarrels on the horizon. On the way to the Land, each man would be looking for a good spot to pitch his tent — a likely source of friction among them. The division of the Land would certainly cause disagreements. And Moses knew this time was drawing closer, for had it not been for the Sin of the Spies, the conquest would have come about instantaneously and miraculously, without weapons or war. Therefore, he chose this occasion to tell them to provide themselves with judges and bailiffs.

בָּעֵת הַהִוא — *At that time.* Moses looked for a *mitzvah* which would provide the people with enough merit to inherit the land without loss of lives. He found that "appointing suitable judges carries with it enough merit to keep Israel alive [without dying in a war of conquest] and to settle them on their land" (*Sanhedrin* 32). *Rashi* quotes this Talmudic passage later in *Devarim*, when the Torah says, "Judges and officers shall you appoint . . . so that you will live and possess the Land that Hashem, your God, gives you" (16:18-20). This is why Moses commanded Israel to appoint suitable judges "at that time," just when they were about to enter the Land.

לֹא־אוּכַל לְבַדִּי שְׂאֵת אֶתְכֶם — *I cannot carry you alone.* Since Moses had already decided that he could not carry the people by himself, why

וְהִנְּכֶם הַיּוֹם כְּכוֹכְבֵי הַשָּׁמַיִם לָרֹב: שני יא יְהוָה א
אֱלֹהֵי אֲבוֹתֵכֶם יֹסֵף עֲלֵיכֶם כָּכֶם אֶלֶף פְּעָמִים יא־יג
וִיבָרֵךְ אֶתְכֶם כַּאֲשֶׁר דִּבֶּר לָכֶם: יב אֵיכָה אֶשָּׂא לְבַדִּי
טָרְחֲכֶם וּמַשַּׂאֲכֶם וְרִיבְכֶם: יג הָבוּ לָכֶם אֲנָשִׁים
חֲכָמִים וּנְבֹנִים וִידֻעִים לְשִׁבְטֵיכֶם וַאֲשִׂימֵם בְּרָאשֵׁיכֶם:

---

does he ask again later, "How can I alone carry your contentiousness?" (v. 12).

The fact is that being a ruler of Israel is similar to being a slave. Even after Moses, the acknowledged ruler of his people, decided that he was unable to bear all their problems and judge all their cases himself, as he declares in this verse, he asks himself what the people will say. Perhaps his "masters" would think he was shirking his duty towards them, and that he was really capable of bearing the burden by himself. Therefore, he asked them if they agreed with him (v. 12). Let them tell him, if they can, how he can bear it all by himself! Only after they answered him, "The thing that you have proposed to do is good" (v. 14), was his mind at ease.

10. וְהִנְּכֶם הַיּוֹם כְּכוֹכְבֵי הַשָּׁמַיִם לָרֹב — *Behold! you are like the stars of heaven in abundance.* "But on that day, were they as the stars in the heaven? Indeed, they were no more than 600,000 [adult men]!" Actually Moses was saying, הַיּוֹם, literally "the day" — "You may be compared to the day; you are everlasting like the sun, the moon, and the stars" (*Rashi*).

In that case, "in abundance" refers to abundant quality, not quantity. But this interpretation makes it difficult to understand why Moses said, "I cannot carry you alone." If he was not referring to their great numbers but to their excellent quality, why was it so hard for him to deal with their disputes by himself?

This may be explained as follows: The greater the "quality" of the litigants who bring their case before a *dayan*, the more trouble it makes for him. Working-class litigants accept the judge's decision unquestioningly, acknowledging that he is a learned rabbi and that they have submitted the case to his judgment. When a more erudite man loses a court case, he looks for grounds to dispute the decision. He might even think he is more capable of deciding the law than the *dayan*, completely forgetting that he is biased in his own favor.

We see that Jethro had advised Moses to ease his workload by accepting only the "big cases" (הַדָּבָר הַגָּדוֹל) and letting others judge the petty disputes (*Shemos* 18:22). *Chazal* point out that הַדָּבָר הַגָּדוֹל also implies "the words of the great" — cases involving distinguished men (*Sanhedrin* 16), along with all the trouble they incur.

Speaking in a lighter vein, we might say that if two litigants have a "run-in" with each other, they cannot hurt anyone but each other, but when two stars collide, they can destroy entire worlds.

1
11-13

behold! you are like the stars of heaven in abundance. [11] May HASHEM, the God of your forefathers, add to you a thousand times yourselves, and bless you as He has spoken of you.
[12] How can I alone carry your contentiousness, your burdens, and your quarrels? [13] Provide for yourselves distinguished men, who are wise, understanding, and well known to your tribes, and I shall appoint them as your heads."

---

11. **ה׳. . . יֹסֵף עֲלֵיכֶם כָּכֶם אֶלֶף פְּעָמִים** — *May Hashem... add to you a thousand times yourselves. Rambam* (*Hilchos Melachim* 11) finds proof in the written Torah for the coming of the Messiah from a passage in *Devarim* which talks about the cities of refuge: "When Hashem will broaden your boundary ... then you shall add three more cities to these three" (19:8-9).

As no mention is found in our history of any such three additional cities ever having been built, and since the Torah does not contain false promises, the Torah must be referring to a future time — the days of the Messiah. In accordance with this line of reasoning, it follows that in this verse Moses blessed the Children of Israel with a thousandfold increase, and that blessing must come true at some time, since false promises are not found in the Torah. Since throughout history, our numbers have not yet reached six hundred million, the fulfillment of this blessing must be reserved for the future, when the Messiah comes.

אֶלֶף פְּעָמִים — *A thousand times.* "[Moses said to them,] 'This is my own [blessing], but God will bless you as He has spoken to you' " (*Rashi*). This seems to imply that the thousandfold blessing was Moses' to give. This is exactly what he had to offer, no more and no less. For if he had had more to give, he would have given it all to Israel. What is the reason for this particular number?

P'nei Yehoshua offers a very good explanation. On two occasions, Hashem said to Moses, "I will make you into a great nation." The first was after the episode of the Golden Calf, and the second after sending the spies into the Holy Land. Hashem's attribute of goodness is always five hundred times greater than His attribute of retribution (*Yoma*, 76a, and *Rashi* ad. loc.). We can assume, therefore, that on each of these occasions God's intention was to build a new nation from Moses five hundred times greater than the number of the Children of Israel whom He was going to destroy — i.e., five hundred times sixty myriads. Since God made this proposition to Moses twice, the promised figure of one thousand times six hundred thousand was bestowed upon him.

God's word, even when spoken conditionally, can never remain completely unfulfilled. Therefore, Moses possessed a blessing "in reserve" of a thousandfold increase over the original sixty myriads of Israel. He now chose to pass that blessing onto the people.

13. **וִידֻעִים לְשִׁבְטֵיכֶם** — *And well known to your tribes.* "[Choose men] who are familiar to you, for if [a man] comes before me wrapped in his *tallis* I do not

א יד וַתַּעֲנוּ אֹתִי וַתֹּאמְרוּ טוֹב־הַדָּבָר אֲשֶׁר־דִּבַּרְתָּ לַעֲשׂוֹת׃
יד־טו טו וָאֶקַּח אֶת־רָאשֵׁי שִׁבְטֵיכֶם אֲנָשִׁים חֲכָמִים וִידֻעִים
וָאֶתֵּן אוֹתָם רָאשִׁים עֲלֵיכֶם שָׂרֵי אֲלָפִים וְשָׂרֵי מֵאוֹת
וְשָׂרֵי חֲמִשִּׁים וְשָׂרֵי עֲשָׂרֹת וְשֹׁטְרִים לְשִׁבְטֵיכֶם׃

---

know who he is or whether he is upright" (*Rashi*). This explanation has puzzled people. Didn't Jethro say to Moses, "You must seek out [such men]," and didn't *Rashi* comment that this would be done "with the *ruach hakodesh* (Divine spirit) that is upon you" (*Shemos* 18:21)?

This discrepancy may be explained as follows: Moses was telling the people to bring him men who were "wise, understanding, and well known to your tribes" for their uprightness, not just anyone who announced his candidacy for the position. He did not want to have to use *ruach hakodesh* to screen out unsuitable candidates and then dismiss them, so he asked the people to bring men who, at the very least, seemed suitable in their eyes.

According to the *Rambam's* interpretation, "well known to your tribes" means "those with whom the people are generally pleased." In this case, "well known" is used in the same manner as it was used when Hashem praised Abraham — "for I have known him" — as an expression of love and affection. In other words, "well known" refers to the well-liked.

15. אֲנָשִׁים חֲכָמִים וִידֻעִים — *Men who were wise and well known.* "But I could not find men who were understanding" (*Rashi*). The Children of Israel may have brought men whom they considered "understanding," but when they were scrutinized by Moses, of whom King David said, "You have made him but little less than the angels" (*Tanchuma, Vayikra* §3), he found them merely "wise." It all depends on who conducts the examination, but in the final analysis, it sufficed in Moses' eyes that they were wise.

⇐§ חֲכָמִים וִידֻעִים — *Wise and well known.* "But I could not find men who were understanding" (*Rashi*). It is surprising that Moses could not find men who were understanding. Granted that it was difficult to find "men of truth, who despise money," for these are indeed few and far between. But how could he fail to find men of understanding among the nation that was called "a wise and discerning people" (4:6)?

Let us define our terms: "Who is wise? He who learns from every person." And who is understanding? He who learns from every event, who is able to extrapolate and retain his observations of an event to apply to subsequent events (see *Chagigah* 14a). For example, *Rashi* quotes the *Sifre* on the word "Hazeroth" in verse 1: "God said to them, 'You should have learned from what I did to Miriam at Hazeroth for speaking *lashon hara*, but instead you spoke against God.' " And because they were lacking this power of extrapolation, God decided that "this was not an understanding people" (*Yeshayahu* 27:11). (I heard this from my nephew, Rabbi Shmuel David Walkin [זצ"ל], who was the Rav of Lukacsz, before moving to Brooklyn.)

[14] *You answered me and said, "The thing that you have proposed to do is good."*

[15] *So I took the heads of your tribes, distinguished men, who were wise and well known, and I appointed them as heads over you, leaders of thousands, leaders of hundreds, leaders of fifties, and leaders of tens, and officers for your tribes.*

Later in *Devarim*, we find the verse, "Surely a wise and discerning people is this great nation" (4:6), which refers to what the nations of the world will say when they see the Jews fulfilling the Torah, "for it is your wisdom and your discernment in the eyes of the peoples." As we learn in *Iyov* (28:28), "Turning away from evil [is an act of] understanding."

רָאשִׁים עֲלֵיכֶם — *As heads over you.* Although they were already "heads of your tribes," i.e., the most highly regarded men of the tribes, they did not actually have any official position in the community. But since Moses was officially appointing them to be "heads over you," the people are obligated to honor them.

שָׂרֵי אֲלָפִים . . . וְשָׂרֵי עֲשָׂרֹת — *Leaders of thousands . . . and leaders of tens.* According to the Vilna Gaon, all these leaders were judges, as the Torah says in *Parashas Yisro*, "they shall judge the people." But they were also assigned special duties: the "leaders of thousands" were officers in time of war; the "leaders of hundreds" were the regular judges; the "leaders of fifties" were called "elders" and their duty was to teach Torah to the people (*Chazal* note that שַׂר חֲמִשִּׁים, "the leader of fifties," was referred to by Yeshayahu (3:3) as שַׂר חֲמָשִׁים, for "he who knows how to debate over the five *Chumashim*," which contain fifty *parashiyos* — *Chagigah* 14); and the "leaders of tens" were the bailiffs. According to this interpretation, "and officers for your tribes" does not refer to an additional appointment, but explains "leaders of tens."

(Yet, I have not succeeded in fully understanding the Gaon's holy words. Regarding the war with Midian, the Torah tells us that "Moses became angry with the officers of the army — the leaders of thousands and the leaders of hundreds." Does this not mean that the "leaders of hundreds" were also army officers?)

When we compute the total number of men appointed, we arrive at the figure of 78,600 — a surprising number of leaders for a camp of 600,000. Apparently, Moses fixed such a number only for that generation, since they were in a state of war during all their wanderings. It was not a strain on the "national budget,"for everyone subsisted on manna and water from Miriam's well, and the leaders worked as volunteers. (See *Oznayim LaTorah* to *Shemos* 18:22 and *Bamidbar* 31:50.)

In later generations, too, the Judges of Israel served without remuneration. They would render decisions until it was time for the morning meal and afterwards work at their trades. Indeed, *Chazal* teach: "If a person takes pay for rendering judgment, his decisions are null and void" (*Kesubos* 105).

טז וָאֲצַוֶּה֙ אֶת־שֹׁפְטֵיכֶ֔ם בָּעֵ֥ת הַהִ֖וא לֵאמֹ֑ר שָׁמֹ֤עַ בֵּין־
אֲחֵיכֶם֙ וּשְׁפַטְתֶּ֣ם צֶ֔דֶק בֵּֽין־אִ֥ישׁ וּבֵין־אָחִ֖יו וּבֵ֥ין גֵּרֽוֹ:
יז לֹֽא־תַכִּ֨ירוּ פָנִ֜ים בַּמִּשְׁפָּ֗ט כַּקָּטֹ֤ן כַּגָּדֹל֙ תִּשְׁמָע֔וּן לֹ֤א
תָג֙וּרוּ֙ מִפְּנֵי־אִ֔ישׁ כִּ֥י הַמִּשְׁפָּ֖ט לֵאלֹהִ֣ים ה֑וּא וְהַדָּבָר֙ אֲשֶׁ֣ר
יִקְשֶׁ֣ה מִכֶּ֔ם תַּקְרִב֥וּן אֵלַ֖י וּשְׁמַעְתִּֽיו: יח וָאֲצַוֶּ֥ה אֶתְכֶ֖ם בָּעֵ֣ת
הַהִ֑וא אֵ֥ת כָּל־הַדְּבָרִ֖ים אֲשֶׁ֥ר תַּעֲשֽׂוּן: יט וַנִּסַּ֣ע מֵחֹרֵ֗ב וַנֵּ֡לֶךְ
אֵ֣ת כָּל־הַמִּדְבָּ֣ר הַגָּדוֹל֩ וְהַנּוֹרָ֨א הַה֜וּא אֲשֶׁ֣ר רְאִיתֶ֗ם דֶּ֚רֶךְ
הַ֣ר הָֽאֱמֹרִ֔י כַּֽאֲשֶׁ֥ר צִוָּ֛ה יְהוָ֥ה אֱלֹהֵ֖ינוּ אֹתָ֑נוּ וַנָּבֹ֕א עַ֖ד קָדֵ֥שׁ
בַּרְנֵֽעַ: כ וָאֹמַ֖ר אֲלֵכֶ֑ם בָּאתֶם֙ עַד־הַ֣ר הָֽאֱמֹרִ֔י אֲשֶׁר־יְהוָ֖ה

---

16. שָׁמֹעַ בֵּין־אֲחֵיכֶם — *Listen among your brethren.* Why does the Torah not
say, "Listen *to* your brethren," instead of using such a peculiar expression?
Chazal understood this wording as a warning to the *beis din* never to hear
what one litigant has to say before the other arrives (*Sanhedrin* 7). Therefore
the next words are "and judge righteously."

§ בֵּין־אֲחֵיכֶם — *Among your brethren.* A judge tends to view himself as
virtuous and the litigants as wicked, especially while they are standing
before him. Nevertheless, the Torah commands judges to relate to the litigants
as "brethren." (See *Oznayim LaTorah* to *Vayikra* 19:15.)

§ וּבֵין גֵּרוֹ — *Or his litigant.* "This means his neighbor" (*Sanhedrin* 7). Based on
this interpretation, we may better understand the first part of the verse,
which says, "I instructed your judges at that time." The Children of Israel were
preparing to decamp and move on ("turn yourselves around and journey" — v.
7). The judges were, therefore, inclined to think that hearing disputes between
neighbors would be a waste of time, since the source of contention would cease
to exist within a day or two when they decamped. For this reason, Moses
cautioned them to judge even cases like these. As *Chazal* teach (*Sanhedrin* 8a;
Avos D'Rav Nassan 10:2), "a case involving a single *prutah* should be just as
important to you as a case involving a hundred dinars." So, too, a case
involving one day or even one hour has the same importance as one involving
a year or more.

17. לֹֽא־תַכִּירוּ פָנִים בַּמִּשְׁפָּט — *You shall not show favoritism in judgment.*
[Literally, to "recognize faces."] "To tip the judgment in favor of someone
he knows" (*Ibn Ezra*).

These words influence the *Rambam* when he says: "The two litigants must
be equal in the eyes and hearts of the judges. And a judge who is not familiar
with either of them or their deeds is considered most likely to render a fair
decision."

With this in mind, we may interpret the verse literally: "You shall not
recognize faces in judgment" — do not try to recognize the faces of the liti-

1
16-20

[16] *I instructed your judges at that time, saying, "Listen among your brethren and judge righteously between a man and his brother or his litigant.* [17] *You shall not show favoritism in judgment, small and great alike shall you hear; you shall not tremble before any man, for the judgment is God's; any matter that is too difficult for you, you shall bring to me and I shall hear it."* [18] *I commanded you at that time all the things that you should do.*

[19] *We journeyed from Horeb and we went through that entire great and awesome Wilderness that you saw, by way of the Amorite mountain, as HASHEM, our God, commanded us, and we came until Kadesh-barnea.* [20] *Then I said to you, "You have come until the Amorite mountain that HASHEM,*

---

gants and see whether you know them; it is better not to even know the people standing before you.

In *Chazal's* view, however, the verse refers to a person whose job is to set up the courts. As *Rashi* explains, he is cautioned to choose only judges who are learned in Torah.

וְהַדָּבָר אֲשֶׁר יִקְשֶׁה מִכֶּם תַּקְרִבוּן אֵלַי וּשְׁמַעְתִּיו — *Any matter that is too difficult for you, you shall bring to me and I shall hear it.* It is hard to understand how the humblest of all men was promising to solve any difficulty, no matter how complex (*Chazal* have discussed this point at length). But we may also explain that the verse refers to a difficult litigant. After Moses told the judges, "You shall not tremble before any man," he added that they should not pervert the Law if a litigant should come "who is too difficult for you" — i.e., if you should find yourselves unable to give a ruling because of him. Rather, "bring [this case] to me and I shall hear it," for I am willing to suffer the slings and arrows of this difficult man.

וְהַדָּבָר אֲשֶׁר יִקְשֶׁה — *Any matter that is too difficult.* Jethro had said, "any major matter," but as we explained previously, according to *Chazal*, Jethro's phrase can also mean, "the words of the great." Actually, they are both one and the same, because the words of a great man are usually words of Torah, and these are indeed the most difficult to analyze and judge.

19. וַנֵּלֶךְ אֵת כָּל־הַמִּדְבָּר הַגָּדוֹל וְהַנּוֹרָא הַהוּא — *And we went through that entire great and awesome Wilderness.* No one ever passed through this Wilderness, because it was full of snakes and scorpions as big as wooden beams. Therefore, everyone would go around it and make the journey from Horeb to Kadesh in eleven days. But you went straight through the Wilderness and found the snakes and scorpions lying dead before you. "אֲשֶׁר רְאִיתֶם, that you saw" — this wonder is what you saw.

אֱלֹהֵינוּ נֹתֵן לָנוּ: כא רְאֵה נָתַן יהוה אֱלֹהֶיךָ לְפָנֶיךָ א
אֶת־הָאָרֶץ עֲלֵה רֵשׁ כַּאֲשֶׁר דִּבֶּר יהוה אֱלֹהֵי אֲבֹתֶיךָ לָךְ כא־כב
אַל־תִּירָא וְאַל־תֵּחָת: שלישי כב וַתִּקְרְבוּן אֵלַי כֻּלְּכֶם
וַתֹּאמְרוּ נִשְׁלְחָה אֲנָשִׁים לְפָנֵינוּ וְיַחְפְּרוּ־לָנוּ אֶת־
הָאָרֶץ וְיָשִׁבוּ אֹתָנוּ דָּבָר אֶת־הַדֶּרֶךְ אֲשֶׁר נַעֲלֶה־בָּהּ וְאֵת

---

21. רְאֵה נָתַן ה׳ . . . לְפָנֶיךָ אֶת־הָאָרֶץ — *See — Hashem . . . has placed the Land before you.* From this miracle you see that God has placed the Land before you. He Who prevented you from being obstructed on your way to the Promised Land by killing the snakes and scorpions in the great and awesome Wilderness will surely drive out the nations who dwell there before you. Therefore, "Go up and possess" — with no one to stand against you, as an heir who takes over his inheritance without disturbance.

22. וַתִּקְרְבוּן אֵלַי כֻּלְּכֶם — *All of you approached me. Rashi* explains that the Israeliates came to Moses in a disorderly fashion. This was not the case at Mount Sinai, when they approached Moses in an orderly fashion, as the Torah explains: "All the heads of your tribes and your elders approached me" (*Devarim* 5:20). At that time they approached Moses in the correct manner. The young showed respect for their elders by sending them ahead, and the elders showed respect for the heads of their tribes, making way for them to go first. But here, as *Rashi* notes, the young people pushed the elders, and the elders pushed the heads of the tribes.

Several reasons may be offered for the difference in *Bnei Yisrael's* behavior:

a) At Mount Sinai, the people were under the influence of the enormous event they had just experienced. They had just heard God's voice speaking to them out of the fire, "Honor your father." In that state of mind, the young ones saw clearly what it meant to honor their fathers and their elders. But at Kadesh-barnea, they had been in a state of "craving" and had been "complaining" for some time, and the elders had been appointed to wage war against these ambitions. The younger men, therefore pushed them, for they feared the elders would have their way.

b) It is the way of the world that the young honor the old in spiritual matters, as in speaking with Moses about receiving the Torah on their behalf. However, when it comes to "worldly" affairs, such as inheriting the Holy Land, the young tend to push the elders aside, saying: "We know more about these things than you do."

c) When it was necessary to approach Moses while he stood in the midst of the great fire on Mount Sinai, the young people sent the elders, who approached God all the time in Torah study and prayer. The young ones themselves stood back, remaining out of danger. Yet when a question of going up the Amorite mountain to make war or avoiding it by sending spies was involved, they pushed the elders aside in their haste, saying, "Let

our God, gives us. 21 *See — HASHEM, your God, has placed the*
Land before you; go up and possess, as HASHEM, God of your
forefathers, has spoken to you. Do not fear and do not lose
resolve."
22 *All of you approached me and said, "Let us send men*
ahead of us and let them spy out the Land for us, and bring
word back to us: the road on which we should ascend and the

---

us send spies ahead of us." For if it came to war, they were the ones who would have to fight. This time, too, they preferred to stay out of danger.

נִשְׁלְחָה אֲנָשִׁים . . . וְיַחְפְּרוּ־לָנוּ אֶת־הָאָרֶץ וְיָשִׁבוּ אֹתָנוּ דָּבָר — *Let us send men . . . and let them spy out the Land for us and bring word back to us.* How did our ancestors dare to propose that they should send spies, a decision normally left to the military leaders? Moreover, how could they say, "and let them . . . bring back word to us: the road on which we should ascend," when God was constantly before them with a pillar of cloud to guide them? *Rashi* points out that there is rarely a road without a crooked course, but they did not need spies on that account. They had the Cloud of God, which "flattened out the high places and raised up the low places" (*Rashi* to *Bamidbar* 10:34). And why send spies at all, when they would journey and encamp "according to the word of Hashem" (*Bamidbar* 9:18)?

The Children of Israel apparently had lost faith in everything they had experienced, when they heard the prophecy of Eldad and Medad: "Moses will die, and Joshua will bring the Children of Israel into the Land" (See *Rashi* to *Bamidbar* 11:26). Their fear only became greater when Moses said in God's name:(v. 21) "See — Hashem, your God, has placed the Land before you; go up and possess, as Hashem, God of your forefathers, has spoken to you." They noticed how Moses spoke in the second person, excluding himself when he said, "[you] go up and possess." They realized that his days were numbered, since he said, "go up" in the immediate, imperative sense. For they already knew that he would die before they entered the Land and Joshua would bring them into the Promised Land.

Their mistake was in assuming that the moment Moses was gone, the heavenly ministrations would cease. They believed that they would now be forced to resort to natural means; no longer would the pillar of cloud go before them by day, nor the pillar of fire by night. As Joshua was only forty-two years old, they thought they should choose one man from each tribe to share the leadership with him. (See our lengthy discussion in this regard in *Parashas Shelach* 13:2, כֹּל נָשִׂיא בָהֶם).

וְיָשִׁבוּ אֹתָנוּ דָּבָר — *And bring word back to us.* "[To tell us] what language they speak" (*Rashi*). Then we will be able to place a man in each army unit who speaks their language, because sometimes it is necessary to interrogate prisoners to learn important facts, such as the approaches to a city, etc.

הֶעָרִים אֲשֶׁר נָבֹא אֲלֵיהֶן: כג וַיִּיטַב בְּעֵינַי הַדָּבָר וָאֶקַּח א
מִכֶּם שְׁנֵים עָשָׂר אֲנָשִׁים אִישׁ אֶחָד לַשָּׁבֶט: כד וַיִּפְנוּ וַיַּעֲלוּ כג־כח
הָהָרָה וַיָּבֹאוּ עַד־נַחַל אֶשְׁכֹּל וַיְרַגְּלוּ אֹתָהּ: כה וַיִּקְחוּ בְיָדָם
מִפְּרִי הָאָרֶץ וַיּוֹרִדוּ אֵלֵינוּ וַיָּשִׁבוּ אֹתָנוּ דָבָר וַיֹּאמְרוּ טוֹבָה
הָאָרֶץ אֲשֶׁר־יְהֹוָה אֱלֹהֵינוּ נֹתֵן לָנוּ: כו וְלֹא אֲבִיתֶם לַעֲלֹת
וַתַּמְרוּ אֶת־פִּי יְהֹוָה אֱלֹהֵיכֶם: כז וַתֵּרָגְנוּ בְאָהֳלֵיכֶם
וַתֹּאמְרוּ בְּשִׂנְאַת יְהֹוָה אֹתָנוּ הוֹצִיאָנוּ מֵאֶרֶץ מִצְרָיִם לָתֵת
אֹתָנוּ בְּיַד הָאֱמֹרִי לְהַשְׁמִידֵנוּ: כח אָנָה | אֲנַחְנוּ עֹלִים

---

23. וַיִּיטַב בְּעֵינַי הַדָּבָר — *The idea was good in my eyes.* "Because all of you were agreed on it" (*Ibn Ezra*). Moses had seen how the people's unity led to receiving the Torah: "and Israel encamped there" — all of the same mind (see *Rashi* on *Shemos* 19:2). He, therefore, thought that the people's unity would again produce something good. Nevertheless, he consulted God, Who told him ambiguously, "Send forth men, if you please" — you send them if you wish, but I am not commanding you to do so. Afterwards, too, God gave them "the opportunity to be misled by the spies' words, so that they would not inherit the Land" (See *Rashi* to *Bamidbar* 13:2).

24. וַיָּבֹאוּ עַד־נַחַל אֶשְׁכֹּל — *They . . . came until the Valley of Eshcol.* This was on their way back, because they certainly did not carry the cluster of fruit for forty days throughout the length and breadth of the Land.

☙ **וַיְרַגְּלוּ אֹתָהּ** — *And spied it out.* They spied out the whole Land, for they schemed to deceive and frighten the people into rebellion against God and Moses, His servant, at the Valley of Eshcol, when they saw the giants and the fortified cities. Then Caleb went to the graves of the Patriarchs to beseech God to save him from their plans. For it was there that he heard the report they were planning to deliver to the Children of Israel.

25. וַיִּקְחוּ בְיָדָם — *They took in their hands.* The fruits were so big that they should have been loaded onto camels and donkeys; as the verse says, "He will tie his donkey to the vine; to the vine branch his donkey's foal" (*Bereishis* 49:11). But because of the danger, they took the fruits "in their hands" and labored mightily to bring them back to the camp.

☙ **טוֹבָה הָאָרֶץ** — *Good is the Land.* Some Sages say that all twelve spies began by uttering the truth: "and indeed it flows with milk and honey." Yet they did not describe it as "the land Hashem, our God, gives us," which were Moses' own words. Others explain that Moses is referring to Joshua and Caleb, who said not only "Good is the Land," but "very, very good." Yet Moses quoted only part of their statement, "Good is the Land."

In *Parashas Shelach*, we explained that the ten spies (excluding Joshua and Caleb) were not particularly praising the Land when they said "indeed [lit., also] it flows with milk and honey." Their intention was to insinuate that Egypt was

cities to which we should come."
23 The idea was good in my eyes, so I took from you twelve
men, one man for each tribe. 24 They turned and ascended the
mountain and came until the Valley of Eshcol, and spied it
out. 25 They took in their hands from the fruit of the Land and
brought it down to us; they brought back word to us and said,
"Good is the Land that HASHEM, our God, gives us!"
26 But you did not wish to ascend, and you rebelled against
the word of HASHEM, your God. 27 You slandered in your
tents and said, "Because of HASHEM's hatred for us did He
take us out of the land of Egypt, to deliver us into the hand
of the Amorite to destroy us. 28 To where shall we ascend?

---

the ultimate land "flowing with milk and honey" (as Dathan and Abiram had claimed in their time), and the Holy Land also possessed this characteristic.

All twelve spies admitted that the Land was good. Two said that it was "very, very good," and ten said that it flowed with milk and honey, but hinted that Egypt was a better land. Moses chose the one common denominator from these conflicting statements, and said merely that they all admitted the Land was good.

As for the spies' statement that this was a "land that devours its inhabitants," that was said later, not in Moses' presence, when the spies saw that the Children of Israel were leaning towards the report of Joshua and Caleb, as well as in God's promise through Moses that the Land was good. Only then did they begin to spread lies about this most desirable of lands.

26. וַתַּמְרוּ אֶת־פִּי ה׳ — *And you rebelled against the word of Hashem.* For it was God who had told them, "Go up and possess."

27. בְּשִׂנְאַת ה׳ אֹתָנוּ . . . לָתֵת אֹתָנוּ בְּיַד הָאֱמֹרִי לְהַשְׁמִידֵנוּ — *Because of Hashem's hatred for us . . . to deliver us into the hand of the Amorite to destroy us.* When Pharaoh said to them: "Look! Evil is opposite your faces!" it meant that he had seen a star whose astrological name is "Evil," a sign of bloodshed and killing, rising to meet them in the Wilderness.

The people had also heard Moses praying to God during the incident of the Golden Calf. In his prayer, he pointed out that if God destroyed the Jewish people, the Egyptians would say that He had brought them out under the influence of the evil star, in order "to kill them in the mountains to annihilate them from the face of the earth" (*Shemos* 32:12).

Perceiving themselves in a desperate position, having just been commanded to go up the mountain and make war with "a people greater and taller than we," which dwelt in cities "fortified to the heavens," they now remembered Pharaoh's words, and began to give credence to them. Their choice of expression here, "Because of Hashem's hatred for us did He take us out of the land of Egypt," echoes Moses' argument that the Egyptians would claim, "With Evil did He take them out."

א
כט־לג

אַחֵ֫ינוּ הֵמַ֫סּוּ אֶת־לְבָבֵ֫נוּ לֵאמֹר עַ֣ם גָּד֤וֹל וָרָם֙ מִמֶּ֔נּוּ
עָרִ֛ים גְּדֹלֹ֥ת וּבְצוּרֹ֖ת בַּשָּׁמָ֑יִם וְגַם־בְּנֵ֥י עֲנָקִ֖ים רָאִ֥ינוּ
שָֽׁם׃ כט וָאֹמַ֖ר אֲלֵכֶ֑ם לֹא־תַעַרְצ֥וּן וְלֹא־תִֽירְא֖וּן מֵהֶֽם׃
ל יְהוָ֤ה אֱלֹהֵיכֶם֙ הַהֹלֵ֣ךְ לִפְנֵיכֶ֔ם ה֖וּא יִלָּחֵ֣ם לָכֶ֑ם כְּ֠כֹל
אֲשֶׁ֨ר עָשָׂ֧ה אִתְּכֶ֛ם בְּמִצְרַ֖יִם לְעֵינֵיכֶֽם׃ לא וּבַמִּדְבָּר֙ אֲשֶׁ֣ר
רָאִ֔יתָ אֲשֶׁ֤ר נְשָׂאֲךָ֙ יְהוָ֣ה אֱלֹהֶ֔יךָ כַּאֲשֶׁ֥ר יִשָּׂא־אִ֖ישׁ
אֶת־בְּנ֑וֹ בְּכָל־הַדֶּ֨רֶךְ֙ אֲשֶׁ֣ר הֲלַכְתֶּ֔ם עַד־בֹּאֲכֶ֖ם עַד־הַמָּק֥וֹם
הַזֶּֽה׃ לב וּבַדָּבָ֖ר הַזֶּ֑ה אֵֽינְכֶם֙ מַאֲמִינִ֔ם בַּיהוָ֖ה אֱלֹהֵיכֶֽם׃
לג הַהֹלֵ֨ךְ לִפְנֵיכֶ֜ם בַּדֶּ֗רֶךְ לָת֥וּר לָכֶ֛ם מָק֖וֹם לַחֲנֹֽתְכֶ֑ם
בָּאֵ֣שׁ ׀ לַ֗יְלָה לַרְאֹֽתְכֶם֙ בַּדֶּ֙רֶךְ֙ אֲשֶׁ֣ר תֵּֽלְכוּ־בָ֔הּ וּבֶעָנָ֖ן יוֹמָֽם׃

---

28. וּבְצוּרֹת בַּשָּׁמָיִם — *And fortified to [*lit., *"in"] the heavens.* This is an example of the Torah using exaggerated language (*Rashi*).

In *Parashas Shelach*, we explained that Moses saw that the Jewish people were entering the Land because of the wickedness of the nations and not because of their righteousness. Therefore, he ordered the spies to investigate the spiritual condition of the Amorites as well — had the measure of their sins been filled? And when he asked, "Are there trees in it or not?" he was asking about the presence of righteous men, who are likened to fruit-bearing trees, whose merit might protect the nation.

The answer they brought back was that far from their measure of sins being full, the people dwelling there were אַנְשֵׁי מִדּוֹת, "huge," or, from a spiritual standpoint, people of good character. Thus there was no hope of defeating them because of their wickedness. The spies implied this by making the exaggerated claim that the Canaanite cities were "fortified in the heavens" — protected from above, because of the lofty spiritual status of their people.

We can also interpret *Rashi's* comment to mean that the Scriptures are simply reporting the exact words of the Children of Israel, full of the overstated descriptions they had heard from the spies.

29. וָאֹמַר אֲלֵכֶם — *Then I said to you.* This is not mentioned at all in *Parashas Shelach*, but *Divrei Torah* are poor in one place and rich in another. Some commentators explain that Moses delivered this speech after "Caleb silenced the people toward Moses," demanding that the people give Moses a chance to speak. Others maintain that Moses gave them this rebuke the next day, when he and Aaron fell on their faces before the congregation. How good it would have been had Moses spoken these words to the people when they first said to him, "Let us send men ahead of us," before all the fighting began! Then perhaps they would have changed their minds.

30. ה' . . . יִלָּחֵם לָכֶם — *Hashem ... shall make war for you.* It is not up to you to fight the entire war. All you must do is start: go up the mountain,

Our brothers have melted our hearts, saying, 'A people greater and taller than we, cities great and fortified to the heavens, and even children of the giant have we seen there!'"

29 *Then I said to you, "Do not be broken and do not fear them!* 30 *HASHEM, your God, Who goes before you — He shall make war for you, like everything He did for you in Egypt, before your eyes.* 31 *And in the Wilderness, as you have seen, that HASHEM, your God, bore you, as a man carries his son, on the entire way that you traveled, until you arrived at this place.* 32 *Yet in this matter you do not believe in HASHEM, your God,* 33 *Who goes before you on the way to seek out for you a place for you to encamp, with fire by night to show you the road that you should travel and with a cloud by day!"*

---

and God "shall make war for you, like everything He did for you in Egypt, before your eyes." For as they stood on the shore of the Sea of Reeds, Moses had said to them, "Do not fear! . . . God will do battle for you" (*Shemos* 14:13-14).

Nothing was required of you then, except belief and trust in God. As soon as one of you jumped into the sea and all the tribes followed him, the sea was split. It is the same now: "Do not be broken and do not fear them! Hashem . . . will make war for you, like everything He did for you" — literally, "together with you," for if you do your part and show your faith by ascending the mountain, then He will do His part and perform miracles for you, as He did "in Egypt, before your eyes."

31. כַּאֲשֶׁר יִשָּׂא־אִישׁ אֶת־בְּנוֹ — *As a man carries his son.* How could it ever enter your minds that "Because of Hashem's hatred for us did He take us out . . . to destroy us?" Heaven forbid! "You have seen, that Hashem, your God, bore you, as a man carries his son, on the entire way . . . until you arrived at this place." On the way, Amalek attacked you and God gave you victory; on the way, which was full of snakes and scorpions, God laid them dead before you. And if He punished you for your sins with the Calf, at Taberah, and at Kibroth-hataavah, this, too, demonstrated His love for you. As the verse says, "You should know in your heart that just as a father will chastise his son, so Hashem, your God, chastises you" (*Devarim* 8:5). He punished you for your own good, not to destroy you.

32. וּבַדָּבָר הַזֶּה — *Yet in this matter.* Regarding God's carrying you "as a man carries his son, . . . you do not believe." Yet, is He not the One Who goes before you in fire by night and in cloud by day, to show you the way and to seek out a place for you to encamp?

א
לד־מ

לד וַיִּשְׁמַע יהוה אֶת־קוֹל דִּבְרֵיכֶם וַיִּקְצֹף וַיִּשָּׁבַע לֵאמֹר:
לה אִם־יִרְאֶה אִישׁ בָּאֲנָשִׁים הָאֵלֶּה הַדּוֹר הָרָע הַזֶּה
אֵת הָאָרֶץ הַטּוֹבָה אֲשֶׁר נִשְׁבַּעְתִּי לָתֵת לַאֲבֹתֵיכֶם:
לו זוּלָתִי כָּלֵב בֶּן־יְפֻנֶּה הוּא יִרְאֶנָּה וְלוֹ־אֶתֵּן אֶת־הָאָרֶץ
אֲשֶׁר דָּרַךְ־בָּהּ וּלְבָנָיו יַעַן אֲשֶׁר מִלֵּא אַחֲרֵי יהוה:
לז גַּם־בִּי הִתְאַנַּף יהוה בִּגְלַלְכֶם לֵאמֹר גַּם־אַתָּה לֹא־
תָבֹא שָׁם: לח יְהוֹשֻׁעַ בִּן־נוּן הָעֹמֵד לְפָנֶיךָ הוּא יָבֹא שָׁמָּה
אֹתוֹ חַזֵּק כִּי־הוּא יַנְחִלֶנָּה אֶת־יִשְׂרָאֵל: רביעי לט וְטַפְּכֶם
אֲשֶׁר אֲמַרְתֶּם לָבַז יִהְיֶה וּבְנֵיכֶם אֲשֶׁר לֹא־יָדְעוּ הַיּוֹם
טוֹב וָרָע הֵמָּה יָבֹאוּ שָׁמָּה וְלָהֶם אֶתְּנֶנָּה וְהֵם יִירָשׁוּהָ:
מ וְאַתֶּם פְּנוּ לָכֶם וּסְעוּ הַמִּדְבָּרָה דֶּרֶךְ יַם־סוּף:

---

34. וַיִּשְׁמַע ה׳ . . . וַיִּקְצֹף וַיִּשָּׁבַע — *Hashem heard . . . and He was incensed and He swore [an oath].* That is, God's attribute of mercy rushed forward and swore the oath before His attribute of justice could demand a worse punishment.

35. אִם־יִרְאֶה אִישׁ בָּאֲנָשִׁים הָאֵלֶּה — *If even a man of these people.* This refers to the spies, who slandered the Holy Land; and "this evil generation" refers to those who believed their slander.

36. זוּלָתִי כָּלֵב . . . הוּא יִרְאֶנָּה — *Except for Caleb . . . he shall see it.* Why is Joshua not mentioned? In *Parashas Shelach*, as well, Joshua is not mentioned the first time God reveals who shall be excluded from punishment: "But My servant Caleb, because . . . he followed Me wholeheartedly" (*Bamidbar* 14:24). The same language is used again here: "because he followed Hashem wholeheartedly." For he aggressively thwarted the slanderers; as the Torah says, "Caleb silenced the people."

Only the second time the Torah speaks about exclusion from punishment does it say, "except for Caleb . . . and Joshua" (*Bamidbar* 14:30). As we explained there, Joshua was treated measure for measure. At first he did not join Caleb in contradicting the other spies, perhaps because he thought they would not listen to him since he was the "servant of Moses." But the second time he rent his garments along with Caleb, and they both said: "The Land is very, very good." This is why the Torah only praises him in the second declaration.

The Torah mentions Joshua as the one who will bring the Children of Israel into the Holy Land. Through his appointment to this mission, he was forgiven for the sin of not joining Caleb at first in "following God wholeheartedly." This explanation is in accordance with *Talmud Yerushalmi* (*Bikkurim* 3:3), which states that "three are forgiven for their sins: one who is appointed [to a position of leadership], a proselyte, and a bridegroom."

37. גַּם־בִּי הִתְאַנַּף ה׳ בִּגְלַלְכֶם — *With me, as well, Hashem became angry because of you.* In verse 13 we find the words, "I shall appoint them as your heads,"

1
34-40

34 HASHEM heard the sound of your words, and He was
incensed and He swore, saying, 35 "If even a man of these
people, this evil generation, shall see the good Land that I
swore to give to your forefathers. 36 Except for Caleb son of
Jephunneh: He shall see it, and to him shall I give the Land on
which he walked, and to his children, because he followed
HASHEM wholeheartedly."
37 With me, as well, HASHEM became angry because of you,
saying: You, too, shall not come there. 38 Joshua son of Nun,
who stands before you, he shall come there; strengthen him,
for he shall cause Israel to inherit it. 39 And as for your small
children, of whom you said, "They will be taken captive,"
and your children who did not know good from evil this day
— they will come there; to them shall I give it and they shall
possess it. 40 And as for you, turn yourselves around and
journey to the Wilderness, toward the Sea of Reeds.

---

which *Rashi* explains may be read as "their guilt shall be upon your heads." For the guilt of the nation is upon the heads of its judges.

Here Moses rebukes the judges for not protesting, for not warning the people, or for making errors in leadership. But Moses also erred in agreeing to send the spies, for he should have immediately responded: "God will make war for you, and the pillar of cloud will show us the way — why should we send spies?" Instead, he even asked the spies to seek additional information that the people had not demanded, such as, "Is it good? And the nation . . . is it strong?" Because of these errors in judgment, he was punished with the decree: "You, too, shall not come there."

But God chose to conceal this to protect Moses' honor, and found another reason not to allow Moses and Aaron to enter the Land — the incident at *Mei Merivah* (the Waters of Stife). However, Moses demonstrated his great humility by revealing the true reason to the people. He desired to do this, as he felt it might console the new generation, bereaved of its parents, with the knowledge that the "shepherd" had fallen where the "flock" had fallen.

Furthermore, at *Mei Merivah*, when Moses said things that would have been better left unsaid, he was also punished for his unintentional sin with the spies (for he thought that if he did not send the spies the people would rise up in rebellion). This was because at the incident of the spies he had left unsaid what should have been said — the words of rebuke which were uttered too late.

38. הָעֹמֵד לְפָנֶיךָ — *Who stands before you.* This is a reference to Joshua being Moses' student, and a student is compared to a son.

40. וּסְעוּ הַמִּדְבָּרָה דֶּרֶךְ יַם־סוּף — *And journey to the Wilderness toward the Sea of Reeds.* The road that leads to the Sea of Reeds is the way back to Egypt! How could Moses say this? Had not the people just said, "Let us appoint a leader

א מא־מה

מא וַתַּעֲנוּ ׀ וַתֹּאמְרוּ אֵלַי חָטָאנוּ לַיהוה אֲנַחְנוּ נַעֲלֶה
וְנִלְחַמְנוּ כְּכֹל אֲשֶׁר־צִוָּנוּ יהוה אֱלֹהֵינוּ וַתַּחְגְּרוּ אִישׁ
אֶת־כְּלֵי מִלְחַמְתּוֹ וַתָּהִינוּ לַעֲלֹת הָהָרָה: מב וַיֹּאמֶר
יהוה אֵלַי אֱמֹר לָהֶם לֹא תַעֲלוּ וְלֹא־תִלָּחֲמוּ כִּי
אֵינֶנִּי בְּקִרְבְּכֶם וְלֹא תִּנָּגְפוּ לִפְנֵי אֹיְבֵיכֶם: מג וָאֲדַבֵּר
אֲלֵיכֶם וְלֹא שְׁמַעְתֶּם וַתַּמְרוּ אֶת־פִּי יהוה וַתָּזִדוּ
וַתַּעֲלוּ הָהָרָה: מד וַיֵּצֵא הָאֱמֹרִי הַיֹּשֵׁב בָּהָר הַהוּא
לִקְרַאתְכֶם וַיִּרְדְּפוּ אֶתְכֶם כַּאֲשֶׁר תַּעֲשֶׂינָה הַדְּבֹרִים
וַיַּכְּתוּ אֶתְכֶם בְּשֵׂעִיר עַד־חָרְמָה: מה וַתָּשֻׁבוּ וַתִּבְכּוּ לִפְנֵי
יהוה וְלֹא־שָׁמַע יהוה בְּקֹלְכֶם וְלֹא הֶאֱזִין אֲלֵיכֶם:

---

and let us return to Egypt" (*Bamidbar* 14:4)? Only after the slandering spies had died in the plague and the people who insisted on ascending to the Land had been struck down did they abandon their evil thought of returning to Egypt. So why does Moses tell them now, in God's name, that they must turn back along the road to the Sea of Reeds — and Egypt?

The Sea of Reeds splits into two gulfs at its northern end, one to the west (the Gulf of Suez) bordering on Egypt at Raamses, and one to the east (the Gulf of Aqaba) which ends at Eilat and Etzion-geber. Between these two gulfs lies the huge Sinai Peninsula, containing Mount Sinai and the wildernesses of Shur, Sin, Sinai, and Paran. The Children of Israel were now being commanded, not to "return" to the Sea of Reeds (the western gulf, which they had already passed through) but to "turn and journey" to a new place — "to the Wilderness toward the Sea of Reeds" — i.e., the eastern arm of the Sea of Reeds, towards Eilat and Etzion-geber. This is how they came to the Mountain of Seir, which is in the vicinity of Etzion-geber. Later, Moses mentions that "we circled Mount Seir for many days" (2:1) and "we passed from our brothers, the children of Esau who dwell in Seir, from the way of the Arabah, from Elath and from Etzion-geber" (2:8). Clearly, then, this phrase refers to the eastern arm of the Sea of Reeds. Hence, whenever this phrase appears in the Torah, it is not translated as "by way of the Sea of Reeds," but rather "toward the Sea of Reeds." Actually, one need only look at a map to see that this is the correct explanation.

41. וַתַּעֲנוּ וַתֹּאמְרוּ אֵלַי חָטָאנוּ לַה׳ — *Then you spoke up and said to me, "We have sinned to Hashem!"* Perhaps by behaving this way they were straying into the ways of idolaters, who customarily confess sins before their priests. This is not the way of Israel, who confess their sins directly before God — after asking forgiveness from the person they have wronged, if it is a sin between man and his neighbor. The Jewish people ultimately realized their error and wept before God. But it was too late, since the sentence had already been passed.

44. כַּאֲשֶׁר תַּעֲשֶׂינָה הַדְּבֹרִים — *As the bees would do.* Bees make honey, but also sting. When the beekeeper goes to collect honey, first he lights a fire with

41 *Then you spoke up and said to me, "We have sinned to*
HASHEM! We shall go up and do battle according to
everything that HASHEM, our God, has commanded us!"
Every man of you girded his weapons of war, and you were
ready to ascend the mountain!
42 *HASHEM said to me: Tell them, "Do not ascend and do*
not do battle, for I am not among you; so that you not be
struck down before your enemies."
43 *So I spoke to you, but you did not listen. You rebelled*
against the word of HASHEM, and you were willful and
climbed the mountain. 44 *The Amorite who dwell on that*
mountain went out against you and pursued you as the bees
would do; they struck you in Seir until Hormah. 45 *Then*
you retreated and wept before HASHEM, but HASHEM did
not listen to your voice and He did not hearken to you.

---

green wood, which sends up a lot of smoke. The bees smell the smoke and run inside the hive and cower, leaving the keeper free to take his honey unmolested. When a stranger comes to steal honey, he cannot make a fire and produce this smoke, lest the keeper see it. He must, therefore, approach the hive unshielded, and the bees fall upon him, stinging him liberally, and preventing him from taking the honey. In the end, he is forced to flee for his life.

So it was with these men who insisted on climbing the mountain. If they had been going to take lawful possession of the Land, having received God's command, "Go up and possess," then the pillar of cloud would have gone before them, with the Ark of the Covenant, from whose rods flashes of fire would go forth to strike Israel's enemies (*Bamidbar Rabbah* 5:1). The Amorites would either have been burnt or would have fled from the Jews like bees from the smoke, and the Jewish people would have been unmolested as they took the "honey" — i.e., the land flowing with it.

But when these willful people barged in unlawfully, they were like thieves seeking to take honey from the hive without a smokescreen. For they went without the pillar of cloud, and "the Ark of God's covenant and Moses did not move from the midst of God's camp." The Amorites fell upon them "like bees" and stung them. Thus they did not get the honey, only the stings.

45. וַתָּשֻׁבוּ וַתִּבְכּוּ לִפְנֵי ה׳ וְלֹא־שָׁמַע ה׳ בְּקֹלְכֶם — *Then you retreated and wept before Hashem, but Hashem did not listen to your voice.* Not even God's attribute of mercy was aroused. Although the Sages teach that "the gates of tears are never locked" before our prayers, it is different once God has sworn a heavenly decree (v. 34). Consequently gates were made, for if the heavens were open wide to tears under *all conditions*, there would be no need for gates to open and close. But when a sentence has been pronounced with a heavenly oath, even the "gates of tears" are hermetically sealed and do not open to receive appeals.

א מו וַתֵּשְׁבוּ בְקָדֵשׁ יָמִים רַבִּים כַּיָּמִים אֲשֶׁר יְשַׁבְתֶּם׃
מו א וַנֵּפֶן וַנִּסַּע הַמִּדְבָּרָה דֶּרֶךְ יַם־סוּף כַּאֲשֶׁר דִּבֶּר יהוה אֵלָי
ב וַנָּסָב אֶת־הַר־שֵׂעִיר יָמִים רַבִּים׃ חמישי ב וַיֹּאמֶר
א־ד יהוה אֵלַי לֵאמֹר׃ ג רַב־לָכֶם סֹב אֶת־הָהָר הַזֶּה פְּנוּ
לָכֶם צָפֹנָה׃ ד וְאֶת־הָעָם צַו לֵאמֹר אַתֶּם עֹבְרִים

---

46. וַתֵּשְׁבוּ בְקָדֵשׁ יָמִים רַבִּים כַּיָּמִים אֲשֶׁר יְשַׁבְתֶּם — *You dwelt in Kadesh for many days, as many days as you dwelt.* The *Rashbam* explains the phrase, "As many days as you dwelt," to means, "as many as you know." But this explanation seems forced. Moreover, if this is what's implied, the verse tells us nothing. *Ibn Ezra* interprets: "As many as the number of days you spent spying out the Land — that is, forty days. The Children of Israel stayed at Kadesh for forty days, until the spies returned" (*Ibn Ezra* and *Mekor Chaim* on the *Ibn Ezra*). But this, too, is a strained explanation.

Rashi, however, explains the verse according to the *Seder Olam*. They dwelt at Kadesh for the exact length of time that they had wandered in the Wilderness. According to this interpretation, the prayers and cries of the Children of Israel were partially effective. God allowed them to wander for only nineteen years and to dwell in a settled fashion in Kadesh for another nineteen years, until all the men of military age had died. In that case, when the verse says, "You dwelt at Kadesh ... as many days as you dwelt," the second "dwelt" means "you spent time." You spent time in the Wilderness, wandering homeless. The first "dwelt" actually means dwelling — at rest — for it is followed by the words "at Kadesh."

The words "for many days" appear to tell us of God's kindness in giving the Children of Israel "many days" of rest, even after their wandering had been decreed. The *Seder Olam* teaches that they wandered in exile for nineteen years and then dwelt at Kadesh for another nineteen years. In other words, after spending nineteen years wandering, God relented and allowed them to spend the next nineteen years quietly at Kadesh. *Rashi* interprets it in the opposite way: that they stayed at Kadesh for the first nineteen years and then wandered in exile for the next nineteen years, finally returning to Kadesh. According to this view, we are obliged to conclude that God also exempted them from His original command, "Tomorrow, turn and journey toward the Wilderness in the direction of the Sea of Reeds" (*Bamidbar* 14:25).

I cannot understand why *Rashi* gave a contrary interpretation to the one found in *Seder Olam*. He may have considered it to be too forced, for accordingly, the Jewish people spent the last nineteen years at Kadesh-barnea. Yet, in the fortieth year of their exodus from Egypt (the thirty-eighth and last year of the punishment) they had suddenly reached the other Kadesh, which is on the border of Edom, where Miriam died on the tenth of Nissan. Moreover, this journey was so long that it was made in nineteen stages, between Rithmah (the place to which the spies were sent, according to *Rashi*) and "the

1 46 *You dwelt in Kadesh for many days, as many days as*
46 *you dwelt.*
2 1 *We turned and journeyed to the Wilderness toward the*
1-4 *Sea of Reeds, as HASHEM spoke to me, and we circled Mount*
Seir for many days.
2 *HASHEM said to me, saying:* 3 *Enough of your circling*
this mountain; turn yourselves northward. 4 *You shall*
command the people, saying, "You are passing through

Wilderness of Zin, which is Kadesh." (These journeys are listed in *Parashas Masei*.)

2.

1. וַנָּסָב אֶת־הַר־שֵׂעִיר יָמִים רַבִּים — *And we circled Mount Seir for many days.* Please refer to our comments to the previous verse. Here we find some support for *Rashi's* view. This verse may be understood to imply that after the Jewish people had dwelt at Kadesh-barnea for nineteen years, they wandered through the Wilderness towards the Sea of Reeds (the "tongue" of the Sea of Reeds, at the site of modern-day Eilat), thus encircling Mount Seir. This encircling procedure took "many days," that is, nineteen years, the same length of time that they dwelt at Kadesh.

◆§ יָמִים רַבִּים — *Many days.* This is the same phrase used in the previous verse: "You dwelt in Kadesh for many days." In both places the phrase has a double meaning: its literal one, or by implication, days of suffering (*Shemos Rabbah*, Ch. 1). For the bad days seem long and the good days seem short; as the Torah says of Jacob, "and they seemed to him a few days because of his love for her" (*Bereishis* 29:20).

3. רַב־לָכֶם סֹב אֶת־הָהָר הַזֶּה — *Enough of your circling this mountain.* This directive informs Moses that they had come around to the furthest point of the southeast border of Edom. They would now turn northward and follow the eastern border of Edom in a northerly direction, without setting foot in Edom itself, for they had been forbidden to do so.

4. וְאֶת־הָעָם צַו — *You shall command the people.* God's command concerning Moab, and even Ammon, the nation which we were forbidden to provoke in any way, was directed only to Moses. It was understood that Moses would see to it that the Jewish people observed the prohibition. Why, then, is there a special warning to "the people" regarding Edom? This was a reward to Esau for his kindness towards Jacob by coming to meet him with four hundred men. Esau himself and his men refrained from laying a hand on Jacob and his family. They neither attempted to rob him, nor seize anything as a "reward for their trouble." Presumably Esau ordered his men not to harm Jacob. Therefore, this commandment is worded measure for measure: "You shall

ב בִּגְבוּל֙ אֲחֵיכֶ֣ם בְּנֵי־עֵשָׂ֔ו הַיֹּשְׁבִ֖ים בְּשֵׂעִ֑יר וְיִֽירְא֣וּ מִכֶּ֔ם
ה־ז וְנִשְׁמַרְתֶּ֖ם מְאֹֽד׃ ה אַל־תִּתְגָּר֣וּ בָ֔ם כִּ֠י לֹא־אֶתֵּ֤ן לָכֶם֙
מֵֽאַרְצָ֔ם עַ֖ד מִדְרַ֣ךְ כַּף־רָ֑גֶל כִּֽי־יְרֻשָּׁ֣ה לְעֵשָׂ֔ו נָתַ֖תִּי אֶת־הַ֥ר
שֵׂעִֽיר׃ ו אֹ֣כֶל תִּשְׁבְּר֧וּ מֵֽאִתָּ֛ם בַּכֶּ֖סֶף וַאֲכַלְתֶּ֑ם וְגַם־מַ֜יִם
תִּכְר֧וּ מֵֽאִתָּ֛ם בַּכֶּ֖סֶף וּשְׁתִיתֶֽם׃ ז כִּי֩ יהוֹה אֱלֹהֶ֜יךָ בֵּֽרַכְךָ֗ בְּכֹל֙

---

command the people ... you should be very careful ... you shall not provoke them."

בִּגְבוּל אֲחֵיכֶם בְּנֵי־עֵשָׂו — *The boundary of your brothers the children of Esau.* The children of Ishmael are also a branch of our genealogical tree, yet we never find Scripture calling them "our brothers." Why, then, does the Torah use this description when referring to the Edomites, who have wronged us more than any other nation? Surely they deserve to be called "our brothers" even less than the Ishmaelites.

The Torah uses this expression for the sole purpose of rewarding Esau measure for measure. For when Jacob came into his hands, Esau spoke kindly to him, saying, "I have plenty, my brother" (*Bereishis* 33:9).

וְיִירְאוּ מִכֶּם — *They will fear you.* The Torah informs us that "Jacob became very frightened, and ... distressed" (ibid. 32:7) at the thought of a possible war with Esau and his men. Just as that fear proved unnecessary, so would the fear of Esau's children be unnecessary, for the Children of Israel would not harm them.

As for Jacob's distress, *Chazal* explain that Jacob was "frightened" lest he be killed, and "distressed" lest he would be forced to kill others. But this is not said of Esau's children, for if they had been given the chance to kill the Children of Israel, they would not have been distressed at all.

וְיִירְאוּ מִכֶּם וְנִשְׁמַרְתֶּם מְאֹד — *They will fear you, but you should be very careful.* When soldiers see that the enemy's troops are afraid, they seize the opportunity to attack. The Torah, therefore, tells the Jewish people to "be very careful" — to resist the temptation.

5. **כִּי לֹא־אֶתֵּן לָכֶם מֵאַרְצָם עַד מִדְרַךְ כַּף־רָגֶל** — *For I shall not give you of their land even the right to set foot.* Of Moab the Torah says, "for I shall not give you an inheritance from their land" (v. 9), and regarding Ammon the Torah speaks in a similar way. Why when speaking of Esau does the Torah add the words "even the right to set foot?"

We must recall that Esau, like Jacob, was an heir to *Eretz Yisrael*, only he chose Seir as his particular portion of the inheritance. (Seir was among the ten lands that God promised to Abraham.) Esau's choice included the proviso that his brother Jacob would take upon himself the debt of "your offspring shall be aliens," and in return Jacob would receive all of *Eretz Yisrael* as his portion.

2 *the boundary of your brothers the children of Esau, who*
5-7 *dwell in Seir; they will fear you, but you should be very*
careful. 5 *You shall not provoke them, for I shall not give you*
of their land even the right to set foot, for as an inheritance to
the children of Esau have I given Mount Seir. 6 *You shall*
purchase food from them for money so that you may eat;
also water shall you buy from them for money so that you
may drink. 7 *For* HASHEM, *your God, has blessed you in all*

The Jewish people now wished to cross Mount Seir on their way to claim their inheritance, the Land of Israel. Did they have the right? According to Rava (*Bava Basra* 7b), when brothers divide an inheritance, they retain the right of passage over each other's land. Thus, the Jewish people had the right to cross Mount Seir on their way to their portion. However, Shmuel maintains (ibid.) that brothers do not retain right of passage. As his view is the accepted one, Rava's opinion isn't even applicable. In fact, R' Nachman added words of caution to Shmuel's ruling: "Be careful of these matters, for they are definite *halachos.*" *Rambam* also concludes that brothers have no right of passage over each other's land (*Hilchos Shecheinim*, Chapter 2).

God, therefore, told Moses that in addition to His not giving the Jewish people a portion in Mount Seir, which is Esau's inheritance, they also had no right to cross his land without permission.

Ammon and Moab had never claimed brotherhood with Israel, nor had they divided any land with them. God had given them homes in the Kenite and Kenizite lands as a gift to keep until the coming of the Messiah. It was, therefore, understood that the Jewish people had no right to pass through their land unauthorized.

6. אֹכֶל תִּשְׁבְּרוּ . . . וַאֲכַלְתֶּם וְגַם־מַיִם . . . וּשְׁתִיתֶם — *You shall purchase food . . . so that you may eat; also water . . . so that you may drink.* Why does the Torah bother mentioning "eating" and "drinking?" What else would people do with food and water?

Melo HaOmer explains that this construction was intended to reassure the people, who might otherwise have feared that the local inhabitants would poison the food and water. God told the Jewish people that these nations feared them and knew they would strike back in response to such an act. Therefore, the Jewish people had no need to fear.

Ka'aras Kesef offers a different explanation: Take only a little, whatever could be consumed on the spot, but do not take provisions for the way. After all, they had lacked nothing for forty years. Why should they begin to worry now?

Yet, I believe that in this verse the Torah is reacting to the slander spoken by the Children of Israel regarding the manna, "Our soul is disgusted with the insubstantial food" (*Bamidbar* 21:5). Undoubtedly, there were those who also found fault with the water from Miriam's well (see *Ha'amek Davar* to

ב מַעֲשֵׂה יָדֶךָ יָדַע לֶכְתְּךָ אֶת־הַמִּדְבָּר הַגָּדֹל הַזֶּה זֶה ׀
ח־יא אַרְבָּעִים שָׁנָה יהוה אֱלֹהֶיךָ עִמָּךְ לֹא חָסַרְתָּ דָּבָר: ח וַנַּעֲבֹר
מֵאֵת אַחֵינוּ בְנֵי־עֵשָׂו הַיֹּשְׁבִים בְּשֵׂעִיר מִדֶּרֶךְ הָעֲרָבָה
מֵאֵילַת וּמֵעֶצְיֹן גָּבֶר וַנֵּפֶן וַנַּעֲבֹר דֶּרֶךְ מִדְבַּר
מוֹאָב: ט וַיֹּאמֶר יהוה אֵלַי אַל־תָּצַר אֶת־מוֹאָב וְאַל־תִּתְגָּר
בָּם מִלְחָמָה כִּי לֹא־אֶתֵּן לְךָ מֵאַרְצוֹ יְרֻשָּׁה כִּי לִבְנֵי־לוֹט
נָתַתִּי אֶת־עָר יְרֻשָּׁה: י הָאֵמִים לְפָנִים יָשְׁבוּ בָהּ עַם גָּדוֹל
וְרַב וָרָם כַּעֲנָקִים: יא רְפָאִים יֵחָשְׁבוּ אַף־הֵם כַּעֲנָקִים

(*Bamidbar* 21:5), in a similar manner to what had occurred after Moses sweetened the water at Marah (refer to our commentary to *Shemos* 15:23). Perhaps the reason Moses asked, "shall we bring forth water for you from this rock?" (*Bamidbar* 20:10), referred to the choice of the rock, lest they complain afterwards that they would have picked a rock which could produce sweeter water!

The Jewish people had been journeying around the border of Edom for some time and were excited by the prospect of buying bread — real bread from the ground, not from the sky — and water — real, natural water. God, therefore, advised them to go ahead and buy some, then eat and drink. Finally they would discover that they had indeed lacked nothing for forty years in the Wilderness, with bread from Heaven and water from Miriam's well. In fact, their Heavenly provisions were superior to "the real thing," since they contained God's blessing and tasted like anything the eater desired, not just like plain bread and water.

וְגַם־מַיִם תִּכְרוּ מֵאִתָּם בַּכֶּסֶף — *Also water shall you buy from them for money.* Why does the Torah make a separate statement about water? Food and water could have been mentioned together in a single sentence; for example: "Food and water shall you purchase from them for money, so that you may eat and drink." And why is the unusual word תִּכְרוּ used here?

The Torah uses this uncommon term to tell us something about water. In order to obtain drinking water, the Jewish people may have considered digging a cistern on Edomite land, without permission. The Torah's expression for digging a cistern is כִּי יִכְרֶה אִישׁ בֹּר (*Shemos* 21:33). The same wording is used here to warn the Jewish people specifically about water. If they want to dig (תִּכְרוּ) for water, they must buy (תִּכְרוּ) the water! Even if a new water supply is produced through your own effort and labor and will be left for the Edomites after you leave, nevertheless such a thing cannot be done without permission and full payment.

בַּכֶּסֶף . . . בַּכֶּסֶף — *For money . . . for money.* This warning is repeated for emphasis. They should not accept gifts from Esau's children, in order not to develop a feeling of closeness with them and become influenced by their behavior.

your handiwork; He knew your way in this great Wilder-
ness; this forty-year period HASHEM, *your God, was with*
you; you did not lack a thing.'' 8 *So we passed from our*
brothers, the children of Esau who dwell in Seir, from the way
of the Arabah, from Elath and from Ezion-geber and we
turned and passed on the way of the Moabite desert.
9 HASHEM *said to me: You shall not distress Moab and you*
shall not provoke war with them, for I shall not give you an
inheritance from their land, for to the children of Lot have I
given Ar as an inheritance. 10 *The Emim dwelled there*
previously, a great and populous people, and tall as the
giants. 11 *They, too, were considered Rephaim, like the giants;*

---

8. וַנַּעֲבֹר מֵאֵת אַחֵינוּ בְנֵי־עֵשָׂו — *So we passed from our brothers, the children of Esau.* And we did no harm whatsoever to them, even though we were capable of doing so. This is parallel to Esau acceding to Jacob's request, ''Let my lord go ahead of his servant'' (*Bereishis* 33:14), and Esau did so without doing Jacob any harm. Yet, Esau acceded partially in response to the rich gifts that Jacob had just sent him, whereas we did not receive any gift from Esau's children. On the contrary, we provided them with benefit, for they reaped great profit from selling us bread and water. Thus, one good turn paid for another, and the slate was now clean between Israel and Edom.

But from that day on Edom have ''done worse to us than all the kingdoms of the earth'' (*Mussaf* of Yom Kippur), having destroyed our Holy Temple and sent us into exile. And Ovadiah prophesied regarding the future: ''As you have done, so shall be done to you; your reward will come down on your head.... Saviors shall arise on Mount Zion to judge the mountain of Esau, and kingship will be God's'' (*Ovadiah* 1:21).

10. הָאֵמִים לְפָנִים יָשְׁבוּ בָהּ — *The Emim dwelled there previously.* This verse appears here lest the Jewish people complain: ''It's all very well for Esau. He gave up all of *Eretz Yisrael*, and chose Mount Seir as his sole inheritance to avoid 'paying his debt' ('Your offspring shall be aliens' — *Bereishis* 15:13). In return, he received his land without fighting many strong nations. But Moab is not our brother, like Esau. How did he earn his own land without fighting for it?''

Therefore, God made sure to record that ''a great and populous people, and tall as the giants'' once dwelt here. Their original name was רְפָאִים (weakening), for whoever saw them felt a weakening in his hands. The Moabites, too, called them אֵמִים (fearsome), for everyone was afraid of them. Yet the Moabites were still able to fight against them and wipe them out. And even Esau, whose land was his promised inheritance, did not obtain it until he had fought the Horites who then inhabited it. So the Jewish people could have no justification for complaining about having to fight for *Eretz Yisrael*.

וְהַמֹּאָבִים יִקְרְאוּ לָהֶם אֵמִים: יב וּבְשֵׂעִיר יָשְׁבוּ הַחֹרִים ב
לְפָנִים וּבְנֵי עֵשָׂו יִירָשׁוּם וַיַּשְׁמִידוּם מִפְּנֵיהֶם וַיֵּשְׁבוּ תַּחְתָּם יב־כב
כַּאֲשֶׁר עָשָׂה יִשְׂרָאֵל לְאֶרֶץ יְרֻשָּׁתוֹ אֲשֶׁר־נָתַן יהוה לָהֶם:
יג עַתָּה קֻמוּ וְעִבְרוּ לָכֶם אֶת־נַחַל זָרֶד וַנַּעֲבֹר אֶת־נַחַל
זָרֶד: יד וְהַיָּמִים אֲשֶׁר־הָלַכְנוּ ׀ מִקָּדֵשׁ בַּרְנֵעַ עַד אֲשֶׁר־
עָבַרְנוּ אֶת־נַחַל זֶרֶד שְׁלֹשִׁים וּשְׁמֹנֶה שָׁנָה עַד־תֹּם
כָּל־הַדּוֹר אַנְשֵׁי הַמִּלְחָמָה מִקֶּרֶב הַמַּחֲנֶה כַּאֲשֶׁר נִשְׁבַּע
יהוה לָהֶם: טו וְגַם יַד־יהוה הָיְתָה בָּם לְהֻמָּם מִקֶּרֶב הַמַּחֲנֶה
עַד תֻּמָּם: טז וַיְהִי כַאֲשֶׁר־תַּמּוּ כָּל־אַנְשֵׁי הַמִּלְחָמָה לָמוּת
מִקֶּרֶב הָעָם: יז וַיְדַבֵּר יהוה אֵלַי לֵאמֹר:
יח אַתָּה עֹבֵר הַיּוֹם אֶת־גְּבוּל מוֹאָב אֶת־עָר: יט וְקָרַבְתָּ מוּל
בְּנֵי עַמּוֹן אַל־תְּצֻרֵם וְאַל־תִּתְגָּר בָּם כִּי לֹא־אֶתֵּן מֵאֶרֶץ
בְּנֵי־עַמּוֹן לְךָ יְרֻשָּׁה כִּי לִבְנֵי־לוֹט נְתַתִּיהָ יְרֻשָּׁה: כ אֶרֶץ־
רְפָאִים תֵּחָשֵׁב אַף־הִוא רְפָאִים יָשְׁבוּ־בָהּ לְפָנִים וְהָעַמֹּנִים
יִקְרְאוּ לָהֶם זַמְזֻמִּים: כא עַם גָּדוֹל וְרַב וָרָם כָּעֲנָקִים
וַיַּשְׁמִידֵם יהוה מִפְּנֵיהֶם וַיִּירָשֻׁם וַיֵּשְׁבוּ תַחְתָּם: כב כַּאֲשֶׁר
עָשָׂה לִבְנֵי עֵשָׂו הַיֹּשְׁבִים בְּשֵׂעִיר אֲשֶׁר הִשְׁמִיד אֶת־הַחֹרִי

---

14. עַד אֲשֶׁר־עָבַרְנוּ אֶת־נַחַל זֶרֶד שְׁלֹשִׁים וּשְׁמֹנֶה שָׁנָה — *Until we crossed Zered Brook were thirty-eight years.* Why did Moses make this calculation at this point? The Children of Israel had come to the edge of their destined land and went on to take Zered Brook away from Sihon. (Later, when it became part of Gad's hereditary land, it was called "Divon of Gad," see *Bamidbar* 21:12.) Thus it was appropriate for Moses to stop now and remind the people that from Kadesh-barnea, the point of the spies's departure, to Zered Brook, on the edge of their inheritance, thirty-eight years had passed. Even though the decree was that "your children will roam in the Wilderness for forty years," God in His mercy counted their time in the Wilderness before the Sin of the Spies — almost two years — as part of the decree.

19. וְקָרַבְתָּ מוּל בְּנֵי עַמּוֹן — *And you shall approach opposite the children of Ammon.* "From here we learn that the land of Ammon lies to the north" (*Rashi*).

I don't think that the Jewish people needed to pass through the land of the children of Ammon. For the land of Sihon was located between Ammon and Moab and consisted of territory, the major part of which had been conquered by him from Ammon and Moab (*Bamidbar* 21:27-29; *Gittin* 38a; see also *Yehoshua* 13:25, *Shoftim* 11:13). So once the Children of Israel had conquered the land of Sihon, it sufficed to open a clear path for them to the Jordan and the Land of Israel. This, then, is why the Torah says, "opposite

2
12-22

and the Moabites called them Emim. 12 *And in Seir the*
Horites dwelled previously, and the children of Esau drove
them away from before themselves and dwelled in their
place, as Israel did to the Land of its inheritance, which
HASHEM gave them. 13 *Now, rise up and get yourselves across*
Zered Brook — so we crossed Zered Brook.

14 *The days that we traveled from Kadesh-barnea until we*
crossed Zered Brook were thirty-eight years, until the end of
the entire generation, the men of war, from the midst of the
camp, as HASHEM swore to them. 15 *Even the hand of HASHEM*
was on them to confound them from amid the camp, until
their end. 16 *So it was that the men of war finished dying from*
amidst the people . . .

17 *HASHEM spoke to me, saying:* 18 *This day you shall cross*
the border of Moab, at Ar, 19 *and you shall approach opposite*
the children of Ammon; you shall not distress them and you
shall not provoke them, for I shall not give any of the land of
the children of Ammon to you as an inheritance, for to the
children of Lot have I given it as an inheritance. 20 *It, too, is*
considered the land of the Rephaim; the Rephaim dwelled in
it previously, and the Ammonites called them Zamzumim.
21 *A great and populous people, and tall as giants, and*
HASHEM destroyed them before them, and they drove them
out and dwelled in their place, 22 *just as he did for the*
children of Esau who dwell in Seir, who destroyed the Horite

---

the children of Ammon," not through their midst. In case the people might take it into their heads to conquer the rest of the country still possessed by the Ammonites, the Torah adds the warning "You shall not distress them and you shall not provoke them."

21-22. וַיַּשְׁמִידֵם ה׳ מִפְּנֵיהֶם. . . . כַּאֲשֶׁר עָשָׂה לִבְנֵי עֵשָׂו . . . אֲשֶׁר הִשְׁמִיד אֶת־הַחֹרִי — *And Hashem destroyed them before them. . . . just as He did for the children of Esau . . . who destroyed the Horite.* The Torah just mentioned (v. 12) how the children of Esau destroyed the Horites; why does it have to repeat this again now? In verses 9-13, the basic context is the Moabites and their ancestral claim to the land of Ar. Seir and the Horites are only an aside. God was not willing to have His name mentioned in such a context. For מוֹאָב signifies מֵאָב, "from my father," a shameless flaunting of an act of incest (see *Rashi* to *Bereishis* 19:37). Therefore, when the Torah mentions that the Zamzumim had been driven out, it also explains how Esau's children drove out the Horites, noting that their success was supernatural, brought about by Divine will. This supernatural conquest occurred so that they would take Mount Seir as theirs and relinquish their claims on *Eretz Yisrael.*

ב מִפְּנֵיהֶם וַיִּירָשֻׁם וַיֵּשְׁבוּ תַחְתָּם עַד הַיּוֹם הַזֶּה: כג וְהָעַוִּים
כג־כט הַיֹּשְׁבִים בַּחֲצֵרִים עַד־עַזָּה כַּפְתֹּרִים הַיֹּצְאִים מִכַּפְתֹּר
הִשְׁמִידֻם וַיֵּשְׁבוּ תַחְתָּם: כד קוּמוּ סְּעוּ וְעִבְרוּ אֶת־נַחַל אַרְנֹן
רְאֵה נָתַתִּי בְיָדְךָ אֶת־סִיחֹן מֶלֶךְ־חֶשְׁבּוֹן הָאֱמֹרִי וְאֶת־
אַרְצוֹ הָחֵל רָשׁ וְהִתְגָּר בּוֹ מִלְחָמָה: כה הַיּוֹם הַזֶּה אָחֵל תֵּת
פַּחְדְּךָ וְיִרְאָתְךָ עַל־פְּנֵי הָעַמִּים תַּחַת כָּל־הַשָּׁמָיִם אֲשֶׁר
יִשְׁמְעוּן שִׁמְעֲךָ וְרָגְזוּ וְחָלוּ מִפָּנֶיךָ: כו וָאֶשְׁלַח מַלְאָכִים
מִמִּדְבַּר קְדֵמוֹת אֶל־סִיחוֹן מֶלֶךְ חֶשְׁבּוֹן דִּבְרֵי שָׁלוֹם
לֵאמֹר: כז אֶעְבְּרָה בְאַרְצֶךָ בַּדֶּרֶךְ בַּדֶּרֶךְ אֵלֵךְ לֹא אָסוּר
יָמִין וּשְׂמֹאול: כח אֹכֶל בַּכֶּסֶף תַּשְׁבִּרֵנִי וְאָכַלְתִּי וּמַיִם בַּכֶּסֶף
תִּתֶּן־לִי וְשָׁתִיתִי רַק אֶעְבְּרָה בְרַגְלָי: כט כַּאֲשֶׁר עָשׂוּ־לִי
בְּנֵי עֵשָׂו הַיֹּשְׁבִים בְּשֵׂעִיר וְהַמּוֹאָבִים הַיֹּשְׁבִים בְּעָר עַד

---

23. וְהָעַוִּים . . . כַּפְתֹּרִים . . . הִשְׁמִידֻם — *As for the Avvim . . . the Caphtorim . . . destroyed them.* The Avvim were descendants of the Philistines. Because of Abraham's oath to Avimelech, the Jewish people were forbidden to take their land. So the Caphtorim came and destroyed the Avvim, in order to allow Israel to take their land from the Caphtorim (*Rashi*).

Ramban mentions Rav's opinion (the autoritative opinion in *Chullin* 60), that the Avvim originally came from Yemen, making them a branch of Esau's descendants. This would make their land off limits until taken by the Caphtorim for a different reason.

But what are all these verses about peoples who were driven out doing here? Judging from the context, it seems to me that their purpose was to encourage the Children of Israel. They still remembered the bad report of the spies, "All the people that we saw in it were huge . . . we were like grasshoppers in our eyes" (*Bamidbar* 13:32-33). Moses recently reiterated their sentiments when he said, (1:28) "A people greater and taller than we"... Now they were about to wage war against Sihon and Og, the giant-kings and kings of the Amorites, "whose height is like that of cedar-trees and mighty as oaks" (*Amos* 2:9). God, therefore, chose to guide them around by the lands of Edom, Moab, and Ammon and tell them that in these lands once lived the Rephaim, Emim, and Zamzumim, "great and populous people, and tall as giants." Nevertheless, God had destroyed them in favor of Edom, Moab, and Ammon, of whom Israel were now afraid. This certainly was no minor accomplishment.

The Caphtorim (כַּפְתֹּרִים) were a pygmy race, not even two feet high (see *Ha'amek Davar* and *Targum Onkelos* ad loc.; *Yechezkel* 27:11 and *Rashi* and *Radak*), and were named after the short and squat buttons (כַּפְתּוֹר) they resembled. Despite their physical appearance, it was God's will that they destroyed the Avvim (עַוִּים), so named because whoever beheld them was struck with עֲוִית, *spasms* (of fear).

before them; they drove them out and dwelled in their place
until this day. 23 *As for the Avvim who dwell in open cities*
until Gaza, the Caphtorim who went out of Caphtor
destroyed them, and dwelled in their place. 24 *Rise up and*
cross Arnon Brook; see! into your hand have I delivered
Sihon king of Heshbon, the Amorite, and his land; begin to
possess it, and provoke war with him. 25 *This day I shall*
begin to place dread and fear of you on the peoples under
the entire heaven, when they hear of your reputation, and
they will tremble and be anxious before you."

26 *I sent messengers from the Wilderness of Kedemoth*
to Sihon king of Heshbon, words of peace, saying, 27 *"Let*
me pass through your land; only on the road shall I go; I
will not stray right or left. 28 *Food shall I purchase for*
money as provisions, and I will eat; and you will give
me water for money, and I shall drink — only let me pass
with my foot-goers; 29 *as the children of Esau who dwell*
in Seir did for me, and the Moabites who dwell in Ar — until

All this was said in order to bolster the hearts of the Children of Israel, so they would not fear their enemies' physical strength.

24. הָחֵל רָשׁ וְהִתְגָּר בּוֹ מִלְחָמָה — *Begin to possess it, and provoke war with him.* The structuring of the verse seems incorrect, since first one wages war and then, after defeating the enemy, one possesses his land. But the order given is how it actually happened. The Jewish people were obliged to go through the Wilderness while they circled the lands of Edom and Moab, for they were forbidden to provoke war with them. They, therefore, went through the Wilderness just past the border until they came to the border of Moab at Arnon Brook ("for Arnon is the border of Moab" — *Bamidbar* 21:13), where the kingdom of Sihon began. Then they came out of the Wilderness and into the settled land around Arnon Brook. Thus God said to Moses, "Begin to possess it" — that is, the land around the brook, and then "provoke war with the Amorites" in order to take possession of their entire land.

25. תַּחַת כָּל־הַשָּׁמָיִם — *Under the entire heaven.* "Which teaches us that the sun stood still for Moses" (*Rashi*). This was to make all peoples aware that God was fighting for Israel against the seven nations, and so that they would not ascribe the victory over Sihon to chance.

29. כַּאֲשֶׁר עָשׂוּ־לִי בְּנֵי עֵשָׂו . . . וְהַמּוֹאָבִים — *As the children of Esau . . . did for me, and the Moabites.* "This did not refer to passing through their land [which the Children of Israel did not do in these two cases], but to selling them food and water" (*Rashi*).

The *Riva* raises a difficulty with *Rashi's* explanation. The Torah decrees: "An Ammonite or a Moabite shall not enter the congregation of Hashem,

ב אֲשֶׁר־אֶעֱבֹר אֶת־הַיַּרְדֵּן אֶל־הָאָרֶץ אֲשֶׁר־יְהוָה אֱלֹהֵינוּ
ל-לז נֹתֵן לָנוּ׃ ל וְלֹא אָבָה סִיחֹן מֶלֶךְ חֶשְׁבּוֹן הַעֲבִרֵנוּ בּוֹ
כִּי־הִקְשָׁה יְהוָה אֱלֹהֶיךָ אֶת־רוּחוֹ וְאִמֵּץ אֶת־לְבָבוֹ לְמַעַן
תִּתּוֹ בְיָדְךָ כַּיּוֹם הַזֶּה׃ ששי לא וַיֹּאמֶר יְהוָה
אֵלַי רְאֵה הַחִלֹּתִי תֵּת לְפָנֶיךָ אֶת־סִיחֹן וְאֶת־אַרְצוֹ הָחֵל
רָשׁ לָרֶשֶׁת אֶת־אַרְצוֹ׃ לב וַיֵּצֵא סִיחֹן לִקְרָאתֵנוּ הוּא
וְכָל־עַמּוֹ לַמִּלְחָמָה יָהְצָה׃ לג וַיִּתְּנֵהוּ יְהוָה אֱלֹהֵינוּ לְפָנֵינוּ
וַנַּךְ אֹתוֹ וְאֶת־בָּנָו וְאֶת־כָּל־עַמּוֹ׃ לד וַנִּלְכֹּד אֶת־כָּל־
עָרָיו בָּעֵת הַהִוא וַנַּחֲרֵם אֶת־כָּל־עִיר מְתִם וְהַנָּשִׁים
וְהַטָּף לֹא הִשְׁאַרְנוּ שָׂרִיד׃ לה רַק הַבְּהֵמָה בָּזַזְנוּ לָנוּ
וּשְׁלַל הֶעָרִים אֲשֶׁר לָכָדְנוּ׃ לו מֵעֲרֹעֵר אֲשֶׁר עַל־שְׂפַת נַחַל
אַרְנֹן וְהָעִיר אֲשֶׁר בַּנַּחַל וְעַד־הַגִּלְעָד לֹא הָיְתָה קִרְיָה
אֲשֶׁר שָׂגְבָה מִמֶּנּוּ אֶת־הַכֹּל נָתַן יְהוָה אֱלֹהֵינוּ לְפָנֵינוּ׃
לז רַק אֶל־אֶרֶץ בְּנֵי־עַמּוֹן לֹא קָרָבְתָּ כָּל־יַד נַחַל יַבֹּק וְעָרֵי
ג הָהָר וְכֹל אֲשֶׁר־צִוָּה יְהוָה אֱלֹהֵינוּ׃ א וַנֵּפֶן וַנַּעַל דֶּרֶךְ
א הַבָּשָׁן וַיֵּצֵא עוֹג מֶלֶךְ־הַבָּשָׁן לִקְרָאתֵנוּ הוּא וְכָל־עַמּוֹ

---

even their tenth generation ... because of the fact that they did not greet you with bread and water ... and because he hired against you Balaam" (*Devarim* 23:4-5). This seems to say that the Moabites did not actually sell the Jewish people food and water. He suggests that Ammonites are excluded from the congregation because they would not sell us food and water, and Moabites because they hired Balaam against us. But the Torah makes it quite clear that "they did not greet you with bread and water," the plural form indicating both peoples, and that "he hired Balaam," the singular implicating only one people, the Moabites.

Bartinura suggests that "greeting us" with food means offering it for free, as hospitality. But the Edomites, our "brothers," also did not offer us free hospitality, and they are only excluded from the congregation until the third generation. (Not to mention that a host usually honors a guest with bread and wine, not water, as Malchizedek did for Abraham.)

It seems to me that the best explanation is that the verse is actually speaking about selling bread and water. The Edomites agreed to sell to the Jewish people, but the Ammonites and Moabites initially refused. In this case, the Jewish people received permission to seize from them whatever food and water they needed (*Yalkut Shimoni I*:765). When the Ammonites and Moabites saw what was happening, they agreed to receive money for what was taken, and thus make the best of a bad situation. Yet their original hatred had been so great, that they were incapable of agreeing to sell anything.

This is why the Torah says that "they did not greet you," to sell you bread

2 *I cross the Jordan to the Land that HASHEM, our God, gives*
30-37 *us."* [30] *But Sihon king of Heshbon was not willing to let us*
pass through it, for HASHEM, your God, hardened his spirit
and made his heart stubborn, in order to give him into your
hand, like this very day.

[31] *HASHEM said to me: See, I have begun to deliver before*
you Sihon and his land; begin to drive out, to possess his land.
[32] *Sihon went out toward us — he and his entire people —*
for battle, to Jahaz. [33] *HASHEM, our God, gave him before us,*
and we smote him and his sons and his entire people. [34] *We*
occupied all his cities at that time, and we destroyed every
populated city, with the women and small children; we did
not leave a survivor. [35] *Only the animals did we loot for*
ourselves, and the booty of the cities that we occupied:
[36] *from Aroer, which is by the shore of Arnon Brook, and the*
city that is by the brook, and until Gilead — there was no city
that was too strong for us; HASHEM, our God, gave everything
before us. [37] *Only to the land of the children of Ammon did*
you not draw near, everywhere near Jabbok Brook and the
cities of the mountain, and everywhere that HASHEM, our God
commanded us.

3 [1] *We turned and ascended by way of the Bashan, and Og*
1 *king of Bashan went out toward us, he and his entire people,*

---

and water, until you took these items from them forcibly. God's command regarding the Edomites was "do not distress them or provoke them." Thus, the Jewish people could not take anything from them forcibly. But there was no need for this, since they voluntarily agreed to sell.

32. לַמִּלְחָמָה יָהְצָה — *For battle, to Jahaz.* According to modern-day maps, this town was located inside the kingdom of Sihon. Evidently, the Jewish people entered Sihon's borders, and only then did they march towards them, meeting them at Jahaz. This is a further detail, which supports the above explanation (v. 24): "Begin to possess it" — even before battle — "and [then go on to] provoke war with him."

37. וְכֹל אֲשֶׁר־צִוָּה ה׳ אֱלֹהֵינוּ — *And everywhere that Hashem our God commanded us.* The Jewish people avoided the Ammon border solely because God had commanded them: "Do not distress them or provoke them."

3.

1. וַנֵּפֶן — *We turned.* The kingdom of Sihon stretched on the west to the Jordan River (as mentioned in *Yehoshua* 13:27 and *Shoftim* 11:22). Thus they could have crossed the Jordan at this time and start the conquest of Canaan. Instead,

לַמִּלְחָמָה אֶדְרֶעִי: ב וַיֹּאמֶר יהוה אֵלַי אַל־תִּירָא אֹתוֹ כִּי ג
בְיָדְךָ נָתַתִּי אֹתוֹ וְאֶת־כָּל־עַמּוֹ וְאֶת־אַרְצוֹ וְעָשִׂיתָ לּוֹ ב־י
כַּאֲשֶׁר עָשִׂיתָ לְסִיחֹן מֶלֶךְ הָאֱמֹרִי אֲשֶׁר יוֹשֵׁב בְּחֶשְׁבּוֹן:
ג וַיִּתֵּן יהוה אֱלֹהֵינוּ בְּיָדֵנוּ גַּם אֶת־עוֹג מֶלֶךְ־הַבָּשָׁן
וְאֶת־כָּל־עַמּוֹ וַנַּכֵּהוּ עַד־בִּלְתִּי הִשְׁאִיר־לוֹ שָׂרִיד: ד וַנִּלְכֹּד
אֶת־כָּל־עָרָיו בָּעֵת הַהִוא לֹא הָיְתָה קִרְיָה אֲשֶׁר לֹא־
לָקַחְנוּ מֵאִתָּם שִׁשִּׁים עִיר כָּל־חֶבֶל אַרְגֹּב מַמְלֶכֶת עוֹג
בַּבָּשָׁן: ה כָּל־אֵלֶּה עָרִים בְּצֻרֹת חוֹמָה גְבֹהָה דְּלָתַיִם
וּבְרִיחַ לְבַד מֵעָרֵי הַפְּרָזִי הַרְבֵּה מְאֹד: ו וַנַּחֲרֵם אוֹתָם
כַּאֲשֶׁר עָשִׂינוּ לְסִיחֹן מֶלֶךְ חֶשְׁבּוֹן הַחֲרֵם כָּל־עִיר מְתִם
הַנָּשִׁים וְהַטָּף: ז וְכָל־הַבְּהֵמָה וּשְׁלַל הֶעָרִים בַּזּוֹנוּ לָנוּ:
ח וַנִּקַּח בָּעֵת הַהִוא אֶת־הָאָרֶץ מִיַּד שְׁנֵי מַלְכֵי הָאֱמֹרִי
אֲשֶׁר בְּעֵבֶר הַיַּרְדֵּן מִנַּחַל אַרְנֹן עַד־הַר חֶרְמוֹן: ט צִידֹנִים
יִקְרְאוּ לְחֶרְמוֹן שִׂרְיֹן וְהָאֱמֹרִי יִקְרְאוּ־לוֹ שְׂנִיר: י כֹּל | עָרֵי

---

they "turned" to a new direction: Bashan, the kingdom of Og. They reasoned that since God had granted them possession of Sihon's lands, Og had become an obvious danger to them. He would certainly try to take Sihon's lands for himself as soon as the Jewish people had crossed the Jordan. They, therefore, felt obliged to rid themselves of Og immediately. Ultimately, God agreed with them, as demonstrated by the following verse.

וַנַּעַל — *And ascended.* The lands of Sihon's kingdom were mostly watercourses and plains (see *Yehoshua* 13), but the Bashan was mainly mountains. The Torah, therefore, uses the term, "ascended."

2. אַל־תִּירָא אֹתוֹ — *Do not fear him.* Usually, when a king has tested his troops and found them victorious in one war, he is not afraid of deploying them again in another battle. Why, then, was Moses afraid after the victory over Sihon and his people?

The reason is that the Jewish people did not take the land of the Emori with their swords, nor did their own strength bring them victory. Rather, God's right arm and the light of His face went before them and defeated the foe. Thus, Moses had reason to be afraid after the war, "lest Israel might have done wrong during the war with Sihon, or dirtied themselves with sin" (*Yalkut Shimoni I*:765). Even though that war took place in Elul, and Yom Kippur had since passed and the goat sent to Azazel had atoned for all the people's sins, nevertheless, "Moses always chose the fear of Heaven for himself" (ibid.). Indeed, *Chazal* tell us that "for Moses, fearing Heaven was no small thing" (*Berachos* 33b). He always was concerned about whether he had properly executed his duty, and he felt the same regarding the people.

3
2-10

for war at Edrei. 2 *HASHEM said to me: Do not fear him, for in*
your hand have I given him and his entire people and his
land, and you shall do to him as you did to Sihon king of the
Amorite, who dwells in Heshbon. 3 *HASHEM, our God, gave*
into our hand also Og king of the Bashan and his entire peo-
ple, and we smote him until no survivor was left of him. 4 *We*
occupied all his cities at that time; there was no city that we
did not take from them — sixty cities, the entire region of
Argob — the kingdom of Og in the Bashan. 5 *All these were*
fortified cities, with a high wall, doors and bar, aside from
open cities, very many. 6 *We destroyed them, as we did to*
Sihon king of Heshbon, destroying every populated city, the
women and small children. 7 *And all the animals and the*
booty of the cities we looted for ourselves. 8 *At that time we*
took the land from the hand of the two kings of the Amorite
that were on the other side of the Jordan, from Arnon Brook
to Mount Hermon — 9 *Sidonians would refer to Hermon as*
Sirion, and the Amorites would call it Senir — 10 *all the cities*

---

6. וַנַּחֲרֵם אוֹתָם . . . הַחֲרֵם כָּל־עִיר מְתִם — *We destroyed them ... destroying every populated city. HaK'sav VeHaKabbalah* asks how the Children of Israel could live in the cities of Bashan if the land was under חֶרֶם, a ban of consecration. Regarding the Canaanites, the Torah tells us that Israel "destroyed them (וַיַּחֲרֵם) [*Rashi* explains that this was accomplished by killing them] and their cities [by consecrating them]" (*Bamidbar* 21:3). But in this verse, the Torah only says, "we destroyed them," meaning that the people were killed. This places the emphasis on destroying the population of "every populated city," signifying that only the population was to be destroyed, not the city itself.

Yalkut Shimoni (*I*:765) teaches that only the people were destroyed, so as not to derive any benefit from them. This certainly explains the issue and answers the question of *HaK'sav V.eHaKabbalah* of how the children of Israel could live in their cities.

8. מִנַּחַל אַרְנֹן עַד־הַר חֶרְמוֹן — *From Arnon Brook to Mount Hermon.* Whenever the Torah says "from here to there," it leaves doubt as to whether the extremes themselves are included or only what is between them. But in this case we have information about the extremes, too. As concerns Arnon Brook, the banks and the dale were captured by the Jewish people as mentioned in the Torah: "and the city that is by the brook" (2:36), and "the brook and the border" (3:16). Regarding Mount Hermon, the Torah goes on to explain the situation:

9. צִידֹנִים יִקְרְאוּ לְחֶרְמוֹן שִׂרְיֹן וְהָאֱמֹרִי יִקְרְאוּ־לוֹ שְׂנִיר — *Sidonians would refer to Hermon as Sirion, and the Amorites would call it Senir.* In other words, the Sidonians, who live on the north flank of Hermon, call their part of the mountain (and perhaps all of it, too) "Sirion." The Amorites, who live on the

ג הַמִּישֹׁר וְכָל־הַגִּלְעָד וְכָל־הַבָּשָׁן עַד־סַלְכָה וְאֶדְרֶעִי עָרֵי
יא־טז מַמְלֶכֶת עוֹג בַּבָּשָׁן: יא כִּי רַק־עוֹג מֶלֶךְ הַבָּשָׁן נִשְׁאַר מִיֶּתֶר
הָרְפָאִים הִנֵּה עַרְשׂוֹ עֶרֶשׂ בַּרְזֶל הֲלֹה הִוא בְּרַבַּת בְּנֵי עַמּוֹן
תֵּשַׁע אַמּוֹת אָרְכָּהּ וְאַרְבַּע אַמּוֹת רָחְבָּהּ בְּאַמַּת־אִישׁ:
יב וְאֶת־הָאָרֶץ הַזֹּאת יָרַשְׁנוּ בָּעֵת הַהִוא מֵעֲרֹעֵר אֲשֶׁר־
עַל־נַחַל אַרְנֹן וַחֲצִי הַר־הַגִּלְעָד וְעָרָיו נָתַתִּי לָראוּבֵנִי
וְלַגָּדִי: יג וְיֶתֶר הַגִּלְעָד וְכָל־הַבָּשָׁן מַמְלֶכֶת עוֹג נָתַתִּי
לַחֲצִי שֵׁבֶט הַמְנַשֶּׁה כֹּל חֶבֶל הָאַרְגֹּב לְכָל־הַבָּשָׁן הַהוּא
יִקָּרֵא אֶרֶץ רְפָאִים: יד יָאִיר בֶּן־מְנַשֶּׁה לָקַח אֶת־כָּל־
חֶבֶל אַרְגֹּב עַד־גְּבוּל הַגְּשׁוּרִי וְהַמַּעֲכָתִי וַיִּקְרָא אֹתָם עַל־
שְׁמוֹ אֶת־הַבָּשָׁן חַוֺּת יָאִיר עַד הַיּוֹם הַזֶּה: שביעי טו וּלְמָכִיר
נָתַתִּי אֶת־הַגִּלְעָד: טז וְלָראוּבֵנִי וְלַגָּדִי נָתַתִּי מִן־הַגִּלְעָד

---

the south flank, call their part (or all) "Senir." Since the Children of Israel took possession only of the Amorite sector and never made war against the Sidonians, they only took Senir, the southern half of Hermon.

A mountain always has a peak, or שִׂיא. In the case of Hermon, this is הַר שִׂיאֹן (Mount Sion), mentioned later: "From Aroer that is by the shore of Arnon Brook until Mount Sion, which is Hermon" (4:48). This means that the Jewish people captured even the eternally snow-covered peak of Hermon, which had been ownerless until then.

(The Sidonians whom the tribe of Dan later fought and dispossessed lived within the borders of Canaan: "they were far from the [other] Sidonians" [*Shoftim* 18:7]. Since they lived on Canaanite land, the Danites had the right to dispossess them.)

11. תֵּשַׁע אַמּוֹת . . . בְּאַמַּת־אִישׁ — *Nine cubits . . . by the cubit of that man.* "By Og's own cubit" (*Rashi*). *Chazal* tell us how enormously tall the giants were, and in relation to Og a mere nine cubits would be nothing. *Rashi* explains that the "cubit of that man" was Og's own cubit, measured by the length of his forearm. A cubit is the distance from the elbow to the tip of the middle finger. Since Og's size was enormous, his bed had to be many times more than nine cubits as measured by ordinary human beings. But Og is gone from the world, and we have no idea how long his forearm was. What, then, is this verse trying to teach us?

Actually, *Ibn Ezra* interprets "the cubit of that man" as meaning any man's cubit. But in this case, what would be the point of using such an expression? It would have been just as good to say "nine cubits" and leave it at that, for the Torah never wastes words. Despite *Rashi's* explanation, his comments are still not easily understood, for why didn't the Torah say "by Og's cubit," and thus avoid all doubt?

of the plain, the entire Gilead, and the entire Bashan until
Salcah and Edrei, the kingdom of Og in the Bashan. [11] *For*
only Og king of the Bashan was left of the remaining
Rephaim — behold! his bed was an iron bed, in Rabbah of the
children of Ammon — nine cubits was its length and four
cubits its width, by the cubit of that man.
[12] *And we possessed that land at that time; from Aroer,*
which is by Arnon Brook, and half of the mountain of Gilead
and its cities did I give to the Reubenite and the Gadite. [13] *The*
rest of the Gilead and the entire Bashan, the kingdom of Og,
did I give to half the tribe of Manasseh, the entire region
of the Argov of the entire Bashan, that is called the land
of Rephaim. [14] *Jair son of Manasseh took the entire region*
of Argov until the border of the Geshurite and the Maacath-
ite, and he named them, the Bashan, after himself, "Hav-
voth-jair," until this day. [15] *To Machir I gave the Gilead.*
[16] *To the Reubenite and the Gadite I gave from the Gilead*

Rashbam offers an appropriate solution. The bed in question was not a bed at all. The word עֶרֶשׂ is used, which normally means a crib. Evidently, says *Rashbam*, Og's infant crib was preserved in Rabbah, and it was nine cubits in length, for that was his height even as a baby. Lest we become confused and imagine that the cubits mentioned are a (normal) baby's cubits, the Torah specifies: "by the cubit of that (grown) man."

16. וְלָראוּבֵנִי וְלַגָּדִי נָתַתִּי — *To the Reubenite and the Gadite I gave* .... The inheritance of these tribes was already enumerated in verse 12. Why does Moses repeat it again now?

After Moses wrote that he gave "the rest of the Gilead and the entire Bashan ... to half the tribe of Manasseh" (v. 13), we are bound to wonder about this apportionment. If Moses gave so much land to half of one tribe, how did he justify giving the kingdom of Sihon to two whole tribes? Moses, therefore, begins to describe the width and extent of Sihon's kingdom: "from the Gilead until Arnon Brook, the midst of the brook ... until ... the border of the children of Ammon, and the Arabah and the Jordan, and its border from Kinnereth to ... the Salt Sea. ..."

In verses 14-15, Moses hints that Yair ben Manasseh and Machir fought with the Amorites of the Arnon region, and captured the region "until the border of the Geshurite and the Maacathite." Far from being jealous, Moses and the people rejoiced to hear that Yair and Machir wanted to take this territory so far from the center of *Eretz Yisrael* for their inheritance and remain there to fight the gentiles of the area. This is actually spelled out in *Yehoshua* (17:1): "The lot fell ... on Machir ben Manasseh, the father of the Gilead, for he was a man of war; so the Gilead and the Bashan became his."

ג וְעַד־נַ֣חַל אַרְנֹ֔ן תּ֥וֹךְ הַנַּ֖חַל וּגְבֻ֑ל וְעַד֙ יַבֹּ֣ק הַנַּ֔חַל גְּב֖וּל בְּנֵ֥י
יז־כב עַמּֽוֹן׃ יז וְהָעֲרָבָ֖ה וְהַיַּרְדֵּ֣ן וּגְבֻ֑ל מִכִּנֶּ֗רֶת וְעַ֨ד יָ֤ם הָעֲרָבָה֙ יָ֣ם
הַמֶּ֔לַח תַּ֛חַת אַשְׁדֹּ֥ת הַפִּסְגָּ֖ה מִזְרָֽחָה׃ יח וָאֲצַ֣ו אֶתְכֶ֔ם בָּעֵ֥ת
הַהִ֖וא לֵאמֹ֑ר יְהוָ֣ה אֱלֹהֵיכֶ֗ם נָתַ֨ן לָכֶ֜ם אֶת־הָאָ֤רֶץ הַזֹּאת֙
לְרִשְׁתָּ֔הּ חֲלוּצִ֣ים תַּֽעַבְר֗וּ לִפְנֵ֛י אֲחֵיכֶ֥ם בְּנֵֽי־יִשְׂרָאֵ֖ל
כָּל־בְּנֵי־חָֽיִל׃ יט רַ֗ק נְשֵׁיכֶ֣ם וְטַפְּכֶם֮ וּמִקְנֵכֶם֒ יָדַ֕עְתִּי כִּֽי־
מִקְנֶ֥ה רַ֖ב לָכֶ֑ם יֵֽשְׁבוּ֙ בְּעָ֣רֵיכֶ֔ם אֲשֶׁ֥ר נָתַ֖תִּי לָכֶֽם׃ מפטיר כ עַ֠ד
אֲשֶׁר־יָנִ֨יחַ יְהוָ֥ה ׀ לַאֲחֵיכֶם֮ כָּכֶם֒ וְיָרְשׁ֣וּ גַם־הֵ֔ם אֶת־הָאָ֕רֶץ
אֲשֶׁ֨ר יְהוָ֧ה אֱלֹהֵיכֶ֛ם נֹתֵ֥ן לָהֶ֖ם בְּעֵ֣בֶר הַיַּרְדֵּ֑ן וְשַׁבְתֶּ֗ם אִ֚ישׁ
לִֽירֻשָּׁת֔וֹ אֲשֶׁ֖ר נָתַ֥תִּי לָכֶֽם׃ כא וְאֶת־יְהוֹשׁ֣וּעַ צִוֵּ֔יתִי בָּעֵ֥ת
הַהִ֖וא לֵאמֹ֑ר עֵינֶ֣יךָ הָרֹאֹ֗ת אֵת֩ כָּל־אֲשֶׁ֨ר עָשָׂ֜ה יְהוָ֤ה
אֱלֹהֵיכֶם֙ לִשְׁנֵי֙ הַמְּלָכִ֣ים הָאֵ֔לֶּה כֵּן־יַעֲשֶׂ֤ה יְהוָה֙ לְכָל־
הַמַּמְלָכ֔וֹת אֲשֶׁ֥ר אַתָּ֖ה עֹבֵ֥ר שָֽׁמָּה׃ כב לֹ֖א תִּֽירָא֑וּם כִּ֚י יְהוָ֣ה
אֱלֹהֵיכֶ֔ם ה֖וּא הַנִּלְחָ֥ם לָכֶֽם׃

---

18. וָאֲצַו אֶתְכֶם . . . חֲלוּצִים תַּעַבְרוּ — *I commanded you . . . armed shall you cross over.* When Moses spoke about the inheritance of Gad, Reuben, and half of Manasseh, not everyone listened attentively. Only those directly concerned in the matter — the Gadites, the Reubenites, and half of Manasseh — paid complete attention. That is why the Torah says now, "I commanded you" — those who gathered close to me and listened to the definition of their own new borders.

19. בְּעָרֵיכֶם אֲשֶׁר נָתַתִּי לָכֶם — *In your cities that I have given you.* The Gadites and Reubenites thought at first that all their men of military age were to cross the Jordan. They, therefore, proposed to build new cities on the banks of the Jordan and settle their women and children there. If enemies would attack, there would be time for the men to come to the rescue. Once Moses explained that only the strongest among them would be required to cross the Jordan to aid their brothers and that the main force of the army would stay behind to guard the land, they decided to let their people stay in the

3 17-22 *until Arnon Brook, the midst of the brook and the border,*
until Jabbok Brook, the border of the children of Ammon,
17 *and the Arabah and the Jordan and its border, from*
Kinnereth to the Arabah Sea, the Salt Sea, below the
waterfalls from the mountaintop, eastward.
18 *I commanded you at that time, saying, "*Hashem*, your*
God, gave you this Land for a possession, armed shall you
cross over before your brethren, the Children of Israel, all the
men of accomplishment. 19 *Only your wives, small children,*
and livestock — I know that you have abundant livestock —
shall dwell in your cities that I have given you. 20 *Until*
HASHEM shall give rest to your brethren like yourselves, and
they, too, shall possess the Land that HASHEM, your God,
gives them on the other side of the Jordan; then you shall
return, every man to his inheritance that I have given you."
21 *I commanded Joshua at that time, saying, "Your eyes*
have seen everything that HASHEM, your God, has done to
these two kings; so will HASHEM do to all the kings where you
cross over. 22 *You shall not fear them, for HASHEM, your God*
— He shall wage war for you."

---

existing cities of Trans-Jordan, in order to be able to guard them. This is what Moses meant by "your cities that I have given you" — all the captured cities of Trans-Jordan, but you need not build new cities.

21. וְאֶת־יְהוֹשׁוּעַ צִוֵּיתִי בָּעֵת הַהִוא — *I commanded Joshua at that time.* "The chronological time sequence is not always maintained in the Torah," and the beginning of the next *parashah,* "I implored Hashem at that time," actually occurred before the command recorded in this verse. When God told Moses, "Go up to this mountain of Abarim ... and you shall be gathered unto your people" (*Bamidbar* 27:12-13), he implored God, "Let me, please, pass over and see the Land." And when God answered him, "Enough for you; do not speak any more to Me about this matter," Moses prayed, "Let God appoint ... a man over the community." Then God told him, "Take Joshua," and Moses laid his hands upon Joshua and commanded him. Only now does the Torah explain what Moses had commanded him then.

פרשת ואתחנן
Parashas Va'eschanan

ג
כג־כד

כג וָאֶתְחַנַּן אֶל־יהוה בָּעֵת הַהִוא לֵאמֹר: כד אֲדֹנָי יֱהֹוִה
אַתָּה הַחִלּוֹתָ לְהַרְאוֹת אֶת־עַבְדְּךָ אֶת־גָּדְלְךָ וְאֶת־יָדְךָ
הַחֲזָקָה אֲשֶׁר מִי־אֵל בַּשָּׁמַיִם וּבָאָרֶץ אֲשֶׁר־יַעֲשֶׂה כְמַעֲשֶׂיךָ

---

23. וָאֶתְחַנַּן — *I implored*. Of the ten types of prayer enumerated in *Sifre*, Moses chose to use חנון, which literally means "begging for a free gift." Why did he specifically choose this mode of prayer at this time? For the first time in his life, the "most humble of all men" was about to ask something for himself, and was unable to think of any merit to advance on his own behalf in justification of his prayer. Thus, he had no choice but to ask for a "free gift" of mercy. As King Solomon says, "A poor man speaks imploringly" (*Mishlei* 18:23), and since Moses saw himself as a pauper when it came to his own merit, he spoke accordingly.

But regarding prayer for the Jewish people, Moses spoke altogether differently: "Why, Hashem, should Your anger flare up against Your people? . . . Relent from Your flaring anger and reconsider the evil against Your people!" (*Shemos* 32:11-12). At that time Moses felt as if he were "a rich man who answers fiercely" (*Mishlei*, ibid.), for he always found merits to advance on behalf of the people. Moreover, as *Chazal* teach us, "If one is asking on behalf of the public, it is as if he can force his way in" (*Bamidbar Rabbah* 21:14).

☙ Many people ask why Moses never prayed on Aaron's behalf that he be allowed to enter the Land of Israel? This would have also solved his own problem. For the *Gemara* explains that whenever one person prays for another person to receive something, the who prays on behalf of his fellow will be answered first when he himself needs the same thing (*Bava Kamma* 92a). I believe that there are two possible answers to this question:

The first is that Moses implored Hashem on his own behalf only after he conquered the kingdoms of Sihon and Og, at which time he thought that the Heavenly oath forbidding him to enter the Land might have been annulled (as *Rashi* explains, *s.v.* בָּעֵת הַהִוא). But Aaron died almost immediately after the incident of the Waters of Strife, before Moses even had any such thought.

The second is that when God announced that Aaron must die, Moses knew that prayer could no longer help. For God told him, "Take Aaron and Elazar his son . . . strip Aaron of his vestments and dress Elazar his son in them; Aaron shall be gathered in and die there" (*Bamidbar* 20:25-26). Clearly the time had arrived for Elazar to be High Priest, and "no reign ever touches another even as much as a hairsbreadth" (*Shabbos* 30a). But when God told Moses, "Go up to this mountain of Abarim . . . and you shall be gathered unto your people" (*Bamidbar* 27:12-13), without naming who would reign after him, Moses saw this as a sign that prayer and supplication might still help. He, therefore, implored God, "Let me cross and see the good Land that is on the other side of the Jordan" (*Devarim* 3:25). But when he continued, "May Hashem . . . appoint a man over the assembly" (*Bamidbar* 27:16), and God answered him, "Take to yourself Joshua" (ibid., 27:18), Moses spoke no more of his desire to cross over the Jordan.

[23] *I implored* HASHEM *at that time, saying,* [24] *"My Lord,*
HASHEM/ELOHIM, *You have begun to show Your servant Your*
greatness and Your strong hand, for what power is there in the
heaven or on the earth that can perform according to Your deeds

---

One may object to this answer, quoting *Chazal's* statement that Moses prayed 515 prayers imploring that he be allowed to enter the Land of Israel, as hinted by the numerical value of וָאֶתְחַנַּן, and not one prayer, as we propose. But the Vilna Gaon (*Aderes Eliahu*, ad loc.) explains *Chazal's* teaching to mean that Moses only offered one prayer, yet in that one prayer, Moses included 515 different supplications.

24. **אַתָּה הַחִלּוֹתָ לְהַרְאוֹת אֶת־עַבְדְּךָ אֶת־גָּדְלְךָ וְאֶת־יָדְךָ הַחֲזָקָה** — *You have begun to show Your servant Your greatness and Your strong hand.* Imagine a general who has fought his king's battles with two mighty monarchs and utterly defeated them, and then hears that the king plans to dismiss him and in his stead appoint one of his own disciples. No doubt the general would argue, "Have I not begun to show His majesty my might and my strong hand by destroying two powerful kings? What hero is there in the land who can perform according to my deeds and my might?"

But the most modest of all men said nothing on his own behalf. He did not argue that the public needed him and his strong hand to fight the thirty-one kings of Canaan. He was sure and confident that all these things came from God, Who is "the Master of War," and Who would certainly send His messengers to conquer the Land. Moses only requested mercy for himself, for he wished to see the Land.

☙ **אַתָּה הַחִלּוֹתָ לְהַרְאוֹת אֶת־עַבְדְּךָ** — *You have begun to show Your servant.* "Taken simply, this would mean the supernatural victories over Sihon and Og, as the Torah says [about that war], 'See, I have begun to deliver before you Sihon and his land' (2:31). [Said Moses,] 'Now show me the war of the thirty-one kings!' " (*Rashi*).

According to this literal approach, "Your greatness" and "Your strong hand" must be interpreted differently from the *Aggadic* approach given earlier by *Rashi*. "Your greatness" would mean the war with Sihon, and "Your strong hand" would mean the war with Og, who was stronger than Sihon — either physically, as he is described by the Torah, or in merits, since he was the one who brought the news of Lot's captivity to Abraham.

☙ **אֶת־גָּדְלְךָ** — *Your greatness.* R' Simlai learns from this phrase that "a man should always set forth God's praises first, and then pray" (*Berachos* 32a). We also find in this verse the source for the Men of the Great Assembly choosing "Great, mighty, and awesome God" as the particular praises to be used to introduce the Silent Devotion. For these are exactly the concepts expressed by Moses on this occasion: "You have begun to show . . . Your *greatness*, and Your strong hand," which is *mighty*, "for what power is there . . . that can perform according to Your deeds," which are *awesome*.

ג וְכִגְבוּרֹתֶךָ: כה אֶעְבְּרָה־נָּא וְאֶרְאֶה אֶת־הָאָרֶץ הַטּוֹבָה
כה־כו אֲשֶׁר בְּעֵבֶר הַיַּרְדֵּן הָהָר הַטּוֹב הַזֶּה וְהַלְּבָנֹן: כו וַיִּתְעַבֵּר
יְהוָה בִּי לְמַעַנְכֶם וְלֹא שָׁמַע אֵלָי וַיֹּאמֶר יְהוָה אֵלַי רַב־לָךְ

---

25. אֶעְבְּרָה־נָּא וְאֶרְאֶה . . . הָהָר הַטּוֹב הַזֶּה וְהַלְּבָנֹן — *Let me now cross and see . . . this good mountain and the Lebanon.* Here is Moses, "skipping lightly" over the war of the thirty-one kings, and going straight, as if on a tourist trip, to see "this good mountain" (Jerusalem) "and the Lebanon" (the Holy Temple, not built until hundreds of years later)!

But, as we mentioned above (v. 23), the Vilna Gaon explains the "515 prayers that Moses prayed" as meaning that Moses' single prayer included within it 515 supplications. Accordingly, there is no difficulty in understanding that this, too, was one of the things Moses requested. He might have prayed that the Heavenly Temple of Fire be brought down to earth right away, and that he and the Children of Israel would cross the Jordan and go straight to Jerusalem for a pilgrim-festival before Hashem. As for the war with the Canaanites, the Torah promises that "no man will covet your land when you go up to appear before Hashem" (*Shemos* 34:24). So, while the people were in Jerusalem at their festival, all seven Canaanite nations would, perforce, be under the Torah's decree, and would vacate the entire country of their own accord. There would never have been any Canaanite war had Moses' prayer been granted.

⊲§ אֶעְבְּרָה־נָּא וְאֶרְאֶה — *Let me now cross and see.* One of Moses' many implications in this prayer may have been that if he could not be allowed to cross the Jordan as a leader, God might still allow him to pass over as a simple citizen. For the exact wording of the decree had been "You will not bring this congregation" (*Bamidbar* 20:12). Thus, the implied intention was, "Let Joshua fight the thirty-one kings, if only I could cross the Jordan and see the Land!"

⊲§ אֶת־הָאָרֶץ הַטּוֹבָה אֲשֶׁר בְּעֵבֶר הַיַּרְדֵּן — *The good Land that is on the other side of the Jordan. Chazal* are divided as to exactly how much of the Trans-Jordan is part of the Holy Land. One of the disputed points is whether or not one brings first-fruits from there (see *Mishnah Bikkurim* 1:10 and *Bartinura*). Even the Sages, who disagree with R' Yosei HaGlili and require us to bring first-fruits, agree with him that "it is not a land flowing with milk and honey," and that the west side of the Jordan is a better land than the east bank (*Vayikra Rabbah* 3). So Moses, who was then on the eastern side, asked to see "the good Land."

⊲§ הָאָרֶץ הַטּוֹבָה — *The good Land.* His intent in saying this was to remind God that although the spies had spoken slander about the Land, he had spoken only *good* about it. Why, then, should he not be allowed to see it?

⊲§ הָהָר הַטּוֹב הַזֶּה וְהַלְּבָנֹן — *This good mountain and the Lebanon.* Once Moses had said "the good Land," he included all the mountains and hills as well. Why, then, did he specifically mention these two?

3 25-26

and according to Your mighty acts? [25] *Let me now cross and*
see the good Land that is on the other side of the Jordan, this
good mountain and the Lebanon."
[26] *But* HASHEM *became angry with me because of you, and*
He did not listen to me; HASHEM *said to me, "It is too much for*

It is their specific mention that led *Chazal* to understand "this good mountain" as meaning Jerusalem and "the Lebanon" as meaning the Holy Temple (see *Rashi*). Furthermore, from the fact that Moses called Jerusalem "*this* good mountain," we may deduce that God had revealed to him the exact location where His Temple would one day be built. But evidently He did not allow Moses to tell the Children of Israel about this, so that the tribes would not all quarrel with one another, each desiring to receive that spot as part of its inheritance.

26. לְמַעַנְכֶם — *Because of you.* The word used here is לְמַעַנְכֶם, literally "for your sake." Moses did not say בִּגְלַלְכֶם, the word which is usually used for the meaning "because of you" as he did previously (1:37), for that would have implied "because of your sins." Instead he said לְמַעַנְכֶם, which means "for your sake, for your good."

At this point, his intent was to placate the Children of Israel, to whom he had just delivered some very bad news. He had told them that he would not be crossing the Jordan with them, nor would he be there to fight the Canaanite kings for them, or to apportion their inheritance. He explained that this had not been his decision at all. Quite the contrary, he had pleaded to be allowed to cross over the river and enter the Land, but God would not accept his prayer.

Yet, Moses told them this was all "for their sake," for their good. For if he were to bring the people into the Land and build the Temple, then at such time that the Children of Israel sinned it would be impossible to destroy the Temple. Without the possibility of destruction and exile, the Jewish people would have to perish for their sins. But if someone else were to build the Temple, things would be different. It could be destroyed on account of the people's sins, thus saving them from annihilation. So it was really for the people's own good that Moses did not bring them into the Land.

Chazal mention other benefits we reaped from this. First, God decreed that Moses should be buried in the valley opposite Baal-peor so that he could atone for the sin of Baal-peor. Secondly, Moses was buried there so that the generation that died in the desert would be granted resurrection with him at the End of Days.

⁂ רַב־לָךְ — *It is too much for you.* This wording could be literally interpreted as "Rabbi for you." When Moses suggested that he might be allowed to enter *Eretz Yisrael* as a simple citizen, a disciple of Joshua, God answered him רַב לָךְ, thus hinting that "being a Rabbi is the job for you," and that he could never be simply a student. The account of Moses' efforts are related in *Midrash Tanchuma* (*Va'eschanan* §6): after Moses learned Torah from Joshua, he said, "Until now I asked for life; but now, my soul is Yours for the taking."

ג אַל־תּוֹסֶף דַּבֵּר אֵלַי עוֹד בַּדָּבָר הַזֶּה: כז עֲלֵה ׀ רֹאשׁ הַפִּסְגָּה
כז־כט וְשָׂא עֵינֶיךָ יָמָּה וְצָפֹנָה וְתֵימָנָה וּמִזְרָחָה וּרְאֵה בְעֵינֶיךָ
כִּי־לֹא תַעֲבֹר אֶת־הַיַּרְדֵּן הַזֶּה: כח וְצַו אֶת־יְהוֹשֻׁעַ וְחַזְּקֵהוּ
וְאַמְּצֵהוּ כִּי־הוּא יַעֲבֹר לִפְנֵי הָעָם הַזֶּה וְהוּא יַנְחִיל אוֹתָם
אֶת־הָאָרֶץ אֲשֶׁר תִּרְאֶה: כט וַנֵּשֶׁב בַּגָּיְא מוּל בֵּית פְּעוֹר:

אַל־תּוֹסֶף דַּבֵּר אֵלַי — *Do not continue to speak to Me.* I saw an explanation of this command in the Vilna Gaon's name. Moses had received a tradition that if he said **נָא** twice in his prayer, that prayer would surely be accepted. This is what he did when he prayed for Miriam: **אֵל נָא רְפָא נָא לָהּ**, "*Please* God, *please* heal her," (*Bamidbar* 12:13). Moses prayed using the double **נָא**, and Miriam was healed. This time, too, he began by saying, **אֶעְבְּרָה נָּא**, "*Please* let me cross over," and he intended to continue with **וְאֶרְאֶה נָּא**, "and *please* let me see." But God warned him, "Do not continue to speak to Me further about this matter" — don't use another **נָא** in your prayer to Me about this, for this time your prayer cannot be accepted.

27. עֲלֵה רֹאשׁ הַפִּסְגָּה . . . וּרְאֵה בְעֵינֶיךָ — *Ascend to the top of the cliff . . . and see with your eyes.* Even though the holy man's prayer was not entirely effective this time — for the Heavenly oath had been sworn and could not be broken — it did achieve partial results. For even the prayer of a simple man "does half the work" (*Vayikra Rabbah* 10:5). Moses had asked, "Let me now cross and see the good Land," and God allowed him to at least see the entire Land from the top of the peak.

וְשָׂא עֵינֶיךָ יָמָּה . . . וּמִזְרָחָה — *And raise your eyes westward ... and eastward.* Why should Moses look eastward, when he was already standing across the Jordan, to the east of the Land? We can explain this on the basis of another verse (34:1-2): "Hashem showed him all the Land ... until הַיָּם הָאַחֲרוֹן, the last sea." (the Mediterranean). This phrase can be read alternatively as הַיּוֹם הָאַחֲרוֹן, *the last day.* The *Sifre* comments that this enigmatic phrase hints that Moses saw the future history of the Jewish people until הַיּוֹם הָאַחֲרוֹן, the End of Days and the Resurrection. In those days, God will give us the lands of the Kenites, the Kenizites, and the Kadmonim, across the Jordan, to be our own. Moses had seen only parts of these lands, namely those sectors of Ammon and Moab that had constituted the kingdom of Sihon. God, therefore, commanded Moses to also look eastward, in order to see the lands that would one day belong to Israel.

וּרְאֵה בְעֵינֶיךָ — *And see with your eyes.* Had our Teacher Moses actually entered *Eretz Yisrael,* he would have "seen" it, i.e., felt its holiness, with every fiber of his being. (In Hebrew, "seeing" is often a term which means "understanding" or "feeling.") But since his prayer was not accepted, God told him that he could only "see with his eyes."

3
27-29

you! Do not continue to speak to Me further about this
matter. [27] *Ascend to the top of the cliff and raise your eyes*
westward, northward, southward, and eastward, and see
with your eyes, for you shall not cross this Jordan. [28] *But you*
shall command Joshua, and strengthen him and give him
resolve, for he shall cross before the people and he shall cause
them to inherit the Land that you will see."
[29] *So we remained in the valley, opposite Beth-peor.*

כִּי־לֹא תַעֲבֹר אֶת־הַיַּרְדֵּן הַזֶּה — *For you shall not cross this Jordan.* Joseph spoke with pride about his native land, saying, "For indeed I was kidnaped from the land of the Hebrews" (*Bereishis* 40:15). He was, therefore, rewarded with burial in his own land. Moses did not admit to his native land. When Jethro's daughters said of him, "An Egyptian man saved us" (*Shemos* 2:19), he heard and was silent. Therefore, he did not merit burial in his land (*Devarim Rabbah* 2:8).

People commonly point out that Moses not only refused to admit his native land, but he also denied his people. For Jethro's daughters called him "an Egyptian man," and that is not only a land but a people. Why was he not punished for this denial as well?

Perhaps we can explain this in accordance with the *Midrash*. When Potiphar saw the Ishmaelites offering Joseph for sale, he said to them, "In all the world the white people sell blacks, and here are black people selling a white man! This is no slave" (*Bereishis Rabbah* 86). Since the Egyptians were even darker-skinned than the Ishmaelites, everyone must have known that the Jethro's daughters weren't referring to Moses as an ethnic Egyptian when they said that "an Egyptian man" had saved them. Clearly he was of the lighter-skinned Hebrews living in Egypt at the time — a resident of the country, but not one of its natives. At this point, Moses should have corrected them and told them that he was not an Egyptian at all, but "from the land of the Hebrews."

28. וְצַו אֶת־יְהוֹשֻׁעַ וְחַזְּקֵהוּ וְאַמְּצֵהוּ — *But you shall command Joshua, and strengthen him and give him resolve.* Joshua had already heard the prophecy of Eldad and Medad: "Moses will die and Joshua will take us into the Land." But he had also heard his teacher praying, "Let me cross and see the good Land that is on the other side." Since he believed that Moses' prayer would be readily accepted, Joshua made no preparations for his future role and remained as he had always been — "the young man who served Moses" — dependent upon his teacher. Therefore, God ordered Moses to "command Joshua, and strengthen him and give him resolve, for he shall cross before the people, and he shall cause them to inherit the Land that you will see."

29. וַנֵּשֶׁב בַּגָּיְא מוּל בֵּית פְּעוֹר — *So we remained in the valley, opposite Beth-peor.* "This alludes to Moses' death and burial, which would take place there" (*Abarbanel*).

ד א וְעַתָּה יִשְׂרָאֵל שְׁמַע אֶל־הַחֻקִּים וְאֶל־הַמִּשְׁפָּטִים אֲשֶׁר
א־ב אָנֹכִי מְלַמֵּד אֶתְכֶם לַעֲשׂוֹת לְמַעַן תִּחְיוּ וּבָאתֶם וִירִשְׁתֶּם
אֶת־הָאָרֶץ אֲשֶׁר יהוה אֱלֹהֵי אֲבֹתֵיכֶם נֹתֵן לָכֶם׃ ב לֹא
תֹסִפוּ עַל־הַדָּבָר אֲשֶׁר אָנֹכִי מְצַוֶּה אֶתְכֶם וְלֹא תִגְרְעוּ מִמֶּנּוּ

This verse provides the ideological foundation for the custom of thoughtful people to buy themselves a grave during their lifetime and to visit the site every now and then, in order to remember their inevitable fate and repent and correct their ways while they are alive. Some even sew their own shroud, and put it on from time to time, for the same reason. For we see that as soon as our Teacher Moses heard God tell him, "Do not continue to speak to Me further about this matter . . . for you shall not cross this Jordan" Moses knew that he would die and be buried in the valley opposite Beth-peor, and did not leave that place until the day he died. "So we remained in the valley . . ." until "he was buried in the valley" (34:6).

29.-4:1. מוּל בֵּית פְּעוֹר. וְעַתָּה יִשְׂרָאֵל שְׁמַע אֶל־הַחֻקִּים — *Opposite Beth-peor. Now, O Israel, listen to the decrees. . . .* Based on the verse, "The name of strange gods you shall not mention nor shall your mouth cause it to be heard" (*Shemos* 23:13), the *Gemara* explains that a person should not use an idol as a marker and should not say, "Wait for me next to such-and-such an idol" (*Sanhedrin* 63b). In view of this *halachah*, how could the Torah have described the place where the Children of Israel stayed as being "opposite Beth [the House of] Peor?"

Another *Gemara* provides the answer. "What do we mean by a *baal teshuvah*, a repentant sinner?" R' Yehudah said, "If one has the opportunity to commit the same sins [that he had committed before — *Rashi*], and it came his way once and then again, and he refrained from it, then he is a *baal teshuvah*." R' Yehudah gave as an example for this behavior the case of the same woman, the same time of year, and the same place (*Yoma* 86b).

Following this train of thought, Moses said to the Children of Israel, "Here we are opposite Beth Peor. We will soon be leaving this place, so you ought to take this opportunity to complete your repentance for the sin you did here, since you are in the same place and the same idol is still there."

Chazal further remark (*Bereishis Rabbah* 35) that וְעַתָּה, "and now" is an expression of repentance. It expresses the thought that the past is over and gone, "and now" we are starting anew. Just so, Moses continues, "And now, Israel, listen to [God's] decrees. . . ."

4.

1. אֲשֶׁר אָנֹכִי מְלַמֵּד אֶתְכֶם לַעֲשׂוֹת — *That I teach you to perform.* From this phrase, we deduce that the chief purpose of מִשְׁנֵה תּוֹרָה (*Devarim*), the "Review of the Torah," is the reiteration by Moses to the Jewish people of the Torah commandments before his death, and his instructions "how to perform"

4 *1 Now, O Israel, listen to the decrees and to the ordinances*
1-2 *that I teach you to perform, so that you may live, and*
you will come and possess the Land that HASHEM, *the God*
of your forefathers, gives you. 2 You shall not add to the
word that I command you, nor shall you subtract from it,

---

the *mitzvos.* (This is, of course, in addition to the commandments which had not yet been given to Israel.)

There was no great need to review the Written Torah, for that was already written down plainly. It would have sufficed for Moses to command the people to read it through on their own. But this was not the case with the explanations and clarifications of each verse contained in the Oral Torah. For at that time, it was forbidden to write them down. (Only owing to the tribulations of Exile, when forgetfulness became common because of their wanderings from place to place, did the Sages of the day allow the Oral Torah to be written down, as an emergency measure.) Since Moses was not sure that everyone had memorized all these clarifications, he "began explaining this Torah" and added rebuke and ethical discourses. In this way, the entire Jewish people would know how to go about fulfilling the commandments — what was practically required to do in order to properly observe each one.

This is immensely important. For example, if the Written Torah says, "Bind them as a sign upon your arm and let them be ornaments between your eyes" (6:8), we still do not know in what way we are to make this sign or these ornaments. Only the Oral Torah teaches us that we must make a pair of *tefillin,* and gives us all the necessary details: the enclosures and the scrolls; how many of each to make; what to write in each; on what material to write: how they should be fastened onto head and arm; and how to make the straps and the knots. Each of these things is hinted at in the Written Torah and can be deduced from its wording. Yet, the deductive process is highly specialized, and requires much scrutiny and study, and must be carried out under the tutelage of a *talmid chacham* who can pass on the received tradition. So it is with every commandment in the Torah; and this was the item of chief importance which Moses taught the people before his death.

2. **לֹא תֹסִפוּ עַל־הַדָּבָר אֲשֶׁר אָנֹכִי מְצַוֶּה אֶתְכֶם וְלֹא תִגְרְעוּ מִמֶּנּוּ** — *You shall not add to the word that I command you, nor shall you subtract from it.* The Jewish people had learned from Moses that it is permissible to add to what appears in the Written Torah (for example, the water-libation during Succos), and also to subtract from it (such as reducing "Forty [times] shall he smite him" to thirty-nine lashes). This, of course, is all done according to the thirteen principles of expounding the Written Torah, the fundamental rules of *halachah.* Moses now emphasized this point by reminding the people that no one may add or subtract from the Torah merely according to his own judgment. It may only be done in accordance with the received tradition and the thirteen hermeneutical principles.

ד לִשְׁמֹר אֶת־מִצְוֹת יְהוָה אֱלֹהֵיכֶם אֲשֶׁר אָנֹכִי מְצַוֶּה
ג־ו אֶתְכֶם: ג עֵינֵיכֶם הָרֹאוֹת אֵת אֲשֶׁר־עָשָׂה יְהוָה בְּבַעַל
פְּעוֹר כִּי כָל־הָאִישׁ אֲשֶׁר הָלַךְ אַחֲרֵי בַעַל־פְּעוֹר הִשְׁמִידוֹ
יְהוָה אֱלֹהֶיךָ מִקִּרְבֶּךָ: ד וְאַתֶּם הַדְּבֵקִים בַּיהוָה אֱלֹהֵיכֶם
חַיִּים כֻּלְּכֶם הַיּוֹם: שני ה רְאֵה ׀ לִמַּדְתִּי אֶתְכֶם חֻקִּים
וּמִשְׁפָּטִים כַּאֲשֶׁר צִוַּנִי יְהוָה אֱלֹהָי לַעֲשׂוֹת כֵּן בְּקֶרֶב הָאָרֶץ
אֲשֶׁר אַתֶּם בָּאִים שָׁמָּה לְרִשְׁתָּהּ: ו וּשְׁמַרְתֶּם וַעֲשִׂיתֶם כִּי
הִוא חָכְמַתְכֶם וּבִינַתְכֶם לְעֵינֵי הָעַמִּים אֲשֶׁר יִשְׁמְעוּן אֵת

---

3. הִשְׁמִידוֹ ה׳ אֱלֹהֶיךָ מִקִּרְבֶּךָ — *Hashem, your God, destroyed him from your midst.* The Torah deliberately uses the phrase "from your midst," lest anyone claim that there were some adherents of Baal-peor who were not destroyed. Thus, the Torah specifies that these idolaters were destroyed "from your midst," teaching us that the gentiles indeed continued to worship Baal-peor. They remain alive, though with no more than a mere animal existence. And God allows them to have many divinities; i.e., they are not punished with death if they worship idols in addition to God Himself.

But this was not the command that God gave to Israel, His holy people. Rather, we must cling to Hashem, our God; for us, there is none besides Him. And if one of us worships idols, God destroys him (provided he cannot be judged by a *beis din,* because of a lack of witnesses or because he received no prior warning). He will be destroyed "from your midst" so that he will not entice others to follow him. Thus Heaven upholds its own oft-repeated warning, "you shall destroy the evil from your midst."

5. כַּאֲשֶׁר צִוַּנִי ה׳ אֱלֹהָי — *As Hashem, my God, has commanded me. Chazal* derive a deeper meaning from Moses' words: "Just as I [have taught you the Torah] for free, so you should teach it free of charge." And why does the verse end with "to do so in the midst of the Land to which you come, to possess it"? So that you should not say that it was possible to teach Torah free of charge only in the Wilderness, where manna was your bread, and Miriam's well faithfully provided you with water, and your clothing never wore out. Rather, Moses cautioned them how it would still be possible to do so "in the Land," which must be worked and guarded and where one must earn a living. As people tend to think this way, Moses admonished them to continue teaching the Torah for free, even after they entered the Land.

☙ **לַעֲשׂוֹת כֵּן בְּקֶרֶב הָאָרֶץ** — *To do so in the midst of the Land.* We have already explained the difficulty of performing the commandments without the Oral Torah (4:1). In this "Review of the Torah," Moses once again teaches the Jewish people "how to do" the commandments, lest they forget the Oral Torah's detailed explanations of the Torah's written commandments.

4
3-6

to observe the commandments of H*ASHEM*, *your God, that I*
command you. 3 *Your eyes have seen what* H*ASHEM did with*
Baal-peor, for every man that followed Baal-peor — H*ASHEM*,
your God, destroyed him from your midst. 4 *But you who*
cling to H*ASHEM*, *your God — you are all alive today.*
5 *See, I have taught you decrees and ordinances, as*
H*ASHEM*, *my God, has commanded me, to do so in the midst*
of the Land to which you come, to possess it. 6 *You shall*
safeguard and perform them, for it is your wisdom and
discernment in the eyes of the peoples, who shall hear

Moses was careful to explain to the people that the commandments which they, Israel, were already performing in the Wilderness may be fulfilled anywhere, not only in the Holy Land. Understand, then, how it was all the more necessary to caution them about the proper performance of commandments that can only be done "in the midst of the Land," *mitzvos* which the people had not even experienced during Moses' lifetime. They needed a basic, intensive course in the practical performance of these commandments, so that they would be ready to observe them when they arrived in the Land.

Therefore, Moses said, "See, I have taught you decrees and ordinances . . . to do so in the midst of the Land . . ." — since you have had no practice in performing them as yet, you must be especially attentive, so that you will know what to do when you enter the Land.

We who live in *Eretz Yisrael* today frequently see what trouble new immigrants have in getting used to commandments. For example, since they were not taught the separation of tithes from produce as children, they are not familiar with its practical application. No wonder, then, that Moses particularly stressed the commandments unique to the Holy Land.

☙ The phrase "to do so in the midst of Land" is an allusion to Korach and his followers. Moses meant to say that they suspected him of not being a genuine emissary of God, and now they are "in the land." In other words, they were swallowed up by the earth. Therefore the verse begins with "See" — recall the vision of what happened then, and know that I "have taught you decrees and ordinances as Hashem, my God, has commanded me."

6. וּשְׁמַרְתֶּם וַעֲשִׂיתֶם כִּי הוּא חָכְמַתְכֶם וּבִינַתְכֶם לְעֵינֵי הָעַמִּים — *You shall safeguard and perform them, for it is your wisdom and discernment in the eyes of the peoples.* This sounds odd. Is this a reason to keep God's laws — so that we should appear wise and discerning in the eyes of the other nations? The intent of the verse is as follows: aside from your actual fulfillment of the commandments, which is good in itself, God's Name will be sanctified in the world. For the nations will say, "Surely a wise and discerning people is this great nation!" Some of them will even become proselytes. By your scrupulous *mitzvah*-observance, God's Name will be sanctified "in the eyes of the peoples."

ד כָּל־הַחֻקִּים הָאֵלֶּה וְאָמְרוּ רַק עַם־חָכָם וְנָבוֹן הַגּוֹי הַגָּדוֹל
ז־ט הַזֶּה: ז כִּי מִי־גוֹי גָדוֹל אֲשֶׁר־לוֹ אֱלֹהִים קְרֹבִים אֵלָיו כַּיהוָה
אֱלֹהֵינוּ בְּכָל־קָרְאֵנוּ אֵלָיו: ח וּמִי גּוֹי גָּדוֹל אֲשֶׁר־לוֹ חֻקִּים
וּמִשְׁפָּטִים צַדִּיקִם כְּכֹל הַתּוֹרָה הַזֹּאת אֲשֶׁר אָנֹכִי נֹתֵן
לִפְנֵיכֶם הַיּוֹם: ט רַק הִשָּׁמֶר לְךָ וּשְׁמֹר נַפְשְׁךָ מְאֹד
פֶּן־תִּשְׁכַּח אֶת־הַדְּבָרִים אֲשֶׁר־רָאוּ עֵינֶיךָ וּפֶן־יָסוּרוּ

יִשְׁמְעוּן אֵת כָּל־הַחֻקִּים הָאֵלֶּה — *Who shall hear all these decrees.* When the nations of the world saw the Jewish people winning victories in a supernatural way, they thought that it was all because of their leader, Moses, the man of God (see *Rashi* on *Bamidbar* 22:4). But when they will see them going on to defeat the thirty-one Canaanite kings after Moses' death, they will say that these victories were because of the Torah's decrees (חֻקִּים), which the Jewish people fulfill even though no man knows the reasons for them. Alternatively, their own failure to understand the חֻקִּים will lead them to think that the Jewish people must be "a wise and discerning people," who know the reasons for these laws. This, they will think, is what brings the Jewish people close to God and causes Him to hear their prayers. They will understand that the victories are because of the Torah's decrees (חֻקִּים), but not because of its ordinances (מִשְׁפָּטִים); for the nations have ordinances as well. Moreover, they do not comprehend the distinction between God's ordinances, which are "entirely righteous," and their own, which were formulated by human beings. Today they build up a "code of justice," and tomorrow they knock it down. Therefore, the verse speaks only of the Torah's decrees.

7. כַּה׳ אֱלֹהֵינוּ בְּכָל־קָרְאֵנוּ אֵלָיו — *As is Hashem, our God, whenever we call to Him.* The more we call upon Him, the closer He comes to us. This explains the custom of reciting the verse לִישׁוּעָתְךָ קִוִּיתִי ה׳, three times, changing the order of the words each time. First we say it as it appears in the Torah: לִישׁוּעָתְךָ קִוִּיתִי ה׳, "For Your salvation do I long, O Hashem" (*Bereishis* 49:18). Once we have called upon Hashem, He becomes closer to us; thus, we can place His name closer to the beginning of the verse and say קִוִּיתִי ה׳ לִישׁוּעָתְךָ, "I long, O Hashem, for Your salvation." After calling to Hashem twice, He is now another step closer to us; thus on the third recitation we put His holy Name first: ה׳ לִישׁוּעָתְךָ קִוִּיתִי, "Hashem, for Your salvation do I long."

9. רַק הִשָּׁמֶר לְךָ וּשְׁמֹר נַפְשְׁךָ מְאֹד פֶּן־תִּשְׁכַּח — *Only beware for yourself and greatly beware for your soul, lest you forget.* There are two ways for the Torah to become forgotten, Heaven forbid. The first way is passive. A father neglects to provide his children with a Torah education; yet, he also does not teach them cynicism and licentiousness. Or perhaps he neglects to support Torah learning; he does not separate tithes from his produce to give to the *Kohanim* and *Leviim*, of whom the Torah says, "They will teach Your ordinances to Jacob and Your Torah to Israel" (*Devarim* 33:10). In our times,

all these decrees and who shall say, "Surely a wise and dis-
cerning people is this great nation!" 7 *For which is a great*
nation that has a God Who is close to it, as is HASHEM, *our*
God, whenever we call to Him? 8 *And which is a great nation*
that has righteous decrees and ordinances, such as this entire
Torah that I place before you this day? 9 *Only beware for*
yourself and greatly beware for your soul, lest you forget the
things that your eyes have beheld and lest you remove them

---

this would mean that he fails to support Torah scholars and their students. For we are specifically commanded to do all this: "Accursed is the one who will not uphold the words of this Torah" (*Devarim* 27:26). *Chazal* derive from this verse that "even if a man has studied and taught, and kept and performed [the Torah], yet if he had the means to support Torah learning and did not do so, then he is included in 'accursed is the one who will not uphold' " (*Vayikra Rabbah* 25). People like this indirectly cause the Torah to be forgotten from Israel, and of them it is said, "Only beware for yourself ... lest you forget."

The second way that the Torah may be forgotten is more active. A father sends his children to schools where Torah has been rejected, and specious viewpoints have taken its place. These schools have teachers who not only do their best "to make [the children] forget Your Torah and compel them to stray from the statutes of Your Will," but even teach them to be enemies of our religion and to fight against our holy Torah. If such an individual has been blessed with wealth and a generous heart, he donates his money to the building and maintenance of these anti-Torah institutions and to similar causes. The Torah is speaking about such a person when it says, "and greatly beware for your soul," for through such actions his soul will be lost to its people and cut off from eternal life, Heaven forbid.

פֶּן־תִּשְׁכַּח אֶת־הַדְּבָרִים אֲשֶׁר־רָאוּ עֵינֶיךָ — *Lest you forget the things that your eyes have beheld.* A progression of ideas that began in verse 6 reaches its full development in this verse. It began with "You shall safeguard and perform them." By doing this we insure that God will be close to us whenever we call to Him, and that His name will be sanctified among the nations, for they will say that the Torah's decrees have made us "a wise and discerning people" and "a great nation" which is close to God and whose prayers are heard.

But Moses continues with one condition, which must be fulfilled before we can "safeguard and perform" and before we approach God in prayer. This stipulation is to ensure that we do everything "in awe, in trepidation, with trembling and shuddering," (*Berachos* 22a), "as on the day when you stood before Hashem, your God, at Horeb" — not as a routine matter of mechanics. When you teach your children, do it with the same feeling you had when you heard the words of the Living God: "awe, trepidation, trembling and shuddering." Vibrate with enthusiasm as you study — you, and your child, and

מִלְּבָבְךָ כֹּל יְמֵי חַיֶּיךָ וְהוֹדַעְתָּם לְבָנֶיךָ וְלִבְנֵי בָנֶיךָ׃ ד
י יוֹם אֲשֶׁר עָמַדְתָּ לִפְנֵי יהוה אֱלֹהֶיךָ בְּחֹרֵב בֶּאֱמֹר י־יב
יהוה אֵלַי הַקְהֶל־לִי אֶת־הָעָם וְאַשְׁמִעֵם אֶת־דְּבָרָי
אֲשֶׁר יִלְמְדוּן לְיִרְאָה אֹתִי כָּל־הַיָּמִים אֲשֶׁר הֵם
חַיִּים עַל־הָאֲדָמָה וְאֶת־בְּנֵיהֶם יְלַמֵּדוּן׃ יא וַתִּקְרְבוּן
וַתַּעַמְדוּן תַּחַת הָהָר וְהָהָר בֹּעֵר בָּאֵשׁ עַד־לֵב הַשָּׁמַיִם
חֹשֶׁךְ עָנָן וַעֲרָפֶל׃ יב וַיְדַבֵּר יהוה אֲלֵיכֶם מִתּוֹךְ הָאֵשׁ

---

your grandchild — as the Chosen People did on that day at Horeb (See *HaDe'ah Ve'HaDibur*, *II*:4:4).

"The beginning of wisdom is the fear of God; good understanding for all those who do them" (*Tehillim* 111:10). In other words, one must first establish fear of God in one's heart before he turns to the study of Torah, the only true wisdom, and the performance of commandments. And how does one establish this fear? By remembering the day we stood at Mount Sinai. Then all nations will recognize the Torah as "good understanding" — "Surely a wise and discerning people is this great nation."

The same thing applies to prayer, as the *Mishnah* teaches: "One may not stand up to pray except in a serious frame of mind" (*Berachos* 30b; deduced in the *Gemara* from the verse, "Serve God with awe.").

אֶת־הַדְּבָרִים אֲשֶׁר־רָאוּ עֵינֶיךָ — *The things that your eyes have beheld.* For at Horeb your eyes saw sounds. They saw the words that issued from the mouth of the Living God as black letters written on white fire. (See verse 11 below: "and the mountain was burning with fire.")

לְבָנֶיךָ וְלִבְנֵי בָנֶיךָ — *To your children and your children's children.* And if they indeed do not depart from your mouth and from the mouths of your children and from the mouths of your children's children, then God has promised, "from now until eternity" — the Torah will never cease from your progeny.

10. אֲשֶׁר הֵם חַיִּים עַל־הָאֲדָמָה — *That they live on the earth.* For there is another life besides the one on this earth.

11. וַתִּקְרְבוּן וַתַּעַמְדוּן תַּחַת הָהָר — *So you approached and stood at the foot of the mountain.* And it is through this merit alone that Israel has "a God Who is close to it . . . whenever we call to Him" (*Yeshayahu* 55:6). If we had not come close to the mountain to hear the voice of the Living God, He would not come close to us to hear our prayers. As King Solomon tells us, "If one turns his ear away from hearing Torah, his prayer also becomes loathsome [to God]" (*Mishlei* 28:9). If we do not want to hear His Word, He will not want to hear our prayers.

וְהָהָר בֹּעֵר בָּאֵשׁ . . . חֹשֶׁךְ — *And the mountain was burning with fire. . . darkness.* Fire gives light, and a little light dispels much darkness — especially the Heavenly fire, which was seen on the altar as bright as the sun

from your heart all the days of your life, and make them
known to your children and your children's children —
10 *the day that you stood before* HASHEM, *your God, at*
Horeb, when HASHEM *said to me, "Gather the people to Me*
and I shall let them hear My words, so that they shall
learn to fear Me all the days that they live on the earth,
and they shall teach their children."
11 *So you approached and stood at the foot of the mount-*
ain, and the mountain was burning with fire up to the
heart of heaven, darkness, cloud, and thick cloud.
12 HASHEM *spoke to you from the midst of the fire;*

(*Yoma* 21b). If light and darkness efface each other, how did they combine for the Giving of the Torah?

We can answer this question by considering the view of Rabbi Shimon Ben Lakish (*Shekalim* 25b), that the Torah which was given to Moses was written in black fire on a parchment of white fire (*Yalkut Shimoni, I,* §280). And it is said of the Giving of the Torah, "From His right hand He presented the fiery Torah to them" (*Devarim* 33:2). In other words, Hashem held the Torah on His right side, and it included both the white fire of the parchment, which gave light, and the black fire of the letters, which caused darkness.

עָנָן וַעֲרָפֶל — *Cloud, and mist.* The entire Jewish people were elevated to a state of prophecy at Mount Sinai but did not reach the level of Moses, "the master of all prophets," who was able to see the glory of God "through a clear window" (*Yevamos* 49b). This is why the Torah says of him, "and Moses approached the mist where God was" (*Shemos* 20:18). In other words, when God spoke face to face with Moses, He was hidden only by a mist; for even Moses did not actually see God's glory, as the Torah says: "For no man shall see Me and live."

The Jewish people, on the other hand, had only attained the level of prophetic vision described as "through a murky window." To them God was revealed as if from behind two coverings — an outer covering of cloud, and an inner one of mist. God said to Moses, "Behold! I come to you in the thickness of the cloud, so that the people will hear as I speak to you" (*Shemos* 19:9), with the intention that when He speaks with Moses there is no need for "the thickness of the cloud;" the mist is sufficient. But the people, who have not reached the level of "prophecy through a clear window," need "the thickness of the cloud" as well.

12. וַיְדַבֵּר ה׳ אֲלֵיכֶם מִתּוֹךְ הָאֵשׁ — *Hashem spoke to you from the midst of the fire.* This is explained by a passage in *Sifre* (*Eikev* 4): "A book and a sword came down from heaven intertwined . . . if you fulfill the Torah, you will be saved from [the sword], and if not, you will be stricken by it." Not only will we be stricken by the sword, but by fire, too; as it is said, "For by the fire of Hashem and by His sword all flesh will be judged" (*Yeshayahu* 66:16). The Torah was,

ד קֹ֛ול דְּבָרִ֖ים אַתֶּ֣ם שֹׁמְעִ֑ים וּתְמוּנָ֛ה אֵינְכֶ֥ם רֹאִ֖ים זוּלָתִ֥י
יג־יד קֹֽול׃ יג וַיַּגֵּ֨ד לָכֶ֜ם אֶת־בְּרִיתֹ֗ו אֲשֶׁ֨ר צִוָּ֤ה אֶתְכֶם֙ לַעֲשֹׂ֔ות
עֲשֶׂ֖רֶת הַדְּבָרִ֑ים וַֽיִּכְתְּבֵ֔ם עַל־שְׁנֵ֖י לֻחֹ֥ות אֲבָנִֽים׃ יד וְאֹתִ֞י
צִוָּ֤ה יהוה֙ בָּעֵ֣ת הַהִ֔וא לְלַמֵּ֣ד אֶתְכֶ֔ם חֻקִּ֖ים וּמִשְׁפָּטִ֑ים
לַעֲשֹׂתְכֶ֣ם אֹתָ֔ם בָּאָ֕רֶץ אֲשֶׁ֥ר אַתֶּ֛ם עֹבְרִ֥ים שָׁ֖מָּה לְרִשְׁתָּֽהּ׃

---

therefore, given in fire: to warn us that those who transgress its commandments will be punished with fire.

אַתֶּם שֹׁמְעִים וּתְמוּנָה אֵינְכֶם רֹאִים — *You were hearing the sound of words, but you were not seeing a form.* (Lit., "You hear [שֹׁמְעִים] the sound of words, but you do not see [אֵינְכֶם רֹאִים] a form.") Here Moses is speaking, not only to the people assembled before him, but also to each and every person in Israel who would be born in all the generations to come. This is why he suddenly shifts into the present tense: because the soul of every Jew from every generation was present at Mount Sinai. Every one of them saw the great event and heard the voice of the Living God speaking to him.

Ever since then, every Jew hears within his heart a voice which says to him, "This is the way — the way of God — which you should follow." As the prophet Isaiah says: "And your ears will hear a voice from behind you, saying, 'This is the way; go upon it' " (*Yeshayah* 30:21). This voice is an echo of the voice that every ear heard on Mount Sinai. Yet no Jew has ever been able to recall in his mind's eye a clear visual image of the great event at Mount Sinai, like the voice of God that he can still hear. Why? Because "you were not seeing a form, only a sound."

Speaking in a lighter vein, this verse may be read as rejecting the statues and pictures which the gentiles place in their homes and houses of worship. They claim that they, too, worship God, and the sight of these images helps keep them in fear of sinning against their religion. Yet God testifies that we heed His Torah even though we have no "holy pictures" to remind us. We "hear the words" even though we do not "see a form" before our eyes.

13. אֶת־בְּרִיתוֹ אֲשֶׁר צִוָּה אֶתְכֶם — *Of His covenant that He commanded you.* This verse says "commanded you," not "sealed with you," as in verse 23. This alludes to what occurred at Mount Sinai, when the people became so frightened at seeing the holy fire, that their souls left them. They changed their minds about accepting the Torah, but then God held the mountain over them like a barrel and threatened to bury them on the spot if they would not keep to their agreement. (See *Tosafos*, *Shabbos* 86.)

עַל־שְׁנֵי לֻחוֹת אֲבָנִים — *On two stone Tablets.* Why not on one tablet? Because the first tablet served as an introduction and preparation for the second tablet. It is impossible to warn people not to kill, not to commit adultery, not to steal, not to bear false witness, not to covet their neighbor's house or wife — all of

4
13-14

you were hearing the sound of words, but you were not seeing a form, only a sound. [13] *He told you of His covenant that He commanded you to observe, the Ten Declarations, and He inscribed them on two stone Tablets.* [14] *HASHEM commanded me at that time to teach you decrees and ordinances, that you shall perform them in the Land to which you cross, to possess it.*

---

which are inclinations that is human nature to desire — without first introducing them to belief in God, love for Him, and awe of Him, as it is said, "The beginning of wisdom is fear of God" (*Tehillim* 111:10).

Everything that is prerequisite to successfully observing the second tablet is found on the first tablet:

- "I am Hashem, your God, Who has taken you out of the land of Egypt, from the house of slavery" — from which we derive the love of God and belief in His wonders and His Providence;
- "You shall not recognize the gods of others in My presence ... for I am Hashem, your God — a jealous God, Who visits the sin of fathers upon children... but Who shows kindness for thousands [of generations] to those who love Me and observe My commandments."
- "You shall not take the Name of Hashem, your God, in vain, for Hashem will not absolve...."
- "Remember the Sabbath day to sanctify it." In *HaDe'ah Ve'HaDibur* (*II*:1), we explained that this commandment is intended to implant the belief in God in our hearts (see verse 10 below). Sabbath observance is entrusted to the parents, who must make sure that their sons and daughters do not desecrate it ("you shall not do any work — you, and your son, and your daughter"). We see, then, that this commandment is also meant to inculcate in children, obedience towards parents in the matter of Torah observance in general, and Sabbath observance in particular.

Thus, everything on the first tablet is aimed at implanting in the Jewish heart belief in the Creator and in His supervision over all the world's inhabitants, and the belief that He does good to those who keep His commandments and punishes those who transgress them. And this is the foundation for the warnings that come on the second tablet.

14. לַעֲשֹׂתְכֶם אֹתָם — *That you shall perform them.* The Hebrew expression here — לַעֲשֹׂתְכֶם אֹתָם — is puzzling. Translated literally, it would read something like, "to make you and to make them." We can better understand the meaning of the phrase after learning the first *Braisa*, which comprises the sixth chapter of *Pirkei Avos*: "Whoever engages in Torah study for its own sake merits many things ... he loves the Omnipresent, he loves [His] creatures ... the Torah clothes him in humility and fear [of God] ... righteous, devout, just, and faithful... ". Torah study, then, if it is done as God commanded, for its own sake, creates a great impression upon any individual, making him into a new man.

ד
טו־יט

טו וְנִשְׁמַרְתֶּ֥ם מְאֹ֖ד לְנַפְשֹׁתֵיכֶ֑ם כִּ֣י לֹ֤א רְאִיתֶם֙ כָּל־תְּמוּנָ֔ה
בְּי֗וֹם דִּבֶּ֨ר יְהוָ֧ה אֲלֵיכֶ֛ם בְּחֹרֵ֖ב מִתּ֥וֹךְ הָאֵֽשׁ׃ טז פֶּ֙ן־תַּ֨שְׁחִת֔וּן
וַעֲשִׂיתֶ֥ם לָכֶ֛ם פֶּ֖סֶל תְּמוּנַ֣ת כָּל־סָ֑מֶל תַּבְנִ֥ית זָכָ֖ר א֥וֹ נְקֵבָֽה׃
יז תַּבְנִ֕ית כָּל־בְּהֵמָ֖ה אֲשֶׁ֣ר בָּאָ֑רֶץ תַּבְנִית֙ כָּל־צִפּ֣וֹר כָּנָ֔ף
אֲשֶׁ֥ר תָּע֖וּף בַּשָּׁמָֽיִם׃ יח תַּבְנִ֕ית כָּל־רֹמֵ֖שׂ בָּאֲדָמָ֑ה תַּבְנִ֛ית
כָּל־דָּגָ֥ה אֲשֶׁר־בַּמַּ֖יִם מִתַּ֥חַת לָאָֽרֶץ׃ יט וּפֶן־תִּשָּׂ֨א עֵינֶ֜יךָ
הַשָּׁמַ֗יְמָה וְֽ֠רָאִיתָ אֶת־הַשֶּׁ֨מֶשׁ וְאֶת־הַיָּרֵ֜חַ וְאֶת־הַכּֽוֹכָבִ֗ים
כֹּ֚ל צְבָ֣א הַשָּׁמַ֔יִם וְנִדַּחְתָּ֛ וְהִשְׁתַּחֲוִ֥יתָ לָהֶ֖ם וַעֲבַדְתָּ֑ם אֲשֶׁ֨ר
חָלַ֜ק יְהוָ֤ה אֱלֹהֶ֙יךָ֙ אֹתָ֔ם לְכֹל֙ הָֽעַמִּ֔ים תַּ֖חַת כָּל־הַשָּׁמָֽיִם׃

I once heard a man boasting to his friend that he "gives all his free time to the Torah." His friend answered him, "That's good. But what has the Torah given to you?" His friend meant to say, has all your study made any recognizable impression on you?

Here Moses is saying, "Hashem commanded me ... to teach you decrees and ordinances, לַעֲשֹׂתְכֶם, to make you," through your learning, into "a wise and discerning people" — to make you into good Jews: humble, God-fearing, righteous, just, and faithful. And all this will come to be, if you study in order לַעֲשׂוֹת אֹתָם, *to perform them* — that is, the commandments.

15. כִּי לֹא רְאִיתֶם כָּל־תְּמוּנָה — *For you did not see any likeness.* Not only did you not see a likeness on the level of prophecy achieved by Moses, of whom the Torah says that Hashem "speaks to him in a clear vision" and "at the image of Hashem does he gaze" (*Bamidbar* 12:8). You did not even see a likeness as if "through a murky window."

Although the Jewish people were raised to prophetic status at the Giving of the Torah, no likeness appeared to them, only a sound, lest they make a statue or image of their vision afterwards and bow down to it. For we must remember that they were not prepared for prophecy by a gradual process of spiritual growth; they only merited hearing God speak to them this one time. But the true prophets, who prepared and made themselves fit for prophecy, were allowed to see images concordant with the subject of their prophecy.

16. פֶּן־תַּשְׁחִתוּן — *Lest you act corruptly.* Everything on the list that follows, "a form of a male or a female ... any animal ... any winged bird ... anything that creeps on the ground ... any fish," reveals the "corruption" of those who would worship such things. They have sunk to such base levels, that they can sanctify and revere creatures lower than themselves. As for those who worship the sun, the moon, and the stars, which are more easily mistaken for heavenly rulers, appointed by the King of kings to govern the lower world ("which Hashem, your God, has apportioned to all the peoples under the

4
15-19

[15] *But you shall greatly beware for your souls, for you did not*
see any likeness on the day HASHEM *spoke to you at Horeb,*
from the midst of the fire, [16] *lest you act corruptly and make*
yourselves a carved image, a likeness of any shape; a form of
a male or a female; [17] *a form of any animal on the earth; a*
form of any winged bird that flies in the heaven; [18] *a form of*
anything that creeps on the ground, a form of any fish that is
in the water under the earth; [19] *and lest you raise your eyes to*
the heaven and you see the sun, and the moon, and the stars
— the entire legion of heaven — and you be drawn astray and
bow to them and worship them, which HASHEM, *your God,*
has apportioned to all the peoples under the entire heaven!

---

entire heaven") — the Torah says of them merely that they have been "drawn astray" v. 19); they have strayed from the path of truth, and have bowed down to idols.

19. וְנִדַּחְתָּ וְהִשְׁתַּחֲוִיתָ לָהֶם — *And you be drawn astray and bow to them.* One who bows down to the sun or the moon is straying from his own common sense. Suppose we saw a man circling around a palace every day, never veering from his path to the left or to the right, never feeling free to stop for a moment or go somewhere else for a change. We would conclude that this man is not the master of the palace, for the master would surely be free to come and go as he pleased; this man, who stays within his circumscribed path, is obviously a servant of the king — a palace guard.

Thus, when we see the sun, moon, and stars, each following an appointed path day after day and year after year, anyone capable of thinking must certainly conclude that these heavenly bodies have a master who has placed each one of them in its orbit and compels each body to follow its course, not permitting any changes in their function.

The *Rambam* wrote that anyone who knows how to make astronomical calculations and does not do so is among those censured by Isaiah: "And they look not upon God's acts, nor have they seen the work of His hands" (*Yeshayahu* 5:12). For if they had looked (deeply and intentionally — see *Malbim* ad loc.) upon God's acts— the sun, moon, and stars and their orbits — they would see that these are "the work of His hands."

אֲשֶׁר חָלַק ה׳ אֱלֹהֶיךָ אֹתָם לְכֹל הָעַמִּים תַּחַת כָּל־הַשָּׁמָיִם — *Which Hashem, your God has apportioned to all the peoples under the entire heaven.* "The ancients maintained the view that every country and every people is ruled by a particular star which influences that country, and every people has its own ruling angel" (*Malbim*). "The peoples," then, are "under [the influence of] the entire heaven;" so it is only natural for them to err and worship their stars and ruling angels. This is the reason that Children of Noah are not punished for worshiping others in addition to God.

כ וְאֶתְכֶם לָקַח יהוה וַיּוֹצִא אֶתְכֶם מִכּוּר הַבַּרְזֶל מִמִּצְרָיִם ד
לִהְיוֹת לוֹ לְעַם נַחֲלָה כַּיּוֹם הַזֶּה: כא וַיהוָה הִתְאַנֶּף־בִּי כ־כה
עַל־דִּבְרֵיכֶם וַיִּשָּׁבַע לְבִלְתִּי עָבְרִי אֶת־הַיַּרְדֵּן וּלְבִלְתִּי־בֹא
אֶל־הָאָרֶץ הַטּוֹבָה אֲשֶׁר יהוָה אֱלֹהֶיךָ נֹתֵן לְךָ נַחֲלָה: כב כִּי
אָנֹכִי מֵת בָּאָרֶץ הַזֹּאת אֵינֶנִּי עֹבֵר אֶת־הַיַּרְדֵּן וְאַתֶּם
עֹבְרִים וִירִשְׁתֶּם אֶת־הָאָרֶץ הַטּוֹבָה הַזֹּאת: כג הִשָּׁמְרוּ לָכֶם
פֶּן־תִּשְׁכְּחוּ אֶת־בְּרִית יהוה אֱלֹהֵיכֶם אֲשֶׁר כָּרַת עִמָּכֶם
וַעֲשִׂיתֶם לָכֶם פֶּסֶל תְּמוּנַת כֹּל אֲשֶׁר צִוְּךָ יהוָה אֱלֹהֶיךָ:
כד כִּי יהוָה אֱלֹהֶיךָ אֵשׁ אֹכְלָה הוּא אֵל קַנָּא:
כה כִּי־תוֹלִיד בָּנִים וּבְנֵי בָנִים וְנוֹשַׁנְתֶּם בָּאָרֶץ וְהִשְׁחַתֶּם

---

20. וְאֶתְכֶם לָקַח ה׳ . . . לִהְיוֹת לוֹ לְעַם נַחֲלָה — *But Hashem has taken you . . . to be a nation of heritage for Him.* We are not under the influence of the stars and we have no ruling angel. God alone is our King, the King of all the world. We merited this status through our ordeal in the "iron crucible" of Egypt, where we were refined like silver, and all our impurities were removed. Our Exodus from Egypt, too, elevated our spiritual level, for it did not occur by chance. The end of the crucible did not just happen; God Himself took us out with signs and wonders. Our faith in Him was so strong that we took it upon ourselves "to be a nation of heritage for Him, as this very day." Therefore we are forbidden to offer service to any angel, force, or star, even if only as an "auxiliary" god in addition to God — "only to Hashem alone!" (*Shemos* 22:19).

21. לְבִלְתִּי עָבְרִי אֶת־הַיַּרְדֵּן — *That I would not cross the Jordan.* And in case I should try to come to the Land without crossing the Jordan (for example, by going around the Dead Sea and coming in through the Negev, or going around the springs of Banyas and entering the Land from the north), God also swore that I would "not come to the good Land" — not by any route.

22. כִּי אָנֹכִי מֵת בָּאָרֶץ הַזֹּאת . . . וְאַתֶּם עֹבְרִים — *For I will die in this land . . . but you are crossing.* Surely you remember that when I was six hours late descending from Mount Sinai you said: "Rise up, make for us gods . . . for this man Moses . . . we do not know what became of him"(*Shemos* 32:1). And so you made the Golden Calf. Now that I am about to leave you and not return, there is certainly room for concern "lest you forget the covenant of Hashem . . . and make yourselves a carved image." Therefore I am warning you about this.

23. וַעֲשִׂיתֶם לָכֶם פֶּסֶל . . . אֲשֶׁר צִוְּךָ ה׳ אֱלֹהֶיךָ — *And you make yourselves a carved image . . . as Hashem, your God, has commanded you.* "As He has commanded you *not to do*" (*Rashi*). Yet this implies that the words "not to do" are missing from the verse. Therefore, some commentators explain that this verse alludes to the Cherubim which God commanded the Jewish people to make on the Ark Cover, and forbade them to make elsewhere.

20 But HASHEM has taken you and withdrawn you from
the iron crucible, from Egypt, to be a nation of heritage for
Him, as this very day.
21 HASHEM became angry with me because of you, and
He swore that I would not cross the Jordan and not come
to the good Land that HASHEM, your God, gives you as a
heritage. 22 For I will die in this land; I am not crossing the
Jordan — but you are crossing and you shall possess this good
Land. 23 Beware for yourselves lest you forget the covenant
of HASHEM, your God, that He has sealed with you, and you
make yourselves a carved image, a likeness of anything, as
HASHEM, your God, has commanded you. 24 For HASHEM,
your God — He is a consuming fire, a jealous God.
25 When you beget children and grandchildren and
will have been long in the Land, you will grow corrupt

An important concept is hidden in this wording. The worst transgressor is the one who thinks he is doing a *mitzvah*, for how will he ever repent? There are indeed idol worshipers who make this mistake, and say that the honor they accord to heavenly bodies, which serve God in His world, is really God's own honor, for He desires that people should honor them, just as a king wishes people to accord honor to his ministers. (This is the *Rambam*'s explanation, in *Hilchos Avodah Zarah*, ch. 1.) Because this idolater makes the error of claiming he is doing a *mitzvah*, he will never abandon his ways.

This is why the verse says, "Beware for yourselves lest you forget the covenant of Hashem" — if not His existence — "and you make yourselves a carved image, a likeness of anything" — in the belief that "Hashem, your God, has commanded you" to accord honor to His 'ministers' which direct the lower world.

25. כִּי־תוֹלִיד בָּנִים וּבְנֵי בָנִים וְנוֹשַׁנְתֶּם בָּאָרֶץ — *When you beget children and grandchildren and will have been long in the Land.* I do not fear for the first generation, says Moses, nor even for the second generation, which saw God's deeds and wonders in Egypt and in the Wilderness, and the miraculous Crossing of the Jordan and conquest of the Land. Nor do I fear even for those among the second generation who did not see all this with their own eyes; for they heard it from their parents, who saw it with their own eyes. But I fear for the third generation, lest, having "been long in the Land," they might actually sink low enough to set up an idol, Heaven forbid; they could forget the decrees and ordinances which they received from their fathers and abandon them. (We find an example of this principle in reverse in the *halachah* that a third-generation Egyptian or Edomite proselyte may enter the congregation of God.)

There is another cause for fear as well. The Adversary is bound to arise to challenge the third generation, to goad them off the path of their fathers, if he

ד וַעֲשִׂיתֶם פֶּסֶל תְּמוּנַת כֹּל וַעֲשִׂיתֶם הָרַע בְּעֵינֵי יְהוָה־
כו־כח אֱלֹהֶיךָ לְהַכְעִיסוֹ: כו הַעִידֹתִי בָכֶם הַיּוֹם אֶת־הַשָּׁמַיִם
וְאֶת־הָאָרֶץ כִּי־אָבֹד תֹּאבֵדוּן מַהֵר מֵעַל הָאָרֶץ אֲשֶׁר
אַתֶּם עֹבְרִים אֶת־הַיַּרְדֵּן שָׁמָּה לְרִשְׁתָּהּ לֹא־תַאֲרִיכֻן יָמִים
עָלֶיהָ כִּי הִשָּׁמֵד תִּשָּׁמֵדוּן: כז וְהֵפִיץ יְהוָה אֶתְכֶם בָּעַמִּים
וְנִשְׁאַרְתֶּם מְתֵי מִסְפָּר בַּגּוֹיִם אֲשֶׁר יְנַהֵג יְהוָה אֶתְכֶם
שָׁמָּה: כח וַעֲבַדְתֶּם־שָׁם אֱלֹהִים מַעֲשֵׂה יְדֵי אָדָם עֵץ וָאֶבֶן
אֲשֶׁר לֹא־יִרְאוּן וְלֹא יִשְׁמְעוּן וְלֹא יֹאכְלוּן וְלֹא יְרִיחֻן:

---

can, so that Torah observance will not last for three consecutive generations. For God's promise was given to us by Isaiah: that if the Torah "will not depart from your mouth, and from the mouths of your children, and from the mouths of your children's children," then "God has said, from now until eternity" it will remain (*Yeshayah* 59:21).

וְהִשְׁחַתֶּם . . . לְהַכְעִיסוֹ — *You will grow corrupt... to anger Him.* From this we learn that the worst punishment that can happen to Israel as a whole — "that you will surely perish quickly from the Land" — is inflicted only for the type of idolatry called "corrupt": that is, the worship of animals. (See above, v. 16, for the difference between "act corruptly" and "going astray.") Furthermore, it is inflicted only when the idolatry was done deliberately just so as to anger God. And so we find this expression used about Ahab's idolatry: "And Ahab did even more, so as to anger Hashem" (*I Melachim*,16:33). That is the significance of "to anger Him" in our present verse.

The present verse also says, "and you will do evil in the eyes of Hashem, your God" — that is, to commit murder and adultery, says the *Ibn Ezra*, for the First Temple was destroyed for the sins of idolatry, sexual immorality, and murder. This, too, is called "angering God," as we see in the *Gemara's* account of King Amon, who had incestuous relations with his mother and said, "I do this for no other purpose than to anger my Creator" (*Sanhedrin* 103b).

The Second Temple was destroyed because of slander and baseless hatred. This, too, concurs with our verse, since the Sages say that slander is the equivalent of idolatry, sexual immorality, and murder, all combined (*Tosefta Peah* ch. 1).

27. וְהֵפִיץ ה׳ אֶתְכֶם בָּעַמִּים — *Hashem will scatter you among the peoples.* There is no anguish like ours, nor is any people in the world scattered and dispersed among the nations like Israel in its downfall. There is no suffering like ours in our exile; it exceeds the limits of anything normal. For just as Hashem did miracles and wonders for us before the eyes of all the nations when we lived up to our purpose, to safeguard the Torah, to be His chosen nation and to receive the most desirable of lands, so were we assailed by troubles both numerous and strange, beyond anything explicable by natural

4
26-28 *and make a carved image of anything, and you will do evil in*
the eyes of HASHEM, your God, to anger Him. [26] *I appoint*
heaven and earth this day to bear witness against you that
you will surely perish quickly from the Land to which you are
crossing the Jordan to possess; you shall not have lengthy
days upon it, for you will be destroyed. [27] *HASHEM will scatter*
you among the peoples, and you will be left few in number
among the nations where HASHEM will lead you. [28] *There you*
will serve gods, the handiwork of man, of wood and stone,
which do not see, and do not hear, and do not eat, and do not
smell.

---

causes, when we strayed from the path and were exiled from our Land. But all this is for our good, to make us return to Him, and then He will return to us and show us His mercy.

וְנִשְׁאַרְתֶּם מְתֵי מִסְפָּר — *And you will be left few in number.* There have indeed been a few cases in world history where conquering nations have sent the peoples they vanquished into exile in other lands. One was Sennacherib, who "mixed up" (בִּלְבֵּל) all the peoples of his empire (see *Yeshayah* 10:13, 36:17, and *Berachos* 28a). But these exiled peoples cannot be said to have "been left" in existence; not even a few of their number retained their nationality and religion. They were assimilated into the nations among whom they lived, and no trace of them remains today. Where are Ammon and Moab, Amalek, Philistia, Assyria, Babylonia, and all the other ancient nations? They have disappeared. But of us the Torah says, "you will be left few in number" — "that is, in each single nation," says the *Ramban*, "for He will scatter us to the four winds, but altogether there remain many of us, praise be to God." And this is in fulfillment of the prophet's words: "For I, Hashem, have not changed, and you, children of Jacob, have not wasted away" (*Malachi* 3:6).

אֲשֶׁר יְנַהֵג ה׳ אֶתְכֶם שָׁמָּה — *Where Hashem will lead you.* It is not the nations who have exiled you with their swords and their bows; it is your own sins that have caused it.

28. וַעֲבַדְתֶּם־שָׁם אֱלֹהִים מַעֲשֵׂה יְדֵי אָדָם עֵץ וָאֶבֶן — *There you will serve gods, the handiwork of man, of wood and stone.* What kind of punishment is this for worshiping idols in the Land of Israel — that they should go and worship idols in the Diaspora? Is this not merely giving them what they wanted?

There are two kinds of idol worship. The first is the kind that was practiced in the days of Enosh, when (as we discussed above) people thought that God had placed the lower world under the control of the heavenly bodies, and therefore it must be His will that they be served and revered, as an earthly king wishes his ministers to be revered. They then began to make images and sculptures representing the stars (as the *Rambam* explains in *Hilchos Avodah Zarah* [ch. 1]) and worshiped them. In the course of time, people's good sense waned

ד
כט־לד

כט וּבִקַּשְׁתֶּם מִשָּׁם אֶת־יהוה אֱלֹהֶיךָ וּמָצָאתָ כִּי תִדְרְשֶׁנּוּ
בְּכָל־לְבָבְךָ וּבְכָל־נַפְשֶׁךָ: ל בַּצַּר לְךָ וּמְצָאוּךָ כֹּל הַדְּבָרִים
הָאֵלֶּה בְּאַחֲרִית הַיָּמִים וְשַׁבְתָּ עַד־יהוה אֱלֹהֶיךָ וְשָׁמַעְתָּ
בְּקֹלוֹ: לא כִּי אֵל רַחוּם יהוה אֱלֹהֶיךָ לֹא יַרְפְּךָ וְלֹא
יַשְׁחִיתֶךָ וְלֹא יִשְׁכַּח אֶת־בְּרִית אֲבֹתֶיךָ אֲשֶׁר נִשְׁבַּע לָהֶם:
לב כִּי שְׁאַל־נָא לְיָמִים רִאשֹׁנִים אֲשֶׁר־הָיוּ לְפָנֶיךָ לְמִן־
הַיּוֹם אֲשֶׁר בָּרָא אֱלֹהִים ׀ אָדָם עַל־הָאָרֶץ וּלְמִקְצֵה
הַשָּׁמַיִם וְעַד־קְצֵה הַשָּׁמָיִם הֲנִהְיָה כַּדָּבָר הַגָּדוֹל הַזֶּה אוֹ
הֲנִשְׁמַע כָּמֹהוּ: לג הֲשָׁמַע עָם קוֹל אֱלֹהִים מְדַבֵּר מִתּוֹךְ־
הָאֵשׁ כַּאֲשֶׁר־שָׁמַעְתָּ אַתָּה וַיֶּחִי: לד אוֹ ׀ הֲנִסָּה אֱלֹהִים
לָבוֹא לָקַחַת לוֹ גוֹי מִקֶּרֶב גּוֹי בְּמַסֹּת בְּאֹתֹת וּבְמוֹפְתִים

---

further: they forgot the Creator, and every person had his own idol of wood or stone to which he bowed down. This is the second type of idol worship.

Our verse is talking about how a person can sink from one level to the other. If you start by making a "carved image of anything" — if you make an idol of a star or some lofty object in the belief that God has given it rulership over the world — then you will have to go into exile among barbarous peoples. Eventually you will, like them, bow down to your own handiwork, sculptures of wood and stone: the coarsest kind of idolatry which comes of ignorance and savagery.

29. ובִקַּשְׁתֶּם מִשָּׁם אֶת־ה׳ — *From there you will seek Hashem.* Exile and poverty (which *Chazal* said is worse than fifty plagues in one's house [*Bava Basra* 116]) will eventually bring you back to *teshuvah* — "from there you will seek Hashem."

ובִקַּשְׁתֶּם מִשָּׁם — *From there you will seek.* Not only will you come to realize Who your God is, but you will also realize that you are "there" — that you are not in your Land. But when you seek your God in prayer, that prayer must ascend from the place that your father Jacob singled out: "This is the Gate of Heaven." You will know that you must direct your prayers to Heaven by way of your own Land, with your face towards the Land of Israel.

32. כִּי שְׁאַל־נָא לְיָמִים רִאשֹׁנִים . . . הֲנִהְיָה כַּדָּבָר הַגָּדוֹל הַזֶּה — *For inquire now regarding the early days. . . Has there ever been anything like this great thing . . . ?* In the verse before this Moses said, "and He will not forget the covenant of your forefathers." This might have prompted people to say, "But suppose God makes a covenant with another people, and forgets His love for your fathers and you, and becomes totally involved in His love for them? Or suppose He makes a new covenant with another people because you broke your covenant with Him?" Therefore this verse comes to say that such a thing could not be: "For inquire now regarding the early days. . . from the day when Hashem created man on the earth, and from one end of heaven to the other end

29 From there you will seek HASHEM, your God, and you will
find Him, if you search for Him with all your heart and all
your soul. 30 When you are in distress and all these things
have befallen you, at the end of days, you will return unto
HASHEM, your God, and hearken to His voice. 31 For HASHEM,
your God, is a merciful God, He will not abandon you nor
destroy you, and He will not forget the covenant of your fore-
fathers that He swore to them. 32 For inquire now regarding
the early days that preceded you, from the day when HASHEM
created man on the earth, and from one end of heaven to the
other end of heaven: Has there ever been anything like this
great thing or has anything like it been heard? 33 Has a people
ever heard the voice of God speaking from the midst of the
fire as you have heard, and survived? 34 Or has any god ever
miraculously come to take for himself a nation from amidst
a nation, with challenges, with signs, and with wonders,

---

of heaven: Has there ever been anything like this great thing or has anything like it been heard? Has a people ever heard the voice of God speaking from the midst of the fire as you have heard . . . ?"

If God were to choose another people as His own — Heaven forbid — He would certainly appear to that people for all the world to see, and speak to them from the midst of the fire as He spoke to us. For that is the way of our God, as Isaiah says: "Not in secret did I speak" [when I gave the Torah — (*Rashi*)] "[or] in a place of darkened land; I did not say to the seed of Jacob, 'Seek Me for naught'" (*Yeshayah* 45:19). No one can say, then, that God has abandoned His people and chosen another people "in secret, in a place of darkened land." And therefore, "Israel is saved through Hashem, an eternal salvation; you will neither be ashamed nor humiliated for all eternity." For in every place and at every time the gates of repentance and redemption are open before us.

34. לָקַחַת לוֹ גוֹי מִקֶּרֶב גּוֹי — *To take for himself a nation from amidst a nation.*

Why does Moses recount these events out of their chronological order, talking first about the Giving of the Torah ("Has a people ever heard. . .") and then, in this verse, about the Exodus from Egypt?

Because the previous verse (32) asks, "Has there ever been anything like this great thing or has anything like it been heard?" If a man asks his friend whether he has ever observed a certain event, he will first ask if his friend has seen such a thing close to his own home, and only afterwards if he has ever heard of such a thing happening elsewhere. So it was natural for Moses to mention the events at Mount Sinai first, since these were the closest, most recent events.

But actually this order is just as it should be. For the main question that Moses is asking is whether a new Torah was ever given to another people, in a glorious assembly of the entire nation who heard the voice of God with their own ears "speaking from the midst of the fire." The answer is No; only then

ד וּבְמִלְחָמָה וּבְיָד חֲזָקָה וּבִזְרוֹעַ נְטוּיָה וּבְמוֹרָאִים גְּדֹלִים
לה־מב כְּכֹל אֲשֶׁר־עָשָׂה לָכֶם יהוה אֱלֹהֵיכֶם בְּמִצְרַיִם לְעֵינֶיךָ:
לה אַתָּה הָרְאֵתָ לָדַעַת כִּי יהוה הוּא הָאֱלֹהִים אֵין עוֹד
מִלְּבַדּוֹ: לו מִן־הַשָּׁמַיִם הִשְׁמִיעֲךָ אֶת־קֹלוֹ לְיַסְּרֶךָּ וְעַל־
הָאָרֶץ הֶרְאֲךָ אֶת־אִשּׁוֹ הַגְּדוֹלָה וּדְבָרָיו שָׁמַעְתָּ מִתּוֹךְ
הָאֵשׁ: לז וְתַחַת כִּי אָהַב אֶת־אֲבֹתֶיךָ וַיִּבְחַר בְּזַרְעוֹ אַחֲרָיו
וַיּוֹצִאֲךָ בְּפָנָיו בְּכֹחוֹ הַגָּדֹל מִמִּצְרָיִם: לח לְהוֹרִישׁ גּוֹיִם
גְּדֹלִים וַעֲצֻמִים מִמְּךָ מִפָּנֶיךָ לַהֲבִיאֲךָ לָתֶת־לְךָ אֶת־אַרְצָם
נַחֲלָה כַּיּוֹם הַזֶּה: לט וְיָדַעְתָּ הַיּוֹם וַהֲשֵׁבֹתָ אֶל־לְבָבֶךָ כִּי
יהוה הוּא הָאֱלֹהִים בַּשָּׁמַיִם מִמַּעַל וְעַל־הָאָרֶץ מִתָּחַת אֵין
עוֹד: מ וְשָׁמַרְתָּ אֶת־חֻקָּיו וְאֶת־מִצְוֹתָיו אֲשֶׁר אָנֹכִי מְצַוְּךָ
הַיּוֹם אֲשֶׁר יִיטַב לְךָ וּלְבָנֶיךָ אַחֲרֶיךָ וּלְמַעַן תַּאֲרִיךְ יָמִים
עַל־הָאֲדָמָה אֲשֶׁר יהוה אֱלֹהֶיךָ נֹתֵן לְךָ כָּל־הַיָּמִים:
שלישי מא אָז יַבְדִּיל מֹשֶׁה שָׁלֹשׁ עָרִים בְּעֵבֶר הַיַּרְדֵּן
מִזְרְחָה שָׁמֶשׁ: מב לָנֻס שָׁמָּה רוֹצֵחַ אֲשֶׁר יִרְצַח אֶת־
רֵעֵהוּ בִּבְלִי־דַעַת וְהוּא לֹא־שֹׂנֵא לוֹ מִתְּמֹל שִׁלְשֹׁם

---

does Moses go on to emphasize that it has never even been tried. We can interpret אוֹ הֲנִסָּה as asking "Or has He tried" — the fact is, says Moses, that God has never even made a נִסָּיוֹן, *a trial* of any other nation towards such an assembly. No other nation has been so enslaved, and so purified, nor has it been redeemed with manifest signs and wonders.

36. מִן־הַשָּׁמַיִם הִשְׁמִיעֲךָ אֶת־קֹלוֹ לְיַסְּרֶךָּ וְעַל־הָאָרֶץ הֶרְאֲךָ — *From heaven He caused you to hear His voice in order to teach you, and on earth He showed you.* At the time of the Giving of the Torah God opened the seven heavens and the seven divisions of *Gehinnom*, revealing all the upper worlds and all the lower worlds, and showed you that "there is none other besides Him" (*Devarim Rabbah*, ed. Margolies, 1:40). How, then, could you worship false gods, which brought you to exile and troubles? Therefore, return to God, and to His *mitzvos*, and He will bring you back from exile and show you mercy.

37. וְתַחַת כִּי אָהַב אֶת־אֲבֹתֶיךָ — *Because He loved your forefathers.* If you should ask, "Why did Israel merit such an honor, unlike all the other nations?", the answer is that it was entirely due to the merit of the Patriarchs, who did God's will and made His Name known in the world.

38. לְהוֹרִישׁ גּוֹיִם גְּדֹלִים וַעֲצֻמִים מִמְּךָ מִפָּנֶיךָ — *To drive away before you nations that are greater and mightier than you.* Not only the Exodus from Egypt was accomplished "with His great strength" — in a supernatural way — but the conquest of the Land, too, will be accomplished supernaturally ("nations that are greater and mightier than you"). This is aimed at strengthening your belief in

and with war, and with a strong hand, and with an outstretched arm, and with greatly awesome deeds, such as everything that HASHEM, *your God, did for you in Egypt before your eyes?* [35] *You have been shown in order to know that* HASHEM, *He is the God! There is none beside Him!*

[36] *From heaven He caused you to hear His voice in order to teach you, and on earth He showed you His great fire, and you heard His words from the midst of the fire,* [37] *because He loved your forefathers, and He chose his offspring after him, and took you out before Himself with His great strength from Egypt;* [38] *to drive away before you nations that are greater and mightier than you, to bring you, to give you their land as an inheritance, as this very day.* [39] *You shall know this day and take to your heart that* HASHEM, *He is the God — in heaven above and on the earth below — there is none other.* [40] *You shall observe His decrees and His commandments that I command you this day, so that He will do good to you and to your children after you, and so that you will prolong your days on the Land that* HASHEM, *your God, gives you, for all the days.*

[41] *Then Moses set aside three cities on the bank of the Jordan, toward the rising sun,* [42] *for a murderer to flee there, who will have killed his fellow without knowledge, but who was not an enemy of his from yesterday and before yesterday —*

God and His Providence over Israel. The ultimate purpose is "to bring you, to give you their land as an inheritance" — a Land that has God's eyes upon it, where you can serve Him and keep His Torah.

39. וְיָדַעְתָּ הַיּוֹם — *You shall know this day.* Perhaps the word "know" can be understood here in the same sense as when God said of Abraham, "For I have known him" (*Bereishis* 18:19). By this He meant "For I have loved him," and the same might well be true here. "You shall love the day" on which you stood before your God at Horeb, and this love will cause you to remember that day all your life, so that fear of God will be upon you and you will not sin.

41-42. אָז יַבְדִּיל מֹשֶׁה שָׁלֹשׁ עָרִים . . . לָנֻס שָׁמָּה — *Then Moses set aside three cities. . . to flee there.* To when is the word, "then" referring? At the time that Moses threatened them with exile from their Land if they should serve other gods, it occurred to him that they might already have forgotten the bitterness of exile (for only those few who had been under twenty years of age at the time of the Exodus and were still living could tell the young something about the taste of exile). Still more, when he thought of those moments in the Wilderness when the Children of Israel had said "Let us appoint a leader and return to Egypt," (*Bamidbar* 14:4), he realized they did not necessarily think of

ד וְנָס אֶל־אַחַת מִן־הֶעָרִים הָאֵל וָחָי: מג אֶת־בֶּצֶר בַּמִּדְבָּר
מג־מז בְּאֶרֶץ הַמִּישֹׁר לָראוּבֵנִי וְאֶת־רָאמֹת בַּגִּלְעָד לַגָּדִי וְאֶת־
גּוֹלָן בַּבָּשָׁן לַמְנַשִּׁי: מד וְזֹאת הַתּוֹרָה אֲשֶׁר־שָׂם מֹשֶׁה לִפְנֵי
בְּנֵי יִשְׂרָאֵל: מה אֵלֶּה הָעֵדֹת וְהַחֻקִּים וְהַמִּשְׁפָּטִים אֲשֶׁר
דִּבֶּר מֹשֶׁה אֶל־בְּנֵי יִשְׂרָאֵל בְּצֵאתָם מִמִּצְרָיִם: מו בְּעֵבֶר
הַיַּרְדֵּן בַּגַּיְא מוּל בֵּית פְּעוֹר בְּאֶרֶץ סִיחֹן מֶלֶךְ הָאֱמֹרִי
אֲשֶׁר יוֹשֵׁב בְּחֶשְׁבּוֹן אֲשֶׁר הִכָּה מֹשֶׁה וּבְנֵי יִשְׂרָאֵל
בְּצֵאתָם מִמִּצְרָיִם: מז וַיִּירְשׁוּ אֶת־אַרְצוֹ וְאֶת־אֶרֶץ ׀ עוֹג

---

exile as such a terrible thing. It was "then" that Moses set aside three cities for persons who had to go into exile after killing someone unintentionally, and described to the people in elaborate detail the conditions of life in exile according to the Oral Torah, which he was of course teaching them at that time.

As we explained in our commentary on *Parashas Masei*, Cities of Refuge have no commerce or industry (so that it will never happen that the "avenger of blood" should go there on business [see *Bamidbar* 35:22-28]). There is no way of earning a living in such a city, so that the exile is reduced to waiting each day for his bread to be given him (as it regularly was by the mother of the *Kohen Gadol*). Yet if he goes in search of a livelihood, thus violating the prohibition of leaving the city, the avenger's sword awaits him. (Perhaps the Torah is here foreshadowing the Pale of Settlement that was decreed for the Jews in Tsarist Russia.) Moses told the people of all this and various other restrictions and complications, too, which are explained in Tractate *Sanhedrin*.

"Then" the Children of Israel realized that if this was what exile among Jews is like (wherein the exile is assured of his life, at least, as long as he stays in the city), then exile among the nations of the world would be as bitter as death. For "it is a well-known *halachah* that Esau hates Jacob," and it is equally well-known in the history of our exile that gentiles sometimes even stage their pogroms right in our own homes.

⋄ **וְנָס אֶל־אַחַת מִן־הֶעָרִים הָאֵל וָחָי** — *Then he shall flee to one of these cities and live.* Why does the Torah say, "to one of these cities"? Would anyone think of fleeing to all three of them at once?

We can explain this after looking at the next verse: "Bezer in the wilderness. . . of the Reubenite; Ramoth in the Gilead of the Gadite; and Golan in the Bashan, of the Manassite." Since "of the Reubenite [לָראוּבֵנִי]" could also be explained as "*for* the Reubenite," and so for the other two cities, people might easily come to think that murderers from the tribe of Reuben must flee *only* to Bezer, those from the tribe of Gad *only* to Ramoth, and those from the tribe of Manasseh to Golan. Therefore Moses expressly states: "he shall flee to *[any] one* of these cities and live"; if an accidental murderer from the tribe of Reuben flees to Ramoth or to Golan, there, too, "he will live." (See our commentary to *Bamidbar* 35:2.)

4
43-47

then he shall flee to one of these cities and live: 43 Bezer in
the wilderness, in the land of the plain, of the Reubenite;
Ramoth in the Gilead, of the Gadite; and Golan in the
Bashan, of the Manassite.

44 This is the teaching that Moses placed before the
Children of Israel. 45 These are the testimonies, the decrees,
and the ordinances that Moses spoke to the Children of
Israel, when they left Egypt, 46 on the bank of the Jordan,
in the valley, opposite Beth-peor, in the land of Sihon,
king of the Amorite, who dwells in Heshbon, whom Moses
and the Children of Israel smote when they went out
of Egypt. 47 They possessed his land and the land of Og

---

44. **וְזֹאת הַתּוֹרָה** — *This is the Torah* [*teaching*]. Our Torah is a Torah of life; for one who clings to it, life is not worth living without the Torah. Therefore if a student of Torah is exiled (for an accidental murder), his teacher is exiled with him, so as to fulfill the Torah's promise: וָחָי, "he will live." As the *Rambam* puts it, "There is no life, for the wise and those who seek wisdom, without Torah study" (*Hilchos Rotzeach* 7:1). This is why the words, "This is the Torah," are placed directly after the passage about the Cities of Refuge, as if to say that this is the kind of Torah that Moses placed before the Children of Israel — a Torah whose students feel that without Torah study life is meaningless.

אֲשֶׁר־שָׂם מֹשֶׁה — *That Moses placed*. This word שָׂם, "placed," is a homonym of סַם, "drug, potion." *Chazal* saw this as a hint that "If one merits it, [the Torah] becomes an elixir of life for him; if he does not merit this, then it becomes an elixir of death for him" (*Yoma* 72b). And why does this allusion appear precisely here? — In anticipation of a question that you might ask: "If the exile whom we discussed above is so attached to his Torah study that he cannot live without it, and even his teacher must go into exile with him, then how did he ever come to shed blood in the first place? Shouldn't the merit of his Torah learning have shielded him from becoming involved in such a terrible accident?"

In this verse, therefore, the Torah hints at the answer: there is also such a thing as Torah study without merit, the kind of study which becomes an elixir of death, causing him to become guilty of murder. But one can only hope that after such a disaster befalls them, both student and teacher will give more thought to their deeds, and while in exile the student will begin to study Torah לִשְׁמָהּ — purely for the sake of fulfilling its commandments, and thus merit the "elixir of life."

46. **מוּל בֵּית פְּעוֹר** — *Opposite Beth-peor*. The people's proximity to Beth-peor is mentioned here to tell us that they were no longer concerned that the Evil Inclination might lead them into idolatry. For now they were constantly occupied with Torah study; and *Chazal* tell us that while one is studying Torah, it protects and saves him from the Evil Inclination (*Sotah* 21a; *Rashi*).

ד מֶלֶךְ־הַבָּשָׁן שְׁנֵי מַלְכֵי הָאֱמֹרִי אֲשֶׁר בְּעֵבֶר הַיַּרְדֵּן מִזְרַח
מח־מט שָׁמֶשׁ: מח מֵעֲרֹעֵר אֲשֶׁר עַל־שְׂפַת־נַחַל אַרְנֹן וְעַד־הַר
שִׂיאֹן הוּא חֶרְמוֹן: מט וְכָל־הָעֲרָבָה עֵבֶר הַיַּרְדֵּן מִזְרָחָה
וְעַד יָם הָעֲרָבָה תַּחַת אַשְׁדֹּת הַפִּסְגָּה:
ה רביעי א וַיִּקְרָא מֹשֶׁה אֶל־כָּל־יִשְׂרָאֵל וַיֹּאמֶר אֲלֵהֶם שְׁמַע
א־ו יִשְׂרָאֵל אֶת־הַחֻקִּים וְאֶת־הַמִּשְׁפָּטִים אֲשֶׁר אָנֹכִי דֹּבֵר
בְּאָזְנֵיכֶם הַיּוֹם וּלְמַדְתֶּם אֹתָם וּשְׁמַרְתֶּם לַעֲשֹׂתָם: ב יהוָה
אֱלֹהֵינוּ כָּרַת עִמָּנוּ בְּרִית בְּחֹרֵב: ג לֹא אֶת־אֲבֹתֵינוּ
כָּרַת יהוָה אֶת־הַבְּרִית הַזֹּאת כִּי אִתָּנוּ אֲנַחְנוּ אֵלֶּה
פֹה הַיּוֹם כֻּלָּנוּ חַיִּים: ד פָּנִים | בְּפָנִים דִּבֶּר יהוָה עִמָּכֶם
בָּהָר מִתּוֹךְ הָאֵשׁ: ה אָנֹכִי עֹמֵד בֵּין־יהוָה וּבֵינֵיכֶם
בָּעֵת הַהִוא לְהַגִּיד לָכֶם אֶת־דְּבַר יהוָה כִּי יְרֵאתֶם מִפְּנֵי
הָאֵשׁ וְלֹא־עֲלִיתֶם בָּהָר לֵאמֹר: ו אָנֹכִי
יהוָה אֱלֹהֶיךָ אֲשֶׁר הוֹצֵאתִיךָ מֵאֶרֶץ מִצְרַיִם מִבֵּית עֲבָדִים:

---

48. וְעַד־הַר שִׂיאֹן הוּא חֶרְמוֹן — *Until Mount Sion, which is Hermon.* This is the northern border of the Trans-Jordan. Mount Hermon is called here by the name שִׂיאֹן to tell you that its peak (שִׂיא) also belongs to the Children of Israel. See above, 3:9.

49. וְכָל־הָעֲרָבָה עֵבֶר הַיַּרְדֵּן מִזְרָחָה וְעַד יָם הָעֲרָבָה — *And the entire Arabah, the eastern bank of the Jordan until the Sea of Arabah.* This is the southern border of the Trans-Jordan. Perhaps the reason why Scripture indicates these borders in such detail, even though we already know them, is to explain a puzzling point about the Cities of Refuge: Why were three Cities of Refuge set aside in Trans-Jordan for the use of two and a half tribes, whereas the same number of cities, not more, were set aside in the land of Canaan for nine and a half tribes?

This question is, in fact, discussed in *Makkos* 9b. We can add that from *Bamidbar* 35:14 clear evidence can be deduced that the number of cities is not dependent on the size of the population, but on the distance between the civilian settlements and the Cities of Refuge. For the Torah stipulated that the Cities of Refuge must be accessible to anyone who had to flee to them, in case he should be pursued by the avenger of the blood. If he were to become exhausted on the way, then he would be overtaken and killed.

Geographically, the Trans-Jordan is nearly as large as the land of Israel, being just as long, from Mount Hermon to the Sea of Arabah, and almost as wide. The quality of the land, however, is not as good, and therefore no more than two and a half tribes could be settled there. But because of its geographical length it needed just as many Cities of Refuge as the Land of Israel.

4 *the king of Bashan, two kings of the Amorite, which are on*
48-49 *the bank of the Jordan, where the sun rises;* [48] *from Aroer*
that is by the shore of Arnon Brook until Mount Sion, which
is Hermon, [49] *and the entire Arabah, the eastern bank of the*
Jordan until the Sea of Arabah, under the waterfalls of the
cliffs.

5 [1] *Moses called all of Israel and said to them: Hear, O Israel,*
1-6 *the decrees and the ordinances that I speak in your ears*
today; learn them, and be careful to perform them. [2] *HASHEM,*
our God, sealed a covenant with us at Horeb. [3] *Not with our*
forefathers did HASHEM seal this covenant, but with us — we
who are here, all of us alive today. [4] *Face to face did HASHEM*
speak with you on the mountain, from amid the fire. [5] *I was*
standing between HASHEM and you at that time, to relate the
word of HASHEM to you — for you were afraid of the fire and
you did not ascend the mountain — saying:

[6] *I am HASHEM, your God, Who has taken you out of the*
land of Egypt, from the house of slavery.

5.

4. **פָּנִים בְּפָנִים דִּבֶּר ה׳ עִמָּכֶם** — *Face to face did Hashem speak with you.* As is well known, this is a very high level of prophecy; but why was nothing said about it at the actual Giving of the Torah?

There seems to be a tinge of rebuke in these words. Now, after the sin of the Golden Calf, the Children of Israel were unable even to gaze upon the face of Moses, the mediator between them and God; whereas, before the sin, "face to face did Hashem speak with you on the mountain, from amid the fire." *Chazal* comment, "See how great is the power of sin!" For while they were free of sin, "the appearance of the glory of Hashem was like a consuming fire on the mountaintop before the eyes of the Children of Israel" (*Shemos* 24:17), yet they were not afraid. But after they sinned they recoiled in fear even from the beams of glory that shone from Moses' face (*Rashi* on *Shemos* 34:30, based on *Bamidbar Rabbah* §11). So here it made sense to mention the fact that God once spoke with them "face to face," whereas at the Giving of the Torah, before they sinned, there was no need to mention what was obvious.

5. **כִּי יְרֵאתֶם מִפְּנֵי הָאֵשׁ וְלֹא־עֲלִיתֶם בָּהָר** — *For you were afraid of the fire and you did not ascend the mountain.* Surely the reason they did not ascend the mountain was because they had been commanded not to.

As we explained in *Parashas Yisro*, the Children of Israel assembled all the way down at the foot of Mount Sinai, and did not even ascend to the part of the mountain that they were permitted to ascend to: "Moses brought the people forth from the camp toward God, and they stood at the bottom of the

ה
ז־יד

ז לֹא־יִהְיֶה לְךָ אֱלֹהִים אֲחֵרִים עַל־פָּנָי: ח לֹא־תַעֲשֶׂה לְךָ
פֶסֶל כָּל־תְּמוּנָה אֲשֶׁר בַּשָּׁמַיִם מִמַּעַל וַאֲשֶׁר בָּאָרֶץ מִתָּחַת
וַאֲשֶׁר בַּמַּיִם מִתַּחַת לָאָרֶץ: ט לֹא־תִשְׁתַּחֲוֶה לָהֶם וְלֹא
תָעָבְדֵם כִּי אָנֹכִי יהוה אֱלֹהֶיךָ אֵל קַנָּא פֹּקֵד עֲוֺן אָבוֹת
עַל־בָּנִים וְעַל־שִׁלֵּשִׁים וְעַל־רִבֵּעִים לְשֹׂנְאָי: י וְעֹשֶׂה חֶסֶד
לַאֲלָפִים לְאֹהֲבַי וּלְשֹׁמְרֵי °מצותו: יא לֹא
תִשָּׂא אֶת־שֵׁם־יהוה אֱלֹהֶיךָ לַשָּׁוְא כִּי לֹא יְנַקֶּה יהוה
אֵת אֲשֶׁר־יִשָּׂא אֶת־שְׁמוֹ לַשָּׁוְא: יב שָׁמוֹר
אֶת־יוֹם הַשַּׁבָּת לְקַדְּשׁוֹ כַּאֲשֶׁר צִוְּךָ יהוה אֱלֹהֶיךָ: יג שֵׁשֶׁת
יָמִים תַּעֲבֹד וְעָשִׂיתָ כָּל־מְלַאכְתֶּךָ: יד וְיוֹם הַשְּׁבִיעִי
שַׁבָּת לַיהוה אֱלֹהֶיךָ לֹא־תַעֲשֶׂה כָל־מְלָאכָה אַתָּה ׀
וּבִנְךָ־וּבִתֶּךָ וְעַבְדְּךָ־וַאֲמָתֶךָ וְשׁוֹרְךָ וַחֲמֹרְךָ וְכָל־בְּהֶמְתֶּךָ
וְגֵרְךָ אֲשֶׁר בִּשְׁעָרֶיךָ לְמַעַן יָנוּחַ עַבְדְּךָ וַאֲמָתְךָ כָּמוֹךָ:

°מִצְוֺתָי ק׳

---

mountain" (*Shemos* 19:17). It does not say, "and he had them stand at the bottom of the mountain," as we might have expected, since it was he who "brought them forth." Moses indeed wished to bring them closer, and assemble them on the permitted area of the mountain itself. It was only their fear of the holy fire that prevented them from ascending even partially, so it was their own decision to assemble at the foot of the mountain.

The *Ramban* agrees with this interpretation, that the verse is referring to the permitted part of the mountain, which the Children of Israel nonetheless refused to ascend.

(In *Parashas Mishpatim* (24:13-18) the words, "and Moses ascended to the Mountain of God" are written three times, corresponding to the three levels of holiness in the *Beis Hamikdash*: the courtyard, the sanctuary, and the Holy of Holies.)

12. שָׁמוֹר — *Safeguard.* The first time the Ten Commandments appear in the Torah, the wording is זָכוֹר אֶת יוֹם הַשַּׁבָּת, "Remember the Sabbath day." As *Rashi* explains, "Both words were spoken in a single utterance, as one word." But, while the Children of Israel were in the Wilderness, they were free from ordinary weekday labor, therefore the Sabbath was marked chiefly by "remembering"; that is, by making *kiddush* over wine and keeping the other positive commandments of the day. The Torah emphasizes this concept in *Parashas Yisro* by recording the word "remember" in that version of the Ten Commandments. But now that they had inherited the lands of Sihon and Og and they were about to enter the Land, where they would be working in their fields and vineyards and cities, the Torah stresses the "safeguarding" aspect of the Sabbath, that is, refraining from all forbidden work.

5
7-14

[7] *You shall not recognize the gods of others in My Presence.*
[8] *You shall not make yourself a carved image of any*
likeness of that which is in the heavens above or on the
earth below or in the water beneath the earth. [9] *You shall*
not prostrate yourself to them nor worship them, for I am
HASHEM, your God — a jealous God, Who visits the sin of
fathers upon children to the third and fourth generations,
for My enemies; [10] *but Who shows kindness for thousands*
[of generations], to those who love Me and observe My
commandments.
[11] *You shall not take the Name of HASHEM, your God,*
in vain, for HASHEM will not absolve anyone who takes
His Name in vain.
[12] *Safeguard the Sabbath day to sanctify it, as HASHEM,*
your God, has commanded you. [13] *Six days shall you la-*
bor and accomplish all your work; [14] *but the seventh day*
is Sabbath to HASHEM, your God; you shall not do any
work — you, your son, your daughter, your slave, your
maidservant, your ox, your donkey, and your every
animal, and your convert within your gates, in order that
your slave and your maidservant may rest like you.

שָׁמוֹר אֶת־יוֹם הַשַּׁבָּת — *Safeguard the Sabbath day.* The word שָׁמוֹר, "safeguard", may also be given the meaning it has in וְאָבִיו שָׁמַר אֶת הַדָּבָר, namely, "his father kept the matter in mind" (*Bereishis* 37:11). One should "keep the Sabbath in mind," waiting eagerly all week for the Sabbath to come and redeem him from the crassness of weekday life, and raise him to a plane where all his acts are as a song of praise to the Creator.

לְקַדְּשׁוֹ — *To sanctify it.* Unfortunately there are many people who look forward to the holy day of rest, only to desecrate it by using it for outings, letter-writing, and the like. For their sake the Torah emphasizes that we must look forward to *Shabbos* in order "to sanctify it." Let the Sabbath day be not merely for physical rest, but for holiness, prayer, Torah study, and introspection.

לְקַדְּשׁוֹ כַּאֲשֶׁר צִוְּךָ ה׳ אֱלֹהֶיךָ — *To sanctify it, as Hashem, your God, has commanded you.* Let it not be just a Sabbath of physical pleasures, a Sabbath of rest for the body alone — after all, the gentiles, too, have their weekly day of rest — but a Sabbath for the soul as well. Give your soul the pleasures of prayer, study, and introspection (see *Shemos* 16:29) "as Hashem, your God, has commanded you" — make it a Sabbath that has no equal among the peoples of the earth.

14. לְמַעַן יָנוּחַ עַבְדְּךָ וַאֲמָתְךָ כָּמוֹךָ — *In order that your slave and your maidservant may rest like you.* Of "your ox and your donkey" the Torah

ה
טו־יח

טו וְזָכַרְתָּ כִּי עֶבֶד הָיִיתָ בְּאֶרֶץ מִצְרַיִם וַיֹּצִאֲךָ יְהוָה אֱלֹהֶיךָ
מִשָּׁם בְּיָד חֲזָקָה וּבִזְרֹעַ נְטוּיָה עַל־כֵּן צִוְּךָ יְהוָה אֱלֹהֶיךָ
לַעֲשׂוֹת אֶת־יוֹם הַשַּׁבָּת: טז כַּבֵּד אֶת־
אָבִיךָ וְאֶת־אִמֶּךָ כַּאֲשֶׁר צִוְּךָ יְהוָה אֱלֹהֶיךָ לְמַעַן ׀ יַאֲרִיכֻן
יָמֶיךָ וּלְמַעַן יִיטַב לָךְ עַל הָאֲדָמָה אֲשֶׁר־יְהוָה אֱלֹהֶיךָ נֹתֵן
לָךְ: יז לֹא תִרְצָח וְלֹא
תִנְאָף וְלֹא תִגְנֹב וְלֹא־
תַעֲנֶה בְרֵעֲךָ עֵד שָׁוְא: יח וְלֹא
תַחְמֹד אֵשֶׁת רֵעֶךָ וְלֹא

---

simply says "that they may rest" (*Shemos* 23:12), omitting the words "like you"; for when we consider the rest experienced by gentile slaves who have been immersed in the *mikveh*, and circumcised in the case of males, there is a significant difference between that and the rest known by animals. Neither slaves nor animals are to be put to work for their master on the Sabbath; but in the case of slaves, the master may not allow them to do forbidden work on the Sabbath even for themselves (as explained in *Orach Chaim* §304), whereas he may let his animals do forbidden work for their own purposes. For example (as the Sages derived in the *Mechilta* on *Shemos* 23:12), an animal may be put out to pasture on the Sabbath to eat grass, even though this involves the forbidden labor of cutting off vegetation from its place of growth. (See also *Shabbos* 122a.)

15. וְזָכַרְתָּ כִּי עֶבֶד הָיִיתָ בְּאֶרֶץ מִצְרַיִם — *And you shall remember that you were a slave in the land of Egypt*. But in the first version of the Ten Commandments the Sabbath is spoken of as a remembrance of the Creation! (See *Shemos* 20:11.)

Now, Moses could not have changed anything in the wording. *Rashi* (*Sanhedrin* 56b) makes this clear: "Moses was not speaking for himself when he recapitulated the Torah and cautioned the people about its commandments; he was repeating it to them as he had received it [from God]. Everything in the second version of the Ten Commandments was written on the Tablets, and so had he heard them on Mount Sinai."

Ha'amek Davar (on v. 19) offers an intriguing explanation. The Children of Israel, he says, did not hear the second version directly from God, only Moses heard it. Evidently, here on the Plains of Moab he chose to bring out and highlight the aspect of Sabbath (that he had heard of on Mt. Sinai) that recalls the Exodus. For now that they had come to a settled country, the factor of keeping the Sabbath because they had been taken out of Egypt would have more significance for them. At Mount Sinai however, before they had reached a settled land, they had not yet fully realized the importance of the Exodus. On the contrary, they had complained several times, "What is this that you have done to us to take us out of Egypt?" (*Shemos* 14:11) or, "If only we had died by

15 *And you shall remember that you were a slave in the land of Egypt, and* HASHEM, *your God, has taken you out from there with a strong hand and an outstretched arm; therefore* HASHEM, *your God, has commanded you to make the Sabbath day.*

16 *Honor your father and your mother, as* HASHEM, *your God, commanded you, so that your days will be lengthened and so that it will be good for you, upon the land that* HASHEM, *your God, gives you.*

17 *You shall not kill; and you shall not commit adultery; and you shall not steal; and you shall not bear vain witness against your fellow.*

18 *And you shall not covet your fellow's wife, you shall not*

---

the hand of Hashem in the land of Egypt," (ibid. 16:3) and so on. Therefore at Mount Sinai the Children of Israel heard the command about the Sabbath only as a remembrance of the Creation, but Moses heard both aspects.

16. כַּבֵּד אֶת־אָבִיךָ וְאֶת־אִמֶּךָ — *Honor your father and your mother* "The extra ו of וְאֶת indicates that an elder brother is also included [i.e., must also be honored]" (*Kesubos* 103a).

It seems to me that this is because the eldest brother usually spends a longer time than his siblings with his father and mother (simply because he is older than the others). Consequently, he must know better than his brothers how to follow his parents' ways, habits, and wishes. Therefore, when they honor him they are inevitably learning to go in their parents' way and to honor them.

This is similar to *Chazal's* teaching that the verse "You shall fear Hashem your God" includes reverence for *talmidei chachamim* (*Pesachim* 22b). Part of the reason for this is that a Torah scholar knows better than an ignorant person how to walk in God's ways and do His will. So by honoring him and imitating his behavior they are indirectly honoring God and learning to do His will.

כַּאֲשֶׁר צִוְּךָ ה׳ אֱלֹהֶיךָ — *As Hashem, your God, commanded you.* Normally, children's love and respect for the parents who brought them into the (present) world grows steadily through the years. The more the child enjoys his life, the more happiness he discovers, then the greater will be his love for the parents who gave him this happy life.

In the plains of Moab, Moses was confronted with children who had suffered greatly from wandering in the desert, all because of their parents' misdeeds. It was their parents who had brought down upon them the decree that "Your children will roam in the Wilderness for forty years and bear [the guilt of] your guilt" (*Bamidbar* 14:33). Therefore Moses stressed what God had told him on Mt. Sinai: that this commandment must be done "as Hashem, your God, commanded you": to honor your parents during their life and afterwards, regardless of how well or ill satisfied you are with your life.

ה תִתְאַוֶּ֜ה בֵּ֣ית רֵעֶ֗ךָ שָׂדֵ֜הוּ וְעַבְדּ֤וֹ וַאֲמָתוֹ֙ שׁוֹר֣וֹ וַחֲמֹר֔וֹ וְכֹ֖ל
יט־כ אֲשֶׁ֥ר לְרֵעֶֽךָ׃ חמישי יט אֶת־הַדְּבָרִ֣ים הָאֵ֗לֶּה דִּבֶּ֨ר
יְהוָ֜ה אֶל־כָּל־קְהַלְכֶ֗ם בָּהָ֗ר מִתּ֤וֹךְ הָאֵשׁ֙ הֶֽעָנָ֣ן וְהָֽעֲרָפֶ֔ל ק֥וֹל
גָּד֖וֹל וְלֹ֣א יָסָ֑ף וַֽיִּכְתְּבֵ֗ם עַל־שְׁנֵי֙ לֻחֹ֣ת אֲבָנִ֔ים וַֽיִּתְּנֵ֖ם אֵלָֽי׃
כ וַיְהִ֗י כְּשָׁמְעֲכֶ֤ם אֶת־הַקּוֹל֙ מִתּ֣וֹךְ הַחֹ֔שֶׁךְ וְהָהָ֖ר בֹּעֵ֣ר בָּאֵ֑שׁ

---

18. וְלֹא תִתְאַוֶּה בֵּית רֵעֶךָ — *You shall not desire your fellow's house. Rashi* (ad loc.) seems to say that לֹא תִתְאַוֶּה is the same as לֹא תַחְמֹד, which is the word used in the Ten Commandments in *Shemos* (see *Sifsei Chachamim*, ad loc.). But the *Mechilta (Yisro)* says, "*You shall not covet* [לֹא תַחְמֹד]; and later on [in *Devarim*] it says, *You shall not desire* [לֹא תִתְאַוֶּה]. This is to make desiring a sin of its own and coveting a sin of its own." The *Rambam*, too, counts "you shall not desire" as a commandment by itself.

The *Minchas Chinuch* (§416) explains that "you shall not covet" is the prohibition of taking anything, even in exchange for money, from someone who does not want to sell it to us. "You shall not desire," he says, goes even further and prohibits us from even longing in our hearts for this object. This concurs with the *Mechilta*, which adds that "if one desires [in his heart], in the end he will covet [by actually taking]; and if he covets, in the end he will rob and loot."

The Torah emphasizes the injunction against "desiring" in the second Ten Commandments, because these were said when the Children of Israel were poised on the banks of the Jordan, ready to cross over and seize material possessions for themselves. (This would be why your neighbor's "field" is mentioned here, but not in the first Ten Commandments.) Now it was necessary to remind them to fight "coveting" while it is only a *feeling* in the heart, before he *acts* upon this desire.

19. אֶת־הַדְּבָרִים הָאֵלֶּה — *These words.* This would seem to say that God spoke all of the Ten Commandments directly "to the entire congregation," and so, in fact, is the opinion of *Chazal* (*Pesikta, Shemos Rabbah, Midrash Chazisa*). Evidence for this is that only at the end of the events at Mt. Sinai did the people come and ask Moses to be their intermediary. (See *Shemos* 20:16.)

But R' Yehoshua ben Levi holds that the entire people heard only the first two commandments directly, and the rest of the commandments were told them by Moses. (This would be why the first two commandments are phrased in the first person: "I am Hashem" and "You shall not... in My presence"; whereas the others are in the third person: "Hashem's name," for example, instead of "My name.") The fact that the people's request that Moses be their intermediary comes only at the end of the episode means nothing, for "there is neither early nor late in the Torah."

The *Rambam* (in the *Guide for the Perplexed*) and the *Ramban* uphold R' Yehoshua ben Levi's opinion, but *Abarbanel* "decides the case" (along with

5
19-20

*desire your fellow's house, his field, his slave, his maidser-
vant, his ox, his donkey, or anything that belongs to your
fellow.*
19 *These words* HASHEM *spoke to your entire congregation
on the mountain, from the midst of the fire, the cloud, and
the thick cloud — a great voice, never to be repeated — and
He inscribed them on two stone Tablets and gave them to
me.*
20 *It happened that when you heard the voice from the
midst of the darkness and the mountain was burning in fire,*

---

the *Ibn Ezra*) in favor of *Chazal's* majority opinion, and argues against R' Yehoshua's position at length.

I find R' Yehoshua's opinion amazing. How was it possible for the people to speak to Moses immediately after the first two commandments? The Torah specifically says that when the request was made, "When you heard the voice... all the heads of your tribes and your elders approached me." But how could they have broken through and climbed up to the Divine Presence, or to where Moses stood on the mountain? Moses had announced to them that the mountain was off limits; anyone who so much as touched it until the *shofar* sounded at the end of God's revelation would incur the death penalty. And in fact the Torah tells us that "the people saw, and trembled, and stood from afar" (*Shemos* 20:15).So they could not have approached Moses with their request until after the entire Ten Commandments had been given, and Moses came down from the mountain. — Still, I only point this out, not in any way presuming to decide between "the lofty mountains" (i.e. *Rambam, Ramban, R' Yehoshua, Abarbanel*, etc.).

☙ קוֹל גָּדוֹל וְלֹא יָסָף — *A great voice, never to be repeated.* To tell you that this Torah will never be imitated or replaced; there will never be another Torah from the Creator Himself.

☙ וְלֹא יָסָף — *Never to be repeated.* There were no echoes to this voice (*Shemos Rabbah*, 29:9), lest some people say that there are two Divine Powers. It would have been easy for people to decide that one god had said, "I am Hashem your God," and the 'other god' (the echo) had answered back, "*I* am Hashem your God."

20. וַיְהִי כְּשָׁמְעֲכֶם אֶת־הַקּוֹל מִתּוֹךְ הַחֹשֶׁךְ — *It happened that when you heard the voice from the midst of the darkness.* "This can be likened to a king who married off his son, and hung black curtains around the canopy, for he foresaw that his son would live with his wife only forty days" (*Yalkut Shimoni*, taken from *Pirkei D'Rabbi Eliezer*). And indeed, forty days afterwards the Children of Israel made the Golden Calf. But on this day, when they saw the "black curtains" of darkness, they took them as a sign that the great fire would consume them. This is why the Torah says, "וַיְהִי" (always an expression of sorrow)... "from the midst of the darkness... You approached me... why should we die when this great fire consumes us?"

ה וַתִּקְרְבוּן אֵלַי כָּל־רָאשֵׁי שִׁבְטֵיכֶם וְזִקְנֵיכֶם׃ כא וַתֹּאמְרוּ הֵן
כא־כו הֶרְאָנוּ יְהוָה אֱלֹהֵינוּ אֶת־כְּבֹדוֹ וְאֶת־גָּדְלוֹ וְאֶת־קֹלוֹ
שָׁמַעְנוּ מִתּוֹךְ הָאֵשׁ הַיּוֹם הַזֶּה רָאִינוּ כִּי־יְדַבֵּר אֱלֹהִים
אֶת־הָאָדָם וָחָי׃ כב וְעַתָּה לָמָּה נָמוּת כִּי תֹאכְלֵנוּ הָאֵשׁ
הַגְּדֹלָה הַזֹּאת אִם־יֹסְפִים ׀ אֲנַחְנוּ לִשְׁמֹעַ אֶת־קוֹל יְהוָה
אֱלֹהֵינוּ עוֹד וָמָתְנוּ׃ כג כִּי מִי כָל־בָּשָׂר אֲשֶׁר שָׁמַע קוֹל
אֱלֹהִים חַיִּים מְדַבֵּר מִתּוֹךְ־הָאֵשׁ כָּמֹנוּ וַיֶּחִי׃ כד קְרַב אַתָּה
וּשֲׁמָע אֵת כָּל־אֲשֶׁר יֹאמַר יְהוָה אֱלֹהֵינוּ וְאַתְּ ׀ תְּדַבֵּר
אֵלֵינוּ אֵת כָּל־אֲשֶׁר יְדַבֵּר יְהוָה אֱלֹהֵינוּ אֵלֶיךָ וְשָׁמַעְנוּ
וְעָשִׂינוּ׃ כה וַיִּשְׁמַע יְהוָה אֶת־קוֹל דִּבְרֵיכֶם בְּדַבֶּרְכֶם אֵלָי
וַיֹּאמֶר יְהוָה אֵלַי שָׁמַעְתִּי אֶת־קוֹל דִּבְרֵי הָעָם הַזֶּה
אֲשֶׁר דִּבְּרוּ אֵלֶיךָ הֵיטִיבוּ כָּל־אֲשֶׁר דִּבֵּרוּ׃ כו מִי־יִתֵּן וְהָיָה
לְבָבָם זֶה לָהֶם לְיִרְאָה אֹתִי וְלִשְׁמֹר אֶת־כָּל־מִצְוֺתַי

---

21. הֵן הֶרְאָנוּ ה׳ אֱלֹהֵינוּ אֶת־כְּבֹדוֹ . . . וְאֶת־קֹלוֹ שָׁמַעְנוּ — *Behold! Hashem our God has shown us His glory... and we have heard His voice.* "R' Levi said, 'Two things Israel asked of God: to see His glory and hear His voice'" (*Shemos Rabbah* §29).

The reason was that in Egypt all the resident nations, including Israel, worshiped a visible god. Now they were being told to worship a God Who was hidden beyond their sight. Therefore they told Moses that they wanted to see their King.

Even the best among people then, who knew the God of heaven and earth and called Him "the God of gods," believed that He did not concern Himself with the material world, having handed it over to the care of His "officers," the stars and planets. They were thus totally unable to believe that God would speak to men, much less grant them prophecy. Therefore they asked Moses to see to it that they would hear God's voice speaking to the lower world.

These two requests of the Children of Israel were granted at the Giving of the Torah. "Hashem our God has shown us His glory" — the fact of His existence — "and we heard His voice." They discovered that in fact "Hashem will speak to a person and he can live" in this material world. And now that they had achieved these two goals, they said to Moses, "You should approach ... and you should speak to us" (v. 24).

24. וְאַתְּ תְּדַבֵּר אֵלֵינוּ — *And you should speak to us.* Why did they address Moses with the word אַתְּ, the feminine form of "you"? *Rashi (q.v.)* explains that Moses was so dismayed at this request of theirs that he "became as weak as a woman."

I think that we can understand *Rashi's* last few words thus: A woman is not merely on the receiving end of creation. She does not just "receive" a seed and

5 *that all the heads of your tribes and your elders approached*
21-26 *me.*
[21] *They said, "Behold! HASHEM, our God, has shown us His*
glory and His greatness, and we have heard His voice from
the midst of the fire; this day we saw that HASHEM will speak
to a person and he can live. [22] *But now, why should we die*
when this great fire consumes us? If we continue to hear the
voice of HASHEM, our God, any longer, we will die! [23] *For is*
there any human that has heard the voice of the Living God
speaking from the midst of the fire, as we have, and lived?
[24] *You should approach and hear whatever HASHEM, our God,*
will say, and you should speak to us whatever HASHEM, our
God, will speak to you — then we shall hear and we shall do."
[25] *HASHEM heard the sound of your words when you spoke*
to me, and HASHEM said to me, "I heard the sound of the words
of this people, that they have spoken to you; they did well in
all that they spoke. [26] *Who can assure that this heart should*
remain theirs, to fear Me and observe all My commandments

---

then have it grow into a baby; she also shapes the growing fetus. For consider: one drop enters her, and in the end a living being is born. No one in the world can tell what will become of this tiny seed: whether it will come to be a child at all, and if so whether male or female, wise or foolish, strong or weak, beautiful or ugly. Only the woman, who grows and shapes this seed, helps develop all of these characteristics to recognizable form. At birth all can see the baby's gender and its physical characteristics, and soon after its mental abilities too, none of which could be recognized in the original seed.

Now, when the Children of Israel heard God's voice speaking from the midst of the fire, their souls fled from them. They could not understand the Divine word nor comprehend what was expected of them, for this was suddenly beyond their comprehension. So they said to Moses, "Since you can listen and understand all this, you approach and hear everything that God has to say. But don't repeat things exactly as you heard them, because we cannot understand these things as they are. Instead, you [אַתְּ] speak to us: do for us what a woman can do, who shapes from a seemingly meaningless drop a lovely child whose nature and gifts can be clearly seen. You, אַתְּ, absorb all that God says, and form it into clear, plain words for us, that we can 'hear and do.'"

We can understand in the same way why the Haggadah says of the son who does not know how to ask, "You — אַתְּ — open the way for him." If this child is so limited in his abilities that, although he sees how different everything is on this *Seder* night, he cannot even think how to ask about it, you make yourself like a woman and shape the words for him into a form he can understand.

26. **מִי־יִתֵּן וְהָיָה לְבָבָם זֶה לָהֶם לְיִרְאָה אֹתִי** — *Who can assure that this heart should remain theirs to fear Me. Chazal* say, "the wicked are controlled by

ה כׇּל־הַיָּמִים לְמַעַן יִיטַב לָהֶם וְלִבְנֵיהֶם לְעֹלָם׃ כז לֵךְ אֱמֹר
כז־ל לָהֶם שׁוּבוּ לָכֶם לְאׇהֳלֵיכֶם׃ כח וְאַתָּה פֹּה עֲמֹד עִמָּדִי
וַאֲדַבְּרָה אֵלֶיךָ אֵת כׇּל־הַמִּצְוָה וְהַחֻקִּים וְהַמִּשְׁפָּטִים אֲשֶׁר
תְּלַמְּדֵם וְעָשׂוּ בָאָרֶץ אֲשֶׁר אָנֹכִי נֹתֵן לָהֶם לְרִשְׁתָּהּ׃
כט וּשְׁמַרְתֶּם לַעֲשׂוֹת כַּאֲשֶׁר צִוָּה יהוה אֱלֹהֵיכֶם אֶתְכֶם
לֹא תָסֻרוּ יָמִין וּשְׂמֹאל׃ ל בְּכׇל־הַדֶּרֶךְ אֲשֶׁר צִוָּה יהוה
אֱלֹהֵיכֶם אֶתְכֶם תֵּלֵכוּ לְמַעַן תִּחְיוּן וְטוֹב לָכֶם וְהַאֲרַכְתֶּם
ו יָמִים בָּאָרֶץ אֲשֶׁר תִּירָשׁוּן׃ א וְזֹאת הַמִּצְוָה הַחֻקִּים
א־ב וְהַמִּשְׁפָּטִים אֲשֶׁר צִוָּה יהוה אֱלֹהֵיכֶם לְלַמֵּד אֶתְכֶם
לַעֲשׂוֹת בָּאָרֶץ אֲשֶׁר אַתֶּם עֹבְרִים שָׁמָּה לְרִשְׁתָּהּ׃ ב לְמַעַן
תִּירָא אֶת־יהוה אֱלֹהֶיךָ לִשְׁמֹר אֶת־כׇּל־חֻקֹּתָיו וּמִצְוֺתָיו
אֲשֶׁר אָנֹכִי מְצַוֶּךָ אַתָּה וּבִנְךָ וּבֶן־בִּנְךָ כֹּל יְמֵי חַיֶּיךָ וּלְמַעַן

---

their heart's feelings: 'Esau said in his heart' (*Bereishis* 27:41), 'Jeroboam said in his heart' (*I Melachim* 12:26), 'Haman said in his heart' (*Esther* 6:6); but the righteous control their heart's feelings: 'she was speaking to her heart' (*I Shmuel* 1:13), 'David said to his heart' (*I Shmuel* 27:1), 'Daniel set upon his heart' (*Daniel* 1:8)" (*Bereishis Rabbah* 34:10).

The heart is the center of desire and of base thoughts, that urge man to do "all that his heart desires." The wicked are compelled to fulfill every urge that comes into their hearts, but the righteous rule their heart ("speaking to her heart"), commanding it not to think sinful thoughts and to stay away from base or forbidden urges. This is why God said, "Who can assure that this heart should remain *theirs*" — if only it would always be yours, under your control, "to fear Me and observe all My commandments!"

27. שובו לָכֶם לְאָהֳלֵיכֶם — *Return to your tents.* It is worth noting that this cue to resume normal family life was said in veiled language ("to your tents"), whereas the temporary prohibition of family life was spoken out directly: "Do not draw near a woman!" (*Shemos* 19:15).

This is because when it comes to *heteirim, permissive rulings*, people are always ready to 'understand' even the slightest hint. But when something has to be prohibited, it is not sufficient to speak in hints, for it will fall on deaf ears. How wonderful if people would listen when the prohibition *is* spelled out!

We can also learn from here that when someone is inspiring the public to observe the laws of family purity, he should ignore those who say that in public such things may only be alluded to in veiled terms. For Moses himself did not use hints; he said in God's own name, in public, "Do not draw near a woman."

28. וְאַתָּה פֹּה עֲמֹד עִמָּדִי — *But as for you, stand here with Me.* Why did God specify "here"? Wasn't "with Me" clear enough?

5 *all the days, so that it should be good for them and for their*
27-30 *children forever?* [27] *Go say to them, 'Return to your tents.'*
[28] *But as for you, stand here with Me and I shall speak to you*
the entire commandment, and the decrees, and the ordinances
that you shall teach them and they shall perform in the Land
that I give them, to possess it."
[29] *You shall be careful to act as HASHEM, your God,*
commanded you, you shall not stray to the right or left. [30] *On*
the entire way that HASHEM, your God, commanded you shall
you go, so that you shall live and it will be good for you, and
you shall prolong your days in the Land that you shall
possess.
6 [1] *This is the commandment, and the decrees, and the*
1-2 *ordinances that HASHEM, your God, commanded to teach you,*
to perform in the Land to which you are crossing, to possess
it, [2] *so that you will fear HASHEM, your God, to observe all His*
decrees and commandments that I command you — you, your
child, and your grandchild — all the days of your life, so that

---

The Children of Israel had told Moses, "You should approach and hear," so until now he had stood between God and the people, to give them a running interpretation of God's word. Since the people were standing at the bottom of the mountain, Moses could not go too far up or he would be out of speaking distance from them. But now that he was to go and hear the Torah by himself, and only afterwards interpret it to the Children of Israel, he could come closer to God than before. Therefore God warned him, "stand *here* with Me": stay in your present place, and do not come any closer than you came during the Giving of the Torah (From *Meir Einei Yesharim* in the name of the *Sfas Emes*).

29. וּשְׁמַרְתֶּם לַעֲשׂוֹת — *You shall be careful to act.* You have vanquished the angels, who demanded that the Torah remain in Heaven, thanks to Moses' avowal that the place for fulfilling the commandments is the material world. Now that you have won the argument, you must observe the commandments!

6.

2. לְמַעַן תִּירָא אֶת־ה' אֱלֹהֶיךָ — *So that you will fear Hashem your God.* It seems to us that the fear of God leads one to observe the commandments. But here the Torah says the opposite: that we must keep the commandments "so that we will fear Hashem." Perhaps the explanation is that the present topic is discussing a particular kind of fear, reverence for God's majestic greatness. This indeed can only be acquired by studying and fulfilling the commandments of the Torah.

ו יַאֲרִכֻן יָמֶיךָ: ג וְשָׁמַעְתָּ יִשְׂרָאֵל וְשָׁמַרְתָּ לַעֲשׂוֹת אֲשֶׁר
ג־ד יִיטַב לְךָ וַאֲשֶׁר תִּרְבּוּן מְאֹד כַּאֲשֶׁר דִּבֶּר יהוה אֱלֹהֵי
אֲבֹתֶיךָ לָךְ אֶרֶץ זָבַת חָלָב וּדְבָשׁ:
ששי ד שְׁמַע יִשְׂרָאֵל יהוה אֱלֹהֵינוּ יהוה ׀ אֶחָד:

---

3. וְשָׁמַרְתָּ לַעֲשׂוֹת אֲשֶׁר יִיטַב לְךָ . . . אֶרֶץ זָבַת חָלָב וּדְבָשׁ — *And beware to perform, so that it will be good for you . . . a land flowing with milk and honey.* When Israel does God's will, then their land flows with milk and honey. But if, Heaven forbid, they do not, the land turns into a desert because of its inhabitants' wickedness. The Torah warns, "Beware . . . lest you turn astray and serve gods of others [God] will restrain the heavens so there will be no rain, and the ground will not yield its produce" (11:16-17). That is what the Torah is saying here: "beware to perform" the commandments, so that your land will remain "a land flowing with milk and honey." For it was about such a land that "Hashem, the God of your forefathers spoke for you"; so do not let your sins turn it into a desert.

4. שְׁמַע יִשְׂרָאֵל — *Hear, O Israel.* Even when it comes to such an evident truth as this, the one who pronounces it has to get the people's attention first. It is necessary to say "Hear, O Israel!" before saying "Hashem is our God, Hashem is the One and Only". Even when announcing such an exalted concept, first one must get the people to listen.

⊛ Our custom is to put our hands over our face while accepting the yoke of the Kingdom of Heaven (*Berachos* 13b), and to close our eyes. It is as if we were hiding from seeing all the evil that is done under the sun: the gentiles living in comfort and the torments of the Chosen People, the righteous who suffer and the wicked who prosper. With eyes closed we proclaim, "Hashem is our God, Hashem is the One and Only," to say that we do not judge by what we see with our mortal eyes. We believe with perfect faith that the God of Israel is One, the ruler of all worlds, Who watches over us with special providence, "the Rock Whose work is perfect, a faithful God without wrongdoing, righteous and just is He."

⊛ "All Israel are responsible one for the other" (*Shevuos* 39a). Therefore, when one of us says the *Shema* he should address therewith the entire Jewish nation, calling to each one of them to accept the Yoke of Heaven. If only a few have come to the synagogue that day, or if one is saying *Shema* alone, he must have in mind how to establish God's kingship throughout the entire Jewish people.

Anyone who accepts the Yoke of Heaven on himself alone, without doing a thing to draw other Jews closer to their Father in Heaven, has not fulfilled this commandment. For the act of accepting the yoke is written thus in the Torah: "Hear, O Israel" — one must do something to make Israel hear.

⊛ Why do we begin our declaration of belief in the One God and acceptance of His kingship with the words שְׁמַע יִשְׂרָאֵל?

6
3-4

your days will be lengthened. [3] *You shall hearken, O Israel, and beware to perform, so that it will be good for you, and so that you will increase very much, as* HASHEM, *the God of your forefathers, spoke for you — a land flowing with milk and honey.*

[4] *Hear, O Israel:* HASHEM *is our God,* HASHEM *is the One*

Perhaps the idea is similar to one we express about the angels in the blessings before the *Shema*: "Then they all accept upon themselves the yoke of Heavenly sovereignty from one another, and grant permission to one another to sanctify the One Who formed them. . ." It is the same with every Jew who wishes to accept upon himself the yoke of God's kingship: as the Sages say: "Not everyone who wishes to make use of the Divine Name may freely do so" (*Berachos* 16b). So first each Jew turns to his fellow Jew, or to the Jewish people as a whole, to receive permission to sanctify the One Who formed them all.

☙ ה׳ אֱלֹהֵינוּ ה׳ אֶחָד — *Hashem is our God, Hashem is the One and Only.* See *Rashi*. We can find a further idea hidden here: God, may His Name be blessed, sometimes behaves towards us according to His attribute of mercy (implied in His Name ה׳), and sometimes according to His attribute of strict justice (implied in His Name אֱלֹהֵנוּ). But regardless of whether it is as ה׳ or אֱלֹהֵנוּ, it is all for our eventual good; ultimately, ה׳ אֶחָד — it all comes from the attribute of mercy.

This is what is behind the teaching that *Chazal* derived from the words בְּכָל מְאֹדֶךָ (v. 5). Based on the similarity between מְאֹד (much) and מִדָּה (measure), they learn that בְּכָל מִדָּה וּמִדָּה שֶׁהוּא מוֹדֵד לְךָ, "with whatever attribute He measures out for you, thank Him greatly" (*Berachos* 54a). Even if you are dealt with the attribute of strict justice, you should accept it with love, for it is all for the good, like the mercy of a father towards his son.

☙ ה׳ אֶחָד — *Hashem is the One and Only.* We bear witness that the Creator, may His Name be blessed, is the only God; not only now, but also for all eternity. And this is why we add, "Blessed is the Name of His glorious kingdom for all eternity."

☙ We affirm, not only that there is no other god but Him, but also that He is the unique Creator, and that the existence of both the upper and the lower worlds is dependent solely on His will.

☙ "The people of Jericho used to bind the *Shema* together (הָיוּ כּוֹרְכִין אֶת שְׁמַע)" (*Pesachim* 56a). The *Bartinura* (basing himself on the *Gemara*) explains this phrase as meaning that "they did not stop between the words אֶחָד and וְאָהַבְתָּ [as they should have]; for one must linger on the word אֶחָד and stop between [the acceptance of] God's kingship and other things."

And what are these "other things"?

"You shall love Hashem, your God, with all your heart, with all your soul . . ."!

We are being shown here that accepting God's kingship is a greater *mitzvah* than loving Him. When one says ה׳ אֶחָד, he should linger on the word אֶחָד, in

ה וְאָֽהַבְתָּ֔ אֵ֖ת יְהוָ֣ה אֱלֹהֶ֑יךָ בְּכָל־לְבָבְךָ֥ וּבְכָל־ ו
נַפְשְׁךָ֖ וּבְכָל־מְאֹדֶֽךָ׃ ו וְהָי֞וּ הַדְּבָרִ֣ים הָאֵ֗לֶּה אֲשֶׁ֨ר אָנֹכִ֧י ה־ח
מְצַוְּךָ֛ הַיּ֖וֹם עַל־לְבָבֶֽךָ׃ ז וְשִׁנַּנְתָּ֣ם לְבָנֶ֔יךָ וְדִבַּרְתָּ֖ בָּ֑ם
בְּשִׁבְתְּךָ֤ בְּבֵיתֶ֙ךָ֙ וּבְלֶכְתְּךָ֣ בַדֶּ֔רֶךְ וּֽבְשָׁכְבְּךָ֖ וּבְקוּמֶֽךָ׃
ח וּקְשַׁרְתָּ֥ם לְא֖וֹת עַל־יָדֶ֑ךָ וְהָי֥וּ לְטֹטָפֹ֖ת בֵּ֥ין עֵינֶֽיךָ׃

---

order not to hasten into the word וְאָהַבְתָּ — for it is not proper to rush from a great *mitzvah* to a smaller one. And from this we can deduce that love of God alone, even with all one's heart and soul, but without accepting the yoke of His kingship, is not of much value.

This should strike a nerve in those who would like to be content with "having faith in their hearts," and who think that this is enough to make them *tzaddikim*, because (they fondly imagine) they have the love of God in their hearts. The truth is that with no active performance of the *mitzvos*, with no acceptance deep in ones heart of the yoke of God's kingship and everything that that entails, their faith and their love are worthless — they are merely "other things."

5. וְאָהַבְתָּ אֵת ה׳ אֱלֹהֶיךָ בְּכָל־לְבָבְךָ וּבְכָל־נַפְשְׁךָ וּבְכָל־מְאֹדֶךָ — *You shall love Hashem, your God, with all your heart, with all your soul, and with all your resources.* "With all your soul," as the Sages explain, means "even if He takes your soul from you." [And "all your resources" they explain as meaning one's worldly possessions.] If we are commanded to love God so much that we are willing even to give up our life for His sake, then why are these words followed by "with all your [worldly] resources?" Surely all of one's worldly assets are worth less to him than his life! As it says in *Iyov*, "All that [a man] has he will give for his life." Does it not go without saying, then, that if he would give his life, he would give his wealth?

R' Eliezer asks this very question in the *Gemara* (see both question and answer, *Berachos* 61b). Perhaps we can offer our own answer, too. Certainly a Jew is obligated to love God with all his heart and all his soul: that is, to love Him until his dying breath, or until his life is taken from him for fulfilling His *mitzvos* (under those specific circumstances in which a Jew is commanded to give his life rather than violate a *mitzvah*). But if we go by this criterion, a Jew can never be sure that his service to God comes up to the proper standard unless he actually faces the challenge of being killed for the sanctification of God's Name — something which does not happen to most of us. If this point can be proven only through death, then how can anyone know while he is alive whether God is pleased with him? How can he be sure, without actually dying, that his good intention at the time of reciting the *Shema*, to give up his life if necessary for the sake of God's Name, is truly honest, and will be considered as good as the deed itself?

In order to solve this problem we are commanded to love God with all our worldly goods. A person's money is his substance; it is the thing that keeps him

6
5-8

and Only. 5 *You shall love* HASHEM, *your God, with all*
your heart, with all your soul, and with all your resources.
6 *And these matters that I command you today shall be*
upon your heart. 7 *You shall teach them thoroughly to*
your children and you shall speak of them while you sit
in your home, while you walk on the way, when you
retire and when you arise. 8 *Bind them as a sign upon*
your arm and let them be ornaments between your eyes.

---

on his feet. If he demonstrates his love for God by giving generously and freely of his resources to Torah-true causes, he can see this as proof that if it came to giving his life he would pass that test too. "You shall love Hashem, your God... with all your soul" — and you can be sure that you really do if you also love Him "with all your worldly resources."

This explanation finds support in the life of King Josiah, "who returned to Hashem with all his heart and with all his soul and with all his resources" (*II Melachim* 23:25). King Josiah was not martyred; the words "with all his soul" are used to describe him because he served God "with all his resources" — he gave lavishly of his own flocks for the people's Pesach and *Yom Tov* sacrifices (*II Divrei Hayamim* 35:7).

7. וְשִׁנַּנְתָּם לְבָנֶיךָ וְדִבַּרְתָּ בָּם — *You shall teach them thoroughly to your children and you shall speak of them.* Would it not have been more fitting to place the words "you shall speak of them" directly after "and these matters . . . shall be upon your heart," since they deal with a single theme? Why, then, are the words, "you shall teach them thoroughly to your children" placed between these two? Shouldn't a man develop his own knowledge, until Torah is the regular subject of his speech, before he tries to teach others?

The reason for the order of these verses is that when the Torah talks about teaching children, it is not talking about education as most people conceive of the word. Torah education does not mean merely providing one's children with knowledge of Judaism, Jewish history, and the like. Chiefly it means implanting in their hearts belief in the God of Israel, love and fear of Him, and, in particular, the tradition that has been handed down from father to son since the generation of the Exodus.

This teaching is the father's responsibility, the only prerequisite being that he feels that "these matters" are "upon his heart"; then whatever words that proceed from his heart will enter the heart of his young son. The father may not argue, "I do not yet have the necessary knowledge to teach my son Torah; first I will fulfill וְדִבַּרְתָּ בָּם — I will become so learned that Torah will be the subject of my everyday conversation — and after that I will teach my son." The Torah places the commandment to teach one's son the foundations of Jewish faith before the commandment to make Torah the subject of one's ordinary conversation — teach your son now, even if you are not yet a Torah scholar!

ו ט וּכְתַבְתָּם עַל־מְזֻזוֹת בֵּיתֶךָ וּבִשְׁעָרֶיךָ: י וְהָיָה
ט־טו כִּי־ יְבִיאֲךָ | יהוה אֱלֹהֶיךָ אֶל־הָאָרֶץ אֲשֶׁר נִשְׁבַּע לַאֲבֹתֶיךָ
לְאַבְרָהָם לְיִצְחָק וּלְיַעֲקֹב לָתֶת לָךְ עָרִים גְּדֹלֹת וְטֹבֹת
אֲשֶׁר לֹא־בָנִיתָ: יא וּבָתִּים מְלֵאִים כָּל־טוּב אֲשֶׁר לֹא־
מִלֵּאתָ וּבֹרֹת חֲצוּבִים אֲשֶׁר לֹא־חָצַבְתָּ כְּרָמִים וְזֵיתִים
אֲשֶׁר לֹא־נָטָעְתָּ וְאָכַלְתָּ וְשָׂבָעְתָּ: יב הִשָּׁמֶר לְךָ פֶּן־
תִּשְׁכַּח אֶת־יהוה אֲשֶׁר הוֹצִיאֲךָ מֵאֶרֶץ מִצְרַיִם מִבֵּית
עֲבָדִים: יג אֶת־יהוה אֱלֹהֶיךָ תִּירָא וְאֹתוֹ תַעֲבֹד וּבִשְׁמוֹ
תִּשָּׁבֵעַ: יד לֹא תֵלְכוּן אַחֲרֵי אֱלֹהִים אֲחֵרִים מֵאֱלֹהֵי
הָעַמִּים אֲשֶׁר סְבִיבוֹתֵיכֶם: טו כִּי אֵל קַנָּא יהוה אֱלֹהֶיךָ
בְּקִרְבֶּךָ פֶּן־יֶחֱרֶה אַף־יהוה אֱלֹהֶיךָ בָּךְ וְהִשְׁמִידְךָ מֵעַל פְּנֵי

---

9. וּכְתַבְתָּם עַל־מְזֻזוֹת בֵּיתֶךָ — *And write them on the doorposts of your house.* The *mitzvah* of *tefillin* is not mentioned here, since it was already mentioned in *Parashas Bo*. But now that they had come to settled lands, Moses saw the right opportunity to tell them about the commandment to place a *mezuzah* on the doorposts of the houses they would build.

⁂ **וּכְתַבְתָּם עַל־מְזֻזוֹת בֵּיתֶךָ וּבִשְׁעָרֶיךָ** — *And write them on the doorposts of your house and upon your gates.* These three *mitzvos*: the *tefillin* of the arm, the *tefillin* of the head, and *mezuzah*, correspond to the *mitzvah* to love God with all your heart, all your soul, and all your worldly resources. This correlation will help us to explain something that many people have wondered about: how can a person be commanded to love someone, when love belongs to the heart and intellect, which cannot be commanded? The *Sifre* also asks this question, and its answer is: "When the Torah says, 'you shall love Hashem, your God, with all your heart,' I do not know for what He should be loved; therefore the Torah tells me, 'and these matters that I command you today shall be upon your heart.' Put them there, for then you will come to know the Holy One, blessed be He, and cleave to His ways."

Following this line of reasoning, we can say that putting on the *tefillin* of the arm, which rests near the heart in order to press the desires and thoughts of the heart into the service of God, is an outward act which helps one to love Him with all one's heart; putting on the *tefillin* of the head, close to the brain, so that the spirit that resides in the brain will be pressed into the service of the God, is an outward act which helps one to love Him with all one's soul; and the *mezuzah* on one's house (which is one's first and most basic possession, as *Chazal* say: "A man should always build a house first and afterwards plant a vineyard" [*Sotah* 41a]) helps to implant love of God with all one's resources.

10. וְהָיָה כִּי־יְבִיאֲךָ ה' — *It shall be that when Hashem . . . brings you. Radak* points out that in *Parashas Bo*, too, these words appear after the people are advised

[9] And write them on the doorposts of your house and upon
your gates.
[10] It shall be that when HASHEM, your God, brings you to
the Land that HASHEM swore to your forefathers, to Abra-
ham, to Isaac, and to Jacob, to give you — great and good
cities that you did not build, [11] houses filled with every good
thing that you did not fill, chiseled cisterns that you did not
chisel, orchards and olive trees that you did not plant — and
you shall eat and be satisfied — [12] beware for yourself lest
you forget HASHEM Who took you out of the land of Egypt,
from the house of slavery. [13] HASHEM, your God, shall you
fear, Him shall you serve, and in His Name shall you swear.
[14] You shall not follow after gods of others, of the gods of the
peoples that are around you. [15] For a jealous God is HASHEM,
your God, among you — lest the wrath of HASHEM, your God,
will flare against you and He destroy you from upon the face

---

of the *mitzvah* of *tefillin* (see *Shemos* 13:9-11). What is the connection between *tefillin* and being brought to the Land? We can find the connection by looking ahead to chapter 28, verse 10: "Then all the peoples of the earth will see that the name of Hashem is proclaimed over you, and they will revere you." *Chazal* explain, "this refers to the *tefillin* of the head" (*Berachos* 6a). In other words, when the peoples of the earth see the *tefillin* on the head of a Jew they are stricken with awe and fear; thus the Jews subdued the Canaanites easily and came in to possess the Land.

11. וּבָתִּים מְלֵאִים כָּל־טוּב — *Houses filled with every good thing. Chazal* comment, "Even pork chops" (*Chullin* 17a). This is certainly odd; is the Torah calling pork chops a "good thing"? We can explain by considering the words of the *Sifra* on *Parashas Kedoshim*: "A person should not say, 'I don't want pork,' but rather, 'I want it, but what can I do? My Father in Heaven has ordered me [not to eat it].'' The Torah is speaking here in the ordinary speech of man and calling even pork chops a "good thing," because it is in the nature of human beings to desire them.

13. אֶת־ה׳ אֱלֹהֶיךָ תִּירָא וְאֹתוֹ תַעֲבֹד וּבִשְׁמוֹ תִּשָּׁבֵעַ — *Hashem, your God, shall you fear, Him shall you serve, and in His Name shall you swear.* You should *fear* God, after seeing the strength of His hand against the Egyptians, who forced you to serve them with hard labor. You should *serve* God, Who released you from that house of bondage, for rather than being servants to Pharaoh, it is actually good for you to be God's servants. And since He brought you to a good Land like this one, you should love Him, and so *swear* your oaths by His Name. For a person who swears to the truth of a statement wants to make his oath as strong as possible, so that he will be believed. If he swears by a certain person's life it is clear that this person's life is as dear to him as his own; if it is well known

ו הָאֲדָמָה׃ טז לֹא תְנַסּוּ אֶת־יהוה אֱלֹהֵיכֶם
טז־כג כַּאֲשֶׁר נִסִּיתֶם בַּמַּסָּה׃ יז שָׁמוֹר תִּשְׁמְרוּן אֶת־מִצְוֹת יהוה
אֱלֹהֵיכֶם וְעֵדֹתָיו וְחֻקָּיו אֲשֶׁר צִוָּךְ׃ יח וְעָשִׂיתָ הַיָּשָׁר וְהַטּוֹב
בְּעֵינֵי יהוה לְמַעַן יִיטַב לָךְ וּבָאתָ וְיָרַשְׁתָּ אֶת־הָאָרֶץ
הַטֹּבָה אֲשֶׁר־נִשְׁבַּע יהוה לַאֲבֹתֶיךָ׃ יט לַהֲדֹף אֶת־כָּל־
אֹיְבֶיךָ מִפָּנֶיךָ כַּאֲשֶׁר דִּבֶּר יהוה׃ כ כִּי־
יִשְׁאָלְךָ בִנְךָ מָחָר לֵאמֹר מָה הָעֵדֹת וְהַחֻקִּים וְהַמִּשְׁפָּטִים
אֲשֶׁר צִוָּה יהוה אֱלֹהֵינוּ אֶתְכֶם׃ כא וְאָמַרְתָּ לְבִנְךָ עֲבָדִים
הָיִינוּ לְפַרְעֹה בְּמִצְרָיִם וַיֹּצִיאֵנוּ יהוה מִמִּצְרַיִם בְּיָד
חֲזָקָה׃ כב וַיִּתֵּן יהוה אוֹתֹת וּמֹפְתִים גְּדֹלִים וְרָעִים ׀
בְּמִצְרַיִם בְּפַרְעֹה וּבְכָל־בֵּיתוֹ לְעֵינֵינוּ׃ כג וְאוֹתָנוּ הוֹצִיא
מִשָּׁם לְמַעַן הָבִיא אֹתָנוּ לָתֶת לָנוּ אֶת־הָאָרֶץ אֲשֶׁר נִשְׁבַּע

---

that he has no love for the person whose life he swears by, he will be scorned and not believed. So when the Torah says "in His Name shall you swear," it is talking about the most devoted and visible kind of love. This love is in return for all the good that God has done for us in giving us a desirable Land after we had been in the miserable bondage of Egypt.

16. לֹא תְנַסּוּ אֶת־ה׳ אֱלֹהֵיכֶם — *You shall not test Hashem, your God*. In case any doubt should enter your heart as to whether the God of your fathers is with you, and you think of testing Him "as you tested Him at Massah," saying "Is Hashem among us or not?" (*Shemos* 17:7) — do not test Him again. Instead, remember what the result was the last time you tried this: "Amalek came" (ibid. v. 8).

20. מָחָר — *Tomorrow*. " 'Tomorrow' can sometimes mean, 'after a certain length of time' " (*Rashi*).

As the *Haggadah* points out, the Torah talks about four sons, and this is the verse that talks about the wise son. It is interesting that of the four, the word "tomorrow" is used only when talking about the wise son and the simple son (of whom the Torah says, "It shall be when your son asks you tomorrow, saying, 'What is this?'" [*Shemos* 13:14]). But when talking of the wicked son ("It shall be that when your children say to you, 'What is this service to you?'" [ibid. 12:26]) and the son who does not know how to ask ("You shall tell your son on that day..." [ibid. 13:8]) the word "tomorrow" does not appear.

I once saw an interpretation of the four sons which goes far to explain how the use of the word "tomorrow" separates the sons into two pairs. According to this view, the son who does not know how to ask has fallen under the influence of the wicked son. Like the wicked son, he denies the Torah, only he "does not know how to ask" the kind of sarcastic and dissident questions that his brother asks. Now, the father, seeing that his son is being corrupted by his wicked brother, should tell him: "It is because of this that Hashem acted on my behalf

6 *of the earth.*
16-23 *16 You shall not test HASHEM, your God, as you tested Him*
at Massah. 17 You shall surely observe the commandments of
HASHEM, your God, and His testimonies and His decrees that
He commanded you. 18 You shall do what is fair and good in
the eyes of HASHEM, so that it will be good for you, and you
shall come and possess the good Land that HASHEM swore to
your forefathers, 19 to thrust away all your enemies from
before you, as HASHEM spoke.
20 If your child asks you tomorrow, saying, "What are the
testimonies and the decrees and the ordinances that HASHEM,
our God, commanded you?"
21 You shall say to your child, "We were slaves to Pharaoh
in Egypt, and HASHEM took us out of Egypt with a strong
hand. 22 HASHEM placed signs and wonders, great and
harmful, against Egypt, against Pharaoh and against his
entire household, before our eyes. 23 And He took us out of
there in order to bring us, to give us the Land that He swore

---

when I left Egypt — for me, not for him" (pointing at the wicked son), "because if he had been there, he would not have been redeemed." Perhaps in this way the father will manage to persuade his son not to follow in his brother's footsteps.

The simple son, on the other hand, follows innocently in the footsteps of his wise brother; only he is not learned enough to distinguish between testimonies and decrees or between decrees and ordinances. He merely wants to know, "What is this?"

Basing ourselves on this interpretation, it is clear why the Torah used the word "tomorrow" as it did. For the wicked son (along with his follower, the one who does not know how to ask) will not wait to make his sarcastic observations "tomorrow," after the years in the desert have been forgotten. He is just as likely to make them "today," while God is still leading His people through the desert on a miraculous or near-miraculous level. Right before Mt. Sinai he is capable of saying, "What is this service to you?" and to make a golden calf and feast before it and cavort around it. He is not the sort to wait until "tomorrow" to speak up.

But the wise son is different (and also the simple son who imitates him): he asks only "tomorrow," when many *halachos* have been forgotten during the period of mourning for Moses, and when all the miracles and wonders are fading into the past. Then he (according to his wisdom, and his companion according to his simplicity) wants to hear from his father the stories of what he saw in the Wilderness, or what he received from his own father of the Oral Tradition, so that he may comprehend why God gave us many *mitzvos* and why He divided them into testimonies, decrees, and ordinances.

23. וְאוֹתָנוּ הוֹצִיא מִשָּׁם. . . לָתֶת לָנוּ אֶת־הָאָרֶץ— *And He took us out of there. . . to give us the Land.* God not only punishes the wicked people of the world, as

ו לַאֲבֹתֵינוּ׃ כד וַיְצַוֵּנוּ יהוה לַעֲשׂוֹת אֶת־כָּל־הַחֻקִּים הָאֵלֶּה
כד־כה לְיִרְאָה אֶת־יהוה אֱלֹהֵינוּ לְטוֹב לָנוּ כָּל־הַיָּמִים לְחַיֹּתֵנוּ
כְּהַיּוֹם הַזֶּה׃ כה וּצְדָקָה תִּהְיֶה־לָּנוּ כִּי־נִשְׁמֹר לַעֲשׂוֹת
אֶת־כָּל־הַמִּצְוָה הַזֹּאת לִפְנֵי יהוה אֱלֹהֵינוּ כַּאֲשֶׁר
ז צִוָּנוּ׃ שביעי א כִּי יְבִיאֲךָ יהוה אֱלֹהֶיךָ אֶל־הָאָרֶץ
א־ה אֲשֶׁר־אַתָּה בָא־שָׁמָּה לְרִשְׁתָּהּ וְנָשַׁל גּוֹיִם־רַבִּים ׀ מִפָּנֶיךָ
הַחִתִּי וְהַגִּרְגָּשִׁי וְהָאֱמֹרִי וְהַכְּנַעֲנִי וְהַפְּרִזִּי וְהַחִוִּי וְהַיְבוּסִי
שִׁבְעָה גוֹיִם רַבִּים וַעֲצוּמִים מִמֶּךָּ׃ ב וּנְתָנָם יהוה אֱלֹהֶיךָ
לְפָנֶיךָ וְהִכִּיתָם הַחֲרֵם תַּחֲרִים אֹתָם לֹא־תִכְרֹת לָהֶם
בְּרִית וְלֹא תְחָנֵּם׃ ג וְלֹא תִתְחַתֵּן בָּם בִּתְּךָ לֹא־תִתֵּן לִבְנוֹ
וּבִתּוֹ לֹא־תִקַּח לִבְנֶךָ׃ ד כִּי־יָסִיר אֶת־בִּנְךָ מֵאַחֲרַי וְעָבְדוּ
אֱלֹהִים אֲחֵרִים וְחָרָה אַף־יהוה בָּכֶם וְהִשְׁמִידְךָ מַהֵר׃
ה כִּי־אִם־כֹּה תַעֲשׂוּ לָהֶם מִזְבְּחֹתֵיהֶם תִּתֹּצוּ וּמַצֵּבֹתָם
תְּשַׁבֵּרוּ וַאֲשֵׁירֵהֶם תְּגַדֵּעוּן וּפְסִילֵיהֶם תִּשְׂרְפוּן בָּאֵשׁ׃

He did to the Egyptians; He also does good to those who fulfill His commandments. Surely, then, it is our obligation to accept His mandates and His decrees, even though we do not know the reasons for them, and to believe that "Hashem commanded us to perform all these decrees . . . *for our good*" (v. 24). Furthermore, keeping these decrees has the effect of bringing a person "to fear Hashem." The outcome will be that the good we gain from fulfilling God's decrees will last "all the days" — of this world — "to give us life" — in the Next World.

7.

1. שִׁבְעָה גוֹיִם — *Seven nations.* Did Moses have to count them for us? Whatever could he be trying to say?

The thought behind this statement might be, as I have explained elsewhere, that the seven species of produce for which *Eretz Yisrael* is praised correspond to the seven lands inherited by the Children of Israel. Apparently each of the seven lands excelled in the production of one of these species. In that case we may say that Scripture is speaking in praise of the Land here, implying that it has all the goodness of seven different lands belonging to seven nations.

We may read a further message behind these words — the alliance of the seven nations against you will soon enough be broken. As a later verse plainly states, "On one road will they go out toward you, and on seven roads will they flee before you" (28:7). This could be why Moses says "seven nations": even though they go to war together as one nation, in battle they will once again be seven separate nations.

גּוֹיִם רַבִּים וַעֲצוּמִים מִמֶּךָּ — *Nations greater and mightier than you.* The thought might occur to you at that time that since one may not depend

6

24-25

to our forefathers. [24] *HASHEM commanded us to perform all*
these decrees, to fear HASHEM, our God, for our good, all the
days, to give us life, as this very day. [25] *And it will be a merit*
for us if we are careful to perform this entire commandment
before HASHEM, our God, as He commanded us.

7

1-5

[1] *When HASHEM, your God, will bring you to the Land to*
which you come to possess it, and many nations will be
thrust away from before you — the Hittite, the Girgashite,
the Amorite, the Canaanite, the Perizzite, the Hivvite, and
the Jebusite — seven nations greater and mightier than you,
[2] *and HASHEM, your God, will deliver them before you, and*
you will smite them — you shall utterly destroy them; you
shall not seal a covenant with them nor shall you show them
favor. [3] *You shall not intermarry with them; you shall not*
give your daughter to his son, and you shall not take his
daughter for your son, [4] *for he will cause your child to turn*
away from after Me and they will worship the gods of others;
then HASHEM's wrath will burn against you, and He will
destroy you quickly. [5] *Rather, so shall you do to them: Their*
altars shall you break apart; their pillars shall you smash;
their sacred trees shall you cut down; and their carved
images shall you burn in fire.

---

outright on miracles, you should devise stratagems, by which you may gain the upper hand over these nations by natural means.

You might consider (erroneously), for example, expanding your numbers while diminishing theirs through intermarriage (God forbid). For after the Canaanite nations have, on the one hand, been seized with awe and fear of the Children of Israel, and on the other hand have come to say, "What a wise and discerning people is this great nation!" — surely they will be glad to join our ranks. No doubt, if one of them has the chance to marry one of our daughters, the "son-in-law" will be "a good Jew," and so will their children be "good Jews." In the same vein you might suppose that if one of us takes "the daughter of a strange god" as a wife for his son, their offspring can still be perfectly good Israelites, faithful to their people. When this becomes a common occurrence, and gentiles begin marrying our children left and right, then the people of Israel will be "enlarged" and become capable of defeating the surrounding nations even by natural means.

The Torah warns us, therefore, "You shall not intermarry with them; you shall not give your daughter to his son, and you shall not take his daughter for your son." For neither their children nor they themselves will be faithful to our religion — and certainly not to our "nationality," because we have no nationality except that defined by the Holy Torah. We must always remember that "not because you are more numerous than all the peoples did Hashem

ז ו כִּ֣י עַ֤ם קָדוֹשׁ֙ אַתָּ֔ה לַיהוָ֖ה אֱלֹהֶ֑יךָ בְּךָ֞ בָּחַ֣ר ׀ יְהוָ֣ה אֱלֹהֶ֗יךָ
ו־יא לִהְי֥וֹת לוֹ֙ לְעַ֣ם סְגֻלָּ֔ה מִכֹּל֙ הָֽעַמִּ֔ים אֲשֶׁ֖ר עַל־פְּנֵ֥י הָאֲדָמָֽה׃
ז לֹ֣א מֵֽרֻבְּכֶ֞ם מִכָּל־הָֽעַמִּ֗ים חָשַׁ֧ק יְהוָ֛ה בָּכֶ֖ם וַיִּבְחַ֣ר בָּכֶ֑ם
כִּֽי־אַתֶּ֥ם הַמְעַ֖ט מִכָּל־הָעַמִּֽים׃ ח כִּי֩ מֵאַהֲבַ֨ת יְהוָ֜ה אֶתְכֶ֗ם
וּמִשָּׁמְר֤וֹ אֶת־הַשְּׁבֻעָה֙ אֲשֶׁ֤ר נִשְׁבַּע֙ לַאֲבֹ֣תֵיכֶ֔ם הוֹצִ֧יא יְהוָ֛ה
אֶתְכֶ֖ם בְּיָ֣ד חֲזָקָ֑ה וַיִּפְדְּךָ֙ מִבֵּ֣ית עֲבָדִ֔ים מִיַּ֖ד פַּרְעֹ֥ה
מֶֽלֶךְ־מִצְרָֽיִם׃ מפטיר ט וְיָדַעְתָּ֕ כִּֽי־יְהוָ֥ה אֱלֹהֶ֖יךָ ה֣וּא
הָאֱלֹהִ֑ים הָאֵל֙ הַֽנֶּאֱמָ֔ן שֹׁמֵ֧ר הַבְּרִ֣ית וְהַחֶ֗סֶד לְאֹהֲבָ֛יו
וּלְשֹׁמְרֵ֥י מִצְוֺתָ֖ו לְאֶ֥לֶף דּֽוֹר׃ י וּמְשַׁלֵּ֧ם לְשֹׂנְאָ֛יו אֶל־פָּנָ֖יו
לְהַאֲבִיד֑וֹ לֹ֤א יְאַחֵר֙ לְשֹׂנְא֔וֹ אֶל־פָּנָ֖יו יְשַׁלֶּם־לֽוֹ׃ יא וְשָׁמַרְתָּ֙
אֶת־הַמִּצְוָ֜ה וְאֶת־הַֽחֻקִּ֣ים וְאֶת־הַמִּשְׁפָּטִ֗ים אֲשֶׁ֨ר אָנֹכִ֧י
מְצַוְּךָ֛ הַיּ֖וֹם לַעֲשׂוֹתָֽם׃

---

desire and choose you, for you are the fewest of all the peoples. Rather because of Hashem's love for you . . ." (vs. 7-8).

7. לֹא מֵרֻבְּכֶם מִכָּל־הָעַמִּים — *Not because you are more numerous than all the peoples.* The meaning here is not "more numerous than all the peoples of the world together," nor even "more numerous than all of the Canaanite peoples," for each single one of the peoples dwelling in Canaan was larger than the people of Israel, as is clearly stated in *Yalkut Shimoni* (*Eikev* §876): ". . . any one of the Seven Nations was [at least] as large and as fierce as all of Israel." If large numbers had been important to God, He would have chosen the Canaanites, or even just one of their peoples. Or, as the Sages derived from this verse, because you make yourselves small and humble, God chose you.

9. וְיָדַעְתָּ — *You must know.* Everything that has happened to you since you left Egypt should tell you that Hashem is הָאֱלֹהִים, *the* God. *Targum Yonassan* renders this as "He is a mighty Judge," that is, He has the power to do good to those who do His will and to punish those who transgress it. And He is also "the faithful God," for one can be mighty without being faithful; one can say and not do. Therefore the Torah adds that God is indeed faithful.

7
6-11

6 For you are a holy people to HASHEM, your God; HASHEM, your God, has chosen you to be for Him a treasured people above all the peoples that are on the face of the earth. 7 Not because you are more numerous than all the peoples did HASHEM desire you and choose you, for you are the fewest of all the peoples. 8 Rather, because of HASHEM's love for you and because He observes the oath that He swore to your forefathers did He take you out with a strong hand and redeem you from the house of slavery, from the hand of Pharaoh, king of Egypt. 9 You must know that HASHEM, your God — He is the God, the faithful God, Who safeguards the covenant and the kindness for those who love Him and for those who observe His commandments, for a thousand generations. 10 And He repays His enemies in his lifetime to make him perish; He shall not delay for His enemy — in his lifetime He shall repay him. 11 You shall observe the commandment, and the decrees and the ordinances that I command you today, to perform them.

שֹׁמֵר הַבְּרִית וְהַחֶסֶד לְאֹהֲבָיו — *Who safeguards the covenant and the kindness for those who love Him.* "This refers to those who do [the *mitzvos*] out of love. 'And for those who observe His commandments' — this refers to those who do them out of fear" (*Rashi*, based on *Sotah* 31a).

Following this line of reason, perhaps we can say that "the covenant and the kindness for those who love Him" refers to the covenant that He sealed with the Patriarchs ("those who love Him"), that He would do "kindness" to their children, but on the condition that they would be, at the very least, "those who observe His commandments" — that they would fulfill them out of fear if nothing more.

A passage in chapter 10 supports this explanation: "Hashem said to me. . . 'Let them come and possess the Land that I swore to their forefathers to give them. Now, O Israel, what does Hashem, your God, ask of you? Only to fear Hashem, your God, to go in all His ways. . ." (10:11-12). That is to say, God had made a covenant and a sworn promise to give the Land to the Patriarchs, who served Him out of love. For the fulfillment of this promise to the fathers, it was sufficient that their children serve Him out of fear. Furthermore, this merit will hold good for "a thousand generations," that is, forever, as the *Ibn Ezra* interprets it.

פרשת עקב
Parashas Eikev

ז יב וְהָיָה | עֵקֶב תִּשְׁמְעוּן אֵת הַמִּשְׁפָּטִים הָאֵלֶּה וּשְׁמַרְתֶּם
יב־יג וַעֲשִׂיתֶם אֹתָם וְשָׁמַר יהוה אֱלֹהֶיךָ לְךָ אֶת־הַבְּרִית
וְאֶת־הַחֶסֶד אֲשֶׁר נִשְׁבַּע לַאֲבֹתֶיךָ: יג וַאֲהֵבְךָ וּבֵרַכְךָ

---

12. וְהָיָה עֵקֶב תִּשְׁמְעוּן — *It will be because you hearken.* (Translation follows *Ramban*.) "Hearken" [תִּשְׁמְעוּן] is written in the plural here, as is וּשְׁמַרְתֶּם, "and observe," and וַעֲשִׂיתֶם, "and perform," later in this verse. But afterwards all the rest of the passage is in the singular, this is very odd.

It would seem that the Torah is suggesting a lesson here: that by studying and observing the commandments, the Children of Israel would become a united entity, to whom God would speak as if to a single man. For, as we have explained elsewhere, Israel is by nature comprised of distinct individuals (as the Torah itself suggests: "A lion's cub is Judah... Benjamin is a wolf... Dan a snake"). Only the belief in one God united the separate tribes as they stood around Jacob's bed and cried out, "God is one!" (*Bereishis Rabbah* §95)

Once again, at the Giving of the Torah we find that וַיִּחַן יִשְׂרָאֵל, "Israel encamped," in the singular, not the plural. For we are not truly a nation except by the power of the Holy Torah. King David said the same: "Hashem will give עֹז" (the Torah) "to His people; Hashem will bless His people with peace" (*Tehillim* 29:11). Only where there is peace, can we find blessing; and so our next verse promises, "He will . . . bless you."

☙ **וְהָיָה עֵקֶב** — *It will be because* [עֵקֶב, literally "on the heels of"]. "If you hearken to the minor commandments that a man crushes בַּעֲקֵבָיו, with his heels" (*Rashi*).

Let no man say that only the head, chief of all man's limbs, need serve God. The opposite is true: "Let all my bones say, 'Hashem, who is like You?'" (*Tehillim* 35:10) Not only the living, feeling flesh, but even the hard, cold bones must serve God. And not only the bones of the head or the spine, but "all my bones," all the way down to the ones in the feet. That is why the Torah says here, "It shall be עֵקֶב, on the heels of your hearkening": if you serve God starting from your heels and all the way up to your head, if you serve Him even with your heels, then "Hashem will safeguard for you the covenant and the kindness."

☙ **וְהָיָה עֵקֶב תִּשְׁמְעוּן** — *It will be because you hearken.* "This is what Scripture says, 'Why do I fear in days of evil? [Because] the sin of my heels [עֲקֵבַי] surrounds me' (*Tehillim* 49:6). Said David, 'Master of the World! I am not afraid because of the major commandments, since they are so grave [that I am bound to have been careful of them]. But I am afraid because of the minor commandments, for I may have transgressed one of them, and I may have omitted doing one of them; and You have said, "Be as careful of a minor commandment as of a major one."' Therefore David said, 'Why do I fear in days of evil?'" (*Tanchuma*, ad loc.).

This Midrash may serve to explain a passage in *Gemara Menachos* (41a), telling how R' Ketina asked an angel, "Is punishment meted out for [not

7
12-13

[12] *This shall be the reward when you hearken to these ordinances, and you observe and perform them; HASHEM, your God, will safeguard for you the covenant and the kindness that He swore to your forefathers.* [13] *He will love you, bless you*

fulfilling] a positive commandment?" and the angel answered him, "In a time when there is anger in Heaven we do mete out punishment [for this]." (The *Tosafos* explain that when a person is obligated to do a positive commandment and refuses to do it, even an earthly *Beis Din* will decree that he be whipped until he either agrees or dies; still more so the *Beis Din* of Heaven will punish him. The *Gemara* here is talking about *mitzvos* such as *tzitzis,* which is not strictly obligatory, since one is not obliged to buy a four-cornered garment so as to then put *tzitzis* on it.)

Now, the *Gemara* does not mention any source or reason for this distinction, that one is punished for not doing positive commandments only in times of Heavenly anger. But from where do we derive this?

It would seem to be clearly stated in King David's words: "Why do I fear in days of evil? [Because] the sin of my heels surrounds me." The *Tanchuma* explains that this chiefly refers to 'minor' positive commandments that King David feared he might not have fulfilled; and he states that he only feared retribution for this possible deficiency "in days of evil," when Heaven is angry and evil comes into the world.

אֶת הַמִּשְׁפָּטִים הָאֵלֶּה — *These ordinances*. The word מִשְׁפָּטִים usually refers to the commandments that apply between man and his fellow. Why did God use this particular word here, when the reference is to the entire Torah?

Because He made the covenant between Him and us in the same way that two men, or two kings, make a mutual covenant. From then on, upholding the covenant is considered a matter "between man and his Fellow," as it were. Therefore God has promised us that if we will observe the commandments between man and his fellow, He will give us measure for measure in return and uphold the covenant between us and Him.

וּשְׁמַרְתֶּם וַעֲשִׂיתֶם אֹתָם וְשָׁמַר ה' אֱלֹהֶיךָ לְךָ . . . — *And you keep* [*observe*] *and do* [*perform*] *them; Hashem, your God will keep* [*safeguard*]. . . Human beings of flesh and blood sometimes "keep" an agreement safe and sound, but do not "do" it. Therefore the Torah insists that we must both "keep and do" the Torah. But if the Holy One, blessed be He, keeps something close to Him, He surely also does it. It is enough, then, to say that "Hashem, your God will keep the covenant for you."

13. וַאֲהֵבְךָ וּבֵרַכְךָ — *He will love you and bless you.* Any blessing that does not stem from love is not a true blessing. Even the *Kohanim*, before they bless the people, recall that God has commanded them "to bless His people Israel with love." And since Balaam blessed Israel with hatred in his heart, all his blessings (except one) turned to curses. So, to reassure us, the Torah first tells

ז וְהִרְבֶּךָ וּבֵרַךְ פְּרִי־בִטְנְךָ וּפְרִי־אַדְמָתֶךָ דְּגָנְךָ וְתִירֹשְׁךָ
יד־טז וְיִצְהָרֶךָ שְׁגַר־אֲלָפֶיךָ וְעַשְׁתְּרֹת צֹאנֶךָ עַל הָאֲדָמָה אֲשֶׁר־
נִשְׁבַּע לַאֲבֹתֶיךָ לָתֶת לָךְ: יד בָּרוּךְ תִּהְיֶה מִכָּל־הָעַמִּים
לֹא־יִהְיֶה בְךָ עָקָר וַעֲקָרָה וּבִבְהֶמְתֶּךָ: טו וְהֵסִיר יהוה מִמְּךָ
כָּל־חֹלִי וְכָל־מַדְוֵי מִצְרַיִם הָרָעִים אֲשֶׁר יָדַעְתָּ לֹא יְשִׂימָם
בָּךְ וּנְתָנָם בְּכָל־שֹׂנְאֶיךָ: טז וְאָכַלְתָּ אֶת־כָּל־הָעַמִּים
אֲשֶׁר יהוה אֱלֹהֶיךָ נֹתֵן לָךְ לֹא־תָחוֹס עֵינְךָ עֲלֵיהֶם

---

us that "He will love you"; and out of that love "He will bless you," a true and full blessing.

וּבֵרַךְ פְּרִי־בִטְנְךָ וּפְרִי־אַדְמָתֶךָ — *And He will bless the fruit of your womb and the fruit of your Land.* A blessing on the fruit of the womb is mentioned here before the blessing of sustenance — to teach you that a man should not hold back from having children even in a time when he does not have "the fruit of the land, grain and wine" with which to sustain his children. He should trust God, Who nourishes and sustains His world. For "when a son comes into the world, bread for him comes with him" (*Niddah* 31b).

14. בָּרוּךְ תִּהְיֶה מִכָּל־הָעַמִּים — *You will be the most blessed of all the peoples.* All the peoples will see that the people of Israel is blessed (not that they will grant us their blessing, as if that were worth anything!). This will not happen because our grain and wine will be blessed with abundance, for that might be no more than chance, or the result of industrial or agricultural skill. Only when they see that there is no one barren among Israel, even among their livestock, nor are there any illnesses or pains afflicting them (which are certainly common enough at present) — then they will understand that this is the hand of God. Then the nations will say that this wonderful people are indeed blessed by God.

15. כָּל־חֹלִי וְכָל־מַדְוֵי — *Every illness and all the maladies...* There is a difference between these two words. A חלי is a passing illness, but a dangerous one: either one recovers or succumbs. But a מַדְוֶה, a 'pain' as its name indicates, is a malady that is usually not at all dangerous but causes one long-term suffering.

וְכָל־מַדְוֵי מִצְרַיִם הָרָעִים . . . וּנְתָנָם בְּכָל־שֹׂנְאֶיךָ — *And all the bad maladies of Egypt... He will put them upon all your foes.* That way they will have a "headache" of their own, and will not sit around all day thinking of how to harm you. The Torah takes the trouble to mention "the bad maladies *of Egypt*," for these had become famous throughout the world, and the mention of them would make the nations afraid to abuse you.

16. וְאָכַלְתָּ אֶת־כָּל־הָעַמִּים — *You will devour all the peoples.* You will destroy them (see *Onkelos*); but only "the peoples that Hashem, your God will

7
14-16

and multiply you, and He will bless the fruit of your womb
and the fruit of your Land; your grain, your wine, and your
oil; the offspring of your cattle and the flocks of your sheep
and goats; on the Land that He swore to your forefathers to
give you. 14 *You will be the most blessed of all the peoples;*
there will be no infertile male or infertile female among you
nor among your animals. 15 *HASHEM will remove from you*
every illness; and all the bad maladies of Egypt that you knew
— He will not put them upon you, but will put them upon all
your foes. 16 *You will devour all the peoples that HASHEM,*
your God, will deliver to you; your eye shall not pity them;

---

deliver" their lands to you. For when Noah divided up the earth among his children, these lands fell in the portion of Shem. But later, in the days of Abraham, the Canaanites went to war and took them away from the children of Shem (see *Rashi* on *Bereishis* 12:6). Now the Canaanites were being required to give the Land back to Israel, Shem's descendants. And if they would not agree to leave the Land (as indeed was the case with the Girgashites), the Children of Israel would be required to destroy them. This was especially so, seeing as these peoples had sinned grievously and had by now incurred the penalty of utter destruction; but all the same, if they were willing to abandon the Land, then their exile would atone for their sins, and perhaps in the future they would better their ways.

לֹא־תָחוֹס עֵינְךָ עֲלֵיהֶם — *Your eye shall not pity them.* Hashem, your God, the wellspring of kindness and mercy, has commanded you to destroy them, for their sins have piled up to the very heavens. You must, therefore, fulfill the commandment to "destroy the evil from your midst" (13:6).

If, despite this, you let your feelings of pity rule you, thinking that you will be more merciful than Heaven itself, know that this is the sort of logic used by idolaters; but "you shall not worship their gods."

This kind of 'mercy' will lead you into idol worship, for the idolaters love to say that their god is more merciful than the "vengeful" God of Israel. But let the record show who is the more prone to robbery, murder, and wickedness: the disciples of this doctrine of 'mercy' (which teaches that their god forgives even those who do not repent — so that they can do whatever they please and count on the 'forgiveness' of the 'merciful god'), or the Holy People, who fear their God and stay far from all evil, knowing that "God will bring every deed into the judgment."

In the end, then, the Jewish people's 'cruelty' towards the wicked peoples of the Land is really mercy: mercy for them, by putting an end to their sins, whether through exile, or, if they insisted on being stubborn, through death; and mercy for the world, by breaking the might of evil-doers. And the so-called 'mercy' of idolaters is really cruelty, since it only leads men into more and more sin: "your eye shall not pity them"!

ז וְלֹא תַעֲבֹד אֶת־אֱלֹהֵיהֶם כִּי־מוֹקֵשׁ הוּא לָךְ: יז כִּי
יז־כב תֹאמַר בִּלְבָבְךָ רַבִּים הַגּוֹיִם הָאֵלֶּה מִמֶּנִּי אֵיכָה אוּכַל
לְהוֹרִישָׁם: יח לֹא תִירָא מֵהֶם זָכֹר תִּזְכֹּר אֵת אֲשֶׁר־
עָשָׂה יְהוָה אֱלֹהֶיךָ לְפַרְעֹה וּלְכָל־מִצְרָיִם: יט הַמַּסֹּת
הַגְּדֹלֹת אֲשֶׁר־רָאוּ עֵינֶיךָ וְהָאֹתֹת וְהַמֹּפְתִים וְהַיָּד הַחֲזָקָה
וְהַזְּרֹעַ הַנְּטוּיָה אֲשֶׁר הוֹצִאֲךָ יְהוָה אֱלֹהֶיךָ כֵּן־יַעֲשֶׂה
יְהוָה אֱלֹהֶיךָ לְכָל־הָעַמִּים אֲשֶׁר־אַתָּה יָרֵא מִפְּנֵיהֶם:
כ וְגַם אֶת־הַצִּרְעָה יְשַׁלַּח יְהוָה אֱלֹהֶיךָ בָּם עַד־אֲבֹד
הַנִּשְׁאָרִים וְהַנִּסְתָּרִים מִפָּנֶיךָ: כא לֹא תַעֲרֹץ מִפְּנֵיהֶם
כִּי־יְהוָה אֱלֹהֶיךָ בְּקִרְבֶּךָ אֵל גָּדוֹל וְנוֹרָא: כב וְנָשַׁל
יְהוָה אֱלֹהֶיךָ אֶת־הַגּוֹיִם הָאֵל מִפָּנֶיךָ מְעַט מְעָט לֹא
תוּכַל כַּלֹּתָם מַהֵר פֶּן־תִּרְבֶּה עָלֶיךָ חַיַּת הַשָּׂדֶה:

---

17. כִּי תֹאמַר בִּלְבָבְךָ — *Perhaps you will say in your heart.* You will not say it out loud, of course — not after the episode of the spies, who were unwilling to go to war and corrupted the entire people, and who, when they finally found some courage and changed their minds, were not accepted as penitents. Of course you are all of one mind in your readiness to cross the Jordan and do battle with these populous nations. But perhaps a doubt will enter your mind: "How will I be able to drive them out? After all, I am outnumbered by far."

However, you have come to know God during these forty years of wandering in the Wilderness, and you believe that He will keep His word and give you the Promised Land; the only question you have is, How? Then the thought may occur to you that you simply have no idea of your own strength, whereas of course God does. Perhaps He knows that Israel is really stronger than all the seven nations put together, and with this strength Israel will defeat them, numerous though they be. After you have won your victories, then, you will naturally tend to say, "My strength and the might of my hand made me all this wealth!" (8:17)

I am warning you, therefore: "Do not fear them!" And not because of some hidden strength in you, known only to God, by virtue of which He commands you to do battle with them. Instead, "You shall remember what Hashem, your God, did to Pharaoh and to all of Egypt . . . Hashem, your God took you out" — and you didn't have to do a thing ("Hashem shall do battle for you, and you shall remain silent" [*Shemos* 14:14]). Just "so shall Hashem, your God, do to all the peoples before whom you fear." Although this time, unlike in Egypt, God commands you to take a role by fighting to the best of your ability, essentially, this war too will be fought by God, the Master of War.

21. אֵל גָּדוֹל וְנוֹרָא — *A great and awesome God.* In the *Shemoneh Esrei* we say, "the great, mighty, and awesome God"; why does the word "mighty" not appear here?

you shall not worship their gods, for it is a snare for you.
17 Perhaps you will say in your heart, "These nations are
more numerous than I; how will I be able to drive them out?"
18 Do not fear them! You shall remember what HASHEM,
your God, did to Pharaoh and to all of Egypt. 19 The great tests
that your eyes saw, and the signs, the wonders, the strong
hand, and the outstretched arm with which HASHEM, *your*
God, took you out — so shall HASHEM, *your God, do to all the*
peoples before whom you fear. 20 Also the hornet-swarm will
HASHEM, *your God, send among them, until the survivors and*
hidden ones perish before you. 21 You shall not be broken
before them, for HASHEM, *your God is among you, a great and*
awesome God.
22 HASHEM, *your God, will thrust these nations from before*
you little by little; you will not be able to annihilate them
quickly, lest the beasts of the field increase against you.

We can explain this according to the interpretation we once offered of the verse, "O God, by Your Name save me, and by Your might vindicate me" (*Tehillim* 54:3). The "might" of which King David is speaking is of an exalted kind, as in "Who is mighty? He who conquers his evil inclination" (*Pirkei Avos* 4:1); when applied to God, this would refer to His attribute of being slow to anger. God exercises this attribute towards good people and even bad people, for they can always repent — but not towards the Canaanites, who sinned so excessively that the gates of repentance were shut before them. This is why God's might is not mentioned here, in relation to the Canaanites. But He is called "great," for the hidden miracles He does for us, and "awesome," for the revealed miracles He does.

22. פֶּן־תִּרְבֶּה עָלֶיךָ חַיַּת הַשָּׂדֶה — *Lest the beasts of the field increase against you.*

"Is it not true that if we do God's will, we need not fear wild animals, as the verse says, 'And the beasts of the field have made peace with you'? But it was revealed before God that they would eventually sin" (*Rashi*).

But these words immediately follow: "Hashem, your God, will deliver them before you, and will confound them with great confusion." If we say that this verse is talking about the future, when the Children of Israel would sin, it does not make sense; why should people come to a worse end than animals?

One possible explanation is that compared to the nations, the Children of Israel would be considered righteous even after they sinned, and through Israel God would purge the Holy Land of the wicked. Wild beasts, on the other hand, are not responsible for their actions; one cannot say, then, that the Children of Israel are "more righteous" than they. Therefore if the Children of Israel sin, wild beasts will overpower them, Heaven forbid.

ז כג וּנְתָנָם יְהוָה אֱלֹהֶיךָ לְפָנֶיךָ וְהָמָם מְהוּמָה גְדֹלָה עַד
כג־כו הִשָּׁמְדָם: כד וְנָתַן מַלְכֵיהֶם בְּיָדֶךָ וְהַאֲבַדְתָּ אֶת־שְׁמָם
מִתַּחַת הַשָּׁמָיִם לֹא־יִתְיַצֵּב אִישׁ בְּפָנֶיךָ עַד הִשְׁמִדְךָ אֹתָם:
כה פְּסִילֵי אֱלֹהֵיהֶם תִּשְׂרְפוּן בָּאֵשׁ לֹא־תַחְמֹד כֶּסֶף וְזָהָב
עֲלֵיהֶם וְלָקַחְתָּ לָךְ פֶּן תִּוָּקֵשׁ בּוֹ כִּי תוֹעֲבַת יְהוָה אֱלֹהֶיךָ
הוּא: כו וְלֹא־תָבִיא תוֹעֵבָה אֶל־בֵּיתֶךָ וְהָיִיתָ חֵרֶם כָּמֹהוּ
שַׁקֵּץ | תְּשַׁקְּצֶנּוּ וְתַעֵב | תְּתַעֲבֶנּוּ כִּי־חֵרֶם הוּא:
ח א כָּל־הַמִּצְוָה אֲשֶׁר אָנֹכִי מְצַוְּךָ הַיּוֹם תִּשְׁמְרוּן לַעֲשׂוֹת
א־ב לְמַעַן תִּחְיוּן וּרְבִיתֶם וּבָאתֶם וִירִשְׁתֶּם אֶת־הָאָרֶץ אֲשֶׁר־
נִשְׁבַּע יְהוָה לַאֲבֹתֵיכֶם: ב וְזָכַרְתָּ אֶת־כָּל־הַדֶּרֶךְ אֲשֶׁר
הוֹלִיכְךָ יְהוָה אֱלֹהֶיךָ זֶה אַרְבָּעִים שָׁנָה בַּמִּדְבָּר לְמַעַן
עַנֹּתְךָ לְנַסֹּתְךָ לָדַעַת אֶת־אֲשֶׁר בִּלְבָבְךָ הֲתִשְׁמֹר מִצְוֹתָו

---

23. וּנְתָנָם ה׳ אֱלֹהֶיךָ לְפָנֶיךָ — *Hashem, your God will deliver them before you.* It will not be as it was in Egypt, where you were slaves and had no experience in battle, and therefore God did all the fighting for you. Now that you are free, it is up to you to fight the Canaanites; but all the same, God will deliver them before you — "and He said, 'Destroy!'" (33:27).

24. וְנָתַן מַלְכֵיהֶם בְּיָדֶךָ — *He will deliver their kings into your hand.* If you were to destroy them while their kings escaped, then you would have cause for concern. For the kings might recover their forces by gathering together the survivors and those who hid, or they might seek help from other peoples, and come to fight you again. Therefore God promises to "deliver their kings into your hand."

8.

1. כָּל־הַמִּצְוָה . . . תִּשְׁמְרוּן לַעֲשׂוֹת לְמַעַן תִּחְיוּן וּרְבִיתֶם . . . וִירִשְׁתֶּם אֶת־הָאָרֶץ — *The entire commandment... you shall observe to perform, so that you may live and increase . . . and possess the Land.* Israel had three worries at this time:

1) That they might continue dying on the night of every *Tishah B'Av*, just as some fifteen thousand of them had died on that night every year since the Sin of the Spies. Only last year they had seen a respite from this punishment, and they still feared it might be repeated this year and thereafter.

2) In Egypt they had multiplied miraculously, despite their bondage; yet during all their forty years of wandering they had not increased, even by natural means. On the contrary, they had numbered 603,550 when they left Egypt (see *Bamidbar* Ch. 1), and when they came to the Land they numbered only 601,730 (ibid. Ch. 26). Not only had they not increased; they had lost 1,820 of their number, which made them very uneasy.

7 23-26
23 *HASHEM, your God, will deliver them before you, and will*
confound them with great confusion, until their destruction.
24 *He will deliver their kings into your hand and you shall*
cause their name to perish from under the heaven; no man
will stand up against you until you have destroyed them.
25 *The carved images of their gods you shall burn in the fire;*
you shall not covet and take for yourself the silver and gold
that is on them, lest you be ensnared by it, for it is an
abomination of HASHEM, your God. 26 *And you shall not bring*
an abomination into your home and become banned like it;
you shall surely loathe it and you shall surely abominate it,
for it is banned.

8 1-2
1 *The entire commandment that I command you today you*
shall observe to perform, so that you may live and increase,
and come and possess the Land that HASHEM swore to
your forefathers. 2 *You shall remember the entire road on*
which HASHEM, your God, led you these forty years in the
Wilderness so as to afflict you, to test you, to know what is in
your heart, whether you would observe His commandments

---

3) They had still not come to rest, or to inherit the Land that had been promised to their forefathers and to them.

Moses said to them, therefore, that it was in their power to remedy all three of these things, on one condition: "The entire commandment that I command you today you shall observe to perform." Then "you will live" — there will be no more mass deaths — and "you will increase" — as it says above, "He will bless the fruit of your womb... there will be no infertile male or infertile female among you" (7:14). And your third desire, too, will be attained shortly: you will "come and possess the Land that Hashem swore to your forefathers."

2. וְזָכַרְתָּ אֶת־כָּל־הַדֶּרֶךְ . . . אַרְבָּעִים שָׁנָה בַּמִּדְבָּר — *You shall remember the entire road... forty years in the Wilderness.* You must be wondering, said Moses, why God did this to us, and why He did not bring us directly from Egypt to the Promised Land, or at any rate immediately after we received the Torah, before we committed the sin of the Golden Calf. But the inheritance of the Land depends on the fulfillment of the Torah's commandments, as we have said: "This shall be your reward when you hearken to these ordinances and you observe to perform them; Hashem, your God, will safeguard for you the covenant... that He swore to your forefathers." (And in *Tehillim* (105:44-45) we find: "He gave them the lands of [other] peoples, and they inherited the toil of nations, so that they might safeguard His statutes and observe His teachings.")

Therefore it was necessary to make you wander in the desert "so as to afflict you, to test you, to know what is in your heart, whether you would observe His commandments or not" — for with your mouth you had already said, "We shall do and we shall hear," but what was in your heart had yet to be revealed.

אִם־לֹֽא: ג וַיְעַנְּךָ֮ וַיַּרְעִבֶ֒ךָ֒ וַיַּֽאֲכִֽלְךָ֤ אֶת־הַמָּן֙ אֲשֶׁ֣ר לֹא־
יָדַ֔עְתָּ וְלֹ֥א יָֽדְע֖וּן אֲבֹתֶ֑יךָ לְמַ֣עַן הוֹדִֽיעֲךָ֗ כִּ֠י לֹ֣א עַל־
הַלֶּ֤חֶם לְבַדּוֹ֙ יִחְיֶ֣ה הָֽאָדָ֔ם כִּ֛י עַל־כָּל־מוֹצָ֥א פִֽי־יְהוָ֖ה
יִחְיֶ֥ה הָֽאָדָֽם: ד שִׂמְלָ֨תְךָ֜ לֹ֤א בָֽלְתָה֙ מֵֽעָלֶ֔יךָ וְרַגְלְךָ֖ לֹ֣א
בָצֵ֑קָה זֶ֖ה אַרְבָּעִ֥ים שָׁנָֽה: ה וְיָֽדַעְתָּ֖ עִם־לְבָבֶ֑ךָ כִּ֗י כַּֽאֲשֶׁ֨ר
יְיַסֵּ֥ר אִישׁ֙ אֶת־בְּנ֔וֹ יְהוָ֥ה אֱלֹהֶ֖יךָ מְיַסְּרֶֽךָּ: ו וְשָׁ֣מַרְתָּ֔ אֶת־
מִצְוֺ֖ת יְהוָ֣ה אֱלֹהֶ֑יךָ לָלֶ֥כֶת בִּדְרָכָ֖יו וּלְיִרְאָ֥ה אֹתֽוֹ: ז כִּ֚י
יְהוָ֣ה אֱלֹהֶ֔יךָ מְבִֽיאֲךָ֖ אֶל־אֶ֣רֶץ טוֹבָ֑ה אֶ֚רֶץ נַ֣חֲלֵי מָ֔יִם עֲיָנֹת֙
וּתְהֹמֹ֔ת יֹֽצְאִ֥ים בַּבִּקְעָ֖ה וּבָהָֽר: ח אֶ֤רֶץ חִטָּה֙ וּשְׂעֹרָ֔ה וְגֶ֥פֶן
וּתְאֵנָ֖ה וְרִמּ֑וֹן אֶֽרֶץ־זֵ֥ית שֶׁ֖מֶן וּדְבָֽשׁ: ט אֶ֚רֶץ אֲשֶׁ֣ר לֹ֣א
בְמִסְכֵּנֻ֗ת תֹּֽאכַל־בָּ֥הּ לֶ֨חֶם֙ לֹֽא־תֶחְסַ֣ר כֹּ֣ל בָּ֑הּ אֶ֚רֶץ אֲשֶׁ֣ר

Since everything is revealed and known to God, we must understand God's
words following עֲקֵדַת יִצְחָק, *the Binding of Isaac*: "For now I know that you are
a God-fearing man" (*Bereishis* 22:12). *Rashi* explains the meaning: "Now I have
something to answer the Adversary and the nations of the world, who wonder
at the affection that I have for you." It is the same here: God tested the Children
of Israel for forty years in the Wilderness in order to show the Satan and the
nations of the world what a high spiritual level His people had reached in the
desert — and to answer them when they wondered why He destroyed the
Canaanites to make way for them.

4. שִׂמְלָֽתְךָ לֹא בָֽלְתָה מֵֽעָלֶיךָ — *Your garment did not wear out upon you.* Why
does it say "upon you?" We might offer this explanation: it is to teach us that
this miracle was due to the spiritual purity and cleanliness of the physical bodies
of the Children of Israel in that generation. For so it is stated in *Pirkei D'Rabbi
Eliezer*: "R. Pinchas says, 'All of that generation who obeyed God achieved a
level of existence like that of the ministering angels; parasites could not touch
them in their lives, nor grave-worms in their deaths" (as quoted in *Yalkut
Shimoni* §831).

Accordingly, when Rabbi bar Bar-Chana discovered the bodies of those who
died in the Wilderness, he found them free of decomposition, their faces still
glowing as in life (*Bava Basra* 73b). Similarly, "your feet did not swell," because
"your shoe did not wear out from on your foot" (29:4), and this was for the same
reason that your garment did not wear out; thus it says, "from on your foot."

8. אֶרֶץ חִטָּה וּשְׂעֹרָה וְגֶפֶן וּתְאֵנָה וְרִמּוֹן אֶֽרֶץ־זֵית שֶׁמֶן וּדְבָשׁ — *A Land of wheat,
barley, grape, fig, and pomegranate; a Land of oil-olives and date-honey.* The
Land of Israel is praised for seven kinds of produce. Five of these are fruits,
whereas only two are grains of the field. This is a tribute to *Eretz Yisrael*,
because at the beginning of the Creation, before man's first sin, it was God's will
that man should live chiefly on the fruit of trees: "Hashem God caused to sprout
from the ground every tree that was pleasing to the sight and good for food. . .

8
3-9

or not. [3] *He afflicted you and let you hunger, then He fed you*
the manna that you did not know, nor did your forefathers
know, in order to make you know that not by bread alone
does man live, rather by everything that emanates from the
mouth of God does man live. [4] *Your garment did not wear out*
upon you and your feet did not swell, these forty years. [5] *You*
should know in your heart that just as a father will chastise
his son, so HASHEM, *your God, chastises you.* [6] *You shall ob-*
serve the commandments of HASHEM, *your God, to go in His*
ways and fear Him. [7] *For* HASHEM, *your God, is bringing you*
to a good Land: a Land with streams of water, of springs and
underground water coming forth in valley and mountain; [8] *a*
Land of wheat, barley, grape, fig, and pomegranate; a Land of
oil-olives and date-honey; [9] *a Land where you will eat bread*
without poverty — you will lack nothing there; a Land whose

Hashem God took the man and placed him in the Garden of Eden . . . 'Of every tree of the garden you may freely eat'" (*Bereishis* 2:9-16).

This was a great advantage for man, since he would not to have to work the land. (For the care of trees and their fruits is nothing compared to the work of the field. As for the phrase "to work it and to guard it" in the passage quoted above, this is explained in *Bereishis Rabbah* Ch. 16 and in *Sifre Parashas Eikev* 11:13 as referring to sacrifices, study, prayer, and observing the Sabbath.) Adam had plenty of free time to contemplate God's works, to study the seven Noahide commandments, and to praise God for His goodness to His creatures. It was only after Adam sinned that God sent him out of the Garden of Eden to work the land and suffer the curse of "By the sweat of your brow shall you eat bread." For eating bread instead of fruit is considered a curse in the light of *Chazal's* observation: "How much Adam had to exert himself before he procured bread to eat" (*Berachos* 58a).

In *Parashas Behar* we learn that one of the reasons for the Sabbatical and Jubilee years is to free men from plowing, sowing, and reaping so that they will have time to study Torah while living on a healthy (if meager, for that is the way of the Torah) diet of fruit, which is available without effort.

Besides this, fruit is pleasanter to look at and better flavored than grains.

This is the praise of *Eretz Yisrael* — it is a Land of fruits. And this is proved by the Torah's words: "When you shall come to the Land and you shall plant any food tree" (*Vayikra* 19:23).

9. לֹא־בְמִסְכֵּנֻת תֹּאכַל־בָּהּ לֶחֶם לֹא־תֶחְסַר כֹּל בָּהּ — *You will eat bread without poverty — you will lack nothing there.* "Not by bread alone does man live", his needs are many. If there were no stone quarries or metal mines in the land, to build buildings with and forge all kinds of tools, the people would have to export much of their bread in order to buy in exchange all their other needs for house and field. Then they would inescapably have to "eat their bread in

ח אֲבָנֶיהָ בַרְזֶל וּמֵהֲרָרֶיהָ תַּחְצֹב נְחֹשֶׁת׃ י וְאָכַלְתָּ וְשָׂבָעְתָּ
י־יד וּבֵרַכְתָּ אֶת־יהוָה אֱלֹהֶיךָ עַל־הָאָרֶץ הַטֹּבָה אֲשֶׁר נָתַן־
לָךְ׃ שני יא הִשָּׁמֶר לְךָ פֶּן־תִּשְׁכַּח אֶת־יהוָה אֱלֹהֶיךָ לְבִלְתִּי
שְׁמֹר מִצְוֹתָיו וּמִשְׁפָּטָיו וְחֻקֹּתָיו אֲשֶׁר אָנֹכִי מְצַוְּךָ הַיּוֹם׃
יב פֶּן־תֹּאכַל וְשָׂבָעְתָּ וּבָתִּים טֹבִים תִּבְנֶה וְיָשָׁבְתָּ׃ יג וּבְקָרְךָ
וְצֹאנְךָ יִרְבְּיֻן וְכֶסֶף וְזָהָב יִרְבֶּה־לָּךְ וְכֹל אֲשֶׁר־לְךָ יִרְבֶּה׃
יד וְרָם לְבָבֶךָ וְשָׁכַחְתָּ אֶת־יהוָה אֱלֹהֶיךָ הַמּוֹצִיאֲךָ מֵאֶרֶץ

---

poverty." Therefore the Torah promises that "you will lack nothing there," seeing as this Land's "stones are iron" (strong and good for building with; or, as some say, under them you will find iron mines) and "from whose mountains you will mine copper." There will be no need to trade bread for stone and metals that you need, and so "you will eat bread without poverty."

לֹא־בְמִסְכֵּנֻת תֹּאכַל־בָּהּ לֶחֶם — *You will eat bread without poverty.* In our days, when someone consults a doctor he is often warned not to eat bread. The doctor will tell him to "eat of every tree of the Garden" — every nutritious food is to be permitted, "only of the Tree of Knowledge" — which was wheat, say some of the Sages (*Sanhedrin* 70b) — "he must not eat," or not much. Yet King David praised "bread, that sustains man's heart" (*Tehillim* 104:15). How can things have become so topsy-turvy, until bread is accused of harming man's health by causing overweight?

Perhaps it is because the wheat of *Eretz Yisrael* is an entirely different breed from that commonly found in the world. (As a matter of fact, *Eretz Yisrael* wheat is presently sold for twice the price of wheat from other lands. People will pay that much for it because it is hard wheat, good for making pasta.) So when the Torah says that "you will eat bread without poverty" it may be hinting (according to *Targum Yonassan*, which interprets "without lack") that you will not have to weigh it out by the ounce, for fear of fatty degeneration of the heart. (Heard from my nephew, R' Shmuel David Walkin [זצ"ל], the Rav of Lukacz, now of Brooklyn.)

10. וּבֵרַכְתָּ אֶת־ה' אֱלֹהֶיךָ — *And bless Hashem, your God.* "Said R' Yehudah, whence do we derive the Grace After Meals from the Torah? As it says, 'You will eat and you will be satisfied, and bless.'' Whence do we derive the blessing before Torah study from the Torah? As it says, 'When I call out the name of Hashem, ascribe greatness to our God' (32:3)." (*Berachos* 21a)

The blessings before eating food and after reading the Torah are Rabbinically instituted, and for that reason they are shorter than their corresponding blessings instituted by the Torah. But why, for that matter, did the Torah decree a blessing only *after* eating food, and only *before* Torah study and reading?

We could suggest that this follows the rule observed in all the בִּרְכוֹת הַנֶּהֱנִין, the blessings said over pleasure derived from the Creation (for the blessing on studying Torah is also of this sort; see *Levush, Orach Chaim* §46). We always

stones are iron and from whose mountains you will mine
copper. 10 *You will eat and you will be satisfied, and bless*
HASHEM, your God, for the good Land that He gave you.
11 *Take care lest you forget HASHEM, your God, by not*
observing His commandments, His ordinances, and His
decrees, which I command you today, 12 *lest you eat and be*
satisfied, and you build good houses and settle, 13 *and your*
cattle and sheep and goats increase, and you increase silver
and gold for yourselves, and everything that you have will
increase — 14 *and your heart will become haughty and you*
will forget HASHEM, your God, Who took you out of the land

---

make the blessing at the time the greatest pleasure is derived from the food, and if there are several kinds of food before us we make the blessing over the choicest kind available.

It therefore makes perfect sense to say the blessing over Torah just before we begin to study, for then our pleasure is at its greatest, as we toss aside the fleeting life of physicality and delve into our eternal life. But when we end our studies for the moment and turn back to our mundane activities — there is no point in saying a blessing then.

With eating the opposite is true. The greatest pleasure our soul has from it all is not when we begin eating but when we finish as *Chazal* say, "Before one prays for Torah to enter into him, let him pray for excessive eating and drinking not to enter him" (*Tanna Devei Eliyahu Rabbah* 26:3, as quoted in *Mesillas Yesharim*). So naturally the blessing (which, according to the *Zohar*, is the principal sustenance of our souls) should be said when we have finished.

Another reason we might suggest is that, if there were a Torah commandment to say a blessing whenever we finish studying, there would no doubt be some people who would hurry through their studies, so as to quickly fulfill the great *mitzvah* of saying the blessing after Torah. But when it comes to eating, there is never such a problem.

11. הִשָּׁמֶר לְךָ פֶּן־תִּשְׁכַּח אֶת־ה׳ אֱלֹהֶיךָ לְבִלְתִּי שְׁמֹר מִצְוֹתָיו — *Take care lest you forget Hashem, your God, by not observing His commandments.* Even if, Heaven forbid, a person forgets God, if he still observes His commandments, the light of the Torah will eventually bring him back to the right path. As *Chazal* say, God said about the generation of the Destruction of the Temple, "Would that they had left Me and kept My Torah! The light that is in it would have brought them back to the good" (*Yerushalmi Chagigah* 1:7). But if a man "forgets Hashem his God, by not observing His commandments," then what can ever bring him back?

12-14. פֶּן־תֹּאכַל וְשָׂבָעְתָּ . . . וְרָם לְבָבֶךָ וְשָׁכַחְתָּ אֶת־ה׳ אֱלֹהֶיךָ — *Lest you eat and be satisfied... and your heart will become haughty and you will forget Hashem, your God.* We might naturally interpret this warning as meaning chiefly "lest you forget Hashem"; but that cannot be, for this very warning has

ח מִצְרַיִם מִבֵּית עֲבָדִים׃ טו הַמּוֹלִיכְךָ בַּמִּדְבָּר ׀ הַגָּדֹל וְהַנּוֹרָא
טו-יט נָחָשׁ ׀ שָׂרָף וְעַקְרָב וְצִמָּאוֹן אֲשֶׁר אֵין־מָיִם הַמּוֹצִיא לְךָ
מַיִם מִצּוּר הַחַלָּמִישׁ׃ טז הַמַּאֲכִלְךָ מָן בַּמִּדְבָּר אֲשֶׁר
לֹא־יָדְעוּן אֲבֹתֶיךָ לְמַעַן עַנֹּתְךָ וּלְמַעַן נַסֹּתֶךָ לְהֵיטִבְךָ
בְּאַחֲרִיתֶךָ׃ יז וְאָמַרְתָּ בִּלְבָבֶךָ כֹּחִי וְעֹצֶם יָדִי עָשָׂה לִי
אֶת־הַחַיִל הַזֶּה׃ יח וְזָכַרְתָּ אֶת־יְהוָה אֱלֹהֶיךָ כִּי הוּא
הַנֹּתֵן לְךָ כֹּחַ לַעֲשׂוֹת חָיִל לְמַעַן הָקִים אֶת־בְּרִיתוֹ
אֲשֶׁר־נִשְׁבַּע לַאֲבֹתֶיךָ כַּיּוֹם הַזֶּה׃
יט וְהָיָה אִם־שָׁכֹחַ תִּשְׁכַּח אֶת־יְהוָה אֱלֹהֶיךָ וְהָלַכְתָּ

---

just been given in the previous verse). It makes better sense, then, to interpret the chief warning as being "lest you eat and be satisfied," for this very thing can be the beginning of sin. As *Chazal* say, "Before a man prays for Torah to enter his body, let him pray for excessive eating and drinking not to enter him" (*Tanna Devei Eliyahu Rabbah* 26:3). The warning is, then, not to "eat and be satisfied," which leads to "your heart will become haughty and you will forget Hashem, your God." Even though we have already just been warned not to forget God (v.11), the Torah now comes to warn us against the Adversary's way: to persuade man to stuff himself with excessive amounts of rich food, which then leads him to forget God.

13. וְכֶסֶף וְזָהָב יִרְבֶּה־לָּךְ — *And silver and gold become abundant for you.* The chief worry is that silver and gold will become abundant "for you," and you will not lend it to your fellowmen and the poor among your people. As we explained in *Shemos* (22:24), the deeper meaning of "If money you should lend" is that "if money" — if you see that you have more money than you need, "you should lend" it to those who do need it. God has given you the portion destined for the poor, to test you and see whether you will faithfully hand it over. Even if "silver and gold become abundant" in your hands, as long as it is not only "for you," and you help others with it, there is no fear that "your heart will become haughty and you will forget."

14. וְרָם לְבָבֶךָ וְשָׁכַחְתָּ אֶת־ה׳ אֱלֹהֶיךָ — *And your heart will become haughty and you will forget Hashem, your God.* A Jewish heart is the tabernacle of the Divine Presence; as the Torah says, "I will dwell in their midst" — בְּתוֹכָם, literally, "within them." Thus a Jew always remembers his God. But if that heart should become haughty and pride comes to settle within it, then the Divine Presence will leave, as *Chazal* tell us, "the Holy One, blessed be He, cannot live with conceited people." The inevitable result is that this type of Jew forgets his God.

14-16. הַמּוֹצִיאֲךָ מֵאֶרֶץ מִצְרַיִם . . . הַמּוֹלִיכְךָ בַּמִּדְבָּר . . . הַמַּאֲכִלְךָ מָן — *Who took you out of the land of Egypt... Who leads you through the... Wilderness... Who feeds you manna.* Once conceit and egotism have made

8
15-19

of Egypt from the house of slavery, [15] *Who leads you through*
the great and awesome Wilderness — of snake, fiery serpent,
and scorpion, and thirst where there was no water — who
brings forth water for you from the rock of flint, [16] *Who feeds*
you manna in the Wilderness, which your forefathers knew
not, in order to afflict you and in order to test you, to do good
for you in your end. [17] *And you may say in your heart, "My*
strength and the might of my hand made me all this wealth!"
[18] *Then you shall remember HASHEM, your God: that it was*
He Who gave you strength to make wealth, in order to
establish His covenant that He swore to your forefathers, as
this day.
[19] *It shall be that if you forget HASHEM, your God, and go*

---

their way into you, man made of clay, your end will be disbelief in God's supervision of this lowly world. For you will begin to daydream about what it would be like if you had created a world — you would not even deign to look at such lowly creatures! So of course you will not be willing to believe that Hashem, your God, took you out of Egypt, and led you through the desert, and brought water for you out of the flint, and fed you all these years — all the things we are here commanded not to forget, and which are the foundations of pure faith. They are the very antithesis of the "religion of egotism."

18. **וְזָכַרְתָּ אֶת־ה׳ אֱלֹהֶיךָ כִּי הוּא הַנֹּתֵן לְךָ כֹּחַ לַעֲשׂוֹת חָיִל** — *Then you shall remember Hashem, your God: that it was He Who gave you strength to make wealth.* Man is not supposed to sit idle. The Torah promises us, "Hashem, your God, will bless you in all that you do" (16:18) and the *Sifre* explains, "Does this mean even if he sits idle? — The Torah says, 'in all that you *do.*'" At the beginning of the Torah we hear of all "that God made לַעֲשׂוֹת, to do," signifying that God created the raw materials and left it to man לַעֲשׂוֹת, to make from them all that is useful. Everything made during the Seven Days of Creation awaits man's finishing touches, for it was God's desire that it should be so.

But man must also remember that God gives him strength to do all this. Let his heart not become haughty, so that he begins to think that God needs him to work and produce. To remind us of this, the Torah prefaces its warning with a demonstration that the opposite is true. At the Exodus from Egypt God brought them great wealth (the loans of the Egyptians and the spoils of the Red Sea) without their lifting a finger to get it. During the forty years in the desert He brought them water from places whence no human power could have brought it, and sent the manna every day; and for all this they did no work at all. Upon remembering this the Children of Israel must know that all comes from God, and they have nothing to boast about.

ח אַחֲרֵי אֱלֹהִים אֲחֵרִים וַעֲבַדְתָּם וְהִשְׁתַּחֲוִיתָ לָהֶם הַעִדֹתִי
כ בָכֶם הַיּוֹם כִּי אָבֹד תֹּאבֵדוּן: כ כַּגּוֹיִם אֲשֶׁר יהוה מַאֲבִיד
מִפְּנֵיכֶם כֵּן תֹּאבֵדוּן עֵקֶב לֹא תִשְׁמְעוּן בְּקוֹל יהוה
אֱלֹהֵיכֶם:
ט א שְׁמַע יִשְׂרָאֵל אַתָּה עֹבֵר הַיּוֹם אֶת־הַיַּרְדֵּן לָבֹא לָרֶשֶׁת
א־ד גּוֹיִם גְּדֹלִים וַעֲצֻמִים מִמֶּךָּ עָרִים גְּדֹלֹת וּבְצֻרֹת בַּשָּׁמָיִם:
ב עַם־גָּדוֹל וָרָם בְּנֵי עֲנָקִים אֲשֶׁר אַתָּה יָדַעְתָּ וְאַתָּה
שָׁמַעְתָּ מִי יִתְיַצֵּב לִפְנֵי בְּנֵי עֲנָק: ג וְיָדַעְתָּ הַיּוֹם כִּי יהוה
אֱלֹהֶיךָ הוּא הָעֹבֵר לְפָנֶיךָ אֵשׁ אֹכְלָה הוּא יַשְׁמִידֵם וְהוּא
יַכְנִיעֵם לְפָנֶיךָ וְהוֹרַשְׁתָּם וְהַאֲבַדְתָּם מַהֵר כַּאֲשֶׁר דִּבֶּר
יהוה לָךְ: שלישי ד אַל־תֹּאמַר בִּלְבָבְךָ בַּהֲדֹף יהוה אֱלֹהֶיךָ
אֹתָם ׀ מִלְּפָנֶיךָ לֵאמֹר בְּצִדְקָתִי הֱבִיאַנִי יהוה לָרֶשֶׁת
אֶת־הָאָרֶץ הַזֹּאת וּבְרִשְׁעַת הַגּוֹיִם הָאֵלֶּה יהוה מוֹרִישָׁם

---

20. **כַּגּוֹיִם אֲשֶׁר ה׳ מַאֲבִיד מִפְּנֵיכֶם** — *Like the nations that Hashem causes to perish before you.* Why this comparison? Because at the moment when success begins to shine upon man — when he has plenty to eat, a fine house to live in, great herds of cattle and an abundance of money, he is not about to believe that if he sins he is lost and all will go down the drain. Therefore the Torah gives him an allegory to consider here: You can see for yourself how rich and content are the nations presently dwelling in the Land. Yet you will witness how God is about to destroy them because of their terrible sins. If they can perish, then you too should fear such a possible end.

But there is a question here. "When the Most High gave the nations inheritance and set forth the peoples' borders," could He not have put aside for His people an uninhabited land such as all other peoples received? Did it have to be only the land of Canaan, with the attendant result that the people of Israel had to go around from nation to nation and wander in the Wilderness, waiting until the "sin of the Amorite was complete" and they could conquer their land?

The answer is that no other land would have done so well for the Holy People, receivers of the Torah and the *mitzvos*. For now they would dwell in a land that had disgorged its former inhabitants, because they had defiled the land with their evil deeds. Thus the Children of Israel would have a reminder right before their eyes to pay heed to their deeds, "that the land may not vomit you out, as it vomited the people that was before you" (*Vayikra* 18:28).

9.

1-3. **שְׁמַע יִשְׂרָאֵל אַתָּה עֹבֵר הַיּוֹם . . . לָרֶשֶׁת גּוֹיִם גְּדֹלִים . . . וְיָדַעְתָּ הַיּוֹם כִּי ה׳ אֱלֹהֶיךָ הוּא הָעֹבֵר לְפָנֶיךָ . . . הוּא יַשְׁמִידֵם** — *Hear, O Israel; today you cross. . . to drive out nations that are greater. . . But you know today that Hashem, your*

8 *after the gods of others, and worship them and prostrate*
20 *yourself to them — I testify against you today that you will*
surely perish,[20] *like the nations that HASHEM causes to perish*
before you, so will you perish because you will not have
hearkened to the voice of HASHEM, your God.
9 [1] *Hear, O Israel, today you cross the Jordan, to come and*
1-4 *drive out nations that are greater and mightier than you,*
cities that are great and fortified up to the heavens, [2] *a great*
and lofty people, children of giants, that you knew and of
whom you have heard, "Who can stand up against the
children of the giant?" [3] *But you know today that HASHEM,*
your God — He crosses before you, a consuming fire; He will
destroy them and He will subjugate them before you; you will
drive them out and cause them to perish quickly, as HASHEM
spoke to you.
[4] *Do not say in your heart, when HASHEM pushes them*
away from before you, saying, "Because of my righteousness
did HASHEM bring me to possess this Land and because of the
wickedness of these nations did HASHEM drive them away

God, He crosses before you... He will destroy them. These words are very like those spoken to the warriors by the *Kohen* anointed for battle, in Chapter 20. And why did Moses see fit to speak in the same way this day? Because after he had mentioned in the previous verse "the nations that Hashem causes to perish before you," the people might have pointed out that these nations had not yet perished, and that they were many, and mightier and better equipped than the Children of Israel. How, then, can they be spoken of as if already defunct?

Moses forestalled this argument by giving the people a promise: that God Himself was crossing the Jordan with them, "God Who is a consuming fire," and that He would destroy the Canaanites Himself. And in that case these wicked people were already doomed, and no one could have any doubts about it.

4. **אַל־תֹּאמַר בִּלְבָבְךָ בַּהֲדֹף ה׳ אֱלֹהֶיךָ אֹתָם . . . בְּצִדְקָתִי הֱבִיאַנִי ה׳ . . . וּבְרִשְׁעַת הַגּוֹיִם הָאֵלֶּה** — *Do not say in your heart, when Hashem pushes them away... Because of my righteousness did Hashem bring me... and because of the wickedness of these nations*. What would be so bad about Israel saying this? One possible answer is that they would probably decide to make do with their present level of Torah and good deeds, since, in combination with the wickedness of the Canaanite peoples, it was sufficient to win the Land for them.

Therefore the Torah had to inform them that, first, the nations' wickedness alone was certainly not enough to win the Land for the Children of Israel, since the Land might disgorge the Canaanites, and still Israel would not be the next inhabitants (this had actually happened in the case of Sodom and Gomorrah). And secondly, the Children of Israel were not in fact sufficiently righteous in

מִפָּנֶיךָ: ה לֹא בְצִדְקָתְךָ וּבְיֹשֶׁר לְבָבְךָ אַתָּה בָא לָרֶשֶׁת ט
אֶת־אַרְצָם כִּי בְּרִשְׁעַת ׀ הַגּוֹיִם הָאֵלֶּה יהוה אֱלֹהֶיךָ ה־יב
מוֹרִישָׁם מִפָּנֶיךָ וּלְמַעַן הָקִים אֶת־הַדָּבָר אֲשֶׁר נִשְׁבַּע יהוה
לַאֲבֹתֶיךָ לְאַבְרָהָם לְיִצְחָק וּלְיַעֲקֹב: ו וְיָדַעְתָּ כִּי לֹא
בְצִדְקָתְךָ יהוה אֱלֹהֶיךָ נֹתֵן לְךָ אֶת־הָאָרֶץ הַטּוֹבָה הַזֹּאת
לְרִשְׁתָּהּ כִּי עַם־קְשֵׁה־עֹרֶף אָתָּה: ז זְכֹר אַל־תִּשְׁכַּח אֵת
אֲשֶׁר־הִקְצַפְתָּ אֶת־יהוה אֱלֹהֶיךָ בַּמִּדְבָּר לְמִן־הַיּוֹם אֲשֶׁר־
יָצָאתָ ׀ מֵאֶרֶץ מִצְרַיִם עַד־בֹּאֲכֶם עַד־הַמָּקוֹם הַזֶּה מַמְרִים
הֱיִיתֶם עִם־יהוה: ח וּבְחֹרֵב הִקְצַפְתֶּם אֶת־יהוה וַיִּתְאַנַּף
יהוה בָּכֶם לְהַשְׁמִיד אֶתְכֶם: ט בַּעֲלֹתִי הָהָרָה לָקַחַת לוּחֹת
הָאֲבָנִים לוּחֹת הַבְּרִית אֲשֶׁר־כָּרַת יהוה עִמָּכֶם וָאֵשֵׁב
בָּהָר אַרְבָּעִים יוֹם וְאַרְבָּעִים לַיְלָה לֶחֶם לֹא אָכַלְתִּי וּמַיִם
לֹא שָׁתִיתִי: י וַיִּתֵּן יהוה אֵלַי אֶת־שְׁנֵי לוּחֹת הָאֲבָנִים
כְּתֻבִים בְּאֶצְבַּע אֱלֹהִים וַעֲלֵיהֶם כְּכָל־הַדְּבָרִים אֲשֶׁר דִּבֶּר
יהוה עִמָּכֶם בָּהָר מִתּוֹךְ הָאֵשׁ בְּיוֹם הַקָּהָל: יא וַיְהִי מִקֵּץ
אַרְבָּעִים יוֹם וְאַרְבָּעִים לַיְלָה נָתַן יהוה אֵלַי אֶת־שְׁנֵי לֻחֹת
הָאֲבָנִים לֻחוֹת הַבְּרִית: יב וַיֹּאמֶר יהוה אֵלַי קוּם רֵד מַהֵר

---

that generation to deserve the goodly Land. God was bringing them there only so as to fulfill the oath He had sworn to the Patriarchs; and if the Children of Israel wanted to stay there very long, they would have to improve their behavior.

7. מַמְרִים הֱיִיתֶם עִם־ה׳ — *You have been rebels against Hashem.* This phrasing needs explanation; for normally one would say that a person rebels *against* another, but the Torah says here that the Children of Israel rebelled עִם, *with* God. What could this mean?

Evidently the Torah has a special lesson in mind here, and perhaps we can discover it in the *Midrash Tanchuma* (*Ki Sisa* §25), which tells us how even on the day that the Children of Israel made the Golden Calf, the manna came down for them, and they went and offered some of it up before their molten image. Here the Torah is reminding us of that deed: God had even then been kind to them, by feeding them His heavenly food on the same day that they made a molten image, and עִם, *with* that very kindness they rebelled against Him by offering it up as an idolatrous sacrifice, thus involving, as it were, God Himself in their rebellion against Him.

Another aspect of עִם is that just when the Children of Israel were more than ever *with* God, having seen His glory and how He led them day by day with the pillars of cloud and fire — even then they were capable of rebelling against Him.

9 *from before you."* [5] *Not because of your righteousness and the*
5-12 *uprightness of your heart are you coming to possess their*
Land, but because of the wickedness of these nations does
HASHEM, your God, drive them away from before you, and in
order to establish the word that HASHEM swore to your
forefathers, to Abraham, to Isaac, and to Jacob. [6] *And you*
should know that not because of your righteousness does
HASHEM, your God, give you this good Land to possess it, for
you are a stiff-necked people.
[7] *Remember, do not forget, that you provoked HASHEM,*
your God, in the Wilderness; from the day you left the land of
Egypt until your arrival at this place, you have been rebels
against HASHEM. [8] *And in Horeb you provoked HASHEM, and*
HASHEM became angry with you to destroy you. [9] *Then I*
ascended the mountain to receive the Tablets of stone, the
Tablets of the covenant that HASHEM sealed with you, and I
remained on the mountain for forty days and forty nights;
bread I did not eat, and water I did not drink. [10] *And HASHEM*
gave me the two stone Tablets, inscribed with the finger of
HASHEM, and on them were all the words that HASHEM spoke
with you on the mountain from the midst of the fire, on the day
of the congregation.
[11] *It was at the end of forty days and forty nights that*
HASHEM gave me the two stone Tablets, the Tablets of the
covenant. [12] *Then HASHEM said to me, "Arise, descend quickly*

---

8. **וּבְחֹרֵב הִקְצַפְתֶּם אֶת־ה׳** — *And in Horeb you provoked Hashem.* In that holy place, where you received the Torah: even there you dared to provoke God and profane the holiness of the place.

9. **לֶחֶם לֹא אָכַלְתִּי וּמַיִם לֹא שָׁתִיתִי** — *Bread I did not eat, and water I did not drink.* You should have shared in my situation and decreed fasting and prayer until I returned safely.

10. **וַיִּתֵּן ה׳ אֵלַי אֶת־שְׁנֵי לוּחֹת הָאֲבָנִים** — *And Hashem gave me the two stone Tablets.* Throughout this passage they are called "*the* stone Tablets"; for they had been created for this single purpose during the Six Days of Creation, as *Chazal* tell us: "the script; the inscription; and the Tablets, were created *Erev Shabbos* at twilight" (*Avos* 5:8). From this the people might deduce how much pain it cost Moses to break them.

12. **קוּם רֵד מַהֵר מִזֶּה** — *Arise, descend quickly from here.* God told him to go "quickly" so as to save what could be saved while there was yet time. But why did He tell him to "descend quickly *from here*," when the important thing was simply to get down to the encampment as quickly as possible?

ט מִזֶּה כִּי שִׁחֵת עַמְּךָ אֲשֶׁר הוֹצֵאתָ מִמִּצְרָיִם סָרוּ מַהֵר מִן־
יג־יד הַדֶּרֶךְ אֲשֶׁר צִוִּיתִם עָשׂוּ לָהֶם מַסֵּכָה: יג וַיֹּאמֶר יהוה אֵלַי
לֵאמֹר רָאִיתִי אֶת־הָעָם הַזֶּה וְהִנֵּה עַם־קְשֵׁה־עֹרֶף הוּא:
יד הֶרֶף מִמֶּנִּי וְאַשְׁמִידֵם וְאֶמְחֶה אֶת־שְׁמָם מִתַּחַת הַשָּׁמָיִם

Here is proof for *Chazal's* statement that as soon as the Children of Israel made the Golden Calf, the angels attempted to harm Moses (*Shemos Rabbah* §41). This would be why God stressed that Moses must "descend quickly from here," for now it was dangerous for Moses to stay in Heaven. So God opened a way for him under the Throne of Glory, by which he descended (*Shemos Rabbah* §42:4).

This was not reported in *Parashas Ki Sisa;* only now Moses revealed to the Children of Israel how his life had been in danger then, and how he braved all dangers for their sake. As for them, not only had they not prayed for their emissary to return safely; even before mourning their 'former' leader — who was dead, according to the Satan's false report — they had quickly chosen a new 'leader' with joyful dancing.

⊱ **עַמְּךָ אֲשֶׁר הוֹצֵאתָ מִמִּצְרָיִם** — *Your people, that you took out of Egypt.* It is easy enough, when talking to Moses, to call the Children of Israel "your people"; but was it Moses who took them out of Egypt? He was not even a willing emissary to their redemption, and God had to force him to accept his position!

The reference here might actually be to a group that can rightly be called "Moses' people": the Mixed Multitude that Moses took out of Egypt along with the Children of Israel, without asking God about it. His intent was to bring them all under the wings of the *Shechinah,* but in fact they were the bad influence that led to making the Golden Calf. Now God was reminding Moses that "*he* had brought *his* people out of Egypt" although this had not been God's will.

13. רָאִיתִי אֶת־הָעָם הַזֶּה וְהִנֵּה עַם־קְשֵׁה־עֹרֶף הוּא — *I have seen this people, and behold, it is a stiff-necked people.* Why did God add the fact that He "had seen this people"? Was it not enough just to say, "it is a stiff-necked people"?

But let us consider: what if God had simply told Moses that the people had "strayed quickly from the way... and made themselves a molten image... Release Me and I shall destroy them"? Then Moses, and all the Children of Israel too (for Moses was told this לֵאמֹר, to pass on to the people) would have had a just complaint. God knows the future, and surely He saw that the Children of Israel would make an image in the Wilderness. Why, then, had He ever taken them out of Egypt?

Moses would have had a further complaint on his own account. Had he not said back in Midian, "Who am I that I should go to Pharaoh and that I should bring the Children of Israel out of Egypt?" — *Chazal* explain his deeper intent: "What merit do they have by which I may bring them out?" (*Shemos Rabbah*

9
13-14

from here, for the people that you took out of Egypt has become corrupt; they have strayed quickly from the way that I commanded them; they have made themselves a molten image."

[13] *HASHEM said to me, saying, "I have seen this people, and behold! it is a stiff-necked people.* [14] *Release Me, and I shall destroy them and erase their name from under the heavens,*

---

§3) — Yet all the same God had sent him, knowing full well that they were going to anger Him with the Golden Calf.

To forestall these arguments, God told Moses right away, "I have seen this people" — a phrase we can understand on the basis of the *Tanchuma*. For the Midrash (*Shemos* §20) explains why God told Moses רָאֹה רָאִיתִי, literally, "Seeing I have seen" (*Shemos* 3:7): "I see with two visions: I have seen the people's pains, and I will redeem them; and 'I have seen this people, and behold, it is a stiff-necked people,' which will one day anger Me with the Golden Calf." *Shemos Rabbah* (ad loc.) further clarifies this point, that God always judges man by his deeds at *that* time, even though He knows that later he will sin.

And this is the point here. I always knew, God said, that they were going to make the Golden Calf, and even so, back then when they believed Moses' message, and circumcised themselves and offered the *Pesach*-sacrifice before the Egyptians' eyes, I redeemed them and gave them the Torah. But now that they have made the Calf, "Release Me and I shall destroy them."

14. וְאַשְׁמִידֵם — *And I shall destroy them. Apparently this means all of them, since* the verse goes on to say, "and I shall make you [Moses]. . . a nation" — that is, only the children of Moses would remain. Even the tribe of Levi, except for Moses' family, was included in God's resolve to destroy the people, although the Torah says of them, "For they have observed Your word and Your covenant they preserved." (*Rashi* explains that "Your word" refers to "You shall not have other gods," for the Levites never committed idolatry, and that "Your covenant" is the covenant of circumcision, for all the males of that tribe were circumcised even while they were still in Egypt.) Why should the righteous die with the evildoers?

The Levites' one sin was that they did not protest when they witnessed the others' wrongdoing, and for this they, too, deserved annihilation. That is what we learn in *Shabbos* (55a): even people so righteous that they have fulfilled the Torah from *alef* to *taf* can be stricken by the punishing angels because they failed to protest. Even though when Hur protested he was killed for it, this still did not exempt the rest of the tribe, for if they had all come out in force against the sinners, as they did later after Moses descended, they could have overcome the three thousand Calf-worshipers. Indeed we find that when Aaron died and the Children of Israel were seized with fear and started back towards Egypt, the tribe of Levi fought against them all until they overcame the deserters and made them resume their journey towards the Land. (This is

וְאֶעֱשֶׂה אוֹתְךָ לְגוֹי־עָצוּם וָרָב מִמֶּנּוּ: טו וָאֵפֶן וָאֵרֵד ט
מִן־הָהָר וְהָהָר בֹּעֵר בָּאֵשׁ וּשְׁנֵי לוּחֹת הַבְּרִית עַל שְׁתֵּי טו־יז
יָדָי: טז וָאֵרֶא וְהִנֵּה חֲטָאתֶם לַיהוָה אֱלֹהֵיכֶם עֲשִׂיתֶם
לָכֶם עֵגֶל מַסֵּכָה סַרְתֶּם מַהֵר מִן־הַדֶּרֶךְ אֲשֶׁר־צִוָּה יהוָה
אֶתְכֶם: יז וָאֶתְפֹּשׂ בִּשְׁנֵי הַלֻּחֹת וָאַשְׁלִכֵם מֵעַל שְׁתֵּי יָדָי

---

explained by *Rashi* on 10:6 below and in *Bamidbar* 26:13, based on the *Talmud Yerushalmi Sotah* 1:10.)

15. וְהָהָר בֹּעֵר בָּאֵשׁ — *As the mountain was burning in fire.* This was a sign that the bond between God and Israel had not yet been broken. I once saw a reason offered for this, namely that God still intended to make a great nation out of Moses. But we can explain the matter without this, since Moses prayed for the people before he descended the mountain, as we find in *Parashas Ki Sisa*, and as a result of his prayer "Hashem relented regarding the evil that He declared He would do to His people" (*Shemos* 32:14). That is, He decided to eradicate only that generation and bring their children to *Eretz Yisrael*. This is why the mountain was burning with fire: after Moses' prayer, surely the bond was not broken.

16. וָאֵרֶא וְהִנֵּה חֲטָאתֶם לַה' — *Then I saw and behold! you had sinned to Hashem.* Why does it say, "I saw"? Shouldn't it have been enough to say, "So I turned and descended from the mountain. . . and behold! you had sinned to Hashem"?

In the Book of *Shemos*, God says to Moses רָאֹה רָאִיתִי ("I have indeed seen. . ."), and *Chazal* derive from this double expression that "God said to Moses, 'You see one vision (i.e., the receiving of the Torah by the Children of Israel, for God revealed to him, 'When you take the people out of Egypt, you will serve God on this mountain'), and I see two visions' (i.e., God also saw that they would make the Golden Calf after being given the Torah)" (*Shemos Rabbah* Ch. 3).

This is what Moses meant when he said "I saw" — "Now I see the 'second vision' to which God was alluding when I stood before Him next to the burning bush."

17. וָאֶתְפֹּשׂ בִּשְׁנֵי הַלֻּחֹת וָאַשְׁלִכֵם מֵעַל שְׁתֵּי יָדָי — *I grasped the two Tablets and threw them from my two hands.* In verse 15 above, Moses emphasizes similarly that he carried the two Tablets in his two hands. True, this was not emphasized in *Parashas Ki Sisa*, where it simply says, "Moses turned and descended from the mountain, with the two Tablets of the Testimony in his hand" (*Shemos* 32:15), and we are given only a hint, in v. 19, that he used both hands: "He threw down the Tablets from his hands" — the phrase "his hands" is actually written as in the singular without a *yud* (ידו), but it is vocalized with the plural form (יָדָו = יָדָיו) and is plural in meaning.

Be this as it may, here in *Devarim* it is stated twice, with strong emphasis,

and I shall make you a mightier, more numerous nation than
they!" 15 *So I turned and descended from the mountain as the*
mountain was burning in fire, and the two Tablets of the
covenant were in my two hands.
16 *Then I saw and behold! you had sinned to* HASHEM,
your God; you made yourselves a molten calf; you strayed
quickly from the way that HASHEM *commanded you.* 17 *I*
grasped the two Tablets and threw them from my two hands,

---

that Moses held the Tablets, and also broke them, with his *two hands*, and since "Moses is true and his Torah is truth," that is how it must have been.

Now that we have established that Moses held the first Tablets in his two hands, we have to try to understand: why does the Torah say quite clearly of the second Tablets, "and he took two stone Tablets in his *hand*" (*Shemos* 34:4), and similarly, "then I ascended the mountain with the two Tablets in my *hand*" (10:3)? Apparently he was holding both Tablets in one hand, despite the fact that the way up a mountain is harder than the way down.

We can offer several reasons. First and most simply, Moses was very depressed on his way down the mountain with the first Tablets; his energy had been drained (see *Berachos* 32) by the bad news he had heard of what was going on below — as it is said, "A dejected spirit will dry up one's strength" (*Mishlei* 17:22). Therefore he had to use both hands, whereas when he made the second Tablets he had been told that God had forgiven Israel for the episode of the Calf and was inviting him to come up and receive a second set of Tablets, and this good news bolstered his strength, as it is said, "Good news invigorates the bones" (ibid. 15:30). Thus he was able to carry them in one hand.

A second reason for the difference: the first Tablets were made by God himself, and had been ready since the Six Days of Creation. (In *Pirkei D'Rabbi Eliezer*, Ch. 46, it says, "The Tablets were not created out of the earth, but out of Heaven.") The writing on them, moreover, was the writing of God engraved into the stone, which was not so when Moses brought the second Tablets up, for then they were still plain, unengraved stones.

Now, since everything is drawn to its source, the Heavenly letters of the first Tablets tended to float upwards from the stone; only because the Tablets were meant to be brought down to earth, the letters were "obliged" to obey Moses and descend the mountain with him. Especially as Moses came closer to earth, the force of gravity began to exert its pull on the heavy Tablets, as anyone versed in physical science can tell you.

Now, we find in *Nedarim* (38a) that Moses was very strong, and the evidence of this is that he broke the Tablets, which were six *tefachim* long, six *tefachim* wide, and three *tefachim* thick; Moses was able to carry them with his own strength and break them merely by throwing them to the ground. From this it would seem that Moses held them in a strong grasp to keep them from falling to the ground, but in *Yerushalmi Taanis* (23a) R' Yochanan says that the Tablets were trying to fly away and because of this Moses held them

ט וָאֲשַׁבְּרֵם לְעֵינֵיכֶם׃ יח וָאֶתְנַפַּל לִפְנֵי יְהוָה כָּרִאשֹׁנָה
יח־כא אַרְבָּעִים יוֹם וְאַרְבָּעִים לַיְלָה לֶחֶם לֹא אָכַלְתִּי וּמַיִם לֹא
שָׁתִיתִי עַל כָּל־חַטַּאתְכֶם אֲשֶׁר חֲטָאתֶם לַעֲשׂוֹת הָרַע
בְּעֵינֵי יְהוָה לְהַכְעִיסוֹ׃ יט כִּי יָגֹרְתִּי מִפְּנֵי הָאַף וְהַחֵמָה אֲשֶׁר
קָצַף יְהוָה עֲלֵיכֶם לְהַשְׁמִיד אֶתְכֶם וַיִּשְׁמַע יְהוָה אֵלַי גַּם
בַּפַּעַם הַהִוא׃ כ וּבְאַהֲרֹן הִתְאַנַּף יְהוָה מְאֹד לְהַשְׁמִידוֹ
וָאֶתְפַּלֵּל גַּם־בְּעַד אַהֲרֹן בָּעֵת הַהִוא׃ כא וְאֶת־חַטַּאתְכֶם
אֲשֶׁר־עֲשִׂיתֶם אֶת־הָעֵגֶל לָקַחְתִּי וָאֶשְׂרֹף אֹתוֹ ׀ בָּאֵשׁ

---

tightly. "These and those are the words of the Living God," for both heavenly and earthly powers caught hold of the Holy Tablets: the upper powers were pulling them upward while the lower powers were pulling them downward. (Perhaps *Chazal* were thinking of this in the wonderful *Aggadah* that tells how the Tablets were six *tefachim* long; Moses caught hold of two *tefachim* and God caught hold of two *tefachim*, and Moses succeeded in wresting them from God's grip.) This is why Moses had to use both hands: one to keep the Tablets from flying upward while he was still in the vicinity of Heaven, and one to keep from dropping them to the ground as he approached the camp.

18. וָאֶתְנַפַּל . . . אַרְבָּעִים יוֹם וְאַרְבָּעִים לַיְלָה לֶחֶם לֹא אָכַלְתִּי וּמַיִם לֹא שָׁתִיתִי — *Then I threw myself down. . . forty days and forty nights — bread I did not eat and water I did not drink.* *Chazal* said, "A person should never deviate from the [local] custom, for Moses ascended to Heaven and did not eat bread, whereas the ministering angels descended to earth and ate bread, as is written: 'and they ate'" (*Bava Metzia* 86b).

My nephew, Rabbi Shmuel David Walkin [זצ"ל], wrote to me as follows: "The *gaon* R' Menachem Ziemba הי"ד once posed this question to me: 'Granted that the angels ate, or appeared to eat, in Abraham's tent, so as not to deviate from the custom. That is well and good, since no mishap resulted from it. But Moses' not eating for forty days is more difficult to comprehend — how could he not eat? It is impossible for a man to exist without eating and drinking; if someone vows to eat nothing for seven days, he immediately incurs the punishment of lashes for making an oath in vain, and he may eat whenever he likes, for his oath is null and void (*Rambam, Hilchos Shevuos* 5:20). How, then, could Moses endanger his life by not eating or drinking for such a long time, just for the sake of not deviating from the custom? This is not among the *mitzvos* we are required to die for; on the contrary, according to several of the *Rishonim*, one is forbidden to forfeit his life in a case where he is not commanded to do so.'

"There are many ways of answering this question. But I just saw in *Oznayim LaTorah* (*Shemos* 24:11) the commentary on the words, 'they gazed at God, yet they ate and drank.' That is, they ate and drank with Moses, who was about to ascend Mount Horeb for a stay of forty days and forty nights without food or

9 *and I smashed them before your eyes.* [18] *Then I threw my-*
18-21 *self down before* HASHEM *as the first time — forty days*
and forty nights — bread I did not eat and water I did
not drink, because of your entire sin that you committed,
to do that which is evil in the eyes of HASHEM, *to anger*
Him, [19] *for I was terrified of the wrath and blazing anger*
with which HASHEM *had been provoked against you to*
destroy you; and HASHEM *hearkened to me that time, as*
well. [20] HASHEM *became very angry with Aaron to destroy*
him, so I prayed also for Aaron at that time. [21] *Your sin that*
you committed — the Calf — I took and burned it in fire,

---

drink; therefore he feasted on God's bounty in preparation, for this feast had the power to sustain him for that length of time. It is just as we find in the case of Elijah, who went for forty days and forty nights without food or drink, and this was by virtue of his consumption of the hoecakes and the jar of water brought to him by the angel from the 'heavenly table' (*I Melachim* 19:5-6). We could certainly say, then, that Moses ate a meal that could sustain him for forty days, so that there would be no need for him to deviate from the custom."

As we wrote in the commentary referred to above, the nobles of Israel ate only in Moses' honor. As for the second and third times Moses ascended the mountain, we find no mention of his eating a feast from God's bounty. Perhaps his strength was so great that he was sustained for these occasions, too, by that one feast.

19. וַיִּשְׁמַע ה' אֵלַי גַּם בַּפַּעַם הַהִוא — *And Hashem hearkened to me that time, as well.* The *Ibn Ezra* remarks that this refers to the fact that Moses had already prayed for the people at the Sea of Reeds and at Marah. But we can explain the phrasing without reaching this far back. For on this very occasion Moses had already prayed for them briefly, "and Hashem relented regarding the evil that He declared He would do to His people"(*Shemos* 32:14): He agreed not to destroy them all at one blow. But He still entertained thoughts of eradicating them, as He did with those who had sinned in the episode of the spies. And now, when Moses threw himself down before God for forty days and forty nights, God heard his prayer "that time, as well," and agreed to put off the evil decree entirely, "until the day that I make My account." And meanwhile God said to Moses, "Go and lead the people to where I have told you." (See *Shemos* 32:34.)

21. אֶת־הָעֵגֶל לָקַחְתִּי וָאֶשְׂרֹף אֹתוֹ בָּאֵשׁ — *The Calf — I took and burned it in fire.* These words are juxtaposed to the mention of Moses' prayer on Aaron's behalf, and his forgiveness, to teach us that only after the Calf was burned did God agree to forgive him. For as long as the sin was still in existence, it came under the category of "the warped which cannot be repaired" (*Koheles* 1:15; see *Chaggigah* 9).

Aaron was righteous and his intention was for the sake of Heaven, and it befitted him as a "lover of peace and pursuer of peace" to give rebuke in a

וָאֶכֹּת אֹתוֹ טָחוֹן הֵיטֵב עַד אֲשֶׁר־דַּק לְעָפָר וָאַשְׁלִךְ ט
אֶת־עֲפָרוֹ אֶל־הַנַּחַל הַיֹּרֵד מִן־הָהָר׃ כב וּבְתַבְעֵרָה וּבְמַסָּה כב־כו
וּבְקִבְרֹת הַתַּאֲוָה מַקְצִפִים הֱיִיתֶם אֶת־יְהוָה׃ כג וּבִשְׁלֹחַ
יְהוָה אֶתְכֶם מִקָּדֵשׁ בַּרְנֵעַ לֵאמֹר עֲלוּ וּרְשׁוּ אֶת־הָאָרֶץ
אֲשֶׁר נָתַתִּי לָכֶם וַתַּמְרוּ אֶת־פִּי יהוה אֱלֹהֵיכֶם וְלֹא
הֶאֱמַנְתֶּם לוֹ וְלֹא שְׁמַעְתֶּם בְּקֹלוֹ׃ כד מַמְרִים הֱיִיתֶם
עִם־יְהוָה מִיּוֹם דַּעְתִּי אֶתְכֶם׃ כה וָאֶתְנַפַּל לִפְנֵי יהוה אֵת
אַרְבָּעִים הַיּוֹם וְאֶת־אַרְבָּעִים הַלַּיְלָה אֲשֶׁר הִתְנַפָּלְתִּי כִּי־
אָמַר יְהוָה לְהַשְׁמִיד אֶתְכֶם׃ כו וָאֶתְפַּלֵּל אֶל־יהוה וָאֹמַר

---

peaceful manner, and thus he had wished to do on this occasion also. Nevertheless, since, as the previous verse stated, "Hashem became very angry with Aaron" — for God is exacting with his pious ones to a hairsbreadth — the forgiveness of his sin and the sin of all the Children of Israel was dependent on the total destruction of the Calf.

23. וַתַּמְרוּ אֶת־פִּי ה׳ — *Then you rebelled against the word of Hashem.* For you did not listen when He told you, "Go up and possess the Land," and "you did not hearken to His voice" when He told you, "Do not ascend" — you went up to battle anyway.

24. מַמְרִים הֱיִיתֶם עִם־ה׳ מִיּוֹם דַּעְתִּי אֶתְכֶם — *You have been rebels against [lit., "with"] Hashem from the day that I knew you.* "This verse begins with the letter *mem* (40) and ends with the letter *mem*, to tell you that throughout the forty years that you were in the Wilderness you were rebels" (*Baal HaTurim*).

These are surprising words, since after all, they put "We will do" before "we will hear" and received the Torah in the Wilderness. Indeed, in *Midrash Rabbah* (on *Shir Hashirim* 1:5) *Chazal* expound the well-known phrase "I am black but comely": "I am black at Marah. . . and comely at Marah. . . black at Rephidim. . . and comely at Rephidim. . . I am black at Horeb, as is said, 'They have made a calf at Horeb,' and comely at Horeb, as is said, 'All that Hashem has spoken we will do and we will hear.' I am black in the Wilderness, as is said, 'How they did rebel against Him in the Wilderness!', and I am comely in the Wilderness, with the building of the Tabernacle. . ." Clearly, then, they were not rebels throughout the entire forty years.

I have read in various commentaries that seeing as the first *mem* in the word מַמְרִים, "rebels," is written small, this might be a hint that they did not really rebel for the entire forty years, which is just what *Chazal* have shown us. And if we take away this first *mem* (as its reduced size indicates we may do), we are left with מְרִים, indicating that the Children of Israel were "teachers" for all the nations of the world, for through the miracles that God did for them upon their Exodus from Egypt all the nations came to recognize

and I pounded it, grinding it well, until it was fine as dust,
and I threw its dust into the brook that descended from the
mountain.
22 *And in Taberah, in Massah, and in Kibroth-hattaavah*
you were provoking HASHEM, 23 *and when* HASHEM *sent you*
from Kadesh-barnea, saying, "Go up and possess the Land
that I gave you" — then you rebelled against the word of
HASHEM, *your God; you did not believe Him and you did not*
hearken to His voice. 24 *You have been rebels against* HASHEM
from the day that I knew you!
25 *I threw myself down before* HASHEM *for the forty days*
and the forty nights that I threw myself down, for HASHEM
had intended to destroy you. 26 *I prayed to* HASHEM *and said,*

God. As Rahab said to Joshua's spies: "we heard that Hashem dried the waters of the Sea of Reeds before you... for Hashem, your God, is God in the heavens above and on the earth below" (*Yehoshua* 2:10-11). And Jethro said likewise: "Now I know that Hashem is greater than all the gods" (*Shemos* 18:11).

One final point: the phrase עִם ה׳, which literally means "with Hashem," implies a partnership with God. That is, with His help and with the wonders He has done for us we have had the ability at times to be "a kingdom of priests and a holy nation," one that can teach [מֹרֶה] all the other nations the reality of God, may His Name be blessed.

25. וָאֶתְנַפַּל לִפְנֵי ה׳ . . . כִּי־אָמַר ה׳ לְהַשְׁמִיד אֶתְכֶם — *I threw myself down before Hashem... for Hashem had intended to destroy you.* According to the *Ramban*, Moses is mentioning for the second time how he threw himself down for forty days and forty nights because of God's initial intention to destroy Israel. But this was already said in verses 18-19: "Then I threw myself down before Hashem... forty days and forty nights... for I was terrified of the wrath and blazing anger with which Hashem had been provoked against you to destroy you."

Why, then, does Moses repeat the statement here? Apparently he meant to say that even after the Calf had been burnt, and the Children of Israel had allowed Moses to burn it, and they seemed to have repented completely, God was not yet willing to forgive this grievous sin — not after He had come to view them as a "stiff-necked people" and knew that they had already tested Him at Massah and were going to sin again at Taberah with idolatrous thoughts... and that they had been rebellious since the day He had taken them out of Egypt. It was extremely necessary, therefore, for Moses to prostrate himself before God in prayer for forty days and forty nights in order to plead with Him to cancel His decision to destroy that generation, even though God had already relented concerning His intention to eradicate the people entirely, Heaven forbid.

ט אֲדֹנָי יֱהֹוִה אַל־תַּשְׁחֵת עַמְּךָ וְנַחֲלָתְךָ אֲשֶׁר פָּדִיתָ בְּגָדְלֶךָ
כז־כט אֲשֶׁר־הוֹצֵאתָ מִמִּצְרַיִם בְּיָד חֲזָקָה: כז זְכֹר לַעֲבָדֶיךָ
לְאַבְרָהָם לְיִצְחָק וּלְיַעֲקֹב אַל־תֵּפֶן אֶל־קְשִׁי הָעָם הַזֶּה
וְאֶל־רִשְׁעוֹ וְאֶל־חַטָּאתוֹ: כח פֶּן־יֹאמְרוּ הָאָרֶץ אֲשֶׁר
הוֹצֵאתָנוּ מִשָּׁם מִבְּלִי יְכֹלֶת יהוה לַהֲבִיאָם אֶל־הָאָרֶץ
אֲשֶׁר־דִּבֶּר לָהֶם וּמִשִּׂנְאָתוֹ אוֹתָם הוֹצִיאָם לַהֲמִתָם
בַּמִּדְבָּר: כט וְהֵם עַמְּךָ וְנַחֲלָתֶךָ אֲשֶׁר הוֹצֵאתָ בְּכֹחֲךָ הַגָּדֹל
וּבִזְרֹעֲךָ הַנְּטוּיָה:
י רביעי א בָּעֵת הַהִוא אָמַר יהוה אֵלַי פְּסָל־לְךָ שְׁנֵי־לוּחֹת
א־ב אֲבָנִים כָּרִאשֹׁנִים וַעֲלֵה אֵלַי הָהָרָה וְעָשִׂיתָ לְּךָ אֲרוֹן
עֵץ: ב וְאֶכְתֹּב עַל־הַלֻּחֹת אֶת־הַדְּבָרִים אֲשֶׁר הָיוּ עַל־

---

27. **זְכֹר לַעֲבָדֶיךָ לְאַבְרָהָם לְיִצְחָק וּלְיַעֲקֹב** — *Remember for the sake of Your servants, for Abraham, for Isaac, and for Jacob.* In the original prayer, as recorded in *Parashas Ki Sisa,* Moses added the words, "to whom You swore by Yourself... 'I shall increase your offspring,'" (*Shemos* 32:13) because then Moses was praying against total eradication of the people; he protested, therefore, that God had sworn to increase their offspring, not wipe them out.

In this prayer, however (according to *Rashi's* view), after God had relented concerning the total eradication of the people, and commuted the sentence to merely wiping out the sinful generation and bringing their children to the Land, it would be out of place to remind God of His oath.

This is why it says "for Israel" in *Ki Sisa* (ibid.) instead of "for Jacob," as it says here: because then, at the time the prayer was uttered, the angels of destruction wanted to attack Moses; therefore he used the name "Israel" to frighten them away. For this was the name God gave to Jacob as a sign that he had "striven with angels and with man and had overcome." In the present verse, however, the angels are no longer threatening Moses, so there is no need to frighten them away.

⌘ **אַל־תֵּפֶן אֶל־קְשִׁי הָעָם הַזֶּה וְאֶל־רִשְׁעוֹ וְאֶל־חַטָּאתוֹ** — *Do not turn to the stubbornness of this people, and to its wickedness and to its sin.* Through the merit of the three holy Patriarchs, Moses prays "Do not turn" to three things: by the merit of Abraham, who used the trait of stubbornness to fight idolatry, "do not turn to the stubbornness of this people"; by the merit of Isaac, who willingly bared his neck to the slaughtering-knife, "do not turn to its wickedness," the iniquities willfully committed; and by the merit of Jacob, who suffered troubles and exile all his life, "do not turn to its sin," those sins committed unintentionally (for exile atones for unintentional sins). This is why the three items are listed from the most serious fault down to the least serious one, although one would expect the opposite: for they are listed in the order of the Patriarchs they correspond to.

9 "My Lord, HASHEM/ELOHIM, do not destroy Your people and
27-29 Your heritage that You redeemed in Your greatness, that You
took out of Egypt with a strong hand. [27] Remember for the
sake of Your servants, for Abraham, for Isaac, and for Jacob;
do not turn to the stubbornness of this people, and to its
wickedness and to its sin, [28] lest the land from which You
took them out will say, 'For lack of HASHEM's ability to bring
them to the Land of which He spoke to them, and because of
His hatred of them did He take them out to let them die in the
Wilderness.' [29] Yet they are Your people and Your heritage,
whom You took out with Your great strength and Your
outstretched arm."*

10 [1] At that time HASHEM said to me, "Carve for yourself
1-2 two stone Tablets like the first ones, and ascend to Me to
the mountain, and make a wooden ark for yourself. [2] And
I shall inscribe on the Tablets the words that were on*

10.

1. פְּסָל-לְךָ שְׁנֵי-לוּחֹת אֲבָנִים . . . וְעָשִׂיתָ לְּךָ אֲרוֹן עֵץ — *Carve for yourself two stone Tablets. . . and make a wooden ark for yourself.* Moses goes on to say, "So I made an Ark of cedarwood and I carved out two stone Tablets." *Rashi* explains (following the *Tanchuma*) that Moses asked, "When I arrive with the Tablets in my hands, where shall I put them?" Therefore he made the Ark before he carved the Tablets. But in that case, why did God place the command to carve the Tablets before the command to make the Ark?

It seems that God was eager to tell Moses the good news that He was appeased and willing to give him a new set of Tablets; He was quick, therefore, to say, "Carve for yourself two stone Tablets." If God had said to Moses first "Make a wooden Ark for yourself," Moses would not yet know what the Ark was for, and meanwhile he would still be worried and pained over the people's sin. Rather than leave Moses suffering for a few seconds longer than necessary, God took care to tell him immediately that he should carve the new Tablets. From this we can learn how we should always try to tell good news to a person promptly and thus bring joy to his heart.

⇐§ וְעָשִׂיתָ לְּךָ אֲרוֹן עֵץ — *And make a wooden ark for yourself.* Why didn't God command Moses to make an ark for the first Tablets? We can answer this by saying that (of course) it was known to God that they were destined to be broken, and in the meantime there was no need of an ark. This is the opinion expressed by the *Ramban*. Alternatively, the *Asarah Ma'amaros* (quoted in *Yalkut Reuveni* on *Parashas Ki Sisa*) says that if we had not corrupted ourselves with the incident of the Calf, the Tablets would never have needed to be stored in an ark, for Moses' hands would have been their holy ark: he would

הַלֻּחֹת הָרִאשֹׁנִים אֲשֶׁר שִׁבַּרְתָּ וְשַׂמְתָּם בָּאָרוֹן: ג וָאַעַשׂ י
אֲרוֹן עֲצֵי שִׁטִּים וָאֶפְסֹל שְׁנֵי־לֻחֹת אֲבָנִים כָּרִאשֹׁנִים וָאַעַל ג־ז
הָהָרָה וּשְׁנֵי הַלֻּחֹת בְּיָדִי: ד וַיִּכְתֹּב עַל־הַלֻּחֹת כַּמִּכְתָּב
הָרִאשׁוֹן אֵת עֲשֶׂרֶת הַדְּבָרִים אֲשֶׁר דִּבֶּר יהוה אֲלֵיכֶם בָּהָר
מִתּוֹךְ הָאֵשׁ בְּיוֹם הַקָּהָל וַיִּתְּנֵם יהוה אֵלָי: ה וָאֵפֶן וָאֵרֵד
מִן־הָהָר וָאָשִׂם אֶת־הַלֻּחֹת בָּאָרוֹן אֲשֶׁר עָשִׂיתִי וַיִּהְיוּ
שָׁם כַּאֲשֶׁר צִוַּנִי יהוה: ו וּבְנֵי יִשְׂרָאֵל נָסְעוּ מִבְּאֵרֹת
בְּנֵי־יַעֲקָן מוֹסֵרָה שָׁם מֵת אַהֲרֹן וַיִּקָּבֵר שָׁם וַיְכַהֵן אֶלְעָזָר
בְּנוֹ תַּחְתָּיו: ז מִשָּׁם נָסְעוּ הַגֻּדְגֹּדָה וּמִן־הַגֻּדְגֹּדָה יָטְבָתָה

---

have gone on carrying them with him wherever he went, and that would have been straight to the Holy Land and the Garden of Eden, our eternal home.

3. וָאַעַשׂ אֲרוֹן עֲצֵי שִׁטִּים — *So I made an Ark of cedarwood.* God told Moses to make "a wooden ark"; in that case, he could have made it of any wood. Why, then, does Moses specify that he made the Ark of cedarwood, and not just any kind of cedar, but שִׁטִּים wood? The *Tanchuma* (*Terumah* §9) explains: "R' Shmuel bar Nachman says, 'There were twenty-four varieties of cedar... and out of them all, the *shittah* alone was chosen... in order to remedy what the people would later do at Shittim [when the men of Israel were seduced by the daughters of Moab]... do not think that this applies only to the Ark made by Moses — any ark that Jews make should have some *shittim* cedarwood in its construction.'"

Moses, our teacher, who was delivering his message of rebuke after the sins of Israel at Shittim had become a reality, alluded to this episode in his mention of *shittim* wood. This was the reason why in *Parashas Ki Sisa* Moses never spoke of the ark he had made for the Tablets — the people knew about it, and there was no need to elaborate on it. But when it came time to give rebuke, he mentioned that he had been commanded to make a wooden ark, and he had made it out of *shittim*...

§ וָאַעַשׂ אֲרוֹן . . . וָאֶפְסֹל שְׁנֵי־לֻחֹת אֲבָנִים — *So I made an Ark... and I carved out two stone Tablets.* At verse 1, above, we mentioned *Rashi's* point that Moses obeyed God's commandments in reverse order, for God said to him first, "Carve for yourself two stone Tablets," and then, "make a wooden ark for yourself." We must find a way of understanding this: how could Moses apply his own reasoning to God's word so as to deviate from it in any way?

Apparently Moses understood that in this case God chose not to put His commands in the order in which they were to be carried out, for the words "make a wooden ark for yourself" come after "and ascend to Me to the mountain." Moses could not make the Ark in the heavenly heights of the mountain, and this fact afforded him a reason to arrange things according to practical necessity. Therefore he made the Ark first, so that he would have a

10
3-7

the first Tablets that you smashed, and you shall place them in the Ark."

³ So I made an Ark of cedarwood and I carved out two stone Tablets like the first ones; then I ascended the mountain with the two Tablets in my hand. ⁴ He inscribed on the Tablets according to the first script, the Ten Statements that HASHEM spoke to you on the mountain from the midst of the fire, on the day of the congregation, and HASHEM gave them to me. ⁵ I turned and descended from the mountain, and I placed the Tablets in the Ark that I had made, and they remained there as HASHEM had commanded.

⁶ The Children of Israel journeyed from Beeroth-bene-jaakan to Moserah; there Aaron died and he was buried there, and Elazar his son ministered in his place. ⁷ From there they journeyed to Gudgod, and from Gudgod to Jotbah,

---

place ready to put the Tablets as soon as he brought them down from the mountain; then he carved the Tablets, and finally he ascended the mountain. But God said, "Carve for yourself two stone Tablets" first, in order to let him know immediately that Israel was back in His good graces, as we explained above.

6. וּבְנֵי יִשְׂרָאֵל נָסְעוּ מִבְּאֵרֹת בְּנֵי־יַעֲקָן מוֹסֵרָה — *The Children of Israel journeyed from Beeroth-bene-jaakan to Moserah.* This passage is positioned just after the placing of the Tablets into the Ark, to inform us that the journey to Moserah after Aaron's death did not have Divine permission, and therefore the Ark and the Tablets did not move from the encampment. As *Rashi* explains here, this was a journey of rebellion, back to Egypt and its idolatry, the opposite direction to that pointed out by the Tablets.

Moses did not say "you journeyed" in this verse, as he has up until now, because only part of the Children of Israel turned back at this point, and therefore it would have been wrong to blame everyone, by saying "you."

וַיְכַהֵן אֶלְעָזָר בְּנוֹ תַּחְתָּיו — *And Elazar his son ministered in his place.* The clouds of glory returned, just as in Aaron's time. Even though it was actually through Moses' merit that they returned, it never occurred to the "most modest of all men" that this might be so, and he accredited it all to Elazar's merit, the High Priest who filled his father's place.

7. מִשָּׁם נָסְעוּ הַגֻּדְגֹּדָה . . . אֶרֶץ נַחֲלֵי מָיִם — *From there they journeyed to Gudgod... a land of brooks of water.* The *Ha'amek Davar* points out several times that even after Miriam's well was restored following her death, through Moses' merit, the water was not as sweet as it had been in her lifetime. That was why the people began to buy water from the Edomites and others.

On this basis we can understand the Torah's reference here. After the rebellious people had repented of their plan to return to Egypt, and mourned intensely for Aaron's recent death as if he had died and been buried there in

י אֶרֶץ נַחֲלֵי מָיִם: ח בָּעֵת הַהִוא הִבְדִּיל יהוה אֶת־שֵׁבֶט
ח-יב הַלֵּוִי לָשֵׂאת אֶת־אֲרוֹן בְּרִית־יהוה לַעֲמֹד לִפְנֵי יהוה
לְשָׁרְתוֹ וּלְבָרֵךְ בִּשְׁמוֹ עַד הַיּוֹם הַזֶּה: ט עַל־כֵּן לֹא־הָיָה
לְלֵוִי חֵלֶק וְנַחֲלָה עִם־אֶחָיו יהוה הוּא נַחֲלָתוֹ כַּאֲשֶׁר
דִּבֶּר יהוה אֱלֹהֶיךָ לוֹ: י וְאָנֹכִי עָמַדְתִּי בָהָר כַּיָּמִים
הָרִאשֹׁנִים אַרְבָּעִים יוֹם וְאַרְבָּעִים לָיְלָה וַיִּשְׁמַע יהוה
אֵלַי גַּם בַּפַּעַם הַהִוא לֹא־אָבָה יהוה הַשְׁחִיתֶךָ:
יא וַיֹּאמֶר יהוה אֵלַי קוּם לֵךְ לְמַסַּע לִפְנֵי הָעָם וְיָבֹאוּ
וְיִירְשׁוּ אֶת־הָאָרֶץ אֲשֶׁר־נִשְׁבַּעְתִּי לַאֲבֹתָם לָתֵת לָהֶם:
חמישי יב וְעַתָּה יִשְׂרָאֵל מָה יהוה אֱלֹהֶיךָ שֹׁאֵל מֵעִמָּךְ
כִּי אִם־לְיִרְאָה אֶת־יהוה אֱלֹהֶיךָ לָלֶכֶת בְּכָל־דְּרָכָיו

Moserah, they achieved atonement for their sin. At once streams of water burst forth for them at Gudgod and Jotbah, as a sign of Heavenly good will and blessing.

8. בָּעֵת הַהִוא הִבְדִּיל ה׳ אֶת־שֵׁבֶט הַלֵּוִי — *At that time, Hashem set apart the tribe of Levi.* This was the third time that the tribe of Levi had demonstrated its loyalty and devotion to the God of Israel and His Torah: in Egypt they kept the covenant of circumcision and rejected idolatry; when the Golden Calf was made, they put their lives on the line to rid Israel of the offenders; and when some of Israel turned back to Egypt after Aaron's death, they chased after the rebels and fought them fiercely until they returned to the camp, at the cost of four entire Levite families being wiped out.

After three times, their quality was proven; and so God now set them forever apart from the rest of Israel, and elevated them in three ways: (1) they would carry the Ark of the Covenant, (2) they would stand before God to serve Him, and (3) they would bless the people in God's name until this very day. — The whole tribe of Levi is being referred to here, which in its entirety includes the *Kohanim;* and some of these things are given only to the *Kohanim* to do. For example, blessing the people in God's name is only for the *Kohanim;* but as for serving before God, some aspects of Divine Service are for the *Kohanim* and some are for the *Leviim,* such as singing while the sacrifices are being offered.

9. עַל־כֵּן לֹא־הָיָה לְלֵוִי חֵלֶק וְנַחֲלָה — *Therefore Levi did not have a share and a heritage.* Because God "set apart the tribe of Levi. . . to stand before Hashem to minister to Him" — because of that they get no share in the Land?

Ordinary people, who see the Land as being everything, would cry out against such treatment: "Is this the Torah and is this its reward? Because the Levites 'kept the covenant'; and, heedless of their own lives, cut down the worshipers of the Baal; and fought with the people who set out to return to Egypt until they all turned back towards *Eretz Yisrael;* because of this they were

10
8-12

a land of brooks of water. [8] *At that time, HASHEM set apart the*
tribe of Levi to carry the Ark of the covenant of HASHEM, to
stand before HASHEM to minister to Him and to bless in His
Name until this day. [9] *Therefore, Levi did not have a share*
and a heritage with his brethren; HASHEM is his heritage, as
HASHEM, your God, had spoken of him.

[10] *I remained on the mountain as on the first days — forty*
days and forty nights — and HASHEM listened to me this time,
as well, and HASHEM did not wish to destroy you. [11] *HASHEM*
said to me, "Arise, go on the journey before the people; let
them come and possess the Land that I swore to their
forefathers to give them."

[12] *Now, O Israel, what does HASHEM, your God, ask of*
you? Only to fear HASHEM, your God, to go in all His ways

---

not to have any land of their own, and would have to depend on the generosity of others and their tithe portions? What a black future for them!"

But the Torah adds, "Hashem is his heritage"; and the Levites themselves would no doubt tell these people, "Though I sit in darkness, God is light for me" (*Michach* 7:8).

12. וְעַתָּה — *Now.* God has granted my request, and He Himself is going with us; and I said in my prayer, "By Your going with us we will be distinguished from any people that is on the face of the earth" — only under those conditions would we be able to be what You wanted us to be, "a treasure from among all the nations." For if You would be going with us, by being close to You we would learn to go in Your ways. So now is certainly the time to learn "what Hashem asks of you, to fear Him and to go in all His ways."

☙ " 'Now' is an expression signifying repentance" (*Bereishis Rabbah* §38). Its significance is, what is past is in the past, and 'now' in the present we must start afresh, like a new-born baby. And as for your sins until now, they will be forgotten and never mentioned again, if from this day on you fear your God and go in all His ways and love Him.

☙ **. . . מָה ה׳ אֱלֹהֶיךָ שֹׁאֵל מֵעִמָּךְ כִּי אִם־לְיִרְאָה אֶת־ה׳ אֱלֹהֶיךָ** — *What does Hashem, your God, ask of you? Only to fear Hashem, your God,. . . Chazal* ask, 'Is the fear of Heaven such a small thing?' and answer, 'Yes! for Moses it was a small thing' (*Berachos* 33b). But "Moses commanded *us* the Torah," and for *us* the fear of Heaven is a great matter indeed. Did he not take this into account?

Perhaps he did not. For when Moses came down from Mt. Sinai with beams of Heavenly light emanating from his face, (*Shemos* 34:30), he saw how all the people were frightened at the sight. He might well have stopped to think, if they feared him so much, how much more must they fear Heaven itself; in which case, for them too "the fear of Heaven was a small thing."

וּלְאַהֲבָ֣ה אֹת֔וֹ וְלַעֲבֹד֙ אֶת־יהוה אֱלֹהֶ֔יךָ בְּכָל־לְבָבְךָ֖
וּבְכָל־נַפְשֶֽׁךָ: יג לִשְׁמֹ֞ר אֶת־מִצְוֺ֤ת יהוה וְאֶת־חֻקֹּתָ֔יו אֲשֶׁ֧ר
אָנֹכִ֛י מְצַוְּךָ֖ הַיּ֑וֹם לְט֖וֹב לָֽךְ: יד הֵ֚ן לַיהוה אֱלֹהֶ֔יךָ הַשָּׁמַ֖יִם
וּשְׁמֵ֣י הַשָּׁמָ֑יִם הָאָ֖רֶץ וְכָל־אֲשֶׁר־בָּֽהּ: טו רַ֧ק בַּאֲבֹתֶ֛יךָ חָשַׁ֥ק
יהוה לְאַהֲבָ֣ה אוֹתָ֑ם וַיִּבְחַ֞ר בְּזַרְעָ֤ם אַחֲרֵיהֶם֙ בָּכֶ֔ם מִכָּל־
הָעַמִּ֖ים כַּיּ֥וֹם הַזֶּֽה: טז וּמַלְתֶּ֕ם אֵ֖ת עָרְלַ֣ת לְבַבְכֶ֑ם וְעָ֨רְפְּכֶ֔ם
לֹ֥א תַקְשׁ֖וּ עֽוֹד: יז כִּ֚י יהוה אֱלֹֽהֵיכֶ֔ם ה֚וּא אֱלֹהֵ֣י הָֽאֱלֹהִ֔ים
וַאֲדֹנֵ֖י הָאֲדֹנִ֑ים הָאֵ֨ל הַגָּדֹ֤ל הַגִּבֹּר֙ וְהַנּוֹרָ֔א אֲשֶׁר֙ לֹא־יִשָּׂ֣א
פָנִ֔ים וְלֹ֥א יִקַּ֖ח שֹֽׁחַד: יח עֹשֶׂ֛ה מִשְׁפַּ֥ט יָת֖וֹם וְאַלְמָנָ֑ה וְאֹהֵ֣ב

⅏ כִּי אִם־לְיִרְאָה אֶת־ה׳ אֱלֹהֶיךָ — *Only to fear Hashem, your God. Abarbanel*
asks what kind of fear the Torah is talking about here. If it is reverence for
God's greatness, this is no small matter even for the greatest of sages. The Torah
could not summarily demand this kind of fear of the entire people, and go even
farther and call it 'a small thing.' But if, alternately, the Torah is talking about
fear of Divine punishment, that is something so basic to life that even animals
have it, for sheep and cattle will flee from wolves or lions. Surely the Torah is
not suggesting that from such a lowly level we should serve God!

Abarbanel gives his answer at length; but I definitely think that the Torah is
talking about fear of Divine punishment. This is something that can be asked
of all Israel, even the simplest among them; but it is a fear based on faith in God
and in just reward and punishment in the Hereafter. It is not the same as an
animal's instinctive fear of a predator standing palpably before it and gnashing
its teeth, a fear that passes as soon as the danger is past. For God asks us to fear
Him at all times, even though He is hidden from our sight and knowledge. We
are expected to fulfill the verse, "I have set Hashem always before me," (*Tehillim*
16:8) and believe that no matter how a man hides, God sees him.

Fear that comes from faith that God sees all our deeds and metes out to us
what we deserve — a faith maintained even while we see the wicked prospering
and the righteous suffering — is no mere animal terror; it is an intellectual
achievement. It is this feat of intellect that God asks of every one of us, and with
it we may serve God to our benefit all our days.

⅏ לְיִרְאָה אֶת־ה׳ אֱלֹהֶיךָ לָלֶכֶת בְּכָל־דְּרָכָיו — *To fear Hashem, your God, to go in
all His ways...* This fear is to lead you to the fulfillment of the Torah's
commandments. Moreover, one of those commandments is to love God, and
from such love will certainly follow service "with all one's heart and all one's
soul" — not mechanical service by rote, so common among those motivated by
fear.

13. לְטוֹב לָךְ — *For your benefit.* All that God asks of you is not for His benefit,
for "if you have been righteous, what are you giving Him?" (*Iyov* 35:7). It
is purely for your sake.

and to love Him, and to serve HASHEM, your God, with all
your heart and with all your soul, 13 *to observe the command-*
ments of HASHEM and His decrees, which I command you
today, for your benefit. 14 *Behold! To HASHEM, your God, are*
the heaven and highest heaven, the earth and everything that
is in it. 15 *Only your forefathers did HASHEM cherish to love*
them, and He chose their offspring after them — you — from
among all the peoples, as this day. 16 *You shall cut away the*
barrier of your heart and no longer stiffen your neck. 17 *For*
HASHEM, your God — He is the God of the powers and the
Lord of the lords, the great, mighty, and awesome God, Who
does not show favor and Who does not accept a bribe. 18 *He*
carries out the judgment of orphan and widow, and loves

---

14. הֵן לַה׳ אֱלֹהֶיךָ הַשָּׁמַיִם וּשְׁמֵי הַשָּׁמָיִם הָאָרֶץ וְכָל־אֲשֶׁר־בָּהּ — *Behold! To Hashem, your God, are the heaven and highest heaven, the earth and everything that is in it.* He had a wide choice when it came to whom He would love: all the hosts of heaven and those that live on earth. Yet all the same. . .

15. רַק בַּאֲבֹתֶיךָ חָשַׁק ה׳ לְאַהֲבָה אוֹתָם וַיִּבְחַר בְּזַרְעָם — *Only your forefathers did Hashem cherish to love them, and He chose their offspring.* This places an obligation upon us: not only to fear this great God, but also to love Him, in return for His loving our fathers and us. As the Torah says, "As water [reflects] face to face, so does man's heart to another heart" (*Mishlei* 27:19). So if we have merited receiving all this love from God, we should love Him in return "with all our heart and all our soul."

16. וּמַלְתֶּם אֵת עָרְלַת לְבַבְכֶם — *You shall cut away the barrier of your heart.* True, "the cast of man's heart is bad from his youth" (*Bereishis* 8:21), but man is given free choice. He can circumcise his heart, removing the evil from it and showering it with uprightness and the fear of Heaven. He can tell his heart that:

17. כִּי ה׳ אֱלֹהֵיכֶם הוּא אֱלֹהֵי הָאֱלֹהִים — *For Hashem, your God, He is the God of the powers.* [The word אֱלֹהִים often means "judges."] He is the Judge of the judges, Who punishes sinners, and "the Lord of lords," Who should be feared.

☙ וְלֹא יִקַּח שֹׁחַד — *Who does not accept a bribe.* What sort of bribe could one offer God? Certainly not silver or gold. Perhaps flattering words? But the Torah itself advises us, "take words with you" (*Hoshea* 14:3), which advice becomes clear when we read further in the verse: "and return to God." It is repentance, not one's words, that helps.

Perhaps giving charity? Indeed, Daniel advised the king, "atone for your sin with charity." *Chazal* say that anyone who gives a coin to a poor man is as if he had sent a gift to the King of kings, blessed be He, and that charity saves one from the judgment of *Gehinnom* (*Bava Basra* 10a). But their intent is that charity

י גֵּר לָתֶת לוֹ לֶחֶם וְשִׂמְלָה: יט וַאֲהַבְתֶּם אֶת־הַגֵּר כִּי־גֵרִים
יט־כב הֱיִיתֶם בְּאֶרֶץ מִצְרָיִם: כ אֶת־יְהוָה אֱלֹהֶיךָ תִּירָא אֹתוֹ
תַעֲבֹד וּבוֹ תִדְבָּק וּבִשְׁמוֹ תִּשָּׁבֵעַ: כא הוּא תְהִלָּתְךָ וְהוּא
אֱלֹהֶיךָ אֲשֶׁר־עָשָׂה אִתְּךָ אֶת־הַגְּדֹלֹת וְאֶת־הַנּוֹרָאֹת
הָאֵלֶּה אֲשֶׁר רָאוּ עֵינֶיךָ: כב בְּשִׁבְעִים נֶפֶשׁ יָרְדוּ אֲבֹתֶיךָ
מִצְרָיְמָה וְעַתָּה שָׂמְךָ יְהוָה אֱלֹהֶיךָ כְּכוֹכְבֵי הַשָּׁמַיִם לָרֹב:
יא א וְאָהַבְתָּ אֵת יְהוָה אֱלֹהֶיךָ וְשָׁמַרְתָּ מִשְׁמַרְתּוֹ וְחֻקֹּתָיו
א־ד וּמִשְׁפָּטָיו וּמִצְוֹתָיו כָּל־הַיָּמִים: ב וִידַעְתֶּם הַיּוֹם כִּי ׀ לֹא
אֶת־בְּנֵיכֶם אֲשֶׁר לֹא־יָדְעוּ וַאֲשֶׁר לֹא־רָאוּ אֶת־מוּסַר
יְהוָה אֱלֹהֵיכֶם אֶת־גָּדְלוֹ אֶת־יָדוֹ הַחֲזָקָה וּזְרֹעוֹ הַנְּטוּיָה:
ג וְאֶת־אֹתֹתָיו וְאֶת־מַעֲשָׂיו אֲשֶׁר עָשָׂה בְּתוֹךְ מִצְרָיִם
לְפַרְעֹה מֶלֶךְ־מִצְרַיִם וּלְכָל־אַרְצוֹ: ד וַאֲשֶׁר עָשָׂה לְחֵיל

---

atones for sins, just as bringing a sacrifice to the Temple atones; and of course, in both cases one must first repent and only then seek atonement. So none of these (neither "words" nor charity) can be called a "bribe," since each is only an adjunct of repentance, which was created before the world itself (*Pesachim* 54a).

Or perhaps this is a bribe consisting of *mitzvos?* But no, the commandments are obligatory for us. And if one tries extra hard and does more than he is strictly obligated to do, this would seem to be far from a bribe. It is no more than what one ought to do, since *Chazal* advise us, "If you have done piles of sins, set against them piles of *mitzvos*" (*Vayikra Rabbah* 21:5).

However, the intent here is that a person might "pile on" his *mitzvos*, thinking that by so doing he will outweigh his sins and gain eternal life despite them. But this "bribe" will not work; he will be punished none the less, unless he repents.

20. אֶת־ה׳ אֱלֹהֶיךָ תִּירָא . . . וּבִשְׁמוֹ תִּשָּׁבֵעַ — *Hashem, your God shall you fear . . . and in His Name shall you swear.* "Said the Holy One, blessed be He: 'Even for the truth you are not entitled to swear by My Name, unless you have all these qualities in you, as the Torah says, "You shall fear Hashem, your God, Him shall you serve, to Him shall you cleave". . . if you have all these qualities you are entitled to swear [by My Name], and if not, you are not entitled'" (*Tanchuma, Mattos* §1).

If a person swears by his own life, he is (at least sometimes) to be believed, since an ordinary person wants to go on living. But if he swears by his fellowman's life, or the king's life, his oath will not be accepted unless it is known that he loves his fellow, or the king, and is utterly devoted to him, so that he would never curse him, or put him to shame by swearing falsely for the sake of money.

Therefore no man may swear by God's Name, even to the truth, unless he has

10
19-22

the proselyte to give him bread and garment. 19 *You shall love*
the proselyte for you were strangers in the land of Egypt.
20 *HASHEM, your God, shall you fear, Him shall you serve, to*
Him shall you cleave, and in His Name shall you swear. 21 *He*
is your praise and He is your God, Who did for you these
great and awesome things that your eyes saw. 22 *With*
seventy souls did your ancestors descend to Egypt, and now
HASHEM, your God, has made you like the stars of heaven for
abundance.

11
1-4

1 *You shall love HASHEM, your God, and you shall safe-*
guard His charge, His decrees, His ordinances, and His com-
mandments, all the days. 2 *You should know today that it is*
not your children who did not know and who did not see the
chastisement of HASHEM, your God, His greatness, His strong
hand, and His outstretched arm; 3 *His signs and His deeds*
that He performed in the midst of Egypt, to Pharaoh, king
of Egypt, and to all his land; 4 *and what He did to the army*

"all these qualities": fear of Heaven and devoted service; since if he doesn't have them, people will say that he doesn't care about the Divine honor and is only swearing to avoid paying his debts — a *chillul Hashem.*

11.

2. **וִידַעְתֶּם הַיּוֹם כִּי לֹא אֶת־בְּנֵיכֶם אֲשֶׁר לֹא־יָדְעוּ וַאֲשֶׁר לֹא־רָאוּ אֶת־מוּסַר ה׳ אֱלֹהֵיכֶם** — *You should know today that it is not your children who did not know and who did not see the chatisement of Hashem, your God.* The end of this exhortation is at verse 7: "Rather it is your own eyes that see all the great work of Hashem, which He did." Moses intended to say by this that all those alive today, at the transmission of the *Mishneh Torah,* who left Egypt and were younger than twenty years of age at the time of the Sin of the Spies know, and upon their acceptance testify that with their "own eyes" they saw "all the great work of Hashem, which He did."

Perhaps if another generation who did not include among themselves יוֹצְאֵי מִצְרַיִם, would have received the Torah, then future generations would have just been satisfied with the miracles and wonders which Hashem performed for us in Egypt, on the Sea and in the Wilderness. Therefore, Moses emphasized that he is transmitting the Torah to those who witnessed *firsthand* Hashem's "chastisement, His greatness, His strong hand. . . His signs and His deeds." It is incumbent upon them to be an example and bequeath to their children and — generation to generation — to their grandchildren all they had witnessed. Thus will our Tradition be upheld and perpetuated from the first generation, who saw with their "own eyes" and through their acceptance of the Torah confirmed and attested to its truth.

מִצְרַ֗יִם לְסוּסָ֤יו וּלְרִכְבּוֹ֙ אֲשֶׁ֨ר הֵצִ֜יף אֶת־מֵ֤י יַם־סוּף֙ עַל־פְּנֵיהֶ֔ם בְּרׇדְפָ֖ם אַחֲרֵיכֶ֑ם וַיְאַבְּדֵ֣ם יְהֹוָ֔ה עַ֖ד הַיּ֥וֹם הַזֶּֽה: ה וַאֲשֶׁ֤ר עָשָׂה֙ לָכֶ֣ם בַּמִּדְבָּ֔ר עַד־בֹּאֲכֶ֖ם עַד־הַמָּק֥וֹם הַזֶּֽה: ו וַאֲשֶׁ֨ר עָשָׂ֜ה לְדָתָ֣ן וְלַאֲבִירָ֗ם בְּנֵ֣י אֱלִיאָב֮ בֶּן־רְאוּבֵן֒ אֲשֶׁ֨ר פָּצְתָ֤ה הָאָ֨רֶץ֙ אֶת־פִּ֔יהָ וַתִּבְלָעֵ֥ם וְאֶת־בָּתֵּיהֶ֖ם וְאֶת־אׇהֳלֵיהֶ֑ם וְאֵ֤ת כׇּל־הַיְקוּם֙ אֲשֶׁ֣ר בְּרַגְלֵיהֶ֔ם בְּקֶ֖רֶב כׇּל־יִשְׂרָאֵֽל: ז כִּ֤י עֵֽינֵיכֶם֙ הָֽרֹאֹ֔ת אֶת־כׇּל־מַעֲשֵׂ֥ה יְהֹוָ֖ה הַגָּדֹ֑ל אֲשֶׁ֖ר עָשָֽׂה: ח וּשְׁמַרְתֶּם֙ אֶת־כׇּל־הַמִּצְוָ֔ה אֲשֶׁ֧ר אָנֹכִ֛י מְצַוְּךָ֖ הַיּ֑וֹם לְמַ֣עַן תֶּחֶזְק֗וּ וּבָאתֶם֙ וִֽירִשְׁתֶּ֣ם אֶת־הָאָ֔רֶץ אֲשֶׁ֥ר אַתֶּ֛ם עֹבְרִ֥ים שָׁ֖מָּה לְרִשְׁתָּֽהּ: ט וּלְמַ֨עַן תַּאֲרִ֤יכוּ יָמִים֙ עַל־הָ֣אֲדָמָ֔ה אֲשֶׁר֩ נִשְׁבַּ֨ע יְהֹוָ֤ה לַאֲבֹֽתֵיכֶם֙ לָתֵ֣ת לָהֶ֔ם וּלְזַרְעָ֑ם אֶ֛רֶץ זָבַ֥ת חָלָ֖ב וּדְבָֽשׁ: שׁשׁי י כִּ֣י הָאָ֗רֶץ אֲשֶׁ֨ר אַתָּ֤ה בָא־שָׁ֨מָּה֙ לְרִשְׁתָּ֔הּ לֹ֣א כְאֶ֤רֶץ מִצְרַ֨יִם֙ הִ֔וא אֲשֶׁ֥ר יְצָאתֶ֖ם מִשָּׁ֑ם אֲשֶׁ֤ר תִּזְרַע֙ אֶֽת־זַרְעֲךָ֔ וְהִשְׁקִ֥יתָ בְרַגְלְךָ֖ כְּגַ֥ן הַיָּרָֽק: יא וְהָאָ֗רֶץ אֲשֶׁ֤ר אַתֶּם֙ עֹבְרִ֥ים שָׁ֨מָּה֙ לְרִשְׁתָּ֔הּ אֶ֥רֶץ הָרִ֖ים וּבְקָעֹ֑ת לִמְטַ֥ר הַשָּׁמַ֖יִם תִּשְׁתֶּה־מָּֽיִם: יב אֶ֕רֶץ אֲשֶׁר־יְהֹוָ֥ה אֱלֹהֶ֖יךָ דֹּרֵ֣שׁ אֹתָ֑הּ תָּמִ֗יד עֵינֵ֨י יְהֹוָ֤ה אֱלֹהֶ֨יךָ֙ בָּ֔הּ מֵֽרֵשִׁית֙ הַשָּׁנָ֔ה וְעַ֖ד אַחֲרִ֥ית שָׁנָֽה: יג וְהָיָ֗ה אִם־שָׁמֹ֤עַ תִּשְׁמְעוּ֙ אֶל־מִצְוֺתַ֔י אֲשֶׁ֧ר אָנֹכִ֛י מְצַוֶּ֥ה אֶתְכֶ֖ם הַיּ֑וֹם לְאַהֲבָ֞ה אֶת־יְהֹוָ֤ה אֱלֹֽהֵיכֶם֙ וּלְעׇבְד֔וֹ בְּכׇל־לְבַבְכֶ֖ם וּבְכׇל־נַפְשְׁכֶֽם: יד וְנָתַתִּ֧י מְטַֽר־אַרְצְכֶ֛ם בְּעִתּ֖וֹ יוֹרֶ֥ה

---

13. וּלְעׇבְד֔וֹ בְּכׇל־לְבַבְכֶ֖ם וּבְכׇל־נַפְשְׁכֶֽם — *And to serve Him with all your heart and with all your soul.* But not "with all your resources (מְאֹדֶךָ)"? I once heard an explanation for this, based on the fact that this passage is in the plural, not in the singular like the *Shema*. There is no fear that the entire people's collective wealth might be dearer to them than their very selves, whereas this is possible in the case of an occasional individual, as *Chazal* said about the *Shema*: "In case there is someone whose money is dearer to him than himself, the Torah says, 'and with all your resources.'"

But I am still not satisfied. After all, the words "with all your resources" could have been placed in our verse before "and with all your soul," as if to say, "not only your possessions, but furthermore you must be ready to give your life." I once heard, however, in the name of the *Kotzker Rebbe* that this is precisely why the words "with all your resources" are left out in this plural-form verse. For if the entire Jewish community were to hand over all their property for the sake of the Torah, the nation's existence would be threatened, and this is already covered by "with all your soul." In the case of an individual, however, even if

11
5-14

of Egypt, to its horses and its riders, over whom He swept the
waters of the Sea of Reeds when they pursued you, and
HASHEM caused them to perish until this day; 5 *and what He*
did for you in the Wilderness, until you came to this place;
6 *and what He did to Dathan and Abiram the sons of Eliab*
son of Reuben, when the earth opened its mouth wide and
swallowed them, and their households, and their tents, and
all the fortunes at their feet, in the midst of all Israel. 7 *Rather*
it is your own eyes that see all the great work of HASHEM,
which He did.

8 *So you shall observe the entire commandment that I*
command you today, so that you will be strong, and you will
come and possess the Land to which you are crossing the
Jordan, to possess it, 9 *and so that you will prolong your days*
on the Land that HASHEM swore to your forefathers to give
them and to their offspring — a land flowing with milk and
honey.

10 *For the Land to which you come, to possess it — it is not*
like the land of Egypt that you left, where you would plant
your seed and water it on foot like a vegetable garden. 11 *But*
the Land to which you cross over to possess it is a Land of
hills and valleys; from the rain of heaven shall you drink
water; 12 *a Land that HASHEM, your God, seeks out; the eyes*
of HASHEM, your God, are always upon it, from the beginning
of the year to year's end.

13 *It will be that if you hearken to My commandments that*
I command you today, to love HASHEM, your God, and to
serve Him with all your heart and with all your soul, 14 *then*
I shall provide rain for your Land in its proper time, the early

---

he were to give all he owns for love of God and His Torah, he could still live on charity, so his life would not be endangered.

14. וְנָתַתִּי מְטַר־אַרְצְכֶם — *Then I shall provide rain for your Land.* Some commentaries I have seen interpret וְנָתַתִּי ("I shall provide") literally, as "I shall give" — as a gift. This view is based on *Chazal's* dictum that there is no reward for *mitzvos* in this world (*Kiddushin* 39b). But how would these commentators interpret "Hashem will make (יִתֵּן) the rain of your Land dust and dirt" (below, 28:24)? Is this also a "gift"?

Let us address the basic issue: reward for *mitzvos* in this world. We find in the *Gemara* that one who hires a laborer must provide his food, and not just meager rations, but meals befitting the children of Abraham, Isaac, and Jacob (*Bava Metzia* 83). Certainly, then, if the Children of Israel fulfill the Torah (that is, if they labor for the "Boss") they are entitled to receive their meals, in addition to

יא וּמַלְקוֹשׁ וְאָסַפְתָּ דְגָנֶךָ וְתִירֹשְׁךָ וְיִצְהָרֶךָ: טו וְנָתַתִּי עֵשֶׂב
טו־יט בְּשָׂדְךָ לִבְהֶמְתֶּךָ וְאָכַלְתָּ וְשָׂבָעְתָּ: טז הִשָּׁמְרוּ לָכֶם פֶּן־
יִפְתֶּה לְבַבְכֶם וְסַרְתֶּם וַעֲבַדְתֶּם אֱלֹהִים אֲחֵרִים
וְהִשְׁתַּחֲוִיתֶם לָהֶם: יז וְחָרָה אַף־יהוה בָּכֶם וְעָצַר אֶת־
הַשָּׁמַיִם וְלֹא־יִהְיֶה מָטָר וְהָאֲדָמָה לֹא תִתֵּן אֶת־יְבוּלָהּ
וַאֲבַדְתֶּם מְהֵרָה מֵעַל הָאָרֶץ הַטֹּבָה אֲשֶׁר יהוה נֹתֵן
לָכֶם: יח וְשַׂמְתֶּם אֶת־דְּבָרַי אֵלֶּה עַל־לְבַבְכֶם וְעַל־
נַפְשְׁכֶם וּקְשַׁרְתֶּם אֹתָם לְאוֹת עַל־יֶדְכֶם וְהָיוּ לְטוֹטָפֹת בֵּין
עֵינֵיכֶם: יט וְלִמַּדְתֶּם אֹתָם אֶת־בְּנֵיכֶם לְדַבֵּר בָּם בְּשִׁבְתְּךָ

---

their "wages," which are paid only in the Next World. Thus, "You will eat and you will be satisfied" is not "the reward for a *mitzvah* in this world"; it is simply a worker's due allowance for sustenance.

וְאָסַפְתָּ דְגָנֶךָ — *You may gather in your grain.* What is an expression in the singular form doing in the middle of a passage that is expressed completely in the plural? It could be there to tell us that no one should say, "I will be all right even though I go according to my own desires; as long as most of the Jewish people are going in God's way and keeping His commandments, the Land is assured of rain in its season."

Indeed, the world, and each individual country in it, is judged according to the majority. But precisely because individuals tend to think this way, the Torah says to each and every Jew — in the singular — "You may gather in your grain" — if you are worthy of it. But if you personally deviate from the way of God and rely on the merit of the majority to bring rain on your field, no such thing will come to pass, for God's providence is individual, too, "giving to a man according to his ways and according to the fruit of his actions" (*Yirmiyah* 32:19). You may gather in your grain. . . if you do not stray from the way of God. "One field shall be given rain, and another field that rain does not fall on shall dry up" (*Amos* 4:7).

15. וְאָכַלְתָּ וְשָׂבָעְתָּ — *You will eat and you will be satisfied.* This compound expression implies something more than what was already mentioned: you will eat to satisfaction not only of your grain, wine, and oil, but also foods such as meat and milk. Furthermore, strong, healthy animals will work your land well so that it will yield good crops.

We can also interpret this phrase to mean that you will have not only oil or wine with your bread, but meat or milk as well.

16. פֶּן־יִפְתֶּה לְבַבְכֶם — *Lest your heart be seduced.* Unwholesome notions originate in the heart, as *Chazal* said: "'Do not wander after your heart' — this means heresy" (*Berachos* 12). There is good reason for this to be so, for physically the heart is the center of the circulatory system, and emotionally it is the seat of base desires — as *Rashi* says, "it is the heart that covets" (*Bamidbar*

11
15-19

and the late rains, that you may gather in your grain, your
wine, and your oil. 15 *I shall provide grass in your field for*
your cattle and you will eat and you will be satisfied.
16 *Beware for yourselves, lest your heart be seduced and you*
turn astray and serve gods of others and prostrate yourselves
to them. 17 *Then the wrath of* HASHEM *will blaze against you;*
He will restrain the heaven so there will be no rain, and the
ground will not yield its produce; and you will be swiftly
banished from the goodly Land that HASHEM *gives you.*
18 *You shall place these words of Mine upon your heart and*
upon your soul; you shall bind them for a sign upon your arm
and let them be an ornament between your eyes. 19 *You shall*
teach them to your children to discuss them, while you sit

15:39). Blinded by desire, the heart says "there is no law and no judge," or else it is led into idolatry, worshiping imaginary gods who are themselves ruled by their passions, while their worshipers imitate their ways with no thought or fear of the true God.

17. אֲשֶׁר ה׳ נֹתֵן לָכֶם — *That Hashem gives you.* Everything is valued based on its quality and price. But there are some things that are valued more according to who gave them. There is a story of a God-fearing Jew who was one of the ministers to a great king. One *Shabbos*, at an assembly of all the important government officials, the king offered him a cigar. In deference to the king's honor, the Jew accepted the cigar, but when the king offered him a match, the Jew said to him, "When one receives a cigar from the king, should he burn it? I would rather keep it as a souvenir." This is the meaning here: you should feel honored that God Himself has given you this Land.

18. וְשַׂמְתֶּם אֶת־דְּבָרַי אֵלֶּה עַל־לְבַבְכֶם — *You shall place these words of Mine upon your heart.* It has often been asked why this verse says, "upon your heart," rather than "in your heart," as in "in your mouth and in your heart" (30:14).

This may be answered by looking at *Chazal's* interpretation of another word here: וְשַׂמְתֶּם, "you shall place." By reading this word as its homonym, סַם תָּם, "a perfect medicine," *Chazal* derived that "The Torah is compared to an elixir of life. Imagine a man who has struck his son harshly and injured him. He then places a dressing on the wound. So said God to the Children of Israel: 'My children, I have created the Evil Inclination'" — a harsh blow — "'and I have created the Torah as a remedy'" (*Kiddushin* 30b). The Torah is like a healing dressing for the wound of the Evil Inclination, and this is what the Torah is hinting to us here: "Place these words of Mine upon your heart" — put the dressing on the wound, and it will not overcome you. In a similar vein the Torah says, "upon your soul" — your mental processes, too, require the "remedy" of the Torah.

יא בְּבֵיתֶ֗ךָ וּבְלֶכְתְּךָ֣ בַדֶּ֔רֶךְ וּֽבְשָׁכְבְּךָ֖ וּבְקוּמֶֽךָ׃ כ וּכְתַבְתָּ֛ם עַל־
כ־כד מְזוּז֥וֹת בֵּיתֶ֖ךָ וּבִשְׁעָרֶֽיךָ׃ כא לְמַ֨עַן יִרְבּ֤וּ יְמֵיכֶם֙ וִימֵ֣י בְנֵיכֶ֔ם
עַ֚ל הָֽאֲדָמָ֔ה אֲשֶׁ֨ר נִשְׁבַּ֧ע יְהוָ֛ה לַאֲבֹתֵיכֶ֖ם לָתֵ֣ת לָהֶ֑ם כִּימֵ֥י
הַשָּׁמַ֖יִם עַל־הָאָֽרֶץ׃ שביעי ומפטיר כב כִּי֩
אִם־שָׁמֹ֨ר תִּשְׁמְר֜וּן אֶת־כָּל־הַמִּצְוָ֣ה הַזֹּ֗את אֲשֶׁ֧ר אָנֹכִ֛י
מְצַוֶּ֥ה אֶתְכֶ֖ם לַעֲשֹׂתָ֑הּ לְאַהֲבָ֞ה אֶת־יְהוָ֧ה אֱלֹהֵיכֶ֛ם לָלֶ֥כֶת
בְּכָל־דְּרָכָ֖יו וּלְדָבְקָה־בֽוֹ׃ כג וְהוֹרִ֧ישׁ יְהוָ֛ה אֶת־כָּל־הַגּוֹיִ֥ם
הָאֵ֖לֶּה מִלִּפְנֵיכֶ֑ם וִירִשְׁתֶּ֣ם גּוֹיִ֔ם גְּדֹלִ֥ים וַעֲצֻמִ֖ים מִכֶּֽם׃
כד כָּל־הַמָּק֗וֹם אֲשֶׁ֨ר תִּדְרֹ֧ךְ כַּף־רַגְלְכֶ֛ם בּ֖וֹ לָכֶ֣ם יִהְיֶ֑ה

---

21. לְמַעַן יִרְבּוּ יְמֵיכֶם — *In order to prolong your days.* If the meaning here were that the Children of Israel will dwell in their Land "like the days of the heaven over the earth" (meaning forever), it would have been enough to say, "In order that you should dwell upon the Land that Hashem has sworn. . . like the days of the heaven over the earth." From the fact that it says instead "in order to prolong your days and the days of your children," we can learn that the meaning is different: "if you will observe this entire commandment. . . to love Hashem, your God,. . . and to cleave to Him" (v. 22), then both you and your posterity will enjoy long life.

Since, as we explained above, these verses are talking about the Messianic Era, let us look once again at the words of a prophet: "For a youth will die a hundred years old. . ." (*Yeshayah* 65:20). In other words, during the Messiah's time if someone dies at the age of one hundred, people will say, "A youth has died." The *Ibn Ezra* comments that in the end the world will return to its original state; that is, people will live for many years as the ancients did, from Adam to Noah.

Now we may examine the phrase "like the days of the heaven over the earth" from a new perspective. The *Talmud Yerushalmi* tells us that the distance between the earth and the sky is a five hundred years' walk, and five hundred years is the sum of the three Patriarchs' life-spans. (Abraham lived 175 years, Isaac 180, and Jacob 147. That adds up to 502 years. When we subtract the first two years of Abraham's life, since he did not recognize the Creator until his third year, we are left with five hundred years (*Yerushalmi Berachos* 1:5). This explains why the verse mentions "the Land that Hashem has sworn to your forefathers," who served Him and made His Name known for five hundred years — "like the days of the heaven over the earth."

כִּימֵי הַשָּׁמַיִם עַל־הָאָרֶץ — *Like the days of the heaven over the earth.* "That is, forever. For if the Children of Israel are exiled, they are destined to return to the Land" (*R' Bachya*).

The Land was given to our forefathers on the condition that we keep God's commandments, and because of our many sins we were exiled from our Land twice. Nevertheless, God promised Abraham, our father, "For all the land that

11
20-24

in your home, while you walk on the way, when you retire
and when you arise. 20 *And you shall write them on the*
doorposts of your house and upon your gates. 21 *In order to*
prolong your days and the days of your children upon the
Land that HASHEM has sworn to your forefathers to give
them, like the days of the heaven over the earth.
22 *For if you will observe this entire commandment that I*
command you, to perform it, to love HASHEM, your God, to
walk in all His ways and to cleave to Him, 23 *HASHEM will*
drive out all these nations from before you, and you will drive
out greater and mightier nations than yourselves. 24 *Every*
place where the sole of your foot will tread shall be yours —

---

you see — to you will I give it, and to your descendants forever" (*Bereishis* 13:15), and God's promise must inevitably come to fruition. This will happen in the Messianic Era, as Amos prophesied: "On that day I shall raise the fallen *succah* of David. . . and I shall plant them on their land and they will no more leave their land that I have given them" (*Amos* 9:11,15). We will never again have to be exiled because of our sins, as Ezekiel prophesied (36:27-28): "And I shall place My spirit among you and I shall bring about that you will go by My decrees, and safeguard and perform My ordinances, and you will dwell in the Land which I gave to your forefathers, and you will be a people to Me, and I shall be a God to you."

22. כִּי אִם־שָׁמֹר תִּשְׁמְרוּן אֶת־כָּל־הַמִּצְוָה הַזֹּאת — *For if you will observe this entire commandment.* When will your days be prolonged "like the days of the heaven over the earth"? When "you will observe this entire commandment."

23. וְהוֹרִישׁ ה' אֶת־כָּל־הַגּוֹיִם הָאֵלֶּה — *Hashem will drive out all these nations.*

Since the Torah says above, "In order to prolong your days and the days of your children," you might think that *Eretz Yisrael* will not be able to contain its population. Therefore this verse comes to promise you that "if you will observe this entire commandment," then the plan mentioned in Chapter 7:22 detailing that "Hashem, your God, will thrust these nations from before you little by little. . . lest the beasts of the field increase against you," will be canceled, and instead "Hashem will drive out all these nations from before you" all at once. For "when the people of Israel do the will of the Omnipresent, they need not be fearful of wild beasts" (*Rashi* on v. 7:22).

24. כָּל־הַמָּקוֹם אֲשֶׁר תִּדְרֹךְ כַּף־רַגְלְכֶם בּוֹ לָכֶם יִהְיֶה — *Every place where the sole of your foot will tread shall be yours.* If it is not enough for you that "I will drive out all these nations [all seven of the Canaanite nations] before you" all at once, then listen to this: "Every place where the sole of your foot will tread shall be yours." "The sole of your foot" is said in the singular, to indicate that if you even tread with one foot upon a place, your enemies will flee and their land will become yours. The expression מִלִּפְנֵיכֶם ("from before you") in the previous

מִן־הַמִּדְבָּ֜ר וְהַלְּבָנ֗וֹן מִן־הַנָּהָ֣ר נְהַר־פְּרָ֗ת וְעַד֙ הַיָּ֣ם הָאַחֲר֔וֹן יא
יִהְיֶ֖ה גְּבֻלְכֶֽם׃ כה לֹא־יִתְיַצֵּ֥ב אִ֖ישׁ בִּפְנֵיכֶ֑ם פַּחְדְּכֶ֨ם כה
וּמוֹרַאֲכֶ֜ם יִתֵּ֣ן ׀ יהוִ֣ה אֱלֹהֵיכֶ֗ם עַל־פְּנֵ֤י כָל־הָאָ֙רֶץ֙ אֲשֶׁ֣ר
תִּדְרְכוּ־בָ֔הּ כַּאֲשֶׁ֖ר דִּבֶּ֥ר לָכֶֽם׃

---

verse, used in preference to בִּפְנֵיכֶם, supports this line of thought; the implication is that they will flee before you even come near or attack them.

מִן־הַמִּדְבָּר — *From the Wilderness.* This is the desert to the south of *Eretz Yisrael*; "the Lebanon" is the northern border. "From the river, the Euphrates River" — according to the maps available today this would be the extreme eastern border of *Eretz Yisrael*; "until the Western [i.e., Mediterranean] Sea" — thus shall be your boundary. This means that the lands of the Kenite, the

11 *from the Wilderness and the Lebanon, from the river, the*
25 *Euphrates River, until the western sea shall be your*
boundary. [25] *No man will stand up against you; Hashem,*
your God, will set your terror and fear on the entire face of
the earth where you will tread, as He spoke to you.

Kenizite, and the Kadmonite (Edom, Ammon, and Moab) are included in our inheritance; this part of it will come to us in the Messianic Era, when God will give us all the lands He promised to Abraham. Actually, our inheritance is not so far off, though the Messiah's coming has been delayed by our many sins. If we were to "observe this entire commandment. . . to love Hashem, your God, to walk in all His ways and to cleave to Him," he would come promptly, '[even] today — if you heed Him!" (*Tehillim* 95:7).

פרשת ראה
Parashas Re'eh

יא
כו־ל

כו רְאֵה אָנֹכִי נֹתֵן לִפְנֵיכֶם הַיּוֹם בְּרָכָה וּקְלָלָה: כז אֶת־
הַבְּרָכָה אֲשֶׁר תִּשְׁמְעוּ אֶל־מִצְוֹת יהוה אֱלֹהֵיכֶם אֲשֶׁר
אָנֹכִי מְצַוֶּה אֶתְכֶם הַיּוֹם: כח וְהַקְּלָלָה אִם־לֹא תִשְׁמְעוּ
אֶל־מִצְוֹת יהוה אֱלֹהֵיכֶם וְסַרְתֶּם מִן־הַדֶּרֶךְ אֲשֶׁר אָנֹכִי
מְצַוֶּה אֶתְכֶם הַיּוֹם לָלֶכֶת אַחֲרֵי אֱלֹהִים אֲחֵרִים אֲשֶׁר
לֹא־יְדַעְתֶּם: כט וְהָיָה כִּי יְבִיאֲךָ יהוה
אֱלֹהֶיךָ אֶל־הָאָרֶץ אֲשֶׁר־אַתָּה בָא־שָׁמָּה לְרִשְׁתָּהּ וְנָתַתָּה
אֶת־הַבְּרָכָה עַל־הַר גְּרִזִּים וְאֶת־הַקְּלָלָה עַל־הַר עֵיבָל:
ל הֲלֹא־הֵמָּה בְּעֵבֶר הַיַּרְדֵּן אַחֲרֵי דֶּרֶךְ מְבוֹא הַשֶּׁמֶשׁ
בְּאֶרֶץ הַכְּנַעֲנִי הַיֹּשֵׁב בָּעֲרָבָה מוּל הַגִּלְגָּל אֵצֶל אֵלוֹנֵי מֹרֶה:

---

26. רְאֵה — *See.* The word רְאֵה is the singular imperative, whereas לִפְנֵיכֶם, "before you" is in the plural. How can we explain this?

Chazal taught us that a person should always view himself as having done an equal number of good deeds and bad ones in his life until now, while the rest of the world is equally divided between righteous and wicked people. Whenever he does a *mitzvah*, then, he tips the balance for himself and for the whole world to the side of merit. If he sins, he brings about the opposite, for the world is judged by the majority of mankind's deeds (*Kiddushin* 40b; see *Rashi* ad loc). We may conclude from this that each and every Jew can act to bring the blessing or the curse on all of Israel.

Therefore רְאֵה, "See," is in the singular, addressed to each individual, whereas "I present before you" is in the plural, for the blessing and the curse are meant for the whole nation of Israel. Not only your own fate, but the fate of the Jewish people, is in the hands of each one of you.

We might further understand from this phrasing that each individual Jew should concern himself, not only with his own observance of the Torah, but with that of the entire Jewish people ("that you hearken" is in the plural). He should not say, "I have saved my own soul, never mind about the others," for every deed affects the balance.

⊲§ אָנֹכִי נֹתֵן לִפְנֵיכֶם — *I present before you.* The humblest of all men surely did not claim ownership of the blessing and the curse. Perhaps this use of the word אָנֹכִי is an allusion to the One who said, אָנֹכִי ה׳ אֱלֹהֶיךָ — "I am Hashem, your God, Who has taken you out of Egypt."

⊲§ בְּרָכָה וּקְלָלָה — *A blessing and a curse.* "Which were pronounced [later] on Mount Gerizim and Mount Ebal" (*Rashi*). These are the blessings and the curses which the Children of Israel were soon to accept upon themselves on the above-mentioned mountains: the blessings, if they heeded God's word, and the curses, if they did not. This was in addition to the blessings and curses pronounced by God in *Parashas Bechukosai*, and the blessings and curses pronounced by Moses in *Parashas Ki Savo*. All in all, then, the blessings and

11
26-30

26 *See, I present before you today a blessing and a curse.* 27 *The blessing: that you hearken to the commandments of* HASHEM, *your God, that I command you today.* 28 *And the curse: if you do not hearken to the commandments of* HASHEM, *your God, and you stray from the path that I command you today, to follow gods of others, that you did not know.*

29 *It shall be that when* HASHEM, *your God, brings you to the Land to which you come, to possess it, then you shall deliver the blessing on Mount Gerizim and the curse on Mount Ebal.* 30 *Are they not on the other side of the Jordan, far, in the direction of the sunset, in the land of the Canaanite, that dwells in the plain, far from Gilgal, near the plain of Moreh?*

---

curses were pronounced three times.

This is the reason why: There are some people who will listen only to the word of God Himself, spoken by one of His prophets. Then there are those whose fear of their teacher is greater than their fear of God, as the Sages said, "May it be His will that you feel the fear of Heaven as you feel the fear of flesh and blood" (*Berachos* 28b). For these people, the blessing of a *tzaddik* is worth more, and his curse is to be feared more intensely, than anything else. Finally, there are those for whom their own word, which they have accepted upon themselves with an oath, is more significant than what the Torah itself says. Therefore the blessings, if the Children of Israel heed God's word, and the curses if they do not, were pronounced in three different ways, by God, by Moses, and by the Children of Israel themselves, so as to address all three possibilities.

27. אֶת־הַבְּרָכָה אֲשֶׁר תִּשְׁמְעוּ — *The blessing: that you hearken.* The Holy One, Blessed be He, desires to give us the blessing; therefore He says decisively, "that you hearken." However, He does not wish the curse to come upon us, Heaven forbid; therefore He does not decide upon it, but merely says, "*if* you do not hearken."

29-30. וְאֶת־הַקְּלָלָה עַל־הַר עֵיבָל. . . אֵצֶל אֵלוֹנֵי מֹרֶה — *And the curse on Mount Ebal . . . near the plain of Moreh?* "That is, Shechem" (*Rashi*). This is the place where our father Abraham called upon God's name for the first time, when he came to the land of Canaan. In this place he called upon God to remove idols from the earth. There you will pronounce the curse upon those who follow other gods.

30. הֲלֹא־הֵמָּה . . . אֵצֶל אֵלוֹנֵי מֹרֶה — *Are they not. . . near the plain of Moreh?* This is the place where our father Abraham built the first altar upon his arrival in the land of Canaan at God's command, as the Torah says: "Abram passed into the land as far as the site of Shechem, until the Plain of Moreh."

יא לא כִּי אַתֶּם עֹבְרִים אֶת־הַיַּרְדֵּן לָבֹא לָרֶשֶׁת אֶת־
לא־לב הָאָרֶץ אֲשֶׁר־יהוה אֱלֹהֵיכֶם נֹתֵן לָכֶם וִירִשְׁתֶּם אֹתָהּ
וִישַׁבְתֶּם־בָּהּ: לב וּשְׁמַרְתֶּם לַעֲשׂוֹת אֵת כָּל־הַחֻקִּים
יב וְאֶת־הַמִּשְׁפָּטִים אֲשֶׁר אָנֹכִי נֹתֵן לִפְנֵיכֶם הַיּוֹם: א אֵלֶּה
א־ג הַחֻקִּים וְהַמִּשְׁפָּטִים אֲשֶׁר תִּשְׁמְרוּן לַעֲשׂוֹת בָּאָרֶץ
אֲשֶׁר נָתַן יהוה אֱלֹהֵי אֲבֹתֶיךָ לְךָ לְרִשְׁתָּהּ כָּל־
הַיָּמִים אֲשֶׁר־אַתֶּם חַיִּים עַל־הָאֲדָמָה: ב אַבֵּד תְּאַבְּדוּן
אֶת־כָּל־הַמְּקֹמוֹת אֲשֶׁר עָבְדוּ־שָׁם הַגּוֹיִם אֲשֶׁר אַתֶּם
יֹרְשִׁים אֹתָם אֶת־אֱלֹהֵיהֶם עַל־הֶהָרִים הָרָמִים וְעַל־
הַגְּבָעוֹת וְתַחַת כָּל־עֵץ רַעֲנָן: ג וְנִתַּצְתֶּם אֶת־מִזְבְּחֹתָם
וְשִׁבַּרְתֶּם אֶת־מַצֵּבֹתָם וַאֲשֵׁרֵיהֶם תִּשְׂרְפוּן בָּאֵשׁ וּפְסִילֵי
אֱלֹהֵיהֶם תְּגַדֵּעוּן וְאִבַּדְתֶּם אֶת־שְׁמָם מִן־הַמָּקוֹם הַהוּא:

There God promised him the inheritance of the land: "Hashem appeared to Abram and said, 'To your offspring I will give this land.' So he built an altar there to Hashem" (*Bereishis* 12:6-7).

This was why God commanded the Children of Israel to build an altar immediately upon crossing the Jordan: to thank Him for keeping this promise. They did indeed build an altar to God there, as we will see in *Parashas Ki Savo*, and they formally accepted the decrees of the Torah with the blessings and the curses — because it was only for the purpose of their keeping the *mitzvos* that God was giving them "the lands of peoples . . . and the toil of nations" (*Tehillim* 105:44).

31. כִּי אַתֶּם עֹבְרִים אֶת־הַיַּרְדֵּן — *For you are crossing the Jordan.* "The miracles at the Jordan will be a sign for you that you will come and possess the Land" (*Rashi*). The Children of Israel were in need of encouragement at that time, for they were about to cross the Jordan and go to war against nations larger and mightier than themselves, without their leader Moses, through whom God had performed so many miracles, for he was destined to die there on the east bank of the Jordan. No longer would they live on the miraculous level to which they had become accustomed, and the clouds of glory would depart, leaving them without guidance and protection.

Moses alludes to this situation in the previous verse, as the *Sifre* explains: דֶּרֶךְ — this is a hint that the Children of Israel should take *a road*, not the open country; הַיֹּשֵׁב — *a settled area*, not a wilderness; בָּעֲרָבָה — on the *plains*, not in the mountains. This directive would take the place of the pillar of cloud which had led their every step from the day they left Egypt until the death of Moses.

At this difficult juncture, Moses commanded the people to accept all the laws of the Torah upon themselves with an oath entailing blessings and curses, immediately upon crossing the Jordan. This, despite the fact that a *beis din* does

11 [31] *For you are crossing the Jordan to come and possess the*
31-32 *Land that* H*ASHEM*, *your God, gives you; you shall possess it*
and you shall settle in it. [32] *You shall be careful to perform all*
the decrees and the ordinances that I present before you
today.
12 [1] *These are the decrees and the ordinances that you shall*
1-3 *observe to perform in the Land that* H*ASHEM*, *the God of your*
forefathers, has given you, to possess it, all the days that you
live on the Land. [2] *You shall utterly destroy all the places*
where the nations that you are driving away worshiped their
gods: on the high mountains and on the hills, and under every
leafy tree. [3] *You shall break apart their altars; you shall*
smash their pillars; and their sacred trees shall you burn in
the fire; their carved images shall you cut down; and you
shall obliterate their names from that place.

---

not make a litigant swear to his statement during the Ten Days of Repentance ("so as not to arouse the powers of judgment during the Days of Judgment," (*Shulchan Aruch, Orach Chaim* §602), so that it would have been best to put off the blessings and curses until after the conquest of the land, a crucial period similar in nature to the Days of Judgment. (Rabbi Yishmael's opinion is, in fact, that the blessings and curses were pronounced only after fourteen years of conquest and division of the Land, but the other Sages disagree, citing the words וְהָיָה בְּעָבְרְכֶם [*Yerushalmi Sotah* 30b]).

In light of all this, Moses saw fit to encourage the Children of Israel with the news that God would perform miracles for them when they crossed the Jordan, although he himself would no longer be with them, and this would be a sign to them that God was still going before them and they would indeed inherit the Land.

12.

3. וְאִבַּדְתֶּם אֶת־שְׁמָם מִן־הַמָּקוֹם הַהוּא — *And you shall obliterate their names from that place.* "By making up derogatory names [for places of idolatry], for example... *Ein Kol* (the Eye of All) should be called *Ein Kotz* (Thorn in the Eye)" (*Rashi*).

But isn't this merely changing the name rather than obliterating the original one? We can explain by considering how people naturally tend to give pejorative names, especially mocking ones, to people or places. This is forbidden, however: "One who calls his friend a derogatory name is counted among those who descend to *Gehinnom* and do not ascend" (*Bava Metzia* 58b), and the spies were punished for spreading an evil report about the trees and stones (*Arachin* 15b). Knowing this, many people take care never to use defamatory names. But here we are talking about idolatry, and "all mockery is forbidden except mockery of idolatry, which is permitted" (*Megillah* 25b).

ד לֹא־תַעֲשׂוּן כֵּן לַיהוָה אֱלֹהֵיכֶם: ה כִּי אִם־אֶל־הַמָּקוֹם

Everyone, then, will gladly call the place where a house of idolatry once stood by its new, derisive name, and thus the old name will fade into oblivion — "you shall obliterate their names."

4. לֹא־תַעֲשׂוּן כֵּן לַה׳ אֱלֹהֵיכֶם — *You shall not do this to Hashem, your God.* The next verse, which reads, "Rather, only at the place that Hashem, your God, will choose," clarifies the basic point this verse is making: it is not fitting for us, who uphold the concept of God's Oneness, to formally worship Him in various places, wherever it may happen to strike our fancy, as the gentiles do with their gods — "rather, only at the place [one place, just as God is One] that Hashem, your God, will choose... to place His Name."

But this verse is adjacent to "you shall obliterate their names," and all the Sages have agreed that, in this *chumash* of Recapitulating the Torah, adjacent verses invite a combined interpretation. *Chazal*, therefore, take these verses as a prohibition against dislodging even a single stone from the Altar or the Sanctuary. Rabbi Yishmael's response to this is, "Is it conceivable that Israel would demolish its own altars? Rather, the verses are saying, 'Do not act as the gentiles do, lest your sins cause the Temple of your forefathers to be destroyed' " (*Rashi*, based on the *Sifre*).

Rabbi Yishmael's words need to be understood in depth. The Torah has already told us, "Beware for yourselves, lest your heart be seduced and you turn astray and serve other gods... and you will be swiftly banished from the goodly Land" (11:16-17); the Torah has also said, "you will grow corrupt and make a carved image ... I appoint heaven and earth to bear witness ... that you will surely perish quickly from the Land ... for you will be destroyed ... Hashem will scatter you among the peoples" (4:25-27). If there are people who have not yet been sufficiently warned by threats of exile from their land, ruin and destruction, what is the point of adding a subtle hint "you shall not do this to Hashem, your God?" What is the use of suggesting that they refrain from emulating the Canaanites, so as not to bring destruction to the Holy Temple? Will they fear for the Temple more than for their own lives ("with all your soul"), and for the loss of their homeland, the source of their livelihood ("with all your resources")?

There are two ways of explaining this seemingly superfluous warning. Firstly: A Jew, however much he may sin, is generally careful not to cut himself off altogether from his roots. Rather, the typical hardened sinner tells himself, "I haven't really done anything wrong. What does God care if I have my desires?" and other such blandishments of the Evil Inclination. But he wishes to repent before he dies, and certainly to die and be buried as a Jew (after living like a *goy*). So when he encounters something which would totally repudiate his connection with the Jewish People, he recoils from going that far. In our times, for example, we see that even people who have cast off the yoke of the Kingdom

[4] *You shall not do this to* HASHEM, *your God.* [5] *Rather, only*

of Heaven and the yoke of the Torah still bring their sons into the covenant of Abraham through circumcision; only one in a thousand would abrogate the *bris*, and why? Because they sense that this would cut them off completely from their people ... and from Him who sealed the covenant, however weak their belief in Him may be.

This element in the makeup of every Jew can be found throughout our history. Moses burned the Calf and dealt with its worshipers before the eyes of all of Israel, including the fence-straddlers among them who sympathized with the debauchery (for they uttered no protest when the Calf was made, and even took off their golden jewelry to make it). Now they all stood by and watched as Moses burned the Calf and punished its worshipers, and why? Because they had all seen him break the Tablets, which was tantamount in their eyes to a breaking off of their relationship with God and an abrogation of their covenant with Him. When they saw how far things had gone, they were taken aback, and allowed Moses to destroy what they had done.

Likewise, we find Ahab, who deliberately set out "to anger Hashem, the God of Israel, more than all the kings of Israel that were before him" (*I Melachim* 16:33). Ahab's smallest sins were like Jeroboam's worst ones; there was not a single furrow in all of *Eretz Yisrael* where he did not erect an idol and prostrate himself to it (*Sanhedrin* 102b). And when Ben-Hadad King of Aram sent him a message saying, "Your silver and gold are mine; and your wives and the best of your children are mine," Ahab answered, "Just as you say, my lord King, I and all that I have are yours." For who can argue with one stronger than himself? But when Ben-Hadad went on to demand "your most precious thing," which, *Chazal* tell us, meant a *Sefer Torah* (ibid.), then Ahab answered, "Everything that you said in your first message I will do, but this thing I cannot do" (*I Melachim* 20:2-9). A war broke out then and there, because Ahab would not hand over his Torah scroll to Ben-Hadad!

Why did Ahab, who sinned and who caused his people to sin, refuse this demand? Because he realized that by giving in he would totally breach the covenant between Israel and the Giver of the Torah. When his very core was touched, he showed more love and devotion for God's Torah than for gold and silver ("with all your resources"), or for wives and children ("with all your heart"); furthermore, he endangered himself by going to war with a mighty conqueror ("with all your soul").

Here in our verse it is the same idea. God gives the Children of Israel a warning aimed at their innermost feelings. Although they have already been threatened with losing the Land, now, while they are engaged in demolishing the altars of idol worshipers, they are threatened with the destruction of their Holy Temple. Let them take it to heart as they knock down each idolatrous stone, that if they sin the tables will be turned and their enemies will demolish

אֲשֶׁר־יִבְחַ֣ר יְהֹוָ֣ה אֱלֹֽהֵיכֶם֮ מִכָּל־שִׁבְטֵיכֶם֒ לָשׂ֥וּם אֶת־
שְׁמ֖וֹ שָׁ֑ם לְשִׁכְנ֥וֹ תִדְרְשׁ֖וּ וּבָ֥אתָ שָֽׁמָּה: ו וַהֲבֵאתֶ֣ם שָׁ֗מָּה
עֹלֹֽתֵיכֶם֙ וְזִבְחֵיכֶ֔ם וְאֵת֙ מַעְשְׂרֹֽתֵיכֶ֔ם וְאֵ֖ת תְּרוּמַ֣ת יֶדְכֶ֑ם
וְנִדְרֵיכֶם֙ וְנִדְבֹ֣תֵיכֶ֔ם וּבְכֹרֹ֖ת בְּקַרְכֶ֥ם וְצֹאנְכֶֽם: ז וַאֲכַלְתֶּם־
שָׁ֗ם לִפְנֵי֙ יְהֹוָ֣ה אֱלֹֽהֵיכֶ֔ם וּשְׂמַחְתֶּם֙ בְּכֹל֙ מִשְׁלַ֣ח יֶדְכֶ֔ם אַתֶּ֖ם

יב
ו־ז

---

the Temple of God, Who chose Israel and gave them His Torah. If nothing else
works, perhaps this will prevent them straying from His path.

A second explanation: We learn from the prophecies of Jeremiah (*Yirmiyah*,
ch. 7) that during the period before the destruction of the Holy Temple there
were sinners who relied on the Temple rites to protect them from the
consequences of their actions, for they thought that God would not destroy His
sanctuary because of our sins and the Land would never be brought to ruin. The
prophet said to them: "Behold, you are putting your trust in lies. . . the thief has
murdered and committed adultery and sworn falsely and brought incense
before an idol. . . and you come and stand before this House and say, 'We are
saved' "?

The Torah itself rebutted this way of thinking when it said, "You shall break
apart their altars . . . You shall not do this to Hashem, your God" — that is, "Do
not let your sins cause the Temple of your forefathers to be destroyed," for if you
act abhorrently God's Sanctuary will not save you. On the contrary, your sins
will cause its destruction. "But if you truly improve your ways. . . I shall dwell
with you in this place . . . forever" (ibid.).

5. כִּי אִם־אֶל־הַמָּקוֹם — *Rather, only at the place.* That is, *one* place for all Israel
to bring sacrifices to God, not many places. "That Hashem, your God, will
choose" — not as a human being would choose, looking with his eyes alone and
choosing the most scenic view in the Land, a place whose beauty will attract
many pilgrims. For then they might come with ulterior motives. As the *Gemara*
tells us (*Pesachim* 8b), the fruits of Ginosar (famed for their sweetness) and the
hot springs of Tiberias are not found in Jerusalem, simply so that pilgrims
should not come just for their sake. God will look to the heart of the Land, which
faces the heavenly Temple. He alone knows how to choose the most sacred spot
to place His Name there.

וּבָאתָ שָׁמָּה — *And come there.* First this verse says "you shall seek out His
Presence" [לְשִׁכְנוֹ תִדְרְשׁוּ] in the plural, and then it says "and come there"
[וּבָאתָ] in the singular. What is the significance of this?

Since the pilgrims go up to Jerusalem to see and to be seen (*Chagigah* 4b), that
is, to appear before the Lord God, they need elaborate spiritual preparation, so
as not to be among those of whom the prophet says, "When you come to see My
Face — who asked this of you, to trample My courtyard?" (*Yeshayah* 1:12). A
person should never say, "All Israel comes to the pilgrim festivals. They are all
beloved, all holy, and all prepared to appear before God. I'll just squeeze in

at the place that HASHEM, *your God, will choose from among*
all your tribes to place His Name shall you seek out His
Presence and come there. 6 *And there shall you bring your*
elevation-offerings and feast-offerings, your tithes and
what you raise up with your hands, your vow offerings
and your free-will offerings, and the firstborn of your cattle
and your flocks. 7 *You shall eat there before* HASHEM, *your*
God, and you shall rejoice with your every undertaking, you

---

among them and no one will notice me." Anticipating this way of thinking, the Torah says, Even though the whole nation is "seeking out His Presence," nonetheless every individual must prepare himself "and come there" as if he were coming alone.

☙ Another reason can be offered for this sudden shift to the singular, when the entire *parashah* has been addressed in the plural. It could well be meant as an allusion to one of the aims of the Holy Temple, i.e., to consolidate all Israel, who are scattered and separated all year, into a single unit, united by the pilgrimage festival, with everyone sacrificing to one God and eating and rejoicing before Him. (For other references to the Temple as a symbol of Israel's unity, see *Bereishis* 46:1, and *Shemos* 26:28.)

6. מַעְשְׂרֹתֵיכֶם — *Your tithes.* This refers to "The animal tithe and the 'second tithe' (מַעֲשֵׂר שֵׁנִי), which are to be eaten within the [city] wall" (*Rashi*). In *Ein Yaakov* (on *Zevachim* 118), a question comes up on this comment of *Rashi's*, since, according to *Rashi's* own interpretation, "you shall seek out His Presence" refers to Shiloh (see *Rashi* on v. 5), and everyone agrees that in Shiloh the people ate the minor sacrifices anywhere within sight of Shiloh. But it would have been better to point out another discrepancy: we find no mention of there having been a wall around Shiloh. The difficulty can be straightened out by explaining it this way: "The place that Hashem, your God, will choose" is Jerusalem, and "you shall seek out His Presence" refers to Shiloh. The 'city wall' *Rashi* speaks of is the wall of Jerusalem; there is no argument over where the minor sacrifices were consumed at Shiloh.

7. וּשְׂמַחְתֶּם בְּכֹל מִשְׁלַח יֶדְכֶם — *And you shall rejoice with your every undertaking.* This could be read not as a promise, but as a commandment. That is, when a person sits at home, he is usually more or less content with his lot. But when he goes out among friends and sees that they have become rich through practicing a certain occupation, then it will probably occur to him that he, too, should try his hand at this lucrative work. A pilgrimage to Jerusalem, then, could cause him to think poorly of his own occupation. The Torah, therefore, admonishes those who make the thrice-yearly pilgrimage and who may meet friends there who are wealthier than they, not to envy them. Let them rather rejoice in practicing their own trade faithfully, for neither poverty nor riches comes from a craft; everything comes from God's Providence. If one

יב וּבָתֵּיכֶם אֲשֶׁר בֵּרַכְךָ יהוה אֱלֹהֶיךָ: ח לֹא תַעֲשׂוּן כְּכֹל
ח-יב אֲשֶׁר אֲנַחְנוּ עֹשִׂים פֹּה הַיּוֹם אִישׁ כָּל־הַיָּשָׁר בְּעֵינָיו: ט כִּי
לֹא־בָאתֶם עַד־עָתָּה אֶל־הַמְּנוּחָה וְאֶל־הַנַּחֲלָה אֲשֶׁר־
יהוה אֱלֹהֶיךָ נֹתֵן לָךְ: י וַעֲבַרְתֶּם אֶת־הַיַּרְדֵּן וִישַׁבְתֶּם
בָּאָרֶץ אֲשֶׁר־יהוה אֱלֹהֵיכֶם מַנְחִיל אֶתְכֶם וְהֵנִיחַ לָכֶם
מִכָּל־אֹיְבֵיכֶם מִסָּבִיב וִישַׁבְתֶּם־בֶּטַח: שני יא וְהָיָה הַמָּקוֹם
אֲשֶׁר־יִבְחַר יהוה אֱלֹהֵיכֶם בּוֹ לְשַׁכֵּן שְׁמוֹ שָׁם שָׁמָּה
תָבִיאוּ אֵת כָּל־אֲשֶׁר אָנֹכִי מְצַוֶּה אֶתְכֶם עוֹלֹתֵיכֶם
וְזִבְחֵיכֶם מַעְשְׂרֹתֵיכֶם וּתְרֻמַת יֶדְכֶם וְכֹל מִבְחַר נִדְרֵיכֶם
אֲשֶׁר תִּדְּרוּ לַיהוה: יב וּשְׂמַחְתֶּם לִפְנֵי יהוה אֱלֹהֵיכֶם

---

wants to get rich, he does not need to change his occupation; he needs to pray to the One to Whom all riches belong.

8. אִישׁ כָּל־הַיָּשָׁר בְּעֵינָיו — *Every man what is proper in his eyes.* Look at the difference between recent generations and the generation of Moses:

In more recent times when we talk about "You shall not do. . . every man what is proper in his eyes," we mean things like theft, robbery, adultery, murder, or even idolatry, whereas in the generation of Moses, it meant that one must not bring a sacrifice to God on a בָּמָה, a private family altar. Private altars were permissible at that time, of course, but here the Torah is referring to someone who brings to a private altar one of those sacrifices which should be offered only at the national altar at Shiloh.

Times change, and we change with them.

9. אֶל־הַמְּנוּחָה — *To the resting place.* This is Shiloh, and "the heritage" is Jerusalem (*Rashi*, from *Zevachim* 119a). As *Chazal* explain, the Tabernacle in Shiloh had a stone building at its base (as it is said: "She brought him to the house of God" [*I Shmuel* 1:24]) with the Tabernacle draperies laid over the top (as it is said: "He abandoned the Tabernacle of Shiloh, the tent where He dwelled among men" [*Tehillim* 78:60]). This house-tent hybrid was meant to tell us that the Children of Israel had come to a resting place for the Tabernacle. It was no longer a tent that must wander on one journey after another; but on the other hand, since the Temple was yet to be built at the place God would choose, a location not yet known to the Children of Israel, they covered the top half of the building with the Tabernacle draperies, signifying a temporary status, for only the Temple would have the status of an eternal heritage.

It still remains to be understood, however, why the Children of Israel declined to use the costly gold-plated planks and silver sockets from the Tabernacle. Why did they hide them away and build walls of stone in their place, whereas they retained the curtains of the original Tabernacle, which were far less valuable than the planks and sockets? Why did they not do the opposite? One answer is that the curtains, which were made by the women of hand-spun goat hair, were very

12
8-12

and your households, as HASHEM, your God, has blessed you.
8 You shall not do everything that we do here today —
[rather,] every man what is proper in his eyes — 9 for you will
not yet have come to the resting place or to the heritage that
HASHEM, your God, gives you.
10 You shall cross the Jordan and settle in the Land that
HASHEM, your God, causes you to inherit, and He will give
you rest from all your enemies all around, and you will dwell
securely.
11 It shall be that the place where HASHEM, your God, will
choose to rest His Name — there shall you bring everything
that I command you: your elevation-offerings and your
feast-offerings, your tithes and what you raise up with your
hands, and the choicest of your vow offerings that you will
vow to HASHEM. 12 You shall rejoice before HASHEM, your God

---

precious in God's eyes, because the women were not ambivalent in their worship. They did not give their jewelry for the Calf, but for the Tabernacle they gave generously (they even gave up the copper mirrors before which they adorned themselves). "Every wise-hearted woman spun with her hands; and they brought the spun yarn of turquoise, purple, and scarlet wool. . . All the women whose hearts inspired them with wisdom spun the goat hair" (*Shemos* 35:25-26). The men, on the other hand, although they too gave generously for the Tabernacle, gave just as generously for the Calf when asked to do so. Therefore the curtains of the righteous women of that generation were retained at the Tabernacle of Shiloh, for they had been made with intentions very pleasing to God.

10. **וַעֲבַרְתֶּם אֶת־הַיַּרְדֵּן** — *You shall cross the Jordan.* This is the first step towards establishing a place for the Altar, i.e., the seven years of conquest and the following seven years of dividing up the Land, during which the Tabernacle was pitched at Gilgal. During this time בָּמוֹת, private altars for family sacrifices, were permitted, since as the Children of Israel were scattered all through the Land and could not as yet bring their sacrifices to Gilgal. The next step was "and settle in the Land": after conquest and settlement the Children of Israel erected the Tent of Meeting (only the curtains; below them was a stone building) at Shiloh. At this point the private altars were prohibited, but only for as long as the Tabernacle of Shiloh stood; when it was reduced to desolation (*Shmuel I*, ch. 4-5), private altars were permitted again. And last came the step of "giving you rest from all your enemies all around," which brought in its wake the obligation to build the Holy Temple "in the place that God chooses," i.e., Jerusalem; and this time its holiness would be eternal.

11. **וְכֹל מִבְחַר נִדְרֵיכֶם** — *And the choicest of your vow-offerings.* In v. 6 above, which refers to the Tabernacle of Shiloh, the Torah mentions "your vow-offerings" without calling them "choicest." What is the reason for the difference?

יב אַתֶּם וּבְנֵיכֶם וּבְנֹתֵיכֶם וְעַבְדֵיכֶם וְאַמְהֹתֵיכֶם וְהַלֵּוִי
יג־יז אֲשֶׁר בְּשַׁעֲרֵיכֶם כִּי אֵין לוֹ חֵלֶק וְנַחֲלָה אִתְּכֶם: יג הִשָּׁמֶר
לְךָ פֶּן־תַּעֲלֶה עֹלֹתֶיךָ בְּכָל־מָקוֹם אֲשֶׁר תִּרְאֶה: יד כִּי
אִם־בַּמָּקוֹם אֲשֶׁר־יִבְחַר יהוה בְּאַחַד שְׁבָטֶיךָ שָׁם תַּעֲלֶה
עֹלֹתֶיךָ וְשָׁם תַּעֲשֶׂה כֹּל אֲשֶׁר אָנֹכִי מְצַוֶּךָּ: טו רַק
בְּכָל־אַוַּת נַפְשְׁךָ תִּזְבַּח ׀ וְאָכַלְתָּ בָשָׂר כְּבִרְכַּת יהוה
אֱלֹהֶיךָ אֲשֶׁר נָתַן־לְךָ בְּכָל־שְׁעָרֶיךָ הַטָּמֵא וְהַטָּהוֹר
יֹאכְלֶנּוּ כַּצְּבִי וְכָאַיָּל: טז רַק הַדָּם לֹא תֹאכֵלוּ עַל־הָאָרֶץ
תִּשְׁפְּכֶנּוּ כַּמָּיִם: יז לֹא־תוּכַל לֶאֱכֹל בִּשְׁעָרֶיךָ מַעְשַׂר דְּגָנְךָ

The key is that the reference in our verse is to "the place that God will choose to rest His name." From the entire Holy Land, God chose the holiest place of all: Mt. Moriah, which stands vis-a-vis the Heavenly Temple, to draw near to us there. We can explain our verse, then, according to the rule that our task is to emulate God's ways: just as He chose the best of places for His "chosen House" to be near to us, we in turn should choose the best and finest of our animals for sacrifice, and thereby draw near to Him.

Actually, nowhere does the Torah state that the obligation to bring a fine animal for sacrifice is greater at the Holy Temple than it was at the Tabernacle of Shiloh. However, we do find Malachi (during the Temple period) complaining of the villain "who has in his flock a [fine] male, and for his vow brings a maimed [beast] to God" (*Malachi* 1:14). On the other hand, during the period before "the rest and the heritage" of the Temple, the Children of Israel were impoverished, as the Torah tells us: "Whenever Israel sowed [grain], Midian and Amalek and the Easterners would rise up upon it. . . and would destroy the land's yield. . . and leave no sustenance among Israel, nor sheep nor cattle nor donkey. . . Israel became greatly impoverished" (*Shoftim* 6:3-4). In that case they could not bring choice animals for their sacrifices; but it was different when the Children of Israel arrived at their "rest and heritage" and built the Chosen House. Then only the best animals could be placed upon the Altar.

15. רַק בְּכָל־אַוַּת נַפְשְׁךָ תִּזְבַּח וְאָכַלְתָּ בָשָׂר — *However, to your heart's desire you may slaughter and eat meat.* The simple meaning is that from this time on unconsecrated animals might be slaughtered to provide meat, and not only those consecrated and brought for sacrifice (in the desert only sacrifice was permitted and only the meat of sacrifices was eaten).

Chazal derive from here a further *halachah:* that if a sacrificial animal has developed a physical defect, so that it cannot be offered, it may be redeemed for its value in money and then slaughtered and eaten. But even after redemption no benefit may be derived from this animal until it is slaughtered: its wool may not be clipped, its milk may not be drunk, and so on. (See *Rashi*.)

This *halachah* seems to be implicit in the wording of our verse: "to your heart's desire you may slaughter and eat meat." The desire of man's heart is to eat

12
13-17

— you, your sons and your daughters, your slaves and your
maidservants, and the Levite who is in your cities, for he
has no share and inheritance with you. 13 *Beware for your-*
self lest you bring up your elevation-offerings in any place
that you see. 14 *Rather, only in the place that* HASHEM *will*
choose, among one of your tribes, there shall you bring up
your elevation-offerings, and there shall you do all that I
command you.

15 *However, to your heart's desire you may slaughter and*
eat meat, according to the blessing that HASHEM, *your God,*
will have given you in all your cities; the contaminated one
and the pure one may eat it, like the deer and the hart. 16 *But*
you shall not eat the blood; you shall pour it onto the earth,
like water.

17 *In your cities, you may not eat: the tithe of your grain,*

---

meat, not to slaughter animals, so that it would have made more sense to put the "heart's desire" right next to "eating meat," which is indeed the wording in v. 20. But in our verse the word "slaughtering" interrupts between the two (and there is even a *piska* diacritical mark after the word תִּזְבַּח to make a further interruption). Evidently, the change in wording makes it clear that when "your heart's desire" is to derive benefit from a defective sacrificial animal that you have redeemed, you must first "slaughter" it, and only then "eat its meat"; you cannot clip its wool or drink its milk while it is yet alive.

16. **עַל־הָאָרֶץ תִּשְׁפְּכֶנּוּ כַּמָּיִם** — *You shall pour it onto the earth, like water.* "To tell you that it does not need to be covered with dirt. Another interpretation: it is like water in that seeds touched by it become capable of impurity" (*Rashi*; see *Sifsei Chachamim*).

This rule, however, applies to all slaughtered domestic animals, not only to defective sacrificial animals (the subject of these verses, see above). What is more, these two *halachos* could just as well be derived from v. 24, where the subject is clearly unconsecrated meat. Evidently we should look for some other meaning here.

It would seem that this verse comes to tell us that the blood of a defective sacrificial animal, once it is redeemed and slaughtered, is permitted for use by man. Thus it says to "pour it onto the earth like water," free for dogs to lick and for the earth to be fertilized by it. We might have thought since when such an animal dies it must be buried, and even when redeemed it is not redeemed for use as dog food, we would have to bury the blood when it is slaughtered, so that no one will benefit from it. By telling us to pour out the blood "onto the earth like water," the Torah is telling us that once we redeem this animal for its meat, even the parts of it that are forbidden to eat (such as blood and *chelev* fat) become permitted for use and benefit, and do not have to be buried.

יב וְתִירֹשְׁךָ וְיִצְהָרֶךָ וּבְכֹרֹת בְּקָרְךָ וְצֹאנֶךָ וְכָל־נְדָרֶיךָ אֲשֶׁר
יח־כ תִּדֹּר וְנִדְבֹתֶיךָ וּתְרוּמַת יָדֶךָ׃ יח כִּי אִם־לִפְנֵי יהוה אֱלֹהֶיךָ
תֹּאכְלֶנּוּ בַּמָּקוֹם אֲשֶׁר יִבְחַר יהוה אֱלֹהֶיךָ בּוֹ אַתָּה וּבִנְךָ
וּבִתֶּךָ וְעַבְדְּךָ וַאֲמָתֶךָ וְהַלֵּוִי אֲשֶׁר בִּשְׁעָרֶיךָ וְשָׂמַחְתָּ לִפְנֵי
יהוה אֱלֹהֶיךָ בְּכֹל מִשְׁלַח יָדֶךָ׃ יט הִשָּׁמֶר לְךָ פֶּן־תַּעֲזֹב
אֶת־הַלֵּוִי כָּל־יָמֶיךָ עַל־אַדְמָתֶךָ׃ כ כִּי־
יַרְחִיב יהוה אֱלֹהֶיךָ אֶת־גְּבֻלְךָ כַּאֲשֶׁר דִּבֶּר־לָךְ וְאָמַרְתָּ
אֹכְלָה בָשָׂר כִּי־תְאַוֶּה נַפְשְׁךָ לֶאֱכֹל בָּשָׂר בְּכָל־אַוַּת נַפְשְׁךָ

---

18. אַתָּה וּבִנְךָ וּבִתֶּךָ — *You, your son, your daughter.* We have spoken several times of how doing a *mitzvah* leads one to the fear of Heaven (and vice versa). That is the case here, too: if you are willing to abandon everything, house and field and, while "you, your son, your daughter, your slave and your maidservant" all go off — taking with you even the Levite, who has no Second Tithe food — to see the Face of the Lord the entire festival and if you do not sit around worrying about what is happening to your house and your livestock, but instead "rejoice before Hashem, your God, in your every undertaking," with absolute faith that He is guarding your every undertaking; — Then this *mitzvah*, partaking as it does of "loving God with all your might," will surely implant the fear of Heaven in your heart; and this in fact is the principal objective of eating Second Tithe food "before Hashem."

20. כִּי־יַרְחִיב ה׳ אֱלֹהֶיךָ אֶת־גְּבֻלְךָ כַּאֲשֶׁר דִּבֶּר־לָךְ — *When Hashem, your God, will broaden your boundary as He spoke to you.* Some say that this is talking about the Messianic Age, when God will add to our boundaries the lands of Kenites, the Kenizites, and the Kadmonites. They view this passage as being in the same vein as the passage concerning the Cities of Refuge (19:8). However, there the text reads "When Hashem will broaden your boundary, as He swore to your forefathers . . . ." Since He promised Abraham to give his children the lands of ten peoples, and in Joshua's day only those of the Seven Peoples were taken, it is obvious that this second verse must refer to the missing three regions, which we will not receive until the Messianic Age.

Our present verse, on the contrary, reads "as He spoke to *you*." God never promised *us* any more than the lands of the Seven Peoples. Besides, if this verse is talking about the fulfillment of the Messianic prophecy, Isaiah clearly states that in those days "the wolf will dwell with the lamb. . . the lion like an ox will eat hay. . . none will do evil nor destroy. . . for the land will be filled with the knowledge of God" (11:6-9). How could it be that man, the pinnacle of Creation, who tries every day to know God even now, would not learn in those days from the beasts of the field to stop desiring meat? Here we are, of course, following R' Yochanan's opinion about the Messianic Era (*Berachos* 34b), but even according to Shmuel, who holds that "there is no difference between this world and the Messianic Era except [the end of] subjugation to the

and your wine, and your oil; the firstborn of your cattle and
your flocks; all your vow offerings that you vow and your
free-will offerings; and what you raise up with your hands.
18 *Rather you shall eat them before* HASHEM, *your God, in the*
place that HASHEM, *your God, will choose — you, your son,*
your daughter, your slave, your maidservant, and the Levite
who is in your cities — and you shall rejoice before HASHEM,
your God, in your every undertaking. 19 *Beware for yourself*
lest you forsake the Levite, all your days on your Land.
20 *When* HASHEM, *your God, will broaden your boundary as*
He spoke to you, and you say, "I would eat meat," for you
will have a desire to eat meat, to your heart's entire desire

---

peoples of the world," it is hard to imagine that the Torah is triumphantly announcing to us — that in those days we will crave meat. (This isn't even news, since secular slaughter was permitted immediately upon entering the Land.)

The main interpretation, then, is *Rashi's* and that of several other commentators: the "broadening" spoken of here is an expansive lifestyle and the increase of material wealth that came with the Conquest.

וְאָמַרְתָּ אֹכְלָה בָשָׂר — *And you say, 'I would eat meat.'* But you should not cry over it, as happened at Kibroth-hattaavah, the Graves of Lust: "The rabble that was among them [in the people's midst] cultivated a craving; the Children of Israel, also wept once more and said, 'Who will feed us meat?'" (*Bamidbar* 11:4) (The circumstances then were hardly ones of liberal lifestyle and material wealth!) A person who cries over not having meat to eat is eating up his own flesh before any other flesh ever enters his mouth. From this we can tell that other interests are operating here: it is not only the lack of meat that is being lamented, as indeed the Torah (loc. cit. and *Rashi*) goes on to make clear.

כִּי־תְאַוֶּה נַפְשְׁךָ לֶאֱכֹל בָּשָׂר — *For you will have a desire to eat meat.* Only meat will you desire, but beware of falling into a general craving for all sorts of things, as happened at Kibroth-hattaavah, where the people "cultivated a craving," i.e., the Evil Inclination of desire struck at them, so that they wept, "Who will feed us meat" — and fish, and cucumbers, and melons, and leeks, and onions and garlic (and all in the desert, where nothing at all grows). And from this they went on to a further stage, of weeping "in their family groups," i.e., over the restrictions of marital purity that prevented them from committing immorality (*Rashi*). Now their real intent came out: it was not lust for flesh that motivated them, but fleshly lusts.

But if, once you are settled and have achieved a liberal lifestyle, you "have a desire to eat meat" — and not more — then "to your heart's entire desire may you eat meat."

יב תֹּאכַל בָּשָׂר׃ כא כִּי־יִרְחַק מִמְּךָ הַמָּקוֹם אֲשֶׁר יִבְחַר יהוה
כא־כז אֱלֹהֶיךָ לָשׂוּם שְׁמוֹ שָׁם וְזָבַחְתָּ מִבְּקָרְךָ וּמִצֹּאנְךָ אֲשֶׁר
נָתַן יהוה לְךָ כַּאֲשֶׁר צִוִּיתִךָ וְאָכַלְתָּ בִּשְׁעָרֶיךָ בְּכֹל אַוַּת
נַפְשֶׁךָ׃ כב אַךְ כַּאֲשֶׁר יֵאָכֵל אֶת־הַצְּבִי וְאֶת־הָאַיָּל כֵּן
תֹּאכְלֶנּוּ הַטָּמֵא וְהַטָּהוֹר יַחְדָּו יֹאכְלֶנּוּ׃ כג רַק חֲזַק לְבִלְתִּי
אֲכֹל הַדָּם כִּי הַדָּם הוּא הַנָּפֶשׁ וְלֹא־תֹאכַל הַנֶּפֶשׁ עִם־
הַבָּשָׂר׃ כד לֹא תֹּאכְלֶנּוּ עַל־הָאָרֶץ תִּשְׁפְּכֶנּוּ כַּמָּיִם׃ כה לֹא
תֹּאכְלֶנּוּ לְמַעַן יִיטַב לְךָ וּלְבָנֶיךָ אַחֲרֶיךָ כִּי־תַעֲשֶׂה הַיָּשָׁר
בְּעֵינֵי יהוה׃ כו רַק קָדָשֶׁיךָ אֲשֶׁר־יִהְיוּ לְךָ וּנְדָרֶיךָ תִּשָּׂא
וּבָאתָ אֶל־הַמָּקוֹם אֲשֶׁר־יִבְחַר יהוה׃ כז וְעָשִׂיתָ עֹלֹתֶיךָ

---

21. כִּי־יִרְחַק מִמְּךָ הַמָּקוֹם — *If the place... will be far from you.* The intent is, "If you are not at present on a high enough spiritual level to eat sacrificial meat — even if you live right in Jerusalem." That the intent is not physical but spiritual distance is attested by the Torah's statements about tithes: "If the road should be too long for you, for you cannot carry [all the produce]," and about the Pesach sacrifice, which mentions those who were "on a far road." In these cases the "road" is mentioned matter-of-factly as being too long, whereas in our verse the "place" is spoken of as being "far from you" — in spiritual status.

23. רַק חֲזַק לְבִלְתִּי אֲכֹל הַדָּם — *Only be strong not to eat the blood.* We tell a man "be strong" in two cases: when he is fighting someone stronger than himself (as the Philistines said to each other, "Who will save us from these mighty gods?... Be strong...!" [*I Shmuel* 4:8-9]), and when he is obliged to fight battle after battle, or a battle on two fronts at once (Joshua had to fight thirty-one kings one after another, and was repeatedly told "Be strong"; Joab, who was attacked from in front and behind simultaneously told Abishai "Be strong and let us grow stronger!" [*II Shmuel* 10:12]).

So it is here. In those days the Evil Inclination tempted man strongly to eat blood, especially because of the prevalent practice of eating a bloody feast in order to attract demons and learn the future from them. Therefore the Torah says, "be strong not to eat the blood."

But even later generations, who are disgusted by the thought of eating blood, need strengthening to avoid eating it, for a Jew must fight 'battle after battle' with blood before he is entitled to put a piece of meat in his mouth. The Torah lists them, one by one: "for the blood it is the [animal's] life" (v. 23) — eating the blood that issues during *shechitah*, while life is leaving the animal, is punishable by the eternal cutting off of the sinner's soul. "You shall not eat the [animal's] life with the meat" (ibid.) — warning us not to eat a limb taken from a living animal (*Rashi*), which still has its blood in it. "You shall not eat it" (v. 24) — warning us not to eat blood that trickles out after *shechitah* (*Rashi*). "You shall not eat it" (v. 25) — warning us not to eat free-flowing blood that

12
21-27

may you eat meat. [21] *If the place that* HASHEM, *your God, will*
choose to place His Name will be far from you, you may
slaughter from your cattle and your flocks that HASHEM *has*
given you, as I have commanded you, and you may eat in
your cities according to your heart's entire desire. [22] *Even as*
the deer and the hart are eaten, so may you eat it, the con-
taminated one and the pure one may eat it together. [23] *Only*
be strong not to eat the blood — for the blood, it is the life —
and you shall not eat the life with the meat. [24] *You shall not*
eat it, you shall pour it onto the ground like water. [25] *You shall*
not eat it, in order that it be well with you and your children
after you, when you do what is right in the eyes of HASHEM.
[26] *Only your sanctities that you will have and your vow*
offerings shall you carry, and come to the place that HASHEM
will choose. [27] *You shall perform your elevation-offerings,*

---

remains within the animal's limbs (*Rashi*). It becomes necessary, then, to soak the meat, and salt it, and rinse it, so as to get out the blood and remove the blood-soaked salt, until finally it is fit to cook.

A Jew has a "face-to-face" battle with blood, to the point where, if he finds a speck of blood in his egg, he throws away the entire egg.

Yet, even though the gentiles see how Jews are repelled by any sort of blood, they do not hesitate, nor do they feel the slightest shame, to bring "blood accusations" against us. This battle, too (an attack from behind) must be fought by us, by convincing just-minded people among the nations that such accusations are groundless.

It could be that this kind of 'blood', too, is included in the Torah's dictum: "Only be strong not to eat the blood," and that the Torah is encouraging us to remember that with the merit of this *mitzvah* "it will be well with you and with your children after you" forever, and the gentiles who spilled your blood will perish.

26. תִּשָּׂא וּבָאתָ אֶל־הַמָּקוֹם — *Shall you carry, and come to the place.* This is very unusual wording; why did the Torah not simply say, ". . . you shall bring to the place etc.," as it does concerning first fruits (*Shemos* 23:19)?

There are three possible explanations:

First, following the simple meaning, the Torah is saving us the trouble of a special trip to Jerusalem just to bring our sacrifices. Since you must come in any event three times a year for the Festivals, "you shall carry" your sacrifices with you when "you come." And if you find it too hard to refrain from meat in between Festivals, secular slaughter is now permitted to you. And as for your sacrifices, you may bring them to God's House on each Festival.

The second explanation follows the *Sifre*, which understands this verse as referring to animals consecrated in foreign lands, which cannot be offered up at a family altar (בָּמָה) or at a pseudo-Temple. The meaning would be, then, that

יב הַבָּשָׂר וְהַדָּם עַל־מִזְבַּח יהוה אֱלֹהֶיךָ וְדַם־זְבָחֶיךָ יִשָּׁפֵךְ
כח־ל עַל־מִזְבַּח יהוה אֱלֹהֶיךָ וְהַבָּשָׂר תֹּאכֵל: כח שְׁמֹר וְשָׁמַעְתָּ
אֵת כָּל־הַדְּבָרִים הָאֵלֶּה אֲשֶׁר אָנֹכִי מְצַוֶּךָּ לְמַעַן יִיטַב
לְךָ וּלְבָנֶיךָ אַחֲרֶיךָ עַד־עוֹלָם כִּי תַעֲשֶׂה הַטּוֹב וְהַיָּשָׁר
בְּעֵינֵי יהוה אֱלֹהֶיךָ: שלישי כט כִּי־יַכְרִית
יהוה אֱלֹהֶיךָ אֶת־הַגּוֹיִם אֲשֶׁר אַתָּה בָא־שָׁמָּה לָרֶשֶׁת
אוֹתָם מִפָּנֶיךָ וְיָרַשְׁתָּ אֹתָם וְיָשַׁבְתָּ בְּאַרְצָם: ל הִשָּׁמֶר לְךָ

---

you must not think that family altars are forbidden only within the Land of Israel. You might assume that in foreign lands, where bringing sacrifices to the Temple involves much greater distance and difficulty (including, perhaps, trouble with the Customs agents), you would be allowed to offer yours at a family altar. Therefore the Torah warns you, "You shall carry them and come to the place that Hashem will choose" — you shall bear the burden and the trouble and bring your sacrifices only to that place.

Third is R' Yehudah's opinion in the *Sifre*, that anyone bringing a sacrifice to the Temple must "carry" the responsibility for his sacrifice until he "comes" to the Chosen House; if the animal dies or is lost or maimed on the way, he must provide another.

28. שְׁמֹר וְשָׁמַעְתָּ אֵת כָּל־הַדְּבָרִים הָאֵלֶּה — *Safeguard [keep] and hearken to all these words [things].* How can one keep something that he hasn't heard yet?

Evidently, "hearkening" (שְׁמִיעָה) means here, as it often does, understanding the explanations for things. The reasons for bringing sacrifices are beyond our comprehension and since there are people who insist on understanding a commandment — with their finite intelligence! — in all its lofty, esoteric wisdom, and only then will they agree to do it, and they ignore all that their brains (destined to become worms some day) cannot fathom — therefore the Torah warns us, "safeguard and hearken." First of all you must keep all these things "that I command you" (taking good notice of Who is commanding you), whether you understand the reason or whether it is hidden from you (for you, man of clay, are as far from perceiving God's thought as east is far from west). And I promise you (says God) that if you "keep" the commandments faithfully and whole-heartedly, then in the end you will "hearken" to the reasons, for they will be revealed to you from Heaven.

29. וְיָרַשְׁתָּ אֹתָם וְיָשַׁבְתָּ בְּאַרְצָם — *And you drive [inherit] them away and settle in their land.* Even if you live "in their land": in a city where the majority are gentiles (or even if the whole Land has a majority of gentiles), you will still be living in *Eretz Yisrael* and not in the Diaspora. And so *Chazal* teach us: "A person should certainly live in *Eretz Yisrael*, even in a city where the majority are gentiles, and not in the Diaspora, even in a city where the majority are Jews. For whoever lives in the Diaspora is like a person who has no God" (*Kesubos* 110b).

12
28-30

the flesh and the blood, upon the Altar of HASHEM*, your God;*
and the blood of your feast-offerings shall be poured upon the
Altar of HASHEM*, your God, and you shall eat the flesh.*
28 *Safeguard and hearken to all these words that I*
command you, in order that it be well with you and your
children after you forever, when you do what is good and
right in the eyes of HASHEM*, your God.*
29 *When* HASHEM*, your God, will cut down the nations*
where you come to drive them away before you, and you drive
them away and settle in their land, 30 *beware for yourself*

☙ Even after you have disinherited them, you must remember that you are living "in their land," which has not lost its name of "the land of Canaan." That is to say, it has been given to you with a condition attached: "If you walk in My laws." As King David expressed it, "He gave them the lands of nations . . . that they might keep His laws and guard His Torah" (*Tehillim* 105:44-45).

☙ וְיָשַׁבְתָּ בְּאַרְצָם — *And settle in their land.* "It is told of R' Elazar ben Shamua and R' Yochanan the Cobbler that they were on the way to Netzivin [in western Babylonia] to learn Torah from R' Yehudah ben Beseira. When they came to Tzeidan [on the border] and remembered *Eretz Yisrael*, they lifted up their eyes and their tears flowed; they tore their clothes and said this verse: 'You drive them away and settle in their land.' They turned and went back to their homes, and said, 'Living in *Eretz Yisrael* is worth all the commandments in the Torah' " (*Sifre*).

Ever since the breaches in the wall of Torah grew, unfortunately even in the Holy Land, owing to our sins, some people have come to think that when we say "the *Shechinah* is in Exile" we mean it literally. They leave the Holy Land and go into the lands of Exile to look for the *Shechinah* there, to serve God and sit in the *yeshivos* in those lands. But once they come to "Tzeidan" — once they come to the first city in the Diaspora, they suffer a great disappointment, and begin to realize that the *Shechinah* has never moved from Its home. It is only in response to our present-day misdeeds that Its face is hidden from us. In private the Divine Presence weeps for Its children who have left the way of Torah, and also for those who have gone "to dwell in the fields of Moab."

There, in that foreign city, they lift up their eyes to look for God, but "whoever lives in the Diaspora is like a person who has no God" (*Kesubos* 110b). How, then, could they study the Torah and keep the commandments better there than in the Holy Land?

"Their tears flowed; they tore their clothes and said this verse: 'You drive [inherit] them away and settle in their land.' They turned and went back to their homes, and said, 'Living in *Eretz Yisrael* is worth all the commandments in the Torah.'" For whoever lives in *Eretz Yisrael* is like a person who has a God (*Kesubos*, loc. cit.). And, since this verse puts two things together (taking over an inheritance and dwelling there), we can learn from it that only if we dwell

פֶּן־תִּנָּקֵשׁ אַחֲרֵיהֶם אַחֲרֵי הִשָּׁמְדָם מִפָּנֶיךָ וּפֶן־תִּדְרֹשׁ יב
לֵאלֹהֵיהֶם לֵאמֹר אֵיכָה יַעַבְדוּ הַגּוֹיִם הָאֵלֶּה אֶת־ לא
אֱלֹהֵיהֶם וְאֶעֱשֶׂה־כֵּן גַּם־אָנִי: לא לֹא־תַעֲשֶׂה כֵן לַיהוָה
אֱלֹהֶיךָ כִּי כָל־תּוֹעֲבַת יהוה אֲשֶׁר שָׂנֵא עָשׂוּ לֵאלֹהֵיהֶם כִּי
גַם אֶת־בְּנֵיהֶם וְאֶת־בְּנֹתֵיהֶם יִשְׂרְפוּ בָאֵשׁ לֵאלֹהֵיהֶם:
א אֵת כָּל־הַדָּבָר אֲשֶׁר אָנֹכִי מְצַוֶּה אֶתְכֶם אֹתוֹ תִשְׁמְרוּ יג
לַעֲשׂוֹת לֹא־תֹסֵף עָלָיו וְלֹא תִגְרַע מִמֶּנּוּ: א

---

in the land are we sure of its inheritance remaining ours. But is that inheritance not also dependent on "If you walk in My laws"? The answer is that if one lives in the Land with the intention that his dwelling is a *mitzvah*, then this constant *mitzvah* will lead him to fulfill all the commandments of the Torah. That is why living in the Land is "worth all the commandments in the Torah."

30. פֶּן־תִּנָּקֵשׁ אַחֲרֵיהֶם אַחֲרֵי הִשָּׁמְדָם מִפָּנֶיךָ — *Lest you be attracted [snared] after them, after they have been destroyed before you.* If a person walks over a pit snare that has been camouflaged with a mat, and falls into the pit and dies of the fall, there is reason to mourn his death, for how could he have known that a pit was there? But imagine a second man, who watches the first man die, and then when the mat has been put back in place goes and walks right over it, and falls and dies. The universal reaction will be that he threw his life away in an act of deliberate suicide.

It is the same with idolatry. There are those who will sigh over the fate of the Amorites, who were destroyed by the deadly snare of idol worship (see 7:16), for they did not know what they were doing. They blindly followed their ancestral tradition, and it led to their final disaster. But you, Israel, if you "are attracted after them, after they have been destroyed before you," after you saw the effects of this "snare" on them, then no one will mourn your passing. Everyone will say that you committed deliberate suicide, since you had been warned and took no heed of the warning: you were shown an example and learned nothing from it.

❧ **אֵיכָה יַעַבְדוּ הַגּוֹיִם הָאֵלֶּה** — *How do these nations worship.* The verb is not in the past tense, עָבְדוּ, as one might expect ("how *did* they worship?") but in the future: how *will* they continue to worship their gods stubbornly even after their fall.

You may well say to yourself that they seem confident in their gods and sure that by worshiping them they will regain their lands. And from this you may advance to the idea of "competing" with them: "I will do the same" so that these gods will not drive me out of their land. But on the other hand, you will say, we must worship God, Who redeemed us from Egyptian bondage and brought us to this good land. So let us strike a compromise. We are commanded to worship God in His Temple, with the four basic services (incense, sacrifice, libation, and prostration), but these gentiles perform many other services before their gods. "I will do the same" for their idols, just to cover all bases.

12
31
lest you be attracted after them after they have been destroy-
ed before you, and lest you seek out their gods, saying, "How
do these nations worship their gods, and even I will do the
same." [31] *You shall not do so to* HASHEM, *your God, for*
everything that is an abomination of HASHEM, *that He hates,*
have they done to their gods; for even their sons and their
daughters have they burned in the fire for their gods.
13
1
[1] *The entire word that I command you, that shall you*
observe to do; you shall not add to it and you shall not subtract
from it.

But conjoining any other god with God is also idolatry, and so the Torah goes to some length to spell out this prohibition.

13.

1. לֹא־תֹסֵף עָלָיו וְלֹא תִגְרַע מִמֶּנּוּ — *You shall not add to it and you shall not subtract [detract] from it.* This warning was already given in v. 4:2 above. Why is it repeated here?

The Vilna Gaon explains that at 4:2 the Torah is referring to adding a new commandment to the six hundred and thirteen that we were given, or deleting one of their number. Here, however, the reference is to adding something to an existing commandment or subtracting something from it, such as putting five, or three, scrolls in a pair of *tefillin* instead of four.

But *Rashi* explains v. 4:2 as referring to "such things as five scrolls in *tefillin* or five kinds of plant in a *lulav*"; and he gives the same explanation here. How would he account for the repetition of this commandment?

We can say on *Rashi's* behalf that no new *halachah* is being given here, but the reason for the *halachah* is being revealed: "do not add" so that "you will not detract," for every addition to the Torah is inevitably a detraction (*Sanhedrin* 29a). And on this account our verse is juxtaposed to the account of how the gentiles used to burn their children in worship of their idols. For God commands us to bring sacrifices "from among the animals," but if we were to suggest adding sacrifices "from among mankind" this would be nothing but murder.

Chazal point out to us the logical conclusion of such 'additions': "'even [גַּם, literally "also"] their sons and their daughters have they burned' — 'also' indicates that they burned their fathers and mothers too" (*Sifre*). So the fathers would burn their sons and daughters so as to find favor and blessing from the idol, and the children, when they grew up and got the upper hand, would burn their fathers and mothers. What ruination!

And what clearer example could there be of how adding to God's commandments always means detracting. What could be wrong, we might think, about adding extra sacrifices to our worship? Even if we don't see it right away, we are not adding but detracting.

יג ב כִּי־יָקוּם בְּקִרְבְּךָ נָבִיא אוֹ חֹלֵם חֲלוֹם וְנָתַן אֵלֶיךָ אוֹת אוֹ
ב־ד מוֹפֵת: ג וּבָא הָאוֹת וְהַמּוֹפֵת אֲשֶׁר־דִּבֶּר אֵלֶיךָ לֵאמֹר נֵלְכָה
אַחֲרֵי אֱלֹהִים אֲחֵרִים אֲשֶׁר לֹא־יְדַעְתָּם וְנָעָבְדֵם: ד לֹא
תִשְׁמַע אֶל־דִּבְרֵי הַנָּבִיא הַהוּא אוֹ אֶל־חוֹלֵם הַחֲלוֹם
הַהוּא כִּי מְנַסֶּה יהוה אֱלֹהֵיכֶם אֶתְכֶם לָדַעַת הֲיִשְׁכֶם
אֹהֲבִים אֶת־יהוה אֱלֹהֵיכֶם בְּכָל־לְבַבְכֶם וּבְכָל־נַפְשְׁכֶם:

2-3. וְנָתַן אֵלֶיךָ אוֹת אוֹ מוֹפֵת . . . נֵלְכָה אַחֲרֵי אֱלֹהִים אֲחֵרִים — *And he will produce to you a sign or a wonder. . . "Let us follow gods of others"*. It seems odd that no mention is made of one who entices the people to say that there is no God. There are two approaches to this question:

One follows the Ramban's *drashos,* in which he explains that in those ancient times few people thought that the world had always existed. The reason was that there were many people then who could rebut this worthless opinion with the history they had heard from their fathers and elders, who in turn had heard from Adam and his descendants how the world was created.

The Deluge, too, was a ready piece of evidence that there is a Master and Creator of the World. Jacob himself studied under Shem son of Noah and heard directly from him how he and his family were saved from the Deluge and lived in the Ark for a year, and how every other living thing had been wiped out for its immorality. Multitudes, then, would have heard all this from Noah's sons and from Jacob, and would know that the world has its Master.

Even in King David's day atheists were referred to as "louts" — "a lout says in his heart" (because he is ashamed to say it out loud) "there is no God" (*Tehillim* 14:1). Any agitator who wanted his enticement to be successful would, therefore, have chosen to say that the world has a Master, but that He is such-and-such an idol.

The second approach is to consider the mentality of a person who believes that the world always existed, that there is no Creator, and that everything follows the laws of nature. Such a person could not possibly produce a sign or a wonder, since that would mean supplanting the laws of nature, which is impossible according to his beliefs.

In these latter-day times, when the scoffers are brazen enough to say out loud that there is no God and all is according to natural law, it is obvious that (in accordance with their belief) they can offer no sign or wonder to bolster their assertion. In that case, the commandment "do not hearken to the words of that prophet . . . for Hashem, your God, is testing you" (v. 4) must no longer apply in our times, since the scoffers have no sign to show. And yet that is not the situation. Our modern-day enticers use the argument that righteous and wicked, pious and impious, all come to the same fate, and often the wicked prosper while the righteous suffer. This, in their view, is a veritable sign that all is according to blind natural law, Heaven forbid.

13
2-4

[2] *If there should stand up in your midst a prophet or a*
dreamer of a dream, and he will produce to you a sign or a
wonder, [3] *and the sign or the wonder comes about, of which he*
spoke to you, saying, "Let us follow gods of others that you did
not know and we shall worship them!" — [4] *do not hearken to*
the words of that prophet or to that dreamer of a dream, for
HASHEM, your God, is testing you to know whether you love
HASHEM, your God, with all your heart and with all your soul.

But the next verses provide us with a fine explanation of why the wicked may prosper while the righteous suffer: "for Hashem, your God, is testing you, to know whether you love Hashem, your God, with all your heart and with all your soul." Whenever we see the wicked succeeding, and despite this remain firm in our faith, we are fulfilling this commandment "not to hearken to the words of that prophet or to that dreamer of a dream."

4. לֹא תִשְׁמַע אֶל־דִּבְרֵי הַנָּבִיא הַהוּא אוֹ אֶל־חוֹלֵם הַחֲלוֹם הַהוּא כִּי מְנַסֶּה ה׳ אֱלֹהֵיכֶם אֶתְכֶם — *Do not hearken to the words of that prophet or to that dreamer of a dream, for Hashem, your God, is testing you.* This verse was used by the community of converts that flourished in the time of the Czars along the shores of the Caspian Sea, to refute the priests sent by the Russian government to attempt their return to the Christian fold. — Their fathers had been Christians for centuries, but suddenly they had seized upon the idea of converting to Judaism, owing to their habit of constantly reading Scripture on the Christian holidays. — The priests began to tell them all of the signs and wonders that the man that Christians worship had done, and asked them, 'Was this not enough to warrant believing in his prophetic message?' But one of the elders answered that this man's prophecy was based upon the Torah of Moses, and there is written, "If there should stand up in your midst a prophet or a dreamer of a dream, and he will produce to you a sign or a wonder . . . Do not hearken to the words of that prophet . . . for Hashem, your God, is testing you." In that case, what use are the signs and wonders that this man showed, seeing as God Himself has warned us not to listen to such a prophet no matter what wonders he performs? (I heard this from the elders of a group of converts when I was in Tzeritzin, now called Stalingrad, visiting my brother, the Gaon R' Yoel זצוק"ל, who was the Rav there and afterwards in Stoipce.)

כִּי מְנַסֶּה ה׳ אֱלֹהֵיכֶם אֶתְכֶם לָדַעַת הֲיִשְׁכֶם אֹהֲבִים אֶת־ה׳ אֱלֹהֵיכֶם בְּכָל־לְבַבְכֶם וּבְכָל־נַפְשְׁכֶם — *For Hashem, your God, is testing you, to know whether you love Hashem, your God, with all your heart and with all your soul.* It is difficult to understand what the connection is between "with all your heart and soul" and a false prophecy. But we can understand if we picture the following scene: it is a drought year, and the false prophet holds out the blandishment that his idol,if worshiped, will bring rain. The people have built the idol and worshiped it, and rain has come down. The Torah warns us about this that "Hashem, your God, is testing you, to know" whether you remember His promise to you: that

יג ה אַחֲרֵי יהוָה אֱלֹהֵיכֶם תֵּלֵכוּ וְאֹתוֹ תִירָאוּ וְאֶת־מִצְוֹתָיו
ה־ח תִּשְׁמֹרוּ וּבְקֹלוֹ תִשְׁמָעוּ וְאֹתוֹ תַעֲבֹדוּ וּבוֹ תִדְבָּקוּן: ו וְהַנָּבִיא
הַהוּא אוֹ חֹלֵם הַחֲלוֹם הַהוּא יוּמָת כִּי דִבֶּר־סָרָה עַל־יהוָה
אֱלֹהֵיכֶם הַמּוֹצִיא אֶתְכֶם ׀ מֵאֶרֶץ מִצְרַיִם וְהַפֹּדְךָ מִבֵּית
עֲבָדִים לְהַדִּיחֲךָ מִן־ הַדֶּרֶךְ אֲשֶׁר צִוְּךָ יהוָה אֱלֹהֶיךָ לָלֶכֶת
בָּהּ וּבִעַרְתָּ הָרָע מִקִּרְבֶּךָ: ז כִּי יְסִיתְךָ
אָחִיךָ בֶן־אִמֶּךָ אוֹ־בִנְךָ אוֹ־בִתְּךָ אוֹ ׀ אֵשֶׁת חֵיקֶךָ אוֹ רֵעֲךָ
אֲשֶׁר כְּנַפְשְׁךָ בַּסֵּתֶר לֵאמֹר נֵלְכָה וְנַעַבְדָה אֱלֹהִים אֲחֵרִים
אֲשֶׁר לֹא יָדַעְתָּ אַתָּה וַאֲבֹתֶיךָ: ח מֵאֱלֹהֵי הָעַמִּים אֲשֶׁר

---

if "you love Hashem, your God, with all your heart and with all your soul, I will provide rain for your land." Do you understand that you have another way, and a sure one, to get rain? If you reject that direction and try others, clearly you do not love your God with all your heart and soul.

Now, God does not need to test man, for everything is revealed before Him. *Rashi* explains that the Binding of Isaac was intended only to show the nations of the world why Abraham was so beloved of God. In our present case we can take what we have just said above, and see the purpose of the test as showing the Children of Israel how far they have fallen from loving God, so that they may understand the real reason why there is no rain.

5. וְאֶת־מִצְוֹתָיו תִּשְׁמֹרוּ — *His commandments shall you observe.* "This is the Torah of Moses. וּבְקֹלוֹ תִשְׁמָעוּ, *And to His voice shall you hearken* — this is the voice of the prophets" (*Rashi*).

The point is that the Torah of Moses comes first; and when should you hearken to the voice of the prophets? Whenever it does not contradict the Torah of Moses. But if the prophet is trying to annul a commandment or add a new one, you may not listen to him. Only in the case where the prophet declares a temporary, *ad hoc* deviation from *halachah* you must listen to him and obey his instructions — provided he does not declare even a momentary concession for idol worship. In that case you may not obey him.

6. כִּי דִבֶּר־סָרָה עַל־ה׳ אֱלֹהֵיכֶם — *For he had spoken perversion against Hashem, your God.* Even though no one has actually committed idolatry, neither the 'prophet' nor those who listened to him, all the same he has incurred the death penalty for having spoken such a perverted 'prophecy.'

7. אוֹ אֵשֶׁת חֵיקֶךָ — *Or the wife of your bosom.* A man ought not to accept advice from his wife in spiritual matters, if she attempts to entice him to worship idols. Still, sometimes a wife will compel her husband to follow her, even when in his heart he disagrees with her. Adam, for example, followed Eve's counsel against his inner promptings. And when Delilah "tormented [Samson] with her words all day long, and compelled him, and his soul tottered towards death, he told her all [that was in] his heart" (*Shoftim* 16:16-17).

5 *HASHEM, your God, shall you follow and Him shall you fear;*
His commandments shall you observe and to His voice shall
you hearken; Him shall you serve and to Him shall you
cleave. 6 *And that prophet and that dreamer of a dream shall*
be put to death, for he had spoken perversion against HASHEM,
your God, Who takes you out of the land of Egypt, and Who
redeems you from the house of slavery, to make you stray
from the path on which HASHEM, your God, has commanded
you to go; and you shall destroy the evil from your midst.
7 *If your brother, the son of your mother, or your son or your*
daughter, or the wife of your bosom, or your friend who is like
your own soul will entice you secretly, saying, "Let us go and
worship the gods of others" — that you did not know, you
nor your forefathers, 8 *from the gods of the peoples that are*

(*Chazal* deduce that she would interrupt intimate relations in order to torment him [*Sotah* 9b].) Even Solomon, the wisest of all men, was led astray by his wives.

That is the reason for this expression, "the wife of your bosom": since she lies in your bosom, she can exert an influence over you even stronger than that of reason and common sense. Therefore the Torah specifically warns man not to let himself be influenced in this way.

אֲשֶׁר כְּנַפְשְׁךָ — *Who is like your own soul.* "This is your father" (*Sifre*). But why was a father not listed first in this passage, as the one whose influence is naturally the strongest? And why is the father mentioned only in veiled language? — Because a father's way is to teach his son to go in the straight path; he does not normally entice his son to worship idols.

In that case, what can we say about some fathers in our times, who hand their sons over to missionaries? This is a disaster that even the Torah chose not to write out explicitly only indirectly.

We can also explain that the indirect mention here is because the Torah goes on to say, "your hand shall be the first against him to kill him" (v. 9). Since a son cannot be made a deputy to strike or slay his father (after all, this can always be done by someone else), the case of a son bringing his father to trial is mentioned only in veiled language.

בַּסֵּתֶר — *Secretly.* No one may be executed except on the testimony of two witnesses before a *Beis Din.* In this case, where the enticement was done in secret, so that there is only one witness to testify (and if the enticer is his relative he is not competent to testify against him at all), how can the commandment "you shall surely kill him" be fulfilled?

From here we learn that if an enticer refuses to speak openly except in private, before one person only, then we must secrete witnesses where they can see and hear everything without his detecting them. When he commits the act

יג סְבִיבֹתֵיכֶם הַקְּרֹבִים אֵלֶיךָ אוֹ הָרְחֹקִים מִמֶּךָּ מִקְצֵה הָאָרֶץ
ט־יב וְעַד־קְצֵה הָאָרֶץ: ט לֹא־תֹאבֶה לוֹ וְלֹא תִשְׁמַע אֵלָיו
וְלֹא־תָחוֹס עֵינְךָ עָלָיו וְלֹא־תַחְמֹל וְלֹא־תְכַסֶּה עָלָיו: י כִּי
הָרֹג תַּהַרְגֶנּוּ יָדְךָ תִּהְיֶה־בּוֹ בָרִאשׁוֹנָה לַהֲמִיתוֹ וְיַד
כָּל־הָעָם בָּאַחֲרֹנָה: יא וּסְקַלְתּוֹ בָאֲבָנִים וָמֵת כִּי בִקֵּשׁ
לְהַדִּיחֲךָ מֵעַל יְהוָה אֱלֹהֶיךָ הַמּוֹצִיאֲךָ מֵאֶרֶץ מִצְרַיִם
מִבֵּית עֲבָדִים: יב וְכָל־יִשְׂרָאֵל יִשְׁמְעוּ וְיִרָאוּן וְלֹא־יוֹסִפוּ

---

of enticement, they must seize him and bring him to judgment. (This tactic of secreting witnesses is used only in regard to an enticer.)

10. יָדְךָ תִּהְיֶה־בּוֹ בָרִאשׁוֹנָה לַהֲמִיתוֹ — *Your hand shall be the first against him to kill him*. "It is a *mitzvah* for the tempted one to put him [the enticer] to death himself" (*Sifre*). The *Rambam* also rules this way in *Hilchos Avodah Zarah* 5:4. Yet the Torah says of capital cases in general, "The hand of the witnesses shall be upon him first to put him to death" (*Devarim* 17:7); furthermore, the one who has been tempted is usually a relative, unacceptable as a witness. And what other example do we have of this, that someone else beside the witnesses is commanded to put a criminal to death?

An answer is found in the words, "The avenger of the blood, he shall kill the murderer" (*Bamidbar* 35:19). The *Meiri* remarks that some commentators hold that every murderer, including one who has been condemned by a *Beis Din*, should be executed at the hands of the "avenger of the blood," for whom this act is a *mitzvah*, and only if the avenger of the blood does not wish to do the killing, then the *Beis Din* carries out the sentence through the witnesses.

Looking now at *Bamidbar* 35:24, "then the assembly shall judge between the assailant and the avenger of the blood," *Chazal* tell us that if the murder victim has no avenger, the *Beis Din* appoints one (*Sanhedrin* 45b). That is, since the murderer can defend himself in court, and look for witnesses and evidence in his favor, the *Beis Din* must bring someone to speak against him, to cross-examine him, thus "avenging" the blood of the victim. This is because of the seriousness of the matter of bloodshed and the obligation to remove killers from the world.

The matter of idolatry is equally serious, and so the Torah appoints the victim of the enticer's attempt as the prosecutor, for the enticer tried to defile him with idolatry, and a defiler is worse than a killer. It is even the victim's duty to secrete witnesses, to bring the offender to court, to testify against him, and then kill him with his own hands, just as the avenger of the blood kills the murderer.

⁂ **יָדְךָ . . . לַהֲמִיתוֹ** — *Your hand. . . to kill him.* If we look carefully at the laws of the enticer and the enticed, and at the language of this passage, it seems as though Moses wanted to atone before his death for the sin of the Calf, or at least to minimize the punishment that hung over the heads of the Children of Israel — for God had said, "on the day that I make My account, I shall bring their sin to account against them."

13 *all around you, those near to you or those far from you, from*
9-12 *one end of the earth to the other end of the earth —* 9 *you shall*
not accede to him and not hearken to him; your eye shall not
take pity on him, you shall not be compassionate nor conceal
him. 10 *Rather, you shall surely kill him; your hand shall be the*
first against him to kill him, and the hand of the entire peo-
ple afterwards. 11 *You shall pelt him with stones and he shall*
die, for he sought to make you stray from near HASHEM, *your*
God, Who takes you out of Egypt, from the house of slav-
ery. 12 *All Israel shall hear and see, and they shall not again*

The Calf, however, had been made by the Mixed Multitude, the hangers-on among them, and all those who worshiped it had been killed either by the Levites or by the plague. Why, then, should God be so angry against the entire people? The answer is very simple: when Moses cried, "Whoever is for Hashem, join me!" only the Levites gathered around him to remove the evil from Israel. Not one Israelite moved, as if the whole matter were no business of theirs.

"On the next day" (after the Calf-worshipers were eradicated, and the Children of Israel displayed their indifference), "Moses said to the people" (to those who were still alive because they had not been among the idolaters) "You have committed a grievous sin!" You, in your indifference, did not come to God's aid, to eradicate those who worshiped the Calf!

Now Moses wished to inflame the hearts of the Children of Israel to be ready to stand up for God's honor if a similar event should come up, to be ready to kill with their own hands anyone who tried to lure them into idolatry, as the Mixed Multitude had done in their time — even if it meant killing one's own brother.

(*Rashi* comments [*Shemos* 32:26-27] that since the whole tribe of Levi was guiltless, yet Moses says to the Levites, "Let every man kill his brother," this must mean a half-brother from a second marriage of a shared mother, because if they shared a common father then the brother would be a Levite like him, and, like him, be guiltless of idolatry. And this is why our present passage says, "If your brother, the son of your mother, or your son or your daughter, etc." Anyone who entices to idolatry is included in this law; but the Torah gives us this list to teach us that supreme self-mastery is demanded here. One must be zealous for God even towards those close to him, including the son of his own mother, the closest to him of all.)

The verse goes on to say "or your friend" — "this is the proselyte," says the *Sifre*, alluding to the first enticers to idolatry after the Exodus, the Mixed Multitude. And the commandment that the enticer be executed not by the witnesses, as in other capital cases, but by the target of his attempted enticement, comes to teach us that if *any* Jew encounters an enticer, he is not to remain indifferent to this evil, nor even to be satisfied with merely bringing the offender to the *Beis Din*, but rather "your hand shall be the first against him to kill him." Thus God's anger against Israel because of the Calf will be appeased.

יג לַעֲשׂוֹת כַּדָּבָר הָרָע הַזֶּה בְּקִרְבֶּךָ: יג כִּי־תִשְׁמַע
יג־טו בְּאַחַת עָרֶיךָ אֲשֶׁר יהוה אֱלֹהֶיךָ נֹתֵן לְךָ לָשֶׁבֶת שָׁם
לֵאמֹר: יד יָצְאוּ אֲנָשִׁים בְּנֵי־בְלִיַּעַל מִקִּרְבֶּךָ וַיַּדִּיחוּ אֶת־
יֹשְׁבֵי עִירָם לֵאמֹר נֵלְכָה וְנַעַבְדָה אֱלֹהִים אֲחֵרִים אֲשֶׁר
לֹא־יְדַעְתֶּם: טו וְדָרַשְׁתָּ וְחָקַרְתָּ וְשָׁאַלְתָּ הֵיטֵב וְהִנֵּה אֱמֶת

---

13. כִּי־תִשְׁמַע — *If. . . you hear.* This entire passage is addressed to the Great *Beis Din* in Jerusalem, for a עִיר הַנִּדַּחַת, a "Wayward City" may be declared only by a *Beis Din* of seventy-one judges (see *Sanhedrin* 2a). It is their duty to deliberate, arrive at a decision, and carry it out.

Now, Jerusalem cannot be declared a Wayward City (see *Bava Kamma* Ch. 2), and this is why our verse says "if you hear," since the Great *Beis Din* is located in the Chamber of Hewn Stone in the Temple, in Jerusalem where the law of Wayward Cities does not apply. A rumor of this nature could only reach them from outside sources. Looking at the *Sifre*, we find that the rabbis derived from the words "if you hear" that the *Beis Din* has no obligation to investigate the cities of Israel on the chance that, God forbid, any of them had gone astray. (This was, in fact, so uncommon that the majority of Sages held that there had never actually been such a case, nor ever would be — although R' Yonassan said he had seen one and sat upon its remains [*Sanhedrin* 71a].)

Once the rumor has reached them, however, the *Beis Din* must investigate immediately. Interpreting our verse along these lines, we can understand *Rashi* with greater precision: first he jumps ahead to the words "in which to dwell," explaining them to mean that Jerusalem is excluded from the law of the Wayward City; only then does he go back to the words "if . . . you hear, saying . . ." That is, כִּי תִשְׁמַע (if you hear) is linked to לֵאמֹר (saying): if you hear people saying that the inhabitants of a particular city have been led astray. But why did *Rashi* twist the verse around? Because in order to explain "if you hear," he first had to make it clear that this case could not come up in Jerusalem itself, and this is why it says, not "if you see" but "if you hear" — if you hear people talking about some other city.

14. יָצְאוּ אֲנָשִׁים — *Men have emerged.* Men, not women and not children, and a minimum of two men, as expressed by the plural form. If the people of a city are led astray in any other way — for example, by one man alone, or by women, or children under *bar mitzvah* age — then the law of the Wayward City does not apply. In such a case those who committed idolatry are judged individually, their execution is by stoning, and their property is transmitted to their heirs.

מִקִּרְבֶּךָ — *From your midst.* The enticers must be from the same tribe as the people they lead astray. "The dwellers of their city" — the enticers must also be residents of that city (all those who have lived there for at least thirty days are considered "dwellers of the city").

do such an evil thing in your midst.
[13] *If, in one of your cities that* HASHEM, *your God, gives you*
in which to dwell, you hear, saying, [14] *"Lawless men have*
emerged from your midst, and they have caused the dwellers
of their city to go astray, saying, 'Let us go and worship the
gods of others, that you have not known' " — [15] *you shall seek*
out and investigate, and inquire well, and behold! it is true,

---

אֲשֶׁר לֹא־יְדַעְתֶּם — *That you have not known.* And even so, you rush into this new "faith" — just to get the yoke of the Kingdom of Heaven off your neck and follow the enticers.

15. וְדָרַשְׁתָּ וְחָקַרְתָּ וְשָׁאַלְתָּ הֵיטֵב — *You shall seek out and investigate, and inquire well.* The *Sifre* says, "You shall *seek out* from the Torah, and *investigate* from the witnesses, and *inquire* from the Talmud [תַּלְמוּד]." This makes no sense at all, for the Torah and the Talmud are one; how can they be spoken of separately? Indeed, the Vilna Gaon presented abundant evidence for his decision to expunge this sentence from the *Sifre* as a scribal error. In the *Yalkut Shimoni*, however, I found the correct reading: ". . . and inquire from the disciples [תַּלְמִידִים]." Apparently the *Rambam* had this reading before him and based his unique approach to the matter of the Wayward City upon it. This would explain why his views are criticized by the *Raavad*, and why even the commentators on the *Rambam* could not find a source for his approach.

In *Hilchos Avodah Zarah* (4:6) the *Rambam* writes, "The Great *Beis Din* sends [representatives] to seek out the facts, and investigates until it is known by clear evidence that the whole city or its majority have gone astray and returned to idolatry. Afterwards [the *Beis Din*] sends two *talmidei chachamim* to them, to warn them and to bring them back [to serving God]. If they repent, good. If they persist in their wrongdoing, the *Beis Din* calls up an army from all of Israel to march against them. Anyone who is condemned by the testimony of two witnesses that he worshiped an idol after being warned against it, is placed aside. If all the idolaters constitute a minority, they are stoned and the rest of the city is saved. If the idolaters constitute a majority, they are brought before the Great *Beis Din*, where they are sentenced and executed by the sword . . . and all the property of the people of that city is burned."

The *Raavad* comments on the statement that "Afterwards they send two *talmidei chachamim* to them, to warn them and to bring them back [to serving God]. If they repent, good." "How good it would be," says the *Raavad*, "if repentance could help them! But I have never found [in the Torah] that repentance helps [i.e., saves one from the court's sentence] after disregarding a warning and committing a deliberate sin."

Indeed, many have asked, where did the *Rambam* get this idea in the first place, that the *Beis Din* sends *talmidei chachamim* to warn the citizens? Apparently he got it from the above-mentioned *Sifre*, where the text reads, "and they inquire from the *talmidim*"; that is, inquire of them whether the

יג נָכ֣וֹן הַדָּבָ֔ר נֶעֶשְׂתָ֛ה הַתּוֹעֵבָ֥ה הַזֹּ֖את בְּקִרְבֶּֽךָ׃ טז הַכֵּ֣ה
טז־יח תַכֶּ֗ה אֶת־יֹשְׁבֵ֛י הָעִ֥יר הַהִ֖וא לְפִי־חָ֑רֶב הַחֲרֵ֨ם אֹתָ֧הּ
וְאֶת־כָּל־אֲשֶׁר־בָּ֛הּ וְאֶת־בְּהֶמְתָּ֖הּ לְפִי־חָֽרֶב׃ יז וְאֶת־כָּל־
שְׁלָלָ֗הּ תִּקְבֹּץ֮ אֶל־תּ֣וֹךְ רְחֹבָהּ֒ וְשָׂרַפְתָּ֣ בָאֵ֡שׁ אֶת־הָעִ֨יר
וְאֶת־כָּל־שְׁלָלָ֜הּ כָּלִ֗יל לַיהוָ֣ה אֱלֹהֶ֑יךָ וְהָיְתָה֙ תֵּ֣ל עוֹלָ֔ם
לֹ֥א תִבָּנֶ֖ה עֽוֹד׃ יח וְלֹֽא־יִדְבַּ֧ק בְּיָדְךָ֛ מְא֖וּמָה מִן־הַחֵ֑רֶם
לְמַ֡עַן יָשׁוּב֩ יְהוָ֨ה מֵחֲר֜וֹן אַפּ֗וֹ וְנָֽתַן־לְךָ֤ רַחֲמִים֙ וְרִחַמְךָ֣

---

citizens took warning and repented. But again, how can repentance help them after they disregarded the earlier warning and worshiped an idol?

In our book of responsa, *Moznayim Lamishpat*, §19, we explained at length that there are two possible cases of a Wayward City: one is individual Jews who indulged in idolatry despite being forewarned; their death is by stoning, and repentance cannot exempt them from punishment in this world; and the other is a Jewish city, all of whose inhabitants, or most of them (according to the rule of "the majority is like the whole"), have gone astray; the Torah says to burn the city and all its property, and it is never to be rebuilt.

The major distinction of the second case is that in this case the wives and children of the idolaters are also killed, so that no memory of them should remain, and that the idolaters themselves are executed, not by stoning, the severest form of execution, but by beheading.

It stands to reason, as well, that the citizens must be forewarned of the burning of their city and all its contents — not necessarily every citizen individually, but a general warning, since the punishment is general. And this is why the *Rambam* writes, "The Great *Beis Din* sends [representatives] to seek out the facts and investigate until it is known by clear evidence" — of course at this point the witnesses are not examined in the presence of the accused, for they might be afraid to testify — "that the whole city or its majority have gone astray and returned to idolatry." Naturally, it is the duty of the delegates to see and hear all the details — were they led astray by two men, were these men from that same city, etc. This was the *Sifre's* meaning when it said, "You shall seek out from the Torah" — first of all, they must determine whether this can be considered a Wayward City according to all the conditions laid down by the Torah; after that they send two *talmidei chachamim* to warn them concerning their general status as a city.

"If they repent, good" — in that case, the city will not be condemned to burning, the women and children will not be killed, nor will the animals. The individuals found guilty of idolatry, however, are condemned to death by stoning, provided that they were forewarned. This solves the problem raised by the *Raavad*.

But "if they persist in their wrongdoing, the *Beis Din* calls up an army from all of Israel to march against them," and when the city has been breached,

13 16-18 *the word is correct, this abomination was committed in your*
midst. 16 *You shall smite the inhabitants of that city with the*
edge of the sword; lay it waste and everything that is in it,
and its animals, with the edge of the sword. 17 *You shall*
gather together all its booty to the midst of its open square,
and you shall burn in fire completely the city and all its booty
to HASHEM, *your God, and it shall be an eternal heap, it shall*
not be rebuilt. 18 *No part of the banned property may adhere*
to your hand, so that HASHEM *will turn back from His*
burning wrath; and He will give you mercy and be merciful

---

many courts are set up (as *Reish Lakish* says in *Sanhedrin* 112a) to condemn the guilty by witness and prior warning. This time the witnesses must speak in the presence of the accused, for now that the city has been conquered they need not fear. This fulfills the condition set forth by the *Sifre*, "and investigate from the witnesses."

If all or most of the citizens are found guilty, they are brought to Jerusalem so that the city as a whole may be condemned as a Wayward City, and there the *Beis Din* must "inquire from the *talmidim*" whether the general warning was delivered, that is, the warning that if they did not repent, their city would be condemned and their memory obliterated. Then the Great *Beis Din* carries out the sentence on the city. If the idolaters were found to constitute a minority, then the city is not judged a Wayward City and the idolaters are condemned as individuals and stoned, and their property goes to their heirs.

Now, if they did no further sin after the warning was delivered, they are not liable to punishment by the *Beis Din*. But what sin would the city as a whole have done after the warning, so as to qualify as a Wayward City? — That of clinging to their civic idol worship and not letting the court deal with the idolaters of their city. And if they repent of this general passion for idolatry once they have been warned of its consequences, and allow the court to punish the actual idol worshipers for their misdeeds, they cannot be declared a Wayward City.

17. לֹא תִבָּנֶה עוֹד — *It shall not be rebuilt.* Just as there are places particularly fit for holiness, so are there places fit for impurity, as *Chazal* said of Peor. Now, if at the site of this city such an event occurred, that an entire congregation turned to idol worship and fought the whole Jewish nation for their perverted ideals, it can be assumed that the nature of the place caused this to happen, and a new Jewish settlement may not be built there.

18. וְנָתַן־לְךָ רַחֲמִים — *And He will give you mercy.* Killing women and children, as the *Rambam* formulated the *halachah*, may seem excessively cruel. Therefore the Torah adds, "and He will give you mercy" — the quality of mercy in your heart will not be hurt by carrying out this commandment.

יג וְהִרְבֶּךָ כַּאֲשֶׁר נִשְׁבַּע לַאֲבֹתֶיךָ: יט כִּי תִשְׁמַע בְּקוֹל יְהוָה
יט אֱלֹהֶיךָ לִשְׁמֹר אֶת־כָּל־מִצְוֺתָיו אֲשֶׁר אָנֹכִי מְצַוְּךָ הַיּוֹם
יד לַעֲשׂוֹת הַיָּשָׁר בְּעֵינֵי יְהוָה אֱלֹהֶיךָ: רביעי א בָּנִים
א־ו אַתֶּם לַיהוָה אֱלֹהֵיכֶם לֹא תִתְגֹּדְדוּ וְלֹא־תָשִׂימוּ קָרְחָה
בֵּין עֵינֵיכֶם לָמֵת: ב כִּי עַם קָדוֹשׁ אַתָּה לַיהוָה אֱלֹהֶיךָ
וּבְךָ בָּחַר יְהוָה לִהְיוֹת לוֹ לְעַם סְגֻלָּה מִכֹּל הָעַמִּים
אֲשֶׁר עַל־פְּנֵי הָאֲדָמָה: ג לֹא תֹאכַל כָּל־תּוֹעֵבָה:
ד זֹאת הַבְּהֵמָה אֲשֶׁר תֹּאכֵלוּ שׁוֹר שֵׂה כְשָׂבִים וְשֵׂה עִזִּים:
ה אַיָּל וּצְבִי וְיַחְמוּר וְאַקּוֹ וְדִישֹׁן וּתְאוֹ וָזָמֶר: ו וְכָל־בְּהֵמָה
מַפְרֶסֶת פַּרְסָה וְשֹׁסַעַת שֶׁסַע שְׁתֵּי פְרָסוֹת מַעֲלַת גֵּרָה

וְהִרְבְּךָ — *And multiply you.* You need not worry over the decrease in the Jewish population brought about by judging the Wayward City, for God will multiply you, "as He swore to your forefathers" at the time of the Binding of Isaac: "I shall... greatly increase your offspring like the stars of the heaven" (*Bereishis* 22:17). This blessing is given to the Children of Israel as they spill their blood for the sanctity of God's Name, that they will have children who light up the whole world with Torah and wisdom "like the stars of the heaven."

14.

1. **בָּנִים אַתֶּם לַה׳ אֱלֹהֵיכֶם לֹא תִתְגֹּדְדוּ** — *You are children to Hashem, your God — you shall not cut yourselves.* This passage is juxtaposed to that above, which says, "and He will give you mercy and be merciful to you," in order to teach us that we should ask for God's mercy, praying to Him with the simplicity of children requesting something from their father. We may also shed tears during our prayer, for perhaps our sins have caused the Gates of Mercy to close, but the Gates of Tears are never closed. But far be it from us to cut ourselves and draw blood, thinking that this will arouse God's mercy, for this is the way of idolatry. We see of the prophets of Baal, who cried on Mount Carmel, "Baal! Answer us!" — "but there was no voice and none to answer... so they cut themselves, according to their law, with swords and spears, until blood flowed over them" (*I Melachim* 18:26-28).

The *Kesef Mishneh* (on *Hilchos Avodah Zarah* 12:6) explains that they did this "so that Baal would be aroused to answer them, according to their distorted way of thinking" (and this is why the *Rambam* writes that one who cuts himself before an idol is subject to lashes, not stoning, because this in itself is not considered worship). But we are not to do this before our God, for He is our Father, and He wants us to pour out our souls to Him, not our blood.

וְלֹא־תָשִׂימוּ קָרְחָה בֵּין עֵינֵיכֶם לָמֵת — *And you shall not make a bald spot between your eyes for a dead person.* It is equally forbidden on any part of

13 to you and multiply you, as He swore to your forefathers,
19 *19 when you hearken to the voice of* HASHEM, *your God, to*
observe all His commandments that I command you today,
to do what is right in the eyes of HASHEM, *your God.*

14 *1 You are children to* HASHEM, *your God — you shall not cut*
1-6 *yourselves and you shall not make a bald spot between your*
eyes for a dead person. 2 For you are a holy people to HASHEM,
your God, and HASHEM *has chosen you for Himself to be a*
treasured people, from among all the peoples on the face of
the earth.

3 You shall not eat any abomination. 4 These are the
animals that you may eat: the ox, sheep, and goat; 5 the hart,
deer, and the yachmur, the akko, dishon, the teo, and the
zamer. 6 And every animal that has a split hoof, which is
completely separated in two hooves, that brings up its cud

---

the head (*Makkos* 20a). Why, then, does the Torah say "between your eyes"? To teach you that when the Torah commands us to put *tefillin* "between your eyes," that too really means higher up on the head, where hair grows. (For this is obviously the case in our present verse, since how could one make a bald spot where no hair grows?) So says the *Ritva.*

Because the point on the hairline which corresponds with the point between the eyes is the central point for all the senses and thoughts in a human being, the gentiles used to make a bald spot there for a dead person, as if to say, 'Since man is destined to die, he has no advantage over an animal, despite his intelligence.' But you are not like that —

2. כִּי עַם קָדוֹשׁ אַתָּה לַה׳ אֱלֹהֶיךָ — *For you are a holy people to Hashem, your God.* And your holiness does not cease at your death, "and Hashem has chosen you for Himself to be a treasured people." "For Himself" — just as He exists forever, so did He choose you to stand before Him not only in this world, but also in the Next World, eternally, "from among all the peoples" whose existence is only "on the face of the earth."

3. כָּל־תּוֹעֵבָה — *Any abomination.* It is well known that eating forbidden foods "clogs the heart," making it unreceptive to Torah; the *gaon* and *tzaddik* R' Chaim of Tzanz wrote that "entire Jewish communities have been virtually lost to the faith because of irresponsible, incompetent slaughterers. As the people filled their stomachs with *treifos*, foreign views took over their minds, and gradually they shed their religious principles and were lost to the holy nation." In the light of this testimony we can see why the Torah, after giving the laws of enticement to idolatry and the Wayward City, warns us against eating impure things, which brings in its wake foreign and even idolatrous thinking that can take entire communities away from our religion.

יד בַּבְּהֵמָה אֹתָהּ תֹּאכֵלוּ: ז אַךְ אֶת־זֶה לֹא תֹאכְלוּ מִמַּעֲלֵי
ז־יז הַגֵּרָה וּמִמַּפְרִיסֵי הַפַּרְסָה הַשְּׁסוּעָה אֶת־הַגָּמָל וְאֶת־
הָאַרְנֶבֶת וְאֶת־הַשָּׁפָן כִּי־מַעֲלֵה גֵרָה הֵמָּה וּפַרְסָה לֹא
הִפְרִיסוּ טְמֵאִים הֵם לָכֶם: ח וְאֶת־הַחֲזִיר כִּי־מַפְרִיס פַּרְסָה
הוּא וְלֹא גֵרָה טָמֵא הוּא לָכֶם מִבְּשָׂרָם לֹא תֹאכֵלוּ
וּבְנִבְלָתָם לֹא תִגָּעוּ: ט אֶת־זֶה תֹּאכְלוּ
מִכֹּל אֲשֶׁר בַּמָּיִם כֹּל אֲשֶׁר־לוֹ סְנַפִּיר וְקַשְׂקֶשֶׂת תֹּאכֵלוּ:
י וְכֹל אֲשֶׁר אֵין־לוֹ סְנַפִּיר וְקַשְׂקֶשֶׂת לֹא תֹאכֵלוּ טָמֵא הוּא
לָכֶם: יא כָּל־צִפּוֹר טְהֹרָה תֹּאכֵלוּ: יב וְזֶה
אֲשֶׁר לֹא־תֹאכְלוּ מֵהֶם הַנֶּשֶׁר וְהַפֶּרֶס וְהָעָזְנִיָּה: יג וְהָרָאָה
וְאֶת־הָאַיָּה וְהַדַּיָּה לְמִינָהּ: יד וְאֵת כָּל־עֹרֵב לְמִינוֹ:
טו וְאֵת בַּת הַיַּעֲנָה וְאֶת־הַתַּחְמָס וְאֶת־הַשָּׁחַף וְאֶת־הַנֵּץ
לְמִינֵהוּ: טז אֶת־הַכּוֹס וְאֶת־הַיַּנְשׁוּף וְהַתִּנְשָׁמֶת: יז וְהַקָּאָת

---

7. וּמִמַּפְרִיסֵי הַפַּרְסָה הַשְּׁסוּעָה — *Or have a completely separated split hoof.* A split hoof qualifies as a sign of a kosher animal only if the two parts of the hoof are completely separate from each other, as the preceding verse specified: "And every animal that has a split hoof, which is completely separated in two hooves . . ." Accordingly, our present verse says, "or have a completely separated split hoof"; that is, even if the hoof is completely separated, if the animal does not chew its cud, it is impure.

This is the simple meaning of the text. But *Chazal* derived an additional, hidden meaning: the Torah, they said, was speaking of an animal called the *shesuah*, whose back was divided into two; it had two spines, and it was impure. *HaKesav Ve'HaKabbalah* mentions that such a creature existed in his time. It had a deep furrow down its back, giving it the appearance of having two backs and two spines. It chewed its cud, and therefore it is very fitting that its name appears alongside those of the camel, the hare, and the hyrax, which chew their cud, but are impure because they lack a split hoof. For the *shesuah*, too, is lacking a split hoof, despite its name, which refers only to its oddly split back.

9. כֹּל אֲשֶׁר־לוֹ סְנַפִּיר וְקַשְׂקֶשֶׂת תֹּאכֵלוּ — *Anything that has fins or scales you may eat.* Signs of *kashrus* are given here, but no names of species. The *Pa'aneach Raza* asks, why did Scripture not list the forbidden or permitted fish, as it did with birds and beasts, instead of only mentioning signs of *kashrus*? The author answers his question by saying that God did not bring the fish to Adam to be named, as He did with the animals and birds. This matter of whether or not Adam named the fish is, however, left in doubt in the *Gemara* (see *Tosafos* ד"ה כל שיש לו, *Chullin* 66b).

In any case, if the Torah had wanted to list all the impure species of fish (so as to remove any doubt in the case of someone encountering a young fish that

among animals — it may you eat. 7 *But this shall you not*
eat from among those that bring up their cud or have a
completely separated split hoof: the camel, the hare, and
the hyrax, for they bring up their cud, but their hoof is not
split — they are unclean to you; 8 *and the pig, for it has a*
split hoof, but not the cud — it is unclean to you; from
their flesh you shall not eat and you shall not touch their
carcasses.

9 *This you may eat of everything that is in the water:*
anything that has fins or scales you may eat. 10 *And anything*
that does not have fins or scales you shall not eat; it is
unclean to you.

11 *Every clean bird, you may eat.* 12 *This is what you shall*
not eat from among them: the nesher, the peres, the ozniah;
13 *the raah, the ayah, and the dayah according to its kind;* 14
and every oreiv according to its kind; 15 *the bas haya'anah,*
the tachmos, the shachaf, and the netz, according to its
kind; 16 *the kos, the yanshuf, and the tinshemes;* 17 *the ka'as,*

---

has not yet grown its scales, or a fish that sheds its scales when it is taken from the water — for these fish are kosher), then the list would be some seven hundred items long. This would be a violation of the principle laid down in the *Gemara*: "A person should always teach his student in the shortest possible way" (*Chullin* 63).

13. וְהָרָאָה — *The raah*. This bird is named for the fact that it sees (רוֹאָה) exceedingly far. *Chazal* say that if it were standing in Babylonia it could see a carcass in the Land of Israel (*Chullin* 63b).

Why did the Holy One, Blessed be He, give such keen vision to an impure bird? In *Maskil LeDavid*, our holy teacher the *Ari* ז"ל is quoted as saying that if a man gazes at women forbidden to him he does harm to that aspect of Heaven which is congruent to man's eyes, and his punishment is that his soul returns to this world in the form of this bird, the *raah*. Indeed it seems a fitting punishment, for he gazed at women without committing any actual deed; he enjoyed just looking. And so it is with the *raah*, in which his soul has returned. It sees a "carcass" — something appetizing, but it is not close at hand, it is very far away, in another country. By the time it flies (דָאָה) there (a play on the word דַיָּה, one of the other names of this bird given in our verse; see *Rashi*), some other bird or animal has arrived there first. Then it asks, 'Where (אַיֵּה) is the carcass that I saw and flew to?' It remains hungry; it will have to be satisfied (דַיָּה) with just having seen it. *Chazal* hinted at this interpretation when they said, "The *daah*, the *raah*, the *dayah*, and the *ayah* are all one bird" (*Chullin*, loc. cit.), and all four names tell us something about the punishment suffered by the soul that has returned in this form.

יד וְאֶת־הָרָחָמָה וְאֶת־הַשָּׁלָךְ: יח וְהַחֲסִידָה וְהָאֲנָפָה לְמִינָהּ
יח־כב וְהַדּוּכִיפַת וְהָעֲטַלֵּף: יט וְכֹל שֶׁרֶץ הָעוֹף טָמֵא הוּא לָכֶם
לֹא יֵאָכֵלוּ: כ כָּל־עוֹף טָהוֹר תֹּאכֵלוּ: כא לֹא תֹאכְלוּ
כָל־נְבֵלָה לַגֵּר אֲשֶׁר־בִּשְׁעָרֶיךָ תִּתְּנֶנָּה וַאֲכָלָהּ אוֹ מָכֹר
לְנָכְרִי כִּי עַם קָדוֹשׁ אַתָּה לַיהוָה אֱלֹהֶיךָ לֹא־תְבַשֵּׁל
גְּדִי בַּחֲלֵב אִמּוֹ:
חמישי כב עַשֵּׂר תְּעַשֵּׂר אֵת כָּל־תְּבוּאַת זַרְעֶךָ הַיֹּצֵא

---

20. כָּל־עוֹף טָהוֹר תֹּאכֵלוּ — *Every clean bird [flying creature] may you eat.* This refers to the kosher species of locust, the signs of which are specified in *Parashas Shemini*. They are not in the category of the preceding verse: "And every flying swarming creature is unclean to you."

21. לַגֵּר . . . תִּתְּנֶנָּה . . . אוֹ מָכֹר לְנָכְרִי — *To the stranger. . . shall you give it. . . or sell it to a gentile.* Why does it say "that he may eat it" after the word "stranger," but not after the word "gentile"? Let us look at what the *Chasam Sofer* writes about this (*Responsa, Yoreh Deah* 19): "Seeing as the internal organs of an animal which became a *neveilah* during slaughtering are forbidden to gentiles, because of the prohibition of a limb taken from a living animal (see *Chullin* 33a and 114, and *Yoreh Deah* §27), one may certainly give such an animal to a *ger toshav*, even 'that he may eat it,' for he has taken upon himself to observe the seven Noahide laws, and he will not eat the internal organs [i.e., only the flesh]. But to a gentile one may sell the carcass without any particular purpose being mentioned, but not expressly for purposes of eating, since then we would definitely be putting a transgression in his way."

What, then, are we to make of the *Pri Chadash*, who states (*Yoreh Deah*, loc. cit., quoted in *Pischei Teshuvah*) that even if an animal becomes *neveilah* during slaughtering, one is permitted to sell the internal organs to a gentile? The *Chasam Sofer* himself writes that this is the prevailing custom, and goes to some pains to find *halachic* justification for the practice. But if the Torah says "that he may eat it" only of the stranger, teaching that we may not sell the animal to a gentile "that he may eat it," then how is it that we sell to gentiles?

The explanation offered by our teacher the *Chasam Sofer* ז"ל is actually not applicable in our times, when any gentile buying an animal's organs is presumably buying them for eating. We can find a good, simple explanation, though, by looking at the *Tosafos* on *Avodah Zarah* 20a, ד"ה ור' מאיר, where the following problem is raised: all the Sages agree that one must try to give the animal as a gift to a *ger toshav* before resorting to selling it to a gentile, either because of Scripture's phrasing or because they reason that one is commanded to help the *ger toshav* with his livelihood. The *Tosafos* expound: "Does this mean that if a person has something to sell, he should give it as a gift to a *ger toshav* rather than sell it to an idolatrous gentile? But even towards a fellow Jew we have no such obligation! We may explain the matter, however, by saying

14
18-22

the rachamah, and the shalach; 18 *the chasidah, and the*
anafah according to its kind, the duchifas and the atalef.
19 *And every flying swarming creature is unclean to you;*
they shall not be eaten. 20 *Every clean bird may you eat.*
21 *You shall not eat any carcass; to the stranger who is in your*
cities shall you give it that he may eat it, or sell it to a gentile,
for you are a holy people to HASHEM, your God; you shall not
cook a kid in its mother's milk.
22 *You shall tithe the entire crop of your planting, the*

---

this *mitzvah* applies specifically to a *neveilah*, since it was nearly worthless to a Jew, for idolatrous gentiles did not commonly live among Jews, but to the righteous stranger it is as valuable as any meat."

Along these lines, we can explain the verse beautifully. "To the stranger who is in your cities shall you give it that he may eat it" — in other words, the stranger will eat it like any other meat, and you will scarcely lose anything by it. And this is why the verse is phrased as it is, not saying, "or sell it to the gentile who is in your cities," for if there were idol-worshiping gentiles in the cities, then the *neveilah* would have a high market value, and in that case there would be no obligation to give it away for free to the *ger toshav*, since even towards a fellow Jew one is not obligated to give without payment.

22. עַשֵּׂר תְּעַשֵּׂר — *You shall tithe.* "Tithe (עַשֵּׂר) so that you will grow rich (תִּתְעַשֵּׁר)," say *Chazal* (*Taanis* 9a), learning this from the redoubled language in this verse. The idea is that you will actually grow rich, not only that others will say you are rich, for how do they know your true financial status? There may be many who say that about you already... but the point here is that you yourself will have no doubt that you have become rich. This is stated outright in *Malachi* 3:10: "Bring all the tithes to the treasure-house, that there may be food in My house... and pray test Me in this matter, if I will not open to you the windows of Heaven and empty out upon you never-ending blessing" From the language of the verse *Chazal* derived the meaning, "until your lips wear out from saying 'Enough!'" (*Shabbos* 32b); that is, until you see for yourselves what extraordinary blessing has come to you.

This is true wealth, as *Chazal* said, "Who is rich? He who rejoices in his portion" (*Avos* 4:1) — for one who has not come to this level will never say "Enough!", and "he who has one hundred dinars wants two hundred". It is this that we ask of God when we say, "You open Your hand, and satisfy the desire of every living thing" (*Tehillim* 145:16). For it is impossible to satisfy man's eye with silver and gold — even in the grave, shards are placed over the eyes, which never knew satiety — therefore we ask that our *desire* be satisfied, that we should be happy with our portion, truly and honestly rich.

⁂ "Tithe so that you will grow rich." The Sages taught that the Holy One, Blessed be He, leaves the portion of the poor on deposit with the rich. (See

הַשָּׂדֶה שָׁנָה שָׁנָה: כג וְאָכַלְתָּ לִפְנֵי | יהוה אֱלֹהֶיךָ בַּמָּקוֹם יד
אֲשֶׁר־יִבְחַר לְשַׁכֵּן שְׁמוֹ שָׁם מַעְשַׂר דְּגָנְךָ תִּירֹשְׁךָ וְיִצְהָרֶךָ כג

HaDe'ah Ve'HaDibbur, II:9, for an explanation of this.) The rich man then supports the poor by giving them their portion which was deposited with him.

A verse in *Parashas Mishpatim* (*Shemos* 22:24), which we explained in its place, says, "When you lend money" — without interest; and if you should ask why you should lend money to a poor man when it is likely that he will not repay before the *shemittah* year, when debts are cancelled, the reason is that he is "the poor person who is *with you*." His portion was deposited with you, and you are the one who must return it to him.

Now, if a man is honest, and returns people's deposits to them "on the first request," then many people will deposit their money with him. So it is with the rich man and the poor man. If the rich man gives the poor man his deposit on the first request, then God's Providence will see to it that more money is deposited with him, since he is honest. "Tithe" for the Levite, the orphan, and the widow; give them their rightful share "so that you will grow rich" — in heaven it will be arranged that many more "deposits" come your way. You will gain the *mitzvah* of *tzedakah*, for you are doing no more than what is just, as the name *tzedakah* implies, by giving each man his own deposit, and "the reward for a *mitzvah* is a *mitzvah*" (*Avos* 4:2). God will give you wealth with which to continue doing kindness and *tzedakah*, for your benefit in this world and the next.

הַיֹּצֵא הַשָּׂדֶה — *The produce of the field* [lit., "the goer forth of the field"]. The normal Hebrew expression would be הַיֹּצֵא מִן הַשָּׂדֶה, "that goes forth *from* the field." The change in wording here can be understood in accordance with the *Tanchuma's* exposition of the verse "Keep, my son, your father's commandment" (*Mishlei* 6:20): "R' Huna says, 'The Patriarchs separated tithes. . . Isaac separated the Second Tithe, as the Torah says: "Isaac sowed. . . and. . . he reaped a hundredfold; thus had Hashem blessed him." (*Bereishis* 26:12) Now, we know that blessing is not found in what is measured, but Isaac measured only in order to separate the tithe.'"

How did R' Huna know that the tithe Isaac took was the Second Tithe? He learned it from the Torah's language: "thus had Hashem blessed him," for out of all the tithes mentioned in the Torah, blessing is specifically mentioned only in connection with the Second Tithe. And where did Isaac eat the Second Tithe? "Before Hashem," in the fixed spot he had chosen for prayer — "Isaac went forth to supplicate in the field" (*Bereishis* 24:63).

Thus we find that in our verse the Torah uses peculiar syntax as an allusion to our father Isaac: "You shall tithe the entire crop of your planting" — as did Isaac, "the goer forth of the field . . . And you shall eat it before Hashem, your God, in the place that He will choose" — as your father Isaac did when he "went forth to . . . the field" to eat the Second Tithe in the spot he had chosen for prayer. And may He Who blessed the Patriarchs bless the children, and may you, too, reap a hundredfold.

14 *produce of the field, year by year.* [23] *And you shall eat it be-*
23 *fore* HASHEM*, your God, in the place that He will choose to rest*
His Name — the tithe of your grain, your wine, and your oil,

---

23. **וְאָכַלְתָּ לִפְנֵי ה׳ אֱלֹהֶיךָ בַּמָּקוֹם אֲשֶׁר־יִבְחַר** — *And you shall eat it before Hashem, your God, in the place that He will choose.* Evidently Scripture is speaking of the Second Tithe in these verses, for in speaking of the First Tithe the Torah said, "You may eat it everywhere" (*Bamidbar* 18:31). But it is difficult to understand, when Second Tithe is consumed by its owners, why does the Torah declare its blessing principally for separating this tithe, and not for separating the First Tithe, which is given to the Levites?

To answer this, we must first understand that the Levites receive their tithe for two reasons. First is that they have no portion of their own in the Land to support themselves, so the tithe, part of the produce of each Israelite, is their portion. Second, it is given them as compensation for their service in the Tabernacle. These two reasons complement each other, for since each Israelite holds the Levite's portion within his own, it is his duty to give it to him, just as a sharecropper gives part of his crops to the landowner. Nor may the 'sharecropper' deduct something from the tithe for his work in the field, since the Levite can set against that the work that he does on behalf of all Israel in the Tabernacle. Certainly, then, there is no reason to promise a blessing to the Israelite for separating the First Tithe, since he is merely settling a debt.

This is not the case with the Second Tithe, which, although it is separated for the purpose of being consumed by the owner, is transported to Jerusalem and eaten there before God. It is eaten not for its own sake, but "so that you will learn to fear Hashem, your God, all the days" (even after you return home). When one eats before God and in fear of Him, one does not eat alone, but invites the poor, the proselyte, the orphan, the widow, and the Levite (who has no Second Tithe).

Thus one does for the first two years of the *shemittah* cycle; in the third year the Second Tithe is replaced by the Tithe of the Poor. The next three years are a repetition of the first three: in the fourth and fifth years, one eats his Second Tithe in Jerusalem; in the sixth year, he gives this tithe to the poor. The seventh year is the *shemittah* year, when all the crops are declared ownerless, and after that the cycle begins anew.

All of this can be very hard for the farmer, who leaves behind in his field the required gifts for the poor every year: gleanings, forgotten sheaves, the 'corner,' fallen fruits, and undeveloped grape clusters. No poor person who approaches his house goes away empty-handed, as it is said, "Let not the poor come back ashamed" (*Tehillim* 74:21). Yet besides all this, two years out of every seven he must also give one-tenth of his produce to the poor. If there is only one poor person in his area, that one person receives the entire tithe.

This is why a Jew must go to Jerusalem for two years straight to eat his Second Tithe — "so that you will learn to fear Hashem, your God" — so that he will have the strength to give the tithe away in the third year, in addition to the five regular gifts left in the field for the poor. And this is why God placed

יד וּבְכֹרֹ֥ת בְּקָרְךָ֖ וְצֹאנֶ֑ךָ לְמַ֣עַן תִּלְמַ֗ד לְיִרְאָ֛ה אֶת־יְהוָ֥ה
כד־כט אֱלֹהֶ֖יךָ כָּל־הַיָּמִֽים׃ כד וְכִֽי־יִרְבֶּ֨ה מִמְּךָ֜ הַדֶּ֗רֶךְ כִּ֣י לֹ֮א
תוּכַל֮ שְׂאֵתוֹ֒ כִּֽי־יִרְחַ֤ק מִמְּךָ֙ הַמָּק֔וֹם אֲשֶׁ֤ר יִבְחַר֙ יְהוָ֣ה
אֱלֹהֶ֔יךָ לָשׂ֥וּם שְׁמ֖וֹ שָׁ֑ם כִּ֥י יְבָרֶכְךָ֖ יְהוָ֥ה אֱלֹהֶֽיךָ׃ כה וְנָתַתָּ֖ה
בַּכָּ֑סֶף וְצַרְתָּ֤ הַכֶּ֙סֶף֙ בְּיָ֣דְךָ֔ וְהָלַכְתָּ֙ אֶל־הַמָּק֔וֹם אֲשֶׁ֥ר
יִבְחַ֛ר יְהוָ֥ה אֱלֹהֶ֖יךָ בּֽוֹ׃ כו וְנָתַתָּ֣ה הַכֶּ֡סֶף בְּכֹל֩ אֲשֶׁר־תְּאַוֶּ֨ה
נַפְשְׁךָ֜ בַּבָּקָ֣ר וּבַצֹּ֗אן וּבַיַּ֙יִן֙ וּבַשֵּׁכָ֔ר וּבְכֹ֛ל אֲשֶׁ֥ר תִּֽשְׁאָלְךָ֖
נַפְשֶׁ֑ךָ וְאָכַ֣לְתָּ שָּׁ֗ם לִפְנֵי֙ יְהוָ֣ה אֱלֹהֶ֔יךָ וְשָׂמַחְתָּ֖ אַתָּ֥ה
וּבֵיתֶֽךָ׃ כז וְהַלֵּוִ֥י אֲשֶׁר־בִּשְׁעָרֶ֖יךָ לֹ֣א תַעַזְבֶ֑נּוּ כִּ֣י אֵ֥ין ל֛וֹ
חֵ֥לֶק וְנַחֲלָ֖ה עִמָּֽךְ׃ כח מִקְצֵ֣ה ׀ שָׁלֹ֣שׁ
שָׁנִ֗ים תּוֹצִיא֙ אֶת־כָּל־מַעְשַׂר֙ תְּבוּאָ֣תְךָ֔ בַּשָּׁנָ֖ה הַהִ֑וא
וְהִנַּחְתָּ֖ בִּשְׁעָרֶֽיךָ׃ כט וּבָ֣א הַלֵּוִ֡י כִּ֣י אֵֽין־ל֩וֹ֩ חֵ֨לֶק וְנַחֲלָ֜ה
עִמָּ֗ךְ וְהַגֵּ֨ר וְהַיָּת֤וֹם וְהָֽאַלְמָנָה֙ אֲשֶׁ֣ר בִּשְׁעָרֶ֔יךָ וְאָכְל֖וּ וְשָׂבֵ֑עוּ
לְמַ֤עַן יְבָרֶכְךָ֙ יְהוָ֣ה אֱלֹהֶ֔יךָ בְּכָל־מַעֲשֵׂ֥ה יָדְךָ֖ אֲשֶׁ֥ר
טו תַּעֲשֶֽׂה׃ ששי א מִקֵּ֥ץ שֶֽׁבַע־שָׁנִ֖ים תַּעֲשֶׂ֥ה
א־ב שְׁמִטָּֽה׃ ב וְזֶה֮ דְּבַ֣ר הַשְּׁמִטָּה֒ שָׁמ֗וֹט כָּל־בַּ֙עַל֙ מַשֵּׁ֣ה יָד֔וֹ
אֲשֶׁ֥ר יַשֶּׁ֖ה בְּרֵעֵ֑הוּ לֹֽא־יִגֹּ֤שׂ אֶת־רֵעֵ֙הוּ֙ וְאֶת־אָחִ֔יו כִּֽי־קָרָ֥א

---

a blessing in His Torah in the passage concerning the Second Tithe and the Tithe of the Poor: "in order that Hashem, your God, will bless you" with the blessing of "tithe so that you will grow rich."

27. וְהַלֵּוִי אֲשֶׁר־בִּשְׁעָרֶיךָ לֹא תַעַזְבֶנּוּ — *You shall not forsake the Levite who is in your cities.* The Levite has no "portion or inheritance," and of course no Second Tithe. The Torah therefore admonishes the landowner not to leave him without sustenance when he goes to Jerusalem, but to take him along and invite him to the table. Some commentators, however, say that this verse refers to the First Tithe.

15.

2. וְזֶה דְּבַר הַשְּׁמִטָּה — *And this is the matter of the remission* [lit., "the word of the *shemittah*"]. This is the matter of remission of debts, which I am adding, says God, to what was said of the Sabbatical year in *Parashas Behar*.

Chazal derived from the language of our verse that when someone wishes to repay a debt during the seventh year, the lender must say to him, "מְשַׁמֵּט אֲנִי, I have let it go" (i.e., he must say "the word of the *shemittah*, the remission"), but if the borrower replies, "Nonetheless" (I offer it to you as a gift), he may accept it; it is sufficient that he has said "the word of the *shemittah*."

14 *and the firstborn of your cattle and your flocks, so that you*
24-29 *will learn to fear* HASHEM, *your God, all the days.* [24] *If the road*
will be too long for you, so that you cannot carry it, because
the place that HASHEM, *your God, will choose to place His*
Name there is far from you, for HASHEM, *your God, will have*
blessed you — [25] *then you may exchange it for money, wrap*
up the money in your hand, and go to the place that HASHEM,
your God, will choose. [26] *You may spend the money for what-*
ever your heart desires — for cattle, for flocks, for wine, or for
alcoholic beverage, or anything that your soul wishes; you
shall eat it there before HASHEM, *your God, and rejoice — you*
and your household. [27] *You shall not forsake the Levite who is*
in your cities, for he has no portion or inheritance with you.
[28] *At the end of three years you shall take out every tithe of*
your crop in that year and set it down within your cities.
[29] *Then the Levite can come — for he has no portion or*
inheritance with you — and the proselyte, the orphan, and the
widow who are in your cities, so they may eat and be
satisfied, in order that HASHEM, *your God, will bless you in all*
your handiwork that you may undertake.
15 [1]*At the end of seven years you shall institute a remission.*
1-2 [2] *This is the matter of the remission: Every creditor shall*
remit his authority over what he has lent his fellow; he shall
not press his fellow or his brother, for He has proclaimed

---

§ לֹא־יִגֹּשׂ אֶת־רֵעֵהוּ וְאֶת־אָחִיו — *He shall not press his fellow or his brother.* It seems fitting to offer an explanation for the question of why the remission of debts was not mentioned along with the rest of the laws of the Sabbatical year in *Parashas Behar*. And why is the time of remission of debts at the end of the Sabbatical year, rather than at its beginning like all the other prohibitions of that year?

Those who observe the *shemittah* are called "strong heroes who do His word" (*Tehillim* 103:20; *Vayikra Rabbah* §1), because *shemittah* is the most difficult commandment in the Torah. Though the Children of Israel are able to refrain from their labors and their business one day a week (unfortunately there are Jews who find even this too difficult), it is hard to do so for a full week, and how much harder it would be for a month! And who ever heard of a commandment like this, that requires an entire people to be idle from their labor and neglect their livelihood for a full year?

Because this commandment is so difficult, the Torah introduces the concept gradually to the Children of Israel. It begins by saying merely, "When you come into the Land... the land shall observe a Sabbath rest for Hashem. For six years you may sow your field... you may gather in its crop" (*Vayikra* 25:2-3) — words which are easily accepted. Only then does the Torah begin to describe

טו שְׁמִטָּה לַיהוָה: ג אֶת־הַנָּכְרִי תִּגֹּשׂ וַאֲשֶׁר יִהְיֶה לְךָ אֶת־
ג־ז אָחִיךָ תַּשְׁמֵט יָדֶךָ: ד אֶפֶס כִּי לֹא יִהְיֶה־בְּךָ אֶבְיוֹן כִּי־בָרֵךְ
יְבָרֶכְךָ יהוה בָּאָרֶץ אֲשֶׁר יהוה אֱלֹהֶיךָ נֹתֵן־לְךָ נַחֲלָה
לְרִשְׁתָּהּ: ה רַק אִם־שָׁמוֹעַ תִּשְׁמַע בְּקוֹל יהוה אֱלֹהֶיךָ
לִשְׁמֹר לַעֲשׂוֹת אֶת־כָּל־הַמִּצְוָה הַזֹּאת אֲשֶׁר אָנֹכִי מְצַוְּךָ
הַיּוֹם: ו כִּי־יהוה אֱלֹהֶיךָ בֵּרַכְךָ כַּאֲשֶׁר דִּבֶּר־לָךְ וְהַעֲבַטְתָּ
גּוֹיִם רַבִּים וְאַתָּה לֹא תַעֲבֹט וּמָשַׁלְתָּ בְּגוֹיִם רַבִּים וּבְךָ לֹא
יִמְשֹׁלוּ: ז כִּי־יִהְיֶה בְךָ אֶבְיוֹן מֵאַחַד אַחֶיךָ
בְּאַחַד שְׁעָרֶיךָ בְּאַרְצְךָ אֲשֶׁר־יהוה אֱלֹהֶיךָ נֹתֵן לָךְ לֹא
תְאַמֵּץ אֶת־לְבָבְךָ וְלֹא תִקְפֹּץ אֶת־יָדְךָ מֵאָחִיךָ הָאֶבְיוֹן:

(v. 4) "the Sabbath of the Land": "your field you shall not sow and your vineyard you shall not prune" (after all, many people like to sit idle). When the Scripture comes to "The aftergrowth of your harvest you shall not reap and the grapes you had set aside for yourself you shall not pick," (v. 5) it immediately adds, "The Sabbath produce of the land shall be yours to eat, for you, for your slave, and for your maidservant; and for your laborer and for your resident who dwell with you. And for your animal and for the beast. . ." In other words, the landowner, his family, and his servants are permitted to eat of the produce, as well as "the destitute of your people." The listener is comforted a little, especially after he hears the promise, "I will ordain a blessing for you in the sixth year and it will yield a crop sufficient for the three-year period" (*Vayikra* 25:21). But the hardest blow is saved for last, when he hears that all the debts owed to him from his brothers and neighbors are lost; he must release them. Human nature makes this thing harder for him than all the other laws of the seventh year (as the *Abarbanel* points out). It is not so much the monetary loss that troubles him as the fact that the money with which he did such a favor for his friend. . . is going to remain with his friend.

To understand this, think of a butcher who has just left the Rabbi's house after being told that the animal in question was not kosher. People will ask why he is not angry at the Rabbi and burning for revenge, as a litigant so often is after losing a case; for after all, the Rabbi has caused him a monetary loss by his decision. But they answer their own question, saying that the butcher can take comfort in knowing that at least no one else gained from his loss, whereas the litigant who "loses his money" through the Rabbi's "injustice" must suffer the additional pain of seeing it go into the other man's pocket, which is worse than the loss of the money itself.

Thus it is with the laws of *shemittah*. While the landowner's fields lie fallow, no one else is benefitting from them, either; on the contrary, next year they will produce crops for him again. As for his vineyard and his orchard, though they are open to all comers, each one takes only what he needs for immediate consumption, and he and his family are doing the same. But here he has done

a remission for HASHEM. 3 *You may press the gentile; but*
over what you have with your brother, you shall remit
your authority. 4 *However, may there be no destitute among*
you; rather HASHEM, *will surely bless you in the Land*
that HASHEM, *your God, will give you as an inheritance,*
to possess it, 5 *only if you will hearken to the voice of* HASHEM,
your God, to observe, to perform this entire commandment
that I command you today. 6 *For* HASHEM, *your God, has*
blessed you as He has told you; you will lend to many
nations, but you will not borrow; and you will dominate
many nations, but they will not dominate you.
7 *If there shall be a destitute person among you, any*
of your brethren in any of your cities, in the Land that
HASHEM, *your God, gives you, you shall not harden your*
heart or close your hand against your destitute brother.

---

a big favor for his friend by lending him a substantial sum of money in his time of need. His friend has done very well for himself with that money, and now, with the Torah's permission, he is exempt from repaying the debt, whereas he, the lender, is not allowed to press him for it, "for He has proclaimed a remission for Hashem." This, the hardest thing of all for a person to accept (concerning which the Torah goes on to admonish, "Beware lest there be a lawless thought in your heart. . ." v. 9), was not said with the other laws in *Parashas Behar*, but was "put off" until Moses' recapitulation of the Torah. Furthermore, the performance of this law is put off until the last day of the Sabbatical year, until the time when he can take comfort in the fact that in just a short while his fields and vineyard will again be absolutely his own.

6. **כִּי־ה׳ אֱלֹהֶיךָ בֵּרַכְךָ כַּאֲשֶׁר דִּבֶּר־לָךְ** — *For Hashem, your God, has blessed you as He has told you.* "And where did He tell you? [When He said,] 'Blessed shall you be in the city'"(*Rashi*). Why did *Rashi* seize upon this particular blessing? Perhaps we may explain it thus: God gives a person certain side benefits in this world according to the quality of his deeds; as a reward for separating *terumah* and tithes, his fields are blessed: "Blessed shall you be in the field." As a reward for remission of debts and giving charity, his business ventures in the city are blessed ("Hashem, your God, will bless you in all your deeds and in your every undertaking" [v. 10]). Therefore *Rashi* defines "blessed you as He has told you," which refers to the reward for remitting debts, as "Blessed shall you be *in the city.*"

7. **לֹא תְאַמֵּץ אֶת־לְבָבְךָ וְלֹא תִקְפֹּץ אֶת־יָדְךָ** — *You shall not harden your heart or close your hand.* "Charity is collected by two" (*Bava Basra* 8b). Although this statement literally means that two men should go around together to collect charity, we may also read it as an allusion to the two parts of a person that must work together to give charity: the hand and the heart. The heart sees the

ח כִּי־פָתֹחַ תִּפְתַּח אֶת־יָדְךָ לוֹ וְהַעֲבֵט תַּעֲבִיטֶנּוּ דֵּי **טו**
מַחְסֹרוֹ אֲשֶׁר יֶחְסַר לוֹ׃ ט הִשָּׁמֶר לְךָ פֶּן־יִהְיֶה דָבָר ח־יב
עִם־לְבָבְךָ בְלִיַּעַל לֵאמֹר קָרְבָה שְׁנַת־הַשֶּׁבַע שְׁנַת
הַשְּׁמִטָּה וְרָעָה עֵינְךָ בְּאָחִיךָ הָאֶבְיוֹן וְלֹא תִתֵּן לוֹ וְקָרָא
עָלֶיךָ אֶל־יהוֹה וְהָיָה בְךָ חֵטְא׃ י נָתוֹן תִּתֵּן לוֹ וְלֹא־יֵרַע
לְבָבְךָ בְּתִתְּךָ לוֹ כִּי בִּגְלַל ׀ הַדָּבָר הַזֶּה יְבָרֶכְךָ יהוָה אֱלֹהֶיךָ
בְּכָל־מַעֲשֶׂךָ וּבְכֹל מִשְׁלַח יָדֶךָ׃ יא כִּי לֹא־יֶחְדַּל אֶבְיוֹן
מִקֶּרֶב הָאָרֶץ עַל־כֵּן אָנֹכִי מְצַוְּךָ לֵאמֹר פָּתֹחַ תִּפְתַּח אֶת־
יָדְךָ לְאָחִיךָ לַעֲנִיֶּךָ וּלְאֶבְיֹנְךָ בְּאַרְצֶךָ׃ יב כִּי־
יִמָּכֵר לְךָ אָחִיךָ הָעִבְרִי אוֹ הָעִבְרִיָּה וַעֲבָדְךָ שֵׁשׁ שָׁנִים

---

condition of the poor and feels pity, but while we are trying to figure out what can be done for their relief, the heart turns from flesh to stone. Therefore the Torah warns, "You shall not harden your heart." We confess this sin on Yom Kippur when we say, "for the sin we have committed before You by hardening the heart." (The *Iyun Tefillah* explains that this refers to letting avarice get the upper hand over generosity.)

Even if the heart remains generous, however, the hand (the "cashier" within a person) also has something to say in the matter, and sometimes a person finds it hard to make his hand give what his heart wants to offer. Therefore the Torah warns, "you shall not... close your hand." The matter may be compared to a judge and a bailiff. One would suppose that the bailiff is obligated to use his stick and his whip to enforce the judge's decision, but in reality he is permitted to wield these tools leniently or harshly, as he sees fit. The Torah says of them, both the judge and the bailiff, "They shall judge the people with righteous judgment" (16:18), for each one of them has the power to pervert or obstruct the law. So it is with the heart and the hand; whether or not a person does charity and kindness depends on both of them, and so the warning comes to them both.

9. וְרָעָה עֵינְךָ בְּאָחִיךָ הָאֶבְיוֹן וְלֹא תִתֵּן לוֹ — *And you will look malevolently upon your destitute brother and refuse to give him.* Why does the verse not simply say, "and you will refuse to give him"? What purpose is served by this lengthy phrasing?

The answer is that this is the way of the miser. In order to justify his own meanness, he accuses the poor man who stands before him of fraud; he says that he has money of his own but wants to live off of others, or that he is young and strong and could earn a living by working if he weren't so lazy, and so on and so forth. The miser will paint a false picture of his destitute brother, even though he knows perfectly well that his brother does not have enough to live on: "and you will look malevolently upon your destitute brother" (i.e., whom you know to be destitute). This is the kind of person King David meant when he said, "You dispatched your mouth for evil, and your tongue adheres to deceit. You sit and

*8 Rather, you shall open your hand to him; you shall lend him
his requirement, whatever is lacking to him. 9 Beware lest
there be a lawless thought in your heart, saying, "The
seventh year approaches, the remission year," and you will
look malevolently upon your destitute brother and refuse to
give him — then he may appeal against you to HASHEM, and
it will be a sin upon you. 10 You shall surely give him, and let
your heart not feel bad when you give him, for in return for
this matter, HASHEM, your God, will bless you in all your
deeds and in your every undertaking. 11 For destitute people
will not cease to exist within the Land; therefore I command
you, saying, "You shall surely open your hand to your
brother, to your poor, and to your destitute in your Land."*
*12 If your brother, a Hebrew man or a Hebrew woman,
will be sold to you, he shall serve you for six years,*

---

speak against your brother..." (*Tehillim* 50:19-20). "And you... refuse to give him," although you know his condition.

10. כִּי בִּגְלַל הַדָּבָר הַזֶּה — *For in return for this matter.* From the word בִּגְלַל in this verse, the *Sifre* derives that "[affluence] is a wheel (גַּלְגַּל) that revolves through the world."

I once saw an instructive parable to explain this point: There was once a man who made his living filling the orders of local storekeepers, bringing them merchandise from the big city in his wagon. One time before Pesach, when the snows were melting and the roads muddy, this supplier found himself in a predicament. His horse was tired, and his wagon was sinking in the mud. He could not possibly reach his home town in time for the holiday unless he lightened his horse's burden by unloading half of the merchandise and leaving it by the roadside. But if he did that, the storekeepers, his steady customers, would be furious with him for not bringing the full amount of merchandise they had ordered for the holiday. How could he face them? Then he had an idea: his wagon's wheels, with the many layers of mud they had picked up, were even heavier than half of his merchandise. If he were to remove them, then his horse would easily be able to bear the weight, and they could race home in good time for the holiday! The man lost no time removing the wheels ... and to his chagrin he found that without them, the poor horse could not pull the wagon even one inch!

So it is with giving charity. When a man sees that his income is limited, he decides that he must not cut back on food, nor on finery for his wife and daughters, but rather on charity. But the Torah hints that charity and acts of kindness are the "wheels" that keep the "wagon" of his income running. "For in return for (בִּגְלַל) this matter" there is a blessing "in all your deeds and in your every undertaking"; but if you "remove your wheels," then your "wagon" will not budge. And so *Chazal* said: "If a man sees that his livelihood is scanty, he should give *tzedakah* with it ... he will not see the signs of poverty again" (*Gittin* 7b).

וּבַשָּׁנָה֙ הַשְּׁבִיעִ֔ת תְּשַׁלְּחֶ֥נּוּ חָפְשִׁ֖י מֵעִמָּ֑ךְ: יג וְכִי־תְשַׁלְּחֶ֤נּוּ חָפְשִׁי֙ מֵעִמָּ֔ךְ לֹ֥א תְשַׁלְּחֶ֖נּוּ רֵיקָֽם: יד הַעֲנֵ֤יק תַּעֲנִיק֙ ל֔וֹ מִצֹּ֣אנְךָ֔ וּמִֽגָּרְנְךָ֖ וּמִיִּקְבֶ֑ךָ אֲשֶׁ֧ר בֵּֽרַכְךָ֛ יהו֥ה אֱלֹהֶ֖יךָ תִּתֶּן־לֽוֹ: טו וְזָ֣כַרְתָּ֗ כִּ֣י עֶ֤בֶד הָיִ֙יתָ֙ בְּאֶ֣רֶץ מִצְרַ֔יִם וַֽיִּפְדְּךָ֖ יהו֣ה אֱלֹהֶ֑יךָ עַל־כֵּ֞ן אָֽנֹכִ֧י מְצַוְּךָ֛ אֶת־הַדָּבָ֥ר הַזֶּ֖ה הַיּֽוֹם: טז וְהָיָה֙ כִּֽי־יֹאמַ֣ר אֵלֶ֔יךָ לֹ֥א אֵצֵ֖א מֵֽעִמָּ֑ךְ כִּ֤י אֲהֵֽבְךָ֙ וְאֶת־בֵּיתֶ֔ךָ כִּי־ט֥וֹב ל֖וֹ עִמָּֽךְ: יז וְלָֽקַחְתָּ֣ אֶת־הַמַּרְצֵ֗עַ וְנָֽתַתָּ֤ה בְאָזְנוֹ֙ וּבַדֶּ֔לֶת וְהָיָ֥ה לְךָ֖ עֶ֣בֶד עוֹלָ֑ם וְאַ֥ף לַֽאֲמָֽתְךָ֖ תַּֽעֲשֶׂה־כֵּֽן: יח לֹֽא־יִקְשֶׁ֣ה בְעֵינֶ֗ךָ בְּשַׁלֵּֽחֲךָ֙ אֹת֤וֹ חָפְשִׁי֙ מֵֽעִמָּ֔ךְ כִּ֗י מִשְׁנֶה֙ שְׂכַ֣ר שָׂכִ֔יר עֲבָֽדְךָ֖ שֵׁ֣שׁ שָׁנִ֑ים וּבֵֽרַכְךָ֙ יהו֣ה אֱלֹהֶ֔יךָ בְּכֹ֖ל אֲשֶׁ֥ר תַּֽעֲשֶֽׂה:

14. הַעֲנֵיק תַּעֲנִיק לוֹ — *Adorn him generously.* The bondsman has been living for six years in the house of his master, who has supported him and his wife and children (*Kiddushin* 22a); if the master sends him away now empty-handed, where will he go and how will he make a living? The Torah does not want him to be forced, for lack of an alternative, into saying, "I love my master and do not wish to leave" if that is not really true, for then he would remain in servitude until the next *Yovel* year. Therefore the Torah commands the master to give the bondsman at least thirty silver shekels (a considerable sum) upon his release.

Anyone buying a Hebrew bondsman, in that case, would take into account that he must give him this sum at the end of his service, and deduct it from the price he pays. This works out well for both of them: the servant will have something with which to start a new life upon his departure from the master's house, and the master, who does not yet know how good a servant he is buying or whether he might run away, will feel better knowing that he has given only a partial payment, holding the rest in reserve to be given when the servant goes free. (There is, however, another opinion that this payment is not part of the servant's compensation, but a charitable gift. See *Mishneh LaMelech* on *Hil. Avadim* ch. 3)

15. וַיִּפְדְּךָ ה' אֱלֹהֶיךָ עַל־כֵּן אָנֹכִי מְצַוְּךָ אֶת־הַדָּבָר הַזֶּה הַיּוֹם — *And Hashem, your God, redeemed you; therefore I command you regarding this matter today.* That is, that you set your Hebrew bondsman free in the seventh year and give him a monetary grant. For if you should be unwilling to do so, you had better remember what God did to Pharaoh when he refused to let Israel go although the time that God had allotted for their servitude was over. God struck Pharaoh with ten plagues, and took Israel away from him with a strong hand; then He took monetary payment from the Egyptians for the Jews (in the form of the gold, silver, and expensive articles that the Jews took out of Egypt with them). He further exacted a second "grant" from them at the Sea of Reeds (where the Jews took the spoils washed up by the waters).

15 *and in the seventh year you shall send him away from you*
13-18 *free.* 13 *But when you send him away free, you shall not*
send him away empty-handed. 14 *Adorn him generously*
from your flocks, from your threshing floor, and from your
wine-cellar; as HASHEM, your God, has blessed you, so
shall you give him. 15 *You shall remember that you were a*
slave in the land of Egypt, and HASHEM, your God, redeem-
ed you; therefore, I command you regarding this matter
today.
16 *In the event he will say to you, "I will not leave you," for*
he loves you and your household, for it is good for him with
you, 17 *then you shall take the awl and put it through his ear*
and the door, and he shall be for you an eternal slave; even to
your maidservant shall you do the same. 18 *It shall not be*
difficult in your eyes when you send him away free from
you, for twice as much as a hired hand — six years — has he
served you; and HASHEM, your God, will bless you in all that
you do.

From this you should understand that you must let the bondsman go free after his allotted six years of service, and also give him a grant of your own good will, for otherwise God has many other ways of freeing him and taking the payment from you. As Jeremiah prophesied: "You did not heed Me, to declare freedom each man for his brother... Behold, I declare freedom for you — to the sword, to plague, and to famine" (*Yirmiyah* 34:17). "Therefore I command you regarding this matter today" — before Jeremiah's prophecy comes true, do this of your own good will and bring a blessing upon yourself.

16. וְהָיָה כִּי־יֹאמַר אֵלֶיךָ — *In the event he will say to you.* When the Torah says וְהָיָה, it always connotes something joyful. It is a joyous occasion for you to have your servant testify that you treat him so well that he sometimes feels as if he were the master of the house. Not only does he receive food and drink of the same quality enjoyed by you, but if you happen to have only one cushion in the house, he sleeps on it while you sleep on straw. And why is this? Because the verse says, "it is good for him with you." *Chazal* explain that this implies certain obligations on the master's part toward the servant: his living conditions must be as good as yours.

This is all very well, but does the servant deserve *better* living conditions than the master? If there is only one cushion, why couldn't master and servant both sleep on straw? Because that would be adopting the pathological selfishness of Sodom, where "what's mine is mine" was the ruling principle. So if you may not use the cushion because you don't have another one for your servant, then why not let him use it? (*Tosafos, Kiddushin* 20a, ד״ה כל quoting the *Yerushalmi*) This is why *Chazal* said, "Whoever buys a Hebrew bondsman is as if he is buying himself a master" (*Kiddushin,* loc. cit.).

טו שביעי יט כָּל־הַבְּכוֹר אֲשֶׁר יִוָּלֵד בִּבְקָרְךָ וּבְצֹאנְךָ הַזָּכָר
יט־כג תַּקְדִּישׁ לַיהוָה אֱלֹהֶיךָ לֹא תַעֲבֹד בִּבְכֹר שׁוֹרֶךָ וְלֹא תָגֹז
בְּכוֹר צֹאנֶךָ: כ לִפְנֵי יהוה אֱלֹהֶיךָ תֹאכְלֶנּוּ שָׁנָה בְשָׁנָה
בַּמָּקוֹם אֲשֶׁר־יִבְחַר יהוה אַתָּה וּבֵיתֶךָ: כא וְכִי־יִהְיֶה בוֹ
מוּם פִּסֵּחַ אוֹ עִוֵּר כֹּל מוּם רָע לֹא תִזְבָּחֶנּוּ לַיהוָה אֱלֹהֶיךָ:
כב בִּשְׁעָרֶיךָ תֹּאכְלֶנּוּ הַטָּמֵא וְהַטָּהוֹר יַחְדָּו כַּצְּבִי וְכָאַיָּל:
כג רַק אֶת־דָּמוֹ לֹא תֹאכֵל עַל־הָאָרֶץ תִּשְׁפְּכֶנּוּ כַּמָּיִם:
טז א שָׁמוֹר אֶת־חֹדֶשׁ הָאָבִיב וְעָשִׂיתָ פֶּסַח לַיהוָה אֱלֹהֶיךָ
א־ב כִּי בְּחֹדֶשׁ הָאָבִיב הוֹצִיאֲךָ יהוה אֱלֹהֶיךָ מִמִּצְרַיִם
לָיְלָה: ב וְזָבַחְתָּ פֶּסַח לַיהוָה אֱלֹהֶיךָ צֹאן וּבָקָר בַּמָּקוֹם

---

19. כָּל־הַבְּכוֹר . . . תַּקְדִּישׁ לַה׳ אֱלֹהֶיךָ — *Every first-born . . . you shall sanctify to Hashem, your God.* Although the firstborn is automatically sanctified from the moment it emerges from the womb, it is still a *mitzvah* to declare it sanctified (*Arachin* 29a).

We can also interpret this phrase simply to mean "you shall not work with the firstborn of your bull nor shear the firstborn of your flock" (as the *Rashbam* explains it), and this prohibition applies not only to the animal's owner (before he hands the animal over to the *Kohen),* but also to the *Kohen.*

16.

1. שָׁמוֹר אֶת־חֹדֶשׁ הָאָבִיב וְעָשִׂיתָ פֶּסַח לַה׳ אֱלֹהֶיךָ — *You shall observe the month of springtime and perform the pesach-offering for Hashem, your God.* In *Parashas Bo* the Torah says, "This month shall be for you . . . the first of the months of the year" (*Shemos* 12:2), and on its fourteenth day the *pesach* is slaughtered. For so the Torah says: ". . . in the first month, saying: 'The Children of Israel shall make the *pesach*-offering in its appointed time. On the fourteenth day of the month . . ." (*Bamidbar* 9:2-3).

Our present verse comes to point out that the "first month," in which the *pesach*-offering is made, must coincide with the ripening of the spring wheat. We declare each month, however, according to the new moon, whereas the spring wheat and all other matters of agriculture are dependent on the solar year, which is some ten days longer than the lunar year. In the year that the Children of Israel left Egypt, the "first month" fell precisely at the season of the spring wheat (for God had the calendar in His personal charge until the time came for Him to give it over to the Sages' charge), but in the second year, only about twenty days of spring-wheat season fell within "the first month." In the third year this was reduced to less than ten days. Therefore God commanded that the fourth year should be expanded, that is, a second month of Adar should be added so that the first month would

15 [19] *Every firstborn male that is born in your cattle and in*
19-23 *your flock, you shall sanctify to* H*ASHEM*, *your God; you shall*
not work with the firstborn of your bull nor shall you shear
the firstborn of your flock. [20] *Before* H*ASHEM*, *your God, shall*
you eat it, year by year, in the place that H*ASHEM will choose,*
you and your household. [21] *If it shall have a blemish —*
lameness or blindness or any serious blemish — you shall not
slaughter it to H*ASHEM*, *your God.* [22] *In your cities shall you*
eat it, the contaminated one and the pure one alike, like the
deer and the hart. [23] *However you shall not eat the blood; you*
shall pour it onto the ground like water.
[1] *You shall observe the month of springtime and perform*
16 *the pesach-offering for* H*ASHEM*, *your God, for in the month*
1-2 *of springtime* H*ASHEM*, *your God, took you out of Egypt at*
night. [2] *You shall slaughter the pesach-offering to* H*ASHEM*,
your God, from the flock, [and also offer] cattle, in the place

---

again coincide with the spring-wheat season, the correct time for the *pesach*-offering. "For in the month of springtime Hashem, your God, took you out of Egypt."

And while we are thanking Him for all the wondrous miracles which He did for us, we should remember to thank Him for this kindness, too, that he took us out of Egypt "in a comfortable season, when it was neither hot nor cold" (*Sifre*).

2. וְזָבַחְתָּ פֶּסַח לַה׳ אֱלֹהֶיךָ צֹאן וּבָקָר — *You shall slaughter the pesach-offering to Hashem, your God, from the flock and [also offer] cattle.* But doesn't the *pesach*-offering come only from the flock (either a lamb or a kid)?

There are two prevailing opinions on how to interpret this. Some say that "You shall slaughter the *pesach*-offering" refers to the lamb or kid offered as the *pesach*, and "the flock and cattle" refers to the additional *chagigah* offering, which may be brought from either. According to others, the verse is divided thus: "You shall the slaughter the *pesach*-offering to Hashem, your God, from the flock" — the *pesach* can only be a lamb or kid — "and cattle" refers to the *chagigah*, which typically is a steer.

There is a problem with the first interpretation. If "the flock and the cattle" both refer to the *chagigah*, then "cattle" should have been mentioned first, for concerning voluntary offerings the Torah states: "from the cattle or from the flock shall you bring your offering." The Torah teaches us always to bring the choicest offering possible; only if one has no cattle should he offer an animal from the flock. The second interpretation seems to work better: "You shall slaughter the *pesach*-offering to Hashem, your God, from the flock" — for the *pesach*-offering may only be from the flock — "and [also offer] cattle," meaning the *chagigah*. And if no cattle are available, then one may bring a *chagigah* from the flock, as with any offering.

טז אֲשֶׁר יִבְחַר יהוה לְשַׁכֵּן שְׁמוֹ שָׁם: ג לֹא־תֹאכַל עָלָיו חָמֵץ
ג־ז שִׁבְעַת יָמִים תֹּאכַל־עָלָיו מַצּוֹת לֶחֶם עֹנִי כִּי בְחִפָּזוֹן
יָצָאתָ מֵאֶרֶץ מִצְרַיִם לְמַעַן תִּזְכֹּר אֶת־יוֹם צֵאתְךָ מֵאֶרֶץ
מִצְרַיִם כֹּל יְמֵי חַיֶּיךָ: ד וְלֹא־יֵרָאֶה לְךָ שְׂאֹר בְּכָל־גְּבֻלְךָ
שִׁבְעַת יָמִים וְלֹא־יָלִין מִן־הַבָּשָׂר אֲשֶׁר תִּזְבַּח בָּעֶרֶב בַּיּוֹם
הָרִאשׁוֹן לַבֹּקֶר: ה לֹא תוּכַל לִזְבֹּחַ אֶת־הַפָּסַח בְּאַחַד
שְׁעָרֶיךָ אֲשֶׁר־יהוה אֱלֹהֶיךָ נֹתֵן לָךְ: ו כִּי אִם־אֶל־הַמָּקוֹם
אֲשֶׁר־יִבְחַר יהוה אֱלֹהֶיךָ לְשַׁכֵּן שְׁמוֹ שָׁם תִּזְבַּח אֶת־
הַפֶּסַח בָּעָרֶב כְּבוֹא הַשֶּׁמֶשׁ מוֹעֵד צֵאתְךָ מִמִּצְרָיִם:
ז וּבִשַּׁלְתָּ וְאָכַלְתָּ בַּמָּקוֹם אֲשֶׁר יִבְחַר יהוה אֱלֹהֶיךָ בּוֹ

---

3. לֶחֶם עֹנִי — *Bread of affliction.* Many interpretations have been given for the term לֶחֶם עֹנִי (see *Pesachim* 36a-b and 115b), and one of them, based on the similarity between עֹנִי, "affliction," and עוֹנִין, "answering," is that we answer many things over the matzos; that is, we recite the full *Hallel* and the *Haggadah* (*Rashi*). But many have asked: since we also say many things over the *pesach*-offering and the *maror* (over the *pesach* we say *Hallel*, and over the *maror* we say the *Haggadah* at the very least), why are they not also called by a similar title?

We might answer by pointing out that "answering" implies saying something out loud or responding to a question. When the Torah commands the father to answer the son, it does so in a two-part statement: "Matzos shall be eaten throughout the seven-day period . . . And you shall tell your son on that day, saying, 'It is because of this that Hashem acted on my behalf when I left Egypt'" (*Shemos* 13:7-8). Although *Chazal* say that "because of this" means that one says this to his son "only at a time when matzos and *maror* are set before him," this is only a definition of the proper time for the *mitzvah* of *Haggadah*. The *Haggadah* is said only "over matzah," for there is no mention of *maror* in this verse: "Matzos shall be eaten. . . and you shall tell your son." The answer to the son's question is, then, "over matzah."

As for the *pesach*-sacrifice, the Torah also says, "And it shall be that when your children say to you, 'What is this service to you?' You shall say, 'It is a *pesach* feast-offering to Hashem. . .'" (*Shemos* 12:26-27). But here the children who ask about the *pesach* are wicked; they exclude themselves from the community by saying "to you." And the evidence of this is that they do not actually ask their fathers anything; they *say* their opinion to them in the guise of a question. They want to teach their degenerate ways to their fathers, rather than learn the way of God from them. We certainly cannot say of the *pesach*, then, that "many things are answered over it," for the wicked son will not be reformed by words. The correct answer for him, as the *Haggadah* says, it to "set his teeth on edge." Inevitably, then, the commandment to tell the child about the Exodus is fulfilled mainly by answering those who ask about the matzah. And

16
3-7

where HASHEM *will choose to rest His Name.* 3 *You shall not*
eat leavened bread with it, for seven days you shall eat
matzos because of it, bread of affliction, for you departed
from the land of Egypt in haste — so that you will remember
the day of your departure from the land of Egypt all the days
of your life.
4 *No leaven of yours shall be seen throughout your*
boundary for seven days, nor shall any of the flesh that you
offer on the afternoon before the first day remain over-
night until morning. 5 *You may not slaughter the pesach-of-*
fering in one of your cities that HASHEM, *your God, gives*
you; 6 *except at the place that* HASHEM, *your God, will choose*
to rest His Name, there shall you slaughter the pesach-offer-
ing in the afternoon, when the sun descends, the appointed
time of your departure from Egypt. 7 *You shall roast it and*
eat it in the place that HASHEM, *your God, will choose,*

---

this is why we find in the *Gemara* that matzah is called "the bread of affliction" because many things are answered over it.

5. לֹא תוּכַל לִזְבֹּחַ אֶת־הַפָּסַח בְּאַחַד שְׁעָרֶיךָ — *You may not slaughter the pesach-offering in one of your cities.* The meaning here is that even at the time when בָּמוֹת, *private altars,* were permitted, it was forbidden to slaughter the *pesach* on one of them. The *Rambam* writes: "From the Tradition we learn that this verse is a warning not to slaughter the *pesach*-offering at a private altar, even at the time when private altars were permitted" (*Hil. Korban Pesach* 1:3).

We have pointed out in various places in our writings that the *pesach*-offering is meant to unite Israel. It is different from other communal, national offerings in that it is not the nation that brings it on behalf of every Jew, but just the opposite: every individual brings it, together with all of Israel, and on behalf of all of Israel. (This is the reason why it is considered a communal offering, enabling it to be slaughtered even on the Sabbath and even if the majority of the people are in a state of spiritual uncleanliness.) This teaches us to be willing to sacrifice ourselves for the sake of all of Israel. Since this national unity is its purpose, it may not be brought on a private altar, even when private altars are permitted.

7. וּבִשַּׁלְתָּ — *You shall cook it.* In *Parashas Bo* the Torah said, "You shall not eat it partially roasted or בָּשֵׁל מְבֻשָּׁל, cooked in water" (*Shemos* 12:9). This tells us that בִּשּׁוּל, "cooking," is a general term that includes roasting over a fire; for the words "in water" had to be added to make it clear that cooking in water is what the Torah forbids. In our present verse the Torah is speaking briefly, and just says "You shall cook it," in order to include in one term both the *pesach*, which must be roasted, and the *chagigah*, which may be cooked using any method, even in water.

טז וּפָנִיתָ בַבֹּקֶר וְהָלַכְתָּ לְאֹהָלֶיךָ׃ ח שֵׁשֶׁת יָמִים תֹּאכַל
ח־יב מַצּוֹת וּבַיּוֹם הַשְּׁבִיעִי עֲצֶרֶת לַיהוָה אֱלֹהֶיךָ לֹא תַעֲשֶׂה
מְלָאכָה׃ ט שִׁבְעָה שָׁבֻעֹת תִּסְפָּר־לָךְ מֵהָחֵל
חֶרְמֵשׁ בַּקָּמָה תָּחֵל לִסְפֹּר שִׁבְעָה שָׁבֻעוֹת׃ י וְעָשִׂיתָ חַג
שָׁבֻעוֹת לַיהוָה אֱלֹהֶיךָ מִסַּת נִדְבַת יָדְךָ אֲשֶׁר תִּתֵּן כַּאֲשֶׁר
יְבָרֶכְךָ יהוָה אֱלֹהֶיךָ׃ יא וְשָׂמַחְתָּ לִפְנֵי ׀ יהוָה אֱלֹהֶיךָ אַתָּה
וּבִנְךָ וּבִתֶּךָ וְעַבְדְּךָ וַאֲמָתֶךָ וְהַלֵּוִי אֲשֶׁר בִּשְׁעָרֶיךָ וְהַגֵּר
וְהַיָּתוֹם וְהָאַלְמָנָה אֲשֶׁר בְּקִרְבֶּךָ בַּמָּקוֹם אֲשֶׁר יִבְחַר יהוָה
אֱלֹהֶיךָ לְשַׁכֵּן שְׁמוֹ שָׁם׃ יב וְזָכַרְתָּ כִּי־עֶבֶד הָיִיתָ בְּמִצְרָיִם
וְשָׁמַרְתָּ וְעָשִׂיתָ אֶת־הַחֻקִּים הָאֵלֶּה׃

⁂ **וּפָנִיתָ בַבֹּקֶר וְהָלַכְתָּ לְאֹהָלֶיךָ** — *And in the morning you may turn back and go to your tents. Chazal* teach that joy is an integral part of every festival; and we express our joy partly by eating the *shelamim* offerings before God (*Pesachim* 109a). If so, how will we fulfill this commandment if we return to our tents in the morning after consuming the *pesach*? The *Meshech Chochmah* answered this question by saying that our verse is talking about the time when private altars were permitted (in the times when the Tabernacle stood at Gilgal, Nob, and Gibeon). Each family, on arriving home, would offer up a *shelamim*, cook it, and eat happily.

But we saw (in v. 5 above) that the Torah said, "You may not slaughter the *pesach*-offering in one of your cities," and the meaning, was that this prohibition applied even in the times of private altars. In other words, this is a general prohibition applying to all times, whether private altars were permitted or not. How, then, could the Torah go on to say, "and in the morning you may turn back and go to your tents," suddenly restricting itself in this clause to the times when private altars were in use? It could easily be misunderstood to mean that even when private altars are prohibited, one may return home on the second day of Pesach and thus fail to fulfill the commandment of rejoicing during the entire festival (since one would be unable to bring any more offerings).

If I may venture to give my own opinion, I would like to say that the crux of the matter lies in that Pesach marks the beginning of the harvest. For those who lived far from Jerusalem it could take as much as fifteen days to reach home after the end of Pesach, and another fifteen days to return to Jerusalem for Shavuos. There would scarcely be time in between for them to harvest their crops. Therefore it seems to me that the Torah's intention here is to be lenient on the issue of rejoicing during Pesach (only of this festival it says, "and in the morning you may turn back"), and allow the pilgrims to return home for the remainder of the festival and express their joy by wearing fresh clothing and drinking aged wine. (See *Pesachim* 71a, and *Tosafos* on *Succah* 42b, ד"ה לולב). According to the *Rashbam's* interpretation, too, one need not stay in Jerusalem for the duration of Pesach. The *Abarbanel* also states, based on our verse, that

16
8-12

and in the morning you may turn back and go to your tents.
8 For a six-day period you shall eat matzos and on the
seventh day shall be an assembly to HASHEM, your God; you
shall not perform any labor.
9 You shall count seven weeks for yourselves; from when
the sickle is first put to the standing crop shall you begin
counting seven weeks. 10 Then you shall observe the festival
of Shavuos for HASHEM, your God; the voluntary offerings
that you give should be commensurate with how much
HASHEM, your God, will have blessed you. 11 You shall rejoice
before HASHEM, your God — you, your son, your daughter,
your slave, your maidservant, the Levite who is in your cities,
the proselyte, the orphan, and the widow who are among you
— in the place that HASHEM, your God, will choose to rest His
Name. 12 You shall remember that you were a slave in Egypt,
and you shall observe and perform these decrees.

---

unlike the case of Succos, there is no obligation during Pesach to spend the entire festival in Jerusalem.

9. שִׁבְעָה שָׁבֻעֹת — *Seven weeks.* Since the people spend the harvest season in the fields, they tend to be unsure what day of the month it is; therefore the Torah said to count seven weeks and to celebrate Shavuos immediately after the counting (*Tur* on the Torah).

12. וְזָכַרְתָּ כִּי־עֶבֶד הָיִיתָ בְּמִצְרָיִם וְשָׁמַרְתָּ וְעָשִׂיתָ אֶת־הַחֻקִּים הָאֵלֶּה — *You shall remember that you were a slave in Egypt, and you shall observe and perform these decrees.* One would think that on Pesach we have חֻקִּים, "decrees" with no clear logical reason, to perform; but not on Shavuos. Why, then, are such "decrees" mentioned here?

But we should stop and consider: could there be any greater חֹק, whose reason is not apparent to our minds, than this? The Torah commands us to return home at the beginning of the harvest after the *Omer*-offering is reaped — and this is a season when, among the gentiles, even those of religious faith do not remain idle from harvesting, even on their religions' days of rest. Then, after just a week or two of work, we are commanded again to make a pilgrimage to Jerusalem for Shavuos, after which there is the journey home to be made once more.

People who lived far from Jerusalem would spend up to a month and a half of the harvest season on the road (fifteen days to return home after Pesach, fifteen days to journey to Jerusalem again, and another fifteen days to go home again). When would they get their harvesting done? Who else could do it for them? — since their sons and daughters, slaves and maidservants, were all rejoicing before God with them. Therefore the Torah admonishes us, "You shall remember that you were a slave in Egypt" (where you constantly had to do the work of others, against your will), "and you shall observe and perform these

טז מפטיר יג חַג הַסֻּכֹּת תַּעֲשֶׂה לְךָ שִׁבְעַת יָמִים בְּאָסְפְּךָ מִגָּרְנְךָ
יג־טז וּמִיִּקְבֶךָ: יד וְשָׂמַחְתָּ בְּחַגֶּךָ אַתָּה וּבִנְךָ וּבִתֶּךָ וְעַבְדְּךָ
וַאֲמָתֶךָ וְהַלֵּוִי וְהַגֵּר וְהַיָּתוֹם וְהָאַלְמָנָה אֲשֶׁר בִּשְׁעָרֶיךָ:
טו שִׁבְעַת יָמִים תָּחֹג לַיהוָה אֱלֹהֶיךָ בַּמָּקוֹם אֲשֶׁר־יִבְחַר
יהוָה כִּי יְבָרֶכְךָ יהוָה אֱלֹהֶיךָ בְּכֹל תְּבוּאָתְךָ וּבְכֹל מַעֲשֵׂה
יָדֶיךָ וְהָיִיתָ אַךְ שָׂמֵחַ: טז שָׁלוֹשׁ פְּעָמִים | בַּשָּׁנָה יֵרָאֶה
כָל־זְכוּרְךָ אֶת־פְּנֵי | יהוָה אֱלֹהֶיךָ בַּמָּקוֹם אֲשֶׁר יִבְחָר

---

decrees" according to the will of "Hashem, our God, Who gives rain, the early rain, and the latter rain in its season; the weeks of the decrees, harvest He shall keep for us" (*Yirmiyah* 5:24). "You shall observe and perform these decrees" (the *Omer* at Pesach and the Two Loaves at Shavuos), which He has decreed for you during the seven weeks of the harvest, and by that merit "the harvest He shall keep for you" ("the harvest will be on time" [*Rashi*)]. You will have enough time to harvest your fields, despite the pilgrimages you make during these weeks.

13. חַג הַסֻּכֹּת — *The festival of Succos.* Rosh Hashanah, Yom Kippur, and Shemini Atzeres are not mentioned, since this passage discusses pilgrimage festivals, which include rejoicing before God. On Rosh Hashanah and Yom Kippur there is no obligation to make a pilgrimage and rejoice in Jerusalem (see *HaDe'ah Ve'HaDibur II*, :26, for a reason for this), and on Shemini Atzeres there is no obligation to rejoice by eating sacrifices — so *Rashi* states explicitly in *Pesachim* 71a (ד"ה ואין שמחה).

Rashi gives a similar interpretation here (see below, v. 15); but the *Tosafos* on *Pesachim* (ibid., ד"ה לילי) write that rejoicing is obligatory not only on the night, but also during the day of Shemini Atzeres. In fact, *Rashi* himself (on *Succah* 48) says the same. According to this reasoning, we would have to say that Shemini Atzeres is part of Succos; and even though *Chazal* say it is a festival in itself, that statement is not absolute, and only applies to certain aspects of *halachah* but not to others (see *Chagigah* 17a). The Torah, after all, says, "Three times a year all your males shall appear," not four times; that is to say that as far as the matter of appearing and bringing offerings is concerned, Shemini Atzeres is one festival with Succos. And since our verse here is talking about the matter of appearing before God, Shemini Atzeres is included in Succos.

בְּאָסְפְּךָ מִגָּרְנְךָ וּמִיִּקְבֶךָ — *When you gather in from your threshing-floor and from your wine cellar.* "Make a succah from the refuse of your threshing-floor and your wine cellar" (*Succah* 12a). The whole point of the festival of Succos, which comes after Yom Kippur, is to join all the back-sliding elements among us with the rest of the Jewish People. Succos comes to unite those who are like "willow branches," which have neither taste nor smell, neither Torah nor good deeds, with the other three species: with those who have either taste or smell, Torah or good deeds, and especially with those who have both taste and smell (the *esrog*). This is so that sins may be forgiven and atoned.

16
13-16

[13] *You shall make the festival of Succos for a seven-day period, when you gather in from your threshing floor and from your wine cellar.* [14] *You shall rejoice on your festival — you, your son, your daughter, your slave, your maidservant, the Levite, the proselyte, the orphan, and the widow who are in your cities.* [15] *A seven-day period shall you celebrate to HASHEM, your God, in the place that HASHEM, your God, will choose, for HASHEM will have blessed you in all your crop and in all your handiwork, and you will be completely joyous.*

[16] *Three times a year all your males should appear before HASHEM, your God, in the place that He will choose:*

It is not only the Four Species that allude to this union, but also the whole festival of Succos, when we bring offerings from the threshing-floor and the wine cellar (fine flour for *minchah* offerings, and wine for libations) — an allusion to the "aristocracy" of Israel — and the refuse, too, is used to serve God, when we roof our *succos* with it.

But this refuse of the Jewish nation requires special care and constant supervision to be part of the *mitzvah* — there are many *halachos* concerning the roofing material (e.g., you must make it afresh, it must not be lying there ready-made; it must not still be connected to the ground, it must not be made of materials which are capable of acquiring spiritual impurity, etc.), none of which applies to the *succah* walls.

15. **וְהָיִיתָ אַךְ שָׂמֵחַ** — *And you will be completely joyous.* From the word אַךְ, translated here as "completely" but literally meaning "only," *Chazal* infer that the Torah means to include the night of Shemini Atzeres in the commandment to rejoice (*Succah* 48).

The use of the word אַךְ may also be seen as an allusion to another place where it appears: "Only [אַךְ] Noah survived" (*Bereishis* 7:23). In this case *Chazal* learned from the word אַךְ that "even he was coughing up blood because of the cold [in the Ark]" (*Bereishis Rabbah* §32; according to another opinion, Noah was maimed by a lion).

The use of the same word indicates a link between the two verses. We can learn here that even in times of trouble, when Israel is "coughing up blood," we are commanded to rejoice in our festival. And this is evident to anyone who listens to the verses we recite during the *Hakafos* of Simchas Torah, when the joy of the festival reaches its peak. Joyfully we cry out to God: "Please, Hashem, save now!" And this is how we are "completely joyous."

16. **יֵרָאֶה כָל־זְכוּרְךָ** — *All your males will appear.* According to the letters written in a Torah scroll, this would mean "All your males will *see* [יִרְאֶה] Hashem's face"; but we read it in the passive voice, as "All your males will appear [יֵרָאֶה, *be seen*] before Hashem."

The *Tosafos*, commenting on this (*Chagigah* 2a, ד"ה יראה), say that one meaning can be learned from the other. First we must derive the lesson from the

טז בְּחַ֧ג הַמַּצּ֛וֹת וּבְחַ֥ג הַשָּׁבֻע֖וֹת וּבְחַ֣ג הַסֻּכּ֑וֹת וְלֹ֧א יֵרָאֶ֛ה
יז אֶת־פְּנֵ֥י יהוָ֖ה רֵיקָֽם׃ יז אִ֖ישׁ כְּמַתְּנַ֣ת יָד֑וֹ כְּבִרְכַּ֛ת יהוָ֥ה
אֱלֹהֶ֖יךָ אֲשֶׁ֥ר נָֽתַן־לָֽךְ׃

---

word as written, and afterwards from the word as read. Thus we find that it is good for a man who enters the Temple court on a pilgrimage festival to concentrate first on "seeing" God's face, insofar as a human being is capable of this; and this vision will surely have a good effect on him, turning his thoughts to repentance and a renewed acceptance of the yoke of the Kingdom of Heaven.

Afterwards he should concentrate on fulfilling the commandment as it is read, to "be seen" before God, for then the Divine Presence will find him clinging wholeheartedly to his God. If he were to do the opposite, concentrating first of all on "appearing" before God, the Divine Presence would find him just as he is, straight from the workaday world, full of trivial thoughts, not as he should be. This is why the pious men of early times used to spend an hour directing their thoughts towards God before they would begin to pray.

וְלֹא יֵרָאֶה אֶת־פְּנֵי ה׳ רֵיקָם — *And he shall not appear before Hashem empty-handed* [רֵיקָם]. That is, without an offering. But the *Yalkut Shimoni*

16 *on the Festival of Matzos, the Festival of Shavuos, and the*
17 *Festival of Succos; and he shall not appear before* HASHEM
empty-handed, [17] *everyone according to what he can give,*
according to the blessing that HASHEM, *your God, gives you.*

---

understands רֵיקָם as meaning "without charity." By combining these two views, we can learn that there is no Temple and no offering if a person comes (even from a distance) to visit this holy place, from which the Divine Presence has never departed, without at least bringing some charity with him.

☙ In *Parashas Mishpatim* the Torah said וְלֹא יֵרָאוּ פָנַי רֵיקָם, "they shall not appear [before] Me [My face] empty-handed" (*Shemos* 23:15). Aside from the simple meaning, a further meaning may be derived from these words: a person who comes empty-handed to a pilgrimage festival will not merit seeing the face of God — "they shall not see My face" if they come "empty-handed." But one who brings a gift to the King of all kings will see the King's face, as it is said: "And I, because of righteousness I shall behold Your face, upon awakening I will be satisfied by Your image" (*Tehillim* 17:15).

פרשת שופטים

Parashas Shoftim

טז יח שֹׁפְטִים וְשֹׁטְרִים תִּתֶּן־לְךָ בְּכָל־שְׁעָרֶיךָ אֲשֶׁר יְהוָה
יח־יט אֱלֹהֶיךָ נֹתֵן לְךָ לִשְׁבָטֶיךָ וְשָׁפְטוּ אֶת־הָעָם מִשְׁפַּט־צֶדֶק׃
יט לֹא־תַטֶּה מִשְׁפָּט לֹא תַכִּיר פָּנִים וְלֹא־תִקַּח שֹׁחַד

---

18. שֹׁפְטִים וְשֹׁטְרִים — *Judges and officers.* The *Raavad* (on *Rambam, Hil. Issurei Mizbeiach* 5:7) explains why this passage is juxtaposed to that of the Festivals: "even though you are obligated to go three times a year to where the *Kohanim* perform the holy service, and there you will be able to inquire about the Torah's laws and statutes, this does not suffice. You must also have judges in all your cities."

It seems clear that saving all questions and disputes for Festival time "does not suffice"; and not merely because of the great number of matters that would descend on Jerusalem at those times from every part of the country. There is also the commandment "not to be seen before God empty-handed," i.e. to bring a sacrifice; and God hates a wrongfully attained sacrifice. So everyone, before he brings his sacrifices on the Festival pilgrimage, must make sure, with the help of his local *Beis Din*, that there is no question of theft on any of his sacrificial animals.

This question could never be settled before the Great *Beis Din* in Jerusalem, since the courts do not sit during festivals. And if it developed after the Festival that someone's sacrifice was indeed not justifiably his own property, then it would be too late, for retroactively the sacrifice would be invalid and hated by God.

תִּתֶּן־לְךָ בְּכָל־שְׁעָרֶיךָ — *Shall you appoint [for yourself] in all your cities* [שְׁעָרֶיךָ, lit. "your gates"]. The word שַׁעַר means either a gate or the gateway it is set in; and from the gate of a city it came to signify the city itself, as in the present verse. This is because a typical city in those days was surrounded by a wall with gates for access.

But "gateway" here also indicates the place where the judges were to sit in each city; every litigant knew to come "to the elders of his city and the gateway of his place" (21:19). Likewise a man's "sister-in-law shall ascend to the gate, to the elders," (25:7) which is just where Boaz went in his time (*Ruth* 4:1).

This seems undemocratic. Should not the judges' place be in the center of the city, equally accessible to all? Two reasons present themselves for this:

First, the *Beis Din* of a city served as its banner and insignia, a token that justice ruled there. Wayfarers who came upon a city in those days feared to enter its gates, lest the inhabitants prove villains or savages at whose hands they would come to grief. So the Children of Israel, who were commanded over and over to love the stranger, placed their courts of justice in the gates of every city, so that every passer-by might know that here he will find shelter and no harm will befall him because justice prevails.

Second, every action of the court, whether adjudication or execution of judgment, must be carried out in a public place in front of the multitudes, so as

[18] *Judges and officers shall you appoint in all your cities*
— which HASHEM, your God, gives you — for your tribes;
and they shall judge the people with righteous judgment.
[19] *You shall not pervert judgment, you shall not respect*
someone's presence, and you shall not accept a bribe,

---

to educate the people to do everything according to law and judgment and to follow the Torah's laws. (As the Torah says, "all Israel will hear and be afraid, and no longer do this sort of evil in your midst" [13:12].) The Torah therefore chose the city gateway for the judges assembly because everyone enters and leaves the city from there, so naturally whatever transpires at that location will be public knowledge.

⸎ תִּתֶּן־לְךָ — *Shall you appoint [for yourself].* There is a story about a great rabbi who was appointed to be the *Rav* of a prominent city. (In those happier days, the *Rav* was chosen exclusively by the aldermen of the community and its president.) When the *Rav* had been in the city only a few days, a beggar came up to him and demanded that the community president be summoned to the court, as he (the beggar) had a charge against him. The *Rav* immediately sent his bailiff to summon the president, but, to his amazement, the president refused to come!

The *Rav* sent the bailiff back with a warning, but the president ignored it. Then a third summons was sent, with the added warning that, if the president did not immediately appear in court, he would be excommunicated.

Suddenly the president stood up, and, calling the aldermen to him, went to call on the *Rav*. "*Mazal tov, Rebbe!*" he cried. "Today you have truly become the *Rav* of this town: you have proven that you will never show preference to anyone, not even to the community president who appointed you." Only then did the *Rav* realize that this whole business had been nothing but a test, to see whether or not he was a true judge before whom all were equal.

This story can help explain the meaning of "Judges and officers shall you appoint *for yourself*." It is an injunction to all those whose task it is to appoint judges: be sure to appoint someone who will be ready to judge you, too, sternly and with no preferential treatment. For then we can hope that "they shall judge the people with righteous judgment."

19. לֹא־תַטֶּה מִשְׁפָּט לֹא תַכִּיר פָּנִים וְלֹא־תִקַּח שֹׁחַד — *You shall not pervert judgment, you shall not respect someone's presence, and you shall not accept a bribe.* We can understand these commandments as applying not only to the judge but to the court officer as well. When he is sent to carry out the court's judgment, he may not pervert justice, nor give deferential treatment to anyone. Neither may he take a bribe in order to "soften" the judgment to be executed (such as to give lashes with a relaxed arm, or the like), or postpone execution of sentence and "interpret" it as he might see fit.

טז כִּ֤י הַשֹּׁחַד֙ יְעַוֵּר֙ עֵינֵ֣י חֲכָמִ֔ים וִֽיסַלֵּ֖ף דִּבְרֵ֥י צַדִּיקִֽם׃ כ צֶ֥דֶק
כ־כא צֶ֖דֶק תִּרְדֹּ֑ף לְמַ֤עַן תִּֽחְיֶה֙ וְיָרַשְׁתָּ֣ אֶת־הָאָ֔רֶץ אֲשֶׁר־יְהוָ֥ה
אֱלֹהֶ֖יךָ נֹתֵ֥ן לָֽךְ׃ כא לֹֽא־תִטַּ֥ע לְךָ֛ אֲשֵׁרָ֖ה

כִּי הַשֹּׁחַד יְעַוֵּר עֵינֵי חֲכָמִים וִיסַלֵּף דִּבְרֵי צַדִּיקִם — *For the bribe will blind the eyes of the wise and make just words crooked.* If the judge takes a bribe before he has even "seen" the case, obviously the bribe will *blind his eyes*, and cause him to err in his evaluation and issue a false judgment.

But even after he has "seen" and reviewed the case and is ready to announce a true judgment on it, should he then, take a bribe to reverse the judgment, it will "make just words crooked." He will find a way to twist the wording of the judgment and spoil its execution, thus making "just words" unjust.

כִּי הַשֹּׁחַד יְעַוֵּר עֵינֵי חֲכָמִים — *For the bribe will blind the eyes of the wise*. Not only does this refer to the "eyes" of his spirit — a mental blindness whereby a bribe influences him to favor the giver — but this Divine decree extends even to physical blindness. As *Chazal* tell us: "no judge who takes bribes dies of old age without going blind" (*Yerushalmi Peah* 37a). This can be deduced by reading the verse in a double sense, not only as a statement of fact but as a warning of retribution, measure for measure.

Bereishis Rabbah (65:7) deduces this from the Torah's statement that "when Isaac grew old, his eyes grew dim": "Said R' Yehudah, 'If [Isaac] took a bribe from someone who was obligated to give it to him, and all the same his eyes grew dim, one who takes a bribe from another who owes him nothing will even more surely go blind.'"

Now, *Chazal* tell us that Isaac asked to be given suffering at the end of his life, saying, "If a man dies without suffering, the Aspect of Strict Justice lies waiting before him" (*Bereishis Rabbah,* loc. cit.). At first this seems strange: why would Isaac, the "perfect sacrifice," fear Divine Justice more than the other Patriarchs, who did not ask for suffering? It was because he feared punishment for the "bribes" that he had received "from someone who was obligated to give it to him" (from Esau who was obligated to honor his father). Because of this he had leaned towards Esau to the point of wishing to give him the blessings.

God answered his request, and Isaac's eyes grew dim. God chose this suffering above all others so as to atone for the spiritual blindness that had come over Isaac in the matter of Esau: measure for measure.

20. לְמַעַן תִּחְיֶה וְיָרַשְׁתָּ אֶת־הָאָרֶץ — *So that you will live, and possess the Land.* "The appointing of judges is important enough to guarantee that Israel will live and remain in their Land" (*Sifre*).

We can understand this Midrash on the basis of another verse: "It will be, when you hearken to these מִשְׁפָּטִים . . ." — 'ordinances,' מִשְׁפָּטִים, are the laws that apply between man and his neighbor — "Hashem, your God, will safe-

for the bribe will blind the eyes of the wise and make just
words crooked. 20 *Righteousness, righteousness shall you*
pursue, so that you will live and possess the Land that
HASHEM, your God, gives you.
21 *You shall not plant for yourselves an idolatrous tree —*

---

guard for you the covenant and the kindness that He swore to your forefathers" (7:12). The lesson here is that God treats us as we treat each other. For example, we find that when R' Yehoshua ben Levi entered Paradise alive and then swore that he would never leave, the Angel of Death ordered him to leave. But God commanded that R' Yehoshua's record be examined: if he had never in his life attempted to attain a *halachic* release from an oath he had taken, then this oath, too, must be treated as inviolable, and he might stay (*Kesubos* 77b).

In the same way, when the Children of Israel keep the Torah's laws that pertain between man and his fellow, keep them faithfully and truly, never abrogating the covenant that lies between them, then God treats them the same way. He upholds the covenant that He swore to their fathers, to give them the Land of Canaan. This is the meaning of *Chazal's* exposition, "The appointing of judges is important enough to guarantee that Israel will live and remain in their Land."

21. לֹא־תִטַּע לְךָ אֲשֵׁרָה — *You shall not plant for yourselves an idolatrous tree.*

The juxtaposition of this verse to that of appointing judges leads to the following deduction in *Sanhedrin* (7b): "Said Reish Lakish, 'Anyone who appoints a judge who is unfit for the job is as if he had planted an *asheirah*-tree among Israel.'"

This analogy is remarkably instructive, for if a person plants a seed, intending it to grow into an *asheirah*-tree, at present his action is quite unnoticeable; and even if he plants it as a sapling, for the time being it doesn't have the look of a tall tree that people worship. But little trees grow into big ones, and in time this innocent-looking sapling will be a full-fledged *asheirah.*

It is the same with an unfit judge. When he is first appointed, he is simply unfit, i.e., incompetent. But R' Yehudah bar Nachmani (*Sanhedrin,* loc. cit.) applied this verse to a judge who has not studied the Law: "Woe to him that says to a tree 'Arise!', to a lifeless stone 'Awake!' Shall he decide the law? He is caught up in gold and silver, and no spirit at all is within him" (*Chavakuk* 2:19).

This was said only about an incompetent judge. Yet in his first days in office such a judge is bound to show preference to rich men, accept "verbal bribes" of flattery, and more. The "seed" or "sapling" of this *asheirah*-tree is growing. Since the unfit judge is "caught up in gold and silver, and no spirit at all is within him," he will certainly end by accepting bribes of money — he will grow into a full-fledged *asheirah*-tree.

טז כָּל־עֵץ אֵצֶל מִזְבַּח יהוה אֱלֹהֶיךָ אֲשֶׁר תַּעֲשֶׂה־
כב לָּךְ: כב וְלֹא־תָקִים לְךָ מַצֵּבָה אֲשֶׁר שָׂנֵא יהוה
יז אֱלֹהֶיךָ: א לֹא־תִזְבַּח לַיהוה אֱלֹהֶיךָ שׁוֹר
א־ג וָשֶׂה אֲשֶׁר יִהְיֶה בוֹ מוּם כֹּל דָּבָר רָע כִּי תוֹעֲבַת יהוה
אֱלֹהֶיךָ הוּא: ב כִּי־יִמָּצֵא בְקִרְבְּךָ בְּאַחַד
שְׁעָרֶיךָ אֲשֶׁר־יהוה אֱלֹהֶיךָ נֹתֵן לָךְ אִישׁ אוֹ־אִשָּׁה אֲשֶׁר
יַעֲשֶׂה אֶת־הָרַע בְּעֵינֵי יהוה־אֱלֹהֶיךָ לַעֲבֹר בְּרִיתוֹ:
ג וַיֵּלֶךְ וַיַּעֲבֹד אֱלֹהִים אֲחֵרִים וַיִּשְׁתַּחוּ לָהֶם וְלַשֶּׁמֶשׁ ׀
אוֹ לַיָּרֵחַ אוֹ לְכָל־צְבָא הַשָּׁמַיִם אֲשֶׁר לֹא־צִוִּיתִי:

---

22. וְלֹא־תָקִים לְךָ מַצֵּבָה אֲשֶׁר שָׂנֵא ה׳ אֱלֹהֶיךָ — *And you shall not erect for yourselves a pillar, which Hashem, your God, hates.* "Even though it was beloved of Him in the days of the Patriarchs, now He hates it, since [the gentiles] have made it a fixed part of their idolatry" (*Rashi*).

But didn't Moses build twelve pillars, one for each tribe (*Shemos* 24:4)? Now, according to those who hold that this was done before the Giving of the Torah, there is no problem, for only when Moses went up to the thick cloud to receive the Torah did God tell him, "And altar of earth shall you make for Me . . . or else an altar of [many] stones shall you make for Me" (ibid. 20:21-22), thereby intimating that He no longer desired a pillar.

This point is clearly stated by *Rashi* on this verse (ד"ה אשר שנא): "He commanded that an altar of earth or stones be made, and this [pillar He announced that] He hated, because it was a custom of the Canaanites." If the announcement came with the command to build an altar of earth, then obviously until then it was permitted to erect a pillar, and that would be why Moses set up twelve of them at the mountain's base.

But according to those who hold that these twelve pillars were erected after the Giving of the Torah, we have a difficulty: how could Moses build them now that they had been prohibited?

We can suggest that this is why the Torah specifically adds the words "for the twelve tribes of Israel" (*Shemos* 24:4). This is an indication that Moses did not sacrifice anything at all on them (only on the altar that he built); they were simply intended as witness that all twelve tribes had entered the Covenant. The *Rashbam* understands them this way. But the *Ha'amek Davar* writes that on the altar communal sacrifices were made, and individuals sacrificed on the pillars. This is no problem, though; it is in accordance with the *Ha'amek Davar's* approach (which he backs up with evidence from the *Gemara*), that this all happened before the Giving of the Torah, as *Rashi* holds.

17.

2. אִישׁ אוֹ־אִשָּׁה — *A man or woman.* Although a city that has been led astray by a woman is not adjudged to be a Wayward City, still, the woman herself

16 *any tree — near the Altar of HASHEM, your God, that you*
22 *shall make for yourself.* [22] *And you shall not erect for*
yourselves a pillar, which HASHEM, your God, hates.
17 [1] *You shall not slaughter for HASHEM, your God, an ox or a*
1-3 *lamb or kid in which there will be a blemish, any bad thing,*
because that is an abomination of HASHEM, your God.
[2] *If there will be found among you in one of your cities,*
which HASHEM, your God gives you, a man or woman who
commits what is evil in the eyes of HASHEM, your God, to
violate His covenant, [3] *and he will go and serve gods of*
others and prostrate himself to them, or to the sun or the
moon or to any host of heaven, which I have not commanded,

---

who has committed idolatry incurs the death penalty (*Sifre*).

3. וַיֵּלֶךְ וַיַּעֲבֹד — *And he will go and serve.* The word וַיֵּלֶךְ, "and he will go," seems unnecessary. In explanation, *Yonassan ben Uzziel* interprets this word in his *Targum* as "and he goes after his Evil Inclination."

But this, too, is not so clear. What is so special about this person going after his *yetzer hara*? What else have we been talking about until now?

It seems clear that in recent chapters we have been talking about people (false prophets, enticers, and the like) who are chiefly interested in entrapping others in the clutches of the Evil Inclination. Here, by adding the word וַיֵּלֶךְ, the Torah signals that it is now talking about a person who gets up and goes away from his hometown to a place where no one knows him, just so as to be free to "serve other gods" all by himself, without enticing or seducing anyone else. Nonetheless, he is not blameless: he too is an idolater and must be put to death.

וַיֵּלֶךְ וַיַּעֲבֹד אֱלֹהִים אֲחֵרִים — *And he will go and serve gods of others.* Anyone who takes that final step, and actually worships a false god, has at this point "gone" and left the Jewish faith and the Jewish people.

וַיִּשְׁתַּחוּ לָהֶם . . . אֲשֶׁר לֹא־צִוִּיתִי — *And prostrate himself to them. . . which I have not commanded.* Surely it ought to say "which I have commanded you not to worship"?

We can understand the present wording according to the *Rambam's* teaching. He explains (*Hil. Avodah Zarah* ch. 2) that the first idolaters were worshipers of stars and constellations, who erroneously thought that God had delegated the governance of this world to the host of heavenly bodies, and so certainly He desired that mankind give them honor. This, they said, was only part of giving honor to God Himself, just as an earthly king expects his officers to be shown honor, since that reflects back on him.

But in truth God had not given any such delegation to the heavenly bodies; on the contrary, as the Torah says, they were created purely to serve mankind. What is more, an earthly king cannot possibly rule his entire nation in person, because of the distances involved and the inherent physical and mental

יז ד וְהֻגַּד־לְךָ וְשָׁמָעְתָּ וְדָרַשְׁתָּ הֵיטֵב וְהִנֵּה אֱמֶת נָכוֹן הַדָּבָר
ד־ז נֶעֶשְׂתָה הַתּוֹעֵבָה הַזֹּאת בְּיִשְׂרָאֵל: ה וְהוֹצֵאתָ אֶת־הָאִישׁ
הַהוּא אוֹ אֶת־הָאִשָּׁה הַהִוא אֲשֶׁר עָשׂוּ אֶת־הַדָּבָר הָרָע
הַזֶּה אֶל־שְׁעָרֶיךָ אֶת־הָאִישׁ אוֹ אֶת־הָאִשָּׁה וּסְקַלְתָּם
בָּאֲבָנִים וָמֵתוּ: ו עַל־פִּי | שְׁנַיִם עֵדִים אוֹ שְׁלֹשָׁה עֵדִים יוּמַת
הַמֵּת לֹא יוּמַת עַל־פִּי עֵד אֶחָד: ז יַד הָעֵדִים תִּהְיֶה־בּוֹ
בָרִאשֹׁנָה לַהֲמִיתוֹ וְיַד כָּל־הָעָם בָּאַחֲרֹנָה וּבִעַרְתָּ הָרָע
מִקִּרְבֶּךָ:

---

limitations of being mere flesh and blood. (As Jethro pointed out to Moses, "You will surely become worn out" [*Shemos* 18:18].) So an earthly king needs officers. But the Holy One, blessed be He, Whose glory fills all the universe, and Who surveys all mankind with a single glance, needs no officers and emissaries; He alone rules the entire universe, without any associates. Clearly, then, there is no reason whatever to give honor to the heavenly bodies.

That is the meaning of this verse: a person might "... prostrate himself to them, or to the sun or the moon or to any host of heaven," under the mistaken assumption that these are the 'king's officers,' and it is part of honoring the King to show them honor, and so the King has commanded — but the truth is "that I have not commanded" any such thing. I never commanded man to prostrate himself to the host of heaven, and anyone who does, even with the intent of honoring Me, is committing idolatry and incurring the death penalty.

6. עַל־פִּי שְׁנַיִם עֵדִים — *By the testimony* [עַל פִּי, literally "by the mouth"] *of two witnesses.* A *piska* mark divides between "by the testimony" and "two witnesses." Interestingly, the same mark divides the same phrase in verse 19:15 below, where the subject is property cases. Surely this signifies something.

It would seem that the pause in the middle of the phrase comes to emphasize that only עַל פִּי, "by the mouth" of a witness do we accept testimony. If the testimony is submitted as a written document it is unacceptable. A live witness is insisted on not only in a capital case; it is the rule in property cases, too, which is why the *piska* mark also appears in v. 19:15.

7. יַד הָעֵדִים תִּהְיֶה־בּוֹ בָרִאשֹׁנָה לַהֲמִיתוֹ — *The hand of the witnesses shall be upon him first to put him to death.* The custom in "enlightened" countries is to have a professional hangman who administers the death sentences issued by the courts. The job of hangman is also considered the most despised occupation that can be, and only evil, cruel men ever accept (for a large salary) this kind of work. Even then, the ruffian who accepts will often make it a condition of acceptance that his identity as the public hangman be kept secret. There have been cases of a hangman keeping the nature of his job secret even from his family.

The Holy Torah, quite surprisingly, assigns this job, which none of us would care to take on professionally, to the witnesses in the case. What sin have they committed, then, to be handed such a dreadful task?

17
4-7

4 and it will be told to you and you will hear; then you shall
investigate well, and behold! it is true, the testimony is correct
— this abomination was done in Israel — 5 then you shall
remove that man or that woman who did this evil thing to
your cities — the man or the woman — and you shall pelt
them with stones, so that they will die. 6 By the testimony of
two witnesses or three witnesses shall the condemned person
die; he shall not die by the testimony of a single witness. 7 The
hand of the witnesses shall be upon him first to put him to
death, and the hand of the entire people afterward, and you
shall destroy the evil from your midst.

We can only understand by delving deeply into the Torah's philosophy of why certain sinners need to be killed — as opposed to the "enlightened" world's understanding of this need.

The light of the Torah's truth is not at all like the ideas of the "civilized" world, that walks in darkness. For the denizens of this material world are not so far removed from comprehending the psyche of the sinner. To a large extent they understand him perfectly, and in certain cases they even sympathize with him and justify what he did in their hearts (for example, they may sympathize with a man who has killed a woman's husband because he and she have "fallen in love"). In that case, in countries where the death penalty exists it is intended only as a means of keeping order, a deterrent, on the chance, for example, that a murderer may go and murder again, in which case no one could be sure of his life.

When the sinner is executed, then, he is being "sacrificed" for the communal good, because it is society's desire not to have such people in the world. But since, deep in its heart, the society that executes him sympathizes with him, and sometimes even justifies him, no one is willing to go and do "the evil deed," no matter how necessary it is.

But the Torah's philosophy is quite different. First of all, execution is only a possibility after search and investigation and thorough examination of the testimony, as well as the sinner's having been warned before his deed; so that a death sentence was the rarest of events, and a *Sanhedrin* that executed even one man in seven was called "a murderous *Sanhedrin*."

Second, according to the Torah a sinner is executed not merely because he is actively dangerous to ordered society, i.e. he may continue to murder or commit other physically disruptive acts. According to Torah law, the death penalty is also incurred by such sinners as adulterers, Sabbath desecrators, and idolaters, who pose no threat to society as such if allowed to live. The underlying reason for execution is that this person is dangerous to the Jewish soul and spirit. Others might learn from him to give themselves over to bodily lusts and tawdry life-goals, and throw off the yoke of the Kingdom of Heaven, becoming lawless scoundrels like him.

ח כִּי יִפָּלֵא מִמְּךָ דָבָר לַמִּשְׁפָּט בֵּין־דָּם ׀ לְדָם בֵּין־דִּין לְדִין יז
וּבֵין נֶגַע לָנֶגַע דִּבְרֵי רִיבֹת בִּשְׁעָרֶיךָ וְקַמְתָּ וְעָלִיתָ אֶל־ ח־י
הַמָּקוֹם אֲשֶׁר יִבְחַר יהוה אֱלֹהֶיךָ בּוֹ: ט וּבָאתָ אֶל־הַכֹּהֲנִים
הַלְוִיִּם וְאֶל־הַשֹּׁפֵט אֲשֶׁר יִהְיֶה בַּיָּמִים הָהֵם וְדָרַשְׁתָּ וְהִגִּידוּ
לְךָ אֵת דְּבַר הַמִּשְׁפָּט: י וְעָשִׂיתָ עַל־פִּי הַדָּבָר אֲשֶׁר יַגִּידוּ
לְךָ מִן־הַמָּקוֹם הַהוּא אֲשֶׁר יִבְחַר יהוה וְשָׁמַרְתָּ לַעֲשׂוֹת

This 'revolutionary' rationale is actually spelled out in the Torah: "and all Israel will see and be afraid, and no longer do this sort of evil thing in your midst" (13:12). Even the repeatedly-used expression, "you shall remove the evil from your midst," may be understood along these lines: that every Jew who assists in executing the sinner will thereby remove the evil from his midst, from the depths of his *own* heart. He will no longer entertain any envy or admiration for sinners that might tempt him to do as they do.

Participation in the execution of such a sinner, who was warned that he would incur the death penalty if he continued, and yet committed an act that God hates before the eyes of witnesses, is an educational experience. Every Jew is obligated to educate himself to keep distant from sin, to remove the evil from his heart that tempts him to do as this sinner has done. Equally, a Jew is obligated to root out any thoughts of sympathy or of vindication that may stir within him when confronted with evil deeds. For they make an impression on him, whether he wills it or not; and without a doubt, the impression is indelibly stamped on the witnesses, who saw the evil deed with their own eyes (hearing is not at all the same thing as seeing [see *Rosh HaShanah* 25b]). The witnesses were the ones who warned the sinner what would happen if he persisted, and it was to them that he answered that he didn't care if he was sentenced to death, he would commit the sin anyway.

A man declares himself willing to give his life for the indulgence of his craving to be free of the Yoke of Heaven! Seeing such an event must make a strong impression on the witnesses, and perhaps a thought will steal into their hearts: "Maybe he should be forgiven?" or some other such ploy of the Evil Inclination. They must, in that case, do something to chase away such thoughts, to remove the evil from themselves. That is why the Torah commands them to use their own hands to carry out the *Sanhedrin's* judgment: "The hand of the witnesses shall be upon him first to put him to death," and afterwards "the hand of the entire people", who have heard about this evil deed — "and all Israel shall hear, and be afraid, and they shall not again do such an evil thing in your midst."

8. **כִּי יִפָּלֵא מִמְּךָ דָבָר . . . וְקַמְתָּ וְעָלִיתָ** — *If a matter of judgment is hidden from you [beyond your understanding] . . . you shall rise up and ascend . . .* If a judge before whom a case has come is not ashamed to tell the litigants, "I don't know; I must inquire about this matter myself before someone greater than I"

[8] *If a matter of judgment is hidden from you, between blood
and blood, between verdict and verdict, between plague and
plague, matters of dispute in your cities — you shall rise
up and ascend to the place that* HASHEM, *your God, shall
choose.* [9] *You shall come to the Kohanim, the Levites, and to
the judge who will be in those days; you shall inquire and
they will tell you the word of judgment.* [10] *You shall do
according to the word that they will tell you, from that
place that* HASHEM *will choose, and you shall be careful to do*

— then that is an indication that this judge has "risen up" out of the baseness of arrogance and "ascended" to a higher level of existence. The Torah promises us that "whoever comes to purify himself will be helped" (*Yoma* 38b), and so it announces here, "you shall rise up and ascend."

בֵּין־דָּם לְדָם — *Between blood and blood.* "— between pure and impure [i.e., *niddah*] blood; 'between verdict and verdict' — between a verdict of innocent and one of guilty; 'between affliction and affliction' — between a pure affliction and an impure [i.e., leprous] one" (*Rashi*).

Chazal tell us that if a teacher once becomes angry with his student and the student keeps silent, he will be granted the wisdom to distinguish between pure and impure blood; and if the teacher becomes upset a second time and still the student keeps silent, he will be granted discernment between property cases and capital cases (*Berachos* 63b). So if we see a *beis din* whose members are not competent to distinguish "between blood and blood, between verdict and verdict," we can suspect that when they were students and their teacher became angry with them, they did not keep silent. As a result, now that they have become judges themselves, they do not know how to distinguish the law in each case.

9. אֶל־הַכֹּהֲנִים הַלְוִיִּם וְאֶל־הַשֹּׁפֵט — *To the Kohanim, the Levites, and to the judge.* According to the *Sifre*, this refers to the Great *Beis Din* that sits in the Chamber of Hewn Stone in the Temple. It is a *mitzvah* to have *Kohanim* and Levites as judges on this *beis din*, for they are especially commanded to teach Torah to Israel, as it says, "They shall teach Your ordinances to Jacob and Your Torah to Israel" (33:10). But this is not actually necessary; even if all its members were Israelites the court could function as usual, for the crown of Torah is free for all to take (see *Yoma* 72a).

10. אֲשֶׁר יַגִּידוּ לְךָ מִן־הַמָּקוֹם הַהוּא — *That they will tell you, from that place.* The Torah has already said, "You shall rise up and ascend to the place that Hashem, your God, shall choose." Why say the same phrase again? To tell you the reason why you must act "according to the word that they will tell you": because it emanates "from that place," the place where God has chosen as His Name's dwelling. Whatever they tell you from the Chamber of Hewn Stone is the word of God.

יז כְּכֹל אֲשֶׁר יוֹרוּךָ: יא עַל־פִּי הַתּוֹרָה אֲשֶׁר יוֹרוּךָ וְעַל־
יא־טו הַמִּשְׁפָּט אֲשֶׁר־יֹאמְרוּ לְךָ תַּעֲשֶׂה לֹא תָסוּר מִן־הַדָּבָר
אֲשֶׁר־יַגִּידוּ לְךָ יָמִין וּשְׂמֹאל: יב וְהָאִישׁ אֲשֶׁר־יַעֲשֶׂה
בְזָדוֹן לְבִלְתִּי שְׁמֹעַ אֶל־הַכֹּהֵן הָעֹמֵד לְשָׁרֶת שָׁם אֶת־
יְהוָה אֱלֹהֶיךָ אוֹ אֶל־הַשֹּׁפֵט וּמֵת הָאִישׁ הַהוּא וּבִעַרְתָּ
הָרָע מִיִּשְׂרָאֵל: יג וְכָל־הָעָם יִשְׁמְעוּ וְיִרָאוּ וְלֹא יְזִידוּן
עוֹד: שני יד כִּי־תָבֹא אֶל־הָאָרֶץ אֲשֶׁר יְהוָה
אֱלֹהֶיךָ נֹתֵן לָךְ וִירִשְׁתָּהּ וְיָשַׁבְתָּה בָּהּ וְאָמַרְתָּ אָשִׂימָה עָלַי
מֶלֶךְ כְּכָל־הַגּוֹיִם אֲשֶׁר סְבִיבֹתָי: טו שׂוֹם תָּשִׂים עָלֶיךָ מֶלֶךְ

---

11. עַל־פִּי הַתּוֹרָה אֲשֶׁר יוֹרוּךָ — *According to the teaching that they will teach you.* Everything that they tell you in explanation of the Torah, according to the meaning of its verses (*Ramban*). "And according to the judgment that they will say to you" — these are the things that they may deduce from exegesis following the methods of expounding the Torah (*Rambam*). "The word that they will tell you" — this is the tradition that they have received, passed down from master to disciple (ibid.).

12. וְהָאִישׁ אֲשֶׁר־יַעֲשֶׂה בְזָדוֹן — *And the man that will act with willfulness [deliberate evil.]* This entire passage has been phrased directly, in the second person ("If a matter of judgment is hidden from you . . . You shall rise up . . . you shall come . . . you shall inquire . . .") — until now. The Torah shows this kind of closeness, and uses this kind of direct speech, only to a man who questions his own understanding, and goes to inquire after God's word, so that he will know how to act once the *Kohen* and the judge that sit in God's house have told him.

It is very different with the man that this verse is talking about. He is an elder, sitting on the *Sub-Sanhedrin* of a town, and he has gone to Jerusalem, to the Temple, to seek the word of God in the Chamber of Hewn Stone. Now he returns to his town — and publicly instructs the people to do the opposite of what the Sages told him! In token of his rebellion, the Torah "no longer recognizes him" so as to speak directly to him in second person. Instead it speaks of "that man" who has acted with deliberate evil. With this the Torah removes the elder's mantle from him, and commands all Israel, "that man shall die."

14. כִּי־תָבֹא . . . אָשִׂימָה עָלַי מֶלֶךְ — *When you come. . . "I will set a king over myself."* This passage is juxtaposed to the mention of "the judge who will be in those days," from which *Chazal* deduced that "Jephthah in his generation is like Samuel in his generation." With this juxtaposition, then, the Torah was warning that the period of the Judges would precede the period of the Kings.

§ כִּי־תָבֹא אֶל־הָאָרֶץ אֲשֶׁר ה׳ אֱלֹהֶיךָ נֹתֵן לָךְ . . . אָשִׂימָה עָלַי מֶלֶךְ — *When you come to the Land that Hashem, your God, gives you. . . "I will set a king over myself."* *Chazal* teach that the people were given three commandments to do when they came to the Land, one of which was to appoint a king over them

17
11-15

according to everything that they will teach you. 11 *Accord-*
ing to the teaching that they will teach you and according to
the judgment that they will say to you, shall you do; you
shall not deviate from the word that they will tell you, right
or left. 12 *And the man that will act with willfulness, not*
listening to the Kohen who stands there to serve H*ASHEM*,
your God, or to the judge, that man shall die, and you shall
destroy the evil from among Israel. 13 *The entire nation shall*
listen and fear, and they shall not act willfully any more.
14 *When you come to the Land that* H*ASHEM*, *your God,*
gives you, and possess it, and settle in it, and you will say,
"I will set a king over myself, like all the nations that
are around me." 15 *You shall surely set over yourself a king*

(*Sanhedrin* 20b). At first glance it would seem to make more sense if they appointed the king before entering the Land, so that he could conduct the war and divide the Land among them.

Moses and Joshua, the faithful shepherds of Israel, were never called "kings," for this very reason, that God did not want to appoint a king over Israel until the Land had been conquered and apportioned. But why not?

Probably because if the people had appointed a king, and he brought them into the Land and conquered it, they would have attributed their success to the king's prowess and bravery and his sagacious tactics. They might even have said that God had done nothing for them, only their king. Therefore God delegated His faithful prophet to carry out the conquest, and failing that, his disciple Joshua. Thus might all Israel know that "from God was this thing." That is why these verses are phrased the way they are: "When you come to the Land that Hashem, your God," — and not any king of your choosing — "gives you, and possess it, and settle in it" — not that the king apportions you fields and vineyards; only then — "you shall surely set over yourself a king."

מֶלֶךְ כְּכָל־הַגּוֹיִם אֲשֶׁר סְבִיבֹתָי — *A king... like all the nations that are around me.* The One who said, "You shall not go in their laws" is now suggesting that Israel will want "a king, like all the nations"? Astounding!

We can suggest that this is actually intended to speak in Israel's favor. For if the nations around the Land of Israel (which presented the chief danger) had been kingless, with no one to unite them and lead them to war against us, we would not have asked for a king at all. But since in fact "all the nations that are around us" had a king, and they all had evil intentions toward us, it was essential for us also to have a king, who would turn the army back and bring it to their gates.

15. שׂוֹם תָּשִׂים עָלֶיךָ מֶלֶךְ — *You shall surely set over yourself a king. Chazal* deduce from here that "the fear of the king must be upon you" (*Kiddushin* 32b). This was no doubt deduced from the expression שׂוֹם תָּשִׂים "set over

אֲשֶׁ֧ר יִבְחַ֛ר יְהֹוָ֥ה אֱלֹהֶ֖יךָ בּ֑וֹ מִקֶּ֣רֶב אַחֶ֗יךָ תָּשִׂ֤ים עָלֶ֙יךָ֙
מֶ֔לֶךְ לֹ֣א תוּכַ֗ל לָתֵ֤ת עָלֶ֙יךָ֙ אִ֣ישׁ נׇכְרִ֔י אֲשֶׁ֥ר לֹֽא־אָחִ֖יךָ
ה֥וּא: טז רַק֩ לֹֽא־יַרְבֶּה־לּ֨וֹ סוּסִ֜ים וְלֹֽא־יָשִׁ֧יב אֶת־הָעָ֣ם
מִצְרַ֗יְמָה לְמַ֙עַן֙ הַרְבּ֣וֹת ס֔וּס וַֽיהֹוָה֙ אָמַ֣ר לָכֶ֔ם לֹ֣א
תֹסִפ֛וּן לָשׁ֥וּב בַּדֶּ֖רֶךְ הַזֶּ֥ה עֽוֹד: יז וְלֹ֤א יַרְבֶּה־לּוֹ֙ נָשִׁ֔ים

yourself a king," as opposed to תִּתֶּן לְךָ, "provide for yourself a king" which we find used by [Samuel the last of] the Judges. (See *I Shmuel* 8:6 and 12:13) Here we have the difference between the period of the Judges and that of the Kings: the Judges did not cast any aura of fear over the people, whereas the Kings did.

So, when Barak went to war against Sisera (*Shoftim*, ch. 4) he had with him only ten thousand men of Zebulun and Naphtali, and Deborah in her song castigated the other tribes for not having rallied around the people's cause. Again, the people of Succoth and Penuel refused to give bread to Gideon's army when they were pursuing the kings of Midian (ch. 7). The reason for such failures was that "there was no king then in Israel," and therefore "each man did what was right in his eyes" (*Shoftim* 17:6), for the people did not fear the Judges.

But when the first King of Israel fought his first war, already then the people arose and came from every part of the country to take part in the war, for "the fear of God" Who had commanded them to set a king over themselves "fell upon the people, and they came forth like a single man" (*I Shmuel* 11:7).

§ מִקֶּרֶב אַחֶיךָ תָּשִׂים עָלֶיךָ מֶלֶךְ — *From among your brethren shall you set a king over yourself.* When prophecy comes to its end, and the question arises who should be the next king, then you must choose a king who has the following qualifications:

He must be "from among your brethren" — a person whose lineage is clear, and who lives in the Land of Israel (*Sifre*). For whoever lives in the Diaspora is like a person who has no God (*Kesubos* 110b), and how could a person like that rule over the Holy Nation?

He must not be "a foreign man [אִישׁ נׇכְרִי] who is not your brother." This does not refer to a gentile — for how could the Children of Israel choose a king from among a gentile people? — but to a Jew who has become "foreign" to the Jewish spirit and Torah, as the verse goes on to say: "who is not your brother." This seemingly redundant phrase (for if he is a gentile, he is certainly not your brother!) indicates that this man's deeds have become foreign to Heaven, so that he is no longer your brother in *mitzvos*. (This interpretation is adopted by *Yonassan ben Uzziel*, who always translates the word נׇכְרִי, "foreigner," as בַּר עַמְמִין, "child of the gentiles," but who here translates אִישׁ נׇכְרִי as גְּבַר חִילּוֹנִי, "a profane man.") If the king does not follow the path of Torah, he may sway the people's hearts away from following God.

And if you see that the king upholds the special commandments that apply to him: "He shall not have too many horses . . . too many wives . . . He shall write for himself two copies of this Torah . . . It shall be with him, and he shall read

17 whom HASHEM, your God, shall choose; from among your
16-17 brethren shall you set a king over yourself; you cannot place
over yourself a foreign man, who is not your brother. 16 Only
he shall not have too many horses for himself, so that he
will not return the people to Egypt in order to increase horses,
for HASHEM has said to you, "You shall no longer return on
this road again." 17 And he shall not have too many wives,

---

from it all the days of his life, so that he will learn to fear Hashem . . . to observe all the words of this Torah . . . so that his heart does not become haughty . . ." — this is a sign that he is the king that God has chosen.

16-17. רַק לֹא־יַרְבֶּה־לּוֹ סוּסִים . . . וְלֹא יַרְבֶּה־לּוֹ נָשִׁים — *Only he shall not have too many horses for himself . . . and he shall not have too many wives.* "King Solomon came and thought himself wiser than God's decree. He said, 'Why did God decree not to have many wives? So that the king's heart would not turn away from Him. I will have many, but my heart will not turn away.' Our Rabbis say that then the letter י from the word יַרְבֶּה rose up to Heaven and prostrated itself before the Holy One, blessed be He, protesting, 'Master of the World, did you not say that no letter of the Torah would ever be nullified? And here is Solomon, who has nullified me!' " (*Shemos Rabbah* 6:1).

This Midrash is puzzling: have there not been many Jewish leaders who have transgressed God's commandments? Yet never did the letters with which those commandments are written rise up to Heaven to protest that they are being nullified by this leader.

We can explain that even if most of the Jewish people transgress a certain commandment, still, as long as there is even one Jew in the world who upholds it, this commandment has not been nullified. But the commandment of "not having too many wives" applies from the start to no one but the king; so if he transgresses it, this commandment has been cancelled out entirely from among the Jewish people. That was why a letter of this verse went to complain before the Master of the World that "Solomon had nullified it."

Chazal also taught a lesson in this Midrash: size does not equal importance. Even though the letter י is the smallest of all the letters, it was sent to complain on behalf of the whole word יַרְבֶּה, because it comes first in the word.

⇐§ לֹא־יַרְבֶּה־לּוֹ סוּסִים — *He shall not have too many horses for himself.* The Torah put this prohibition of many horses before that of many wives, because the matter of horses involves the well-being of the entire people, as the Torah goes on to point out: "so that he will not return the people to Egypt in order to increase horses." But as for taking many wives, that would only harm the king himself.

The order of injunctions might also be a logical one: a newly-appointed king would doubtless concern himself first of all with the country's security, which he must guarantee with cavalry and chariots, and only later would he turn to his personal concerns.

יז וְלֹא יָסוּר לְבָבוֹ וְכֶסֶף וְזָהָב לֹא יַרְבֶּה־לּוֹ מְאֹד:
יח־כ יח וְהָיָה כְשִׁבְתּוֹ עַל כִּסֵּא מַמְלַכְתּוֹ וְכָתַב לוֹ אֶת־
מִשְׁנֵה הַתּוֹרָה הַזֹּאת עַל־סֵפֶר מִלִּפְנֵי הַכֹּהֲנִים הַלְוִיִּם:
יט וְהָיְתָה עִמּוֹ וְקָרָא בוֹ כָּל־יְמֵי חַיָּיו לְמַעַן יִלְמַד
לְיִרְאָה אֶת־יהוה אֱלֹהָיו לִשְׁמֹר אֶת־כָּל־דִּבְרֵי הַתּוֹרָה
הַזֹּאת וְאֶת־הַחֻקִּים הָאֵלֶּה לַעֲשֹׂתָם: כ לְבִלְתִּי רוּם־לְבָבוֹ

---

17. וְלֹא יַרְבֶּה־לּוֹ נָשִׁים וְלֹא יָסוּר לְבָבוֹ — *And he shall not have too many wives so that his heart not turn astray.* As is said: "Harlotry and old and new wine seize upon [man's] heart" (*Hoshea* 4:11). The reason for this prohibition, then, is that the king himself, being so occupied with wives, will find his heart turning away from God's Torah, and from the business of ruling his kingdom as well. And in *Mishlei* (31:4) it says, "Let kings not drink wine, and for nobles no strong drink; lest he drink, and forget what is written, and pervert the judgment of all the poor."

18. וְכָתַב לוֹ אֶת־מִשְׁנֵה הַתּוֹרָה הַזֹּאת עַל־סֵפֶר מִלִּפְנֵי הַכֹּהֲנִים הַלְוִיִּם — *He shall write for himself two copies of this Torah in a book, from before the Kohanim, the Levites.* Those who would falsify the Torah in every generation (the Sadducees, for example), always sought a way to the heart of Israel's king or leader, hoping to persuade him to adopt their "Torah," and through him to subvert the religious faith of the entire Jewish people. Therefore the Torah cautions that the king himself should write two copies of the Torah, in the presence of the *Kohanim*, to whom Moses handed over the Torah originally, as the Torah says: "Moses wrote this Torah and gave it to the *Kohanim*, the sons of Levi" (31:9), so that they would safeguard it against forgery. This, too, is why they were commanded to place the Torah "at the side of the Ark of the covenant of Hashem, and it shall be there for you as a witness" (31:26). "There" is the Holy of Holies, where no one may enter and it would not be tampered with. The *Rambam* writes, "[The king's scroll] is proofread against the Torah scroll of the Outer Temple Court, according to the ruling of the Great *Beis Din* of seventy Sages" (*Hilchos Sefer Torah* 7:2). The *Rambam* specifically mentions the Torah scroll written by the king, because there were many who might wish to falsify it.

19. וְהָיְתָה עִמּוֹ וְקָרָא בוֹ — *It shall be with him, and he shall read in it.* The commentators have pointed out the grammatical inconsistency here: the phrase begins with a feminine verb (הָיְתָה), but it ends with a masculine form (בּוֹ). This can be explained in the light of the interpretation of the *Tosafos*, which says that the Torah scroll that was worn perpetually by the king, sewn onto his sleeve, contained only the Ten Commandments, that is, only a single *parashah* of the Torah. Since פָּרָשָׁה is a feminine noun, "it shall be with him" is written in the feminine gender. But the second scroll that the king wrote contained the complete Torah, and therefore would be called a סֵפֶר, which is a masculine noun.

17 18-20 *so that his heart not turn astray; and he shall not greatly*
increase silver and gold for himself. [18] *It shall be that when he*
sits on the throne of his kingdom, he shall write for himself
two copies of this Torah in a book, from before the Kohanim,
the Levites. [19] *It shall be with him, and he shall read in it all*
the days of his life, so that he will learn to fear HASHEM, *his*
God, to observe all the words of this Torah and these decrees,
to perform them, [20] *so that his heart does not become haughty*

(This was the Torah written by the king "in a book" [עַל סֵפֶר] in the presence of the *Kohanim*, so that no one could falsify it.) Since *sefer* is masculine, the words "in it" are in the masculine gender. (I received this explanation in a letter from my nephew, the *gaon* R' Shmuel David Walkin [זצ"ל], formerly *Av Beis Din* of Lukacz, now in Brooklyn.)

לְמַעַן יִלְמַד לְיִרְאָה אֶת־ה׳ אֱלֹהָיו — *So that he will learn to fear Hashem, his God.* Why does the Torah single out the king for its discussion of fear of God, when that is something required of everyone?

Two reasons may be offered. First, based on the *Midrash Hagadol,* which teaches "Woe to authority, for it removes the fear of Heaven from those who hold it," we can say that the Torah is cautioning the king to counteract this tendency by studying Torah constantly all his life.

Second, world history, and the history of the Jews in particular, teach us that a king who strays from the way of God gradually turns the hearts of his people, too, away from God (and the reverse is also true). Thus the Torah is warning the king not to be "a sinner who also causes the populace to sin," God forbid.

19-20. וְקָרָא בוֹ . . . לְמַעַן יִלְמַד לְיִרְאָה אֶת־ה׳ אֱלֹהָיו לִשְׁמֹר אֶת־כָּל־דִּבְרֵי הַתּוֹרָה הַזֹּאת . . . לַעֲשֹׂתָם. לְבִלְתִּי רוּם־לְבָבוֹ — *And he shall read in it . . . so that he will learn to fear Hashem, his God, to observe all the words of this Torah . . . to perform them, so that his heart does not become haughty.* If he studies the Torah in order to observe and perform its commandments, that is "Torah for its own sake." It is certain, then, that he will not come to look down on his brothers, as R' Meir said: "Whoever engages in Torah study for its own sake merits many things . . . [The Torah] clothes him in humility and fear [of God]" (*Pirkei Avos* 6:1).

Furthermore, his heart will "not turn from the commandment right or left," as *Chazal* say, "One who studies in order to practice is given the means to study and to teach, to observe and to practice" (ibid., 4:6), so that "he will prolong years over his kingdom" as *Chazal* say, "[The Torah] gives him kingship and dominion" (ibid., 6:1).

לְמַעַן יִלְמַד לְיִרְאָה אֶת־ה׳ אֱלֹהָיו . . . לְבִלְתִּי רוּם־לְבָבוֹ מֵאֶחָיו — *So that he will learn to fear Hashem, his God . . . so that his heart does not become haughty over his brethren.* A king who knows that there is One above him "Higher than the high," and fears God, will not become haughty over his brethren.

יז מֵאֶחָיו וּלְבִלְתִּי סוּר מִן־הַמִּצְוָה יָמִין וּשְׂמֹאול
כ לְמַעַן יַאֲרִיךְ יָמִים עַל־מַמְלַכְתּוֹ הוּא וּבָנָיו בְּקֶרֶב
יח יִשְׂרָאֵל׃ שלישי א לֹא־יִהְיֶה לַכֹּהֲנִים הַלְוִיִּם
א־ג כָּל־שֵׁבֶט לֵוִי חֵלֶק וְנַחֲלָה עִם־יִשְׂרָאֵל אִשֵּׁי יהוה
וְנַחֲלָתוֹ יֹאכֵלוּן׃ ב וְנַחֲלָה לֹא־יִהְיֶה־לּוֹ בְּקֶרֶב אֶחָיו
יהוה הוּא נַחֲלָתוֹ כַּאֲשֶׁר דִּבֶּר־לוֹ׃ ג וְזֶה
יִהְיֶה מִשְׁפַּט הַכֹּהֲנִים מֵאֵת הָעָם מֵאֵת זֹבְחֵי הַזֶּבַח
אִם־שׁוֹר אִם־שֶׂה וְנָתַן לַכֹּהֵן הַזְּרֹעַ וְהַלְּחָיַיִם וְהַקֵּבָה׃

---

20. לְבִלְתִּי רוּם־לְבָבוֹ מֵאֶחָיו — *So that his heart does not become haughty over his brethren.* Over his brethren, who accord him the honor due to kings. Let not pride steal into his heart, telling him that he is superhuman, not a mortal man, and that he will reign forever. Rather he must study Torah diligently and learn from it that all men stem from the same source: they were taken from the dust of earth and are destined to return to the dust of the earth. Then he will not look down on his subjects, his fellow men.

ּ§ לְבִלְתִּי רוּם־לְבָבוֹ מֵאֶחָיו וּלְבִלְתִּי סוּר מִן־הַמִּצְוָה יָמִין וּשְׂמֹאול — *So that his heart does not become haughty over his brethren and not turn from the commandment right or left.* The Torah's prohibition against pride and haughtiness (according to the *Ramban's* interpretation) comes before that of not turning from the commandments right or left, in order to teach you that a person infected with the trait of pride is incapable of fulfilling the Torah's commandments properly, without deviating from them in some way. (I heard this from my son, the *gaon* R' Elchanan (שליט"א) [זצ"ל], formerly *Av Beis Din* of Zalodak, now in Jerusalem.)

18.

1. לֹא־יִהְיֶה לַכֹּהֲנִים הַלְוִיִּם . . . חֵלֶק וְנַחֲלָה עִם־יִשְׂרָאֵל — *There shall not be for the Kohanim, the Levites . . . a portion and an inheritance with Israel.* This is a directive to the Israelites that they should not envy the *Kohanim* on account of "the fire-offerings of Hashem and His inheritance that they shall eat." Conversely, it is meant to encourage the *Kohanim*: "He shall not have an inheritance among his brethren"; but why not? Because "Hashem is his inheritance, as He spoke to him." There is no inheritance better than this.

3. וְזֶה יִהְיֶה מִשְׁפַּט הַכֹּהֲנִים מֵאֵת הָעָם — *This shall be the due of the Kohanim from the people.* From the people, not from the king, as is the custom of the gentiles, as the Torah says: "Only the land of the priests he did not buy, since the priests had a stipend from Pharaoh, and they lived off their stipend that Pharaoh had given them; therefore they did not sell their land" (*Bereishis* 47:22). In other words, among the gentiles the priests had two sources of livelihood: a portion of the land and also a stipend from the king, thus doubling their income.

17 *over his brethren and not turn from the commandment right or*
20 *left, so that he will prolong years over his kingdom, he and his*
18 *sons amid Israel.*
1-3 [1] *There shall not be for the Kohanim, the Levites — the entire*
tribe of Levi — a portion and an inheritance with Israel; the
fire-offerings of HASHEM and His inheritance shall they eat. [2] *He*
shall not have an inheritance among his brethren; HASHEM is his
inheritance, as He spoke to him.
[3] *This shall be the due of the Kohanim from the people,*
from those who perform a slaughter, whether of an ox or of the
flock: he shall give the Kohen the foreleg, the jaw, and the maw.

Not so with the priests of Jacob. They must serve as an example of modest living, to the entire nation, being content with the necessities of life. And even this meager income must come "from the people," not from the king (which is why this passage is juxtaposed to the passage concerning the king). In this way the *Kohanim* would not be sycophants to the king, but would always be on the side of the people in case the king should oppress them. The *Kohanim* give their priestly blessing of peace to the people out of love, whereas in countries where revolutionaries have succeeded in dethroning their kings, the priests of the various religions are persecuted as "enemies of the people" because they side with the monarchy. If only they knew that they have no reason to persecute the priests of the Jewish religion, for they have always been commanded to live with the people and "from the people," not from the king and for the king.

הַזְּרֹעַ וְהַלְּחָיַיִם וְהַקֵּבָה — *The foreleg, the jaw, and the maw.* See *Rashi* (based on the *Sifre*) for why these particular parts were chosen.

Another reason might be offered, starting by asking why Jacob prayed "If God . . . will give me bread to eat" (*Bereishis* 28:20). Surely it would have been enough to say "if God will give me bread," since we all know that bread is for eating. But suppose a person has bread and his stomach does not function properly, so that he cannot digest the bread. Then it certainly is no good to him. Therefore Jacob prayed for "bread" that he would be able "to eat."

Eating requires hands, a mouth, and a stomach — hands for conveying the food to the mouth, teeth to chew it well for easy digestion, and a healthy stomach to digest it. Now looking at the next verse, we see that it says, "The first of your grain . . . shall you give him." By the merit of tithes the crops are blessed, but what good is a blessing on the grain if, God forbid, the owner of the field becomes ill, too weak even to put food in his mouth and digest it? Therefore the Israelites were commanded to give the foreleg, the jaw, and the maw to the *Kohen*, and by the merit of this *mitzvah* they would have everything they needed to eat their grain: a hand to put it in their mouth, jaws with which to chew it, and a stomach to digest it and bring strength to the whole body.

יח
ד-י

ד רֵאשִׁ֨ית דְּגָֽנְךָ֜ תִּֽירֹשְׁךָ֣ וְיִצְהָרֶ֗ךָ וְרֵאשִׁ֤ית גֵּז
צֹֽאנְךָ֖ תִּתֶּן־לֽוֹ: ה כִּ֣י ב֗וֹ בָּחַ֛ר יהוה אֱלֹהֶ֖יךָ מִכָּל־
שְׁבָטֶ֑יךָ לַֽעֲמֹ֨ד לְשָׁרֵ֧ת בְּשֵׁם־יהוה ה֛וּא וּבָנָ֖יו כָּל־
הַיָּמִֽים: רביעי ו וְכִֽי־יָבֹ֨א הַלֵּוִ֜י מֵֽאַחַ֤ד שְׁעָרֶ֨יךָ֙
מִכָּל־יִשְׂרָאֵ֔ל אֲשֶׁר־ה֥וּא גָּ֖ר שָׁ֑ם וּבָא֙ בְּכָל־אַוַּ֣ת נַפְשׁ֔וֹ
אֶל־הַמָּק֖וֹם אֲשֶׁר־יִבְחַ֥ר יהוה: ז וְשֵׁרֵ֕ת בְּשֵׁ֖ם יהוה אֱלֹהָ֑יו
כְּכָל־אֶחָיו֙ הַֽלְוִיִּ֔ם הָֽעֹמְדִ֥ים שָׁ֖ם לִפְנֵ֥י יהוה: ח חֵ֤לֶק
כְּחֵ֖לֶק יֹאכֵ֑לוּ לְבַ֥ד מִמְכָּרָ֖יו עַל־הָֽאָבֽוֹת: ט כִּ֤י
אַתָּה֙ בָּ֣א אֶל־הָאָ֔רֶץ אֲשֶׁר־יהוה אֱלֹהֶ֖יךָ נֹתֵ֣ן לָ֑ךְ לֹֽא־
תִלְמַ֣ד לַֽעֲשׂ֔וֹת כְּתֽוֹעֲבֹ֖ת הַגּוֹיִ֥ם הָהֵֽם: י לֹֽא־יִמָּצֵ֣א

6-7. וְכִֽי־יָבֹא הַלֵּוִי . . . וְשֵׁרֵת בְּשֵׁם ה' — *When the Levite will come . . . then he shall minister in the name of Hashem.* "You might think that this passage is talking about any member of the tribe of Levi, but the Torah says 'he shall minister'; it is talking about a Levite who is eligible for service [in the Temple, i.e., a *Kohen*], excluding the [ordinary] Levites who are ineligible for service" (*Sifre*).

According to *Chazal* (*Yevamos* 86b), there are twenty-four places in the Torah where the *Kohanim* are called "Levites." Our present verse, which is one of the twenty-four, comes to teach us that a *Kohen* who owes an offering may bring it at any time (even when he is not on duty in the Temple), sacrifice it and eat it, and its hide belongs to him. Similarly, when *Kohanim* come to Jerusalem for a pilgrimage festival, bringing the appropriate offerings with them, each one may offer his own animal on the altar (see *Rashi*).

According to this view, the whole present passage is talking about *Kohanim*, not about ordinary Levites. But the *Torah Temimah* poses a difficulty (based on *Arachin* 11a): *Chazal* deduce from this passage that the Temple choir is a Torah obligation, not only a Rabbinic one, since verse 7 says "Then he shall minister [וְשֵׁרֵת] in the name of Hashem." "What is ministration [שֵׁרוּת] in the name of God?" *Chazal* ask. "We may conclude that it is song [שִׁירָה]." But the duty of singing in the Temple belongs to the Levites, not the *Kohanim*! Having pointed out this discrepancy, the *Torah Temimah* remarks that it needs further study and moves on.

Actually, this question is posed in the *Shitah Mekubetzes* in the name of R' Elchanan, who answers it on the basis of *Tosefos HaRosh*. When the *Sifre* excludes Levites from the message of this verse — says the *Rosh* — that is on the basis of the single word וְשֵׁרֵת, "he shall minister," for of course essentially speaking the Temple ministry is in the hands of the *Kohanim*. But the *Gemara* in *Arachin* is considering a different context: the compound phrase וְשֵׁרֵת בְּשֵׁם ה', "he shall minister in the name of God." This would indicate, not the generality of Temple service but one unique kind: service "in the name of God," which, says the *Gemara*, is the sacred song, and that particular kind of ministry is given over to the Levites.

4 The first of your grain, wine, and oil, and the first of the shear-
ing of your flock shall you give him. 5 For him has HASHEM
chosen from among all your tribes, to stand and minister in
the name of HASHEM, *him and his sons, all the days.*
6 When the Levite will come from one of your cities, from
all of Israel, where he sojourns, and he comes with all the
desire of his soul to the place that HASHEM *will choose, 7 then*
he shall minister in the name of HASHEM, *his God, like all of*
his brethren, the Levites, who stand there before HASHEM.
8 Portion for portion shall they eat, except for what was
transacted by the forefathers.
9 When you come to the Land that HASHEM, *your God,*
gives you, you shall not learn to act according to the
abominations of those nations. 10 There shall not be found

This passage, then, begins by talking about the entire tribe of Levi (and therefore *Kohanim* are referred to here as "Levites," since the initial topic is the entire tribe). Any of this tribe may come to the Temple as he pleases, "and minister" generally speaking, referring only to *Kohanim*, who may offer their personal sacrifices whenever they come. Or he may minister specifically "in the name of God," referring to the Levite choir, their unique ministry in the Temple, which we now discover is a Torah obligation. Each of them may do just like "his brethren, the Levites, who stand there before God," respectively like his fellow *Kohanim* or his fellow Levites. (The *Rambam* understands this passage in the same way, as is clear in the *Mishneh Torah*.)

Only when we come to v. 8, "Portion for portion," does the subject definitely change to *Kohanim* alone.

8. חֵלֶק כְּחֵלֶק יֹאכֵלוּ — *Portion for portion shall they eat.* From this point on the Torah is speaking only of *Kohanim*, for the sacrifices may not be eaten by Levites. *Rashi*, based on the *Sifre*, says that the entire passage is talking only about *Kohanim*, but based on what is said in *Arachin* (see the previous commentary), and on the words of the *Rambam* and the *Rosh*, it seems clear that until now the passage has been talking about both *Kohanim* and Levites, since the Levites also minister in the Temple with their song.

According to this view, only the end of the passage, that is, our present verse, speaks exclusively of *Kohanim*. And so says the *Rambam* explicitly: "And from where do we know that the Torah is speaking only of *Kohanim*? From the words, 'Portion for portion shall they eat,' for there are no gifts in the Temple to be eaten except by *Kohanim*" (*Hilchos Klei HaMikdash* 5:6). The *Rambam* did not bring his evidence from the words "he shall minister" in the previous verse, because in his view they refer to the Levites as well.

9. כִּי אַתָּה בָּא אֶל־הָאָרֶץ . . . לֹא־תִלְמַד לַעֲשׂוֹת כְּתוֹעֲבֹת הַגּוֹיִם הָהֵם — *When you come to the Land . . . you shall not learn to act according to the abominations*

יח בְּךָ מַעֲבִיר בְּנוֹ־וּבִתּוֹ בָּאֵשׁ קֹסֵם קְסָמִים מְעוֹנֵן וּמְנַחֵשׁ
יא־יד וּמְכַשֵּׁף: יא וְחֹבֵר חָבֶר וְשֹׁאֵל אוֹב וְיִדְּעֹנִי וְדֹרֵשׁ אֶל־
הַמֵּתִים: יב כִּי־תוֹעֲבַת יְהֹוָה כָּל־עֹשֵׂה אֵלֶּה וּבִגְלַל
הַתּוֹעֵבֹת הָאֵלֶּה יְהֹוָה אֱלֹהֶיךָ מוֹרִישׁ אוֹתָם מִפָּנֶיךָ:
יג תָּמִים תִּהְיֶה עִם יְהֹוָה אֱלֹהֶיךָ: חמישי יד כִּי ׀ הַגּוֹיִם
הָאֵלֶּה אֲשֶׁר אַתָּה יוֹרֵשׁ אוֹתָם אֶל־מְעֹנְנִים וְאֶל־
קֹסְמִים יִשְׁמָעוּ וְאַתָּה לֹא כֵן נָתַן לְךָ יְהֹוָה אֱלֹהֶיךָ:

---

of those nations. Why is it that in *Parashas Acharei Mos* the Torah says, "Do not perform the practice of the land of Egypt . . . and do not perform the practice of the land of Canaan" (*Vayikra* 18:3), whereas here Egypt is not mentioned, even though Egypt, too, was full of sorcery? This can be explained in two ways: first, these words are being said during the final days of Moses' life, and the new generation had by now forgotten the sorcery they had seen in Egypt.

Second, according to the *Ha'amek Davar*, "since *Eretz Yisrael* has only brief periods of rain, upon which the livelihood of her inhabitants depends, it is necessary to know when the rainfall will be, so as not to be too late in sowing, nor to sow too long before the rain. The seven nations used to use various means of divination, some preferring one method, others another method to determine rainfall. That is why this specific warning was issued to the Children of Israel, 'when you come to the Land.' " This makes our question easy to answer: in Egypt there was no need to divine the time of rainfall, since there is no rainfall there; therefore the Children of Israel were warned only against the abominations that the Canaanites practiced in this area.

10. מַעֲבִיר בְּנוֹ־וּבִתּוֹ בָּאֵשׁ — *One who causes his son or daughter to pass through the fire.* This person does not seem to belong among the practitioners listed here: the astrologer, the one who reads omens, and the sorcerer. But I have found the explanation in the *sefarim.* The idolatrous priests used to promise that anyone who delivered his children over to the Molech would thereby make a covenant with it (and this is why the child would be passed between two bonfires, in the manner of those who seal a covenant [see *Rashi* below, 29:11]). Afterwards, the priests said, the god would come to this man and reveal the future to him.

The *Ramban* writes that "sorcerer" is a general term, and the others listed here are specific categories of sorcerer. The *Abarbanel* disagrees, arguing that if that were the case, the Torah would have put the general term ('sorcerer') first and listed the categories afterwards. He also states the opinion that in those days, one who wanted to make a name for himself as a "seer," that is, to demonstrate his connection with the forces of impurity, would hand his children over to the Molech; therefore this "practitioner" is mentioned first, as a general term.

12. כִּי־תוֹעֲבַת ה׳ כָּל־עֹשֵׂה אֵלֶּה — *For anyone who does these is an abomination of Hashem.* These were the self-appointed wise men who would use the

18
11-14

among you one who causes his son or daughter to pass
through the fire, one who practices divinations, an astrologer,
one who reads omens, a sorcerer; 11 *or an animal charmer, one*
who inquires of Ov or Yidoni, or one who consults the dead.
12 *For anyone who does these is an abomination of* HASHEM,
and because of these abominations HASHEM, *your God,*
banishes [the nations] from before you. 13 *You shall be*
wholehearted with HASHEM, *your God.* 14 *For these nations*
that you are possessing — they hearkened to astrologers and
diviners; but as for you — not so has HASHEM, *your God,*
given for you.

---

forces of impurity against His decrees, denying the authority of the angels whom He appointed to preside over the forces of nature.

13. תָּמִים תִּהְיֶה עִם ה׳ אֱלֹהֶיךָ — *You shall be wholehearted with Hashem, your God*. According to the line of reasoning we took in verse 9, where we quoted the *Ha'amek Davar* as saying that knowledge of when the rains would fall was extremely vital, this admonition (which is also a reassurance) now comes: "Be wholehearted" (trust God to guard you from all kinds of disasters, if you will only be) "with Hashem, your God."

◆ תָּמִים תִּהְיֶה — *You shall be wholehearted.* Even though this may be very difficult (for after all, you do need to know what to do and when to sow), still, you must act wholeheartedly as far as you are able. Then God will come to your aid, for the Torah says to do this "with Hashem, your God." And *Chazal* say, "one who comes to purify himself is helped" (*Yoma* 38b).

We can learn more about this from King David. In his song to God, he said "I was wholehearted *for* Him" (*II Shmuel*, 22:24), whereas in *Tehillim* he says, "I was wholehearted *with* Him" (18:24). The *Malbim*, in the preface to his commentary on this psalm, writes that the song in *Shmuel* was composed first, and later on, when David compiled all his songs of praise into the book of *Tehillim*, he made some emendations to this song. According to this, we may conclude that at first David did not know that God had helped him to achieve the trait of wholeheartedness, and so he said "I was wholehearted *for* Him" — I trusted only in God and in His commandments. But towards the end of his life David realized that he had achieved wholeheartedness *with* God's help, and therefore he changed his phrasing to "I was wholehearted *with* Him."

14. וְאַתָּה לֹא כֵן נָתַן לְךָ ה׳ אֱלֹהֶיךָ — *But as for you — not so has Hashem, your God, provided for you.* You are forbidden to listen to astrologers or to soothsayers. But then you might complain, "They at least have a way of asking their questions, but I? I have none" (*Sifre*). The *Ohr HaChaim* amplifies the complaint: this situation would result in the gentiles being greatly advanced in techniques of knowing the future, while Israel would not be so equipped. Therefore the Torah goes on to say: (continues at v. 15).

יח טו נָבִיא מִקִּרְבְּךָ מֵאַחֶיךָ כָּמֹנִי יָקִים לְךָ יהוה אֱלֹהֶיךָ אֵלָיו
טו־כ תִּשְׁמָעוּן: טז כְּכֹל אֲשֶׁר־שָׁאַלְתָּ מֵעִם יהוה אֱלֹהֶיךָ בְּחֹרֵב
בְּיוֹם הַקָּהָל לֵאמֹר לֹא אֹסֵף לִשְׁמֹעַ אֶת־קוֹל יהוה אֱלֹהָי
וְאֶת־הָאֵשׁ הַגְּדֹלָה הַזֹּאת לֹא־אֶרְאֶה עוֹד וְלֹא אָמוּת:
יז וַיֹּאמֶר יהוה אֵלָי הֵיטִיבוּ אֲשֶׁר דִּבֵּרוּ: יח נָבִיא אָקִים
לָהֶם מִקֶּרֶב אֲחֵיהֶם כָּמוֹךָ וְנָתַתִּי דְבָרַי בְּפִיו וְדִבֶּר אֲלֵיהֶם
אֵת כָּל־אֲשֶׁר אֲצַוֶּנּוּ: יט וְהָיָה הָאִישׁ אֲשֶׁר לֹא־יִשְׁמַע אֶל־
דְּבָרַי אֲשֶׁר יְדַבֵּר בִּשְׁמִי אָנֹכִי אֶדְרֹשׁ מֵעִמּוֹ: כ אַךְ הַנָּבִיא
אֲשֶׁר יָזִיד לְדַבֵּר דָּבָר בִּשְׁמִי אֵת אֲשֶׁר לֹא־צִוִּיתִיו לְדַבֵּר
וַאֲשֶׁר יְדַבֵּר בְּשֵׁם אֱלֹהִים אֲחֵרִים וּמֵת הַנָּבִיא הַהוּא:

---

15. נָבִיא . . . יָקִים לְךָ ה׳ אֱלֹהֶיךָ אֵלָיו תִּשְׁמָעוּן — *A prophet. . . shall Hashem, your God, establish for you — to him shall you hearken.* Here was a great privilege for the Children of Israel, that they would know the future through a prophet of God, whose words are all truth and justice, rather than relying on astrologers and soothsayers.

If the gentiles today were practicing such abominations as reading omens, soothsaying, and raising the dead, this would at least show that they believed in life after death. The dead would also tell their summoners what they were being judged for in *Gehinnom* (*Gittin* 56b-57a); and the spirit called up with an *ov* would refuse the summons on Shabbos (*Sanhedrin* 65b). All this would serve a purpose in strengthening their faith in reward and punishment after death.

Today, on the contrary, every principle of faith is denied, and darkness covers the earth, even among those nations who once boasted of their strong faith. So the question remains: why have the forces of impurity been quiescent for many generations? Why are there no necromancers nor any who seek answers from the dead, and the whole realm of sorcery is seemingly gone from the world?

It seems to me that this, too, can be answered according to what we said on the previous verse. God promised us that we would not be on a lower level than the nations of the world. If the time comes when prophecy must withdraw from Israel, then if the power of divination were to remain with the gentiles, the nations of the world would be on a higher level than Israel, for they would have a way of predicting the future which the Torah has forbidden to us. Therefore the practice of divination has gradually been forgotten among the gentiles (gradually, for even after prophecy had departed from Israel, traces of it still remained in the form of a *bas kol* or *ruach hakodesh*, until the latter generations proved unworthy even of these [*Sotah* 48b]), so that the gentiles would not be on a higher level than Israel.

20. אַךְ הַנָּבִיא אֲשֶׁר יָזִיד לְדַבֵּר דָּבָר בִּשְׁמִי אֵת אֲשֶׁר לֹא־צִוִּיתִיו — *But the prophet who willfully shall speak a word in My name, that which I have not com-*

18
15-20

[15] *A prophet from your midst, from your brethren, like me,*
shall HASHEM, your God, establish for you — to him shall you
hearken. [16] *According to all that you asked of HASHEM, your*
God, in Horeb on the day of the congregation, saying, "I can
no longer hear the voice of HASHEM, my God, and this great
fire I can longer see, so that I shall not die."

[17] *Then HASHEM said to me: They have done well in what*
they have said. [18] *I will establish a prophet for them from*
among their brethren, like you, and I will place My words in
his mouth; He shall speak to them everything that I will
command him. [19] *And it shall be that the man who will not*
hearken to My words that he shall speak in My name, I will
exact from him. [20] *But the prophet who willfully shall speak*
a word in My name, that which I have not commanded him
to speak, or who shall speak in the name of the gods of others
— that prophet shall die.

---

manded him. "But I commanded it to his fellow-prophet" (*Rashi*). Everyone knows that "Whoever repeats a thing in the name of the one who said it brings redemption to the world, as it is said: 'And Esther said to the king in the name of Mordechai' " (*Pirkei Avos* 6:6; *Esther* 2:22). Nevertheless, there are those who are not careful about this, and wrap themselves in a *tallis* that is not theirs; they find a "good *vort*" in a book and repeat it — in their own name.

Perhaps this is because they have not seen what the *Yalkut Shimoni* on *Mishlei* (§938) says about this: "'There are six whom God hates' (*Mishlei* 6: 16), and these are they: idolatry, illicit relations, murder... and one who repeats a thing in the name of one who did not say it [originally], for he brings a curse to the world." The *Yalkut Shimoni* offers no supporting evidence for this identification from the Scriptures, but it seems probable that it is based on the words here in our verse, "that which I have not commanded him," which imply "but I commanded to his fellow prophet." The *Sifre* adds: "Like Chananyah ben Azor, who would hear the words of Jeremiah prophesying in the upper marketplace, and go and 'prophesy' in the lower marketplace."

Now, if Chananyah had said these words in the name of the one who said them first — "Thus says Hashem, through his prophet Jeremiah" — he would have been doing a *mitzvah* by publicizing Jeremiah's prophecy, and also bringing redemption to the world. But because he said them in God's name, as if he himself had become a prophet, he made himself hateful to God, as if he had committed idolatry.

This last is also attested to by our verse: "But the prophet who willfully shall speak a word in My name, that which I have not commanded him to speak, or who shall speak in the name of the gods of others — that prophet shall die." We see that these two are considered equivalent, the one who speaks a word in

יח כא וְכִי תֹאמַר בִּלְבָבֶךָ אֵיכָה נֵדַע אֶת־הַדָּבָר אֲשֶׁר לֹא־
כא־כב דִבְּרוֹ יהוה: כב אֲשֶׁר יְדַבֵּר הַנָּבִיא בְּשֵׁם יהוה וְלֹא־יִהְיֶה
הַדָּבָר וְלֹא יָבֹא הוּא הַדָּבָר אֲשֶׁר לֹא־דִבְּרוֹ יהוה בְּזָדוֹן
יט דִּבְּרוֹ הַנָּבִיא לֹא תָגוּר מִמֶּנּוּ: א כִּי־יַכְרִית
א־ב יהוה אֱלֹהֶיךָ אֶת־הַגּוֹיִם אֲשֶׁר יהוה אֱלֹהֶיךָ נֹתֵן לְךָ
אֶת־אַרְצָם וִירִשְׁתָּם וְיָשַׁבְתָּ בְעָרֵיהֶם וּבְבָתֵּיהֶם: ב שָׁלוֹשׁ
עָרִים תַּבְדִּיל לָךְ בְּתוֹךְ אַרְצְךָ אֲשֶׁר יהוה אֱלֹהֶיךָ נֹתֵן לְךָ

God's name that God has not commanded to him (but to his fellow prophet), and the one who speaks in the name of other gods.

But still one could advance such a sophistry as arguing that all this applies specifically to prophecy. Chananyah wanted to make himself an "established prophet," and since all his words (which he had heard from Jeremiah) came true, the natural result would be that people would rely on him as a true prophet. But when someone hears a "vort" on *halachah* or *aggadah* from his *rebbe* or his friend, and then goes on to repeat it as if it were his own, no harm comes of it (seemingly). What, then, made *Chazal* decide that such a person brings a curse to the world, and why did they count him among the "six whom God hates," together with those who commit idolatry, illicit relations, and murder?

Furthermore, we might ask why *Chazal* chose the word "curse." Since whoever repeats a thing in the name of the one who said it brings redemption to the world, it would seem more logical to say that whoever does the opposite brings the opposite effect to the world, that is, servitude or exile.

It would appear that they learned the point in question from the episode when Rebecca sent Jacob instead of his brother Esau to receive Isaac's blessing. When Jacob said to Isaac, "I have done as you told me" (*Bereishis* 27:19), he was speaking words not in the name of the one who said them, words "which I have not commanded him, but have commanded another." Even though Jacob was obliged to do this so that the wicked Esau would not receive the blessings, nevertheless, as the commentators explain, if Isaac (who was unaware of Esau's wicked deeds because of his blindness) had felt Jacob's hands and realized that he was speaking things that had been said not to him but to Esau, he would have cursed Jacob, as the Torah says, "I will bring upon myself a curse" (ibid. v. 12).

Thus we see that not only in the matter of prophecy, but any time a person says a thing in the name of one who did not say it, he brings a curse, not only on himself, as Jacob said, but on the whole world. For if Isaac had blessed Esau the world would have gone straight to its ruination. May the Merciful One save us from this, and incline our hearts to say everything in the name of the one who said it — even secular things, for every word of wisdom is given to a person from Heaven, and is part of his portion of the Torah. And thus may we bring redemption to the world.

18 [21] *When you say in your heart, "How can we know the*
21-22 *word that HASHEM has not spoken?"* [22] *If the prophet will*
speak in the Name of HASHEM and that thing will not occur
and not come about — that is the word that HASHEM has not
spoken; with willfulness has the prophet spoken it, you
should not fear him.
19 [1] *When HASHEM, your God, will cut down the nations*
1-2 *whose Land HASHEM, your God, gives you, and you will*
possess them, and you will settle in their cities and in their
houses, [2] *you shall separate three cities for yourselves in the*
midst of your Land, which HASHEM, your God, gives you

19.

2. תַּבְדִּיל לָךְ — *You shall separate ... for yourselves.* "And not for others" (*Sifre*). That is to say, a gentile who kills accidentally cannot atone for his deed by going into exile; he must die.

Interpreting the verse in its simple sense, we can say that "for yourselves" means at your service, for even though all forty-two cities that the Children of Israel gave to the Levites to dwell in (see *Bamidbar* 35) also took in accidental murderers, there is a difference between these cities and the Cities of Refuge. Since the forty-two cities were given exclusively to the Levites, certainly the killer who flees to one of them must pay rent to the Levites (and this is a problem for the killer, since he is in exile, in a place where he has no source of livelihood except from the mother of the *Kohen Gadol*, who would provide the killers with food and clothing [see *Makkos* 11a]).

The six Cities of Refuge, on the other hand (three in the Trans-Jordan and three to the west of the Jordan), though they also served as dwelling-places for the Levites, were chiefly given for any Israelite to flee to if the disaster of accidentally killing someone should befall him. One who fled there would not have to pay rent to the Levites, and thus the Torah says, "You shall separate ... for yourselves." This idea is confirmed by the verse in *Parashas Masei* which says, "the six Cities of Refuge that you shall provide for a murderer to flee there" (*Bamidbar* 35:6); that is to say, they are chiefly Cities of Refuge, but Levites dwell there in order to teach Torah to the exiles. (It must have been for a reason that human lives were lost at their hands; they most likely committed some sin which brought this tragedy in its wake, as the Torah says, "the consequence of a sin is a sin" [*Pirkei Avos* 4:2]. Through Torah study in exile they will return to God's way and their sin will be atoned.)

What is more, the matter taken up in the next verse, "Prepare the way for yourself," dealing with providing good roads to the cities of refuge and posting signs at crossroads to show the way, applies only to the six Cities of Refuge, which are open and free to anyone who has taken life unintentionally, whether he is poor or rich. But no such commandments apply to the roads leading to

יט לְרִשְׁתָּהּ: ג תָּכִין לְךָ הַדֶּרֶךְ וְשִׁלַּשְׁתָּ אֶת־גְּבוּל אַרְצְךָ אֲשֶׁר
ג־י יַנְחִילְךָ יהוה אֱלֹהֶיךָ וְהָיָה לָנוּס שָׁמָּה כָּל־רֹצֵחַ: ד וְזֶה
דְּבַר הָרֹצֵחַ אֲשֶׁר־יָנוּס שָׁמָּה וָחָי אֲשֶׁר יַכֶּה אֶת־רֵעֵהוּ
בִּבְלִי־דַעַת וְהוּא לֹא־שֹׂנֵא לוֹ מִתְּמֹל שִׁלְשֹׁם: ה וַאֲשֶׁר
יָבֹא אֶת־רֵעֵהוּ בַיַּעַר לַחְטֹב עֵצִים וְנִדְּחָה יָדוֹ בַגַּרְזֶן
לִכְרֹת הָעֵץ וְנָשַׁל הַבַּרְזֶל מִן־הָעֵץ וּמָצָא אֶת־רֵעֵהוּ וָמֵת
הוּא יָנוּס אֶל־אַחַת הֶעָרִים־הָאֵלֶּה וָחָי: ו פֶּן־יִרְדֹּף גֹּאֵל
הַדָּם אַחֲרֵי הָרֹצֵחַ כִּי יֵחַם לְבָבוֹ וְהִשִּׂיגוֹ כִּי־יִרְבֶּה הַדֶּרֶךְ
וְהִכָּהוּ נָפֶשׁ וְלוֹ אֵין מִשְׁפַּט־מָוֶת כִּי לֹא שֹׂנֵא הוּא לוֹ
מִתְּמוֹל שִׁלְשׁוֹם: ז עַל־כֵּן אָנֹכִי מְצַוְּךָ לֵאמֹר שָׁלֹשׁ עָרִים
תַּבְדִּיל לָךְ: ח וְאִם־יַרְחִיב יהוה אֱלֹהֶיךָ אֶת־גְּבֻלְךָ כַּאֲשֶׁר
נִשְׁבַּע לַאֲבֹתֶיךָ וְנָתַן לְךָ אֶת־כָּל־הָאָרֶץ אֲשֶׁר דִּבֶּר לָתֵת
לַאֲבֹתֶיךָ: ט כִּי־תִשְׁמֹר אֶת־כָּל־הַמִּצְוָה הַזֹּאת לַעֲשֹׂתָהּ
אֲשֶׁר אָנֹכִי מְצַוְּךָ הַיּוֹם לְאַהֲבָה אֶת־יהוה אֱלֹהֶיךָ וְלָלֶכֶת
בִּדְרָכָיו כָּל־הַיָּמִים וְיָסַפְתָּ לְךָ עוֹד שָׁלֹשׁ עָרִים עַל הַשָּׁלֹשׁ
הָאֵלֶּה: י וְלֹא יִשָּׁפֵךְ דָּם נָקִי בְּקֶרֶב אַרְצְךָ אֲשֶׁר יהוה
אֱלֹהֶיךָ נֹתֵן לְךָ נַחֲלָה וְהָיָה עָלֶיךָ דָּמִים:

---

other Levite cities, although they also take in unintentional murderers, for a poor man or one of average means could not afford to rent a dwelling-place there. And if the killer should think of fleeing to the nearest Levite city for the time being, and afterwards move to a City of Refuge where he can live for free, he will find it impossible, for he must stay in the first city that took him in for the rest of his days or until the death of the *Kohen Gadol.* If he moves to another city the redeemer of the blood is permitted by the Torah to kill him. (See *Bamidbar* 35:19.)

3. **וְהָיָה לָנוּס שָׁמָּה** — *And it shall be ... to flee there.* "So that he should not wander in exile from city to city" (*Sifre*). The *Malbim* interprets this as meaning that the killer should go straight to a City of Refuge, and not move from city to city until he reaches a City of Refuge. Therefore there should be a direct road to the City of Refuge which does not pass through any other cities on the way.

Now, this is a most impractical idea; to provide a direct road from each town or village to a City of Refuge, passing through no other town. It would seem more plausible to say that "to flee there" means that the killer should remain in the first City of Refuge that he comes to (as *Chazal* expounded, "'that he has fled *there*' — *there* will be his dwelling, *there* will be his death, *there* will be his burial" [*Makkos* 11b]); he must not flee again from there to another City of Refuge. This fits the *Sifre's* interpretation, that he should not wander

19
3-10

to possess it. 3 Prepare the way for yourself, and divide into
three parts the boundary of the Land that HASHEM, *your God,*
causes you to inherit; and it shall be for any murderer to flee
there. 4 This is the matter of the murderer who shall flee there
and live: One who will strike his fellow without knowledge,
and he did not hate him from yesterday or before yesterday;
5 or who will come with his fellow into the forest to hew trees,
and his hand swings the axe to cut the tree, and the iron slips
from the wood and finds his fellow and he dies, he shall flee
to one of these cities and live, 6 lest the redeemer of the blood
will chase after the murderer, for his heart will be hot, and he
will overtake him for the way was long, and he shall strike
him mortally — and there is no judgment of death upon him,
for he did not hate him from yesterday and before yesterday.
7 Therefore I command you, saying: You shall separate three
cities for yourselves.

8 When HASHEM *will broaden your boundary, as He swore*
to your forefathers, and He will give you the entire Land that
he spoke to your forefathers to give, 9 when you observe this
entire commandment to perform it — which I command you
today — to love HASHEM, *your God, and to walk in His ways*
all the years, then you shall add three more cities to these
three. 10 Innocent blood shall not be shed in the midst of your
Land that HASHEM, *your God, gives you as an inheritance, for*
then blood will be upon you.

---

from city to city. And if he does so, and the redeemer of the blood finds him in another City of Refuge and kills him, the redeemer is free of guilt.

4. וְזֶה דְּבַר הָרֹצֵחַ אֲשֶׁר־יָנוּס שָׁמָּה וָחָי — *This is the matter of the murderer who shall flee there and live.* Although all killers flee to the Cities of Refuge, not all are taken in. Only those who killed unintentionally and bore no previous hatred toward the victim "shall flee there and live."

6. פֶּן־יִרְדֹּף גֹּאֵל הַדָּם אַחֲרֵי הָרֹצֵחַ — *Lest the redeemer of the blood will chase after the murderer.* Concerning "the redemption of blood" of which the Torah speaks (which is a great contrast to the custom among backward peoples, whereby the relatives of the victim ambush the murderer and kill him without due process of law), see *Bamidbar* 35:19,25.

10. וְלֹא יִשָּׁפֵךְ דָּם נָקִי בְּקֶרֶב אַרְצְךָ אֲשֶׁר ה׳ אֱלֹהֶיךָ נֹתֵן לְךָ נַחֲלָה וְהָיָה עָלֶיךָ דָּמִים — *Innocent blood shall not be shed in the midst of your Land that Hashem, your God, gives you as an inheritance, for then blood will be upon you.* That is, if we fail to prepare the way to the Cities of Refuge, and the unintentional killer takes too long on his way, so that the redeemer of blood catches up with him

יט יא וְכִי־יִהְיֶה אִישׁ שֹׂנֵא לְרֵעֵהוּ וְאָרַב לוֹ וְקָם עָלָיו וְהִכָּהוּ
יא־יד נֶפֶשׁ וָמֵת וְנָס אֶל־אַחַת הֶעָרִים הָאֵל: יב וְשָׁלְחוּ זִקְנֵי
עִירוֹ וְלָקְחוּ אֹתוֹ מִשָּׁם וְנָתְנוּ אֹתוֹ בְּיַד גֹּאֵל הַדָּם וָמֵת:
יג לֹא־תָחוֹס עֵינְךָ עָלָיו וּבִעַרְתָּ דַם־הַנָּקִי מִיִּשְׂרָאֵל
וְטוֹב לָךְ: ששי יד לֹא תַסִּיג גְּבוּל רֵעֲךָ אֲשֶׁר

---

and strikes him down. The redeemer is not sentenced to death; the blood is upon the people of Israel.

This applies specifically "in the midst of your Land that Hashem, your God, gives you as an inheritance." But if the Children of Israel should conquer other lands, no blood will be upon them if they have no Cities of Refuge there (with the exception of the Kenite, Kenizite, and Kadmonite lands, which are part of their inheritance, as promised to the Patriarchs).

But this entire matter requires an explanation. Why is a sin of omission which leads indirectly to bloodshed, such as our case here or the case of the murdered man whose killer cannot be found (21:1-9), considered a "blood taint" upon the entire Jewish people?

At the end of this *parashah*, in the passage on the heifer whose neck is axed, (עֶגְלָה עֲרוּפָה) the elders ask "Atone for Your people Israel that You have redeemed, O Hashem: Do not place innocent blood in the midst of Your people Israel," (21:8). The *Sifre* expounds: "'that you have redeemed, O Hashem' — this teaches that the heifer atones for the [redeemed] generation of the Exodus. [How?] 'Atone for Your people' — these are the living; 'that You have redeemed'— this teaches that the dead [i.e., the redeemed generation, that of the Exodus] need atonement; we must conclude, then, that if anyone spills blood [the effects of] his sin extends to the generation of the Exodus. [Why?] 'that You have redeemed' — You redeemed us on condition that there be no murderers among us."

These are very surprising words. Why did God make the condition, on redeeming us from Egypt, that there be no murderers among us, but no conditions about any other kind of sin?

We may answer this by pointing out first of all that the most serious sins of all are idolatry, illicit sexual relations, and murder. When the Adversary came to speak against the Children of Israel at the time of the Exodus, he charged that they were no better than the Egyptians: "These worship idols, and those worship idols." And indeed, the Children of Israel were sunk in idolatry while in Egypt. On the other hand however, the Jews, unlike the Egyptians, were very careful about sexual morality — there was only one woman (Shulamis bas Divri) who failed in this matter, and her shame was publicized in the Scriptures (See *Shemos Rabbah*, ch. 1, and *Vayikra Rabbah*, ch. 32).

As for murder, we find in the Scriptures that there were murderers and slanderers among the Children of Israel (Dathan and Abiram and their faction) when Moses went out of Pharaoh's palace to see the condition of his brothers.

19
11-14

[11] *But if there will be a man who hates his fellow, and ambushes him and rises up against him, and strikes him mortally and he dies, and he flees to one of these cities —* [12] *then the elders of his city shall send and take him from there and place him in the hand of the redeemer of the blood, and he shall die.* [13] *Your eye shall not pity him; you shall remove the innocent blood from Israel; and it shall be good for you.*

[14] *You shall not move a boundary of your fellow, which*

At the burning bush, when God appointed him to redeem Israel, he replied "Master of the World, how can I enter a den of robbers and murderers?" (*Shemos Rabbah*, ch. 3). In this case, the Children of Israel were guilty of two out of the three most serious sins.

Once their redeemer came to them, however, they were cured of their habit of slander and talebearing, for we see that for the entire twelve months prior to the redemption (the whole period of the Ten Plagues), they kept silent about God's promise that "Each woman shall request from her neighbor ... silver vessels, golden vessels, and garments... and you shall empty out Egypt" (*Shemos* 3:22). Not one person revealed this secret to the Egyptians, not even Dathan and Abiram (*Yalkut Shimoni* §172). But their "recovery" from slander (which is as serious as bloodshed [*Arachin* 15b] was not complete; all their journeying in the Wilderness was tainted by strife and quarreling. Therefore, in order to tip the scales to the side of merit and redeem Israel from Egypt, God laid down the condition that there be no murderers among them. And in accordance with this condition, we must keep the Land of Israel free even of indirectly caused bloodshed (keeping in mind that slander is often an indirect cause of bloodshed).

14. **לֹא תַסִּיג גְּבוּל רֵעֲךָ** — *You shall not move a boundary of your fellow.* "Has not the Torah already told us not to steal? [And is not moving back a boundary marker to encroach upon your neighbor's land also a form of stealing?] This teaches, then, that one who encroaches on his neighbor's property violates [not one but] two negative commandments. Perhaps this applies even outside of the Land of Israel? [No,] the Torah says, 'in your inheritance that you shall inherit.' In the Land of Israel he transgresses two negative commandments; outside of the Land he transgresses only one'" (*Sifre*).

Apparently the commandment not to move a boundary marker applies only in *Eretz Yisrael*, which Moses and Joshua apportioned everlastingly among the Children of Israel, and this is why the Torah says, "which the early ones marked out, in your inheritance that you shall inherit, in the Land that Hashem, your God, gives you to possess it." This is similar to the distinction we made concerning the Cities of Refuge (see commentary on v. 2 and v. 10 above), and in token of this the prohibition of moving a boundary is juxtaposed to the passage on the Cities of Refuge. Neither of these two commandments applies to conquered lands, even those conquered lands that are considered part of *Eretz*

גָּבְלוּ רִאשֹׁנִים בְּנַחֲלָתְךָ אֲשֶׁר תִּנְחַל בָּאָרֶץ אֲשֶׁר יְהוָה יט
אֱלֹהֶיךָ נֹתֵן לְךָ לְרִשְׁתָּהּ׃ טו לֹא־יָקוּם טו־טז
עֵד אֶחָד בְּאִישׁ לְכָל־עָוֺן וּלְכָל־חַטָּאת בְּכָל־חֵטְא
אֲשֶׁר יֶחֱטָא עַל־פִּי ׀ שְׁנֵי עֵדִים אוֹ עַל־פִּי שְׁלֹשָׁה־עֵדִים
יָקוּם דָּבָר׃ טז כִּי־יָקוּם עֵד־חָמָס בְּאִישׁ לַעֲנוֹת בּוֹ סָרָה׃

Yisrael in other respects. There is no obligation to designate new Cities of Refuge in these areas, nor is there any specific prohibition of moving a boundary marker in addition to the existing prohibition of stealing.

15. עַל־פִּי שְׁנֵי עֵדִים אוֹ עַל־פִּי שְׁלֹשָׁה־עֵדִים — *According to two witnesses or according to three witnesses.* The Torah says עַל פִּי, "by the mouth of," that is, according to their oral testimony and not according to a written statement. The witnesses are not to send their testimony to the court in writing because that would make it impossible to examine them. (Our practice of sometimes accepting an affidavit instead of a live witness is a Rabbinic ordinance designed to streamline the handling of property cases, with the intention that wealthy people should not fear lending to the needy. So the Sages decreed: "[The testimony] of witnesses who have signed an affidavit is equivalent to testimony examined in the court.")

Chazal further interpreted our verse to mean that the testimony must not come from an interpreter; that is, the witness cannot give evidence in a language not understood by the judges, because then the interpreter would become a witness offering second-hand evidence.

16. כִּי־יָקוּם עֵד־חָמָס בְּאִישׁ — *If a false witness stands against a man.* The reference is specifically to witnesses who are proven to have conspired at giving false testimony. Thus: If two witnesses testified that a man committed a transgression punishable by death or lashes, or that he owes someone money, and the sentence is pronounced, and then two more witnesses appear who contradict the first witnesses, claiming that the accused was with them at the stated time of the "crime" and so could not have done what he is accused of having done, then both testimonies are null and void. Even if two witnesses gave the first testimony and a hundred gave the second, or vice versa, all evidence from both sides is null and void, and everyone involved, both the accused and the witnesses, is exempt from punishment.

But suppose the second pair of witnesses comes to the court and says to the first pair, "How can you say that on such-and-such a day, at such-and-such a time and place, this man committed such-and-such a transgression? You were with us at that time at a different place!" In this case the Torah believes the second pair of witnesses, and the first pair now goes on trial as conspiring witnesses. Of them the Torah says, "You shall do to him as he conspired to do to his fellow" (v. 19); that is, the accused is exonerated and the witnesses who conspired against him are punished by death, lashes, or a

19 *the early ones marked out, in your inheritance that you shall*
15-16 *inherit, in the Land that* HASHEM, *your God, gives you to*
possess it.
15 *A single witness shall not stand up against any man for*
any iniquity or for any error, regarding any sin that he may
commit; according to two witnesses or according to three
witnesses shall a matter be confirmed. 16 *If a false witness*
stands against a man to speak up spuriously against him,

---

monetary payment, whatever penalty they were trying to impose upon the man they accused.

But in what respect does the second case differ from the first? The difference is that in the second case, the second pair of witnesses does not testify concerning the actual matter which the first pair has brought before the court. — If they did, there would be no more reason to believe them than to believe the first pair, so both testimonies would be null and void. — They come instead to testify that the first witnesses are unqualified to give evidence. It is just as if they testified about them that they had desecrated the Sabbath, or committed robbery, or done anything else that disqualifies them as witnesses.

Here, therefore the second pair of witnesses is considered credible, since the first pair now occupies the position of the accused, and any testimony they may offer about themselves is not acceptable. Since the two pairs are not equally credible, the second pair's word is believed against the first pair's — not only to cancel out their testimony, but to carry out the judgment against them, of "doing to him as he conspired to do to his fellow." If the sentence was to be death they are executed, if it was lashes they are lashed, and so on.

Chazal add that this ruling is an innovation of the Torah's, to believe the second witnesses and carry out the sentence against the first (see *Bava Kamma* 72 and *Tosafos* ad loc. ד"ה אין לך).

The phrase "a false witness" refers to two witnesses, as *Chazal* explain: Since in v. 15 the Torah commands that "A single witness shall not stand up," we can derive from this that whenever the Torah speaks of "a witness" with no number designated, the meaning is at least two witnesses. In v. 18, too, though the Torah uses the singular form, the meaning is two witnesses. But why does the Torah use the singular form when it says, "You shall do to him as he conspired to do to his fellow"? Why not "You shall do to them"? To teach us that the witnesses are not considered conspirators unless witnesses come to prove that all of them had conspired; if only one is proven a conspirator, or if there were a hundred of them and all of them are proven conspirators except one, then they are not judged as conspiring witnesses. Therefore the Torah says, "You shall do to him . . .", for they are considered as one man in this matter. If they did not all conspire together, they are exempt from punishment.

יז וְעָמְדוּ שְׁנֵי־הָאֲנָשִׁים אֲשֶׁר־לָהֶם הָרִיב לִפְנֵי יְהוָה יט
לִפְנֵי הַכֹּהֲנִים וְהַשֹּׁפְטִים אֲשֶׁר יִהְיוּ בַּיָּמִים הָהֵם: יז־כא
יח וְדָרְשׁוּ הַשֹּׁפְטִים הֵיטֵב וְהִנֵּה עֵד־שֶׁקֶר הָעֵד שֶׁקֶר עָנָה
בְאָחִיו: יט וַעֲשִׂיתֶם לוֹ כַּאֲשֶׁר זָמַם לַעֲשׂוֹת לְאָחִיו
וּבִעַרְתָּ הָרָע מִקִּרְבֶּךָ: כ וְהַנִּשְׁאָרִים יִשְׁמְעוּ וְיִרָאוּ וְלֹא־
יֹסִפוּ לַעֲשׂוֹת עוֹד כַּדָּבָר הָרָע הַזֶּה בְּקִרְבֶּךָ: כא וְלֹא
תָחוֹס עֵינֶךָ נֶפֶשׁ בְּנֶפֶשׁ עַיִן בְּעַיִן שֵׁן בְּשֵׁן יָד בְּיָד כ
רֶגֶל בְּרָגֶל: א כִּי־תֵצֵא לַמִּלְחָמָה עַל־אֹיְבֶךָ א

---

17. וְעָמְדוּ שְׁנֵי־הָאֲנָשִׁים אֲשֶׁר־לָהֶם הָרִיב לִפְנֵי ה׳ — *Then the two men who have [lit., "whose is"] the grievance shall stand before Hashem.* Interpreting the verse in its simplest sense, we could say that the whole verse is talking about the witnesses who have come under suspicion of conspiracy, and the Torah calls them "men" rather than "witnesses," for they have lost their status as witnesses and become merely "men." And they have become not simply men, but "the men who have the grievance," for now all the trouble is completely theirs: they have become the defendants, and the punishment they conspired to inflict on another has now come back to them.

18. וְדָרְשׁוּ הַשֹּׁפְטִים — *The judges shall inquire.* Although the previous verse said that the witnesses "shall stand ... before the *Kohanim* and the judges," it is better that the investigation be done by the judges, who do not have other duties, rather than by the *Kohanim*, who are busy with their duties in the Temple and their other special duties. As the saying goes, "I have never been beaten except by one who plied a single trade" (*Mishlei Yisrael* 3673).

וְהִנֵּה עֵד־שֶׁקֶר — *And behold! the testimony [witness] was false testimony [witness.]* The witness is a false witness, for he could not have seen what happened, having been elsewhere at the time. The testimony itself is not necessarily false; it may have happened as the witness stated, and then again it may not have happened that way. It is the witness himself who is false, and that makes him subject to the sentence, "You shall do to him as he conspired to do . . ."

19. וַעֲשִׂיתֶם לוֹ כַּאֲשֶׁר זָמַם לַעֲשׂוֹת לְאָחִיו — *You shall do to him as he conspired to do to his fellow.* The Tradition teaches: "[Do to him] as he conspired to do, not as he did." That is, if the accused has already been executed, then if the conspirators are discovered now, they are not executed. But if the accused has not yet been executed (only sentenced), and then the conspirators are discovered, they are executed.

Although we might say that if they succeeded in their plot and the accused was killed, that is all the more reason for them to be killed, still, according to Torah law they are not punished. More precisely, they are not punished if the case involves an alleged corporal or capital offense, but in a civil case they are punished, by being required to pay the sum that they conspired to make their

19 *17 then the two men [and those] who have the grievance shall*
17-21 *stand before HASHEM, before the Kohanim and the judges*
who will be in those days. 18 The judges shall inquire
thoroughly, and behold! the testimony was false testimony;
he spoke up falsely against his fellow. 19 You shall do to him
as he conspired to do to his fellow, and you shall destroy the
evil from your midst. 20 And those who remain shall hearken
and fear; and they shall not continue again to do such an evil
thing in your midst. 21 Your eye shall not pity; life for life, eye
20 *for eye, tooth for tooth, hand for hand, foot for foot.*
1 *1 When you go out to the battle against your enemy,*

---

victim pay. Even if the alleged "borrower" has already "repaid" the sum, then the "lender" must return it to him, and he will then receive the same sum of money from the conspirators, for in the realm of property law we administer punishment on a more wide-ranging basis (see *Tosafos* on *Bava Kamma* 4b, ד״ה ועדים).

The *Rambam* writes (*Hil. Eidus* 20:2) that even in a case involving punishment by lashes, we do not apply the principle of "as he conspired, not as he did." So even if the accused has already received lashes, the conspirators now receive lashes, too. This is supported by one interpretation of why "if he has been killed, they are not killed." By this interpretation, if the accused were still alive, he might confess the truth of their charges when he saw innocent people being taken away for execution. There is no room for this doubt in a case of lashes; since the accused is alive, if he does not confess, then they are subject to lashes.

20. וְהַנִּשְׁאָרִים יִשְׁמְעוּ וְיִרָאוּ — *And those who remain shall hearken and fear.* "There must be an announcement that so-and-so and so-and-so are to be executed because they were shown up as conspirators in court" (*Rashi*). We may infer from this that such an announcement is necessary only in a capital case, and that only concerning such a case does the Torah say "and those who remain shall hearken and fear." But the *Rambam* writes (*Hil. Eidus* 18:7): "[The punishment of] conspiring witnesses requires an announcement . . . A letter is sent out to every city saying that so-and-so and so-and-so testified such-and-such, were found to be conspirators, and were put to death, or received lashes, in our presence, or we penalized them with a fine of such-and-such a sum, as the Torah says, 'And those who remain shall hearken and fear.'" In other words, even cases involving lashes or monetary settlements require an announcement, and the principle of "they shall hearken and fear" is relevant here, too — especially because by means of the announcement the conspirators will be publicized as people disqualified to testify in the future.

21. עַיִן בְּעַיִן — *Eye for eye*. "This means a monetary payment, as does 'tooth for tooth,' etc." (*Rashi*).

According to R' Chiya, our deduction that "eye for eye" means a monetary payment rather than an actual eye is derived chiefly from the following phrase,

כ וְרָאִיתָ סוּס וָרֶכֶב עַם רַב מִמְּךָ לֹא תִירָא מֵהֶם כִּי־
ב־ד יְהוָה אֱלֹהֶיךָ עִמָּךְ הַמַּעַלְךָ מֵאֶרֶץ מִצְרָיִם: ב וְהָיָה
כְּקָרָבְכֶם אֶל־הַמִּלְחָמָה וְנִגַּשׁ הַכֹּהֵן וְדִבֶּר אֶל־הָעָם:
ג וְאָמַר אֲלֵהֶם שְׁמַע יִשְׂרָאֵל אַתֶּם קְרֵבִים הַיּוֹם לַמִּלְחָמָה
עַל־אֹיְבֵיכֶם אַל־יֵרַךְ לְבַבְכֶם אַל־תִּירְאוּ וְאַל־תַּחְפְּזוּ
וְאַל־תַּעַרְצוּ מִפְּנֵיהֶם: ד כִּי יְהוָה אֱלֹהֵיכֶם הַהֹלֵךְ עִמָּכֶם

"hand for hand" (יָד בְּיָד, literally, "hand in hand"), for these words are seemingly superfluous, since the previous verse spelled out that "You shall do to him as he conspired to do." What could "hand for hand" mean, says R' Chiya, but something that is given from hand to hand? (*Bava Kamma* 84a; *Kesubos* 32b, see *Tosafos* ad loc. ד"ה מכדי).

The Torah chose to emphasize this principle of "eye for eye means money" here, in the passage on conspiring witnesses, so that it would be adjacent to the passage that follows: "When you go out to battle. . ." This is to let you know that besides the reasons listed in *Bava Kamma* against a literal interpretation of "eye for eye," there is another major reason: not to increase the number of disabled Jews and thus decrease our nation's power of self-defense.

We find an example of this in *Yerushalmi Taanis* (4:5). The Rabbis sent emissaries with a message for Bar Kochba (who would accept into his army only the most courageous men, brave enough to bite off one of their own fingers): "How long will you go on disfiguring Israel?" And indeed, *Rashi* comments on the following verse that a man missing any part of his body may not go out to war.

20.

1. וְרָאִיתָ סוּס וָרֶכֶב — *And you see horse and chariot.* See the passage concerning the king (above, 17:16). Even though it is the king's duty to see to the security of the nation, the Torah forbids him to have many horses, but rather only enough for his own chariot. (*Yerushalmi Sanhedrin* (2:1) gives the maximum limit.) This is why the Torah says here, "And you see horse and chariot" — for this is something you do not often use, especially not in war.

2. וְהָיָה כְּקָרָבְכֶם אֶל־הַמִּלְחָמָה — *It shall be that when you draw near to the war.* The word כְּקָרָבְכֶם has כ as its prefix, giving the meaning "at the first moment of approach," rather than ב, which would give the meaning "when (at any time when) you approach." The idea intended here, then, is "when you arrive at the border" (and so the *Sifre* renders it). That is, when the moment comes to depart from the Holy Land.

Now, since there may be some soldiers among you who must return home (those who have planted a vineyard, betrothed a woman, or are fearful and fainthearted), they ought not to leave the Land of Israel, in that case, since the Torah prohibits leaving the Land needlessly, or indeed at all except under certain

and you see horse and chariot — a people more numerous
than you — you shall not fear them, for HASHEM, *your God, is*
with you, Who brought you up from the land of Egypt. 2 *It*
shall be that when you draw near to the war, the Kohen shall
approach and speak to the people.
3 *He shall say to them, "Hear, O Israel, you are coming near*
to the battle against your enemies; let your heart not be faint;
do not be afraid, do not panic, and do not be broken before
them. 4 *For* HASHEM, *your God, is the One Who goes with you,*

---

circumstances. Now is the time for the *Kohen* to address the people, and order those who should return home to turn back. (This follows the *Rambam's* interpretation [found in *Hil. Melachim* 7:2], that at the border the *Kohen* tells those who should go back to do so.)

3. שְׁמַע יִשְׂרָאֵל — *Hear, O Israel.* "Even if you have no merit but that of reciting the *Shema*, that is enough for God to save you" (*Rashi*). *Rashi* is quoting R' Yochanan in the name of R' Shimon Bar Yochai (*Sotah* 42a). This is a corollary of R' Shimon's view, that even if one merely recites the *Shema* morning and evening he has fulfilled the Torah's injunction, "Let not this Torah pass from your lips." Although it is forbidden to mention this opinion in front of an *am ha'aretz* (lest he decide to neglect the Torah entirely), still, in time of war when the men are burdened with fighting it is enough to recite the *Shema*.

We may learn more about this from the words of the angel to Joshua: "Now I have come" (*Yehoshua* 5:14). "*Now* I have come" to remind you about Torah study; but when they were burdened with the war they were exempt from Torah study (*Megillah* 3a-b, *Eiruvin* 63b, and *Rashi* ad loc.).

In *Sotah* (loc. cit.) R' Yochanan goes on to say that Goliath used to confront the Jewish camp every morning and evening in order to prevent them from reciting the *Shema*. He hoped to defeat them by denying them this merit. Likewise, *Chazal* said that Jerusalem was only destroyed because the people neglected to recite the *Shema* morning and evening (*Shabbos* 119b).

עַל־אֹיְבֵיכֶם — *Against your enemies.* "— who will have no mercy on you if you should fall into their hands" (*Rashi*, based on *Sotah* 42a). In case the Children of Israel should say, "Why provoke them, then, if they will have no mercy on us once we fall into their hands?" the *Sifre* adds, "so that the cities of Israel should not be laid waste." In other words, if we do not go to war against them in their lands, they will come to war against us in our Land, and the cities of Israel will be laid waste. (In *Sotah* 44b, such a war is described as "cutting down the gentiles before they come up against [the Jews].") Therefore we have no alternative, and this "no alternative" situation spurred the warriors on. As Yoav said when he saw that he was attacked from in front and from behind, "be strong and let us strengthen each other, for our people and for the cities of our God!" (*II Shmuel*, 10:12).

כ לְהִלָּחֵ֥ם לָכֶ֛ם עִם־אֹיְבֵיכֶ֖ם לְהוֹשִׁ֥יעַ אֶתְכֶֽם׃ ה וְדִבְּר֣וּ
ה־יא הַשֹּֽׁטְרִים֮ אֶל־הָעָ֣ם לֵאמֹר֒ מִֽי־הָאִ֞ישׁ אֲשֶׁ֨ר בָּנָ֤ה בַֽיִת־חָדָשׁ֙
וְלֹ֣א חֲנָכ֔וֹ יֵלֵ֖ךְ וְיָשֹׁ֣ב לְבֵית֑וֹ פֶּן־יָמוּת֙ בַּמִּלְחָמָ֔ה וְאִ֥ישׁ
אַחֵ֖ר יַחְנְכֶֽנּוּ׃ ו וּמִֽי־הָאִ֞ישׁ אֲשֶׁ֨ר נָטַ֥ע כֶּ֙רֶם֙ וְלֹ֣א חִלְּל֔וֹ יֵלֵ֖ךְ
וְיָשֹׁ֣ב לְבֵית֑וֹ פֶּן־יָמוּת֙ בַּמִּלְחָמָ֔ה וְאִ֥ישׁ אַחֵ֖ר יְחַלְּלֶֽנּוּ׃
ז וּמִֽי־הָאִ֞ישׁ אֲשֶׁ֨ר אֵרַ֤שׂ אִשָּׁה֙ וְלֹ֣א לְקָחָ֔הּ יֵלֵ֖ךְ וְיָשֹׁ֣ב
לְבֵית֑וֹ פֶּן־יָמוּת֙ בַּמִּלְחָמָ֔ה וְאִ֥ישׁ אַחֵ֖ר יִקָּחֶֽנָּה׃ ח וְיָסְפ֣וּ
הַשֹּֽׁטְרִים֮ לְדַבֵּ֣ר אֶל־הָעָם֒ וְאָמְר֗וּ מִי־הָאִ֤ישׁ הַיָּרֵא֙ וְרַ֣ךְ
הַלֵּבָ֔ב יֵלֵ֖ךְ וְיָשֹׁ֣ב לְבֵית֑וֹ וְלֹ֥א יִמַּ֛ס אֶת־לְבַ֥ב אֶחָ֖יו כִּלְבָבֽוֹ׃
ט וְהָיָ֛ה כְּכַלֹּ֥ת הַשֹּׁטְרִ֖ים לְדַבֵּ֣ר אֶל־הָעָ֑ם וּפָֽקְד֛וּ שָׂרֵ֥י
צְבָא֖וֹת בְּרֹ֥אשׁ הָעָֽם׃ שביעי י כִּֽי־תִקְרַ֣ב
אֶל־עִ֔יר לְהִלָּחֵ֖ם עָלֶ֑יהָ וְקָרָ֥אתָ אֵלֶ֖יהָ לְשָׁלֽוֹם׃ יא וְהָיָה֙
אִם־שָׁל֣וֹם תַּֽעַנְךָ֔ וּפָתְחָ֖ה לָ֑ךְ וְהָיָ֞ה כָּל־הָעָ֣ם הַנִּמְצָא־

---

4. לְהִלָּחֵם לָכֶם עִם־אֹיְבֵיכֶם לְהוֹשִׁיעַ אֶתְכֶם — *To fight for you with your enemies, to save you.* In time of war, it is not only the enemy one needs to be saved from. There is also hunger and heat stroke (see *Tosafos* on *Kesubos* 30 ד"ה הכל, who state that in war a man cannot protect himself properly from the heat), and disease, and all the other disasters that come during war. To indicate this the Torah first says "to fight for you with your enemies" and then "to save you" — not only from them but from all harm.

5. השֹּטְרִים — *The officers. Onkelos* translates שֹׁטְרִים as סָרְכַיָּא, "commanders," whereas in the opening verse of this *Parashah* (16:18), he renders the word as פֻּרְעָנִין, "bailiffs." Why should the same word be translated differently in these two cases?

The earlier verse is talking about the officers who enforce the decision of the court "with rod and whip," using physical force if necessary to ensure that the judge's ruling is carried out (*Rashi* ad loc.). Therefore *Onkelos* calls them פֻּרְעָנִין, literally "those who deliver punishment," since they coerce those who refuse to submit to the judge's decision.

Officers of war, however, are in charge of the spiritual purity of the Jewish army, lest there be among them "a man who is fearful and fainthearted" (who is disqualified for army service, so that he should not "melt the heart of his fellows, like his heart"), or those who are worried about their house, their vineyard, or their bride, so that they would be unable to concentrate on fighting Israel's enemies. These officers are charged with a task that does not require the use of force; therefore *Onkelos* is justified in describing them as סָרְכַיָּא, "commanding officers" (*Aruch, s.v.* סרך). However, *Targum Yonassan* does not make this distinction and uses the term סָרְכַיָּא in both places.

But there are further reasons supporting *Onkelos's* opinion: the officers of the

20
5-11

to fight for you with your enemies, to save you."
5 Then the officers shall speak to the people, saying, "Who
is the man who has built a new house and has not inaugurated
it? Let him go and return to his house, lest he die in the war
and another man will inaugurate it. 6 And who is the man
who has planted a vineyard and not redeemed it? Let him go
and return to his house, lest he die in the war and another man
will redeem it. 7 And who is the man who has betrothed a
woman and not married her? Let him go and return to his
house, lest he die in the war and another man will marry her."
8 The officers shall continue speaking to the people and
say, "Who is the man who is fearful and fainthearted? Let
him go and return to his house, and let him not melt the heart
of his fellows, like his heart." 9 When the officers have
finished speaking to the people, the leaders of the legions shall
take command at the head of the people.
10 When you draw near to a city to wage war against it, you
shall call out to it for peace. 11 It shall be that if it responds to
you in peace and opens for you, then the entire people found

---

court do not endanger themselves in their work, whereas the officers of the army, besides purging the army of any defect, also take part in the fighting and endanger themselves. For this they deserve a title of honor.

8. וַיָּסְפוּ הַשֹּׁטְרִים לְדַבֵּר — *The officers shall continue speaking.* See *Rashi*, who explains that the first three questions are the *Kohen's*, though it is the officer who announces them out loud, but the fourth question, "Who is the man who is fearful and fainthearted?" is entirely the officer's own. Since the *Kohen* has to say "Let your heart not be faint," it is not fitting that he should say to them, "Who is the man who is fearful and fainthearted." Therefore the officer says this, speaking for himself.

9. וְהָיָה כְּכַלֹּת הַשֹּׁטְרִים לְדַבֵּר אֶל־הָעָם וּפָקְדוּ שָׂרֵי צְבָאוֹת — *When the officers have finished speaking to the people, the leaders of the legions shall take command.* If the leaders were to take their places at the head of the people before the announcement, "Who is the man who is fearful?... Let him go and return to his house," one of the commanders might fall into that category but decide not to reveal it, so as not to lose his honorable position. This would be particularly undesirable, because a fearful commander could certainly "melt the hearts" of the entire camp. Therefore all the fainthearted are eliminated from the camp first, and then commanders are appointed. (But the *Yerushalmi* holds that they are appointed first.)

10. וְקָרָאתָ אֵלֶיהָ לְשָׁלוֹם — *You shall call out to it for peace.* "Scripture is talking about optional wars" (*Rashi*). But the *Ramban* writes that the call for peace applies even in an obligatory war, that is to say, even in a war against the seven

בָּהּ יִהְיוּ לְךָ לָמַס וַעֲבָדוּךָ: יב וְאִם־לֹא תַשְׁלִים עִמָּךְ כ
וְעָשְׂתָה עִמְּךָ מִלְחָמָה וְצַרְתָּ עָלֶיהָ: יג וּנְתָנָהּ יהוה אֱלֹהֶיךָ יב־יד
בְּיָדֶךָ וְהִכִּיתָ אֶת־כָּל־זְכוּרָהּ לְפִי־חָרֶב: יד רַק הַנָּשִׁים וְהַטַּף

Canaanite nations. For we see that Moses called out for peace to Sihon, king of the Amorites.

In support of *Rashi's* opinion (which is based on the *Sifre*), we can say that Moses' message to Sihon was not the usual offer of peace in exchange for tributary status. This was the message: "Let me pass through your land. . . until we pass through your border" (*Bamidbar* 21:22), given in *Devarim* as "Let me pass through your land. . . until I cross the Jordan to the Land that Hashem, our God, gives us" (2:27-29). This is not an ultimatum, like the call for peace in our passage here; it was a simple request.

There is a deeper point here. In the above-mentioned passage, Moses says: "I sent messengers from the Wilderness of Kedemoth to Sihon . . ." Many commentators have asked, why did Moses bother sending messengers at all? If Sihon had allowed the Children of Israel to pass through his land, would they then have refrained from conquering it?

This is our explanation: At the western edge of the Wilderness there was a city called Kedemoth, which was part of Reuben's inheritance (*I Divrei Hayamim*, 6:64). The Wilderness of Kedemoth was named for this city. The Torah emphasizes that it was from here that Moses sent out his messengers of peace, because this was before God said to him, "Begin to possess it" (2:24), which was Moses' signal that he was now permitted to leave the Wilderness and take over the edge of Sihon's land. Moses had thought at the time that he had to request the right of passage from Sihon!

And this answers the commentators' question. Of course this seeming "call for peace" from Moses to Sihon proves nothing with regard to the call for peace to the seven nations mandated by the Torah. (Although when it comes to actual *halachah*, the *Rambam* rules in accordance with the *Ramban's* opinion.)

11. וַעֲבָדוּךָ — *And they shall serve you.* Slavery came into the world through Noah's curse upon Canaan, the son of Ham: "A slave of slaves shall he be to his brothers." But why would Noah have wanted to curse his own offspring?

Noah saw that the corruption which had brought on the flood, namely sexual immorality, had already reappeared in the human race (for Ham engaged in marital relations while in the Ark, which had been forbidden even to the animals, and now he had castrated, or sodomized, his own father). Noah knew that if this corruption were to spread, terrible punishment would descend upon the world (for even though God had sworn never to flood the entire world again, He has many means of exacting the penalty from those who violate His will, such as the rain of fire and brimstone on Sodom, or the Sea of Reeds for the Egyptians).

Noah further realized that since Ham had demonstrated such utter contempt

20 *within it shall be as tribute for you, and they shall serve*
12-14 *you.* [12] *But if it does not make peace with you, but makes*
war with you, you shall besiege it. [13] *HASHEM, your God, shall*
deliver it into your hand, and you shall smite all its males by
the blade of the sword. [14] *Only the women, the small children,*

---

for his father, there was no one to teach him to mend his ways. He therefore decided to put this corrupt son and his descendants under the "guardianship" of his other sons, Shem and Japheth and their offspring, who had remained guiltless. The children of Ham could never be reformed by mere words, so Noah handed them over as slaves, to be chastised by the rod of Shem and Japheth.

Now, during the period between Noah's death and the conquest of the Land by the Children of Israel, the Canaanite slaves had broken free of their bondage, and during Abraham's time they had even seized the Land from the children of Shem, who had received it as his portion when Noah divided the world among his sons. Later on the Egyptians, another branch of the Hamite family, actually enslaved the Children of Israel, the choicest of Shem's descendants, for two hundred and ten years, so oppressing their spirits that they came to worship Egyptian gods.

The Egyptians received the punishment they deserved, and the Children of Israel went free, received the Torah, and returned to their Land, which had been conquered by the Canaanites. Noah had wanted the Canaanites, and indeed all who followed their destructive ways (even if they were descendants of his other sons), to be subjugated to the children of Shem and Japheth, who at least observed the "seven commandments of the children of Noah." But very few were left at this time who still kept these seven commandments, without which man is no better than an animal (in fact he is worse).

The Children of Israel, who had taken upon themselves the yoke of the Kingdom of Heaven and the 613 commandments, were not up to the task of teaching knowledge of God to the whole world "while standing on one foot." Nevertheless they were commanded to physically subjugate their neighbors at the very least (those people with whom they had regular dealings), so that they would also have some spiritual influence on them.

Thus the servitude of the Canaanites was for their own good, for the salvation of their souls. And so *Chazal* expounded: not only tribute and service must the Children of Israel demand from them, but also a commitment to the seven commandments of the children of Noah. And this was also for the good of the Chosen People: "so that they will not teach you to act according to all their abominations that they performed for their gods, so that you will sin to Hashem, your God," (v. 18). For this was Noah's purpose in making Shem and Japheth "guardians" over the descendants of Canaan.

13. וּנְתָנָהּ ה׳ אֱלֹהֶיךָ בְּיָדֶךָ — *Hashem, your God, shall deliver it into your hand.*

"If you have done all that has been mentioned above, in the end God will deliver it into your hand" (*Rashi*).

כ וְהַבְּהֵמָה וְכֹל אֲשֶׁר יִהְיֶה בָעִיר כָּל־שְׁלָלָהּ תָּבֹז לָךְ וְאָכַלְתָּ
טו־יט אֶת־שְׁלַל אֹיְבֶיךָ אֲשֶׁר נָתַן יהוה אֱלֹהֶיךָ לָךְ: טו כֵּן תַּעֲשֶׂה
לְכָל־הֶעָרִים הָרְחֹקֹת מִמְּךָ מְאֹד אֲשֶׁר לֹא־מֵעָרֵי הַגּוֹיִם־
הָאֵלֶּה הֵנָּה: טז רַק מֵעָרֵי הָעַמִּים הָאֵלֶּה אֲשֶׁר יהוה אֱלֹהֶיךָ
נֹתֵן לְךָ נַחֲלָה לֹא תְחַיֶּה כָּל־נְשָׁמָה: יז כִּי־הַחֲרֵם תַּחֲרִימֵם
הַחִתִּי וְהָאֱמֹרִי הַכְּנַעֲנִי וְהַפְּרִזִּי הַחִוִּי וְהַיְבוּסִי כַּאֲשֶׁר צִוְּךָ
יהוה אֱלֹהֶיךָ: יח לְמַעַן אֲשֶׁר לֹא־יְלַמְּדוּ אֶתְכֶם לַעֲשׂוֹת
כְּכֹל תּוֹעֲבֹתָם אֲשֶׁר עָשׂוּ לֵאלֹהֵיהֶם וַחֲטָאתֶם לַיהוה
אֱלֹהֵיכֶם: יט כִּי־תָצוּר אֶל־עִיר יָמִים רַבִּים
לְהִלָּחֵם עָלֶיהָ לְתָפְשָׂהּ לֹא־תַשְׁחִית אֶת־עֵצָהּ לִנְדֹּחַ עָלָיו
גַּרְזֶן כִּי מִמֶּנּוּ תֹאכֵל וְאֹתוֹ לֹא תִכְרֹת כִּי הָאָדָם עֵץ הַשָּׂדֶה

As a matter of fact, this whole passage is talking about optional wars. Even so, if you go out to such a war with the intent to rid the immediate area of idols, so that you will not be corrupted by them, this intent suffices for God to deliver the entire city into your power.

19. כִּי הָאָדָם עֵץ הַשָּׂדֶה — *Is the tree of the field a man...?* [This could just as well be read, "for man is a tree of the field."] We find man compared to a tree, and trees to man, in several places in Scripture ("I am Hashem, I bow down the lofty tree and raise high the lowly tree" [*Yechezkel* 17:24]; "See, I am a withered tree" [*Yeshayah* 56:3]). We find this again in *Chazal* ("the custom was, when a child was born, to plant a cedar" [*Gittin* 57a]; "Tree, tree, with what shall I bless you?" [*Taanis* 5b]). Such a comparison demands an explanation.

It seems to me that all that man needs for sustenance, health, and longevity, God has provided him in trees. Immediately after the Creation God planted the Garden of Eden, in which "He brought forth every tree pleasing to see and good for food, also the Tree of Life in the midst of the garden, and the Tree of Knowledge of Good and Bad." And "there He placed the man He had formed" (*Bereishis* 2:8,9).

True, He commanded the man not to eat of the Tree of Knowledge. But some say that this tree was the grapevine (*Berachos* 40a), and that God intended for man to squeeze its grapes for the first time as Sabbath approached and make Kiddush on the juice; afterwards it would be permitted to him. Only Adam chose not to wait; he ate its fruit when it was still forbidden.

However this may be, certainly it was not for nothing that God planted the Trees of Life and Knowledge in the Garden. Beyond a doubt He intended them to influence the development of man's intellect and longevity in some definite way. It was only after man sinned that he was banished from the Garden "to work the soil from which he was taken" (*Bereishis* 3:19) But God's intent had been for trees to be man's faithful companions, to supply his needs after only a slight effort on his part and to stimulate his intellectual development by their

20
15-19

the animals, and everything that will be in the city — all
its booty — may you plunder for yourselves; you shall eat
the booty of your enemies, which HASHEM, your God, gave
you. 15 *So shall you do to all the cities that are very distant*
from you, which are not of the cities of these nations. 16 *But*
from the cities of these peoples that HASHEM, your God,
gives you as an inheritance, you shall not allow any person
to live. 17 *Rather you shall utterly destroy them: the Hittite,*
the Amorite, the Canaanite, the Perizzite, the Hivvite, and
the Jebusite, as HASHEM, your God has commanded you,
18 *so that they will not teach you to act according to all their*
abominations that they performed for their gods, so that
you will sin to HASHEM, your God.
19 *When you besiege a city for many days to wage war*
against it to seize it, do not destroy its trees by swinging
an axe against them, for from it you will eat, and you
shall not cut it down; a man is the tree of the field

---

sight, fragrance, and taste. "Said Rava, 'Wine and spices have sharpened my wits'" (*Yoma* 76b); and "Wine is the revealer of [the Torah's] secrets" (*Zohar III*:39a). Similarly, every holy event is marked by *Kiddush* over a cup of wine.

Even after Adam's sin, it is still good to plant trees. *Chazal* tell us that "a man should build a house and plant a vineyard, and then marry" (*Sotah* 44a) — it is good for him to make his living from trees. Doctors, too, recommend eating plenty of fruit.

Indeed, just as man is the finest of living creatures, trees are the finest sort of plant life. And from this comes the Torah's comparison between the two and its demand to spare the life of trees. (For the Torah prohibits the cutting of fruit trees not only during a siege but at all times and places.) This, too, would explain the severe punishment incurred by one who cuts down a fruit tree: "Said R' Chanina, 'The only reason my son Shivchah died was that he cut down a fig tree before its time [i.e., before it was old enough to have stopped producing]'" (*Bava Kamma* 95b).

It was also the Creator's intent that man should play the role of a *talmid chacham* and the trees of the Garden the roles of his "supporter" and "teacher" of knowledge and life. Therefore we are commanded to "give respect" to fruit trees and look to their continued existence. This will serve as background to explain *Chazal's* exposition: "What does the Torah mean by 'For man is a tree of the field'? Is man a tree? No; it is because the Torah says [of such a tree] 'for from it you eat, so you shall not cut it down." And [of a shade tree] it says, 'it you may destroy and cut down.' How is this to be applied? If [a person] is a proper *talmid chacham*, 'from him you shall eat, and you shall not cut him down'; and if not, 'him you may destroy and cut down'" (*Taanis* 7a).

ב
כ

לָבֹא מִפָּנֶיךָ בַּמָּצְוֹר: כ רַ֫ק עֵ֣ץ אֲשֶׁר־תֵּדַ֞ע כִּ֣י לֹא־עֵ֤ץ
מַאֲכָל֙ ה֔וּא אֹת֖וֹ תַשְׁחִ֣ית וְכָרָ֑תָּ וּבָנִ֣יתָ מָצ֗וֹר עַל־הָעִיר֙
אֲשֶׁר־הִ֨וא עֹשָׂ֧ה עִמְּךָ֛ מִלְחָמָ֖ה עַ֥ד רִדְתָּֽהּ:

כא

א־ו

א כִּי־יִמָּצֵ֣א חָלָ֗ל בָּאֲדָמָה֙ אֲשֶׁר֩ יהו֨ה אֱלֹהֶ֜יךָ נֹתֵ֤ן לְךָ֙
לְרִשְׁתָּ֔הּ נֹפֵ֖ל בַּשָּׂדֶ֑ה לֹ֥א נוֹדַ֖ע מִ֥י הִכָּֽהוּ: ב וְיָצְא֥וּ זְקֵנֶ֖יךָ
וְשֹׁפְטֶ֑יךָ וּמָדְדוּ֙ אֶל־הֶ֣עָרִ֔ים אֲשֶׁ֖ר סְבִיבֹ֥ת הֶחָלָֽל: ג וְהָיָ֣ה
הָעִ֔יר הַקְּרֹבָ֖ה אֶל־הֶחָלָ֑ל וְלָקְח֡וּ זִקְנֵי֩ הָעִ֨יר הַהִ֜וא
עֶגְלַ֣ת בָּקָ֗ר אֲשֶׁ֤ר לֹֽא־עֻבַּד֙ בָּ֔הּ אֲשֶׁ֥ר לֹא־מָשְׁכָ֖ה בְּעֹֽל:
ד וְהוֹרִ֡דוּ זִקְנֵי֩ הָעִ֨יר הַהִ֤וא אֶת־הָֽעֶגְלָה֙ אֶל־נַ֣חַל אֵיתָ֔ן
אֲשֶׁ֛ר לֹא־יֵעָבֵ֥ד בּ֖וֹ וְלֹ֣א יִזָּרֵ֑עַ וְעָֽרְפוּ־שָׁ֥ם אֶת־הָעֶגְלָ֖ה
בַּנָּֽחַל: ה וְנִגְּשׁ֣וּ הַכֹּֽהֲנִים֮ בְּנֵ֣י לֵוִי֒ כִּ֣י בָ֗ם בָּחַ֞ר יהו֤ה
אֱלֹהֶ֨יךָ֙ לְשָׁ֣רְת֔וֹ וּלְבָרֵ֖ךְ בְּשֵׁ֣ם יהו֑ה וְעַל־פִּיהֶ֥ם יִהְיֶ֖ה
כָּל־רִ֥יב וְכָל־נָֽגַע: ו וְכֹ֗ל זִקְנֵי֙ הָעִ֣יר הַהִ֔וא הַקְּרֹבִ֖ים
אֶל־הֶחָלָ֑ל יִרְחֲצוּ֙ אֶת־יְדֵיהֶ֔ם עַל־הָעֶגְלָ֖ה הָעֲרוּפָֽה

The comparison is clear: a *talmid chacham* is like a fruitful tree. The *Sifre* makes it clearer: "'For man is a tree of the field' — man's life comes from the trees of the field." That is, the trees are his "supporters," so that he may fulfill the purpose of his creation: to be a *talmid chacham*.

21.

3. וְהָיָ֣ה הָעִ֔יר הַקְּרֹבָ֖ה אֶל־הֶחָלָ֑ל וְלָקְח֡וּ זִקְנֵי֩ הָעִ֨יר הַהִ֜וא עֶגְלַ֣ת בָּקָ֗ר — *It shall be that the city nearest the corpse, the elders of that city shall take a heifer.* "That city" needs a special atonement, and much introspection, concerning its elders.

וְלָקְח֡וּ זִקְנֵי֩ הָעִ֨יר הַהִ֜וא ــ — *The elders of that city shall take.* Look and see what a difference there is between God's perfect Torah and the customs of other nations:

When a body is found and there is no evidence of the murderer's identity, the usual procedure is for the elders and judges to go and search — among the poor. Then they beat and terrorize anybody who seems suspect to them, so that he should admit that he spilled this blood.

But the Torah directs the elders and judges to look, not for suspects to mistreat, but for the root of the sin (since it cannot be established who committed it). And it further instructs them that what they are looking for may well be within themselves. Perhaps they have not educated their generation properly, and the murderer acted because of their negligence. So they must bring an atonement and confess, "Our hands have not spilled this blood, and our eyes did not see." This solemn ceremony should influence the people to stay away from anything remotely connected with bloodshed, and to uncover the murderer's identity and remove the stain of innocent blood from Israel.

20 *that it should enter the siege before you?* [20] *Only a tree that*
20 *you know is not a food tree, it you may destroy and cut down,*
and build a bulwark against the city that makes war with
you, until it is conquered.
21 [1] *If a corpse will be found on the land that* HASHEM, *your*
1-6 *God, gives you to possess it, fallen in the field, it was not*
known who smote him, [2] *your elders and judges shall go out*
and measure toward the cities that are around the corpse. [3] *It*
shall be that the city nearest the corpse, the elders of that city
shall take a heifer, with which no work has been done, which
has not pulled with a yoke. [4] *The elders of that city shall*
bring the heifer down to a harsh valley, which cannot be
worked and cannot be sown, and they shall axe the back of
its neck in the valley. [5] *The Kohanim, the offspring of Levi,*
shall approach, for them has HASHEM, *your God, chosen to*
minister to Him and to bless with the Name of HASHEM, *and*
according to their word shall be every grievance and every
plague.
[6] *All the elders of that city, who are closest to the corpse,*
shall wash their hands over the heifer that was axed in the

אֲשֶׁר לֹא־עֻבַּד בָּהּ — *With which no work has been done.* Perhaps there is a hint here, that the elders of this city have not been a good influence on its citizens. They have not "worked" on the people, guiding them towards love of their fellow man (since it is assumed that the murderer was one of their own). This is a heifer "with which no work has been done."

אֲשֶׁר לֹא־מָשְׁכָה בְּעֹל — *Which has not pulled with a yoke.* But there is another possibility. Perhaps the elders "worked" at their holy task faithfully, and did everything in their power to bring up a reverent, God-fearing generation. In this case "the city" is at fault for "not having pulled with the yoke" and absorbed the lessons which the elders taught them.

Yet even in this case, "the city's" atonement is upon the elders. They must wash their hands over the heifer's blood (symbol of the murdered man's blood) and confess, "Our hands have not spilled this blood," but also "our eyes" — the eyes of the whole community — "did not see"....

6. **וְכֹל זִקְנֵי הָעִיר הַהִוא . . . יִרְחֲצוּ אֶת־יְדֵיהֶם** — *All the elders of that city . . . shall wash their hands.* Why should all the people of the city not do this? As far as guilt for the actual murder is concerned they all have a part, since we assume that the murderer came from the city closest to the body.

The most likely answer is that in this case the murderer himself would certainly join in, and announce that "our hands have not spilled this blood," so as to clear himself of suspicion (see *Sanhedrin* 43b, and *Rashi*). For that matter, even if he confessed at this point, the *halachah* is that a man cannot be believed

כא °שָׁפְכוּ בַּנָּחַל: מפטיר ז וְעָנוּ וְאָמְרוּ יָדֵינוּ לֹא °שפכה אֶת־הַדָּם הַזֶּה
ז־ט וְעֵינֵינוּ לֹא רָאוּ: ח כַּפֵּר לְעַמְּךָ יִשְׂרָאֵל אֲשֶׁר־פָּדִיתָ יהוה
וְאַל־תִּתֵּן דָּם נָקִי בְּקֶרֶב עַמְּךָ יִשְׂרָאֵל וְנִכַּפֵּר לָהֶם הַדָּם:
ט וְאַתָּה תְּבַעֵר הַדָּם הַנָּקִי מִקִּרְבֶּךָ כִּי־תַעֲשֶׂה הַיָּשָׁר בְּעֵינֵי
יהוה:

---

if he incriminates himself (*Sanhedrin* 9b). On such a basis we could not spill his blood, so as to atone for the Land and the innocent blood that has been shed upon it.

7. יָדֵינוּ לֹא שָׁפְכוּ — *Our hands have not spilled*. The word "spilled" is pronounced שָׁפְכוּ, in the plural just like "hands," yet it is written שָׁפְכָה, as if it were singular. Why is this?

The lesson hinted at here may be that people give food to the poor with only one hand; but a murderer pursues his "profession" with both hands. The written

21
7-9

*valley. [7] They shall speak up and say, "Our hands have not
spilled this blood, and our eyes did not see. [8] Atone for Your
people Israel that You have redeemed, O* HASHEM*: Do not
place innocent blood in the midst of Your people Israel!"
Then the blood shall be atoned for them.*

*[9] But you shall remove the innocent blood from your midst
when you do what is upright in the eyes of* HASHEM.

---

form, then, suggests that perhaps the only real suspicion on the people of the city is that they did not give charity (with one hand) to the murdered man — not that they murdered him with both hands!

וְעֵינֵינוּ לֹא רָאוּ — *And our eyes did not see.* Although "our eyes did not see," no act of atonement is prescribed for this. For the eyes could not be guilty in this case, since they do not give charity. They only report what they have seen in the heart and mind. But all of man's thoughts find expression through the hands; therefore they must be washed.

פרשת כי תצא

Parashas Ki Seitzei

י כִּֽי־תֵצֵ֥א לַמִּלְחָמָ֖ה עַל־אֹיְבֶ֑יךָ וּנְתָנ֞וֹ יהוה אֱלֹהֶ֛יךָ כא
בְּיָדֶ֖ךָ וְשָׁבִ֥יתָ שִׁבְיֽוֹ׃ יא וְרָאִיתָ֙ בַּשִּׁבְיָ֔ה אֵ֖שֶׁת יְפַת־תֹּ֑אַר י־יא

10-11. כִּי־תֵצֵא לַמִּלְחָמָה עַל־אֹיְבֶיךָ וּנְתָנוֹ ה׳ אֱלֹהֶיךָ בְּיָדֶךָ וְשָׁבִיתָ שִׁבְיוֹ. וְרָאִיתָ בַּשִּׁבְיָה אֵשֶׁת יְפַת־תֹּאַר וְחָשַׁקְתָּ בָהּ — *When you will go out to war against your enemies, and Hashem, your God, will deliver them into your hand, and you will capture its captivity; and you will see among its captivity a woman who is beautiful of form, and you will desire her.* The purpose of all these introductory phrases is to encourage the men to refrain from such a deed. One should consider that God is the "Man of War," and it is He Who gave you the might and the strength to overcome your enemies and take captives: "Hashem your God will deliver them into your hand, and you will capture its captivity." Here you are, returning home from war alive and well, with an abundance of booty, and crowned with victory. The proper response would be to offer a thanksgiving-offering (*todah*) immediately in God's honor. And in fact, you have a "sacrifice" ready to go and an "altar" prepared to sacrifice it on. You should slaughter the evil inclination which has assaulted you and incited you to look upon women and pick from among them the most attractive one.

Doing this is considered the equivalent of offering a thanksgiving-offering, and so *Chazal* explain the verse, "He who offers a thanksgiving-offering honors Me" (*Tehillim* 50:23) — "Whoever sacrifices [i.e., slaughters] his evil inclination and confesses is considered as having honored God in both worlds" (*Sanhedrin* 43).

And what if you do not do all this? What if you follow your evil inclination? (For even though the Torah permits you this woman, that is only in recognition of base human inclinations, to give you a permitted way to take this woman so that you will not take her in sin — once you have aroused your thoughts in this direction!) Your punishment will be immediately meted out in the form of a rebellious son (*Rashi*), a punishment which perfectly fits the crime. For a son should be grateful to his father who gave him life, raised and educated him, and provided all his needs. Yet rather than be grateful, a rebellious son turns from the ways of his fathers — from God's way — and rebels against them. He indulges in "permissible" behavior: he gorges on meat and wine, and steals, not from others, God forbid, but from his own father. The Torah testifies that such a son will ultimately deplete his father's money, and then rob others to support his habits. And so he drags his father's name into his sins, just as his father did to his Father in Heaven.

10. כִּי־תֵצֵא לַמִּלְחָמָה — *When you will go out to war*. The Torah is teaching us military strategy here. If you have to conduct a war, then you should "*go out* to war": you should try to do your fighting either in the enemy's territory or in no-man's-land. You should not wait until the enemy comes to do battle in your own territory; by the time he has been defeated, he will have destroyed your cities in the process, God forbid.

21
10-11

[10] *When you will go out to war against your enemies, and* H*ASHEM, your God, will deliver them into your hand, and you will capture its captivity;* [11] *and you will see among its captivity a woman who is beautiful of form,*

עַל־אֹיְבֶךָ — *Against your enemies*. And not against the neighbors with whom you have always lived peacefully. If a minor dispute has arisen with them, it can easily be settled. Don't rush to fight; no good ever comes of it.

It could be that this verse is intended to exclude war among Jews from the rules given in this passage. And in fact we find this in the war between the kingdoms of Judah and Israel (see *Rashi* on 20:13) described in *Divrei Hayamim II*,28. In that instance, the prophet Oded rebuked the victors. He ordered them not to take the defeated Judeans as slaves and maidservants, and the people of Shomron obeyed and returned the captives to Judah.

Evidently, then, in this verse the Torah teaches us that if, God forbid, there should be a war between Jews, the law permitting taking captives of war and the 'woman who is beautiful of form (the *yefas to'ar*) do not apply, and it remains forbidden to take a Jewish woman against her will and without a *halachic* marriage ceremony.

ונְתָנוֹ ה' אֱלֹהֶיךָ בְּיָדֶךָ וְשָׁבִיתָ שִׁבְיוֹ — *And Hashem your God, will deliver them into your hand and you will capture its captivity*. Even before the enemy is defeated, captives may fall into your hands during the course of battle, but then no leniency is allowed in matters concerning the female captives, seeing as many have fallen prey to base temptations of this sort. (The incident of Judith and Holofernes is sufficient to prove this point.) The Torah grants permission (in consideration of man's *yetzer*) to take a *yefas to'ar* only after the danger of battle has passed: "Hashem your God will deliver them into your hand" — first — and only then "you will see . . . a woman who is beautiful of form."

11. וְרָאִיתָ בַּשִּׁבְיָה — *And you will see among its captivity*. Here is a hint to support *Chazal*'s dictum that the Torah only permitted the *yefas to'ar* in consideration of the evil inclination. From the words "and you will *see* among its captivity" we learn that this desire is the work of the heavenly Adversary, for "the evil inclination can only seize upon what the eyes [עֵינָיו] see" (*Sotah* 8).

Now, *Chazal* learn from the word עֵינָיו, which literally means "his eyes," that the reference is to the eyes of the evil inclination, and not to what one's own eyes see. "He is the evil inclination, he is the Adversary, he is the Angel of Death, he is all full of eyes" (*Avodah Zarah* 20), so when he comes to make man stumble, he is not coming with just two eyes. He sees in front, behind and to all sides; and he tries to have his victim see what he, the Adversary, wants him to see, even when he is preoccupied with other matters. That is the significance of "seeing among the captives": even though you are busy, hurrying to return home, the evil angel is at his work. Not only do "you see," but also "you will desire her" — "even if she is not beautiful of form" (*Sifre*). For when the evil inclination is

כא וְחָשַׁקְתָּ בָּהּ וְלָקַחְתָּ לְךָ לְאִשָּׁה׃ יב וַהֲבֵאתָהּ אֶל־תּוֹךְ
יב־יד בֵּיתֶךָ וְגִלְּחָה אֶת־רֹאשָׁהּ וְעָשְׂתָה אֶת־צִפָּרְנֶיהָ׃ יג וְהֵסִירָה
אֶת־שִׂמְלַת שִׁבְיָהּ מֵעָלֶיהָ וְיָשְׁבָה בְּבֵיתֶךָ וּבָכְתָה אֶת־
אָבִיהָ וְאֶת־אִמָּהּ יֶרַח יָמִים וְאַחַר כֵּן תָּבוֹא אֵלֶיהָ וּבְעַלְתָּהּ
וְהָיְתָה לְךָ לְאִשָּׁה׃ יד וְהָיָה אִם־לֹא חָפַצְתָּ בָּהּ וְשִׁלַּחְתָּהּ
לְנַפְשָׁהּ וּמָכֹר לֹא־תִמְכְּרֶנָּה בַּכָּסֶף לֹא־תִתְעַמֵּר בָּהּ

---

at work, you do not see with your own eyes but with his, and in the Adversary's eyes the *yefas to'ar* is 'beautifully' suited for his purpose — to bring you to sin.

וְחָשַׁקְתָּ בָּהּ — *And you will desire her*. Young people are often entirely convinced that the only possible way to get married is by 'falling in love,' not through matchmakers and arranged matches. But the Torah warns us that a marriage which results only from "and you will desire her," from the eye seeing and the heart desiring, sometimes ends with "it shall be that if you do not desire her, then you shall send her on her own." The desire will pass, and then both husband and wife will open their eyes and see that their backgrounds are entirely different and their natures and temperaments are not suited, making life together impossible. The only remaining option is "and you will send her on her own." Unfortunately, we see that in our times, when the *yetzer hara* is the matchmaker and some people decide to marry based only on "and you will desire her" and she for him, the incidence of divorce has greatly increased among Jews. First they get married for 'love' — and shortly afterwards they separate in open hatred, God forbid (as in the case of Amnon and Tamar). Desire and what they mistakenly call 'love' ruin the unfortunate couple's judgment, leading people who are worlds apart to marry, only to find that they cannot live together. As a man told me whose daughter 'fell in love' with someone entirely unsuited for her, "even his worst enemy would not have suggested a match for his daughter as bad as the one she arranged for herself"!

But in fact, the entire issue of marriage and married life is divinely inspired. *Chazal* tell us that the Divine Presence dwells between a man (אִישׁ) and a woman (אִשָּׁה), and in token of this God put the letter י in the word אִישׁ and ה in the word אִשָּׁה, which two letters spell one of His Names (*Sotah* 4). Unfortunately, in our topsy-turvy generation the Divine Presence is expelled from many Jewish homes by secular lifestyles: and when you take י־ה out of אִישׁ and אִשָּׁה, only אֵשׁ remains: two burning fires. May God bless His nation with peace.

וְלָקַחְתָּ לְךָ לְאִשָּׁה — *You may take her to yourself for a wife*. "The Torah only spoke in consideration of the evil inclination; for if God did not permit this woman, the man would marry her even though she was forbidden" (*Rashi*). This is difficult to understand. The danger of the evil inclination overpowering man and causing him to sin is present whenever something is

21
12-14

and you will desire her, you may take her to yourself for a
wife. 12 *You shall bring her to the midst of your house; she shall*
shave her head and let her nails grow. 13 *She shall re-*
move the garment of her captivity from upon herself and sit
in your house and she shall weep for her father and her moth-
er for a full month; thereafter you may come to her and live
with her, and she shall be a wife to you. 14 *But it shall be that*
if you do not desire her, then you shall send her on her own, but
you may not sell her for money; you shall not enslave her,

---

forbidden, and especially in sexual matters. Yet God did not issue a blanket exemption for all prohibitions, just to pacify the evil inclination! Why is the case of the *yefas to'ar* different?

We can suggest that this *halachah* is not intended as appeasement for the evil inclination but as a 'medicine' against it. Consider how puzzling this case is: according to *halachah*, only those who are guiltless of any transgression, even a rabbinic one, may go out to war. (According to R' Yosei HaGlili, this is in fact the context of "a man who is fearful and fainthearted" [20:8].) What could have happened to the untainted righteous man, who set out to battle, to topple him into the trap laid by the evil inclination?

War, and the accompanying leniencies about forbidden foods mandated by the Torah during war, have had a negative influence on him. This was compounded by the gentile harlots who adorn themselves to attract the enemy soldiers, at a time when he is separated from his wife. "When the maidservants are immodest and woo the men, enticing them to sin, even though [the men] sin they are held to have been under duress" (*Tosafos, Gittin* 41).

The chances that one will sin under such circumstances are high; and once a man has sinned he loses his spiritual 'balance,' and the *yetzer* can take him over, for "one sin leads to another." This is why the Torah only permitted a *yefas to'ar* when she has been brought to the man's own home, since then he is reunited with his wife. When she arrives there, this harlot must remove her attractive clothing and make herself ugly by shaving her head and growing her nails, and by spending a month crying for her parents. In most cases, this will be enough to cure the infatuation: "it shall be that if you do not desire her, then you shall send her on her own." This is the meaning of *Chazal*'s statement that the Torah spoke here only in consideration of the evil inclination: it provides a 'prescription' against its lures.

12. וַהֲבֵאתָהּ אֶל־תּוֹךְ בֵּיתֶךָ — *You shall bring her to the midst of your house.* Where you will teach her Jewish laws and customs prior to conversion.

14. וְהָיָה אִם־לֹא חָפַצְתָּ בָּהּ — *But it shall be that if you do not desire her.* "The word וְהָיָה expresses joy" (*Bereishis Rabbah* 42:3). If one conquers his evil inclination and chooses not to marry a *yefas to'ar*, saving his family from the potential troubles of a rebellious son, it is truly a joyous occasion!

כא תַּחַת אֲשֶׁר עִנִּיתָהּ׃ טו כִּי־תִהְיֶיןָ לְאִישׁ
טו־יט שְׁתֵּי נָשִׁים הָאַחַת אֲהוּבָה וְהָאַחַת שְׂנוּאָה וְיָלְדוּ־לוֹ
בָנִים הָאֲהוּבָה וְהַשְּׂנוּאָה וְהָיָה הַבֵּן הַבְּכֹר לַשְּׂנִיאָה׃
טז וְהָיָה בְּיוֹם הַנְחִילוֹ אֶת־בָּנָיו אֵת אֲשֶׁר־יִהְיֶה לוֹ לֹא
יוּכַל לְבַכֵּר אֶת־בֶּן־הָאֲהוּבָה עַל־פְּנֵי בֶן־הַשְּׂנוּאָה הַבְּכֹר׃
יז כִּי אֶת־הַבְּכֹר בֶּן־הַשְּׂנוּאָה יַכִּיר לָתֶת לוֹ פִּי שְׁנַיִם
בְּכֹל אֲשֶׁר־יִמָּצֵא לוֹ כִּי־הוּא רֵאשִׁית אֹנוֹ לוֹ מִשְׁפַּט
הַבְּכֹרָה׃ יח כִּי־יִהְיֶה לְאִישׁ בֵּן סוֹרֵר
וּמוֹרֶה אֵינֶנּוּ שֹׁמֵעַ בְּקוֹל אָבִיו וּבְקוֹל אִמּוֹ וְיִסְּרוּ אֹתוֹ
וְלֹא יִשְׁמַע אֲלֵיהֶם׃ יט וְתָפְשׂוּ בוֹ אָבִיו וְאִמּוֹ וְהוֹצִיאוּ

---

15. כִּי־תִהְיֶיןָ לְאִישׁ שְׁתֵּי נָשִׁים — *If a man will have two wives*. *Chazal* point out the conspicuous joining of this *parashah* to the previous one, deducing from it that a man who marries a *yefas to'ar* will ultimately find himself the father of a rebellious son.

We could suggest that these three things: the *yefas to'ar*, the sons of the beloved and hated wives, and the rebellious son, are all related. The first speaks of the man who succeeds in overcoming his *yetzer:* "if you do not desire her." The next deals with a man who did not overcome temptation and married the *yefas to'ar*. Now his Jewish wife has become the "hated one," so much so that he is willing to grant the favored wife's demand and give her son the status of firstborn. The Torah does not allow him to do so: "he *cannot* give the right of the firstborn" (not merely "he should not"). Even if he should attempt to do so his action is void, and the son of the hated wife retains his rights.

Next in the sequence is the plight of parents who did not have the good fortune to die before their son degenerated completely. Now they must bring their rebellious son to the elders of the city to be stoned.

☙ **וְהָיָה הַבֵּן הַבְּכֹר לַשְּׂנִיאָה** — *And the firstborn son is the hated one's*. The Torah is decreeing that in the event that a man has two wives, one beloved and one hated, the hated wife will surely bear the firstborn son. And so it was in the case of Leah: "Hashem saw that Leah was unloved, so He opened her womb; but Rachel remained barren" (*Bereishis* 29:31).

16. וְהָיָה בְּיוֹם הַנְחִילוֹ אֶת־בָּנָיו — *Then it shall be that on the day that he causes his sons to inherit*. The Torah is not really pleased with a father who favors the son of his beloved wife over that of the hated one even during his lifetime. One should never favor one child over the others: "For two yards of cloth that Jacob gave to Joseph beyond what his other sons received, his brothers envied him, with the ultimate outcome that our fathers went down to Egypt" (*Shabbos* 10).

Now, since a man is not obligated by the Torah to support his [grown] sons, a father may do as he pleases with his money — while he lives. But "on the day

21
15-19

because you have afflicted her.
15 If a man will have two wives, one beloved and one hated,
and they bear him sons, the beloved one and the hated one, and
the firstborn son is the hated one's; 16 then it shall be that on
the day that he causes his sons to inherit whatever will be his,
he cannot give the right of the firstborn to the son of the belov-
ed one ahead of the son of the hated one, the firstborn. 17 Rath-
er, he must recognize the firstborn, the son of the hated one, to
give him the double portion in all that is found with him; for
he is his initial vigor, to him is the right of the firstborn.
18 If a man will have a wayward and rebellious son, who
does not hearken to the voice of his father and the voice of his
mother, and they discipline him, but he does not hearken to
them; 19 then his father and mother shall grasp him and take

---

that he causes his son to inherit," if he wants to invoke the Torah's law of inheritance but change it to suit himself (such as making it favor the beloved wife's son), he has no power to do so; he must act in accordance with the *halachah*. (Though even on his death-bed he can distribute his money as he sees fit by giving it as a gift.)

17. כִּי אֶת־הַבְּכֹר בֶּן־הַשְּׂנוּאָה יַכִּיר — *Rather he must recognize the firstborn, the son of the hated one.* Although the Torah has already told us that "he cannot give the right of the firstborn to the son of the beloved one," we might think that the father can treat both sons equally, giving each an equal share of the inheritance. So the Torah specifically tells us that "he must recognize the firstborn, the son of the hated one, to give him the double portion."

18. כִּי־יִהְיֶה לְאִישׁ — *If a man will have*. Even though the rebellious son does not obey his mother any more than he does his father, the Torah puts the blame on the father: "if a *man* will have" a rebellious son. This is because it was the father's particular obligation to teach his son Torah, to rebuke him, and to educate him in proper behavior.

אֵינֶנּוּ שֹׁמֵעַ בְּקוֹל אָבִיו וּבְקוֹל אִמּוֹ — *Who does not hearken to the voice of his father and the voice of his mother.* Apparently, he did not listen "to the voice of his father" whenever his mother defended him (as often happens with mothers); nor did he listen to "the voice of his mother" whenever his father defended him. And that is why "voice" is written twice in this verse. But then the Torah goes on seemingly to repeat itself: "and they discipline him, but he does not hearken to them." The words *they* and *them* indicate that even when both parents were in agreement about his misbehavior, he still would not listen!

19. וְתָפְשׂוּ בוֹ אָבִיו וְאִמּוֹ — *Then his father and mother shall grasp him.* How great is the corruption of the rebellious son, and what a glutton and drunkard he must be, when even his own mother brings him with her own

כא אֹתוֹ אֶל־זִקְנֵי עִירוֹ וְאֶל־שַׁעַר מְקֹמוֹ: כ וְאָמְרוּ אֶל־
כ־כג זִקְנֵי עִירוֹ בְּנֵנוּ זֶה סוֹרֵר וּמֹרֶה אֵינֶנּוּ שֹׁמֵעַ בְּקֹלֵנוּ
זוֹלֵל וְסֹבֵא: כא וּרְגָמֻהוּ כָּל־אַנְשֵׁי עִירוֹ בָאֲבָנִים
וָמֵת וּבִעַרְתָּ הָרָע מִקִּרְבֶּךָ וְכָל־יִשְׂרָאֵל יִשְׁמְעוּ
וְיִרָאוּ: שני כב וְכִי־יִהְיֶה בְאִישׁ חֵטְא מִשְׁפַּט־מָוֶת
וְהוּמָת וְתָלִיתָ אֹתוֹ עַל־עֵץ: כג לֹא־תָלִין נִבְלָתוֹ עַל־הָעֵץ

---

hands to the court to be stoned. This despite the fact that she is from a non-Jewish background, with lower moral standards, and, being a woman, is naturally more merciful. For if either of the parents does not agree, he is not killed.

אֶל־זִקְנֵי עִירוֹ וְאֶל־שַׁעַר מְקֹמוֹ — *To the elders of his city and the gate of his place.* The Torah does not mention "their (the parents') city" and "their place"; it says "his." The blame for the rebellious son's sins is not cast upon the parents after they personally hand him over to the court. For this reason the rebellious son is not stoned at the door of his parents' home; they cannot be taunted with the dismal results of their child-rearing efforts, since they rebuked him and had the courage to bring him to the *Beis Din.*

22. וְהוּמָת וְתָלִיתָ אֹתוֹ עַל־עֵץ — *He shall be put to death, and you shall hang him on a gallows.* We might think the person to be executed should be hung while he is alive, but the Torah says "he shall be put to death [first] and you shall hang him [after he is dead]." The lesson clearly is that one who has been sentenced to death by strangulation must not be killed by hanging. — Certainly not by the barbaric custom of hanging by the hands (as mentioned in *Eichah* [5]: "princes were hung by their hands") in which the accused struggles with death for days. There is no crueler death than this. — But even executing the accused by hanging him on a gallows with a rope around his neck, as is customary among the enlightened gentile nations, is forbidden by the Torah.

The Torah's commandment of execution by strangulation is fulfilled thus: "They sink him in manure up to his knees, then place a coarse scarf inside a soft scarf and wind this around his neck. One [witness] pulls the scarf to one side, and the other pulls it to his side, until he expires" (*Sanhedrin* 52).

It seems to me that the reason we do not perform strangulation by means of hanging is because when a person is hanged he actually kills himself: his body weighs down on the rope and he chokes. We cannot do this for two reasons. First, because in this way the condemned man kills himself, and the Torah's commandment of execution must be carried out by the witnesses. Second, because we may not demand of the condemned man that he help us to kill him, neither with his body nor with his money. *Chazal* say that "the rock with which he is stoned, the tree on which he is hung, the sword with which he is killed and the scarf with which he is strangled, all must belong to the community. Why? Because if they were his property, we cannot tell him, 'go and bring these, and

21
20-23

him out to the elders of his city and the gate of his place.
[20] They shall say to the elders of his city, "This son of ours is
wayward and rebellious; he does not hearken to our voice; he
is a glutton and a drunkard." [21] All the men of his city shall
pelt him with stones and he shall die; and you shall remove
the evil from your midst; and all Israel shall hear and they
shall fear.
[22] If a man shall have committed a sin whose judgment is
death, he shall be put to death, and you shall hang him on a
gallows. [23] You shall not leave his body overnight on the
gallows, rather you shall surely bury him on that day, for a

---

kill yourself'" (*Sanhedrin* 43a). It is therefore not permissible to utilize his body weight so that he should thereby kill himself by hanging.

וְתָלִיתָ אֹתוֹ עַל־עֵץ — *And you shall hang him on a gallows*. The specific word used is עֵץ, literally a *tree*. And why? Because a person is like a tree, as the Torah says, "For man *is* a tree of the field" (*Ibn Ezra* 20:19). Just as the tree upon which the accused is hung is uprooted before its time (since it must be pulled up and buried with the body: *Sanhedrin* 46b), so has this man been uprooted before his time as a result of his sin.

23. לֹא־תָלִין נִבְלָתוֹ עַל־הָעֵץ — *You shall not leave his body overnight on the gallows*. *Chazal* learn from here that one who leaves a body unburied has transgressed a negative commandment; however, if the burial is postponed to bring greater honor to the deceased, it is not a transgression (*Sanhedrin* 46a).

Our obligation to give honor to the deceased needs some explanation. Love of honor is an ugly characteristic, and it is in fact one of the three things that drive a man from the world. Now that the deceased has departed this world and gone to worms, dust and ashes, he sees that all the honor he received in the upside-down world he has just left is utterly worthless. What need has he, who has settled his accounts with this transitory world, of "the last honors" bestowed on him?

We can answer this question with the Midrash, which tells us that when a person dies, God tells the angels: "So-and-So has died; go out and ask if he was righteous." How amazing! For all man's deeds, good and bad, are recorded in Heaven. Why, then, must the angels go and investigate whether this man was righteous or not?

The idea here seems to be derived from the fact that man's chief purpose on earth is to sanctify God's name publicly, by serving as a positive example in the service of God and good human relations. Therefore, the greatest virtue one can have in God's estimation is to have sanctified His name, and conversely, the worst sin is to have desecrated God's name, Heaven forbid, by leading others to learn evil conduct. On the day a man dies and must face Heavenly judgment, God intimates to the angels that much depends on what people say about the

כב כִּֽי־קָב֨וֹר תִּקְבְּרֶ֜נּוּ בַּיּ֣וֹם הַה֗וּא כִּֽי־קִלְלַ֥ת אֱלֹהִ֖ים תָּל֑וּי
א־ד וְלֹ֤א תְטַמֵּא֙ אֶת־אַדְמָ֣תְךָ֔ אֲשֶׁר֙ יְהוָ֣ה אֱלֹהֶ֔יךָ נֹתֵ֥ן לְךָ֖
נַחֲלָֽה׃ א לֹֽא־תִרְאֶה֩ אֶת־שׁ֨וֹר אָחִ֜יךָ א֤וֹ
אֶת־שֵׂיוֹ֙ נִדָּחִ֔ים וְהִתְעַלַּמְתָּ֖ מֵהֶ֑ם הָשֵׁ֥ב תְּשִׁיבֵ֖ם לְאָחִֽיךָ׃
ב וְאִם־לֹ֨א קָר֥וֹב אָחִ֛יךָ אֵלֶ֖יךָ וְלֹ֣א יְדַעְתּ֑וֹ וַאֲסַפְתּ֗וֹ
אֶל־תּ֣וֹךְ בֵּיתֶ֔ךָ וְהָיָ֣ה עִמְּךָ֗ עַ֣ד דְּרֹ֤שׁ אָחִ֙יךָ֙ אֹת֔וֹ וַהֲשֵׁבֹת֖וֹ
לֽוֹ׃ ג וְכֵ֧ן תַּעֲשֶׂ֣ה לַחֲמֹר֗וֹ וְכֵ֣ן תַּעֲשֶׂה֮ לְשִׂמְלָתוֹ֒ וְכֵ֣ן תַּעֲשֶׂ֗ה
לְכָל־אֲבֵדַ֥ת אָחִ֛יךָ אֲשֶׁר־תֹּאבַ֥ד מִמֶּ֖נּוּ וּמְצָאתָ֑הּ לֹ֥א
תוּכַ֖ל לְהִתְעַלֵּֽם׃ ד לֹֽא־תִרְאֶה֩ אֶת־חֲמ֨וֹר
אָחִ֜יךָ א֤וֹ שׁוֹרוֹ֙ נֹפְלִ֣ים בַּדֶּ֔רֶךְ וְהִתְעַלַּמְתָּ֖ מֵהֶ֑ם הָקֵ֥ם

---

deceased (which shows what they learned from him in his lifetime). If they say he was righteous, and detail what they saw in him and learned from him, then even if he sinned in private at times — without causing a public desecration of God's name — he deserves to be pardoned.

In that case it is a good thing for the deceased if the angels hear, at the time of his death, that he is being honored, eulogized, and praised for his piety and good deeds. This is bound to help them to decide that he had indeed sanctified God's name during his lifetime. Therefore, the final honors, eulogies, and honest praise that is bestowed upon a man after his death is not false honor, but a means of defending him before the Heavenly Court and helping him gain eternal life in the World to Come.

כִּי־קָבוֹר תִּקְבְּרֶנּוּ — *You shall surely bury him. Chazal* learn from this double phrasing, קָבוֹר תִּקְבְּרֶנּוּ, that the rock with which he was stoned, the pole on which he was hung, the scarf with which he was strangled, and the sword with which he was killed also have to be buried. But not in the same grave with him; they are buried in a hole specially dug near the grave (*Sanhedrin* 45b). The inference is clear: תִּקְבְּרֶנּוּ, "You shall bury him," refers to the accused, and קָבוֹר indicates a second 'grave' for the articles used in the execution.

22.

1. **לֹא־תִרְאֶה אֶת־שׁוֹר אָחִיךָ** — *You shall not see the ox of your brother*. In *Parashas Mishpatim* the Torah talks about "the ox of your *enemy*." There *Chazal* explain that the commandment to return lost objects is being presented as a fine means of "subduing the evil inclination" and ultimately making peace between the loser and finder. Here the phrasing is deliberately changed, so that you should not think that it applies only to what is lost by your enemy, or that its purpose is only to foster peace. The words "the ox of your brother" make it clear that returning *any* lost object is a positive commandment. The intent behind mentioning "the ox of your enemy" was to lay down the rule that if one

hanging person is a curse of God, and you shall not
contaminate your Land, which HASHEM, your God, gives you
as an inheritance.
1 *You shall not see the ox of your brother or his sheep or goat*
cast off, and hide yourself from them; you shall surely return
them to your brother. 2 *If your brother is not near you and you*
do not know him, then gather it inside your house, and it shall
remain with you until your brother inquires after it, and you
return it to him. 3 *So shall you do for his donkey, so shall you*
do for his garment, and so shall you do for any lost article of
your brother that may become lost from him and you find it;
you shall not hide yourself.
4 *You shall not see the donkey of your brother or his ox fall-*
ing on the road and hide yourself from them; you shall surely

---

must choose between returning an article lost by his friend and one lost by his enemy, the enemy's article takes precedence, because of the added element of "subduing the evil inclination" and making peace.

וְהִתְעַלַּמְתָּ מֵהֶם — *And hide yourself from them.* In verse 3 we are warned, "you shall not hide yourself." *Chazal* (*Bava Metzia* 30a) explain the apparent contradiction: there are times when the finder should "hide himself," i.e., ignore the lost object. For example, this is the case if he is an elder, for whom it would be undignified to deal with returning lost animals. The logic is that if it would be undignified for the finder to retrieve the article even if it was his own, he is not obligated to do so for someone else. For this reason the subject of returning lost objects follows that of "you shall not leave his body overnight": both deal with the necessity of preserving human dignity.

2. וְאִם־לֹא קָרוֹב אָחִיךָ אֵלֶיךָ וְלֹא יְדַעְתּוֹ — *If your brother is not near you and you do not know him*. Even if he is far away and you do not know him, he is still your brother.

The letter ו in וְלֹא can also mean "or," and here we can see it as separating two possibilities. If you "do not know" who the owner is, then it is obvious that you must "gather the ox inside your house" until "your brother inquires after it"; otherwise it would be impossible to fulfill the commandment of returning lost objects. Or, if you know him but he is "not near you," in this case too you may simply "gather it inside your house . . . until your brother inquires after it." You are not obligated to return the item to the owner's home, although of course if possible you should inform him of its whereabouts.

לֹא קָרוֹב אָחִיךָ — *Your brother is not near you.* The Torah uses the longer phrase "not near you," rather than the single word "distant," for how can one Jew be "distant" from another?

כב תָּקִים עִמּוֹ: ה לֹא־יִהְיֶה כְלִי־גֶבֶר עַל־אִשָּׁה
ה־ז וְלֹא־יִלְבַּשׁ גֶּבֶר שִׂמְלַת אִשָּׁה כִּי תוֹעֲבַת יהוה אֱלֹהֶיךָ
כָּל־עֹשֵׂה אֵלֶּה:
ו כִּי יִקָּרֵא קַן־צִפּוֹר ׀ לְפָנֶיךָ בַּדֶּרֶךְ בְּכָל־עֵץ ׀ אוֹ
עַל־הָאָרֶץ אֶפְרֹחִים אוֹ בֵיצִים וְהָאֵם רֹבֶצֶת עַל־
הָאֶפְרֹחִים אוֹ עַל־הַבֵּיצִים לֹא־תִקַּח הָאֵם עַל־
הַבָּנִים: ז שַׁלֵּחַ תְּשַׁלַּח אֶת־הָאֵם וְאֶת־הַבָּנִים תִּקַּח־לָךְ

---

6. **כִּי יִקָּרֵא קַן־צִפּוֹר לְפָנֶיךָ** — *If a bird's nest happens to be before you.* The Torah always equates beasts and birds: both are not usually under man's control, the laws of covering the blood after slaughter are the same for both, and the *chelev* of both is permissible to eat. Yet the commandment of *shiluach hakein* applies only to birds; if we find a doe lying with her young, we may take both her and her young without hesitation.

This is because the nature of birds is different from that of other beasts in God's creation. Birds lay eggs and roost on them until the chicks finally emerge. Other species that we come in contact with bear live young who resemble their parents immediately at birth. In keeping with this disparity, God granted the bird an inordinate love for its young which extends even to the eggs. Even though she sees only an inanimate object before her, and one which bears no resemblance to her, the mother bird devotes herself single-mindedly to the preservation and well-being of her eggs, roosting on them for weeks, barely eating or drinking herself, keeping them warm at all times, until the day she at long last sees her chicks emerge from the shell.

It follows that her anguish must be enormous, when the object of her devotion is taken from her; for her sorrow over harm befalling her young is bound to be proportional to the love for them that God instilled in her. This is why the Torah repeats the words "the young birds or the eggs" twice: to indicate that the bird's love for her young is strong even when the offspring are merely lifeless eggs.

It could be objected that "if someone says [in his prayer] 'even to a bird's nest Your mercy reaches,' he must be silenced, for [this *mitzvah* is not mercy] but the King's decree" (*Megillah* 25a). But this applies only if the man says it as part of his prayer, that is, if he declares that for him the absolute reason for this *mitzvah* is mercy. Of him God says, "one who speaks lies cannot stand before Me" (*Tehillim* 101:7). But there are seventy facets to the Torah, and one may speak of many reasons for a *mitzvah* as long as he does not imagine one of them to be absolute. (See *Tosfos Yom Tov* on *Berachos* 5:3.)

◆§ **בְּכָל־עֵץ** — *On any tree*. The word "any" might seem to be superfluous, God forbid. Possibly it is a veiled reference to the Midrashic teaching that the reward for the *mitzvah* of *shiluach hakein*, the most 'minor' of *mitzvos*, is

22
5-7

stand them up, with him.

5 *Male garb shall not be on a woman, and a man shall not wear a feminine garment, for anyone who does so is an abomination of* HASHEM.

6 *If a bird's nest happens to be before you on the road, on any tree or on the ground — young birds or eggs — and the mother is roosting on the young birds or the eggs, you shall not take the mother with the young.*
7 *You shall surely send away the mother and take the young for yourself,*

---

equal to that of honoring one's parents, the most 'major' of them: "so that it will be good for you and will prolong your days." This being said, the reward for the other commandments are not specified, so that we will be motivated to observe all of them, and not choose only the 'major' ones, since the Torah has equated the reward for both 'major' and 'minor' *mitzvos.*

The Midrash explains the logic with a parable: A king hired workers to plant a field with many kinds of trees, without telling them how much he would pay for planting each kind of tree. At the day's end, the king presented a worker who had planted a simple, common tree with an entire gold coin as payment. The other workers were surprised; if the payment for a simple tree was so great, how much more so for a valuable tree! The king's tactic proved most effective: the following day they all went to work with increased energy and will to work.

Rabbeinu Bachya explains that the commandments are like fruit-bearing trees, with some fruits of better quality than others. Knowing that the reward for fulfilling an easy commandment like *shiluach hakein* is that "it will be good for you and will prolong your days" should serve as motivation for us to invest effort in every one of the "trees" — the 248 positive commandments, 'minor' as well as 'major'.

⋄§ **וְהָאֵם רֹבֶצֶת** — *And the mother is roosting.* The *halachos* of *shiluach hakein* apply when the mother bird is actually roosting on the eggs or hovering over them, not when she is flying overhead with her wings not touching the nest (*Chullin* 140b). But the natural tendency of a bird is to fly away as soon as a human being approaches. Why, in the scenario of *shiluach hakein*, does the mother bird not escape and save herself? Because of her tremendous love for her offspring— she is "roosting on the young birds or the eggs." The Torah does not allow man to exploit the bird's love for her chicks in order to trap her: it commands us, "send away the mother," who could have saved herself but did not. Birds may be caught with nets and traps, but not because of their devotion to their offspring. This is indicated in the *Rambam's Hilchos Shechitah* (13:7): "The Torah only forbade us to trap her when she cannot fly away because of her offspring, on which she is roosting to prevent them from being taken; as it is written, 'And the mother is roosting on the young birds'."

כב לְמַעַן יִיטַב לָךְ וְהַאֲרַכְתָּ יָמִים׃ שלישי ח כִּי
ח־ט תִבְנֶה בַּיִת חָדָשׁ וְעָשִׂיתָ מַעֲקֶה לְגַגֶּךָ וְלֹא־תָשִׂים דָּמִים
בְּבֵיתֶךָ כִּי־יִפֹּל הַנֹּפֵל מִמֶּנּוּ׃ ט לֹא־תִזְרַע כַּרְמְךָ כִּלְאָיִם

---

7. **לְמַעַן יִיטַב לָךְ וְהַאֲרַכְתָּ יָמִים** — *So that it will be good for you and will prolong your days*. It is well known that the commandments of *shiluach hakein* and honoring one's parents are the only ones for which the Torah specifies what the reward will be, and that the reward for both is the same: length of days. But why are these two commandments singled out in this way, and why does so easy a commandment and such a difficult one share the same reward?

It is because the two are related. The mother bird must be sent away free, because rather than escape and save herself when her nest is approached by humans, she risks her life out of love for her young. The Torah, therefore, forbids us to seize her and thereby exploit her meritorious behavior. (It is permissible to catch her the normal way, with a snare [*Chullin* 141b]). The two commandments, then, have a common element of respect for parents who are even willing to endanger themselves to raise their children and preserve the species. Honoring one's parents may seem to us the gravest of obligations, and *shiluach hakein* the slightest, but that is only because of our superficial view of things. In fact, deeper reflection can show us that *shiluach hakein* is actually a graver matter than honoring parents.

Consider, one who honors his parents "repays" them, albeit minimally, for all they do for him until he reaches maturity and independence. However, if this same person should happen to find a bird's nest, he may not take the mother, even if she actually belongs to him and fled from his hatchery, and even if she is nesting on his property. Although this bird has never benefited him in the least he is forbidden to take her simply because she is a mother who is raising her children. He personally gains nothing from her devoted child-rearing, yet must still restrain himself. He will surely find this difficult, though no such difficulty exists with honoring his parents. Therefore this *mitzvah* shares the same reward with honoring parents.

❧ "R' Yaakov interpreted thus: 'So that it will be good for you in the World to Come, and so that your days will be prolonged in the World to Come'" (*Chullin* 142a). Elisha ben Avuyah became *Acher*, "a different man," and denied the entire Torah after seeing a man climb a ladder at his father's request to send away a mother bird and take the fledglings. The obedient son fell off the ladder on his way down and was killed. *Chazal* comment that had *Acher* known the correct interpretation of this verse as R' Yaakov (his grandson) did, he would not have sinned (*Chullin*, loc. cit.).

And why did he not interpret the verses properly? Because he read heretical literature (*Chagigah* 15b). Heretics do not believe in the resurrection of the dead, and apparently *Acher* picked up this opinion from his reading. He

so that it will be good for you and will prolong your days.
[8] *If you build a new house, you shall make a fence for your*
roof, so that you will not place blood in your house if a fallen
one falls from it.
[9] *You shall not sow your vineyard with a mixture, lest the*

---

could only understand "so that your days will be prolonged" as referring to long life in this world: the soul remaining in the physical body for many years. Since the soul (a concept in which heretics profess to believe) is in any case eternal, "long life" could only, to their mind, mean physical life before death.

When *Acher* saw a man die while fulfilling the two commandments for which the Torah promises "long life," he denied the Torah's truth. But we who believe in the actual physical resurrection of the dead know that there can be long life, in which the soul remains in the body, in the World to Come.

8. כִּי תִבְנֶה בַּיִת חָדָשׁ — *If you build a new house*. An old house also needs a parapet around its roof. Why, then, does the Torah talk specifically of a new house? We can answer this by considering *Chazal's* insight (quoted by *Rashi*): "If you have fulfilled the commandment of *shiluach hakein,* you will ultimately build a new house" — blessed with long life, you will outlive your house rather than the other way around, and so will have to build a new one — "and then you will fulfill the commandment of building a fence around the roof. For one *mitzvah* brings another in its wake." (See *Pirkei Avos* 4:2.)

כִּי־יִפֹּל הַנֹּפֵל מִמֶּנּוּ — *If a fallen one falls from it*. A homeowner uses his roof more than anyone else, and it is human nature to be more concerned with preserving one's own life than another's. Why, then, does the Torah warn the homeowner that someone else might fall off his roof? Why not warn him about the danger to himself?

It is because this verse is talking about a man who has built a new home through the merit of having fulfilled the commandment of *shiluach hakein.* He has seen the realization of *Chazal's* promise, so he also feels assured of a long life, as promised him in the Torah. What does he need a parapet for? he thinks. Therefore the Torah warns him not to "place [the guilt of] blood in your house", for even if he is not going to fall off his roof, someone else might, and he would then be held responsible.

9. לֹא־תִזְרַע כַּרְמְךָ כִּלְאָיִם — *You shall not sow your vineyard with a mixture*. The Torah has already told us "do not plant your field with a mixture" (*Vayikra* 19:19), meaning various kinds of grain together. The present verse adds that if one adds grape seeds to the mixture of grains, so that there is also a vineyard here, he is now transgressing two negative commandments.

כב פֶּן־תִּקְדַּשׁ הַמְלֵאָה הַזֶּרַע אֲשֶׁר תִּזְרָע וּתְבוּאַת
י־טו הַכָּרֶם: י לֹא־תַחֲרֹשׁ בְּשׁוֹר־וּבַחֲמֹר יַחְדָּו: יא לֹא
תִלְבַּשׁ שַׁעַטְנֵז צֶמֶר וּפִשְׁתִּים יַחְדָּו: יב גְּדִלִים
תַּעֲשֶׂה־לָּךְ עַל־אַרְבַּע כַּנְפוֹת כְּסוּתְךָ אֲשֶׁר תְּכַסֶּה־
בָּהּ: יג כִּי־יִקַּח אִישׁ אִשָּׁה וּבָא אֵלֶיהָ וּשְׂנֵאָהּ:
יד וְשָׂם לָהּ עֲלִילֹת דְּבָרִים וְהוֹצִא עָלֶיהָ שֵׁם רָע
וְאָמַר אֶת־הָאִשָּׁה הַזֹּאת לָקַחְתִּי וָאֶקְרַב אֵלֶיהָ וְלֹא־
מָצָאתִי לָהּ בְּתוּלִים: טו וְלָקַח אֲבִי הַנַּעֲרָ וְאִמָּהּ

---

10. בְּשׁוֹר־וּבַחֲמֹר יַחְדָּו — *With an ox and a donkey together.* "This is because an ox chews its cud, and [if they were yoked together] the donkey would feel anguish at hearing the ox eat [when he cannot]" (*Baalei Tosafos*). But why, then, is this prohibition only during ploughing or other types of labor? Why did the Torah not forbid putting an ox and donkey together in the same barn?

The answer might be that in a barn, usually all the animals are given food at the same time, so that the donkey, too, is eating; or else the donkey is not so near the ox as when they are yoked together, and so does not hear it chewing its cud.

Ultimately, though, this is a *chok*, a commandment for which the reason has not been revealed, and which we are not to question nor try to assign it a definitive rationale.

11. צֶמֶר וּפִשְׁתִּים יַחְדָּו — *Wool and linen together*. This, too, is a *chok*, a Torah law for which the reason has not been revealed and whose underlying reasons one should not seek.

Interestingly enough, however, in my youth I read that when the electric train system of Kiev was built, the train would not run on one street. The engineers who checked the problem discovered that it was not the train but the cable on that street which was made of a mixture of wool and linen. Not finding any other cause for the train's failure, they replaced the cable with one of pure linen — and the train ran perfectly, causing quite a furor at the time. Apparently, wool and linen do not mix well. Who knows what else may be found behind this mixture which the Torah has forbidden?

12. גְּדִלִים — *Twisted threads*. This topic is placed immediately following the prohibition of *shaatnez* to teach us that in fulfillment of the commandment of *tzitzis* one may even put woolen fringes on a linen garment. A possible reason why this is permissible can be found in the *Baalei Tosafos'* explanation for the prohibition of *shaatnez*:

The Temple curtains were made of mixed linen and wool, as was the clothing of the High Priest. We may not wear clothing of similar construction, just as it is forbidden to make incense of the kind used in the Holy Temple. But in a garment worn to fulfill a positive commandment — ציצית, a fringed garment — the Torah permits this mixture for the sake of the *mitzvah*, since *techeiles*, the blue dye commanded by the Torah, only holds fast in wool.

agrowth of the seed that you plant and the produce of the
vineyard become forbidden.
[10] *You shall not plow with an ox and a donkey together.*
[11] *You shall not wear combined fibers, wool and linen together.*
[12] *You shall make for yourselves twisted threads on the*
four corners of your garment with which you cover yourself.
[13] *If a man marries a wife, and comes to her and hates her,*
[14] *and he makes a wanton accusation against her, spreading*
a bad name against her, and he said, "I married this woman,
and I came near to her and I did not find signs of virginity on
her." [15] *Then the father of the girl and her mother should take*

עַל־אַרְבַּע כַּנְפוֹת כְּסוּתְךָ — *On the four corners of your garment.* I heard from my older brother, the saintly *Gaon* R' Yoel Sorotzkin (Rav of Stalingrad and later of Stoipce, Lithuania), that a lesson awaits us in the Torah's command to put fringes on "the four corners of your garment." The Torah intends to teach us that a Jew should be only "on the corners of the garment," i.e., material life. He should not be "all over the garment": he should be satisfied with a modest lifestyle, and not pursue wealth and luxurious living. Only then can he be certain of fulfilling all of the Torah's commandments. This explains how the commandment of *tzitzis* is equivalent to all the other commandments combined, as the Torah says, "You will see them and remember *all* of God's commandments" (*Menachos* 43b).

13-14. כִּי־יִקַּח אִישׁ אִשָּׁה . . . וְלֹא־מָצָאתִי לָהּ בְּתוּלִים — *If a man marries a wife . . . and I did not find signs of virginity on her.* Why does the topic of punishment for immoral behavior follow the commandment to wear fringed garments? To teach us that anyone who scrupulously fulfills the commandment of *tzitzis* will be saved from falling into such behavior: "You will see [the fringes] . . . and you will not stray. . . after your eyes" (*Bamidbar* 15:39). As *Chazal* explain, "after your eyes" refers to sinful thoughts (*Berachos* 12b).

14. וְשָׂם לָהּ עֲלִילֹת דְּבָרִים וְהוֹצִא עָלֶיהָ שֵׁם רָע — *And he makes a wanton accusation against her, spreading a bad name against her.* The phrasing of this verse is difficult to understand. The husband maintains that he did not find the signs of virginity (the *Gemara* [*Kesubos* 46a] stipulates that he must also bring witnesses that she behaved immorally). Why does the Torah react by saying decisively that he has made "a wanton accusation against her, spreading a bad name against her"? And then, later on (v. 20), the Torah talks of the case "if this matter was true — signs of virginity were not found on the girl"?

The answer is that we are to learn from here how very modest Jewish daughters are. Even before the facts are checked, the Torah decides that it must be that the husband hates his wife and has therefore accused her falsely. Only if the girl's parents cannot refute the witnesses' testimony against their daughter is she put to death. Such an occurrence is a rarity.

וְהוֹצִ֜יאוּ אֶת־בְּתוּלֵ֧י הַֽנַּעֲרָ֛ אֶל־זִקְנֵ֥י הָעִ֖יר הַשָּֽׁעְרָה: טז וְאָמַ֛ר אֲבִ֥י הַֽנַּעֲרָ֖ אֶל־הַזְּקֵנִ֑ים אֶת־בִּתִּ֗י נָתַ֜תִּי לָאִ֥ישׁ הַזֶּ֛ה לְאִשָּׁ֖ה וַיִּשְׂנָאֶֽהָ: יז וְהִנֵּה־ה֡וּא שָׂם֩ עֲלִילֹ֨ת דְּבָרִ֜ים לֵאמֹ֗ר לֹֽא־מָצָ֤אתִי לְבִתְּךָ֙ בְּתוּלִ֔ים וְאֵ֖לֶּה בְּתוּלֵ֣י בִתִּ֑י וּפָֽרְשׂוּ֙ הַשִּׂמְלָ֔ה לִפְנֵ֖י זִקְנֵ֥י הָעִֽיר: יח וְלָֽקְח֛וּ זִקְנֵ֥י הָֽעִיר־הַהִ֖וא אֶת־הָאִ֑ישׁ וְיִסְּר֖וּ אֹתֽוֹ: יט וְעָֽנְשׁ֣וּ אֹת֡וֹ מֵ֣אָה כֶסֶף֩ וְנָֽתְנ֨וּ לַֽאֲבִ֜י הַֽנַּעֲרָ֗ה כִּ֤י הוֹצִיא֙ שֵׁ֣ם רָ֔ע עַ֖ל בְּתוּלַ֣ת יִשְׂרָאֵ֑ל וְלוֹ־תִֽהְיֶ֣ה לְאִשָּׁ֔ה לֹֽא־יוּכַ֥ל לְשַׁלְּחָ֖הּ כָּל־יָמָֽיו: כ וְאִם־אֱמֶ֣ת הָיָ֔ה הַדָּבָ֖ר הַזֶּ֑ה לֹֽא־נִמְצְא֥וּ בְתוּלִ֖ים לַֽנַּעֲרָֽ: כא וְהוֹצִ֨יאוּ אֶת־הַֽנַּעֲרָ֜ אֶל־פֶּ֣תַח בֵּית־אָבִ֗יהָ וּסְקָל֩וּהָ֩ אַנְשֵׁ֨י עִירָ֤הּ בָּֽאֲבָנִים֙ וָמֵ֔תָה כִּֽי־עָשְׂתָ֤ה נְבָלָה֙ בְּיִשְׂרָאֵ֔ל לִזְנ֖וֹת בֵּ֣ית אָבִ֑יהָ וּבִֽעַרְתָּ֥ הָרָ֖ע מִקִּרְבֶּֽךָ: כב כִּֽי־יִמָּצֵ֣א אִ֗ישׁ שֹׁכֵ֣ב ׀ עִם־אִשָּׁ֣ה בְעֻֽלַת־בַּ֗עַל וּמֵ֙תוּ֙ גַּם־שְׁנֵיהֶ֔ם הָאִ֛ישׁ הַשֹּׁכֵ֥ב עִם־הָֽאִשָּׁ֖ה וְהָֽאִשָּׁ֑ה וּבִֽעַרְתָּ֥ הָרָ֖ע מִיִּשְׂרָאֵֽל: כג כִּ֤י יִֽהְיֶה֙ נַֽעֲרָ֣ בְתוּלָ֔ה מְאֹֽרָשָׂ֖ה לְאִ֑ישׁ וּמְצָאָ֥הּ אִ֛ישׁ בָּעִ֖יר וְשָׁכַ֥ב עִמָּֽהּ: כד וְהֽוֹצֵאתֶ֞ם אֶת־שְׁנֵיהֶ֗ם אֶל־שַׁ֙עַר֙ ׀ הָעִ֣יר הַהִ֔וא וּסְקַלְתֶּ֥ם אֹתָ֛ם

---

17. וְהִנֵּה־ה֡וּא שָׂם֩ עֲלִילֹ֨ת דְּבָרִ֜ים . . . וְאֵ֖לֶּה בְּתוּלֵ֣י בִתִּ֑י — *Now behold! he made a wanton accusation . . . but these are the signs of virginity of my daughter.* Why must the father repeat the husband's words? Would it not be enough for him to say just the last thing, "these are the signs of my daughter's virginity"?

When the husband made his accusation (when he "spread a bad name against her") he did so not in court but publicly, in order to humiliate her. The father's words express a complaint to the court about the husband's behavior: the "wanton accusation and bad name" which he has circulated about his daughter humiliate not only her, but her father as well. The husband has shamed him publicly and should be punished.

19. וְעָֽנְשׁ֣וּ אֹת֡וֹ מֵ֣אָה כֶסֶף֩ — *And they shall fine him one hundred silver [shekels].* One who assaults an unmarried woman is only fined fifty silver shekels. Why is the fine greater in this instance?

Chazal explain that one who spreads an accusation is worse than one who actually commits the crime (*Arachin* 15a). They may have meant by this that assaulting a girl causes pain and humiliation, but only to her and her father. However, one who accuses a betrothed Jewish girl of immoral behavior while she is still living in her father's home defiles the good name of *all* modest Jewish daughters. It is only fair that he be fined double. For with his false accusation he has "issued slander against a virgin of Israel", leaving room for other nations

22
16-24

and bring proofs of the girl's virginity to the elders of the city,
to the gate. 16 *The father of the girl should say to the elders, "I*
gave my daughter to this man as a wife, and he hated her.
17 *Now, behold! he made a wanton accusation against her,*
saying, 'I did not find signs of virginity on your daughter' —
but these are the signs of virginity of my daughter!" And
they should spread out the sheet before the elders of the city.
18 *The elders of the city shall take that man and punish*
him. 19 *And they shall fine him one hundred silver [shekels]*
and give them to the father of the girl, for he had issued a
slander against a virgin of Israel, and she shall remain with
him as a wife; he cannot divorce her all his days.
20 *But if this matter was true — signs of virginity were not*
found on the girl — 21 *then they shall take the girl to the*
entrance of her father's house and the people of her city shall
pelt her with stones and she shall die, for she had committed
an outrage in Israel, to commit adultery in her father's house,
and you shall remove the evil from your midst.
22 *If a man will be found lying with a woman who is*
married to a husband, then both of them shall die, the man
who lay with the woman and the woman; and you shall
remove the evil from Israel.
23 *If there will be a virgin girl who is betrothed to a man,*
and a man finds her in the city and lies with her, 24 *then you*
shall take them both to the gate of that city and pelt them

---

to claim that Jewish daughters are as immodest as any others, God forbid. Thus he has slandered not only his own wife, but Jewish women in general.

21. כִּי־עָשְׂתָה נְבָלָה בְּיִשְׂרָאֵל לִזְנוֹת בֵּית אָבִיהָ —*For she had committed an outrage in Israel, to commit adultery in her father's house*. Why is a betrothed girl who behaved immorally stoned, rather than strangled as in the case of a married woman who sinned? Because she has "committed an outrage in Israel" by giving Jewish girls a bad name. Now people will say that, like gentile girls, they do not keep themselves virgins until their marriage.

22. וּמֵתוּ גַּם־שְׁנֵיהֶם — *Then both of them shall die*. *Chazal's* exposition of the phrase "both of them" appears in *Rashi*. A possible, simpler explanation for the use of these words is that in the case of a betrothed girl who sins, only she is put to death, presumably because it is not known who the adulterer was, or else he has run away. In this case, both the man and the woman are to be killed.

24. וְהוֹצֵאתֶם אֶת־שְׁנֵיהֶם — *Then you shall take them both*. In the passage, above, about a husband who accuses his newlywed wife of immoral behavior, no mention is made of the adulterer, while in this case the Torah specifies

כב בָּאֲבָנִים וָמֵתוּ אֶת־הַנַּעֲרָ עַל־דְּבַר אֲשֶׁר לֹא־צָעֲקָה בָעִיר
כה־כט וְאֶת־הָאִישׁ עַל־דְּבַר אֲשֶׁר־עִנָּה אֶת־אֵשֶׁת רֵעֵהוּ וּבִעַרְתָּ
הָרָע מִקִּרְבֶּךָ׃ כה וְאִם־בַּשָּׂדֶה יִמְצָא הָאִישׁ
אֶת־הַנַּעֲרָ הַמְאֹרָשָׂה וְהֶחֱזִיק־בָּהּ הָאִישׁ וְשָׁכַב עִמָּהּ וּמֵת
הָאִישׁ אֲשֶׁר־שָׁכַב עִמָּהּ לְבַדּוֹ׃ כו וְלַנַּעֲרָ לֹא־תַעֲשֶׂה דָבָר
אֵין לַנַּעֲרָ חֵטְא מָוֶת כִּי כַּאֲשֶׁר יָקוּם אִישׁ עַל־רֵעֵהוּ
וּרְצָחוֹ נֶפֶשׁ כֵּן הַדָּבָר הַזֶּה׃ כז כִּי בַשָּׂדֶה מְצָאָהּ צָעֲקָה
הַנַּעֲרָ הַמְאֹרָשָׂה וְאֵין מוֹשִׁיעַ לָהּ׃ כח כִּי־
יִמְצָא אִישׁ נַעֲרָ בְתוּלָה אֲשֶׁר לֹא־אֹרָשָׂה וּתְפָשָׂהּ וְשָׁכַב
עִמָּהּ וְנִמְצָאוּ׃ כט וְנָתַן הָאִישׁ הַשֹּׁכֵב עִמָּהּ לַאֲבִי הַנַּעֲרָ
חֲמִשִּׁים כָּסֶף וְלוֹ־תִהְיֶה לְאִשָּׁה תַּחַת אֲשֶׁר עִנָּהּ לֹא־יוּכַל
כג שַׁלְּחָהּ כָּל־יָמָיו׃ א לֹא־יִקַּח אִישׁ אֶת־
א־ג אֵשֶׁת אָבִיו וְלֹא יְגַלֶּה כְּנַף אָבִיו׃ ב לֹא־יָבֹא
פְצוּעַ־דַּכָּה וּכְרוּת שָׁפְכָה בִּקְהַל יהוה׃ ג לֹא־
יָבֹא מַמְזֵר בִּקְהַל יהוה גַּם דּוֹר עֲשִׂירִי לֹא־יָבֹא לוֹ בִּקְהַל

---

that both the man and woman are stoned at the city gate. Why is this so? (This question is found in the *Minchas Chinuch*.) Logic would dictate that the adulterer is also stoned, but at the city gate and not at the door of the girl's father's home. The reason for this is that the girl is stoned there to shame her father for not having supervised her properly. But it is preferable to stone the adulterer at the city gate, so as to publicize the harsh death of an adulterer.

23.

2. לֹא־יָבֹא פְּצוּעַ־דַּכָּה וּכְרוּת שָׁפְכָה בִּקְהַל ה׳ — *A man with crushed testicles or a severed organ shall not enter the congregation of Hashem*. The damage referred to here was inflicted by human hands, and is so severe that the victim can no longer father children (*Sefer Hachinuch*, Commandment 559). There are two reasons for this prohibition: First, because, owing to his condition, such a person's wife may be unfaithful to him, and bring *mamzeirim* into the world. Second, because the Jewish people are commanded to increase the number of servants of God on earth ("The Jewish nation was dispersed in exile only so that they would be joined by righteous converts" [*Pesachim* 67b]).

The *Maharsha* (*Beitzah* 5, and see *Karnei Re'em*) adds that immediately after the Giving of the Torah the people were told, "return to your tents." In addition to the commandment of "be fruitful and multiply," in this way they were taught the special commandment of *onah*, the minimal times for marital relations. The point was to make the people aware that in their capacity as a holy nation and a kingdom of priests, they are to enhance God's glory on earth by giving birth

22 *with stones and they shall die: the girl because of the fact*
25-29 *that she did not cry out in the city, and the man because of*
the fact that he afflicted the wife of his fellow; and you shall
remove the evil from your midst.
25 *But if it is in the field that the man will find the betrothed*
girl, and the man will seize her and lie with her, only the man
who lies with her shall die. 26 *But you shall do nothing to the*
girl, for the girl has committed no capital sin, for like a man
who rises up against his fellow and murders him, so is this
thing; 27 *for he found her in the field, the betrothed girl cried*
out, but she had no savior.
28 *If a man will find a virgin maiden who was not*
betrothed, and takes hold of her and lies with her, and they
are discovered, 29 *then the man who lay with her shall give*
the father of the girl fifty silver [shekels], and she shall
become his wife, because he had afflicted her; he cannot
divorce her all his life.
23 1 *A man shall not marry the wife of his father; and he shall*
1-3 *not uncover the robe of his father.* 2 *A man with crushed*
testicles or a severed organ shall not enter the congregation of
HASHEM.
3 *A mamzer shall not enter the congregation of HASHEM,*
even his tenth generation shall not enter the congregation of

---

to many more Jewish servants of God. This is why someone suffering from either of these impairments, who cannot reproduce, may not marry a Jewish woman who could otherwise bear children.

3. **לֹא־יָבֹא מַמְזֵר בִּקְהַל ה׳** — *A mamzer shall not enter the congregation of Hashem*. A man and woman who engage in forbidden relations suffer *kares:* they are excised from the source of life. (A *mamzer* is a child born only of a forbidden union punishable by *kares*, excision.) And when does this happen but at the moment of conception, so crucial to their unborn child.

Such parents are incapable of transmitting anything from the wellspring of Israel, the source of eternal life, to their child. Therefore such children will usually be brazen and impudent, and most will inherit their father's slyness, using it to sin and then cover their tracks (*Yerushalmi Kiddushin* 40b; see *Korban Haeidah* and *P'nei Moshe*). The Torah has placed them and their descendants permanently outside the Jewish nation, unlike a righteous convert from among the gentiles. They are most like the seven nations who originally inhabited the Land of Canaan, of whom the Torah said, "do not intermarry with them." (I found in the *Yalkut Reuveni*, quoting from *Midrash Rabbah Parashas Nasso*, that מַמְזֵר is מוּם זָר, "the blemish of something foreign to the Torah" — much the same as the reason for not marrying into the Canaanite nations.)

כג יְהוָה׃ ד לֹא־יָבֹא עַמּוֹנִי וּמוֹאָבִי בִּקְהַל יְהוָה
ד־ח גַּם דּוֹר עֲשִׂירִי לֹא־יָבֹא לָהֶם בִּקְהַל יְהוָה עַד־עוֹלָם׃
ה עַל־דְּבַר אֲשֶׁר לֹא־קִדְּמוּ אֶתְכֶם בַּלֶּחֶם וּבַמַּיִם בַּדֶּרֶךְ
בְּצֵאתְכֶם מִמִּצְרָיִם וַאֲשֶׁר שָׂכַר עָלֶיךָ אֶת־בִּלְעָם בֶּן־
בְּעוֹר מִפְּתוֹר אֲרַם נַהֲרַיִם לְקַלְלֶךָּ׃ ו וְלֹא־אָבָה יְהוָה
אֱלֹהֶיךָ לִשְׁמֹעַ אֶל־בִּלְעָם וַיַּהֲפֹךְ יְהוָה אֱלֹהֶיךָ לְּךָ אֶת־
הַקְּלָלָה לִבְרָכָה כִּי אֲהֵבְךָ יְהוָה אֱלֹהֶיךָ׃ ז לֹא־תִדְרֹשׁ
שְׁלֹמָם וְטֹבָתָם כָּל־יָמֶיךָ לְעוֹלָם׃ רביעי ח לֹא־

But aside from his marital status, a *mamzer* is obligated to keep the Torah like any other Jew, and if he learns Torah, "a learned *mamzer* takes precedence over an ignorant High Priest" (*Horayos* 13). What is more, in the World to Come *mamzerim* will be permitted to marry (*Yerushalmi Kiddushin* 41b). It is also possible for a *mamzer* to free his children from their forbidden status so that they will be able to marry Jews. This is done by buying a maidservant and having children with her. The children will have the *halachic* status of slaves, so that if he frees them, they are permitted to marry into the Jewish nation (*Yevamos* 78a).

גַּם דּוֹר עֲשִׂירִי לֹא־יָבֹא לוֹ בִּקְהַל ה׳ — *Even his tenth generation shall not enter the congregation of Hashem*. "Merciful" people ask a simpleton's question: True, the *mamzer*'s parents brought him into the world in a despicable and hateful fashion, but why should the innocent child be penalized? Why must he and all his future descendants remain outside the Jewish community through no fault of their own? In answer, consider the following parallel:

Those who suffer from certain types of hereditary diseases — tuberculosis, leprosy, and the like — are cautioned by their physicians not to marry, especially not to a partner who shares the same illness. Not only would it be detrimental to their own delicate health, but their offspring stand to inherit the disease. If, despite the doctor's warnings, the patients do marry and have children, or if healthy parents behave in a manner which the Torah cautions can result in damage to the fetus (see *Kesubos* 77b) — does anyone ask why the innocent child must suffer because his parents conceived him in defiance of medical advice? And if this is true of physical ills, it is even more true of spiritual ills, against which we were warned.

The Torah warned us against forbidden relationships and informed us that not only the sinners themselves will be cut off from the Jewish nation, but children born of their union will be *mamzeirim* for all future generations. It is the parents who have cut their children's souls off from the World to Come and separated them from the Jewish people.

4. לֹא־יָבֹא עַמּוֹנִי . . . עַד־עוֹלָם — *An Ammonite . . . shall not enter. . . to eternity*. This is also true of a *mamzer*, whose forbidden status endures "to eternity."

HASHEM.
4 *An Ammonite or Moabite shall not enter the congregation*
of HASHEM, even their tenth generation shall not enter the
congregation of HASHEM, to eternity, 5 *because of the fact that*
they did not greet you with bread and water on the road
when you were leaving Egypt, and because he hired against
you Balaam son of Beor, of Pethor, Aram Naharaim, to curse
you. 6 *But HASHEM, your God, refused to listen to Balaam, and*
HASHEM, your God, reversed the curse to a blessing for you,
because HASHEM, your God, loved you. 7 *You shall not seek*
their peace or welfare, all your days, forever.

However, these words are not explicitly used in his case, because in the World to Come the *mamzeirim* will become permitted to marry.

5. וַאֲשֶׁר שָׂכַר — *Because he hired*. The singular ("he hired") is used, because it refers only to Moab. "Because . . . *they* did not greet you" is in the plural, as it refers to both Ammon and Moab.

6. וַיַּהֲפֹךְ ה׳ אֱלֹהֶיךָ לְּךָ אֶת־הַקְּלָלָה לִבְרָכָה כִּי אֲהֵבְךָ ה׳ אֱלֹהֶיךָ — *Hashem, your God, reversed the curse to a blessing for you, because Hashem, your God, loved you*. Nowhere else do we find such a reason offered for God's having been kind towards us. How are we to understand this statement?

It could be suggested that an explanation is being hinted at here, as to why God did not save the Jewish people from the plague which killed twenty-four thousand of them in the wake of Balaam's scheme to entice the Jews into immoral behavior. After all, if God turned Balaam's curse into a blessing, why were they not saved at a later date from the plague brought about through his intrigues?

The answer lies in the fact that "Hashem your God loved you" as long as the Jews in Shittim did not lapse into immoral behavior, which God despises. In this verse כִּי means "when" — God turned curses into blessings *when He loved you* (see *Bereishis* 6:2 for a similar usage of כִּי).

When Balaam came to curse the Jews, he found that the doors of their homes did not face each other, so that no one would look at his neighbor's wife ("How goodly are your tents, O Jacob.") On that occasion curse became blessing. But at Shittim, Balaam's schemes succeeded, because "the God of this people hates immorality."

7. לֹא־תִדְרֹשׁ שְׁלֹמָם . . . לְעוֹלָם — *You shall not seek their peace . . . forever*. The *Sifre* uses the double phrasing לְעוֹלְמֵי עוֹלָמִים, "forever and ever." Why the emphasis?

Abraham risked his life to do battle with four kings in order to save his nephew Lot. Lot also owned sheep, cattle and tents, thanks to his association with Abraham (*Bereishis* 13 and *Bereishis Rabbah* §41). If Lot's descendants repaid Abraham's kindness with evil to his descendants, they can well be described as "one who repays good with evil," and in that case "bad will not

כג תְתַעֵב אֲדֹמִי כִּי אָחִיךָ הוּא לֹא־תְתַעֵב מִצְרִי כִּי־גֵר הָיִיתָ
ח־יג בְאַרְצוֹ: ט בָּנִים אֲשֶׁר־יִוָּלְדוּ לָהֶם דּוֹר שְׁלִישִׁי יָבֹא לָהֶם
בִּקְהַל יהוה: י כִּי־תֵצֵא מַחֲנֶה עַל־אֹיְבֶיךָ
וְנִשְׁמַרְתָּ מִכֹּל דָּבָר רָע: יא כִּי־יִהְיֶה בְךָ אִישׁ אֲשֶׁר
לֹא־יִהְיֶה טָהוֹר מִקְּרֵה־לָיְלָה וְיָצָא אֶל־מִחוּץ לַמַּחֲנֶה לֹא
יָבֹא אֶל־תּוֹךְ הַמַּחֲנֶה: יב וְהָיָה לִפְנוֹת־עֶרֶב יִרְחַץ בַּמָּיִם
וּכְבֹא הַשֶּׁמֶשׁ יָבֹא אֶל־תּוֹךְ הַמַּחֲנֶה: יג וְיָד תִּהְיֶה לְךָ מִחוּץ

---

depart from his home" (*Mishlei* 17:13). That is why the *Sifre* uses double phraseology for emphasis. This is intended to show us that the Torah means "forever" literally, and not only (as לְעוֹלָם sometimes means) until the next Jubilee year.

8. לֹא־תְתַעֵב אֲדֹמִי . . . לֹא־תְתַעֵב מִצְרִי — *You shall not reject an Edomite. . . you shall not reject an Egyptian*. Edomites and Egyptians share the same *halachic* status. At this point we had already been strangers in Egypt, and God was fully aware that we would be strangers in the lands of Edom in the future. Therefore it is forbidden to abominate either of these two nations, and after three generations converts from both Egypt and Edom may marry into the Jewish community.

☙ לֹא־תְתַעֵב מִצְרִי כִּי־גֵר הָיִיתָ בְאַרְצוֹ — *You shall not reject an Egyptian, for you were a sojourner in his land*. This refers to the welcome offered to Jacob and his family on their arrival in Egypt, including the grant of choice territory in which to settle. But this state of affairs lasted only for one generation. After the last of Jacob's children passed away, the Egyptians enslaved the Jews for three generations, as God had told Abraham at the Covenant Between the Parts: "the fourth generation will return here." In keeping with this, the Torah decreed that "children who are born to them in the third generation may enter the congregation of Hashem", just as the third generation of Jews to be enslaved was the one which left Egypt.

The Egyptians and the Edomites share the same status because while they both enslaved the Jews, this was only bodily servitude. But the descendants of Lot caused the Jews to sin, and one who causes another to sin is worse even than one who kills him (see *Rashi*).

10. כִּי־תֵצֵא מַחֲנֶה עַל־אֹיְבֶיךָ — *When a camp goes out against your enemies*. "You must only go out against your enemies" (*Sifre*). This verse comes to exclude civil war from Divine auspices (such as the one between the kingdoms of Judah and Israel — see *Rashi* on *Sifre* 20:3). In such a case, even if you "guard against anything evil" God will not "walk in the midst of your camp to rescue you." A war between Jews is inherently evil in God's eyes, and one cannot "guard against anything evil" in a situation which is intrinsically evil.

☙ מִכֹּל דָּבָר רָע — *Anything evil*. "It is known to be the custom in military camps to eat all abominations, to steal and rob, and to commit adultery and

23
8-13

8 *You shall not reject an Edomite, for he is your brother;*
you shall not reject an Egyptian, for you were a sojourner in
his land. 9 *Children who are born to them in the third*
generation may enter the congregation of HASHEM.
10 *When a camp goes out against your enemies, you shall*
guard against anything evil. 11 *If there will be among you a*
man who will not be clean because of a nocturnal occurrence,
he shall go outside the camp; he shall not enter the midst
of the camp. 12 *When it will be toward evening, he shall im-*
merse himself in the water, and when the sun sets, he may
enter the midst of the camp. 13 *You shall have a place outside*

---

any other outrages without shame. Even one who is honest by nature will become cruel and wrathful when the camp goes out against an enemy. Therefore the Torah warns him, 'you shall guard against anything evil' " (*Ramban*).

Even though Jews who go to war must be entirely free of sin — those who are afraid because of their sins must return home from the battlefield — the Torah found it necessary to issue a warning to keep away from "anything evil." Why?

Because during the course of the battle soldiers are sometimes left with nothing to eat. In such a case the Torah permits them to eat foods which are otherwise forbidden to Jews. But this will engender in them bad qualities, and they are then liable to commit any sin (see *Oznayim LaTorah, Vayikra* 11:43). Therefore the Torah must warn even a camp of righteous Jews to keep away from such foods.

11. אֲשֶׁר לֹא־יִהְיֶה טָהוֹר — *Who will not be clean.* In our commentary on *Bereishis* 7:8 we explained that before the giving of the Torah, when there were no special laws concerning impure animals, the Torah used the longer phrase "animals which are not pure", to avoid the repugnant word טָמֵא. But once the Torah was given, anything which it defined as impure is openly called just that. Why, then, does this verse use the lengthier phrase "who will not be clean"?

There are two possible answers. The first is that the Torah has already warned that in the camp of Israel, where God's presence dwells, "you shall guard against anything evil" — even unbecoming speech or thought. To illustrate this the Torah avoided using the offensive word טָמֵא in this verse.

A second reason is that when speaking of righteous people, like these men who are free of all sin and are now risking their lives to defend the Jewish people, the Torah did not want to use the word טָמֵא. The circumlocution "who will not be clean" indicates that the impurity mentioned here does not cling to this man, and all he needs is immersion in a *mikveh*.

12. וּכְבֹא הַשֶּׁמֶשׁ יָבֹא אֶל־תּוֹךְ הַמַּחֲנֶה — *And when the sun sets, he may enter the midst of the camp*. It is a marvelous thing that every Jewish soldier who goes out with the camp must be cleansed of any impurity whose source is in his own body, even though he was in any case impure through contact with dead bodies. Until he immersed himself he may not enter the camp to fight God's battles.

כג לַמַּחֲנֶה וְיָצָאתָ שָׁמָּה חוּץ: יד וְיָתֵד תִּהְיֶה לְךָ עַל־אֲזֵנֶךָ
יד־טז וְהָיָה בְּשִׁבְתְּךָ חוּץ וְחָפַרְתָּה בָהּ וְשַׁבְתָּ וְכִסִּיתָ אֶת־צֵאָתֶךָ:
טו כִּי יהוה אֱלֹהֶיךָ מִתְהַלֵּךְ ׀ בְּקֶרֶב מַחֲנֶךָ לְהַצִּילְךָ וְלָתֵת
אֹיְבֶיךָ לְפָנֶיךָ וְהָיָה מַחֲנֶיךָ קָדוֹשׁ וְלֹא־יִרְאֶה בְךָ עֶרְוַת דָּבָר
וְשָׁב מֵאַחֲרֶיךָ: טז לֹא־תַסְגִּיר עֶבֶד אֶל־אֲדֹנָיו

This might not be so surprising, since the Holy Ark was present in the army camp, granting it the same *halachic* status as the Levites' encampment in the desert. But even in the Levite encampment, a person who had immersed himself that same day, and would only be completely purified at sunset, was permitted to enter; and here the Torah says that only "when the sun sets he may enter the midst of the camp"!

Possibly this is because it is better for one who has left the camp to re-enter it "when the sun sets", so that no one will realize that he had a "nocturnal occurrence" and it will not be talked about. For the Torah warns the men of the camp, "you shall guard against *anything* [דָּבָר] evil" — any evil דִּבּוּר, *speech.*

14. וְיָתֵד תִּהְיֶה לְךָ עַל־אֲזֵנֶךָ — *You shall have a shovel in addition to your weapons.* The *Gemara* in *Kesubos* learns from this verse that one's fingers are shaped like a peg, so that it will be easy to plug up his ears when one is in danger of hearing unseemly speech. This veiled reference follows the Torah's instructions to "guard against anything [דָּבָר] evil" — not to talk any evil talk [דִּבּוּר], and as a further warning to listeners to block their ears against hearing such talk.

וְכִסִּיתָ אֶת־צֵאָתֶךָ — *And cover your excrement.* This would be understandable if the rules given here applied to a regular army camp. But according to those commentators who explain that these verses refer to the camp of the Jews in the desert, there seems to be a difficulty. For in the desert the Jews ate manna which was entirely absorbed in their bodies, so that there were no body wastes.

It could be said that this commandment refers to wastes derived from ordinary food which the Jews in the desert purchased from gentile peddlars. *Chazal* tell us (*Eruvin* 55) that in the desert the Jews did not relieve themselves in front of the camp or to the side of it, only behind it, which indicates that they did relieve themselves in the desert.

But if this commandment was in force in the desert, how can it be that Moses only informed the Jews of it before his death? We may answer that they began to purchase food from gentile peddlars only when they neared settled lands — which occurred towards the end of Moses' life — and that is when he taught them this commandment.

15. וְהָיָה מַחֲנֶיךָ קָדוֹשׁ וְלֹא־יִרְאֶה בְךָ עֶרְוַת דָּבָר — *So your camp shall be holy, so that He will not see a shameful thing among you.* This verse first talks about the entire "camp," and then concludes by talking about "you." The lesson hinted at is that if every individual Jew strives to be free of "shameful things", then our entire camp will be holy.

the camp, and to it you shall go out. 14 *You shall have a shovel*
in addition to your weapons, and it will be that when you sit
outside, you shall dig with it; you shall go back and cover
your excrement. 15 *For* HASHEM, *your God, walks in the midst*
of your camp to rescue you and to deliver your enemies
before you; so your camp shall be holy, so that He will not see
a shameful thing among you and turn away from behind you.
16 *You shall not turn over to his master a slave who is*

וְלֹא־יִרְאֶה בְךָ עֶרְוַת דָּבָר — *So that He will not see a shameful thing among you*. This verse immediately follows "and it will be that when you sit outside", as an indication of *Chazal's* teaching that one should also be modest in the lavatory, keeping oneself covered there as well.

וְלֹא־יִרְאֶה בְךָ עֶרְוַת דָּבָר — *So that he will not see a shameful thing among you. Chazal* learn from this verse that one may not recite the *Shema* in front of parts of the body that are normally covered. This does not mean only in front of another person's exposed body, which naturally tends to arouse desire. No; the Torah says, "He will not see a shameful thing among *you*": one may not say *Shema* even if he himself is not properly covered. And so *Chazal* teach: "a man cannot separate *challah* while he is undressed" (*Challah* 2:3).

16. לֹא־תַסְגִּיר עֶבֶד אֶל־אֲדֹנָיו — *You shall not turn over to his master a slave. Onkelos* understands this as referring to "a slave who belongs to a gentile." But (according to this opinion) if he belongs to a Jew one is obligated to return him just like any other "lost object" — just as one must return a lost ox or donkey, for he is the master's property. Even though we do not in any case return lost articles to gentiles, the Torah here adds a specific prohibition against returning a lost slave.

But in the *Gemara* (*Gittin* 45a), *Chazal* state that even a Canaanite slave belonging to a Jew may not be returned to his master if this Jew is living outside the Holy Land and his slave has fled to the Holy Land. This is because the obligation to settle the Land applies even to a Canaanite slave who has been circumcised and immersed himself with the intent of becoming a Jew's slave (*Gittin*, ibid.). This *halachah* is in keeping with *Chazal's* statement that even a Canaanite maidservant who lives in the Holy Land is assured of entering the World to Come.

עֶבֶד אֶל־אֲדֹנָיו — *To his master a slave.* As we said above, according to *Chazal* (*Gittin* 45a) the slave referred to is a Canaanite and the master is Jewish. According to the *Rambam* (*Hilchos Avadim* 8:10), not only do we not return him to slavery, we should attempt to persuade his master to accept a promissory note until the slave obtains enough funds to redeem himself. If the master does not wish to accept even this arrangement, the court annuls his claim to the slave, who now goes free.

Apparently the *Rambam* learns from the words "who is rescued from his master to you," that the servant's intentions in running off were pure: he wanted

כג אֲשֶׁר־יִנָּצֵל אֵלֶיךָ מֵעִם אֲדֹנָיו: יז עִמְּךָ יֵשֵׁב בְּקִרְבְּךָ
יז־יט בַּמָּקוֹם אֲשֶׁר־יִבְחַר בְּאַחַד שְׁעָרֶיךָ בַּטּוֹב לוֹ לֹא
תּוֹנֶנּוּ: יח לֹא־תִהְיֶה קְדֵשָׁה מִבְּנוֹת יִשְׂרָאֵל
וְלֹא־יִהְיֶה קָדֵשׁ מִבְּנֵי יִשְׂרָאֵל: יט לֹא־תָבִיא אֶתְנַן זוֹנָה

---

to fulfill the commandments which are applicable only in the Holy Land. This is why he left his master, who lives in the Diaspora — he fled "to you." If his intention was merely to rid himself of a harsh master, he would have gone to some other country, escaping both from his master and his obligation to keep the Torah at the same time. If he chose Zion to run to, he has also chosen the One Who dwells in Zion, His people, and His Torah. The *Rambam* writes (ibid., *halachah* 11) that "this convert who escaped to the Holy Land is a righteous convert." And since one who wishes for purity is aided by Heaven (*Shabbos* 104a), we too must help him obtain his liberty, so that he will become fully obligated in all the commandments, instead of his limited obligations as a slave. He began by taking on the commandments fulfilled only in the Holy Land, but one who achieves a little purity on his own will be purified greatly (see *Yoma* 39a).

17. עִמְּךָ יֵשֵׁב בְּקִרְבְּךָ בַּמָּקוֹם אֲשֶׁר־יִבְחַר בְּאַחַד שְׁעָרֶיךָ — *He shall dwell with you in your midst, in whatever place he will choose in one of your cities*. This commandment serves to indict the gentile nations. Even a runaway Canaanite slave who escapes to the Holy Land may live anywhere in the land he chooses, "in one of your cities which is beneficial to him." There are no limitations or objections to his settling wherever he pleases. Yet when the Jews "escaped to [the gentile nations]" from harsh masters, the gentiles confined them to ghettos and the Pale of Settlement. If a Canaanite slave who ran away from his lawful master is granted such freedom, how much more should free Jews, the princely sons of Abraham, Isaac and Jacob, be granted! As the prophet Jeremiah (2:) cried, "Is Israel a slave?"

⊱ לֹא תּוֹנֶנּוּ — *You shall not taunt him*. According to the *Sifre*, this means verbal taunts. The Torah forbids us all to abuse each other verbally (*Vayikra* 25:17), but it doubles the prohibition in the case of a convert (*Vayikra* 19:33). For besides the kind of abuse that can be hurled against anyone, a convert is open to additional insults, such as, "Remember what you used to do? Remember how you worshiped idols and ate pork?" This necessitates an additional warning against talking in such a way.

Now, a slave who escaped from his master to the Holy Land is open to the type of remark Naval made to David's servants (*I Shmuel* 25:10): "There are many servants these days who rebel each against his master." Comments such as this cast doubt on the sincerity of the former slave's motives, and call for yet a third warning in this verse: "You shall not taunt him." Thus the *Rambam* states definitively that one who taunts a former slave who has converted actually transgresses three separate prohibitions: "Do not taunt each other; Do not taunt a convert; And you shall not taunt him."

23
17-19

rescued from his master to you. 17 *He shall dwell with you in*
your midst, in whatever place he will choose in one of your
cities, which is beneficial to him; you shall not taunt him.
18 *There shall not be a promiscuous woman among the*
daughters of Israel, and there shall not be a promiscuous man
among the sons of Israel. 19 *You shall not bring a harlot's hire*

ஃ In our times, when there are no Canaanite slaves, it is difficult to transgress this prohibition, which applies to such a slave who has fled from his master. However, the Adversary has found a way to offer his "customers" the opportunity to transgress this commandment, even during our own "era of freedom and liberty."

The Jewish people in our times have not yet been privileged to receive the Holy Land in its entirety, nor to enter it freely, led by our Messiah. Instead, a trickle of immigrants sneaked their way in at first, followed by the waves of immigration known as the "*aliyot*" to the western part of the Land. With time, the members of the various "*aliyot*" began to provoke each other. The *aliyah* of the *Chalutzim* boasted that they were the first to revive the desolate land. They worked it with their sweat, and it was for this noble cause that they had come to the Holy Land. They looked down on other "*aliyot*," who, they maintained, had come not out of love of the land but to escape persecution in their former homes. They mockingly called the Jews who came from pre-war Poland "Gravsky's *aliyah*," after the anti-Semitic Polish finance minister who made the lives of Polish Jews a misery with oppressive taxes. Refugees from Germany, and later from all of Europe, were looked down upon as "Hitler's *aliyah*."

Dear brothers, let us not fight among ourselves! The Torah tells us not to cause pain to a Canaanite slave, even just with words (hard as it may be to believe that his motivation for escape was strictly love of the Holy Land and the Torah). If he has come to live in the Holy Land, we may not suspect him of simply wishing to rid himself of a harsh master; we are to judge him favorably. In fact, we can first examine the motivation of our own ancestors, who left Egypt to escape Pharaoh's enslavement, and who at times protested to Moses, "what have you done to us, that you took us out of Egypt!" Some sincere soul-searching on the part of the *Chalutzim* would uncover the facts, if they were not too embarrassed to admit them: it was actually anti-Semitism which gave birth to the ideal of "returning home" to the Holy Land. It was their good fortune to leave Europe before the volcano erupted.

Yet it was God Who planted the idea in their minds to leave in time. For at times קוֹל ה׳ בֶּהָדָר, God's voice is heard "in glory"; at other times קוֹל ה׳ בַּכֹּח, His voice is heard "in strength." Finally, there are those for whom God's voice is only heard when קוֹל ה׳ שׁוֹבֵר אֲרָזִים "it breaks cedars"(*Tehillim* 29).

19. אֶתְנַן זוֹנָה — *A harlot's hire*. A harlot profanes sanctity: "If the daughter of a Kohen desecrates herself through adultery, she desecrates her father" (*Vayikra* 21:9). On the other hand, *Chazal* tell us that refraining from immorality

כג וּמְחִיר כֶּלֶב בֵּית יהוָה אֱלֹהֶיךָ לְכָל־נֶדֶר כִּי תוֹעֲבַת יהוָה
כ אֱלֹהֶיךָ גַּם־שְׁנֵיהֶם׃ כ לֹא־תַשִּׁיךְ לְאָחִיךָ

leads one to sanctity. Obviously, then, one may not bring a harlot's hire to the Holy Temple.

וּמְחִיר כֶּלֶב . . . כִּי תוֹעֲבַת ה' אֱלֹהֶיךָ — *Or the exchange for a dog... are an abomination of Hashem, your God*. We can understand why "a harlot's hire" is unacceptable, as God despises immorality, but what harm has an innocent dog done which would make even the barter exchanged for him forbidden for use in the Holy Temple?

A possible answer is that the Torah wants to show us how loathsome treachery and spying are in God's eyes. For dogs are the greatest informers of all against other animals, their own 'comrades.' To explain: God gave Adam "rule over the fish of the sea and the birds in the sky," and told Noah that "all that creeps... will be for food for you." In *Tehillim* (8:7-8) we learn that "everything You placed under man's feet, sheep and cattle." But at the same time, God gave all living creatures the will and the strength to flee from man and save themselves from his nets and traps.

Some animals choose willingly to become domesticated and serve man. He provides for all their needs — food and dwelling — but in return works them, and slaughters them for food. Other animals prefer to be free, and keep clear of human beings. They provide for themselves entirely, and in doing so face great difficulties (especially in winter); but they are free. No one works them, no one slaughters them.

If man wants these animals, he must hunt them from afar, while they, aware of the imminent danger, can and do run and hide from his arrows. But the dog, the beast who made friends with man, accompanies its master on the hunt, and uses its highly developed sense of smell to sniff out hidden animals, whom it proudly delivers to death. The dog "involves himself in a fight not his own" (*Mishlei* 26:17) and betrays its fellow beast, who had longed for a life of liberty. Then, spy that he is, the dog receives a hunk of meat from his master as a reward.

God despises such a 'profession,' for indeed He allowed man to eat meat, but He also allowed the animals to protect themselves. Therefore the dog, no less than the harlot, is "an abomination of God."

This is why our verse is juxtaposed to the two preceding ones: the "harlot's hire" is related to "there shall not be a promiscuous woman," and "the exchange for a dog" to "you shall not turn over to his master a slave." True, the master is right, and the slave is his property, but who told you to get involved in such a business, like a dog who constantly hands over its fellow beasts to the hunters?

וּמְחִיר כֶּלֶב — *The exchange for a dog*. There is an additional reason for this prohibition. We find that of all the animals and beasts on earth, man "made friends" with the "most brazen of all beasts" (*Beitzah* 25b) — the dog. He

23
20 *or the exchange for a dog to the House of HASHEM, your*
God, for any vow, for both of them are an abomination
of HASHEM, your God.
20 *You shall not cause your brother to take interest,*

---

fondles him, gives him the finest food and drink, talks to him, finds him pleasurable, and spends his leisure time with him. He treats him like a pampered child.

If a dog's master were to use the money he spends on his pet to help support orphans or homeless vagabonds, there would be much fewer hungry, abandoned people in this world. Such people, then, can be described as "those who slaughter man and kiss calves" (*Hoshea* 13). In Jewish ethics, one is described as "slaughtering man" if he sees a hungry person but does not share his food with him (the elders' declaration of innocence, "our hands did not spill this blood nor did our eyes see" [*Devarim* 21:7] is explained by *Rashi* as meaning "we did not see him and let him go without food"). Yet these same people "kiss calves" — they kiss, and still more, feed the animal they have chosen as their companion.

If one really wants the affection of an animal, why not befriend a pure animal which harms no one, as the prophet Nathan described in his rebuke to King David? The prophet told of a poor man and his lone lamb: "It ate of his bread and drank from his cup and lay in his bosom, and was like a daughter to him" (*II Shmuel*,12:3)." Why, then, do people choose the company of impudent dogs? For the very reason that they *are* impudent and wicked, and guard their masters against thieves and murderers.

However, given free rein, a dog does not limit itself to attacking dangerous intruders. It barks at, pounces on and bites anyone who nears its master's home, even attacking passersby in the street. The government is forced to impose restrictions, insisting that dogs who are dangerous be muzzled when on the streets, and led by their masters on a leash; otherwise there are serious penalties.

Chazal went further, and, basing themselves on the verse "So that you will not place blood in your house" (22:8), forbade raising a vicious dog in one's home even if it is chained, "because it bites and barks and causes women to miscarry from fright" (*Bava Kamma* 79b and *Rashi*). (An ordinary dog may be kept if it is chained.) Rabbi Eliezer the Great says that one who raises dogs is like one who raises pigs, which has the practical ramification that he comes under the same curse as one who raises pigs (*Bava Kamma* 82b).

It is only permissible to raise a dog if one lives near the border, because it functions as a "weapon" against enemies, and even then it must be tied by day and released only at night. A dog, then, according to the Torah is a destructive force, like a sword or iron, and even worse than them, for a dog is a living creature capable of movement.

The Torah cautions us: "You passed your sword over it (the altar) and defiled it" (*Shemos* 20:25). *Rashi* explains that the altar is meant to lengthen man's life, whereas iron, of which weapons are made, cuts it short. The altar brings peace among men, and iron does just the opposite. It is for this very reason that it is

נֶ֫שֶׁךְ כֶּ֫סֶף נֶ֫שֶׁךְ אֹ֫כֶל נֶ֫שֶׁךְ כָּל־דָּבָ֖ר אֲשֶׁ֥ר יִשָּֽׁךְ: כא לַנָּכְרִ֣י

תַשִּׁ֔יךְ וּלְאָחִ֖יךָ לֹ֣א תַשִּׁ֑יךְ לְמַ֙עַן֙ יְבָרֶכְךָ֜ יהוה אֱלֹהֶ֗יךָ

בְּכֹל֙ מִשְׁלַ֣ח יָדֶ֔ךָ עַל־הָאָ֕רֶץ אֲשֶׁר־אַתָּ֥ה בָא־שָׁ֖מָּה

לְרִשְׁתָּֽהּ: כב כִּֽי־תִדֹּ֥ר נֶ֙דֶר֙ לַֽיהוה֙ אֱלֹהֶ֔יךָ

לֹ֤א תְאַחֵר֙ לְשַׁלְּמ֔וֹ כִּֽי־דָרֹ֨שׁ יִדְרְשֶׁ֜נּוּ יהוה אֱלֹהֶ֙יךָ֙ מֵֽעִמָּ֔ךְ

וְהָיָ֥ה בְךָ֖ חֵֽטְא: כג וְכִ֥י תֶחְדַּ֖ל לִנְדֹּ֑ר לֹֽא־יִהְיֶ֥ה בְךָ֖ חֵֽטְא:

כד מוֹצָ֥א שְׂפָתֶ֖יךָ תִּשְׁמֹ֣ר וְעָשִׂ֑יתָ כַּֽאֲשֶׁ֙ר נָדַ֜רְתָּ לַֽיהוה

אֱלֹהֶ֗יךָ נְדָבָה֙ אֲשֶׁ֣ר דִּבַּ֔רְתָּ בְּפִֽיךָ: חמישי כה כִּ֤י

תָבֹא֙ בְּכֶ֣רֶם רֵעֶ֔ךָ וְאָֽכַלְתָּ֧ עֲנָבִ֛ים כְּנַפְשְׁךָ֖ שָׂבְעֶ֑ךָ וְאֶֽל־

כֶּלְיְךָ֖ לֹ֥א תִתֵּֽן: כו כִּ֤י תָבֹא֙ בְּקָמַ֣ת

רֵעֶ֔ךָ וְקָֽטַפְתָּ֥ מְלִילֹ֖ת בְּיָדֶ֑ךָ וְחֶרְמֵשׁ֙ לֹ֣א תָנִ֔יף עַ֖ל קָמַ֥ת

רֵעֶֽךָ: א כִּֽי־יִקַּ֥ח אִ֛ישׁ אִשָּׁ֖ה וּבְעָלָ֑הּ

---

forbidden "to bring the exchange for a dog to the House of Hashem." A dog
cuts short man's life and causes hatred between men, and so cannot be brought,
even indirectly, upon the altar which serves the opposite purpose. Perhaps this
is why this topic precedes that of "do not take interest from [lit., 'bite'] your
brother," as the dog has the fiercest bite of them all.

21. לְמַעַן יְבָרֶכְךָ ה׳ אֱלֹהֶיךָ בְּכֹל מִשְׁלַח יָדֶךָ עַל־הָאָרֶץ — *So that Hashem, your God,*
will bless you in your every undertaking on the Land. This blessing refers
to the two types of interest previously mentioned: both "interest of money or
interest of food." Money is usually loaned for business undertakings, while
food is usually borrowed by a farmer whose fields have suffered blight. The
Torah blesses one who does either form of kindness without asking for
recompense: God will bless you "measure for measure," both "in your every
undertaking" and "on the land."

◆§ אֲשֶׁר־אַתָּה בָא־שָׁמָּה לְרִשְׁתָּהּ — *To which you are coming to possess it.* "As a
reward for your coming there, you will inherit it" (*Sifre*). But why is this
promise mentioned here?

A wealthy person may well decide that he is better off living outside the
Holy Land. There he can lend out his money to gentiles at interest, while in
the Holy Land he would have nothing to do with his money, as it is forbidden to lend money at interest to fellow Jews. And if this person has no
means of support, he will spend all his money and ultimately return to the
Diaspora with empty hands. This is why the Torah promises people who think
this way that "you are coming to possess it," even without making loans at
interest.

22. וְהָיָה בְךָ חֵטְא — *There will be a sin in you.* The word חֵטְא here signifies 'lack,
loss': this man's punishment will be through lack and loss that will be
suffered by his wife and children. And so we find in the case of Jacob: when he

23
21-26 *interest of money or interest of food, interest of anything*
that he may take as interest. 21 *You may cause a gentile to*
take interest, but you may not cause your brother to take
interest, so that HASHEM, *your God, will bless you in your*
every undertaking on the Land to which you are coming, to
possess it.
22 *When you make a vow to* HASHEM, *your God, you shall*
not be late in paying it, for HASHEM, *your God, will demand it*
of you, and there will be a sin in you. 23 *If you refrain from*
vowing, there will be no sin in you. 24 *You shall observe and*
carry out what emerges from your lips, just as you vowed a
voluntary gift to HASHEM, *your God, whatever you spoke*
with your mouth.
25 *When you come into the vineyard of your fellow, you*
may eat grapes as is your desire, to your fill, but you may not
put into your vessel.
26 *When you come into the standing grain of your fellow,*
you may pluck from the ears with your hand, but you may
24 *not lift a sickle against the standing grain of your fellow.*
1 1 *If a man marries a woman and lives with her, and*

---

delayed in paying a vow, he was punished with the incident of Dinah and with the death of Rachel (see *Bereishis* 31:13 and *Rashi*).

24. מוֹצָא שְׂפָתֶיךָ תִּשְׁמֹר וְעָשִׂיתָ כַּאֲשֶׁר נָדַרְתָּ לַה' אֱלֹהֶיךָ נְדָבָה *You shall observe and carry out what emerges from your lips, just as you vowed a voluntary gift to Hashem, Your God.* One who vows runs the risk of transgressing "you shall not be late in paying it." If so, then, we might wonder how it is possible to vow to become a Nazirite or to dedicate a sacrifice.

The answer is that in this verse כַּאֲשֶׁר means "[like] at the time" (See *Shemos* 17:11 for a similar usage of the word): at the time when you make your vow to God, fulfill it right away. Do as Hillel the Elder did: He would bring an unsanctified animal to the Temple courtyard, sanctify it right there, and slaughter it immediately (*Nedarim* 9). This leaves no room for problems of delaying payment of the vow.

25. כְּנַפְשְׁךָ שָׂבְעֶךָ — *As is your desire, to your fill*. This verse refers to a laborer (*Rashi*, based on *Bava Metzia* 87b). Even if he comes to work satisfied, but would still like to eat grapes, he may — as *Chazal* say, "There is always room for sweets" (*Eruvin* 82b). If he arrives on the job full, he may eat "as he wishes." If he arrives hungry, he may eat his fill, but not to excess.

26. וְחֶרְמֵשׁ לֹא תָנִיף עַל קָמַת רֵעֶךָ — *You may not lift a sickle against the standing grain of your fellow*. It is self-evident that a laborer may eat grain in the field, just as he would be permitted to eat grapes had he been working in a vineyard. Here the Torah means to forbid him to "*lift a sickle* against the

כד וְהָיָה אִם־לֹא תִמְצָא־חֵן בְּעֵינָיו כִּי־מָצָא בָהּ עֶרְוַת דָּבָר
ב־ה וְכָתַב לָהּ סֵפֶר כְּרִיתֻת וְנָתַן בְּיָדָהּ וְשִׁלְּחָהּ מִבֵּיתוֹ: ב וְיָצְאָה
מִבֵּיתוֹ וְהָלְכָה וְהָיְתָה לְאִישׁ־אַחֵר: ג וּשְׂנֵאָהּ הָאִישׁ
הָאַחֲרוֹן וְכָתַב לָהּ סֵפֶר כְּרִיתֻת וְנָתַן בְּיָדָהּ וְשִׁלְּחָהּ מִבֵּיתוֹ
אוֹ כִי יָמוּת הָאִישׁ הָאַחֲרוֹן אֲשֶׁר־לְקָחָהּ לוֹ לְאִשָּׁה: ד לֹא־
יוּכַל בַּעְלָהּ הָרִאשׁוֹן אֲשֶׁר־שִׁלְּחָהּ לָשׁוּב לְקַחְתָּהּ לִהְיוֹת
לוֹ לְאִשָּׁה אַחֲרֵי אֲשֶׁר הֻטַּמָּאָה כִּי־תוֹעֵבָה הִוא לִפְנֵי
יְהוָה וְלֹא תַחֲטִיא אֶת־הָאָרֶץ אֲשֶׁר יְהוָה אֱלֹהֶיךָ נֹתֵן לְךָ
נַחֲלָה: ששי ה כִּי־יִקַּח אִישׁ אִשָּׁה חֲדָשָׁה לֹא יֵצֵא

---

standing grain of his fellow" in order to eat it. A number of reasons have been offered for this.

The *Rambam* writes that doing so would involve the laborer wasting time that should be spent on his work.

According to the *Ha'amek Davar*, a sickle cuts a large quantity of grain, and some might be left over. If this is the reason, though, it is no problem at all: the field's owner is in any case harvesting the grain now. Cannot the laborer simply add his leftover grain to all the rest?

It would seem to me that there are two reasons for this prohibition. The first is to prevent the field's owner from becoming annoyed with his worker. The owner, who is usually present during the harvesting, would be angry if he saw the laborer cutting large amounts of grain for his own use — and possibly even to take home, illegitimately.

Then again, a laborer should not get into the habit of "lifting his sickle against his fellow's grain." To prevent this, he must cut grain for his own use differently than he would normally: he may pluck the grain by hand where the Torah allows him to. He should also be careful not to pick grain to eat when he is not working in that particular field, or when he is working with another type of crop: "When he works with grapes, he should not eat figs" (*Sifre*).

24.

1. וְהָיָה — *And it will be*. "The word וְהָיָה expresses joy" (*Bereishis Rabbah* 42:3); for it is good news if, when a man finds that his wife has behaved immorally, he is displeased. It is preferable for him to divorce such a woman, rather than reconcile himself to wrongdoing.

This verse does not refer to the type of actions for which the Torah obligates a husband to divorce his wife, but to 'ugly' behavior, such as leaving her hair uncovered, weaving in the marketplace in a way which exposes her arms, wearing slit sleeves, and bathing in the same place that men bathe. Such behavior does not obligate him to divorce her, but it is a *mitzvah* for him to do so (*Gittin* 90a-b).

24
2-5

it will be that she will not find favor in his eyes, for he found in her a matter of immorality, and he wrote her a bill of divorce and presented it into her hand, and sent her from his house,
[2] *and she left his house and went and married another man,*
[3] *and the latter man hated her and wrote her a bill of divorce and presented it into her hand and sent her from his house, or the latter man who married her to himself will die —*
[4] *her first husband who divorced her shall not again take her to become his wife, after she had been defiled, for it is an abomination before HASHEM. You shall not bring sin upon the Land that HASHEM, your God, gives you as an inheritance.*
[5] *When a man marries a new wife, he shall not go out*

---

2. **וְיָצְאָה מִבֵּיתוֹ** — *And she left his house*. As *Chazal* tell us, "A man who divorces his wife should not continue to live in the same courtyard with her, lest they come to immoral behavior." The wife is the one who must move, for it is more difficult for the man to move than for the woman (*Kesubos* 27b-28a, following the *Rambam*'s text in כ"ז הל' איסורי ביאה פכ"א הל'; see also the commentary of the *Maggid Mishnah*).

וְהָלְכָה — *And (she) went*. To a place where no one knows her. After her first husband divorced her because of her ugly behavior, she remarried. The second husband should have inquired into the reasons for her previous divorce. Since he was not concerned about it, the Torah calls him "*another* man" — not like the first husband.

3. **וּשְׂנֵאָהּ הָאִישׁ הָאַחֲרוֹן** — *And the latter man hated her*. After he got to know her behavior.

וְשִׁלְּחָהּ מִבֵּיתוֹ — *And sent her from his house*. In this verse the Torah does not say "and she left," since this time she did not go to a place where no one knows her. Instead, she set her sights on someone who already knew her: her first husband, who now 'regrets' having "expelled wickedness from his home." and would marry her again if he could.

4. **אַחֲרֵי אֲשֶׁר הֻטַּמָּאָה כִּי־תוֹעֵבָה הִוא לִפְנֵי ה'** — *After she had been defiled, for it is an abomination before Hashem*. The *Sefer Hachinuch* (Commandment 580) writes: "It is akin to adultery for a woman to leave one husband and go to another, and then return to the first one." The *Sforno* (similarly to the *Ramban*) further explains: "This is an opening to adultery. A man will divorce his wife at the adulterer's request so that he can live with her for a time, and then her first husband will remarry her." Had the Torah permitted a man to remarry his wife after she had married another and then been divorced, adulterers would swap wives by means of *halachic* marriages and divorces: degenerates within the letter of the law.

Chazal explain "after she had been defiled" as referring to a married woman who has committed adultery, and is now forbidden to her husband.

בַּצָּבָא וְלֹא־יַעֲבֹר עָלָיו לְכָל־דָּבָר נָקִי יִהְיֶה לְבֵיתוֹ שָׁנָה כד
אֶחָת וְשִׂמַּח אֶת־אִשְׁתּוֹ אֲשֶׁר־לָקָח: ו לֹא־יַחֲבֹל רֵחַיִם ו־ח
וָרָכֶב כִּי־נֶפֶשׁ הוּא חֹבֵל: ז כִּי־יִמָּצֵא אִישׁ
גֹּנֵב נֶפֶשׁ מֵאֶחָיו מִבְּנֵי יִשְׂרָאֵל וְהִתְעַמֶּר־בּוֹ וּמְכָרוֹ וּמֵת
הַגַּנָּב הַהוּא וּבִעַרְתָּ הָרָע מִקִּרְבֶּךָ: ח הִשָּׁמֶר
בְּנֶגַע־הַצָּרַעַת לִשְׁמֹר מְאֹד וְלַעֲשׂוֹת כְּכֹל אֲשֶׁר־
יוֹרוּ אֶתְכֶם הַכֹּהֲנִים הַלְוִיִּם כַּאֲשֶׁר צִוִּיתִם תִּשְׁמְרוּ

---

6. לֹא־יַחֲבֹל רֵחַיִם וָרָכֶב — *One shall not take* [or, *give*] *an upper or lower millstone as a pledge*. Why does this verse follow "he shall be free for his home for one year, and he shall gladden his wife whom he has married"? To teach us that there must be a limit to the bridegroom's joy. He is freed from military service, and is exempt from all communal duties, but he certainly must not pledge away the tools of his trade to finance the celebration! "He shall not give his upper and lower millstones as a pledge" to gladden his new wife. If he does, he will end up a pauper when the lender comes to claim the pledge — a heavy price to pay for overdoing the festivities.

Mention should be made here of an unfortunate custom which has grown up in recent years. People of moderate means, and even truly poor people, pledge all they own to borrow money and make lavish affairs for hundreds of guests in expensive halls for any sort of occasion in the family, especially for a bar mitzvah, wedding or engagement. An apartment and furniture, clothing and jewelry are all purchased with no thought given to expense. Not only do these people exhaust their own modest means, they must go around asking donations for *"hachnassas kallah,"* or even *"hachnassas chassan."* Yet this too is not enough to provide for all the luxuries, until the celebrants go bankrupt and leave unpaid all the debts incurred for all those "necessities."

7. וּמֵת הַגַּנָּב הַהוּא — *That kidnaper shall die*. Why does the Torah say *"that* kidnaper"? Initially, the gentile nations had no interest in accepting the Torah because of the prohibitions against murder, adultery, and robbery. When these same nations became cultured and civilized, they began to "steal" a few of the rational commandments, and grudgingly conceded the latter half of the Ten Commandments. However, when these enlightened gentiles wanted to brutally murder Jews and seize their possessions, they invented clever ways to "steal" from the Torah and falsify its commandments to suit their own purposes and justify the killing.

It is well known that the worst oppressors have always been those who had learned some Torah and found in it excuses to justify the horrors they committed against our people. The arch-murderer Nevuzaradan of Babylon killed 94,000 Jews on one stone, claiming that he was avenging the death of the prophet Zechariah.

24
6-8
to the army, nor shall it obligate him for any matter; he shall
be free for his home for one year, and he shall gladden his wife
whom he has married.
6 *One shall not take an upper or lower millstone as a pledge,*
for he would be taking a life as a pledge.
7 *If a man is found kidnaping a person of his brethren among*
the Children of Israel, and he enslaves him and sells him, that
kidnaper shall die, and you shall remove the evil from your
midst.
8 *Beware of a tzaraas affliction, to be very careful and to act;*
according to everything that the Kohanim, the Levites, shall
teach you — as I have commanded them — you shall be careful

Another horrible example of this perversion is the Roman governor who lived at the time of the Destruction of the Second Temple. Thirsty for the blood of the great men of the time, he convened the Ten Martyrs' as judges to judge the ten Tribes of Israel for selling Joseph. The general was certain that they would judge truthfully. He did not inform them that they personally were to be the defendants.

They were to judge the case not according to Roman law, but by the holy Torah law, given straight from Heaven! How do we punish one who kidnaps a person, one of his brothers among the Children of Israel, and he enslaves him and sells him? The supposed kidnapers — Jacob's sons — were no longer alive; said the general, "were they alive, I would judge them before you. Instead you will bear the sin of your fathers." The judges would replace the absent defendants! And they had given the Torah's verdict truly: "That kidnaper shall die." This was enough for the Roman butcher to brutally murder his entire "panel of judges" (from the *selichos* in the *Yom Kippur Mussaf*).

But these martyrs found a hint to the monster's end in the words of the Torah itself: "*That* kidnaper" — who stole words of the Torah and abused them — "shall die!" Not only will he die a temporary, bodily death, but an eternal one, and his end will be "among the corpses of those who sinned against Me, for their worms will not die and their fire will not go out, and they will be an eternal disgrace for all flesh."

8. **הִשָּׁמֶר בְּנֶגַע־הַצָּרַעַת** — *Beware of a tzaraas affliction.* The three separate warnings regarding *tzaraas* ("Beware of a *tzaraas* affliction"; "Be very careful"; and "You shall be careful to perform") correspond to the three things that become defiled with *tzaraas* in order: one's skin, his clothing, and his house.

The *Rambam* seems to reverse the order given in the Torah (*Tum'as Tzaraas*, 16:10; see *Vayikra* 14:34 for the reason). He writes that the walls of a slanderer's home will become leprous. If he mends his ways, the house will be restored to normal. If he continues to sin until the house has to be destroyed, the clothing he wears will become leprous. If he still does not repent after his clothing has been burnt, his own skin will be affected.

כד לַעֲשֽׂוֹת׃ ט זָכ֕וֹר אֵ֧ת אֲשֶׁר־עָשָׂ֛ה יהוה אֱלֹהֶ֖יךָ לְמִרְיָ֑ם
ט־טו בַּדֶּ֖רֶךְ בְּצֵאתְכֶ֥ם מִמִּצְרָֽיִם׃ י כִּֽי־תַשֶּׁ֥ה
בְרֵֽעֲךָ֖ מַשַּׁ֣את מְא֑וּמָה לֹֽא־תָבֹ֥א אֶל־בֵּית֖וֹ לַעֲבֹ֥ט עֲבֹטֽוֹ׃
יא בַּח֖וּץ תַּעֲמֹ֑ד וְהָאִ֗ישׁ אֲשֶׁ֤ר אַתָּה֙ נֹשֶׁ֣ה ב֔וֹ יוֹצִ֥יא אֵלֶ֛יךָ
אֶת־הָעֲב֖וֹט הַחֽוּצָה׃ יב וְאִם־אִ֥ישׁ עָנִ֖י ה֑וּא לֹ֥א תִשְׁכַּ֖ב
בַּעֲבֹטֽוֹ׃ יג הָשֵׁב֩ תָּשִׁ֨יב ל֤וֹ אֶֽת־הָעֲבוֹט֙ כְּב֣וֹא הַשֶּׁ֔מֶשׁ
וְשָׁכַ֥ב בְּשַׂלְמָת֖וֹ וּבֵֽרְכֶ֑ךָּ וּלְךָ֙ תִּהְיֶ֣ה צְדָקָ֔ה לִפְנֵ֖י יהוה
אֱלֹהֶֽיךָ׃ שביעי יד לֹא־תַעֲשֹׁ֥ק שָׂכִ֖יר עָנִ֣י
וְאֶבְי֑וֹן מֵֽאַחֶ֕יךָ א֧וֹ מִגֵּרְךָ֛ אֲשֶׁ֥ר בְּאַרְצְךָ֖ בִּשְׁעָרֶֽיךָ׃
טו בְּיוֹמוֹ֩ תִתֵּ֨ן שְׂכָר֜וֹ וְלֹא־תָב֧וֹא עָלָ֣יו הַשֶּׁ֗מֶשׁ כִּ֤י עָנִי֙ ה֔וּא

We find, then, that according to both views, leprosy in clothing (which is mentioned in the Torah after leprosy of the skin) comes after one has spoken slander once and, instead of repenting, goes ahead and speaks more. This is why such a person is told by the Torah to "be very careful": if one has become accustomed to sinning, he no longer sees anything wrong with his actions, making it difficult to repent. (See also the *Sifre*, which explains this verse as referring to leprosy in people, clothing, and houses.)

9. זָכוֹר אֵת אֲשֶׁר־עָשָׂה ה׳ אֱלֹהֶיךָ לְמִרְיָם בַּדֶּרֶךְ — *Remember what Hashem, your God did to Miriam on the way*. Consider what happened to the prophetess Miriam, who spoke against her brother. She was older than he and raised him on her knees. She had risked her life to save his. She did not say anything bad about him; she merely made a mistake in equating him to the other prophets. He personally did not mind at all, as 'the man Moses was very humble', yet all the same she was immediately punished with *tzaraas*. How much more so, then, will the wicked, foolish people who speak abundant, exaggerated tales be punished! (*Rambam, Tum'as Tzaraas*, chapter 16).

בַּדֶּרֶךְ בְּצֵאתְכֶם מִמִּצְרָיִם — *On the way, when you were leaving Egypt*. Even though the Jews were on their way out of Egypt, "Miriam was quarantined outside the camp for seven days, and the people did not journey until Miriam was brought in" (*Bamidbar* 12:15). From here we learn to "be very careful to perform" all the laws concerning *tzaraas*, whether to quarantine a person or to declare him impure, even if it involves great financial loss.

11. וְהָאִישׁ — *And the man*. *Chazal* explain that this refers both to the previous words and the following words. In its context with the preceding words it means, "You shall stand outside with *the man*," that is, the court bailiff, who also is not permitted to come into the borrower's home to claim the pledge. In its context with the following words it means, "And the man to whom you lend shall bring the security to you outside."

24 *to perform.* 9 *Remember what* HASHEM, *your God, did to*
9-15 *Miriam on the way, when you were leaving Egypt.*
10 *When you make your fellow a loan of any amount,*
you shall not enter his home to take security for it. 11 *You*
shall stand outside; and the man to whom you lend shall
bring the security to you outside. 12 *If that man is poor,*
you shall not sleep with his security. 13 *You shall return the*
security to him when the sun sets, and he will sleep in his
garment and bless you, and for you it will be an act of
righteousness before HASHEM, *your God.*
14 *You shall not cheat a poor or destitute hired person*
among your brethren, or a proselyte who is in your Land,
or one who is in your cities. 15 *On that day shall you pay*
his hire; the sun shall not set upon him, for he is poor,

In a lighter vein, we can consider that אִישׁ means a man of worth and respect (as in the usage "אִישׁי כֹּהֵן גָּדוֹל," or David's statement to Abner "you are an אִישׁ" [*I Shmuel*, 26:15]). The Torah, then, could be hinting to us not to be too sure that a borrower will bring his pledge out of his own volition. If he is an אִישׁ, he will remember your kindness in helping him out when he was in trouble, and will bring out the pledge. However, it is also possible that he will conveniently forget all about it, and take advantage of his privileged position as an important person whose home cannot be entered to claim the pledge; he may leave you waiting outside endlessly. In such a case *Rabbeinu Bachya* says that the court forces the borrower to fulfill the positive commandment of repaying a loan, and sells his land to pay off the lender.

12. וְאִם־אִישׁ עָנִי הוּא לֹא תִשְׁכַּב בַּעֲבֹטוֹ — *If that man is poor, you shall not sleep with his security*. Why does the Torah not say simply "if he is poor"? Why is the additional word אִישׁ, 'man,' used?

The use of the word אִישׁ says something about the character of the person in question. If he is a 'man' of worth and good character, an appreciative person, he will return the pledge to the lender in the morning himself. Yet there may be those who do return the pledge the first time or two, but regret it the following day. If the Torah allows this man "to sleep in his garment" every night, he will not return it to the lender even by day. The *Minchas Chinuch* (Commandments 585 and 587) explains that if the borrower does not return the security to the lender, the lender may take possession of it forcibly. This is what is meant by "if he is a poor אִישׁ, he may sleep in his garment."

וְאִם־אִישׁ עָנִי הוּא — *If that man is poor*. The word אִישׁ also implies a man of means. In our case, the borrower may own a considerable amount of land, but the pillow which the lender took as security is his only one. If he is poor in regard to the particular item which he gave as security on a loan, the lender

כד וְאֵלָיו הוּא נֹשֵׂא אֶת־נַפְשׁוֹ וְלֹא־יִקְרָא עָלֶיךָ אֶל־יהוה וְהָיָה
טז־יט בְךָ חֵטְא׃ טז לֹא־יוּמְתוּ אָבוֹת עַל־בָּנִים וּבָנִים
לֹא־יוּמְתוּ עַל־אָבוֹת אִישׁ בְּחֶטְאוֹ יוּמָתוּ׃ יז לֹא
תַטֶּה מִשְׁפַּט גֵּר יָתוֹם וְלֹא תַחֲבֹל בֶּגֶד אַלְמָנָה׃ יח וְזָכַרְתָּ כִּי
עֶבֶד הָיִיתָ בְּמִצְרַיִם וַיִּפְדְּךָ יהוה אֱלֹהֶיךָ מִשָּׁם עַל־כֵּן אָנֹכִי
מְצַוְּךָ לַעֲשׂוֹת אֶת־הַדָּבָר הַזֶּה׃ יט כִּי תִקְצֹר
קְצִירְךָ בְשָׂדֶךָ וְשָׁכַחְתָּ עֹמֶר בַּשָּׂדֶה לֹא תָשׁוּב לְקַחְתּוֹ

---

must return "his nightclothes to him for use at night, and his daytime apparel for use during the day" (*Sifre* and *Ramban*).

15. וְאֵלָיו הוּא נֹשֵׂא אֶת־נַפְשׁוֹ — *And his life depends on it*. "Why did this man climb up a ramp, suspend himself from a tree, and put his life on the line, if not for his wages?" (*Bava Metzia* 112a).

This verse is speaking about a night laborer (who must be paid before the end of the following day), which would usually mean a night watchman, who may be in danger from potential intruders. Nevertheless, *Chazal* emphasize that even daytime work can be dangerous, for example to climb a ramp or hang from a tree. But the employer still transgresses the prohibition of withholding pay when there is no danger at all involved in the work; for *Chazal* interpret "his נֶפֶשׁ, his soul depends on it" as "something for which he gives his soul." *Rashi* explains that this means anything to which the worker obligates himself, even if the job is not especially difficult or dangerous. For a person's soul is his free will, and if he gives that up and obligates himself to others, we say that "his soul depends on it."

⁂ וְלֹא־יִקְרָא עָלֶיךָ אֶל־ה׳ וְהָיָה בְךָ חֵטְא — *Let him not call out against you to Hashem, for it shall be a sin in you*. If a person asks the Heavenly Court to judge his case, he himself will receive punishment first for his own sins; but that is provided he had legal recourse in the earthly Court. The case of a hungry worker who asks his employer for payment, when the employer has the money but withholds it, cannot be judged by an earthly *Beis Din*. The reason for this is that by the time the worker submits his case and the employer is summoned to the court, the twelve hours allowed by the Torah for payment will have passed. Therefore it is permissible (although according to the *Sifre* it is not a positive commandment) for the worker to ask for judgment from the Heavenly Court. If he does so, he has not committed a sin; it is the employer who withheld his pay who has sinned.

17. וְלֹא תַחֲבֹל בֶּגֶד אַלְמָנָה — *You shall not take the garment of a widow as a pledge*. Had this *halachah* immediately followed that of returning a poor person's pledge, we would agree with the opinion of Rabbi Shimon bar Yochai, who says that the Torah is speaking here only about a poor widow, while it would be permissible to take a pledge from a wealthy widow. However, the

24
16-19

and his life depends on it; let him not call out against you to HASHEM, for it shall be a sin in you.

[16] *Fathers shall not be put to death because of sons, and sons shall not be put to death because of fathers; a man should be put to death for his own sin.*

[17] *You shall not pervert the judgment of a proselyte or orphan, and you shall not take the garment of a widow as a pledge.* [18] *You shall remember that you were a slave in Egypt, and HASHEM, your God, redeemed you from there; therefore I command you to do this thing.*

[19] *When you reap your harvest in your field, and you forget a bundle in the field, you shall not turn back to take it;*

---

halachah follows the opinion of the Sages, who prohibit taking a pledge even from a wealthy widow; and that is why the *halachah* regarding a widow follows that of a convert and an orphan. There is a special prohibition not to "pervert their judgment" because they have no one to defend them. From here we see that one may not take a pledge even from a wealthy widow, because she does not have a husband to protect her.

18. **עֶבֶד הָיִיתָ בְּמִצְרַיִם וַיִּפְדְּךָ ה׳ אֱלֹהֶיךָ** — *You were a slave in Egypt, and Hashem, your God, redeemed you.* When the Jews were slaves in Egypt, they cried out to God and He had mercy on them (*Shemos* ch. 2). Therefore He asks that the Jews themselves have mercy on the weak and oppressed.

19. **כִּי תִקְצֹר קְצִירְךָ** — *When you reap your harvest.* The laws of the forgotten sheaf do not apply to a worker who is cutting wheat in someone else's field. He may not "forget" a sheaf. If the workers forgot some wheat, but not the owner of the field, it is not considered forgotten.

וְשָׁכַחְתָּ עֹמֶר בַּשָּׂדֶה לֹא תָשׁוּב לְקַחְתּוֹ — *And you forget a bundle in the field, you shall not turn back to take it.* When the Torah speaks about the commandment to leave behind olives and grapes, no mention is made of a blessing for doing so. Only for leaving behind a forgotten sheaf of wheat are we promised that "Hashem will bless you in all your handiwork." Why is that case different?

A bundle of wheat represents a considerable investment of hard work, much greater than what was put in to growing grapes or olives. It is hard to give away the product of so much labor. This is why the Torah promises a special blessing for doing so, since "the greater the difficulty, the greater the reward" (*Avos* 5:26) This is not the case with the gleanings of vineyard and orchard, because one has not as yet invested that much effort in the harvesting. (The effort he put into planting the trees is already in the past and forgotten.)

כד לַגֵּר לַיָּתוֹם וְלָאַלְמָנָה יִהְיֶה לְמַעַן יְבָרֶכְךָ יהוה אֱלֹהֶיךָ
כ־כב בְּכֹל מַעֲשֵׂה יָדֶיךָ: כ כִּי תַחְבֹּט זֵיתְךָ לֹא
תְפַאֵר אַחֲרֶיךָ לַגֵּר לַיָּתוֹם וְלָאַלְמָנָה יִהְיֶה: כא כִּי
תִבְצֹר כַּרְמְךָ לֹא תְעוֹלֵל אַחֲרֶיךָ לַגֵּר לַיָּתוֹם וְלָאַלְמָנָה
יִהְיֶה: כב וְזָכַרְתָּ כִּי־עֶבֶד הָיִיתָ בְּאֶרֶץ מִצְרָיִם עַל־כֵּן
כה אָנֹכִי מְצַוְּךָ לַעֲשׂוֹת אֶת־הַדָּבָר הַזֶּה: א כִּי־
א־ב יִהְיֶה רִיב בֵּין אֲנָשִׁים וְנִגְּשׁוּ אֶל־הַמִּשְׁפָּט וּשְׁפָטוּם
וְהִצְדִּיקוּ אֶת־הַצַּדִּיק וְהִרְשִׁיעוּ אֶת־הָרָשָׁע: ב וְהָיָה
אִם־בִּן הַכּוֹת הָרָשָׁע וְהִפִּילוֹ הַשֹּׁפֵט וְהִכָּהוּ לְפָנָיו

---

20. כִּי תַחְבֹּט זֵיתְךָ — *When you beat your olive tree*. Olive picking is called "beating," because the trees are beaten with sticks until the olives fall off. This is different than the procedure used in harvesting other fruits, which would be ruined by this method. Olives, which are hard, are processed by being pressed in a vat with heavy beams to soften them and release the oil. The way they are removed from the tree is part of the softening process.

אַחֲרֶיךָ — *Behind you*. It would have been enough to say "do not remove all the splendor," meaning that you must leave behind some of every tree's produce — *its splendor* — as the unreaped 'corner.' Why is the additional "behind you" necessary?

Chazal explain that it refers to שִׁכְחָה, the part of a crop which was forgotten and must be left behind for the poor (*Sifre*). Thus, when one has begun picking the olives from the bottom branches and then moves up to a new set of branches, forgetting in the process some of the olives on the bottom branches, what remains is considered שִׁכְחָה and is left for the poor. The same is true of grapes in a vineyard, where the words "behind you" are also used.

21. כִּי תִבְצֹר כַּרְמְךָ לֹא תְעוֹלֵל — *When you harvest your vineyard you shall not glean*. It would seem that the wording "do not harvest the עוֹלֵלוֹת (not fully developed grapes) of your vineyard, leave them for the poor" would have been more appropriate. But in fact, the words "do not glean" teach us that at any time other than during the harvest, the owner of the vineyard may cut branches of vines that have עוֹלֵלוֹת on them, and this is not considered stealing from the poor. Only during the harvest must the עוֹלֵלוֹת be left behind for the benefit of the poor (*Tosafos s.v.* כך מידל, *Moed Katan* 4b).

כִּי תִבְצֹר כַּרְמְךָ — *When you harvest your vineyard*. *Tosefta Pe'ah* (ch. 2) points out that the owner of a vineyard gives four gifts to the poor: fallen fruit, undeveloped clusters, forgotten clusters, and the 'corner.' Three gifts are given from wheat: gleanings, forgotten sheaves, and the 'corner.' Only two are given from a tree: forgotten branches and 'corner.' Why does the Torah require twice as much from a grapevine as from other trees?

24 *it shall be for the proselyte, the orphan, and the widow, so*
20-22 *that HASHEM, your God, will bless you in all your handiwork.*
[20] *When you beat your olive tree, do not remove all the*
splendor behind you; it shall be for the proselyte, the orphan,
and the widow. [21] *When you harvest your vineyard, you*
shall not glean behind you; it shall be for the proselyte,
the orphan, and the widow. [22] *You shall remember that*
you were a slave in the land of Egypt, therefore I com-
mand you to do this thing.
25 [1] *When there will be a grievance between people, and*
1-2 *they approach the court, and they judge them, and they*
vindicate the righteous one and find the wicked one guilty;
[2] *it will be that if the wicked one is liable to lashes, the*
judge shall cast him down and strike him, before him,

In the *Tanchuma* on Parashas *Noach* we find that when Noah set about planting a vineyard, the Adversary himself volunteered as a partner, knowing as he did that wine leads man to sin. Noah accepted the offer. He did the planting, and the Adversary brought the blood of sheep, lions, pigs, and monkeys as fertilizer (see the *Tanchuma* as to why these particular animals were chosen.) *Bereishis Rabbah* (ch. 36) concludes that the Adversary warned Noah not to "encroach upon his (the Adversary's) portion," i.e., not to drink excessively. If he did, the Adversary would injure him.

The Torah's message to vineyard owners is to give away twice as much of their produce as they would with another tree. This will minimize their wine consumption, and keep them from "encroaching on the portion of the Adversary." Also, this double gift to the poor will make the giver worthy of protection from the Adversary.

25.

2. וְהִפִּילוֹ הַשֹּׁפֵט וְהִכָּהוּ לְפָנָיו — *The judge shall cast him down and strike him, before him*. The judge orders the court's bailiff to cast the convicted man down and strike him. If the judge himself was to do the flogging, the Torah would not have said "before him."

After the bailiff casts the man down, he stretches him out on the whipping post, so that he will be bent over during the flogging, not standing or lying on the ground. For part of the flogging must be administered over his heart, which is only possible when he is bent over and stretched out on the whipping post. The judge must be present to observe every blow and see if it was properly administered, and if the recipient is physically capable of tolerating more. — The Torah does not tell the court to kill him, only to flog him; he must remain alive when it is over. Therefore, the flogging must be done in the presence of the judge, because the bailiff cannot assess the situation accurately.

כה כְּדֵ֥י רִשְׁעָת֖וֹ בְּמִסְפָּֽר׃ ג אַרְבָּעִ֥ים יַכֶּ֖נּוּ לֹ֣א יֹסִ֑יף פֶּן־יֹסִ֨יף
ג לְהַכֹּת֤וֹ עַל־אֵ֙לֶּה֙ מַכָּ֣ה רַבָּ֔ה וְנִקְלָ֥ה אָחִ֖יךָ לְעֵינֶֽיךָ׃

---

§ **כְּדֵי רִשְׁעָתוֹ** — *According to his wickedness*. This is difficult to understand, as there is no practical difference between "major" wickedness and "minor"; anyone "incurring lashes" receives thirty-nine lashes. Some, indeed, say that for a major offense the lashes are administered with the flogger's full strength, while for a minor offense the blows are light. But we do not find this differentiation mentioned in the *halachah*.

It seems to me that what is open to consideration is the state of the offender's health (this would prove that his ability to tolerate the lashes must be assessed). The main reason for flogging a sinner is to weaken his pride and physical strength, the two factors which led him to sin. A healthy person gets more than others (although no more than thirty-nine), to subdue him to future compliance with the laws of the Torah (as the judge whispers to him during the flogging). For a weak person, fewer lashes will do the job. "According to his wickedness," then, means according to his physical strength, which must be broken to keep him from further sin.

§ **כְּדֵי רִשְׁעָתוֹ בְּמִסְפָּר** — *According to his wickedness, by a count*. From this verse and the one that follows, we learn what each of the three judges is to do during the process of the punishment. The senior judge reads out the verse "If you do not obey... God will beat you exceedingly...." (This is also what is meant by "according to his wickedness"; the judge mentions his wickedness.) Meanwhile, the second judge counts the number of lashes given.

3. אַרְבָּעִים יַכֶּנּוּ — *Forty shall he strike him*. The third judge says "Hit him!"

§ Why does the specification "by a count" come before this? If the intention was literally forty, it should say "forty shall he strike him, by a count." The reverse order indicates that "by a count of forty" he should be stricken, meaning a count approaching forty. This is the tradition of *Chazal*. For it is possible to err and administer an additional lash. If this should happen and the sinner dies from it, the court's deputy would have to go into exile as an inadvertent murderer. To avoid this, the Torah tells us to give one lash less, so as not to transgress the prohibition "do not add (to the commandments)."

Another tradition of *Chazal* regarding the process of flogging is that one third of the lashes are struck on the sinner's chest ("he shall strike him before him"), and two thirds from behind, one on each shoulder. (*Chazal* base this on the words "according to his wickedness by a count." 'A count', a plural term, implies a minimum of two.) Likewise, the tradition teaches that the number of lashes given must be divisible by three. For example, if he was sentenced to twenty, he receives eighteen. *Rabbeinu Bachya* writes that the term "strike" is used three times: "and strike him before him"; "forty shall he strike him"; and "lest he strike him." "And strike him before him" means a

25
3 *according to his wickedness, by a count.* [3] *Forty shall he strike him, he shall not add; lest he strike him an additional blow beyond these, and your brother will be degraded in your eyes.*

---

third on the front part of his body, with the remaining two thirds on the back of his body.

וְנִקְלָה אָחִיךָ לְעֵינֶיךָ — *And your brother will be degraded in your eyes*. From here we learn that if the sinner loses bowel control on account of the flogging, he does not receive any further lashes (*Sifre*). "Degraded" means humiliated, and if such a thing happens to him it is a public humiliation. After this, he is once again your brother. Why is this so?

We explained previously (*s.v.* "according to his wickedness") that the purpose of the lashes is to break the sinner's pride and physical strength, which led him to sin. If the flogging has weakened him to the point that he loses control over his bodily functions, and has caused him the humiliation of such an occurrence, the degradation contributes to his repentance and atonement. *Chazal* tell us that "one who sins and is ashamed of it is forgiven for all his sins" (*Berachos* 12b). In this instance, then, after his degradation he is once again considered "your brother."

וְנִקְלָה אָחִיךָ — *And your brother will be degraded*. "Anyone who was liable to excision and was flogged by the court is thereby freed from the sentence of excision, as is written, 'and your brother will be degraded'— after he is flogged, he is as your brother" (*Makkos* 23a).

The *Meir Einei Yesharim* offers this thought in the name of R' Dovid Moshe of Tchortkov: *Chazal* decreed thirty-nine lashes instead of the forty mentioned in the Torah, so as to prevent the sinner from absolving himself entirely of his sin and thinking that he has already been punished in full by the flogging. Through the abolition of that one lash, the sinner will feel that he has not had a full atonement for his sin and must still repent.

אָחִיךָ — *Your brother*. Now that he is freed from excision, he is your brother once again (see *Megillah* 7). We can learn from this how precious suffering is, in that it spares us from the punishment of the World to Come. For God's judgment is very deep ("Your judgment is like the great depths"). What are forty lashes compared to the punishment of excision, in which one's soul is irrevocably cut off from the World to Come?

If one steals a penny in this world, amends can still be made. But in the World to Come, if the theft has still not been returned the thief is left with a serious crime on his hands.

"Rav Chisda explained the verse, 'Thank God, for He is good' thus: Thank God for collecting man's debts with His good (the good He has bestowed on him: *Rashbam*). A wealthy man pays with his ox, a poor man with his sheep, an orphan with his egg, and a widow with her hen." (*Pesachim* 118b) The financial loss atones for bodily punishment. Why? Because suffering in this

כה ד לֹא־תַחְסֹם שׁוֹר בְּדִישׁוֹ׃ ה כִּי־יֵשְׁבוּ
ד־ט אַחִים יַחְדָּו וּמֵת אַחַד מֵהֶם וּבֵן אֵין־לוֹ לֹא־תִהְיֶה
אֵשֶׁת־הַמֵּת הַחוּצָה לְאִישׁ זָר יְבָמָהּ יָבֹא עָלֶיהָ וּלְקָחָהּ לוֹ
לְאִשָּׁה וְיִבְּמָהּ׃ ו וְהָיָה הַבְּכוֹר אֲשֶׁר תֵּלֵד יָקוּם עַל־שֵׁם
אָחִיו הַמֵּת וְלֹא־יִמָּחֶה שְׁמוֹ מִיִּשְׂרָאֵל׃ ז וְאִם־לֹא יַחְפֹּץ
הָאִישׁ לָקַחַת אֶת־יְבִמְתּוֹ וְעָלְתָה יְבִמְתּוֹ הַשַּׁעְרָה אֶל־
הַזְּקֵנִים וְאָמְרָה מֵאֵן יְבָמִי לְהָקִים לְאָחִיו שֵׁם בְּיִשְׂרָאֵל
לֹא אָבָה יַבְּמִי׃ ח וְקָרְאוּ־לוֹ זִקְנֵי־עִירוֹ וְדִבְּרוּ אֵלָיו וְעָמַד
וְאָמַר לֹא חָפַצְתִּי לְקַחְתָּהּ׃ ט וְנִגְּשָׁה יְבִמְתּוֹ אֵלָיו לְעֵינֵי

---

world arouses man to repentance, and nothing stands in the way of repentance. But if one stubbornly refuses to repent even to the very end, it will be too late to change one's mind in the World to Come, where the punishment handed out will be on an infinitely greater scale.

5. **כִּי־יֵשְׁבוּ אַחִים יַחְדָּו** — *When brothers dwell together*. We can explain "together" as meaning in the same courtyard, or in the same city or country, or we can explain it as in the same world: that they were alive at the same time. The latter interpretation would exclude a brother who was born after a childless older brother's death, which *Chazal* call "a brother who was not in his [[the deceased brother's]] world." If the elder brother leaves a widow, not only does the commandment of levirate marriage not apply here to the younger brother, he is prohibited on pain of excision to marry the widow, as if the deceased brother had had children.

The most that "together" could mean would be that the brothers had lived in one courtyard; and by progression, in one city, or one country. But if this had been the Torah's intent, it would have specified the same courtyard, city or country. Since the Torah did not specify, we must take the rule that "If you grasp too much, you cannot hold it; if you grasp a little, you can hold on to it" (*Yoma* 80a). We must give "together" its minimal meaning, which is together in the same lifetime.

☙ **לֹא־תִהְיֶה אֵשֶׁת־הַמֵּת הַחוּצָה לְאִישׁ זָר** — *The wife of the deceased shall not marry outside to a strange man*. Some explain that this is mandated by compassion for the widow. It would be hard on her to leave the home in which she had lived happily with her late husband, expelled by his brothers after his death. But this explanation does not seem likely. Any widow who has no children from her husband, even if he left children from another wife (which would free the childless widow from the obligation of levirate marriage), is liable to such a fate. Also, the verse concludes by specifying "a strange man." Even if there is another man who is willing to marry her and make his home hers, she is still bound to her late husband's brother. It seems, then, that the main reason for this prohibition

25
4-9

[4] *You shall not muzzle an ox in its threshing.*

[5] *When brothers dwell together and one of them dies, and he has no child, the wife of the deceased shall not marry outside to a strange man; her brother-in-law shall come to her, and take her to himself as a wife, and perform levirate marriage.* [6] *It shall be that the firstborn — if she can bear — shall succeed to the name of his dead brother, so that his name not be blotted out from Israel.* [7] *But if the man will not wish to marry his sister-in law, then his sister-in-law shall ascend to the gate, to the elders, and she shall say, "My brother-in-law refuses to establish a name for his brother in Israel, he did not consent to perform levirate marriage with me."*

[8] *Then the elders of his city shall summon him and speak to him, and he shall stand and say, "I do not wish to marry her."*

[9] *Then his sister-in-law shall approach him before the eyes*

---

is to benefit the deceased, so that "his name shall not be blotted out from Israel."

וּלְקָחָהּ לוֹ לְאִשָּׁה — *And take her to himself as a wife*. Once he has married her, she is his wife in every way. Divorce would require a *get* and he is permitted to remarry her afterwards, for by the act of levirate marriage the prohibition of a brother's wife is eliminated (*Yevamos* 19a).

6. וְהָיָה הַבְּכוֹר — *It shall be that the firstborn*. It is a positive commandment for the firstborn (or the oldest among the brothers) to perform levirate marriage. That is why "It shall be that the firstborn" immediately follows "performs levirate marriage"; the reference is to the question of which of the brothers should marry the widow. If the firstborn does not want to, the other brothers, in descending age order, are approached.

Since the Torah says "when brothers dwell together" — meaning that they were alive at the same time — it seems logical that the brother who spent more time in this world with the deceased is better able to "establish a name for his dead brother," so that the dead brother's soul will return in the child born to him and the widow.

9. וְחָלְצָה נַעֲלוֹ מֵעַל רַגְלוֹ — *She shall remove his shoe from on his foot*. The *Rashbam* writes that this is done "in order for her to acquire his dead brother's inheritance from him." But this is not very comprehensible, for the widow does not acquire anything from her brother-in-law by the process of removing his shoe. What is more, she automatically receives the amount promised her in her marriage contract from her late husband's estate. Also, in the practice of taking possession by removing a shoe, it is the wearer of the shoe who removes it, not the other party, as we see in *Megillas Ruth*: "A man removes his shoe and gives it to his neighbor" (*Ruth* 4:7-8).

כה הַזְּקֵנִים וְחָלְצָה נַעֲלוֹ מֵעַל רַגְלוֹ וְיָרְקָה בְּפָנָיו וְעָנְתָה
י־יד וְאָמְרָה כָּכָה יֵעָשֶׂה לָאִישׁ אֲשֶׁר לֹא־יִבְנֶה אֶת־בֵּית אָחִיו׃
י וְנִקְרָא שְׁמוֹ בְּיִשְׂרָאֵל בֵּית חֲלוּץ הַנָּעַל׃ יא כִּי־
יִנָּצוּ אֲנָשִׁים יַחְדָּו אִישׁ וְאָחִיו וְקָרְבָה אֵשֶׁת הָאֶחָד לְהַצִּיל
אֶת־אִישָׁהּ מִיַּד מַכֵּהוּ וְשָׁלְחָה יָדָהּ וְהֶחֱזִיקָה בִּמְבֻשָׁיו׃
יב וְקַצֹּתָה אֶת־כַּפָּהּ לֹא תָחוֹס עֵינֶךָ׃ יג לֹא־
יִהְיֶה לְךָ בְּכִיסְךָ אֶבֶן וָאָבֶן גְּדוֹלָה וּקְטַנָּה׃ יד לֹא־יִהְיֶה לְךָ

The whole matter of levirate marriage and *chalitzah* is among the secrets of the Torah. The Kabbalistic sages tell us that the deceased's soul is spiritually refined even through removing the shoe and the spitting which accompanies it. I heard the following incident from the *gaon* R' Tzvi Rabinowitz of blessed memory, the son of R' Yitzchak Elchonon Spektor, who succeeded him in the Kovno rabbinate:

R' Tzvi was in St. Petersburg for one of the rabbinical assemblies called from time to time by the Czarist government. (The supposed purpose of these meetings was to clarify various "questions" about the Jewish religion. What usually happened was that the committee members had to defend themselves against anti-Semitic attacks on the Talmud and its alleged negative stance towards gentiles). R' Tzvi was approached by the secularist editor of a Jewish Russian-language periodical aimed at hurrying along the process of Jewish assimilation. He suggested that R' Tzvi use his position as head of the committee to annul the commandment of *chalitzah*, since — to his mind, at least — it was meaningless and made Jews look bad in gentile eyes, particularly the detail of spitting on the ground.

At that time a major conference of Russia's leading doctors was meeting in St. Petersburg. R' Tzvi told the editor that he, as chairman of the rabbinical committee, could do nothing about his suggestion, and advised him to turn to the chairman of the medical conference. The editor was taken aback; what did *chalitzah* have to do with medicine? R' Tzvi told him that rather than try to annul *chalitzah*, he would do better to influence all the doctors in Russia to annul death! Then, of course, there would be no need for *chalitzah*.

"But that's impossible!" protested the editor.

"So is your plan," replied R' Tzvi. "The Torah's laws are eternal, like the heavens and the earth. Since medical science cannot explain what death is, or where the deceased's life force, mind, and soul go to when he dies, we had better obey those laws of the Torah related to man's soul and eternal life after death."

The editor could think of nothing to say to this, and he walked away empty-handed.

⸎ With this act, it is as if she is telling him, "Do not tell yourself that your brother died when his soul left his body. If you had re-built his house and

25
10-14

of the elders; she shall remove his shoe from on his foot and spit before him; she shall speak up and say, "So is done to the man who will not build the house of his brother." 10 *Then his name shall be proclaimed in Israel, "The house of the one whose shoe was removed!"*

11 *If men fight with one another, a man and his brother, and the wife of one of them approaches to rescue her husband from the hand of the one who is striking him, and she stretches out her hand and grasps his embarrassing place,*
12 *you shall cut off her hand; your eye shall not show pity.*

13 *You shall not have in your pouch a weight and a weight — a large one and a small one.* 14 *And you shall not have*

---

given him a son, he would have been 'one who left behind a son like himself and is not called dead' (*Bava Basra* 116a). It is only today, when you refuse to rebuild your brother's house and he remains childless, that he is truly dead (see the *Maharsha*'s commentary on *Bava Basra*, loc. cit.). Therefore you must remove your shoes and mourn for him again. Even if you do not feel that this is so, I do, and I am removing your shoe, since you are the one who caused this situation."

10. **בֵּית חֲלוּץ הַנָּעַל** — *The house of the one whose shoe was removed*. All the brothers are asked in turn to perform levirate marriage. Only if they all refuse does one of them perform *chalitzah* on behalf of all the brothers. This is why their whole family is known as "the house of the one whose shoe was removed."

11. **כִּי־יִנָּצוּ אֲנָשִׁים יַחְדָּו אִישׁ וְאָחִיו** — *If men fight with one another, a man and his brother*. The first verse in this chapter discusses a fight between strangers: "When there shall be a grievance between people, they shall approach for justice." If the two people involved in the fight are unrelated, they can take their grievance to court without coming to blows. But if "a man and his brother fight with one another," it will become necessary to "rescue him"; the word **נִצִּים** used in this verse means a fight which comes to blows. (See *Shemos* 2:13 and 21:22 for similar usage of this word).

This verse hints at the phenomenon that brothers who fight injure each other even more than strangers who fight. Brothers know each other's inner depths; as a result, they know all too well how to hurt each other verbally, a situation that leads to blows. We find this concept in Abraham's words to Lot: "Let there not be a fight between us . . . for we are brothers (*Bereishis* 13)." An argument between brothers is likely to develop into a fistfight.

13. **לֹא־יִהְיֶה לְךָ בְּכִיסְךָ אֶבֶן וָאָבֶן** — *You shall not have in your pouch a weight and a weight*. In the following verse the Torah says "do not have in your *house* a measure and a measure," while for weights the Torah says "in your *pouch*." This hints at *Chazal's* teaching that merchants keep their weights in

כה בְּבֵיתְךָ אֵיפָה וְאֵיפָה גְּדוֹלָה וּקְטַנָּה: טו אֶבֶן שְׁלֵמָה וָצֶדֶק
טו־יט יִהְיֶה־לָּךְ אֵיפָה שְׁלֵמָה וָצֶדֶק יִהְיֶה־לָּךְ לְמַעַן יַאֲרִיכוּ יָמֶיךָ
עַל הָאֲדָמָה אֲשֶׁר־יְהוָה אֱלֹהֶיךָ נֹתֵן לָךְ: טז כִּי תוֹעֲבַת יְהוָה
אֱלֹהֶיךָ כָּל־עֹשֵׂה אֵלֶּה כֹּל עֹשֵׂה עָוֶל:
מפטיר יז זָכוֹר אֵת אֲשֶׁר־עָשָׂה לְךָ עֲמָלֵק בַּדֶּרֶךְ בְּצֵאתְכֶם
מִמִּצְרָיִם: יח אֲשֶׁר קָרְךָ בַּדֶּרֶךְ וַיְזַנֵּב בְּךָ כָּל־הַנֶּחֱשָׁלִים
אַחֲרֶיךָ וְאַתָּה עָיֵף וְיָגֵעַ וְלֹא יָרֵא אֱלֹהִים: יט וְהָיָה בְּהָנִיחַ
יְהוָה אֱלֹהֶיךָ ׀ לְךָ מִכָּל־אֹיְבֶיךָ מִסָּבִיב בָּאָרֶץ אֲשֶׁר
יְהוָה־אֱלֹהֶיךָ נֹתֵן לְךָ נַחֲלָה לְרִשְׁתָּהּ תִּמְחֶה אֶת־זֵכֶר
עֲמָלֵק מִתַּחַת הַשָּׁמָיִם לֹא תִּשְׁכָּח:

---

leather pouches, to prevent them from wearing down, which would decrease their weight (*Shabbos* 79a). The word כִּיס in this verse means 'pouch' rather than 'pocket', as people are not in the habit of keeping their weights in the pockets of their clothing.

18. אֲשֶׁר קָרְךָ בַּדֶּרֶךְ — *That he happened upon you on the way*. *Rashi* explains קָרְךָ as being related to the word קַר, 'cold': "Amalek cooled off the boiling [enthusiasm] of the Jews." They set out enthusiastically to receive the Torah, and Amalek cooled them off on the way.

וַיְזַנֵּב בְּךָ — *And he struck those of you who were hindmost*. "The Amalekites cut off the foreskins of the Jews and threw them up to the heavens, saying, 'This is what You chose? Take what You chose!'" (*Tanchuma, Ki Seitzei* §9).

Before the giving of the Torah, the only difference between the Jews and the non-Jews was the commandment of circumcision. Thus, on the one hand, the Amalekites were cursing the One Above, and on the other hand, intentionally made a mockery of the commandment in the Jews' eyes, and just as they were about to receive the Torah. This fits with what Akilas told Emperor Hadrian: "A person who is not circumcised can never learn Torah" *(Tanchuma, Mishpatim* §5) This is why the descendants of Esau gave up circumcision (which they had learned from Isaac): so that none of them would ever turn to Torah, which they despised. When Amalek was angry with the Jewish people for preparing to receive the Torah, they took out their anger on their circumcision, the very thing which enabled them to receive it.

in your house a measure and a measure — a large one and a
small one. 15 *A perfect and honest weight shall you have, a*
perfect and honest measure shall you have, so that your days
shall be lengthened on the Land that HASHEM, *your God,*
gives you. 16 *For an abomination of* HASHEM, *your God, are all*
who do this, all who act corruptly.
17 *Remember what Amalek did to you, on the way when*
you were leaving Egypt, 18 *that he happened upon you on the*
way, and he struck those of you who were hindmost, all the
weaklings at your rear, when you were faint and exhausted,
and he did not fear God. 19 *It shall be that when* HASHEM, *your*
God, gives you rest from all your enemies all around, in the
Land that HASHEM, *your God, gives you as an inheritance to*
possess it, you shall wipe out the memory of Amalek from
under the heaven — you shall not forget!

וְאַתָּה עָיֵף — *When you were faint.* "Faint with thirst and exhausted from travel" (*Rashi*). Amalek thought that with the Jews in such a condition, their blasphemy would fall on receptive ears. But while the Jews did fight with Moses there over the water supply, they repented and went on to Sinai to receive the Torah.

19. תִּמְחֶה אֶת־זֵכֶר עֲמָלֵק — *You shall wipe out the memory of Amalek.* Why did God give over the task of wiping out Amalek to us? At the time of the Generation of the Flood, God said "*I* will wipe out man." He did not give the job to Noah! Indeed, in *Parashas Beshalach* God does say "*I* will wipe out the memory of Amalek," but if anything this only emphasizes the question. Does He need our help? The smallest word of God is more than enough to destroy the memory of Amalek, unaided!

This verse teaches us that the war with Amalek is the eternal war of the Adversary against those who serve God, a war which has been going on since the first generation on earth and will continue on to the last, "until the dawn [of Redemption] breaks." It is for this war that God created the world: the Adversary incites man to sin; man overpowers him and is rewarded. Therefore the Jews are commanded to battle Amalek ("*you* shall wipe out the memory of Amalek"). But once we take up the struggle, God helps us ("*I* shall wipe out the memory of Amalek"). The time will come ("when the dawn breaks") that God will "wipe out the memory of Amalek from under the Heavens," so that not even a remnant of them will survive ("I will remove the concealed one [[the Evil Inclination]] from you" — *Yoel* 2:20 and *Rashi*). God will slaughter the evil inclination, which is the Angel of Death, and His name alone will be exalted on that day.

פרשת כי תבוא
Parashas Ki Savo

א וְהָיָה֙ כִּֽי־תָב֣וֹא אֶל־הָאָ֔רֶץ אֲשֶׁר֙ יהוה אֱלֹהֶ֔יךָ נֹתֵ֥ן
לְךָ֖ נַחֲלָ֑ה וִֽירִשְׁתָּ֖הּ וְיָשַׁ֥בְתָּ בָּֽהּ: ב וְלָקַחְתָּ֞ מֵרֵאשִׁ֣ית ׀
כָּל־פְּרִ֣י הָאֲדָמָ֗ה אֲשֶׁ֨ר תָּבִ֥יא מֵֽאַרְצְךָ֮ אֲשֶׁ֣ר יהוה אֱלֹהֶ֣יךָ
נֹתֵ֣ן לָךְ֒ וְשַׂמְתָּ֣ בַטֶּ֔נֶא וְהָ֣לַכְתָּ֔ אֶל־הַמָּק֔וֹם אֲשֶׁ֤ר יִבְחַר֙
יהוה אֱלֹהֶ֔יךָ לְשַׁכֵּ֥ן שְׁמ֖וֹ שָֽׁם: ג וּבָאתָ֙ אֶל־הַכֹּהֵ֔ן
אֲשֶׁ֥ר יִֽהְיֶ֖ה בַּיָּמִ֣ים הָהֵ֑ם וְאָמַרְתָּ֣ אֵלָ֗יו הִגַּ֤דְתִּי הַיּוֹם֙
לַֽיהוה אֱלֹהֶ֔יךָ כִּי־בָ֨אתִי֙ אֶל־הָאָ֔רֶץ אֲשֶׁ֨ר נִשְׁבַּ֧ע יהוה

26.

1-2. וִֽירִשְׁתָּהּ וְיָשַׁבְתָּ בָּהּ. וְלָקַחְתָּ מֵרֵאשִׁית כָּל־פְּרִי הָאֲדָמָה — *And you possess it and dwell in it, that you shall take of the first of every fruit of the ground.* We see from these verses that the primary fulfillment of settling the Holy Land is working its sacred soil. Anyone who lives there will presumably have "fruit of the ground that you bring in from your Land" from which to bring *bikkurim*, first-fruits (see commentary on verse 2).

2. פְּרִי הָאֲדָמָה אֲשֶׁר תָּבִיא מֵאַרְצֶךָ — *Fruit of the ground that you bring in from your Land.* This verse is not talking about how "you will bring" first-fruits to the Holy Temple, for that whole matter has not been mentioned yet. It refers to what "you will bring forth" with the sweat of your brow, with ploughing, planting, watering, weeding and more, "from your land." After all this hard work you ought to understand that the fruits "that you bring in from your Land" are what "Hashem, your God, gives you." ("That Hashem, your God, gives you" does not refer to the Land, for v. 1 has already mentioned "the Land that Hashem, your God, gives you." The second use of this phrase must refer to the Land's fruits.)

It is not man's strength which brings him success. It is God Who gives rain, sun and dew at the right time, causing the fruits to grow.

3. וּבָאתָ אֶל־הַכֹּהֵן — *You shall come to . . . the Kohen.* We do not go to the *Kohen* to make the first-fruit declaration to him, for the declaration is addressed to God ("then you shall call out and say before Hashem"). Instead, we ask the *Kohen* for permission to thank God and make the declaration, following the example of the angels: "They grant permission to one another to sanctify the One who formed them," and "they receive permission from one another." Prior to bringing first-fruits, we thank Hashem for bringing us to the Holy Land and for His kindness and the miracles He performed for the Jewish people. Before doing so, it is respectful behavior before God to ask permission first from the *Kohen* who serves Him. This is why a short address to the *Kohen*, asking his permission to praise God, precedes the main declaration to God.

אֲשֶׁר יִהְיֶה בַּיָּמִים הָהֵם — *To whomever will be . . . in those days.* "All you have is the Kohen who lives in your own days" (*Sifre*). During the process of

26
1-3

[1] *It will be when you enter the Land that* HASHEM, *your*
God, gives you as an inheritance, and you possess it, and
dwell in it, [2] *that you shall take of the first of every fruit of*
the ground that you bring in from your Land that HASHEM,
your God, gives you, and you shall put it in a basket and go to
the place that HASHEM, *your God, will choose, to make His*
Name rest there.
[3] *You shall come to whomever will be the Kohen in those*
days, and you shall say to him, "I declare today to HASHEM,
your God, that I have come to the Land that HASHEM *swore*

---

bringing first-fruits, a great deal of honor is lavished on the *Kohen*. The bearer of the first-fruits tells him, "I declare today to Hashem, *your God*," and asks his permission before thanking God for the Holy Land and its fruits. In light of this, one might think that this could only refer to Elazar or Pinchas, who were famous for their piety and truly deserved such an honor.

Yet this is not the case, and so the Torah added the words "whomever will be the *Kohen* in those days" and *Chazal* explain that one has only the *Kohen* who lives in his own time. If we feel that the *Kohanim* are not what they used to be, we should remember that neither we nor the rest of the nation are what previous generations were! The level of the *Kohen* suits the level of the people as a whole.

הִגַּדְתִּי הַיּוֹם — *I declare today*. Literally the words mean, "I have declared today." Why does this verse use the past tense when nothing has been said as yet, and the speaker is just beginning his declaration?

When the Jews brought first-fruits to Jerusalem, they came in large, festive groups, singing and rejoicing (this was unlike the case of the other priestly gifts, which the *Kohen* had to go and get for himself). This joyous procession was in itself a declaration. "The firmament tells of His handiwork . . . there is no speech and there are no words" (*Tehillim* 19:2,4) — deeds can speak louder than words. By the act of bringing the first-fruits with great fanfare, the bearer declares that "I have come to the Land that Hashem, your God, swore to our forefathers. He Who knows man's thoughts surely understands and appreciates my gratitude, and knows why I undertook the difficult trip to Jerusalem. But it is God's will that we thank Him aloud, publicly and openly, so that all the nations may know of the kindness God has done for His people. Therefore, honored *Kohen Gadol*, I am ready and at your service to express my thanks to God verbally."

הִגַּדְתִּי הַיּוֹם לַה' אֱלֹהֶיךָ — *I declare today to Hashem, your God*. By saying "*your* God," the bearer of the first-fruits seems to be excluding himself. When the wicked son in the *Haggadah* says "what is this service for you," *Chazal* comment, "for you, and not for him; the wicked son excludes himself from the community." Why does the bringer of first-fruits use similar language?

The wicked son is addressing his own brothers, one a simpleton and the other unable even to ask a question, and along with them various other

כו לַאֲבֹתֵ֖ינוּ לָ֥תֶת לָֽנוּ׃ ד וְלָקַ֧ח הַכֹּהֵ֛ן הַטֶּ֖נֶא מִיָּדֶ֑ךָ וְהִ֨נִּיח֔וֹ לִפְנֵ֕י
ד־ח מִזְבַּ֖ח יְהוָ֥ה אֱלֹהֶֽיךָ׃ ה וְעָנִ֨יתָ וְאָמַרְתָּ֜ לִפְנֵ֣י ׀ יְהוָ֣ה אֱלֹהֶ֗יךָ
אֲרַמִּי֙ אֹבֵ֣ד אָבִ֔י וַיֵּ֣רֶד מִצְרַ֔יְמָה וַיָּ֥גָר שָׁ֖ם בִּמְתֵ֣י מְעָ֑ט וַֽיְהִי־
שָׁ֕ם לְג֥וֹי גָּד֖וֹל עָצ֥וּם וָרָֽב׃ ו וַיָּרֵ֧עוּ אֹתָ֛נוּ הַמִּצְרִ֖ים וַיְעַנּ֑וּנוּ
וַיִּתְּנ֥וּ עָלֵ֖ינוּ עֲבֹדָ֥ה קָשָֽׁה׃ ז וַנִּצְעַ֕ק אֶל־יְהוָ֖ה אֱלֹהֵ֣י אֲבֹתֵ֑ינוּ
וַיִּשְׁמַ֤ע יְהוָה֙ אֶת־קֹלֵ֔נוּ וַיַּ֧רְא אֶת־עָנְיֵ֛נוּ וְאֶת־עֲמָלֵ֖נוּ וְאֶת־
לַחֲצֵֽנוּ׃ ח וַיּוֹצִאֵ֤נוּ יְהוָה֙ מִמִּצְרַ֔יִם בְּיָ֤ד חֲזָקָה֙ וּבִזְרֹ֣עַ נְטוּיָ֔ה

---

run-of-the-mill men and women. So when he says "for you," he could only mean "and not for me." But the farmer who comes to the Holy Temple and sees the *Kohanim* involved in God's service (according to *Yonassan Ben Uzziel* these verses refer to the High Priest himself) obviously is going to speak humbly to the *Kohen*. He tells him, "you serve God all day in His Holy Temple and are close to Him. I have come to learn from you how to serve Hashem, your God, how to thank Him and worship Him." We find that Jacob used similar language in speaking to Isaac: "For Hashem, your God, arranged it [game] for me" (*Bereishis* 27:20). Bringing a gift of first-fruits to the *Kohen*, as Jacob brought stew to Isaac, also shows respect for him as a servant of God.

4. וְלָקַח הַכֹּהֵן הַטֶּנֶא מִיָּדֶךָ — *The Kohen shall take the basket from your hand.* "To wave it. The *Kohen* puts his hand under the hand of the owner and waves [the basket]" (*Rashi*). In the blessings of Moses to the Jewish people, he mentioned the job of the *Kohanim* as being to "teach Your laws to Jacob and Your Torah to Israel." In addition, another important task is hinted at in the commandment for the *Kohen* to wave the first-fruits. If the *Kohen* sees that the people's hands have become too weighty and cumbersome to be moved about in God's service (in sacred matters and acts of charity), then the *Kohen* should "place his hand under theirs and move them about."

5. אֲרַמִּי אֹבֵד אָבִי וַיֵּרֶד מִצְרַיְמָה — *An Aramean tried to destroy my forefather, he descended to Egypt*. The only other countries affected by the Egyptian famine of Joseph's time were Phoenicia, Arabia, and Palestine (*Bereishis Rabbah* 90:6). Why, then, did Jacob not send his sons to their grandfather in Aram to obtain food? Because "An Aramean tried to destroy my forefather" and wanted "to uproot everything" (*Sifre*). Therefore Jacob was afraid to send his sons to Laban, out of fear that he would either kill them or influence them to turn away from God. The only option left was to "descend to Egypt."

וַיָּגָר שָׁם — *And sojourned there*. Jacob did not go to Egypt to savor his position as the viceroy's father. He only went to sojourn there temporarily, because of the famine in Canaan (*Yalkut Shimoni*, beg. of *Ki Savo*).

וַיְהִי־שָׁם לְגוֹי גָּדוֹל — *And there he became a great nation.* Of all the many miracles God performed for the Jews in Egypt, the greatest and most important (as discussed in the beginning of *Shemos* and *Bamidbar*) was their

26
4-8

to our forefathers to give us." [4] *The Kohen shall take the*
basket from your hand, and lay it before the Altar of
HASHEM, your God.
[5] *Then you shall call out and say before HASHEM, your God,*
"An Aramean tried to destroy my forefather. He descended
to Egypt and sojourned there, few in number, and there he
became a nation — great, strong, and numerous. [6] *The*
Egyptians mistreated us and afflicted us, and placed hard
work upon us.[7] *Then we cried out to HASHEM, the God of our*
forefathers, and HASHEM heard our voice and saw our af-
fliction, our travail, and our oppression. [8] *HASHEM took us out*
of Egypt with a strong hand and with an outstretched arm,

---

rate of reproduction. At a natural rate of birth, the seventy original members of Jacob's family could have grown into an extended family of perhaps two thousand people during their two hundred and ten years in Egypt. This would have been far too few people to merit the Divine Presence, which never rests on less than twenty-two thousand people. They could not have received the Torah nor taken possession of the Holy Land. They would have been outnumbered not only by the wild animals, but also by the Canaanite nations, who would have gotten together and destroyed them. God did a great kindness and an open miracle by enormously increasing their numbers in Egypt. From seventy people He made them into more than two million (see an amazing calculation in *Shemos* 1:7), who received the Torah and took possession of the Holy Land.

6. וַיְעַנּוּנוּ — *And afflicted us.* They "afflicted us" when they "placed hard work upon us." The Egyptians gave men's jobs to the women and women's jobs to the men (*Shemos Rabbah*, ch. 1). Their intention in doing so was not to have "hard work" done for them that they did not want to do themselves, but simply to torture their Jewish slaves.

7. וַנִּצְעַק אֶל־ה׳ אֱלֹהֵי אֲבֹתֵינוּ — *Then we cried out to Hashem, the God of our forefathers*. What possible good could be accomplished by their outcry? God had made a treaty with our forefathers that the Egyptians would enslave the Jews for four hundred years, and the time was not yet up.

The Jews counted on two new factors in their cries to God: First, that there were now many, many people enslaved ("he became a great nation there"), and second, that the enslavement was excruciatingly hard ("they afflicted us and placed hard work on us"). This explains the sequence of the last few verses.

8. בְּיָד חֲזָקָה — *With a strong hand*. "This is the plague of pestilence. 'An outstretched arm' is the sword. 'With great awesomeness' is the revelation of the Divine Presence" (Passover *Haggadah*). The revelation of the Divine Presence alone, without the preliminaries of plague and sword, would not have made the slightest impression on the Egyptians, and they would not have let the Jews leave based only on וּבְמֹרָא גָּדֹל, *with great awesomeness.*

כו וּבְמֹרָא גָּדֹל וּבְאֹתוֹת וּבְמֹפְתִים: ט וַיְבִאֵנוּ אֶל־הַמָּקוֹם
ט־יב הַזֶּה וַיִּתֶּן־לָנוּ אֶת־הָאָרֶץ הַזֹּאת אֶרֶץ זָבַת חָלָב וּדְבָשׁ:
י וְעַתָּה הִנֵּה הֵבֵאתִי אֶת־רֵאשִׁית פְּרִי הָאֲדָמָה אֲשֶׁר־
נָתַתָּה לִּי יהוה וְהִנַּחְתּוֹ לִפְנֵי יהוה אֱלֹהֶיךָ וְהִשְׁתַּחֲוִיתָ
לִפְנֵי יהוה אֱלֹהֶיךָ: יא וְשָׂמַחְתָּ בְכָל־הַטּוֹב אֲשֶׁר נָתַן־
לְךָ יהוה אֱלֹהֶיךָ וּלְבֵיתֶךָ אַתָּה וְהַלֵּוִי וְהַגֵּר אֲשֶׁר
בְּקִרְבֶּךָ: שני יב כִּי תְכַלֶּה לַעְשֵׂר אֶת־כָּל־
מַעְשַׂר תְּבוּאָתְךָ בַּשָּׁנָה הַשְּׁלִישִׁת שְׁנַת הַמַּעֲשֵׂר וְנָתַתָּה

We find a similar phenomenon with Balaam, the evil prophet: "God opened Balaam's eyes and he saw an angel of God standing in the road with his sword outstretched in his hand" (*Bamidbar* 22:31). The appearance of an angel without a drawn sword would not have made any impression on such a wicked person as Balaam. In our present case too, it was only after the preliminaries of plague and sword that the Egyptians would be impressed by the Divine Presence.

10. וְעַתָּה — *And now*. When I (the bearer of the first-fruits) consider the circumstances under which God "brought us to this place," and all the troubles which overtook us on the way, and how He saved us, despite all the times our forefathers tested Him during their forty years in the desert — I am filled with feelings of remorse and repentance for their deeds (the word וְעַתָּה is always indicative of repentance [*Bereishis Rabbah* §38). "And now, behold! I have brought the first fruit of the ground" (unlike the other priestly gifts, which the *Kohen* must go out and get himself), as a special token of thanks to Him who 'brought us to this place'.

וְהִנַּחְתּוֹ לִפְנֵי ה׳ אֱלֹהֶיךָ — *And you shall lay it before Hashem, your God*. The bearer is to "lay the first-fruits before God," and the *Kohen* then receives them as a gift from God (not from the bearer).

11. אַתָּה וְהַלֵּוִי וְהַגֵּר — *You and the Levite and the proselyte*. The Torah does not tell us here to gladden the Levite and the convert at one's own table, as the owner of the first-fruits himself gets no physical enjoyment from the fruits. He only "lays them before God." The joy here is spiritual, with songs and praise to God for the privilege of bringing the first fruits to His house. The donor's own home is still almost empty at this point, which is why no mention is made here of gladdening orphans and widows.

Instead, the Torah teaches us here that a Levite can also enjoy this elevated level of joy if he planted fruits in a Levite city. A convert who purchased land (so that it is now his, until the Jubilee year) also brings first-fruits, even if he cannot make the declaration, since it says "the Land which Hashem swore to our forefathers" (*Bikkurim* 1:4).

According to the *Rambam*, though, a convert not only brings first-fruits but also makes the declaration. How can he say "to our forefathers"? Because

26
9-12

with great awesomeness, and with signs and with wonders.
9 *He brought us to this place, and He gave us this Land, a*
Land flowing with milk and honey. 10 *And now, behold! I*
have brought the first fruit of the ground that You have given me, O HASHEM!" *And you shall lay it before* HASHEM, *your God, and you shall prostrate yourself before* HASHEM, *your God.*
11 *You shall be glad with all the goodness that* HASHEM,
your God, has given you and your household — you and the Levite and the proselyte who is in your midst.
12 *When you have finished tithing every tithe of your*
produce in the third year, the year of the tithe, you shall give

---

the land was given to Abraham, who is as much the father of converts as of born Jews.

The reason converts do not have a share in the Holy Land is because Abraham was told "I will give this land to your descendants" before he was told "I have made you the father of many nations" (meaning the father of all those who believe in God and His Torah). Thus there is no reason why converts cannot say "the God of our fathers" both in prayer and in the first-fruits declaration.

12. כִּי תְכַלֶּה לַעְשֵׂר . . . בַּשָּׁנָה הַשְּׁלִישִׁת שְׁנַת הַמַּעֲשֵׂר — *When you have finished tithing... in the third year, the year of the tithe*. The tithe for the poor is given in the third year, rather than the מַעֲשֵׂר שֵׁנִי, *Second Tithe*. The Torah has already commanded us in *Parashas Re'eh* (14:28) to give the tithe for the poor and remove all tithes from the house (בִּעוּר מַעַשְׂרוֹת) in the third year of the Sabbatical cycle. What is new here is the commandment of the Tithe Confession ("I have removed the sanctity from the house"). Why does this commandment follow that of first-fruits, rather than being included with the laws of tithing? Because the Tithe Confession, like the first-fruits declaration, must be done "before Hashem," in the Holy Temple.

כִּי תְכַלֶּה לַעְשֵׂר — *When you have finished tithing*. The first stage in giving the various agricultural gifts and tithes is the bringing of first-fruits. The conclusion is the Tithe Confession said on *Erev Pesach* in the fourth and seventh years of the Sabbatical cycle, after having "removed the holy things from the house" — having given all the various gifts as dictated by the Torah. At the very beginning, when giving first-fruits, we thank God and bow before Him. And at what point do we pray "gaze down... and bless Your people Israel, and the ground" (v. 15)? Solely when "you have finished tithing." Only when we can declare that we have done what was necessary and given what we were commanded to give, do we have sufficient merit on which to base a request for God's blessing.

בַּשָּׁנָה הַשְּׁלִישִׁת שְׁנַת הַמַּעֲשֵׂר — *In the third year, the year of the tithe*. If the Torah had only said "in the third year," we would not have known that it

כו לַלֵּוִי לַגֵּר לַיָּתוֹם וְלָאַלְמָנָה וְאָכְלוּ בִשְׁעָרֶיךָ וְשָׂבֵעוּ:
יג יג וְאָמַרְתָּ לִפְנֵי יהוה אֱלֹהֶיךָ בִּעַרְתִּי הַקֹּדֶשׁ מִן־הַבַּיִת וְגַם
נְתַתִּיו לַלֵּוִי וְלַגֵּר לַיָּתוֹם וְלָאַלְמָנָה כְּכָל־מִצְוָתְךָ אֲשֶׁר

---

is necessary to remove tithes from the house in the sixth year as well as the third year (or to be exact, on *Erev Pesach* of the following year). From the additional words "the year of the tithe" we learn that if in the third year the tithe for the poor is followed by removal of tithes, then in the sixth year, in which we give "the [same] tithe," we must do the same.

שְׁנַת הַמַּעֲשֵׂר — *The year of the tithe*. The tithe for the poor is here called "the" tithe. Why this distinction?

The owner of a field suffers no loss through the Second Tithe, as in any case he has to go to Jerusalem for the Festivals, and has to prepare food for his stay. But to give away a tenth of one's produce to the poor — that, unfortunately, is something people find very difficult. This is why the tithe for the poor is called "the" tithe in this verse. (Even giving the tithe to the Levite is less of a struggle than giving the tithe for the poor, for we can well appreciate that the portion of the Holy Land which should have gone to the Levite is in our possession, so the Levite is entitled to a share of our crop.)

The Second Tithe is given in the first, second, fourth and fifth years of the Sabbatical cycle. The tithe for the poor is given in the third and sixth years of the cycle. The purpose of the Second Tithe is explicit in the Torah: "That you will learn to fear Hashem, your God, all the days" (14:23). We are to separate one tenth of our produce four times in the Sabbatical cycle, so that we will consume that tenth before God (in Jerusalem), without any worries, and so "learn to fear God all our days." The purpose of the tithe for the poor is self-explanatory: to provide for the poor, the convert and the orphan.

The fact that the Second Tithe is separated four times in the seven-year cycle, and the tithe for the poor only twice, teaches us something. One should be more concerned with his own soul, its purity and progress, with learning to fear God through spending time in His House and learning Torah from the Sages in the *Sanhedrin* chambers — even more than with supporting the poor.

It stands to reason that one who has a pure soul and feeling heart, and who fears God, will in any case feed and clothe the poor, and not ignore them. Since the destruction of the Temple, people's understanding of others has diminished, and there is not enough concern for the support of Torah scholars. (There are certainly few enough who leave their homes and businesses to spend one tenth of the year in God's house, the Yeshivah, to "learn to fear Him".)

The generosity inherent in the Jewish heart is now entirely directed to "the convert, the orphan and the widow." In this area we outshine the gentiles. But with fear of God on the wane in society at large as well as among Jews, who knows what effect this lack of support for scholars will have on traditional Jewish goodheartedness? When there is no Second Tithe four times in a

26 *to the Levite, to the proselyte, to the orphan, and to the*
13 *widow, and they shall eat in your cities and be satisfied.*
[13] *Then you shall say before* HASHEM, *your God, "I have removed the holy things from the house, and I have also given it to the Levite, to the proselyte, to the orphan, and to the widow, according to whatever commandment You*

Sabbatical, to support the learned Levite, who can say if the tithe for the poor will survive at least twice in a Sabbatical?

13. וְאָמַרְתָּ לִפְנֵי ה' אֱלֹהֶיךָ — *Then you shall say before Hashem, your God.*

Chazal call this a confession; one "confesses" to having fulfilled all the laws of the various tithes. It would seem that a confession which is not about any type of sin is a matter of no importance. Yet on closer examination, we find just the opposite. It is easier to tell God "We have been guilty, we have done treason," than to announce to Him, "I did everything as You commanded me," especially when this is about tithes and charity.

If a person says "we have been guilty, we have done treason," and that is indeed true, then he need only confess his sins, regret them, and ask for forgiveness. If it is an exaggeration, and he has not actually done what he has confessed to, he will not be punished for his exaggeration, for there is no one so righteous that he has never sinned at all. But how careful one has to be when telling Him Who knows all man's deeds and thoughts "I did everything as You commanded me!"

בִּעַרְתִּי הַקֹּדֶשׁ מִן־הַבַּיִת ◆ — *I have removed the holy things from the house.*

Why do *Chazal* call this statement a "confession"? Ordinarily, confession means detailing one's sins before God and asking for forgiveness. Nowhere else in the Torah do we find this sort of self-congratulation for having fulfilled a commandment, nor do we ever find that it should be called 'confession.'

Moreover, I once saw how the Rizhiner Rebbe, of blessed memory, explained the words "You remember all that is forgotten" in the *Rosh Hashanah* prayers. This does not merely mean that whatever man remembers, God certainly remembers. It means that God's way is to remember the very things that man does and then forgets about. For example, if one sins and forgets his sin, God will surely remember to punish him for it. Similarly, if one does a good deed and forgets it, or minimizes its importance (thinking, "What have I done, after all? I only did my duty"), God will remember it in all its goodness. This is the meaning of "remembering all that is forgotten."

But those things that man remembers, God 'forgets,' as it were. So, if one does a good deed and remembers to praise himself for it at every opportunity, God will 'forget' that good deed. And on the other hand, if one sins and remembers it constantly, ("my sin is before me always" [*Tehillim* 51:5]), then God will "forget" that sin.

In light of this, it is difficult to understand the statement made in these verses: "I have removed the holy things from the house, and I have also given it to the

צִוִּיתָ֫נִי לֹא־עָבַ֤רְתִּי מִמִּצְוֺתֶ֙יךָ֙ וְלֹ֣א שָׁכָ֔חְתִּי: יד לֹא־אָכַ֧לְתִּי
בְאֹנִ֣י מִמֶּ֗נּוּ וְלֹא־בִעַ֤רְתִּי מִמֶּ֙נּוּ֙ בְּטָמֵ֔א וְלֹא־נָתַ֥תִּי מִמֶּ֖נּוּ
לְמֵ֑ת שָׁמַ֗עְתִּי בְּק֙וֹל֙ יהו֣ה אֱלֹהָ֔י עָשִׂ֕יתִי כְּכֹ֖ל אֲשֶׁ֥ר צִוִּיתָֽנִי:
טו הַשְׁקִ֩יפָה֩ מִמְּע֨וֹן קָדְשְׁךָ֜ מִן־הַשָּׁמַ֗יִם וּבָרֵ֤ךְ אֶֽת־עַמְּךָ֙
אֶת־יִשְׂרָאֵ֔ל וְאֵת֙ הָֽאֲדָמָ֔ה אֲשֶׁ֥ר נָתַ֖תָּה לָ֑נוּ כַּֽאֲשֶׁ֤ר נִשְׁבַּ֙עְתָּ֙
לַֽאֲבֹתֵ֔ינוּ אֶ֛רֶץ זָבַ֥ת חָלָ֖ב וּדְבָֽשׁ: שלישי טז הַיּ֣וֹם
הַזֶּ֡ה יהו֣ה אֱלֹהֶ֩יךָ֩ מְצַוְּךָ֨ לַֽעֲשׂ֜וֹת אֶת־הַֽחֻקִּ֤ים הָאֵ֙לֶּה֙ וְאֶת־
הַמִּשְׁפָּטִ֔ים וְשָֽׁמַרְתָּ֤ וְעָשִׂ֙יתָ֙ אוֹתָ֔ם בְּכָל־לְבָֽבְךָ֖ וּבְכָל־נַפְשֶֽׁךָ:

Levite, to the proselyte, to the orphan, and to the widow, according to whatever commandment You commanded me... I have acted according to everything You commanded me." Perhaps we can say that it is good to praise oneself on this occasion so that others will hear about it and do the same. Similarly, although it is forbidden to test God, regarding tithes the Torah says, "test Me in this matter" (*Malachi* 3:10). In the same vein, then, the act of charity done with tithes should be publicized, so that others will learn to give as well.

14. לֹא־אָכַלְתִּי בְאֹנִי מִמֶּנּוּ — *I have not eaten of it in my intense mourning.* The purpose of eating the Second Tithe in Jerusalem is to "learn to fear God" while in the Holy City in the company of sages and scholars, and to learn Torah with the special joy achieved through fulfilling God's commandments. A mourner is incapable of achieving either of these two things.

15. הַשְׁקִיפָה מִמְּעוֹן קָדְשְׁךָ . . . וּבָרֵךְ אֶת־עַמְּךָ אֶת־יִשְׂרָאֵל — *Gaze down from Your holy abode. . . and bless* Your *people Israel.* Rashi (on *Bereishis* 18:16) writes that every time the word הַשְׁקָפָה appears in the Torah it has a negative connotation, with the exception of this verse. The reason is the tremendous merit of the agricultural gifts to the poor, which is so great that it transforms Divine anger into mercy. This needs some explanation: if the word הַשְׁקָפָה signifies 'gazing with ill intent,' why does the Torah tell us to use it in the Tithe Confession, when asking for blessing?

We can say that from time to time God gazes (הַשְׁקָפָה) scrutinizingly on His world, or on a nation, or an individual. Since there are very few truly righteous people, and in fact most people are steeped in ignorance and sin, this scrutiny is bound to have bad results, for who can stand before God's judgment? But since the merit of gifts to the poor turns Divine anger into mercy, the Torah reveals to us the secret that the occasion of the Tithe Confession ("I have also given it to the Levite and to the proselyte and to the orphan and to the widow according to whatever commandment You commanded me") is a good time to ask God to turn His scrutiny towards us: now, at this moment of His mercy. Even if He finds that things are not entirely as they should be, the merit of charity will cause Him to be filled with mercy for us, and to "Bless His people Israel and the ground that He gave us," so that it will remain "a Land flowing with milk and honey as He swore to our forefathers."

26 14-16 *commanded me; I have not transgressed any of your com-*
mandments, and I have not forgotten. [14] *I have not eaten of it*
in my intense mourning, I did not consume it in a state of con-
tamination, and I did not give of it for the needs of the dead;
I have hearkened to the voice of HASHEM, *my God; I have*
acted according to everything You commanded me. [15] *Gaze*
down from Your holy abode, from the heavens, and bless Your
people Israel, and the ground that You gave us, as You swore
to our forefathers, a Land flowing with milk and honey."
[16] *This day,* HASHEM, *your God, commands you to perform*
these decrees and the statutes, and you shall observe and
perform them with all your heart and with all your soul.

⌘ There is a firmament in the heavens where the angels sing praise to God at night, and remain silent during the day out of respect for Israel. It is called מָעוֹן (*Chagigah* 12b). Why do we ask God to bless Israel specifically from the holy abode called מָעוֹן?

Because there, not only will no accusations be made against Israel by the angels, but the angels will actually rejoice in the blessing to be bestowed on the Jews. (See the *Maharsha's* explanation in *Chagigah*, stating that the angels are the ones who confer blessing at God's command.)

The *Sifre* explains that this blessing is that of having sons and daughters. Now, the angels cannot sing before God in the heavenly מָעוֹן until the Jews first sing to Him on earth (*Chullin* 91b). Therefore, the angels certainly want the Jews to multiply, so that there will always be people to sing on earth, enabling the angels to fulfill the purpose of their own creation by singing to God in heaven.

We similarly explained in *HaDe'ah Ve'HaDibur* (*I*:4) that the blessing שֶׁהַשִּׂמְחָה בִּמְעוֹנוֹ ("In Whose dwelling is joy") is said only at marriages because the angels in the Heavenly Dwelling rejoice when a new Jewish family is founded, insuring that there will be more Jews on earth who will first sing God's praises on earth, enabling the angels to sing praises in the מָעוֹן in heaven.

16. הַיּוֹם הַזֶּה ה׳ אֱלֹהֶיךָ מְצַוְּךָ לַעֲשׂוֹת אֶת־הַחֻקִּים הָאֵלֶּה — *This day, Hashem, your God, commands you to perform these decrees.* "They should be new in your eyes every day, as if you had just been commanded to do them today" (*Rashi*). Why did Moses choose to say these words at this particular point in time?

We can explain this in keeping with the fact that this *Chumash* of Repetition of the Torah is replete with chastisement and rebuke, mixed with the account of our people's experiences since the exodus from Egypt until the passing of Moses. Only in the *parashios* of *Re'eh*, *Shoftim*, *Ki Seitzei*, and part of *Ki Savo*, does Moses repeat some of the commandments of the Torah, or teach commandments which he heard at Mount Sinai and for various reasons had not yet taught the people. When he finished the review of the commandments and turned back to chastisement and rebuke once again, he now warned the Jewish people that the words of the Torah should always be new in their eyes.

יז אֶת־יְהוָה הֶאֱמַרְתָּ הַיּוֹם לִהְיוֹת לְךָ לֵאלֹהִים וְלָלֶכֶת **כו**
בִּדְרָכָיו וְלִשְׁמֹר חֻקָּיו וּמִצְוֹתָיו וּמִשְׁפָּטָיו וְלִשְׁמֹעַ בְּקֹלוֹ: **יז־יט**
יח וַיהוָה הֶאֱמִירְךָ הַיּוֹם לִהְיוֹת לוֹ לְעַם סְגֻלָּה כַּאֲשֶׁר
דִּבֶּר־לָךְ וְלִשְׁמֹר כָּל־מִצְוֹתָיו: יט וּלְתִתְּךָ עֶלְיוֹן עַל כָּל־
הַגּוֹיִם אֲשֶׁר עָשָׂה לִתְהִלָּה וּלְשֵׁם וּלְתִפְאָרֶת וְלִהְיֹתְךָ
עַם־קָדֹשׁ לַיהוָה אֱלֹהֶיךָ כַּאֲשֶׁר דִּבֵּר:
רביעי א וַיְצַו מֹשֶׁה וְזִקְנֵי יִשְׂרָאֵל אֶת־הָעָם לֵאמֹר שָׁמֹר **כז**
אֶת־כָּל־הַמִּצְוָה אֲשֶׁר אָנֹכִי מְצַוֶּה אֶתְכֶם הַיּוֹם: ב וְהָיָה **א־ד**
בַּיּוֹם אֲשֶׁר תַּעַבְרוּ אֶת־הַיַּרְדֵּן אֶל־הָאָרֶץ אֲשֶׁר־יְהוָה
אֱלֹהֶיךָ נֹתֵן לָךְ וַהֲקֵמֹתָ לְךָ אֲבָנִים גְּדֹלוֹת וְשַׂדְתָּ אֹתָם
בַּשִּׂיד: ג וְכָתַבְתָּ עֲלֵיהֶן אֶת־כָּל־דִּבְרֵי הַתּוֹרָה הַזֹּאת
בְּעָבְרֶךָ לְמַעַן אֲשֶׁר תָּבֹא אֶל־הָאָרֶץ אֲשֶׁר־יְהוָה אֱלֹהֶיךָ ׀
נֹתֵן לְךָ אֶרֶץ זָבַת חָלָב וּדְבַשׁ כַּאֲשֶׁר דִּבֶּר יְהוָה
אֱלֹהֵי־אֲבֹתֶיךָ לָךְ: ד וְהָיָה בְּעָבְרְכֶם אֶת־הַיַּרְדֵּן תָּקִימוּ

17-18. אֶת־ה׳ הֶאֱמַרְתָּ הַיּוֹם לִהְיוֹת לְךָ לֵאלֹהִים . . . וַה׳ הֶאֱמִירְךָ הַיּוֹם לִהְיוֹת לוֹ לְעַם סְגֻלָּה — *You have distinguished Hashem today to be a God for you . . . And Hashem has distinguished you today to be for Him a treasured people.* God always provides us first with all our needs, and then we fulfill commandments with them, as we see in *Iyov* (41:3): "Who came before Me, that I should reward him?" God gives us a house, and then we affix a *mezuzah* and build a parapet on the roof; He gives us a field and we give the gifts of its produce to the *Kohen*, the Levite and the poor; He gives us a son and we circumcise him and redeem the firstborn. But in this one instance, God demands that we first "distinguish Him to be our God," accepting His sovereignty and the yoke of His commandments, and only then will He distinguish us to be His treasured people. For everything depends on Heaven except for fear of Heaven. Only when we first make the effort to purify ourselves does God help us to keep all His commandments.

18. וַה׳ הֶאֱמִירְךָ . . . וְלִשְׁמֹר כָּל־מִצְוֹתָיו — *Hashem has distinguished you . . . and to observe all His commandments.* From this verse we deduce that one who is obligated to fulfill a commandment and does so is greater than one who is not obligated and fulfills the commandment anyway. If we have already "distinguished Hashem . . . to observe all His commandments," what purpose does it serve for God to "distinguish (*you*) us . . . to observe all His commandments," seeing as we are already observing them? It serves to make us "those who are obligated to fulfill the commandments and do so," a higher level than the one we had occupied when we voluntarily agreed to observe the commandments.

26 17 You have distinguished HASHEM today to be a God for you,
17-19 *and to walk in His ways, and to observe His decrees, His*
commandments, and His statutes, and to hearken to His
voice. 18 *And* HASHEM *has distinguished you today to be for*
Him a treasured people, as He spoke to you, and to observe all
His commandments, 19 *and to make you supreme over all the*
nations that He made, for praise, for renown, and for
splendor, and so that you will be a holy people to HASHEM,
your God, as He spoke.
27 1 *Moses and the elders of Israel commanded the people,*
1-4 *saying, "Observe the entire commandment that I command*
you this day. 2 *It shall be on the day that you cross the Jordan*
to the Land that HASHEM, *your God, gives you, you shall set*
up great stones and you shall coat them with plaster. 3 *You*
shall inscribe on them all the words of this Torah, when you
cross over, so that you may enter the Land that HASHEM,
your God, gives you, a Land flowing with milk and honey,
as HASHEM, *the God of your forefathers, spoke about you.*
4 *It shall be that when you cross the Jordan, you shall erect*

27.

1. שְׁמֹר אֶת־כָּל־הַמִּצְוָה — *Observe the entire commandment*. That is, all the commandments in the Torah.

3. וְכָתַבְתָּ עֲלֵיהֶן אֶת־כָּל־דִּבְרֵי הַתּוֹרָה הַזֹּאת — *You shall inscribe on them all the words of this Torah*. Some commentators explain that the people inscribed the Torah's commandments and prohibitions on the stones. But the *Ramban* writes that "all the words of this Torah" is meant literally: everything from "In the beginning" to "before the eyes of all Israel" was inscribed on these stones, making the feat a miracle.

The *Ralbag*, however, writes (on *Yehoshua* 8:31) that if the stone altar discussed here was the same size as the altar in the Second Temple, it would be nothing out of the ordinary for the entire Torah, written in medium-sized letters, to fit on it. But whatever the case, the entire Torah written out seventy times in seventy languages (the meaning of "well clarified") could only have fit on the stones through a miracle. And this miracle had to be, so that the nations would believe that the Torah is Divine and that every word in it, starting from the account of Creation, is completely true.

Perhaps this is why the Torah says "great stones," without any exact size or weight. And in fact, when Joshua commanded twelve people to take stones, no mention is made (in either Chapter 4 or Chapter 8 in *Yehoshua*) that the stones had to be large ones. The words "great stones," then, mean that the stones

כז אֶת־הָאֲבָנִים הָאֵלֶּה אֲשֶׁר אָנֹכִי מְצַוֶּה אֶתְכֶם הַיּוֹם בְּהַר
ה־ו עֵיבָל וְשַׂדְתָּ אוֹתָם בַּשִּׂיד: ה וּבָנִיתָ שָּׁם מִזְבֵּחַ לַיהוָה
אֱלֹהֶיךָ מִזְבַּח אֲבָנִים לֹא־תָנִיף עֲלֵיהֶם בַּרְזֶל: ו אֲבָנִים
שְׁלֵמוֹת תִּבְנֶה אֶת־מִזְבַּח יהוָה אֱלֹהֶיךָ וְהַעֲלִיתָ עָלָיו

---

demonstrate the greatness of God and His Torah, by the very fact that such ordinary stones held so much writing.

4. בְּהַר עֵיבָל — *On Mount Ebal*. Why were the Jewish people told, on the day they crossed the Jordan River, to go to Mount Ebal, more than a hundred and fifty miles (seventy *parsaot*) away in the heart of enemy territory, build an altar there, write the Torah on its stones in seventy languages, and return to the camp in Gilgal that same day, after reading out the blessings and curses (*Sotah* 34a)? Why was all this bother necessary? Also, the trip into enemy territory was likely to be dangerous, and the enemy might say that these would-be conquerors who are retracing their footsteps "are confused in the land."

We can suggest three reasons for this trip. First, the Jews were obligated to announce to the entire world that they were coming to the Holy Land not as conquerors of a foreign land by force, but by the command of Him Who created all lands. That command was written in the Torah, and would now be miraculously inscribed on the stones set up in the heart of the land. This was done on the very day they crossed the Jordan, before they even unsheathed a sword.

A second reason is that when Abraham, at God's order, arrived in the Holy Land, his first move was to "pass through the land until the place of Shechem, until Alon Moreh ... and God appeared to Abraham and said, 'To your descendants I will give this land.' He built an altar there, to God Who appeared to Him" (*Bereishis* 12:6-8). Therefore, God wanted Abraham's descendants, who followed in his footsteps, to do as he had done when they reached the Promised Land. Their first stop was also to be in Shechem, where they would build an altar to recall God's having fulfilled His promise, as Abraham had done to memorialize God's promise to give the land to his descendants.

Finally, the Jews had to know that they were coming to the Holy Land in order to keep the Torah. This is why they had to go to Shechem, the site of God's promise to Abraham, that same day, and accept Torah observance on themselves with blessings and curses.

☙ Why not on Mount Gerizim, where the blessings were proclaimed? We can say that it was because God foresaw that in the future the Samaritans would dispute the sanctity of Jerusalem and the site of the Holy Temple, claiming that the true site for the Altar should be the "mount of blessing" (Mount Gerizim). In order to refute their contention, God instructed the Jews to build the first altar specifically on Mount Ebal, to show that Mount Gerizim has no special sanctity or primacy.

27
5-6

these stones, of which I command you today, on Mount Ebal,
and you shall coat them with plaster. [5] *There you shall build*
an altar for HASHEM, *your God, an altar of stones; you shall*
not raise iron upon them. [6] *Of whole stones shall you build*
the altar of HASHEM, *your God, and you shall bring upon it*

We can also say that God wanted to appease the tribes who were told to stand on Mount Ebal, where the curses were read. The mountain where they stood was the site of the altar, and the sacrifices would atone for them and protect them.

⁂ וְשַׂדְתָּ אוֹתָם בַּשִּׂיד — *You shall coat them with plaster*. The use of a שׂ in the spelling of שִׂיד (plaster) instead of the usual one, סִיד, is surprising. The spelling שִׂיד probably means high quality plaster used for dishes and toys, which is suitable for inscribing with writing, while סִיד is ordinary plaster used for building.

The *Alshich* sees the spelling used in this verse as a veiled reference to the Name of God שַׁדַּי. This particular Name indicates God's attribute of self-limitation, as *Chazal* explain, "He said to His world, 'דַּי, enough.' " Here too, the word שִׂיד implies that the stones were big enough (דַּי) to hold the entire Torah in seventy languages.

⁂ According to Rabbi Yehudah (*Sotah* 35b), they first wrote the Torah on the stones, and then plastered over the writing. Responsa *Panim Meiros* (*I*, §33) writes that this was not considered erasing God's name, because the plaster could be peeled off at any time to reveal the letters. (This is in fact what the scribes sent by the nations to copy the Torah did).

The *Panim Meiros* also raises the question of why it was necessary at all to coat the stones with plaster. He suggests that it might have been done as protection against the rains, which could erase the writing. But I find this surprising. Plaster would not serve as protection against rain; it would be washed away. Also, the tenth of Nissan, when the Jews crossed the Jordan, is not the rainy season in the Holy Land.

It seems to me that we can answer the question as follows: the nations had not accepted the Torah, and it was clear that they were not about to accept it now, either. God only wanted to inform them of the basic concepts of the creation of the world and God's rulership over it, to forestall them from calling the Children of Israel robbers. The Torah itself is "the inheritance of the community of Jacob," and we are forbidden to teach it to non-Jews. Had the Jews written the Torah openly on the stones for the nations to come and copy, it would have looked as if they were actively teaching them Torah. This would be a disaster: *Maseches Sofrim* (1:7-8) tells that when the Sages translated the Torah into Greek for King Ptolemy, it was as tragic a day for the Jewish people as the day that the Golden Calf was made. *Megillas Taanis* relates that darkness descended on the world for three days on that occasion.

עוֹלֹת לַיהוָה אֱלֹהֶיךָ: ז וְזָבַחְתָּ שְׁלָמִים וְאָכַלְתָּ שָּׁם וְשָׂמַחְתָּ **כז**
לִפְנֵי יהוָה אֱלֹהֶיךָ: ח וְכָתַבְתָּ עַל־הָאֲבָנִים אֶת־כָּל־דִּבְרֵי ז־יד
הַתּוֹרָה הַזֹּאת בַּאֵר הֵיטֵב: ט וַיְדַבֵּר מֹשֶׁה וְהַכֹּהֲנִים הַלְוִיִּם
אֶל־כָּל־יִשְׂרָאֵל לֵאמֹר הַסְכֵּת ׀ וּשְׁמַע יִשְׂרָאֵל הַיּוֹם
הַזֶּה נִהְיֵיתָ לְעָם לַיהוָה אֱלֹהֶיךָ: י וְשָׁמַעְתָּ בְּקוֹל יהוָה
אֱלֹהֶיךָ וְעָשִׂיתָ אֶת־מִצְוֹתָו וְאֶת־חֻקָּיו אֲשֶׁר אָנֹכִי מְצַוְּךָ
הַיּוֹם: חמישי יא וַיְצַו מֹשֶׁה אֶת־הָעָם בַּיּוֹם הַהוּא
לֵאמֹר: יב אֵלֶּה יַעַמְדוּ לְבָרֵךְ אֶת־הָעָם עַל־הַר גְּרִזִּים
בְּעָבְרְכֶם אֶת־הַיַּרְדֵּן שִׁמְעוֹן וְלֵוִי וִיהוּדָה וְיִשָּׂשכָר וְיוֹסֵף
וּבִנְיָמִן: יג וְאֵלֶּה יַעַמְדוּ עַל־הַקְּלָלָה בְּהַר עֵיבָל רְאוּבֵן גָּד
וְאָשֵׁר וּזְבוּלֻן דָּן וְנַפְתָּלִי: יד וְעָנוּ הַלְוִיִּם וְאָמְרוּ אֶל־כָּל־

So even though God was commanding the Children of Israel to write the Torah for the nations' use, He also commanded them to cover it over, so that they should not teach it directly. Only then did He put into the heart of each nation to inquire after it, and they removed the plaster and copied the Torah for themselves.

7. וְשָׂמַחְתָּ לִפְנֵי ה׳ אֱלֹהֶיךָ — *And you shall be glad before Hashem, your God*. On Mount Ebal, the "mount of curses," we are to learn to rejoice in the suffering which may come our way (God forbid) because of our sins. (The Holy Land is in any case only acquired through suffering.) We should know that the suffering is for our own benefit, like the punishment meted out by a father to his son. It is for our own ultimate good, and as such should be accepted joyfully.

9. הַיּוֹם הַזֶּה — *This day*. The day that you establish the Covenant again, this time willingly and with complete awareness of what you are agreeing to, namely keeping the entire Torah: "You have become a people to Hashem, your God."

The Jewish people are divided among themselves. Each tribe has its own characteristics, as Jacob emphasized in his blessings to them: Reuben is hasty as water, Judah is a lion, Issachar is a donkey who bears a burden, Dan a snake, Naphtali a deer, and Benjamin a wolf. In *HaDe'ah Ve'HaDibur* we explained at length that Jacob was very frightened that because of his sons' different natures they would not be able to unite into one nation. Only when he found one significant internal common bond between them — their faith in one God and the desire to serve Him — and when they all cried out together at his deathbed, "'Hear, (our father) Israel, Hashem is our God, Hashem the One and Only'; just as there is only one God in your heart, so is there only one God in all of our hearts" — only then Jacob saw that his offspring were all good and true men. It was then that he bestowed a joint blessing on all his sons together (*Bereishis Rabbah* §98). It was also then that he knew that after receiving the Torah from the One and Only God, they would become one nation.

27
7-14

elevation-offerings to HASHEM, your God. [7] You shall slaughter peace-offerings and eat there, and you shall be glad before HASHEM, your God. [8] You shall inscribe on the stones all the words of this Torah, well clarified."

[9] Moses and the Kohanim, the Levites, spoke to all Israel, saying, "Be attentive and hear, O Israel: This day you have become a people to HASHEM, your God. [10] You shall hearken to the voice of HASHEM, your God, and you shall perform all His commandments and His decrees, which I command you today."

[11] Moses commanded the people on that day, saying,
[12] "These shall stand to bless the people on Mount Gerizim, when you have crossed the Jordan: Simeon, Levi, Judah, Issachar, Joseph, and Benjamin. [13] And these shall stand for the curse on Mount Ebal: Reuben, Gad, Asher, Zebulun, Dan, and Naphtali. [14] The Levites shall speak up and say to every

---

This is what Moses said on the day the covenant was made in the plains of Moab: "This day you have become a nation." What is it that unites you? "Hashem, your God,." As Rabbeinu Saadyah Gaon said, "Our nation is only a nation through [the influence of] our holy Torah."

13. **וּזְבוּלֻן** — *And Zebulun*. We have already mentioned the partnership between Issachar who learns Torah and Zebulun who supports him. It is very difficult to understand why these two "twin" tribes were separated here, with each tribe on a different mountain.

In *HaDe'ah Ve'HaDibur* (*I*:4) we explained at length *Chazal*'s teaching that God wants these two "partners" to live together in love and fraternity, as brothers do who share the same mother (who naturally love each other). This is why Zebulun was born to Leah, who was actually supposed to have only four sons and who stopped bearing children after Judah's birth. Leah went on to give birth to Issachar, the Torah scholar, as a reward for giving up Reuben's *dudaim* flowers to her sister and rival Rachel. After that she had to give birth also to Zebulun, the supporter of Torah study, to indicate that the relationship between Torah scholar and Torah supporter should be one of love, like that of brothers from the same mother.

The *Abarbanel* explains that the twelve curses in this *parashah* correspond to the twelve tribes. He finds that each curse refers to the specific tribe whose progenitor or progeny was lax in the fulfillment of the commandment in question, be it positive or negative.

Following this general concept (although not actually in keeping with the opinion of the *Abarbanel*), we may say that "accursed is the one who will not uphold the words of this Torah" refers to Zebulun, the historical supporter of Torah, or more correctly, to the "Zebuluns" in every generation. (This is in keeping with the exposition of the *Yerushalmi* on this verse: even if one learned

כז אִישׁ יִשְׂרָאֵל קוֹל רָם: טו אָרוּר הָאִישׁ אֲשֶׁר
טו־כ יַעֲשֶׂה פֶסֶל וּמַסֵּכָה תּוֹעֲבַת יהוה מַעֲשֵׂה יְדֵי חָרָשׁ וְשָׂם
בַּסָּתֶר וְעָנוּ כָל־הָעָם וְאָמְרוּ אָמֵן: טז אָרוּר מַקְלֶה
אָבִיו וְאִמּוֹ וְאָמַר כָּל־הָעָם אָמֵן: יז אָרוּר מַסִּיג
גְּבוּל רֵעֵהוּ וְאָמַר כָּל־הָעָם אָמֵן: יח אָרוּר מַשְׁגֶּה
עִוֵּר בַּדָּרֶךְ וְאָמַר כָּל־הָעָם אָמֵן: יט אָרוּר מַטֶּה
מִשְׁפַּט גֵּר־יָתוֹם וְאַלְמָנָה וְאָמַר כָּל־הָעָם אָמֵן: כ אָרוּר
שֹׁכֵב עִם־אֵשֶׁת אָבִיו כִּי גִלָּה כְּנַף אָבִיו וְאָמַר כָּל־הָעָם

---

and taught [Torah], and fulfilled its commandments, yet was able to support Torah study and did not do so, he is "accursed [as] one who will not uphold the words of this Torah.") A "Zebulun" of this type is an embezzler, taking all the profits for himself while throwing "Issachar" a few paltry crumbs instead of his rightful half. What is more, he also distances himself physically from his partner. This is against God's wish that these "twin brothers" should live together, both in this world and the next, for Zebulun is to learn from Issachar's exemplary behavior, while Issachar should see Zebulun's devoted business dealings and receive his share from him in full.

This explains the dramatic rebuke against Zebulun for distancing himself from his partner. If Issachar is on one mountain, Zebulun chooses to live on another (to prevent Issachar from seeing just how much he is making, and to spare himself having to learn from Issachar's Torah lifestyle), with a gaping valley lying between them. However, God's holy Ark is in that valley, surrounded by the priests and Levites who face Mount Ebal, where Zebulun is.

Those priests and Levites loudly announce, "Accursed is one who will not uphold the words of this Torah." Realize, Zebulun, that the mountain you stand on, far from Issachar, is the "mount of curses." Do not allow your evil inclination to sway you into thinking that you are 'supporting Torah' by donating trifling sums to yeshivos from time to time. Know that God's Ark, and the priests and Levites in that valley that stretches between you and the Torah scholar, are counting all the crumbs you occasionally throw to your supposed partner, Issachar (who gives up his whole life for Torah study, and is prepared to share half of it with you, if you would only support him truly and faithfully). God is well aware of how much you are earning, and how much you really owe Issachar.

If you, "Zebulun," want to earn eternal life, build a "bridge" across the chasm between Mount Ebal and Mount Gerizim, so that you can be close to your brother "Issachar," to learn from his ways and see how and from what he lives. When the time comes, you will cross this bridge over to the mount of blessing to merit eternal life in the World to Come.

15. אָרוּר הָאִישׁ אֲשֶׁר יַעֲשֶׂה פֶסֶל וּמַסֵּכָה תּוֹעֲבַת ה׳ — *Accursed is the man who will make a graven or molten image, an abomination of Hashem.* According to

27
15-20

man of Israel, in a loud voice:
[15] *'Accursed is the man who will make a graven or molten*
image, an abomination of HASHEM*, a craftsman's handiwork,*
and emplace it in secret.' And the entire people shall speak
up and say, 'Amen.'
[16] *'Accursed is one who degrades his father or mother.'*
And the entire people shall say, 'Amen.'
[17] *'Accursed is one who moves the boundary of his fellow.'*
And the entire people shall say, 'Amen.'
[18] *'Accursed is one who causes a blind person to go astray*
on the road.' And the entire people shall say, 'Amen.'
[19] *'Accursed is one who perverts a judgment of a proselyte,*
orphan, or widow.' And the entire people shall say, 'Amen.'
[20] *'Accursed is one who lies with the wife of his father, for*
he will have uncovered the robe of his father.' And the entire
people shall say, 'Amen.'

---

the commentaries, all the curses in this *parashah* refer to sins committed in private. The curses were proclaimed before the covenant in the plains of Moab, where the Jewish people accepted collective responsibility for one another, meaning that they would eliminate transgressors by means of the laws and statutes of the Torah. But this referred only to sins committed openly, not privately: "The hidden [sins] are for Hashem, our God," (He will punish those who transgress in private) "but the revealed [sins] are ours and our children's forever, to carry out" (against those who sin publicly) "all the words of this Torah" (29:28).

This is why God commanded the entire Jewish nation to say "amen" to the curses proclaimed by the priests and Levites who surrounded God's holy Ark, against those who sin in private. This curse will arouse God's judgment against them so that they will be punished during their lifetime.

מַעֲשֵׂה יְדֵי חָרָשׁ וְשָׂם בַּסָּתֶר — *A craftsman's handiwork, and emplace it in secret*. One who wishes to make an idol will commission an expert craftsman to produce an impressive piece of work, rather than do an amateurish job on his own: "The idol was cast by a craftsman and a smith hammered it of gold, and a silversmith made silver chains . . . he will choose wood that does not rot, and seek a wise craftsman to prepare an idol which will not collapse" (*Yeshayah* 40:19-20). This is the meaning of "accursed is the man who will make" by himself "a graven or molten image, an abomination of Hashem," which he would really have preferred to have made as "a craftsman's handiwork" as the gentiles do, but he was afraid to do it publicly, "and emplace it in secret," to avoid being stoned in accordance with Torah law. Since he does the deed in secret, he is the one who is cursed, and the people as a whole are innocent of any responsibility for his actions. (*Chazal's* expositions on this subject are well known, but it seems that this is the simple explanation of the verse.)

כז אָמֵן: כא אָרוּר שֹׁכֵב עִם־כָּל־בְּהֵמָה וְאָמַר כָּל־הָעָם
כא־כו אָמֵן: כב אָרוּר שֹׁכֵב עִם־אֲחֹתוֹ בַּת־אָבִיו אוֹ בַת־
אִמּוֹ וְאָמַר כָּל־הָעָם אָמֵן: כג אָרוּר שֹׁכֵב עִם־
חֹתַנְתּוֹ וְאָמַר כָּל־הָעָם אָמֵן: כד אָרוּר מַכֵּה
רֵעֵהוּ בַּסָּתֶר וְאָמַר כָּל־הָעָם אָמֵן: כה אָרוּר
לֹקֵחַ שֹׁחַד לְהַכּוֹת נֶפֶשׁ דָּם נָקִי וְאָמַר כָּל־הָעָם
אָמֵן: כו אָרוּר אֲשֶׁר לֹא־יָקִים אֶת־דִּבְרֵי
הַתּוֹרָה־הַזֹּאת לַעֲשׂוֹת אוֹתָם וְאָמַר כָּל־הָעָם אָמֵן:
כח א וְהָיָה אִם־שָׁמוֹעַ תִּשְׁמַע בְּקוֹל יהוה אֱלֹהֶיךָ לִשְׁמֹר
א־ז לַעֲשׂוֹת אֶת־כָּל־מִצְוֹתָיו אֲשֶׁר אָנֹכִי מְצַוְּךָ הַיּוֹם וּנְתָנְךָ
יהוה אֱלֹהֶיךָ עֶלְיוֹן עַל כָּל־גּוֹיֵי הָאָרֶץ: ב וּבָאוּ עָלֶיךָ
כָּל־הַבְּרָכוֹת הָאֵלֶּה וְהִשִּׂיגֻךָ כִּי תִשְׁמַע בְּקוֹל יהוה אֱלֹהֶיךָ:
ג בָּרוּךְ אַתָּה בָּעִיר וּבָרוּךְ אַתָּה בַּשָּׂדֶה: ד בָּרוּךְ פְּרִי־בִטְנְךָ
וּפְרִי אַדְמָתְךָ וּפְרִי בְהֶמְתֶּךָ שְׁגַר אֲלָפֶיךָ וְעַשְׁתְּרוֹת צֹאנֶךָ:
ה בָּרוּךְ טַנְאֲךָ וּמִשְׁאַרְתֶּךָ: ו בָּרוּךְ אַתָּה בְּבֹאֶךָ וּבָרוּךְ אַתָּה
בְּצֵאתֶךָ: ששי ז יִתֵּן יהוה אֶת־אֹיְבֶיךָ הַקָּמִים עָלֶיךָ נִגָּפִים

28.

1. לִשְׁמֹר לַעֲשׂוֹת — *To observe, to perform.* "To observe" refers to the negative commandments. "To perform" refers to the positive commandments.

2. וּבָאוּ עָלֶיךָ כָּל־הַבְּרָכוֹת הָאֵלֶּה וְהִשִּׂיגֻךָ — *All these blessings will come upon you and overtake you.* This verse can be explained according to the *Sifre*'s commentary on *Parashas Eikev* (11:12). If the Jews were completely righteous on *Rosh Hashanah* and it was decreed that they should receive abundant rainfall, but later they sinned, God will still send the rain. However, it will come at an inopportune time, or will fall on the desert and into the ocean. But "All these blessings ... will overtake you" means that you will actually enjoy the blessings. When? "If you hearken to the voice of Hashem, your God." The blessing will find you in a state in which "you hearken".

⁂ **וּבָאוּ עָלֶיךָ** — *Will come upon you.* All the blessings and curses which were said by Moses were phrased in the singular. The blessings and curses in *Vayikra* are, however, in the plural: "If you will follow [תֵּלֵכוּ] My laws . . . your rain [גִּשְׁמֵיכֶם] in its time . . . and if you do not listen [תִשְׁמְעוּ] to Me . . . I will assign upon you [עֲלֵיכֶם]." (*Vayikra* 26:3-4,14,16) Why the difference?

We may say that once the Children of Israel accepted collective responsibility for the Torah, in the plains of Moab, thereafter even when an individual sinned

27 21 *'Accursed is one who lies with any animal.' And the*
21-26 *entire people shall say, 'Amen.'*
22 *'Accursed is one who lies with his sister, the daughter of*
his father or the daughter of his mother.' And the entire
people shall say, 'Amen.'
23 *'Accursed is one who lies with his mother-in-law.' And*
the entire people shall say, 'Amen.'
24 *'Accursed is one who strikes his fellow stealthily.' And*
the entire people shall say, 'Amen.'
25 *'Accursed is one who takes a bribe to kill a person of*
innocent blood.' And the entire people shall say, 'Amen.'
26 *'Accursed is one who will not uphold the words of this*
Torah, to perform them.' And the entire people shall say,
'Amen.' "
28 1 *It shall be that if you hearken to the voice of* HASHEM,
1-7 *your God, to observe, to perform all of His commandments*
that I command you this day, then HASHEM, *your God, will*
make you supreme over all the nations of the earth. 2 *All*
these blessings will come upon you and overtake you, if you
hearken to the voice of HASHEM, *your God:*
3 *Blessed shall you be in the city and blessed shall you be*
in the field. 4 *Blessed shall be the fruit of your womb, and*
the fruit of your ground, and the fruit of your animals; the
offspring of your cattle and the flocks of your sheep and
goats. 5 *Blessed shall be your fruit basket and your knead-*
ing bowl. 6 *Blessed shall you be when you come in and*
blessed shall you be when you go out. 7 HASHEM *shall cause*
your enemies who rise up against you to be struck down

---

publicly the sin was the responsibility of the community as a whole, if they did not rebuke him and punish him according to Torah law. This is why the blessings and curses are now worded in the singular form.

5. בָּרוּךְ טַנְאֲךָ וּמִשְׁאַרְתֶּךָ — *Blessed shall be your fruit basket and your kneading bowl*. The gifts given to the priest and to the poor begin with a basket of fruit ("and you shall put [the first-fruits] in a basket") and conclude in the kneading-bowl (*challah*, whose obligation occurs when the dough is kneaded). Therefore, the Torah tells us that the blessing will come upon everything from the "basket" until the "bowl."

7. אֹיְבֶיךָ הַקָּמִים עָלֶיךָ — *Your enemies who rise up against you*. The implication is that it is not worthwhile calling down curses on an enemy who does not rise up against you. This is only logical, as "it is a known rule that Esau hates Jacob." It would be impossible to curse all the enemies of the Jews, because there are so many of them.

כח לְפָנֶיךָ בְּדֶרֶךְ אֶחָד יֵצְאוּ אֵלֶיךָ וּבְשִׁבְעָה דְרָכִים יָנוּסוּ
ח־יג לְפָנֶיךָ׃ ח יְצַו יְהוָה אִתְּךָ אֶת־הַבְּרָכָה בַּאֲסָמֶיךָ וּבְכֹל
מִשְׁלַח יָדֶךָ וּבֵרַכְךָ בָּאָרֶץ אֲשֶׁר־יְהוָה אֱלֹהֶיךָ נֹתֵן לָךְ׃
ט יְקִימְךָ יְהוָה לוֹ לְעַם קָדוֹשׁ כַּאֲשֶׁר נִשְׁבַּע־לָךְ כִּי תִשְׁמֹר
אֶת־מִצְוֹת יְהוָה אֱלֹהֶיךָ וְהָלַכְתָּ בִּדְרָכָיו׃ י וְרָאוּ כָּל־
עַמֵּי הָאָרֶץ כִּי שֵׁם יְהוָה נִקְרָא עָלֶיךָ וְיָרְאוּ מִמֶּךָּ׃
יא וְהוֹתִרְךָ יְהוָה לְטוֹבָה בִּפְרִי בִטְנְךָ וּבִפְרִי בְהֶמְתְּךָ
וּבִפְרִי אַדְמָתֶךָ עַל הָאֲדָמָה אֲשֶׁר נִשְׁבַּע יְהוָה לַאֲבֹתֶיךָ
לָתֶת לָךְ׃ יב יִפְתַּח יְהוָה ׀ לְךָ אֶת־אוֹצָרוֹ הַטּוֹב אֶת־
הַשָּׁמַיִם לָתֵת מְטַר־אַרְצְךָ בְּעִתּוֹ וּלְבָרֵךְ אֵת כָּל־מַעֲשֵׂה
יָדֶךָ וְהִלְוִיתָ גּוֹיִם רַבִּים וְאַתָּה לֹא תִלְוֶה׃ יג וּנְתָנְךָ יְהוָה
לְרֹאשׁ וְלֹא לְזָנָב וְהָיִיתָ רַק לְמַעְלָה וְלֹא תִהְיֶה לְמָטָּה
כִּי־תִשְׁמַע אֶל־מִצְוֹת ׀ יְהוָה אֱלֹהֶיךָ אֲשֶׁר אָנֹכִי מְצַוְּךָ

❧ **בְּדֶרֶךְ אֶחָד יֵצְאוּ אֵלֶיךָ** — *On one road will they go out toward you.* Their officers will lose their wisdom, and they will not split up their army into camps when they go out to war (as Jacob did). They also will not set up an ambush at their enemy's rear (as Joshua did at Ai). Instead they will all go out towards you on one road, and thus cause their own downfall.

❧ **וּבְשִׁבְעָה דְרָכִים יָנוּסוּ לְפָנֶיךָ** — *And on seven roads will they flee before you.* When they retreat, they will not do so all together in an orderly fashion, covered by their rear guard. Instead, "they will flee on seven roads," in total disorder and exposed to attack, enabling you to inflict many casualties.

9. יְקִימְךָ ה׳ לוֹ לְעַם קָדוֹשׁ — *Hashem will confirm you for Himself as a holy people.* If you will not only "observe the commandments of Hashem, your God," but also "go in His ways" — just as He is merciful and compassionate, so must you be — then He "will confirm you for Himself as a holy people." If you "observe the commandments" and no more, that will only bring you to the level of being "supreme over all the nations" (verse 1).

10. וְיָרְאוּ מִמֶּךָּ — *And they will revere you.* Superiority breeds envy, and at times also strife and war. But if "all the peoples of the earth see that the Name of Hashem is proclaimed over you" as a nation 'holy to God', "they will revere (literally 'fear') you" and not go to war with you.

12. לָתֵת מְטַר־אַרְצְךָ בְּעִתּוֹ וּלְבָרֵךְ אֵת כָּל־מַעֲשֵׂה יָדֶךָ — *To provide rain for your Land in its time, and to bless all your handiwork.* As *Chazal* say, "Great is a day of rain, for even a penny in one's pocket is blessed on that day" (*Taanis* 8b). *Rashi* explains that even handiwork which does not require rain is blessed on such a day.

before you; on one road will they go out toward you and on
seven roads will they flee before you. 8 *HASHEM will*
command the blessing for you in your storehouses and your
every undertaking; and He will bless you in the Land that
HASHEM, your God, gives you. 9 *HASHEM will confirm you for*
Himself as a holy people, as He swore to you — if you observe
the commandments of HASHEM, your God, and you go in His
ways. 10 *Then all the peoples of the earth will see that the*
Name of HASHEM is proclaimed over you, and they will
revere you. 11 *HASHEM shall give you bountiful goodness, in*
the fruit of your womb and the fruit of your animals and the
fruit of your ground, on the ground that HASHEM swore to
your forefathers to give you. 12 *HASHEM shall open for you His*
storehouse of goodness, the heavens, to provide rain for your
Land in its time, and to bless all your handiwork; you shall
lend to many nations, but you shall not borrow. 13 *HASHEM*
shall place you as a head and not as a tail; you shall be only
above and you shall not be below — if you hearken to the
commandments of HASHEM, your God, that I command you

---

13. וְהָיִיתָ רַק לְמַעְלָה — *And you shall be only above*. You will always and forever be "only above." "You shall not be below" ever, under any circumstances, "if you hearken to the commandments of Hashem, your God . . . to observe and to perform."

When wrestlers compete, the winner does not subdue his opponent all at once. The two roll on the ground, and the one who was on top may later be on the bottom. So too in a war between two nations: during the course of the war, the victor may also taste the bitterness of defeat when the enemy has a triumph (which later turns out to have been only temporary). When the victor is on the bottom, he is in despair until he finally overcomes his enemy altogether. God promises us that if we observe His commandments we will be "only above," and never taste the bitterness and despair of being "below" for even one moment.

וְלֹא תִהְיֶה לְמָטָּה — *And you shall not be below*. There are people who are "above" only in this world, which is an upside-down world, where superior people are below and inferior people are on top. But in the World to Come, where things are clear and just, those same people who were on top here come out "below."

The words "you shall be only above" mean both in this world and the next: you will not be below even in the World to Come. This will happen when "you hearken to the commandments of Hashem, your God . . . to observe and to perform," as *Chazal* say, "as for us (Torah scholars), as we are held in esteem here, so we are there" (*Bava Basra* 10b).

כח הַיּוֹם לִשְׁמֹר וְלַעֲשׂוֹת׃ יד וְלֹא תָסוּר מִכָּל־הַדְּבָרִים אֲשֶׁר
יד־כג אָנֹכִי מְצַוֶּה אֶתְכֶם הַיּוֹם יָמִין וּשְׂמֹאול לָלֶכֶת אַחֲרֵי אֱלֹהִים
אֲחֵרִים לְעָבְדָם׃
טו וְהָיָה אִם־לֹא תִשְׁמַע בְּקוֹל יהוה אֱלֹהֶיךָ לִשְׁמֹר לַעֲשׂוֹת
אֶת־כָּל־מִצְוֹתָיו וְחֻקֹּתָיו אֲשֶׁר אָנֹכִי מְצַוְּךָ הַיּוֹם וּבָאוּ עָלֶיךָ
כָּל־הַקְּלָלוֹת הָאֵלֶּה וְהִשִּׂיגוּךָ׃ טז אָרוּר אַתָּה בָּעִיר וְאָרוּר
אַתָּה בַּשָּׂדֶה׃ יז אָרוּר טַנְאֲךָ וּמִשְׁאַרְתֶּךָ׃ יח אָרוּר פְּרִי־
בִטְנְךָ וּפְרִי אַדְמָתֶךָ שְׁגַר אֲלָפֶיךָ וְעַשְׁתְּרֹת צֹאנֶךָ׃ יט אָרוּר
אַתָּה בְּבֹאֶךָ וְאָרוּר אַתָּה בְּצֵאתֶךָ׃ כ יְשַׁלַּח יהוה ׀ בְּךָ
אֶת־הַמְּאֵרָה אֶת־הַמְּהוּמָה וְאֶת־הַמִּגְעֶרֶת בְּכָל־מִשְׁלַח
יָדְךָ אֲשֶׁר תַּעֲשֶׂה עַד הִשָּׁמֶדְךָ וְעַד־אֲבָדְךָ מַהֵר מִפְּנֵי רֹעַ
מַעֲלָלֶיךָ אֲשֶׁר עֲזַבְתָּנִי׃ כא יַדְבֵּק יהוה בְּךָ אֶת־הַדָּבֶר עַד
כַּלֹּתוֹ אֹתְךָ מֵעַל הָאֲדָמָה אֲשֶׁר־אַתָּה בָא־שָׁמָּה לְרִשְׁתָּהּ׃
כב יַכְּכָה יהוה בַּשַּׁחֶפֶת וּבַקַּדַּחַת וּבַדַּלֶּקֶת וּבַחַרְחֻר
וּבַחֶרֶב וּבַשִּׁדָּפוֹן וּבַיֵּרָקוֹן וּרְדָפוּךָ עַד אָבְדֶךָ׃ כג וְהָיוּ שָׁמֶיךָ
אֲשֶׁר עַל־רֹאשְׁךָ נְחֹשֶׁת וְהָאָרֶץ אֲשֶׁר־תַּחְתֶּיךָ בַּרְזֶל׃

---

14. וְלֹא תָסוּר . . . יָמִין וּשְׂמֹאול — *And you do not turn away... right or left.* The slightest deviation from the way of God can cause one to "follow other gods, to worship them." *Chazal* teach us that "this is the method used by the Evil Inclination: today he tells one, 'Do this,' and the next day he tells him, 'Do that', until eventually he tells him, 'Go worship idols', and he does" (*Shabbos* 105b).

15. וְהִשִּׂיגוּךָ — *And overtake you*. Those who turn away from God are wont to say, "Evil will not hurry to overtake us because of our sins" (*Amos* 9:10). They will even boast that they know tactics to ward off potential trouble, just as the Generation of the Dispersion did. They built a tower "to support the sky" and prevent it from collapsing and so causing another Deluge. This is why the additional word וְהִשִּׂיגוּךָ, "overtake you," is included in the curses, for "there is neither wisdom nor understanding nor counsel before Hashem" (*Mishlei* 21:30). (However, people do not look for ways to ward off blessing. But we have already explained why the Torah says that the blessings will "overtake you.")

The Torah does not place the word "overtake you" at the beginning of the present verse ("All these curses shall overtake you if you do not hearken to the voice of Hashem"), because the power of repentance is well known. If the Jewish people repent, the curses certainly will not overtake them.

17. אָרוּר טַנְאֲךָ וּמִשְׁאַרְתֶּךָ — *Accursed will be your fruit basket and your kneading bowl*. If you will not believe in God and His Divine Providence, nor that He provides food for all mankind, you will find it only natural to

today, to observe and to perform; 14 *and you do not turn*
away from any of the words that I command you this day,
right or left, to follow gods of others, to worship them.
15 *But it will be that if you do not hearken to the voice of*
HASHEM, your God, to observe, to perform all His command-
ments and all His decrees that I command you today, then all
these curses will come upon you and overtake you:
16 *Accursed will you be in the city and accursed will you be*
in the field. 17 *Accursed will be your fruit basket and your*
kneading bowl. 18 *Accursed will be the fruit of your womb*
and the fruit of your ground, the offspring of your cattle and
the flocks of your sheep and goats. 19 *Accursed will you be*
when you come in and accursed will you be when you go out.
20 *HASHEM will send in your midst attrition, confusion, and*
worry, in your every undertaking that you will do, until
you are destroyed, and until you are quickly annihilated,
because of the evil of your deeds, for having forsaken Me.
21 *HASHEM will attach the plague to you, until it consumes*
you from upon the ground to which you are coming, to
possess it. 22 *HASHEM will strike you with fever, with swell-*
ing lesions, with burning heat, with thirst, and with sword;
and with wind blasts and with withering — and they will
pursue you until your destruction. 23 *Your heavens over your*
head will be copper and the land beneath you will be iron.

---

willfully limit the number of children you bear. This is why "accursed will be the fruit of your womb" immediately follows this verse.

18. **אָרוּר פְּרִי־בִטְנְךָ** — *Accursed will be the fruit of your womb*. The blessing for "fruit of the womb" precedes that of "fruit of the ground," while here the order is reversed. Why is this so? We can say that this order allows for more anguish: at the same time that one is blessed with children, his house will be empty. The children will ask for food, and he will have none to give them.

20. **עַד־הִשָּׁמֶדְךָ** — *Until you are destroyed*. The commentary *HaKsav Ve'HaKabbalah* proves that the word "עַד" as used here is not inclusive. Rather, it means "up to but not including."

23. **וְהָיוּ שָׁמֶיךָ אֲשֶׁר עַל־רֹאשְׁךָ נְחֹשֶׁת** — *Your heavens over your head will be copper*. Why does the Torah use the specific wording "your heavens over your head"?

We can say that because the curses in this *parashah* are in the singular, they refer to a situation like the one in *Amos* (4:7): "One field shall be given rain, and another field that rain does not fall on shall dry up." This is why the Torah speaks to the individual: "*Your* heavens over *your* head will be copper," while

כח
כד־לג

כד יִתֵּן יְהוָה אֶת־מְטַר אַרְצְךָ אָבָק וְעָפָר מִן־הַשָּׁמַיִם יֵרֵד
עָלֶיךָ עַד הִשָּׁמְדָךְ: כה יִתֶּנְךָ יְהוָה ׀ נִגָּף לִפְנֵי אֹיְבֶיךָ בְּדֶרֶךְ
אֶחָד תֵּצֵא אֵלָיו וּבְשִׁבְעָה דְרָכִים תָּנוּס לְפָנָיו וְהָיִיתָ לְזַעֲוָה
לְכֹל מַמְלְכוֹת הָאָרֶץ: כו וְהָיְתָה נִבְלָתְךָ לְמַאֲכָל לְכָל־עוֹף
הַשָּׁמַיִם וּלְבֶהֱמַת הָאָרֶץ וְאֵין מַחֲרִיד: כז יַכְּכָה יְהוָה בִּשְׁחִין
מִצְרַיִם °ובעפלים וּבַגָּרָב וּבֶחָרֶס אֲשֶׁר לֹא־תוּכַל לְהֵרָפֵא: °וּבַטְּחֹרִים ק׳
כח יַכְּכָה יְהוָה בְּשִׁגָּעוֹן וּבְעִוָּרוֹן וּבְתִמְהוֹן לֵבָב: כט וְהָיִיתָ
מְמַשֵּׁשׁ בַּצָּהֳרַיִם כַּאֲשֶׁר יְמַשֵּׁשׁ הָעִוֵּר בָּאֲפֵלָה וְלֹא תַצְלִיחַ
אֶת־דְּרָכֶיךָ וְהָיִיתָ אַךְ עָשׁוּק וְגָזוּל כָּל־הַיָּמִים וְאֵין מוֹשִׁיעַ:
ל אִשָּׁה תְאָרֵשׂ וְאִישׁ אַחֵר °ישגלנה בַּיִת תִּבְנֶה וְלֹא־תֵשֵׁב °יִשְׁכָּבֶנָּה ק׳
בּוֹ כֶּרֶם תִּטַּע וְלֹא תְחַלְּלֶנּוּ: לא שׁוֹרְךָ טָבוּחַ לְעֵינֶיךָ וְלֹא
תֹאכַל מִמֶּנּוּ חֲמֹרְךָ גָּזוּל מִלְּפָנֶיךָ וְלֹא יָשׁוּב לָךְ צֹאנְךָ
נְתֻנוֹת לְאֹיְבֶיךָ וְאֵין לְךָ מוֹשִׁיעַ: לב בָּנֶיךָ וּבְנֹתֶיךָ נְתֻנִים
לְעַם אַחֵר וְעֵינֶיךָ רֹאוֹת וְכָלוֹת אֲלֵיהֶם כָּל־הַיּוֹם וְאֵין לְאֵל
יָדֶךָ: לג פְּרִי אַדְמָתְךָ וְכָל־יְגִיעֲךָ יֹאכַל עַם אֲשֶׁר לֹא־יָדָעְתָּ

---

the heavens over the head of your Torah-observant neighbor will produce bountiful rains. Similarly, "the land beneath *you* will be iron," but your neighbor's land will be watered.

In *Vayikra*, however, the curses are all in the plural, so the words "over your head" and "beneath you" are not used.

24. יִתֵּן ה׳ אֶת־מְטַר אַרְצְךָ אָבָק וְעָפָר — *Hashem will make the rain of your Land dust and dirt*. You might ask, "Is a day of rain not as terrible as the Day of Judgment? If the world did not need rain, we would pray for mercy and abolish [rainy days]" (*Taanis* 8b; *Rashi* explains that rain is bothersome, as it hinders people from coming and going). One might think that if there were no rain, we might go hungry, but at least we would not suffer the discomforts rain involves. Therefore the Torah says, "Hashem will make the rain of your Land dust and dirt, from the heaven it will descend upon you." You will have the troubles that come with rain, but not the benefits it brings.

32. בָּנֶיךָ וּבְנֹתֶיךָ נְתֻנִים לְעַם אַחֵר — *Your sons and daughters will be given to another people*. *Chazal* explain that this refers to a stepmother. The children's mother will die, and a stepmother will raise them. Apparently, the Sages learn this from the words "and your eyes will see and pine in vain for them all day long." If they were literally taken into captivity, the father would not "see them all day." But the wording is appropriate for sons and daughters who are suffering at the hand of their father's second wife. Actual captivity is in fact discussed in v. 41: "You will bear sons and daughters, but they will not be yours, for they will go into captivity."

28
24-33

24 HASHEM will make the rain of your Land dust and dirt;
from the heaven it will descend upon you until you are
destroyed. 25 HASHEM will cause you to be struck down before
your enemies; on one road you will go out against him, but on
seven roads will you flee before him; and you will be a cause
of terror to all the kingdoms of the earth. 26 Your carcass will
be food for every bird of the sky and animal of the earth, and
nothing will frighten them. 27 HASHEM will strike you with
the boils of Egypt, with hemorrhoids, with wet boils and dry
boils, of which you cannot be cured. 28 HASHEM will strike
you with madness and with blindness, and with confounding
of the heart. 29 You will grope at noontime as a blind man
gropes in the darkness, but you will not succeed on your way;
you will be only cheated and robbed all the days, and there
will be no savior. 30 You will betroth a woman, but another
man will lie with her; you will build a house, but you will
not dwell in it; you will plant a vineyard, but you will not
redeem it. 31 Your ox will be slaughtered before your eyes,
but you will not eat from it; your donkey will be robbed
from before you, but it will not return to you; your flocks
will be given to your enemies, and you will have no savior.
32 Your sons and daughters will be given to another people —
and your eyes will see and pine in vain for them all day
long, but your hand will be powerless. 33 A nation unknown to
you will devour the fruit of your ground and all your labor,

☙ See the previous commentary. However, since one woman cannot possibly be called "another people" (see the commentaries of *Ramban* and *Malbim* on the verse "you shall not sell her to foreign nation" [*Shemos* 21:8]), this interpretation can be no more than tangential to the verse's foremost meaning.

As for that principal meaning, we may say that the troubles and suffering of the Jews in their days of misery and poverty have caused their children to stray from the path of Torah. They come under harmful influences, and some give up Judaism entirely, assimilating into the non-Jewish world: "Your sons and daughters will be given to another people — and your eyes (which are still illumined with the light of Torah) will see and pine in vain for them all day, and your hand will be powerless."

How many tragic cases do we see today of sons and daughters who left their righteous parents for another nation! And how many sons and daughters do we see who were given over by their barely-believing parents to "another people" and a foreign faith for a crust of bread! The eyes of the Jewish people "see and pine in vain for them all day," and they *can* help these distant, helpless brothers! May God send us the prophet Elijah to bring the hearts of fathers back to their

כח
לד־מט

וְהָיִיתָ רַק עָשׁוּק וְרָצוּץ כָּל־הַיָּמִים: לד וְהָיִיתָ מְשֻׁגָּע
מִמַּרְאֵה עֵינֶיךָ אֲשֶׁר תִּרְאֶה: לה יַכְּכָה יהוה בִּשְׁחִין רָע
עַל־הַבִּרְכַּיִם וְעַל־הַשֹּׁקַיִם אֲשֶׁר לֹא־תוּכַל לְהֵרָפֵא מִכַּף
רַגְלְךָ וְעַד קָדְקֳדֶךָ: לו יוֹלֵךְ יהוה אֹתְךָ וְאֶת־מַלְכְּךָ אֲשֶׁר
תָּקִים עָלֶיךָ אֶל־גּוֹי אֲשֶׁר לֹא־יָדַעְתָּ אַתָּה וַאֲבֹתֶיךָ וְעָבַדְתָּ
שָּׁם אֱלֹהִים אֲחֵרִים עֵץ וָאָבֶן: לז וְהָיִיתָ לְשַׁמָּה לְמָשָׁל
וְלִשְׁנִינָה בְּכֹל הָעַמִּים אֲשֶׁר־יְנַהֶגְךָ יהוה שָׁמָּה: לח זֶרַע
רַב תּוֹצִיא הַשָּׂדֶה וּמְעַט תֶּאֱסֹף כִּי יַחְסְלֶנּוּ הָאַרְבֶּה:
לט כְּרָמִים תִּטַּע וְעָבָדְתָּ וְיַיִן לֹא־תִשְׁתֶּה וְלֹא תֶאֱגֹר כִּי
תֹאכְלֶנּוּ הַתֹּלָעַת: מ זֵיתִים יִהְיוּ לְךָ בְּכָל־גְּבוּלֶךָ וְשֶׁמֶן לֹא
תָסוּךְ כִּי יִשַּׁל זֵיתֶךָ: מא בָּנִים וּבָנוֹת תּוֹלִיד וְלֹא־יִהְיוּ לָךְ כִּי
יֵלְכוּ בַּשֶּׁבִי: מב כָּל־עֵצְךָ וּפְרִי אַדְמָתֶךָ יְיָרֵשׁ הַצְּלָצַל:
מג הַגֵּר אֲשֶׁר בְּקִרְבְּךָ יַעֲלֶה עָלֶיךָ מַעְלָה מָּעְלָה וְאַתָּה
תֵרֵד מַטָּה מָּטָּה: מד הוּא יַלְוְךָ וְאַתָּה לֹא תַלְוֶנּוּ הוּא יִהְיֶה
לְרֹאשׁ וְאַתָּה תִּהְיֶה לְזָנָב: מה וּבָאוּ עָלֶיךָ כָּל־הַקְּלָלוֹת
הָאֵלֶּה וּרְדָפוּךָ וְהִשִּׂיגוּךָ עַד הִשָּׁמְדָךְ כִּי־לֹא שָׁמַעְתָּ בְּקוֹל
יהוה אֱלֹהֶיךָ לִשְׁמֹר מִצְוֹתָיו וְחֻקֹּתָיו אֲשֶׁר צִוָּךְ: מו וְהָיוּ בְךָ
לְאוֹת וּלְמוֹפֵת וּבְזַרְעֲךָ עַד־עוֹלָם: מז תַּחַת אֲשֶׁר לֹא־
עָבַדְתָּ אֶת־יהוה אֱלֹהֶיךָ בְּשִׂמְחָה וּבְטוּב לֵבָב מֵרֹב כֹּל:
מח וְעָבַדְתָּ אֶת־אֹיְבֶיךָ אֲשֶׁר יְשַׁלְּחֶנּוּ יהוה בָּךְ בְּרָעָב
וּבְצָמָא וּבְעֵירֹם וּבְחֹסֶר כֹּל וְנָתַן עֹל בַּרְזֶל עַל־צַוָּארֶךָ עַד
הִשְׁמִידוֹ אֹתָךְ: מט יִשָּׂא יהוה עָלֶיךָ גּוֹי מֵרָחֹק מִקְצֵה
הָאָרֶץ כַּאֲשֶׁר יִדְאֶה הַנָּשֶׁר גּוֹי אֲשֶׁר לֹא־תִשְׁמַע לְשֹׁנוֹ:

---

children, and the hearts of children back to their fathers, and to bring us the news of the Messiah's arrival.

34. וְהָיִיתָ מְשֻׁגָּע מִמַּרְאֵה עֵינֶיךָ אֲשֶׁר תִּרְאֶה — *You will go mad from the sight of your eyes that you will see*. A person has the option of closing his eyes to avoid seeing sights which pain him excessively. This is why the Torah adds the words "that you will see." The situation will be such that "you will see" against your will, and not be able to look away.

39. וְיַיִן לֹא־תִשְׁתֶּה — *You will not drink wine*. You may say that you will store the wine to age, thus increasing its value. But the verse says "and you will not . . . gather in."

40. וְשֶׁמֶן לֹא תָסוּךְ — *You will not anoint with oil*. We see from here that oil's chief use is as a lubricant. It is only suitable for consumption as part of a mixture.

28
34-49

and you will be only cheated and downtrodden all the days.
34 You will go mad from the sight of your eyes that you will
see. 35 HASHEM will strike you with a foul boil, on the knees
and on the legs, that cannot be cured, from the sole of your
foot to your crown. 36 HASHEM will lead you and your king
whom you will set up over yourself to a nation you never
knew — neither you nor your forefathers — and there you
will work for the gods of others — of wood and of stone. 37 You
will be a source of astonishment, a parable, and a conversa-
tion piece, among all the peoples where HASHEM will lead
you. 38 You will take abundant seed out to the field, but you
will harvest little, for the locust will devour it. 39 You will
plant vineyards and work them, but you will not drink wine
and you will not gather in, for the worm will eat it. 40 You will
have olive trees throughout your boundaries, but you will not
anoint with oil, for your olives will drop. 41 You will bear sons
and daughters, but they will not be yours, for they will go into
captivity. 42 All your trees and the fruits of your ground, the
chirping locust will impoverish. 43 The stranger who is among
you will ascend higher and higher, while you will descend
lower and lower. 44 He will lend to you, but you will not lend
to him; he will be a head, but you will be a tail. 45 All these
curses will come upon you and pursue you and overtake you,
until you are destroyed, because you will not have hearkened
to the voice of HASHEM, your God, to observe His command-
ments and decrees that He commanded you. 46 They will be a
sign and a wonder, in you and in your offspring, forever,
47 because you did not serve HASHEM, your God, amid
gladness and goodness of heart, when everything was
abundant. 48 So you will serve your enemies whom HASHEM
will send against you, in hunger and in thirst, in nakedness
and without anything; and he will put an iron yoke on your
neck, until he destroys you. 49 HASHEM will carry against
you a nation from afar, from the end of the earth, as an eagle
will swoop, a nation whose language you will not understand,

---

43. הַגֵּר אֲשֶׁר בְּקִרְבְּךָ יַעֲלֶה עָלֶיךָ מַעְלָה מָּעְלָה — *The stranger who is among you will ascend higher and higher*. His ascent will not be due to his own superiority, but only because "you will descend lower and lower."

44. הוּא יִהְיֶה לְרֹאשׁ — *He will be a head*. It is not that he will be worthy of such an exalted position; it is only because "you will be a tail" that he will be your head.

נ גּוֹי עַז פָּנִים אֲשֶׁר לֹא־יִשָּׂא פָנִים֙ לְזָקֵ֔ן וְנַ֖עַר לֹ֥א יָחֹֽן: נא וְאָכַ֣ל פְּרִ֣י בְהֶמְתְּךָ֘ וּפְרִי־אַדְמָֽתְךָ֒ עַ֣ד הִשָּֽׁמְדָ֔ךְ אֲשֶׁ֣ר לֹֽא־יַשְׁאִ֣יר לְךָ֗ דָּגָן֙ תִּיר֣וֹשׁ וְיִצְהָ֔ר שְׁגַ֥ר אֲלָפֶ֖יךָ וְעַשְׁתְּרֹ֣ת צֹאנֶ֑ךָ עַ֥ד הַאֲבִיד֖וֹ אֹתָֽךְ: נב וְהֵצַ֨ר לְךָ֜ בְּכָל־שְׁעָרֶ֗יךָ עַ֣ד רֶ֤דֶת חֹמֹתֶ֨יךָ֙ הַגְּבֹהֹ֣ת וְהַבְּצֻרֹ֔ת אֲשֶׁ֥ר אַתָּ֛ה בֹּטֵ֥חַ בָּהֵ֖ן בְּכָל־אַרְצֶ֑ךָ וְהֵצַ֤ר לְךָ֙ בְּכָל־שְׁעָרֶ֔יךָ בְּכָ֨ל־אַרְצְךָ֔ אֲשֶׁ֥ר נָתַ֛ן יְהֹוָ֥ה אֱלֹהֶ֖יךָ לָֽךְ: נג וְאָכַלְתָּ֣ פְרִֽי־בִטְנְךָ֗ בְּשַׂ֤ר בָּנֶ֨יךָ֙ וּבְנֹתֶ֔יךָ אֲשֶׁ֥ר נָֽתַן־לְךָ֖ יְהֹוָ֣ה אֱלֹהֶ֑יךָ בְּמָצוֹר֙ וּבְמָצ֔וֹק אֲשֶׁר־יָצִ֥יק לְךָ֖ אֹיְבֶֽךָ: נד הָאִישׁ֙ הָרַ֣ךְ בְּךָ֔ וְהֶעָנֹ֖ג מְאֹ֑ד תֵּרַ֨ע עֵינ֤וֹ בְאָחִיו֙ וּבְאֵ֣שֶׁת חֵיק֔וֹ וּבְיֶ֥תֶר בָּנָ֖יו אֲשֶׁ֥ר יוֹתִֽיר: נה מִתֵּ֣ת | לְאַחַ֣ד מֵהֶ֗ם מִבְּשַׂ֤ר בָּנָיו֙ אֲשֶׁ֣ר יֹאכֵ֔ל מִבְּלִ֥י הִשְׁאִֽיר־ל֖וֹ כֹּ֑ל בְּמָצוֹר֙ וּבְמָצ֔וֹק אֲשֶׁ֨ר יָצִ֥יק לְךָ֛ אֹיִבְךָ֖ בְּכָל־שְׁעָרֶֽיךָ: נו הָרַכָּ֨ה בְךָ֜ וְהָֽעֲנֻגָּ֗ה אֲשֶׁ֨ר לֹֽא־נִסְּתָ֤ה כַף־רַגְלָהּ֙ הַצֵּ֣ג עַל־הָאָ֔רֶץ מֵהִתְעַנֵּ֖ג וּמֵרֹ֑ךְ תֵּרַ֤ע עֵינָהּ֙ בְּאִ֣ישׁ חֵיקָ֔הּ וּבִבְנָ֖הּ וּבְבִתָּֽהּ: נז וּֽבְשִׁלְיָתָ֞הּ הַיּוֹצֵ֣ת | מִבֵּ֣ין רַגְלֶ֗יהָ וּבְבָנֶ֨יהָ֙ אֲשֶׁ֣ר תֵּלֵ֔ד כִּֽי־תֹֽאכְלֵ֥ם בְּחֹֽסֶר־כֹּ֖ל בַּסָּ֑תֶר בְּמָצוֹר֙ וּבְמָצ֔וֹק אֲשֶׁ֨ר יָצִ֥יק לְךָ֛ אֹיִבְךָ֖ בִּשְׁעָרֶֽיךָ: נח אִם־לֹ֣א תִשְׁמֹ֗ר לַֽעֲשׂוֹת֙ אֶת־כָּל־דִּבְרֵי֙ הַתּוֹרָ֣ה הַזֹּ֔את הַכְּתֻבִ֖ים בַּסֵּ֣פֶר הַזֶּ֑ה לְ֠יִרְאָ֠ה אֶת־הַשֵּׁ֞ם הַנִּכְבָּ֤ד וְהַנּוֹרָא֙ הַזֶּ֔ה אֵ֖ת יְהֹוָ֥ה אֱלֹהֶֽיךָ: נט וְהִפְלָ֤א יְהֹוָה֙ אֶת־מַכֹּ֣תְךָ֔ וְאֵ֖ת מַכּ֣וֹת זַרְעֶ֑ךָ מַכּ֤וֹת גְּדֹלֹת֙ וְנֶ֣אֱמָנ֔וֹת וָֽחֳלָיִ֥ם רָעִ֖ים וְנֶֽאֱמָנִֽים: ס וְהֵשִׁ֣יב בְּךָ֗ אֵ֚ת כָּל־מַדְוֵ֣ה מִצְרַ֔יִם אֲשֶׁ֥ר יָגֹ֖רְתָּ מִפְּנֵיהֶ֑ם וְדָֽבְק֖וּ בָּֽךְ: סא גַּ֤ם כָּל־חֳלִי֙ וְכָל־מַכָּ֔ה אֲשֶׁר֙ לֹ֣א כָת֔וּב בְּסֵ֖פֶר הַתּוֹרָ֣ה הַזֹּ֑את יַעְלֵ֤ם יְהֹוָה֙ עָלֶ֔יךָ עַ֖ד הִשָּֽׁמְדָֽךְ: סב וְנִשְׁאַרְתֶּם֙ בִּמְתֵ֣י מְעָ֔ט תַּ֚חַת אֲשֶׁ֣ר הֱיִיתֶ֔ם כְּכֽוֹכְבֵ֥י הַשָּׁמַ֖יִם לָרֹ֑ב כִּי־לֹ֣א שָׁמַ֔עְתָּ בְּק֖וֹל יְהֹוָ֥ה אֱלֹהֶֽיךָ: סג וְהָיָ֗ה כַּֽאֲשֶׁר־שָׂ֤שׂ יְהֹוָה֙ עֲלֵיכֶ֔ם לְהֵיטִ֥יב אֶתְכֶם֙

---

53. בְּשַׂ֤ר בָּנֶ֨יךָ֙ וּבְנֹתֶ֔יךָ אֲשֶׁ֥ר נָֽתַן־לְךָ֖ ה' אֱלֹהֶ֑יךָ — *The flesh of your sons and daughters which Hashem, your God, had given you.* You do not own your children, and you have no right to slaughter them and eat their flesh. They do not belong to you; "Hashem, your God, had given [them to] you."

54. הָאִישׁ . . . תֵּרַ֨ע עֵינ֤וֹ בְאָחִיו֙ — *The man. . . will turn selfish against his brother.* Why does the Torah not say (in v. 56) that women will also turn against their brothers? Because a woman's closeness to her brothers in any case diminishes at the time of her marriage, as we see from the verse "his virgin sister who is close to him, who has not been wed" (*Vayikra* 21:3). See also the commentaries of the *Abarbanel* and *Oznayim LaTorah* in *Vayikra*.

28
50-63

*[50] a brazen nation that will not be respectful to the old nor
gracious to the young. [51] It will devour the fruit of your
animals and the fruit of your ground, until you are destroyed
— it will not leave you grain, wine, or oil, offspring of your
cattle or flocks of your sheep and goats — until it causes you
to perish. [52] It will besiege you in all your cities, until the
collapse of your high and fortified walls in which you trusted
throughout your Land; it will besiege you in all your cities, in
all your Land, which HASHEM, your God, has given you.
[53] You will eat the fruit of your womb — the flesh of your sons
and daughters, which HASHEM, your God, had given you — in
the siege and distress that your enemy will distress you.
[54] The man among you who is tender and very delicate will
turn selfish against his brother and the wife of his bosom, and
against the remaining children that he has let survive, [55] not
to give even one of them of the flesh of his children that he
will eat, not leaving anything for him, in the siege and
distress that your enemy will distress you in all your cities.
[56] The tender and delicate woman among you, who had never
tried to set the sole of her foot on the ground, because of delic-
acy and tenderness, will turn selfish against the husband of
her bosom, and against her son and daughter, [57] against the
afterbirth that emerges from between her legs, and against
her children whom she will bear — for she will eat them in
secret for lack of anything, in the siege and distress that your
enemy will distress you in your cities. [58] If you will not be
careful to perform all the words of this Torah that are written
in this Book, to fear this honored and awesome Name:
HASHEM, your God, [59] then HASHEM will make extraordinary
your blows and the blows of your offspring — great and
faithful blows, and evil and faithful illnesses. [60] He will bring
back upon you all the sufferings of Egypt, of which you were
terrified, and they will cleave to you. [61] Even any illness and
any blow that is not written in this Book of the Torah,
HASHEM will bring upon you, until you are destroyed. [62] You
will be left few in number, instead of having been like the
stars of heaven in abundance, for you will not have
hearkened to the voice of HASHEM, your God. [63] And it will
be that just as HASHEM rejoiced over you to benefit you*

---

59. וְהִפְלָא ה׳ אֶת־מַכֹּתְךָ — *Hashem will make wondrous [extraordinary] your blows*. The blows will come in a wondrous way, as suggested in v. 46.

כח וּלְהַרְבּ֣וֹת אֶתְכֶ֔ם כֵּ֣ן יָשִׂ֤ישׂ יהוה֙ עֲלֵיכֶ֔ם לְהַאֲבִ֥יד אֶתְכֶ֖ם

סד-סט וּלְהַשְׁמִ֣יד אֶתְכֶ֑ם וְנִסַּחְתֶּם֙ מֵעַ֣ל הָ֣אֲדָמָ֔ה אֲשֶׁר־אַתָּ֥ה בָא־שָׁ֖מָּה לְרִשְׁתָּֽהּ: סד וֶהֱפִֽיצְךָ֤ יהוה֙ בְּכָל־הָ֣עַמִּ֔ים מִקְצֵ֥ה הָאָ֖רֶץ וְעַד־קְצֵ֣ה הָאָ֑רֶץ וְעָבַ֣דְתָּ שָּׁ֗ם אֱלֹהִ֤ים אֲחֵרִים֙ אֲשֶׁ֣ר לֹא־יָדַ֔עְתָּ אַתָּ֥ה וַאֲבֹתֶ֖יךָ עֵ֥ץ וָאָֽבֶן: סה וּבַגּוֹיִ֤ם הָהֵם֙ לֹ֣א תַרְגִּ֔יעַ וְלֹא־יִהְיֶ֥ה מָנ֖וֹחַ לְכַף־רַגְלֶ֑ךָ וְנָתַן֩ יהוה֨ לְךָ֥ שָׁם֙ לֵ֣ב רַגָּ֔ז וְכִלְי֥וֹן עֵינַ֖יִם וְדַֽאֲב֥וֹן נָֽפֶשׁ: סו וְהָי֣וּ חַיֶּ֗יךָ תְּלֻאִ֥ים לְךָ֙ מִנֶּ֔גֶד וּפָֽחַדְתָּ֙ לַ֣יְלָה וְיוֹמָ֔ם וְלֹ֥א תַֽאֲמִ֖ין בְּחַיֶּֽיךָ: סז בַּבֹּ֤קֶר תֹּאמַר֙ מִֽי־יִתֵּ֣ן עֶ֔רֶב וּבָעֶ֥רֶב תֹּאמַ֖ר מִֽי־יִתֵּ֣ן בֹּ֑קֶר מִפַּ֤חַד לְבָֽבְךָ֙ אֲשֶׁ֣ר תִּפְחָ֔ד וּמִמַּרְאֵ֥ה עֵינֶ֖יךָ אֲשֶׁ֥ר תִּרְאֶֽה: סח וֶהֱשִֽׁיבְךָ֨ יהוה֥ ׀ מִצְרַ֘יִם֮ בָּֽאֳנִיּוֹת֒ בַּדֶּ֙רֶךְ֙ אֲשֶׁ֣ר אָמַ֣רְתִּי לְךָ֔ לֹא־תֹסִ֥יף ע֖וֹד לִרְאֹתָ֑הּ וְהִתְמַכַּרְתֶּ֨ם שָׁ֧ם לְאֹיְבֶ֛יךָ לַֽעֲבָדִ֥ים וְלִשְׁפָח֖וֹת וְאֵ֥ין קֹנֶֽה: סט אֵ֣לֶּה דִבְרֵ֣י הַבְּרִ֗ית אֲשֶׁר־צִוָּ֤ה יהוה֙ אֶת־מֹשֶׁ֔ה לִכְרֹ֥ת אֶת־בְּנֵ֖י יִשְׂרָאֵ֑ל בְּאֶ֖רֶץ מוֹאָ֑ב מִלְּבַ֣ד הַבְּרִ֔ית אֲשֶׁר־כָּרַ֥ת אִתָּ֖ם בְּחֹרֵֽב:

כט

א שביעי וַיִּקְרָ֥א מֹשֶׁ֖ה אֶל־כָּל־יִשְׂרָאֵ֑ל וַיֹּ֣אמֶר אֲלֵהֶ֔ם אַתֶּ֣ם

---

68. וֶהֱשִֽׁיבְךָ ה׳ מִצְרַיִם בָּאֳנִיּוֹת — *Hashem will return you to Egypt in ships*. Egypt was famous for its slave market. You will be brought there by boat to keep you in good enough shape to attract potential buyers. However, God will also "bring back upon you all the sufferings of Egypt, of which you were terrified, and they will cleave to you" (v. 60). The Egyptians, who have tasted the bitterness of those afflictions, will surely be afraid of contamination. Therefore no one will want to buy you, and you will be left alone. But since you will have no means of support, you "will offer yourselves for sale." You will actually try to sell yourselves, but there will be no buyers.

Perhaps the Torah emphasizes that you will go "in ships" so that you will be like the sea travelers described in *Tehillim* (107:23-24), who "see the deeds of Hashem and His wonders in the watery deep," and are inspired to repent. (This is why the word וֶהֱשִֽׁיבְךָ, which means both 'return' and 'move to repentance', is used). *Chazal* tell us that most sailors are pious (*Kiddushin* 82a). *Rashi* explains that since seafarers are constantly exposed to danger, they are always full of trepidation.

◆ בָּאֳנִיּוֹת בַּדֶּרֶךְ אֲשֶׁר אָמַרְתִּי לְךָ לֹא־תֹסִיף עוֹד לִרְאֹתָהּ — *In ships, on the road of which I said to you, "You shall never again see it."* Some commentators explain that the prohibition of returning to Egypt applies only to a return by the same way that we took to leave it (this might be derived from the words "on the road of which I said to you, 'You shall never again see it'"). But this is difficult to understand. If the Jews left Egypt by way of the Red

28 *and multiply you, so* HASHEM *will cause them to rejoice over*
64-69 *you to make you perish and to destroy you; and you will be*
torn from upon the ground to which you come to possess it.
64 HASHEM *will scatter you among all the peoples, from the end*
of the earth to the end of the earth, and there you will work for
gods of others, whom you did not know — you or your
forefathers — of wood and of stone. 65 *And among those*
nations you will not be tranquil, there will be no rest for the sole
of your foot; there HASHEM *will give you a trembling heart,*
longing of eyes, and suffering of soul. 66 *Your life will hang in*
the balance, and you will be frightened night and day, and you
will not be sure of your livelihood. 67 *In the morning you will*
say, "Who can give back last night!" And in the evening you
will say, "Who can give back this morning!" — for the fright
of your heart that you will fear and the sight of your eyes that
you will see. 68 HASHEM *will return you to Egypt in ships, on the*
road of which I said to you, "You shall never again see it!"
And there you will offer yourselves for sale to your enemies
as slaves and maidservants — but there will be no buyer!
69 *These are the words of the covenant that* HASHEM *com-*
manded Moses to seal with the Children of Israel in the land
of Moab, beside the covenant that He sealed with them in
29 *Horeb.*
1 1 *Moses summoned all of Israel and said to them, "You have*

Sea, which split open for them, how could anyone possibly return the same way?

Perhaps this is why the verse specifies "in ships": that particular leg of the journey will be made by boat. This would then be the Divine way of pointing out to them that when the Jewish people accepted God's sovereignty, He liberated them from Egypt and split the Red Sea for them. Now that they have rebelled against Him, they are being exiled to Egypt once again, and this time by ship.

But if they should decide to be Pharaoh's servants, and thereby cease being God's servants, the Torah warns them, "there will be no buyer!" This is similar to the idea expressed in the prophet *Yechezkel* (20:32-33): "The thought you entertain ... 'Let us be like the nations, like the families of the world' ... 'As I live,' says Hashem, 'but with a strong hand ... I will rule over you.'"

29.

1. **וַיִּקְרָא מֹשֶׁה אֶל־כָּל־יִשְׂרָאֵל** — *Moses summoned all of Israel*. We have already explained that because the Jews "turned green" when they heard the curses, there were those who slipped away, one by one, to avoid hearing them. This is why Moses summoned them back and spoke words of appeasement.

כט רְאִיתֶם אֵת כָּל־אֲשֶׁר עָשָׂה יהוה לְעֵינֵיכֶם בְּאֶרֶץ מִצְרַיִם
ב־ח לְפַרְעֹה וּלְכָל־עֲבָדָיו וּלְכָל־אַרְצוֹ: ב הַמַּסּוֹת הַגְּדֹלֹת
אֲשֶׁר רָאוּ עֵינֶיךָ הָאֹתֹת וְהַמֹּפְתִים הַגְּדֹלִים הָהֵם:
ג וְלֹא־נָתַן יהוה לָכֶם לֵב לָדַעַת וְעֵינַיִם לִרְאוֹת וְאָזְנַיִם
לִשְׁמֹעַ עַד הַיּוֹם הַזֶּה: ד וָאוֹלֵךְ אֶתְכֶם אַרְבָּעִים שָׁנָה
בַּמִּדְבָּר לֹא־בָלוּ שַׂלְמֹתֵיכֶם מֵעֲלֵיכֶם וְנַעַלְךָ לֹא־בָלְתָה
מֵעַל רַגְלֶךָ: ה לֶחֶם לֹא אֲכַלְתֶּם וְיַיִן וְשֵׁכָר לֹא שְׁתִיתֶם
לְמַעַן תֵּדְעוּ כִּי אֲנִי יהוה אֱלֹהֵיכֶם: מפטיר ו וַתָּבֹאוּ
אֶל־הַמָּקוֹם הַזֶּה וַיֵּצֵא סִיחֹן מֶלֶךְ־חֶשְׁבּוֹן וְעוֹג מֶלֶךְ־
הַבָּשָׁן לִקְרָאתֵנוּ לַמִּלְחָמָה וַנַּכֵּם: ז וַנִּקַּח אֶת־אַרְצָם
וַנִּתְּנָהּ לְנַחֲלָה לָרְאוּבֵנִי וְלַגָּדִי וְלַחֲצִי שֵׁבֶט הַמְנַשִּׁי:
ח וּשְׁמַרְתֶּם אֶת־דִּבְרֵי הַבְּרִית הַזֹּאת וַעֲשִׂיתֶם אֹתָם לְמַעַן
תַּשְׂכִּילוּ אֵת כָּל־אֲשֶׁר תַּעֲשׂוּן:

---

2. הַמַּסּוֹת הַגְּדֹלֹת אֲשֶׁר רָאוּ עֵינֶיךָ הָאֹתֹת וְהַמֹּפְתִים הַגְּדֹלִים הָהֵם — *The great trials that your eyes beheld, those great signs and wonders*. The Jews must surely have wondered why Moses was cursing them on his last day on earth. Usually before someone dies, he blesses his children and disciples (as Moses indeed did before he died).

Moses wanted the Jews to understand his terrible fear lest they stray from the proper path. Perhaps all the wonders God had performed for them in Egypt, His judgment against the Egyptians, and the miracles He did openly before their eyes, still were not sufficient for them to remain true to Him. Had they been wise enough to understand God's greatness and His kindness towards them, these things would have sufficed, and they would not have needed the rebuke and the curses. However —

3. וְלֹא־נָתַן ה׳ לָכֶם לֵב לָדַעַת — *But Hashem did not give you a heart [with which] to know*. And this was only because you did not ask God to grant it to you when He said, "that their heart should remain theirs, to fear Me and observe all My commandments" (*Devarim* 5:26). Had you asked, God would have helped you, as He helps all who make the effort to purify themselves. The result of your refusal to ask for help was that you sinned and disobeyed God with the sins of the Golden Calf and the Spies.

☙ וְאָזְנַיִם לִשְׁמֹעַ — *Ears to hear*. At the time of the Giving of the Torah, the Jews were elevated to the level of angels. "The entire nation saw the thunder... and the sound of the *shofar*" (*Shemos* 20:15). *Rashi* explains (based on the *Mechilta*) that "they saw what is normally heard, which is impossible in any

seen everything that HASHEM *did before your eyes in the land*
of Egypt, to Pharaoh and to all his servants and to all his land
— 2 *the great trials that your eyes beheld, those great signs and*
wonders. 3 *But* HASHEM *did not give you a heart to know, or*
eyes to see, or ears to hear until this day. 4 *I led you for forty*
years in the Wilderness, your garment did not wear out from
on you, and your shoe did not wear out from on your foot.
5 *Bread you did not eat and wine or intoxicant you did not*
drink, so that you would know that I am HASHEM*, your God.*
6 *Then you arrived at this place, and Sihon, king of Heshbon,*
and Og, king of Bashan, went out toward us to battle, and we
smote them. 7 *We took their land and gave it as an inheritance*
to the Reubenite, the Gadite, and to half the tribe of the
Manassite. 8 *You shall observe the words of this covenant, so*
that you will succeed in all that you do."

---

other place." They *saw* then what we can only perceive through hearing: the upper realms of spirituality.

This now makes clear what Moses is telling them: had you asked of God at Mount Sinai that your hearts should always entertain the fear of Him, as they did at the Giving of the Torah, you would have "eyes to see" even those realms, which normally can only be heard. And even if your prayers had been only halfway accepted, you would at least have reached the level of having "ears to hear," to keep and fulfill God's commandments. But even this much you have lacked "until this day." Therefore you must bend an "ear that hears the rebuke [that brings] life," for "one who hears rebuke acquires [an understanding] heart" (*Mishlei* 15:31-32).

4. וָאוֹלֵךְ אֶתְכֶם אַרְבָּעִים שָׁנָה בַּמִּדְבָּר — *I led you for forty years in the Wilderness.* Until that entire generation [of the Exodus] died out. The second generation also saw miracles in the desert: "your garment did not wear out . . . and your shoe did not wear out. . ."

7. וַנִּקַּח אֶת־אַרְצָם וַנִּתְּנָהּ לְנַחֲלָה לָראוּבֵנִי — *We took their land and gave it as an inheritance to the Reubenite.* The promise that was given to the Jewish people, to give them "an inheritance of field and vineyard," was now approaching fulfillment: they were about to cross the Jordan River to take possession of the entire Promised Land. It follows, then, that the time had come for them to have a "heart [with which] to know, eyes to see, and ears to hear." It also follows that there was every hope that the covenant (with oath and vow) which they contracted this day would endure.

פרשת נצבים
Parashas Nitzavim

כט ט אַתֶּם נִצָּבִים הַיּוֹם כֻּלְּכֶם לִפְנֵי יהוה אֱלֹהֵיכֶם רָאשֵׁיכֶם
ט־יב שִׁבְטֵיכֶם זִקְנֵיכֶם וְשֹׁטְרֵיכֶם כֹּל אִישׁ יִשְׂרָאֵל: י טַפְּכֶם
נְשֵׁיכֶם וְגֵרְךָ אֲשֶׁר בְּקֶרֶב מַחֲנֶיךָ מֵחֹטֵב עֵצֶיךָ עַד שֹׁאֵב
מֵימֶיךָ: יא לְעָבְרְךָ בִּבְרִית יהוה אֱלֹהֶיךָ וּבְאָלָתוֹ אֲשֶׁר יהוה
אֱלֹהֶיךָ כֹּרֵת עִמְּךָ הַיּוֹם: שני יב לְמַעַן הָקִים־אֹתְךָ הַיּוֹם לוֹ
לְעָם וְהוּא יִהְיֶה־לְּךָ לֵאלֹהִים כַּאֲשֶׁר דִּבֶּר־לָךְ וְכַאֲשֶׁר

9-10. רָאשֵׁיכֶם שִׁבְטֵיכֶם זִקְנֵיכֶם וְשֹׁטְרֵיכֶם כֹּל אִישׁ יִשְׂרָאֵל . . . וְגֵרְךָ — *The heads of your tribes, your elders, and your officers — all the men of Israel . . . and your proselyte*. It would have sufficed to say "all the men of Israel and your proselyte are standing before Hashem." We find similar expressions in many places. Why was all this detailed enumeration necessary here?

We may say that when a simple person vows to accept all his obligations as a Jew, that is not the same thing as what the head of a tribe, an elder, or an officer must accept upon himself. The latter take on not only the obligations of a private individual, but also the additional responsibilities inherent in the loyal, honest, and dedicated fulfillment of their public roles. We find this concept in the *Zichronos* of the *Rosh Hashanah* prayers, when we consider: "A person's enterprise and [the discharge of] his office, and the consequences of man's footsteps." A person standing in prayer on *Rosh Hashanah* may have enough merits to be acquitted from "the consequences of man's footsteps." But if he holds a public position — as a Rabbi, for example — "his office" requires him to account for the deeds of those under his jurisdiction. Was he a good influence on them?

(This is similar to the exposition of *Chazal* on the verse "I shall appoint them as your heads" (*Devarim* 1:13): that the heads of the community are responsible for the people's guilt. We can likewise explain the words "when a leader sins" (*Vayikra* 4:22). What is his sin? At times it is not his own sin but the sin of the people. He is responsible for their wrongdoing.)

The same is true of an earthly kingdom. When a king is crowned, all his subjects swear allegiance to their new ruler. Then, when the king appoints one of his subjects to a specific position, this man must swear again to fulfill his task faithfully. When Moses had the Jewish people swear before his death to keep the Torah, he enumerated all their different ranks, calling on each one to swear to fulfill his *specific* obligation, each according to his rank and the task assigned him.

10. טַפְּכֶם נְשֵׁיכֶם — *Your small children, your women*. In the present verse children are mentioned before women, while when describing the commandment of *Hakhel* (*Devarim* 31:12) the order is reversed.

We may explain this difference by considering the different contexts. This verse concerns the establishment of the covenant to keep the commandments, and therefore it mentions first those who are obligated to keep all the command-

29 [9] *You are standing today, all of you, before HASHEM, your*
9-12 *God: the heads of your tribes, your elders, and your officers*
— all the men of Israel; [10] your small children, your women,
and your proselyte who is in the midst of your camp, from
the hewer of your wood to the drawer of your water, [11] for
you to pass into the covenant of HASHEM, your God, and into
His imprecation that HASHEM, your God, seals with you
today, [12] in order to establish you today as a people to Him
and that He be a God to you, as He spoke to you and as He

---

ments in the Torah. Women are not obligated to keep positive commandments whose fulfillment is tied to specific times. The male children, on the other hand, will be obligated to keep the Torah in its entirety — including time-specific commandments — when they grow up. And since the covenant was made to last for all time, including even souls as yet unborn, therefore the children, who would in the future be more fully obligated than women, are mentioned first.

The commandment of *Hakhel*, on the other hand, involves gathering together to hear words of Torah. The women hear and understand, and fulfill what applies to them. The children, though, do not understand what is being read. Their parents only bring them along to be rewarded for doing so. This is why women are listed before children regarding *Hakhel*.

§ בְּקֶרֶב מַחֲנֶיךָ — *In the midst of your camp*. We can understand this as praise for the converts who chose to join the Jewish people during their wanderings in the desert. The words "in the midst of your camp" highlight their stature: they suffered along with us in the desert camps. This is why they are mentioned before the wood-choppers and water-carriers who converted out of fear. Those who have the greatest stature are mentioned first.

§ מֵחֹטֵב עֵצֶיךָ עַד שֹׁאֵב מֵימֶיךָ — *From the hewer of your wood to the drawer of your water*. The Torah always mentions the wood-choppers before the water-carriers. This is because no particular skill is required to draw water. But to chop wood, and exercise the necessary caution to avoid harming others or oneself in the process, does require skill and experience.

12. לְמַעַן הָקִים־אֹתְךָ הַיּוֹם לוֹ לְעָם וְהוּא יִהְיֶה־לְּךָ לֵאלֹהִים — *In order to establish you today as a people to Him and that He be a God to you*. God always first provides us with our material needs, which we then utilize for our "sacrifices" to fulfill His commandments. He gives us a *tallis*, and we put *tzitzis* on it; He gives us a house and we put a parapet on its roof and a *mezuzah* on the doorpost; He gives us a son and we circumcise him. But in spiritual matters the order is reversed. We must make the first move, because "everything is in the hands of Heaven except for the fear of Heaven." This is why the Torah says here first "in order to establish you ... as a people to Him," and then "He will be a God for you."

כט נִשְׁבַּע לַאֲבֹתֶיךָ לְאַבְרָהָם לְיִצְחָק וּלְיַעֲקֹב: יג וְלֹא אִתְּכֶם
יג־יז לְבַדְּכֶם אָנֹכִי כֹּרֵת אֶת־הַבְּרִית הַזֹּאת וְאֶת־הָאָלָה הַזֹּאת:
יד כִּי אֶת־אֲשֶׁר יֶשְׁנוֹ פֹּה עִמָּנוּ עֹמֵד הַיּוֹם לִפְנֵי יְהוָה
אֱלֹהֵינוּ וְאֵת אֲשֶׁר אֵינֶנּוּ פֹּה עִמָּנוּ הַיּוֹם: שלישי טו כִּי־
אַתֶּם יְדַעְתֶּם אֵת אֲשֶׁר־יָשַׁבְנוּ בְּאֶרֶץ מִצְרָיִם וְאֵת אֲשֶׁר־
עָבַרְנוּ בְּקֶרֶב הַגּוֹיִם אֲשֶׁר עֲבַרְתֶּם: טז וַתִּרְאוּ אֶת־
שִׁקּוּצֵיהֶם וְאֵת גִּלֻּלֵיהֶם עֵץ וָאֶבֶן כֶּסֶף וְזָהָב אֲשֶׁר עִמָּהֶם:
יז פֶּן־יֵשׁ בָּכֶם אִישׁ אוֹ־אִשָּׁה אוֹ מִשְׁפָּחָה אוֹ־שֵׁבֶט

---

14. וְאֵת אֲשֶׁר אֵינֶנּוּ פֹּה עִמָּנוּ הַיּוֹם — *With whoever is not here with us today*. We learn from these words that all the souls which would be born in future generations also participated in this covenant (*Rashi*). This is why the word "*standing* with us today" is not used regarding them.

The *Abarbanel* raises a difficulty: what worth does a vow have when made by disembodied souls? "The dead are free of obligation to fulfill commandments" (*Shabbos* 30a). The only valid vow is one made by a living person comprised of both body and soul. (See the *Abarbanel*'s commentary.)

In answer, it would seem that a vow is something related to the soul, for we see in *Parashas Mattos* that a person can "swear an oath to establish a prohibition upon his soul [עַל נַפְשׁוֹ]" (*Bamidbar* 30:3). We also find in *Daniel* (12:7) that the "man dressed in linen" swore by "the Life of the worlds"; thus angels, who have no body, can swear. Similarly, the souls of all future generations, who were present at the contracting of this covenant, could take an oath to fulfill it when they came to reside on earth.

15. כִּי־אַתֶּם יְדַעְתֶּם אֵת אֲשֶׁר־יָשַׁבְנוּ בְּאֶרֶץ מִצְרָיִם וְאֵת אֲשֶׁר־עָבַרְנוּ בְּקֶרֶב הַגּוֹיִם — *For you know how we dwelled in the land of Egypt and how we passed through the midst of the nations*. Some people have a slower grasp, and will only assimilate the norms of a new country after an extended stay. Others pick things up quickly: as soon as they pass through and see new customs they become excited, and what they see will make a lasting impression. (We find this with Amatziah, who fought with Edom, and then brought home an Edomite idol and worshiped it [*II Divrei Hayamim*, ch. 25).

Moses pointed out to the Jews that now both concerns were present. They had lived in Egypt, among idol worshipers, for many years. They had also passed through the lands of many nations and seen their "new" forms of idol worship, which they may have found attractive. Therefore the danger was great, and Moses had to warn them and administer an oath to them.

☙ וְאֵת אֲשֶׁר־עָבַרְנוּ בְּקֶרֶב הַגּוֹיִם אֲשֶׁר עֲבַרְתֶּם — *And how we passed through the midst of the nations through whom you passed*. The phrasing of this verse appears to be redundant. Also, while the verse begins in first person plural ("we passed") it changes to second person plural ("you passed").

29
13-17

swore to your forefathers, to Abraham, to Isaac, and to Jacob.
13 Not with you alone do I seal this covenant and this
imprecation, 14 but with whoever is here, standing with us
today before HASHEM, *our God, and with whoever is not*
here with us today.
15 For you know how we dwelled in the land of Egypt
and how we passed through the midst of the nations
through whom you passed. 16 And you saw their abomi-
nations and their detestable idols — of wood and stone,
of silver and gold that were with them. 17 Perhaps there
is among you a man or woman, or a family or tribe,

The choice of words seems to emphasize that while there was room for concern that someone might have been attracted to the idol worship of the nations through whom "we passed," it is an even more serious concern that such a person may have absorbed harmful ideas in the places through which "*you* (the people) passed" [alone], unaccompanied by Moses and the Holy Ark, which did not leave the camp.

When some of the people said "let us choose a leader (an idol) and return to Egypt," and when Aaron died and they traveled five encampments back, they were alone. It was only after a difficult battle that the Levites brought them back. Also, when the nation went astray in Shittim and adopted the worship of Baal-peor (an idol), they left the camp and were free of the fear of their teacher (Moses), which was like the fear of God. Under such circumstances, they were capable of absorbing "a root flourishing with gall and wormwood."

17. איש או־אִשָּׁה — *A man or woman*. The Torah always speaks in the masculine gender. Yet we find that when discussing idol worship, in several places the Torah specifically mentions women. Perhaps this is because women had a special leaning towards idol worship, as we find in *Yirmiyah* (44:17-19): the women sacrificed to the work of the heavens and would not hear of giving it up.

We can also say that of the people who had lived in Egypt, "not one of them was left." (The only exceptions were those aged under twenty or over eighty [*Bava Basra* 121b].) But the women were not included in the decree of punishment for the Sin of the Spies (*Bamidbar* 26:64). There were many women who had lived in Egypt still present at the time of the covenant, and they needed a special warning.

☙ We know that the Torah does not obligate us to force others to accept our holy faith, or even to try to persuade them to do so. When Abraham "called out in the name of God," and Isaac and Jacob did the same, and they all always maintained a "yeshivah," it was only so as to teach wandering souls to recognize God and accept the seven Noahide commandments, without which a person is worse than a beast of prey. But God forbid that we get involved in what the

כט אֲשֶׁר לְבָבוֹ פֹנֶה הַיּוֹם מֵעִם יהוה אֱלֹהֵינוּ לָלֶכֶת לַעֲבֹד
יח־כ אֶת־אֱלֹהֵי הַגּוֹיִם הָהֵם פֶּן־יֵשׁ בָּכֶם שֹׁרֶשׁ פֹּרֶה רֹאשׁ
וְלַעֲנָה: יח וְהָיָה בְּשָׁמְעוֹ אֶת־דִּבְרֵי הָאָלָה הַזֹּאת וְהִתְבָּרֵךְ
בִּלְבָבוֹ לֵאמֹר שָׁלוֹם יִהְיֶה־לִּי כִּי בִּשְׁרִרוּת לִבִּי אֵלֵךְ לְמַעַן
סְפוֹת הָרָוָה אֶת־הַצְּמֵאָה: יט לֹא־יֹאבֶה יהוה סְלֹחַ לוֹ
כִּי אָז יֶעְשַׁן אַף־יהוה וְקִנְאָתוֹ בָּאִישׁ הַהוּא וְרָבְצָה בּוֹ
כָּל־הָאָלָה הַכְּתוּבָה בַּסֵּפֶר הַזֶּה וּמָחָה יהוה אֶת־שְׁמוֹ
מִתַּחַת הַשָּׁמָיִם: כ וְהִבְדִּילוֹ יהוה לְרָעָה מִכֹּל שִׁבְטֵי
יִשְׂרָאֵל כְּכֹל אָלוֹת הַבְּרִית הַכְּתוּבָה בְּסֵפֶר הַתּוֹרָה הַזֶּה:

---

gentiles call 'missionary work': the entrapping of souls through coercion or persuasion.

Yet at the same time, we may not give up on even one man or woman who is Jewish either by birth or through willing conversion, who was tempted into evil ways by the Adversary and his emissaries and now worships idols. We are obligated to bring him back to the Jewish faith, even by force if necessary, and needless to say through rebuke. We see the great pains Moses took to bring back even the single individual "whose heart turns away today from being with Hashem, our God, to go and serve the gods of those nations."

This is a clear and open rebuke to those who could protest, and save lost Jewish brothers, young and old, from the claws of the missionaries, and yet do nothing. This plague has grown rampant in recent generations, yet no one lifts a finger to stop it. May God in His mercy open the eyes of the blind to see that there is none other than Him.

אֲשֶׁר לְבָבוֹ פֹנֶה הַיּוֹם מֵעִם ה׳ אֱלֹהֵינוּ לָלֶכֶת לַעֲבֹד אֶת־אֱלֹהֵי הַגּוֹיִם הָהֵם — *Whose heart turns away today from being with Hashem, our God, to go and serve the gods of those nations*. The sin of idol worship is unique in that one is punished not only for an actual deed, but even for intent, as the Torah tells us: "to seize the Jewish people by their hearts" (*Yechezkel* 14:5). The reason is that a person who has considered idolatry will ultimately worship idols actively. For this is the way the evil inclination operates: today he tells one, 'do this', and tomorrow he tells him, 'do that', until he tells him, 'go worship idols', and he goes and worships them (*Shabbos* 105b). This man, "whose heart turns away *today*" is the one who will eventually "go and serve the gods of those nations." He is the first candidate to be enticed by the evil inclination "tomorrow" to go worship idols, as indeed he will. This is why Moses warned this type of person in particular to be careful of what he does.

שֹׁרֶשׁ פֹּרֶה רֹאשׁ וְלַעֲנָה — *A root flourishing with gall and wormwood*. This verse is talking about a person who at the moment is not considering idol worship, but who, however, does not believe in God and His Providence. The verse explains: what is "the root flourishing with gall and wormwood"? It is that

whose heart turns away today from being with HASHEM, our
God, to go and serve the gods of those nations; perhaps there
is among you a root flourishing with gall and wormwood.
18 *And it will be that when he hears the words of this*
imprecation, he will bless himself in his heart, saying, "Peace
will be with me, though I walk as my heart sees fit" —
thereby adding the watered upon the thirsty.
19 *HASHEM will not be willing to forgive him, for then*
HASHEM's anger and jealousy will smoke against that man,
and the entire imprecation written in this Book will come
down upon him, and HASHEM will erase his name from under
heaven. 20 *HASHEM will set him aside for evil from among all*
the tribes of Israel, like all the imprecations of the covenant
that is written in this Book of the Torah.

"he will bless himself in his heart, saying, 'peace will be with me when I walk as my heart sees fit'" — and he has no fear of God. Even if he does not believe in idols and does not worship them, if he does not believe in God and his Providence, "Hashem will not be willing to forgive him."

19. **יֶעְשַׁן אַף־ה'** — *Hashem's anger... will smoke*. This refers to one who has no faith at all. It is God's *jealousy* that will be directed against one who goes to worship other gods: "They would provoke His jealousy with strangers" (*Devarim* 32:16). We find a similar concept in the prophet *Yechezkel* (8:3): "the image of jealousy."

וְרָבְצָה בּוֹ כָּל־הָאָלָה הַכְּתוּבָה בַּסֵּפֶר הַזֶּה — *And the entire imprecation written in this Book will come down upon him.* This passage started with "when he hears the words of this [oral] imprecation"; why does it then go on to mention "the imprecation written in this Book"? If this man of small faith says "peace will be with me" when he hears a curse pronounced orally, how will writing it down impress him?

Perhaps we can look into the precise wording of this passage and find a different intent from the apparent one. The unbeliever blesses himself when he hears "the words of this imprecation," one which was only delivered orally and is not written in the Torah at all. According to a book I saw, quoting a Midrash, this curse was that the *tzaddikim* of the generation would die. In that case, the man "whose heart turns away from being with God" will not be bothered at all by such a curse. For him it only means that now he will be able to "walk as his heart sees fit," and "peace will be with him," since there will be none left to rebuke him and protest his waywardness.

That is why the Torah warns, "God will not be willing to forgive him" — He will not let this man have any opportunity to repent, and why? Because, as *Chazal* tell us, "Anyone who denigrates *talmidei chachamim*" by being pleased at the prospect of their death "has a wound beyond the power of healing"

כא וְאָמַ֞ר הַדּ֣וֹר הָאַחֲר֗וֹן בְּנֵיכֶם֙ אֲשֶׁ֤ר יָק֙וּמוּ֙ מֵאַחֲרֵיכֶ֔ם
וְהַ֨נָּכְרִ֔י אֲשֶׁ֥ר יָבֹ֖א מֵאֶ֣רֶץ רְחוֹקָ֑ה וְ֠רָאוּ אֶת־מַכּ֞וֹת הָאָ֤רֶץ
הַהִוא֙ וְאֶת־תַּ֣חֲלֻאֶ֔יהָ אֲשֶׁר־חִלָּ֥ה יְהוָ֖ה בָּֽהּ׃ כב גָּפְרִ֣ית
וָמֶלַח֮ שְׂרֵפָ֣ה כָל־אַרְצָהּ֒ לֹ֤א תִזָּרַע֙ וְלֹ֣א תַצְמִ֔חַ וְלֹא־יַעֲלֶ֥ה
°וּצְבוֹיִם ק׳ בָ֖הּ כָּל־עֵ֑שֶׂב כְּֽמַהְפֵּכַ֞ת סְדֹ֤ם וַעֲמֹרָה֙ אַדְמָ֣ה °וצביים אֲשֶׁר֙
הָפַ֣ךְ יְהוָ֔ה בְּאַפּ֖וֹ וּבַחֲמָתֽוֹ׃ כג וְאָֽמְרוּ֙ כָּל־הַגּוֹיִ֔ם עַל־מֶ֨ה
עָשָׂ֧ה יְהוָ֛ה כָּ֖כָה לָאָ֣רֶץ הַזֹּ֑את מֶ֥ה חֳרִ֛י הָאַ֥ף הַגָּד֖וֹל הַזֶּֽה׃
כד וְאָ֣מְר֔וּ עַ֚ל אֲשֶׁ֣ר עָֽזְב֔וּ אֶת־בְּרִ֥ית יְהוָ֖ה אֱלֹהֵ֣י אֲבֹתָ֑ם
אֲשֶׁר֙ כָּרַ֣ת עִמָּ֔ם בְּהוֹצִיא֥וֹ אֹתָ֖ם מֵאֶ֥רֶץ מִצְרָֽיִם׃ כה וַיֵּֽלְכ֗וּ
וַיַּֽעַבְדוּ֙ אֱלֹהִ֣ים אֲחֵרִ֔ים וַיִּֽשְׁתַּחֲו֖וּ לָהֶ֑ם אֱלֹהִים֙ אֲשֶׁ֣ר
לֹא־יְדָע֔וּם וְלֹ֥א חָלַ֖ק לָהֶֽם׃ כו וַיִּֽחַר־אַ֥ף יְהוָ֖ה בָּאָ֣רֶץ הַהִ֑וא

(*Shabbos* 119b). His spiritual wound cannot be healed, because there is no one who can teach him the ways of repentance.

Furthermore, if the unwritten curse, the death of the righteous, does not impress this man, he must reflect that "the entire imprecation *written in this Book* will come down upon him."

21. בְּנֵיכֶם אֲשֶׁר יָקוּמוּ מֵאַחֲרֵיכֶם — *Your children who will arise after you*. These children will have as much of an idea about the land of their fathers and its present "illnesses" as "the foreigners who will come from a distant land." They will be the "last generation" of the exile, because by then most of the Jewish people will be on the verge of assimilation. They will be submerged in the forty-nine levels of impurity, like our ancestors in Egypt. And then God will redeem them, in order to fulfill His promise: "For I am Hashem, I have not changed, and you, the children of Jacob, have not died out" (*Malachi* 3:6).

☙ אֶת־מַכּוֹת הָאָרֶץ הַהִוא — *The plagues of that Land*. The blows delivered to the Jewish people will not arouse that much surprise, for they could be attributed to coincidence. After all, people are like the grass in the field: some blossom and others wilt (*Eruvin* 54a). The same is true of nations: one rises, the other falls. But that a land famous for its lushness and fertility ("flowing with milk and honey") should be overturned like Sodom and Gomorrah, "sulphur and salt, a conflagration of the entire Land" — this will arouse great wonder.

22. שְׂרֵפָה כָל־אַרְצָהּ — *A conflagration of the entire Land*. This refers not only to the capital city, residence of the officers and deputies who were the first to sin. It includes the entire Land, whose inhabitants followed these officers blindly, like a beast in the valley. This is what happened in Sodom and Gomorrah, capitals of the Jordan plain: "The outcry of Sodom and Gomorrah is great, and their sin is very heavy" (*Bereishis* 18:20). Even though they were only provincial cities who followed the lead of Sodom and Gomorrah, Admah and Zeboiim were destroyed along with them.

29
21-26

21 *The later generation will say — your children who will*
arise after you and the foreigner who will come from a distant
land — when they will see the plagues of that Land and its
illnesses with which HASHEM *has afflicted it:* 22 *"Sulphur and*
salt, a conflagration of the entire Land, it cannot be sown and
it cannot sprout, and no grass shall rise up on it; like the
upheaval of Sodom and Gomorrah, Admah and Zeboiim,
which HASHEM *overturned in His anger and wrath."* 23 *And*
all the nations will say, "For what reason did HASHEM *do so to*
this Land; why this wrathfulness of great anger?"
24 *And they will say, "Because they forsook the covenant of*
HASHEM, *the God of their forefathers, that He sealed with*
them when He took them out of the land of Egypt; 25 *and*
they went and served the gods of others and prostrated them-
selves to them — gods that they knew not and He did not
apportion to them. 26 *So God's anger flared against that land,*

---

23. **וְאָמְרוּ כָּל־הַגּוֹיִם** — *And all the nations will say*. This question will be raised by "your children," and by the "foreigner who will come from a distant land." Those who are nearby will have gradually become accustomed to the plagues of the land, while "a guest who visits for just a moment sees every fault." But afterwards, why it is that the land of Israel is so unusually desolate will become a question asked by all the nations.

§ The idea seems to be that "the foreigner who will come from a distant land" is the leader of those nations which do not believe in God. Together with our children, many of whom were raised under the influence of their doctrines, they will not mention God's name in their wonder over the destruction of the land. ("With which Hashem has afflicted it" and "which Hashem overturned" are the Torah's expression, not that of the nations.)

But "all the nations" mentioned in this verse do believe in God and His Providence (this is why they are not called "foreigner," since they have not become foreign to God and His ways). They therefore mention God's name in their questions and expressions of wonder: "For what reason did Hashem do so to this Land; why this wrathfulness of great anger?" This is why God illuminated their eyes, allowing them to see the correct answer: "Because they forsook the covenant of Hashem, the God of their forefathers."

25. **וַיַּעַבְדוּ אֱלֹהִים אֲחֵרִים** — *And served other gods*. Such an answer is not fitting, coming from the mouths of "all the nations" who worship idols along with God. Therefore the Torah has them adding that these were "gods that they knew not and He did not apportion to them." In other words, "It is all right for us to worship these gods, for God" (so they imagine) "has apportioned to us the worship of this star or another and to receive our blessing through the heavenly spheres. But He never apportioned such worship to the

כט לְהָבִיא עָלֶיהָ אֶת־כָּל־הַקְּלָלָה הַכְּתוּבָה בַּסֵּפֶר הַזֶּה:
כז־כח כז וַיִּתְּשֵׁם יהוה מֵעַל אַדְמָתָם בְּאַף וּבְחֵמָה וּבְקֶצֶף גָּדוֹל
וַיַּשְׁלִכֵם אֶל־אֶרֶץ אַחֶרֶת כַּיּוֹם הַזֶּה: כח הַנִּסְתָּרֹת לַיהוָה
אֱלֹהֵינוּ וְהַנִּגְלֹת לָנוּ וּלְבָנֵינוּ עַד־עוֹלָם לַעֲשׂוֹת אֶת־כָּל־
ל דִּבְרֵי הַתּוֹרָה הַזֹּאת: רביעי שני כשהן מחוברין א וְהָיָה
א־ג כִּי־יָבֹאוּ עָלֶיךָ כָּל־הַדְּבָרִים הָאֵלֶּה הַבְּרָכָה וְהַקְּלָלָה אֲשֶׁר
נָתַתִּי לְפָנֶיךָ וַהֲשֵׁבֹתָ אֶל־לְבָבֶךָ בְּכָל־הַגּוֹיִם אֲשֶׁר הִדִּיחֲךָ
יהוה אֱלֹהֶיךָ שָׁמָּה: ב וְשַׁבְתָּ עַד־יהוה אֱלֹהֶיךָ וְשָׁמַעְתָּ
בְקֹלוֹ כְּכֹל אֲשֶׁר־אָנֹכִי מְצַוְּךָ הַיּוֹם אַתָּה וּבָנֶיךָ בְּכָל־לְבָבְךָ
וּבְכָל־נַפְשֶׁךָ: ג וְשָׁב יהוה אֱלֹהֶיךָ אֶת־שְׁבוּתְךָ וְרִחֲמֶךָ

Jews! He made a covenant with them that they would worship Him alone, and *that* is why they have been punished for idol worship."

27. וַיִּתְּשֵׁם ה' מֵעַל אַדְמָתָם — *And Hashem removed them from upon their soil.* This is not like the destruction of Sodom, which was overturned together with all its inhabitants. The Holy Land was punished by itself, and then the Jewish people were punished by themselves, enabling the people to survive.

וַיַּשְׁלִכֵם אֶל־אֶרֶץ אַחֶרֶת — *And He cast them to another land*. You may ask what good this exile will do. After all, when the Jews live among the nations, they also worship other gods which "He did not apportion to them." However, the punishment for idol worship committed in other lands is not as great, for the Holy Land is the King's palace, and "God's eyes are upon it from the beginning of the year until the end of the year."

וַיַּשְׁלִכֵם — *And He cast them*. Why is the word וַיַּשְׁלִכֵם written with a large letter *lamed?* Seeing as the nations themselves will someday admit that God did us a kindness in exiling us from our land to live among the gentiles, rather than destroying us for our sins, the Torah wants to teach us another purpose behind our exile. This large *lamed* suggests that exile is intended *to teach* (לְלַמֵּד) wandering souls wisdom. As *Chazal* tell us, God only exiled the Jews among the nations so that they would be joined by righteous converts (*Pesachim* 87b). The Jews in exile are to spread the belief in one God among the nations. Indeed, the word וַיַּשְׁלִכֵם itself, with its letters rearranged, can be read as וְיֵשׁ לָכֶם ל', "you have [a mission of] *lamed*, to teach" the world about the unity of God.

30.

1. וְהָיָה כִי־יָבֹאוּ עָלֶיךָ כָּל־הַדְּבָרִים הָאֵלֶּה הַבְּרָכָה וְהַקְּלָלָה — *It will be that when all these things come upon you, the blessing and the curse*. The blessing alone will not teach you to behave righteously. The Evil Inclination will convince you that it was your good luck which got you a "land flowing with milk and honey"

29 *to bring upon it the entire curse that is written in this Book;*
27-28 [27] *and* HASHEM *removed them from upon their soil, with*
anger, with wrath, and with great fury, and He cast them to
another land, as this very day!"
[28] *The hidden [sins] are for* HASHEM, *our God, but the*
revealed [sins] are for us and our children forever, to carry out
all the words of this Torah.
30 [1] *It will be that when all these things come upon you — the*
1-3 *blessing and the curse that I have presented before you —*
then you will take it to your heart among all the nations where
HASHEM, *your God, has dispersed you;* [2] *and you will return*
unto HASHEM, *your God, and listen to His voice, according to*
everything that I command you today, you and your children,
with all your heart and all your soul. [3] *Then Hashem, your*
God, will bring back your captivity and have mercy upon you,

---

and caused things to go well with you. And if you experienced the curse alone, you would attribute it to your land being lean and dry.

But when you receive blessing for observing the Torah and curses when you do not (and sometimes under supernatural circumstances) — only then will you "take it to your heart . . . and you will return unto Hashem. . . with all your heart and all your soul."

1-3. וַהֲשֵׁבֹתָ אֶל־לְבָבֶךָ . . . וְשַׁבְתָּ עַד־ה׳ . . . וְשָׁב ה׳ אֱלֹהֶיךָ אֶת־שְׁבוּתְךָ — *Then you will take it to your heart . . . and you will return unto Hashem . . . then Hashem, your God, will bring back your captivity*. These words were not said conditionally: "if you will take it to heart . . . then God will bring back . . ." Rather, they are said with certainty. They are a faithful promise to the Jewish people that they will return to God, their Refuge and Redeemer.

2. וְשַׁבְתָּ עַד־ה׳ אֱלֹהֶיךָ . . . אַתָּה וּבָנֶיךָ — *And you will return unto Hashem your God . . . you and your children*. A penitent person must realize that prior to his return to Torah observance, he schooled his children in blasphemy and sin. Therefore, his first obligation is to rectify what he has corrupted: he must make every effort to bring his children to repentance as well.

☙ אַתָּה וּבָנֶיךָ — *You and your children*. The phrasing of this verse speaks favorably of the parents. But in the final generation, there will be families where the parents will be on the verge of assimilation, while their children will be Divinely inspired to return to Torah. These children will fight with their irreligious parents, trying to bring them to Judaism as well. This is what the prophet *Malachi* describes: "He will bring the hearts of fathers back to their children" (3:24). So "before the coming of the great and awesome day of God" (3:23), there will be cases of irreligious fathers returning to their righteous sons. There will also be instances where the opposite will be necessary; "the heart of (straying) sons will return to their fathers" (3:24). May it happen speedily, in our times.

ל וְשָׁ֥ב וְקִבֶּצְךָ֙ מִכָּל־הָ֣עַמִּ֔ים אֲשֶׁ֧ר הֱפִֽיצְךָ֛ יהוָ֥ה אֱלֹהֶ֖יךָ
ד־יב שָֽׁמָּה׃ ד אִם־יִהְיֶ֥ה נִֽדַּחֲךָ֖ בִּקְצֵ֣ה הַשָּׁמָ֑יִם מִשָּׁ֗ם יְקַבֶּצְךָ֙
יהוָ֣ה אֱלֹהֶ֔יךָ וּמִשָּׁ֖ם יִקָּחֶֽךָ׃ ה וֶהֱבִֽיאֲךָ֞ יהוָ֣ה אֱלֹהֶ֗יךָ אֶל־
הָאָ֛רֶץ אֲשֶׁר־יָרְשׁ֥וּ אֲבֹתֶ֖יךָ וִֽירִשְׁתָּ֑הּ וְהֵיטִבְךָ֥ וְהִרְבְּךָ֖
מֵאֲבֹתֶֽיךָ׃ ו וּמָ֨ל יהוָ֧ה אֱלֹהֶ֛יךָ אֶת־לְבָבְךָ֖ וְאֶת־לְבַ֣ב זַרְעֶ֑ךָ
לְאַהֲבָ֞ה אֶת־יהוָ֧ה אֱלֹהֶ֛יךָ בְּכָל־לְבָבְךָ֥ וּבְכָל־נַפְשְׁךָ֖ לְמַ֥עַן
חַיֶּֽיךָ׃ חמישי שלישי כשהן מחוברין ז וְנָתַן֙
יהוָ֣ה אֱלֹהֶ֔יךָ אֵ֥ת כָּל־הָאָל֖וֹת הָאֵ֑לֶּה עַל־אֹיְבֶ֥יךָ וְעַל־
שֹׂנְאֶ֖יךָ אֲשֶׁ֥ר רְדָפֽוּךָ׃ ח וְאַתָּ֣ה תָשׁ֔וּב וְשָׁמַעְתָּ֖ בְּק֣וֹל
יהוָ֑ה וְעָשִׂ֙יתָ֙ אֶת־כָּל־מִצְוֺתָ֔יו אֲשֶׁ֛ר אָנֹכִ֥י מְצַוְּךָ֖ הַיּֽוֹם׃
ט וְהוֹתִֽירְךָ֩ יהוָ֨ה אֱלֹהֶ֜יךָ בְּכֹ֣ל ׀ מַעֲשֵׂ֣ה יָדֶ֗ךָ בִּפְרִ֨י בִטְנְךָ֜
וּבִפְרִ֧י בְהֶמְתְּךָ֛ וּבִפְרִ֥י אַדְמָתְךָ֖ לְטֹבָ֑ה כִּ֣י ׀ יָשׁ֣וּב יהוָ֗ה
לָשׂ֤וּשׂ עָלֶ֙יךָ֙ לְט֔וֹב כַּאֲשֶׁר־שָׂ֖שׂ עַל־אֲבֹתֶֽיךָ׃ י כִּ֣י תִשְׁמַ֗ע
בְּקוֹל֙ יהוָ֣ה אֱלֹהֶ֔יךָ לִשְׁמֹ֤ר מִצְוֺתָיו֙ וְחֻקֹּתָ֔יו הַכְּתוּבָ֕ה
בְּסֵ֖פֶר הַתּוֹרָ֣ה הַזֶּ֑ה כִּ֤י תָשׁוּב֙ אֶל־יהוָ֣ה אֱלֹהֶ֔יךָ בְּכָל־לְבָבְךָ֖
וּבְכָל־נַפְשֶֽׁךָ׃ ששי יא כִּ֚י הַמִּצְוָ֣ה הַזֹּ֔את
אֲשֶׁ֛ר אָנֹכִ֥י מְצַוְּךָ֖ הַיּ֑וֹם לֹֽא־נִפְלֵ֥את הִוא֙ מִמְּךָ֔ וְלֹ֥א רְחֹקָ֖ה
הִֽוא׃ יב לֹ֥א בַשָּׁמַ֖יִם הִ֑וא לֵאמֹ֗ר מִ֣י יַעֲלֶה־לָּ֤נוּ הַשָּׁמַ֙יְמָה֙

---

6. וּמָל ה׳ אֱלֹהֶיךָ אֶת־לְבָבְךָ וְאֶת־לְבַב זַרְעֶךָ לְאַהֲבָה אֶת־ה׳ אֱלֹהֶיךָ — *Hashem, your God, will circumcise your heart and the heart of your offspring, to love Hashem, your God*. What a wonderful promise! For one may choose to be personally righteous and love God, yet not be able to influence his children one way or the other. People have sacrificed everything to raise their children to Torah observance and love of God, and not been successful in their efforts. Here the Torah promises us success.

7. עַל־אֹיְבֶיךָ . . . אֲשֶׁר רְדָפוּךָ — *Upon your enemies . . . who pursued you*. Because they will pursue you to an even greater extent than God decreed. This is made explicit by the prophet *Zechariah* (1:15): "I am greatly angered at the tranquil nations, in that I was a little angry with My nation, and they helped the evil." Similarly, the commentators explain that the plagues came upon the Egyptians because they harmed the Jews more than God had decreed, out of their own wickedness and cruel intentions.

9. כִּי יָשׁוּב ה׳ לָשׂוּשׂ עָלֶיךָ לְטוֹב כַּאֲשֶׁר־שָׂשׂ עַל־אֲבֹתֶיךָ — *When Hashem will return to rejoice over you for good, as He rejoiced over your forefathers*. This will take place in the future generations, when people will be as righteous as the Patriarchs of Israel. The words "He will do good to you and make you more numerous than your forefathers" (v. 5) refer to a generation of repentance, for

30 *and He will gather you in from all the peoples to which*
4-12 *HASHEM, your God, has scattered you.* [4] *If your dispersed will*
be at the ends of heaven, from there HASHEM, your God, will
gather you in and from there He will take you. [5] *HASHEM,*
your God, will bring you to the Land that your forefathers
possessed and you shall possess it; He will do good to you and
make you more numerous than your forefathers. [6] *HASHEM,*
your God, will circumcise your heart and the heart of your
offspring, to love HASHEM, your God, with all your heart
and with all your soul, that you may live.
[7] *HASHEM, your God, will place all these imprecations upon*
your enemies and those who hate you, who pursued you.
[8] *You shall return and listen to the voice of HASHEM, and*
perform all His commandments that I command you today.
[9] *HASHEM will make you abundant in all your handiwork —*
in the fruit of your womb, the fruit of your animals, and the
fruit of your Land — for good, when HASHEM will return to
rejoice over you for good, as He rejoiced over your fore-
fathers, [10] *when you listen to the voice of HASHEM, your God,*
to observe His commandments and His decrees, that are
written in this Book of the Torah, when you shall return to
HASHEM, your God, with all your heart and all your soul.
[11] *For this commandment that I command you today — it*
is not hidden from you and it is not distant. [12] *It is not in hea-*
ven, [for you] to say, "Who can ascend to the heaven for us

"in the place where penitents stand, even the totally righteous cannot stand" (*Berachos* 34b).

10. כִּי תָשׁוּב אֶל־ה׳ אֱלֹהֶיךָ בְּכָל־לְבָבְךָ וּבְכָל־נַפְשֶׁךָ — *When you shall return to Hashem, your God, with all your heart and all your soul*. The words "with all your heart and all your soul" are used three times in these verses in reference to repentance (vs. 2,6,10). It seems to me that in v. 2 this expression refers to thoughts of repentance, and the desire to obey God and return to Him "with all your heart and all your soul." But this sort of penitence will be born of fear, after the advent of the curses and the exile "among all the nations where Hashem, your God, has dispersed you."

In v. 6 we find a promise. After God gathers all the scattered Jews and brings them to the Holy Land, where they will be free of oppressors, they will be granted Divine assistance in returning to God out of love: "Hashem, your God, will circumcise your heart . . . to love Hashem, your God, with all your heart and all your soul."

Next, the Torah promises (v. 10) that "when you listen to the voice of Hashem, your God, to observe His commandments," you will then be privileged

וְיִקָּחֶהָ לָּנוּ וְיַשְׁמִעֵנוּ אֹתָהּ וְנַעֲשֶׂנָּה: יג וְלֹא־מֵעֵבֶר לַיָּם הִוא
לֵאמֹר מִי יַעֲבָר־לָנוּ אֶל־עֵבֶר הַיָּם וְיִקָּחֶהָ לָּנוּ וְיַשְׁמִעֵנוּ
אֹתָהּ וְנַעֲשֶׂנָּה: יד כִּי־קָרוֹב אֵלֶיךָ הַדָּבָר מְאֹד בְּפִיךָ וּבִלְבָבְךָ
לַעֲשֹׂתוֹ: שביעי ומפטיר רביעי כשהן מחוברין טו רְאֵה
נָתַתִּי לְפָנֶיךָ הַיּוֹם אֶת־הַחַיִּים וְאֶת־הַטּוֹב וְאֶת־הַמָּוֶת
וְאֶת־הָרָע: טז אֲשֶׁר אָנֹכִי מְצַוְּךָ הַיּוֹם לְאַהֲבָה אֶת־יהוה
אֱלֹהֶיךָ לָלֶכֶת בִּדְרָכָיו וְלִשְׁמֹר מִצְוֺתָיו וְחֻקֹּתָיו וּמִשְׁפָּטָיו
וְחָיִיתָ וְרָבִיתָ וּבֵרַכְךָ יהוה אֱלֹהֶיךָ בָּאָרֶץ אֲשֶׁר־אַתָּה
בָא־שָׁמָּה לְרִשְׁתָּהּ: יז וְאִם־יִפְנֶה לְבָבְךָ וְלֹא תִשְׁמָע וְנִדַּחְתָּ
וְהִשְׁתַּחֲוִיתָ לֵאלֹהִים אֲחֵרִים וַעֲבַדְתָּם: יח הִגַּדְתִּי לָכֶם
הַיּוֹם כִּי אָבֹד תֹּאבֵדוּן לֹא־תַאֲרִיכֻן יָמִים עַל־הָאֲדָמָה אֲשֶׁר
אַתָּה עֹבֵר אֶת־הַיַּרְדֵּן לָבוֹא שָׁמָּה לְרִשְׁתָּהּ: יט הַעִדֹתִי בָכֶם
הַיּוֹם אֶת־הַשָּׁמַיִם וְאֶת־הָאָרֶץ הַחַיִּים וְהַמָּוֶת נָתַתִּי לְפָנֶיךָ
הַבְּרָכָה וְהַקְּלָלָה וּבָחַרְתָּ בַּחַיִּים לְמַעַן תִּחְיֶה אַתָּה וְזַרְעֶךָ:
כ לְאַהֲבָה אֶת־יהוה אֱלֹהֶיךָ לִשְׁמֹעַ בְּקֹלוֹ וּלְדָבְקָה־בוֹ כִּי
הוּא חַיֶּיךָ וְאֹרֶךְ יָמֶיךָ לָשֶׁבֶת עַל־הָאֲדָמָה אֲשֶׁר נִשְׁבַּע
יהוה לַאֲבֹתֶיךָ לְאַבְרָהָם לְיִצְחָק וּלְיַעֲקֹב לָתֵת לָהֶם:

---

to "return to Hashem, your God, with all your heart and all your soul," this time without Divine assistance, and while living securely in your own land. This repentance will neither be born of fear nor attained with heavenly aid. It will come purely from personal conviction.

17. וְאִם־יִפְנֶה לְבָבְךָ וְלֹא תִשְׁמָע — *But if your heart will stray and you will not listen*. "God made man straight" (*Koheles* 7:29). If anyone does not listen to His commandments, his heart has "strayed" off to the side — as *Koheles* says: "but they sought out many calculations." We can also explain the words "lest your hearts be seduced" (*Devarim* 11:16) in this same fashion.

An Insight on Haftaras Nitzavim

(*Yeshayah* 61:11): [See p. 414]

כֵּן ה׳ אֱלֹהִים יַצְמִיחַ צְדָקָה וּתְהִלָּה נֶגֶד כָּל־הַגּוֹיִם — *So shall Hashem/Elohim cause righteousness and praise to grow in the face of all the nations*. The recipient of charity is embarrassed both in front of the giver and in front of other people; he is obliged to take charity rather than earn his own keep. As Daniel said (9:7), "Yours, Hashem, is the *tzedakah*, and ours is the shamefacedness."

Sometimes the recipient can excuse himself, claiming ill health, or explaining that he was unable to find employment. But how can we possibly offer such excuses to God when we request His charity and kindness? How can we pray for life and livelihood when our hands are not only empty of good deeds, but

and take it for us, so that we can listen to it and perform it?"
13 Nor is it across the sea, [for you] to say, "Who can cross to
the other side of the sea for us and take it for us, so that we
can listen to it and perform it?" 14 Rather, the matter is very
near to you — in your mouth and your heart — to perform it.
15 See — I have placed before you today the life and the
good, and the death and the evil, 16 that which I command
you today, to love HASHEM*, your God, to walk in His ways, to*
observe His commandments, His decrees, and His ordi-
nances; then you will live and you will multiply, and
HASHEM*, your God, will bless you in the Land to which you*
come, to possess it. 17 But if your heart will stray and you will
not listen, and you are led astray, and you prostrate yourself
to strange gods and serve them, 18 I tell you today that you
will surely be lost; you will not lengthen your days upon the
Land that you cross the Jordan to come there, to possess it. 19 I
call heaven and earth today to bear witness against you: I
have placed life and death before you, blessing and curse;
and you shall choose life, so that you will live, you and your
offspring — 20 to love HASHEM*, your God, to listen to His voice*
and to cleave to Him, for He is your life and the length of your
days, to dwell upon the land that HASHEM *swore to your*
forefathers, to Abraham, to Isaac, and to Jacob, to give them.

---

are actually tainted with sin? We cannot excuse ourselves that we had nowhere to "work and earn" (i.e., to keep the Torah), because "the Torah is not in Heaven." We have the strength in our hearts to keep the entire Torah. We can "earn our own sustenance" with commandments fulfilled, and be counted among those who are strong of heart and are far from needing charity.

What is more, we cannot complain of weakness or illness which kept us away from the service of God. When it came to serving the Adversary, and committing sins and abominations despised by God, we had plenty of energy! We could have used that same energy to serve God and fulfill His commandments. When we repeat Daniel's words in the *Selichos* prayers, we add, "What complaint can we make? What can we say? What can we declare? What justification can we offer?" When we have no excuses while asking for God's charity, we are shamefaced.

But this is only the case when we do the spiritual stock-taking ourselves. In the future God will hold a Torah scroll in His arms and take stock of His world. He will then say, "Let everyone who busied himself with this [i.e., the Torah] come and take his reward" (*Avodah Zarah* 2a). When God takes stock of the Jewish people in the presence of the gentile nations, the result will be that "your people are all righteous; they shall inherit the land forever." The nations will see and testify on behalf of the Jews that they kept the Torah, and that they deserve the reward held in God's arms, for "even the sinners of Israel are as full of *mitzvos* as a pomegranate is full of seeds" (*Eruvin* 19a).

In fact, this reward is also in the category of charity and kindness on God's part ("Yours, Hashem, is kindness, for You reward each man in accordance with his deeds" [*Tehillim* 62:13]), since everything belongs to God, and "Who came before Me, that I should reward him?"(*Iyov* 41:3). But before all the nations, who have no part in it, there is nothing shameful or embarrassing about this reward; it is all "charity and praise."

This is comparable to a man planting a half a cup of seed and reaping a hundred bushels. Here is charity on God's part towards the planter, but there is also an element of praise for him, for he is receiving the reward of his toil, not merely a gift. "For the land will give out its foliage, and like a garden sprout forth its seeds. So shall Hashem, your God, make charity and praise spring forth in the presence of all the nations."

פרשת וילך

Parashas Vayeilech

לא
א־ט

א וַיֵּלֶךְ מֹשֶׁה וַיְדַבֵּר אֶת־הַדְּבָרִים הָאֵלֶּה אֶל־כָּל־יִשְׂרָאֵל׃
ב וַיֹּאמֶר אֲלֵהֶם בֶּן־מֵאָה וְעֶשְׂרִים שָׁנָה אָנֹכִי הַיּוֹם לֹא־
אוּכַל עוֹד לָצֵאת וְלָבוֹא וַיהוה אָמַר אֵלַי לֹא תַעֲבֹר אֶת־
הַיַּרְדֵּן הַזֶּה׃ ג יהוה אֱלֹהֶיךָ הוּא ׀ עֹבֵר לְפָנֶיךָ הוּא־יַשְׁמִיד
אֶת־הַגּוֹיִם הָאֵלֶּה מִלְּפָנֶיךָ וִירִשְׁתָּם יְהוֹשֻׁעַ הוּא עֹבֵר
לְפָנֶיךָ כַּאֲשֶׁר דִּבֶּר יהוה׃ שני ד וְעָשָׂה יהוה לָהֶם כַּאֲשֶׁר
עָשָׂה לְסִיחוֹן וּלְעוֹג מַלְכֵי הָאֱמֹרִי וּלְאַרְצָם אֲשֶׁר הִשְׁמִיד
אֹתָם׃ ה וּנְתָנָם יהוה לִפְנֵיכֶם וַעֲשִׂיתֶם לָהֶם כְּכָל־הַמִּצְוָה
אֲשֶׁר צִוִּיתִי אֶתְכֶם׃ ו חִזְקוּ וְאִמְצוּ אַל־תִּירְאוּ וְאַל־תַּעַרְצוּ
מִפְּנֵיהֶם כִּי ׀ יהוה אֱלֹהֶיךָ הוּא הַהֹלֵךְ עִמָּךְ לֹא יַרְפְּךָ וְלֹא
יַעַזְבֶךָּ׃ שלישי חמישי כשהן מחוברין ז וַיִּקְרָא מֹשֶׁה
לִיהוֹשֻׁעַ וַיֹּאמֶר אֵלָיו לְעֵינֵי כָל־יִשְׂרָאֵל חֲזַק וֶאֱמָץ כִּי
אַתָּה תָּבוֹא אֶת־הָעָם הַזֶּה אֶל־הָאָרֶץ אֲשֶׁר נִשְׁבַּע יהוה
לַאֲבֹתָם לָתֵת לָהֶם וְאַתָּה תַּנְחִילֶנָּה אוֹתָם׃ ח וַיהוה הוּא ׀
הַהֹלֵךְ לְפָנֶיךָ הוּא יִהְיֶה עִמָּךְ לֹא יַרְפְּךָ וְלֹא יַעַזְבֶךָּ
לֹא תִירָא וְלֹא תֵחָת׃ ט וַיִּכְתֹּב מֹשֶׁה אֶת־הַתּוֹרָה הַזֹּאת
וַיִּתְּנָהּ אֶל־הַכֹּהֲנִים בְּנֵי לֵוִי הַנֹּשְׂאִים אֶת־אֲרוֹן בְּרִית יהוה

31.

1. וַיֵּלֶךְ מֹשֶׁה — *Moses went*. We see here how exceptionally humble Moses was. When he prepared to ask the people if they were willing to accept Joshua's leadership after his death, he did not send Joshua (who stood to gain from all this) away so that he could speak to them in his tent. Instead, on the last day of his life, at the age of a hundred and twenty, the leader of the entire nation troubled himself to go out to the people, while his disciple Joshua stayed behind in the tent. Can one possibly find such humility in any non-Jewish king, from the time of the Creation of the world up to this day?

2. לֹא־אוּכַל עוֹד לָצֵאת וְלָבוֹא — *I can no longer go out and come in*. When Moses asked God to "appoint . . . a man over the congregation . . . who will take them out and bring them in," he added that without such a leader, the people would be "like sheep who have no shepherd" (*Bamidbar* 27:16-17). This is why he now told the Jews that from today onward, when Moses no longer has permission to "go out and come in," they must see to it that they have a new leader. He also told them that in God's eyes, Joshua was the right one to replace him.

3. ה׳ אֱלֹהֶיךָ הוּא עֹבֵר לְפָנֶיךָ . . . יְהוֹשֻׁעַ הוּא עֹבֵר לְפָנֶיךָ — *Hashem, your God, He will cross before you. . . Joshua, he shall cross over before you*. Why does the verse first say that God will cross before you, and then that Joshua will cross before you? *Onkelos* explains that, more precisely, "the word of God" (מֵימְרֵהּ)

31
1-9

1 *Moses went and spoke these words to all of Israel.* 2 *He said*
to them, "I am a hundred and twenty years old today; I can
no longer go out and come in, for HASHEM *has said to me, 'You*
shall not cross this Jordan.' 3 HASHEM, *your God — He will*
cross before you; He will destroy these nations from before
you, and you shall possess them; Joshua — he shall cross over
before you, as HASHEM *has spoken.* 4 HASHEM *will do to them*
as He did to Sihon and Og, the kings of the Amorite, and their
land, which He destroyed, 5 *and* HASHEM *gave them before*
you; and you shall do to them according to the entire
commandment that I have commanded you. 6 *Be strong and*
courageous, do not be afraid and do not be broken before them,
for HASHEM, *your God — it is He Who goes before you, He will*
not release you nor will He forsake you."
7 *Moses summoned Joshua and said to him before the eyes*
of all Israel, "Be strong and courageous, for you shall come
with this people to the Land that HASHEM *swore to give them,*
and you shall cause them to inherit it. 8 HASHEM *— it is He*
Who goes before you; He will be with you; He will not release
you nor will He forsake you; do not be afraid and do not be
dismayed."
9 *Moses wrote this Torah and gave it to the Kohanim, the*
sons of Levi, the bearers of the Ark of the covenant of HASHEM,

---

would cross before them. This interpretation is easy to understand, for we cannot say that God would literally cross before them in place of Moses. Rather, Moses promised the Jewish people that the word of God, which until now had been in Moses' mouth when he led them in war, would still be with them: "The word of Hashem, your God, will cross before you," as *Onkelos* interprets.

Moses then further explained to them where God's word would be from now on: in Joshua's mouth — "Joshua, he shall cross over before you." Joshua would now lead them in war, at God's command, "as Hashem has spoken".

7. וַיִּקְרָא מֹשֶׁה לִיהוֹשֻׁעַ וַיֹּאמֶר אֵלָיו לְעֵינֵי כָל־יִשְׂרָאֵל — *Moses summoned Joshua and said to him before the eyes of all Israel*. After he had consulted with the people about Joshua's appointment, Moses handed over the leadership to him "before the eyes of all Israel."

9. וַיִּכְתֹּב מֹשֶׁה אֶת־הַתּוֹרָה הַזֹּאת — *Moses wrote this Torah*. Why did Moses interrupt Joshua's installation as the people's new leader to speak about the giving of the Torah to the priests and elders, and about the commandment of *Hakhel*? (This commandment is fulfilled by the king reading *Deuteronomy* out loud to the entire nation on the first day of *Chol HaMoed* Succos, that followed a Sabbatical year.) Why did he speak about these things before God issued His command to Joshua, which would complete his appointment as Moses' successor?

לא וְאֶל־כָּל־זִקְנֵי יִשְׂרָאֵל׃ רביעי י וַיְצַו מֹשֶׁה אוֹתָם לֵאמֹר
י־יב מִקֵּץ ׀ שֶׁבַע שָׁנִים בְּמֹעֵד שְׁנַת הַשְּׁמִטָּה בְּחַג הַסֻּכּוֹת׃
יא בְּבוֹא כָל־יִשְׂרָאֵל לֵרָאוֹת אֶת־פְּנֵי יְהוָה אֱלֹהֶיךָ בַּמָּקוֹם
אֲשֶׁר יִבְחָר תִּקְרָא אֶת־הַתּוֹרָה הַזֹּאת נֶגֶד כָּל־יִשְׂרָאֵל
בְּאָזְנֵיהֶם׃ יב הַקְהֵל אֶת־הָעָם הָאֲנָשִׁים וְהַנָּשִׁים וְהַטַּף וְגֵרְךָ

We may say that this was to prevent Joshua (and the judges and kings who would follow him) from saying that a Jewish leader's *only* responsibilities are to conquer the Holy Land, divide it among the people, and protect the people from their enemies. This is why Moses immediately told Joshua that he must see to it that the people learn Torah and fulfill its commandments. He must, practically speaking, make sure that the priests, Levites, and elders, teach the people Torah constantly (since it would be impracticable for the king himself to be constantly occupied with teaching). In addition, once every seven years the king must gather the entire Jewish people in the Holy Temple, and personally read to them from the Torah. This would help the Jews to honor the Torah, and thus be willing to learn it from the priests, Levites, and elders.

10-11. בְּמֹעֵד שְׁנַת הַשְּׁמִטָּה בְּחַג הַסֻּכּוֹת . . . תִּקְרָא אֶת־הַתּוֹרָה הַזֹּאת נֶגֶד כָּל־יִשְׂרָאֵל — *At the time of the Sabbatical year, during the Succos festival . . . you shall read this Torah before all Israel*. Why on Succos? Why not on Passover or Shavuos?

Succos is called "the Festival of the Harvest" (*Shemos* 34:22). Even though the holiday is called *Succos* in remembrance of the "booths" in which God caused the Jewish people to dwell when they left Egypt, it is at the same time the harvest festival. (All the Torah holidays are also celebrations of nature. Passover is the spring festival, and Shavuos the holiday of the first-fruits. See *HaDe'ah VeHaDibur II*:4)

During the Sabbatical year, when there is no harvest, one might think that there is also no joy on Succos. But during the Sabbatical year, when the Jews were free from their agricultural work, they increased their Torah study and their involvement in the commandments. And at the end of the year there was a *spiritual* "harvest festival." To enhance the importance and joyfulness of this "harvest," the King himself would personally read "this Torah" (i.e., *Sefer Devarim*) to the nation in the place where God had chosen to have His Name dwell. The purpose of this *Hakhel* was to teach the Jewish people the enormous value of studying Torah and observing its commandments, so that they would make the effort to find time for regular Torah study, even during the six years of work: "so that they will learn, and they shall fear Hashem, your God, and be careful to perform all the words of this Torah . . . all the days that you live on the land" (v. 12-13)." Although the land must be worked and cared for, we still must make every effort to "learn and to teach, to observe and to perform [the Torah]."

and to all the elders of Israel.

[10] *Moses commanded them, saying, " At the end of seven years, at the time of the Sabbatical year, during the Succos festival,* [11] *when all Israel comes to appear before* HASHEM, *your God, in the place that He will choose, you shall read this Torah before all Israel, in their ears,* [12] *Gather together the people — the men, the women, and the small children, and your stranger*

---

10. שְׁנַת הַשְּׁמִטָּה בְּחַג הַסֻּכּוֹת — *The Sabbatical year, during the Succos festival.* There is another possible reason why *Hakhel* is held at the end of the Sabbatical year. When God wanted to instill His fear into the hearts of the Jewish people (especially in "their children who do not know" [v. 13]), He chose an opportune time to do so: the end of the Sabbatical year, when the people had let their fields lie fallow for an entire year, and eaten the whole time of God's blessing from the sixth year.

(This is similar to recounting the Exodus from Egypt specifically while we have matzah and bitter herbs before us. These two things testify to the miracles and wonders that God did for our ancestors when He took them out of Egypt.)

The Torah tells us "I will ordain My blessing for you in the sixth year, and it will yield a crop sufficient for the three-year period" (*Vayikra* 25:21). Not only will there be grain enough to eat in the eighth year (until the new crop ripens), but also enough with which to sow the fields. The sight of this great miracle, and of the fulfillment of the promise given in the Torah, will make it easier to read the people the Torah, "so that they will hear and so that they will learn, and they shall fear Hashem, your God . . . and their children who do not know (the miracles) they shall hear and they shall learn to fear Hashem, your God, all the days."

11. בְּבוֹא כָל־יִשְׂרָאֵל לֵרָאוֹת אֶת־פְּנֵי ה׳ אֱלֹהֶיךָ — *When all Israel comes to appear before Hashem, your God.* We may learn from this verse that if it is possible to combine two gatherings and hold them at once, one should do so. One should not trouble the people to assemble twice if it can be avoided.

12. וְהַטַּף — *And the small children.* This term includes also the suckling infants. We find this meaning of the word טַף in the Torah's account of Dathan and Abiram (*Bamidbar* 16:27). On the words וּנְשֵׁיהֶם וּבְנֵיהֶם וְטַפָּם, "with their wives, children, and infants," *Rashi* comments, "How terrible is controversy, because of which even suckling infants perished."

The *Ramban* writes, however, that in the present verse, "the small children" does not refer to suckling infants, for the verse says "so that they will learn," which of course an infant is too young to do. Even if we say that the reference is to their future, today's infants will certainly have forgotten by then anything that they heard at this time.

But the *Talmud Yerushalmi* (at the end of the first chapter of *Yevamos*) tells of the *Tanna* R' Yehoshua's mother, who would take his crib to the synagogue so that his ears would hear words of Torah. It seems, then, that even tiny

לא אֲשֶׁר בִּשְׁעָרֶיךָ לְמַעַן יִשְׁמְעוּ וּלְמַעַן יִלְמְדוּ וְיָרְאוּ אֶת־
יג־טז יְהוָה אֱלֹהֵיכֶם וְשָׁמְרוּ לַעֲשׂוֹת אֶת־כָּל־דִּבְרֵי הַתּוֹרָה
הַזֹּאת: יג וּבְנֵיהֶם אֲשֶׁר לֹא־יָדְעוּ יִשְׁמְעוּ וְלָמְדוּ לְיִרְאָה
אֶת־יְהוָה אֱלֹהֵיכֶם כָּל־הַיָּמִים אֲשֶׁר אַתֶּם חַיִּים עַל־
הָאֲדָמָה אֲשֶׁר אַתֶּם עֹבְרִים אֶת־הַיַּרְדֵּן שָׁמָּה לְרִשְׁתָּהּ:
חמישי ששי כשהן מחוברין יד וַיֹּאמֶר יְהוָה אֶל־מֹשֶׁה הֵן קָרְבוּ
יָמֶיךָ לָמוּת קְרָא אֶת־יְהוֹשֻׁעַ וְהִתְיַצְּבוּ בְּאֹהֶל מוֹעֵד
וַאֲצַוֶּנּוּ וַיֵּלֶךְ מֹשֶׁה וִיהוֹשֻׁעַ וַיִּתְיַצְּבוּ בְּאֹהֶל מוֹעֵד: טו וַיֵּרָא
יְהוָה בָּאֹהֶל בְּעַמּוּד עָנָן וַיַּעֲמֹד עַמּוּד הֶעָנָן עַל־פֶּתַח
הָאֹהֶל: טז וַיֹּאמֶר יְהוָה אֶל־מֹשֶׁה הִנְּךָ שֹׁכֵב עִם־אֲבֹתֶיךָ

---

infants benefit from hearing words of Torah. "Why do the טַף, the small children come? So that those who bring them will have a reward" (*Chagigah* 3a). If the parents bring along their young children with the intent of R' Yehoshua's mother, they too will be rewarded.

וּלְמַעַן יִלְמְדוּ וְיָרְאוּ אֶת־ה' אֱלֹהֵיכֶם וְשָׁמְרוּ לַעֲשׂוֹת — *So that they will learn, and they shall fear Hashem, your God, and be careful to perform*. Fear of God cannot exist without Torah study, as *Chazal* tell us: "a boor cannot be fearful of sin (*Avos* 2:6)"; and Torah observance without fear of God will not stand the test of time.

13. יִשְׁמְעוּ — *They shall hear*. The previous verse also says "so that they will hear." But it was only those who stood close to the platform who had the privilege of actually hearing the king read the Torah; those far away did not. The *Rambam* writes: "One who cannot hear (because he is far away [*Lechem Mishneh*]) must think over in his mind what is being read, remembering that the Torah decreed it solely to strengthen the true faith. He should see himself as if he was being commanded right now to keep the Torah, and as if he was hearing it from God, for the king is God's messenger to proclaim His words."

"Listening" [יִשְׁמְעוּ], as it often does, also means "understanding" in this case. Those present at *Hakhel* had to *understand* before Whom they stood, and what was the purpose of their presence there. This type of comprehension is possible even for "their children who do not know" what is being read before them. They will understand that all of Israel has gathered to hear the word of God from the king; that the Torah is the essence of the Jews' life. Through this experience they will learn to fear God "all the days."

14. הֵן קָרְבוּ יָמֶיךָ לָמוּת — *Behold your days are drawing near to die*. "Righteous people are considered to be alive even after their death" (*Berachos* 18a). It is only the days which man was given for perfecting himself on earth which draw to a close. This happens either because the *tzaddik* has already attained

who is in your cities — so that they will hear and so that they
will learn, and they shall fear HASHEM, *your God, and be*
careful to perform all the words of this Torah. [13] *And their*
children who do not know — they shall hear and they shall
learn to fear HASHEM, *your God, all the days that you live on*
the land to which you are crossing the Jordan, to possess it."
[14] HASHEM *spoke to Moses, "Behold, your days are drawing*
near to die; summon Joshua, and both of you shall stand in the
Tent of Meeting, and I shall instruct him." So Moses and
Joshua went and stood in the Tent of Meeting.
[15] HASHEM *appeared in the Tent, in a pillar of cloud, and the*
pillar of cloud stood by the entrance of the Tent. [16] HASHEM
said to Moses, "Behold, you will lie with your forefathers,

---

perfection, or because "one reign never impinges on another." In this instance, it was time for Joshua to take over leadership of the people.

קְרָא אֶת־יְהוֹשֻׁעַ . . . וַאֲצַוֶּנּוּ — *Summon Joshua . . . and I shall instruct him.* Actually, God first instructed the people through Moses and rebuked them, and commanded Moses to write down "this song" (v. 19) and teach it to the Jews. Only afterwards did God instruct Joshua.

We can learn from this that before instructing a leader of the people and preparing him for his new task, one should first instruct the people and guide them in the way of Torah. Only then will they respect the leader, who bears the banner of Torah. Without this preliminary preparation, it is possible that they will not obey him.

This is why the Torah interrupted the narrative of Joshua's installation with the commandment of *Hakhel*, the purpose of which is to strengthen our faith and enhance the honor of the Torah in the people's eyes. From *Hakhel* the nation will learn to honor the bearer of the Torah's banner.

15. וַיַּעֲמֹד עַמּוּד הֶעָנָן עַל־פֶּתַח הָאֹהֶל — *And the pillar of cloud stood by the entrance of the Tent.* According to the simple explanation of the verse, Moses and Joshua stood at the entrance of the tent as they were commanded. The Divine Presence also appeared in the Tent of Meeting, in the pillar of cloud. Why, then, did the pillar of cloud go and stand at the entrance of the Tent?

The commentators have found this difficult to answer. However, it would seem that the answer is related to the warning given here: If the Jewish nation should "stray after the gods of the foreigners of the Land . . . "My anger will flare against it on that day. . . and I will conceal My face from them." God wanted to demonstrate this literally, by having the pillar of cloud, which represents God's glory, leave Moses and Joshua in the Tent of Meeting and go and stand at the entrance of the Tent.

We find a similar occurrence at the time of the destruction of the Temple, when God's Presence traveled from the Cherubim to the threshold (*Rosh*

וְקָם הָעָם הַזֶּה וְזָנָה ׀ אַחֲרֵי ׀ אֱלֹהֵי נֵכַר־הָאָרֶץ אֲשֶׁר הוּא לא
בָא־שָׁמָּה בְּקִרְבּוֹ וַעֲזָבַנִי וְהֵפֵר אֶת־בְּרִיתִי אֲשֶׁר כָּרַתִּי יז־כד
אִתּוֹ: יז וְחָרָה אַפִּי בוֹ בַיּוֹם־הַהוּא וַעֲזַבְתִּים וְהִסְתַּרְתִּי פָנַי
מֵהֶם וְהָיָה לֶאֱכֹל וּמְצָאֻהוּ רָעוֹת רַבּוֹת וְצָרוֹת וְאָמַר בַּיּוֹם
הַהוּא הֲלֹא עַל כִּי־אֵין אֱלֹהַי בְּקִרְבִּי מְצָאוּנִי הָרָעוֹת
הָאֵלֶּה: יח וְאָנֹכִי הַסְתֵּר אַסְתִּיר פָּנַי בַּיּוֹם הַהוּא עַל כָּל־
הָרָעָה אֲשֶׁר עָשָׂה כִּי פָנָה אֶל־אֱלֹהִים אֲחֵרִים: יט וְעַתָּה
כִּתְבוּ לָכֶם אֶת־הַשִּׁירָה הַזֹּאת וְלַמְּדָהּ אֶת־בְּנֵי־יִשְׂרָאֵל
שִׂימָהּ בְּפִיהֶם לְמַעַן תִּהְיֶה־לִּי הַשִּׁירָה הַזֹּאת לְעֵד בִּבְנֵי
יִשְׂרָאֵל: ששי שביעי כשהן מחוברין כ כִּי־אֲבִיאֶנּוּ אֶל־הָאֲדָמָה ׀
אֲשֶׁר־נִשְׁבַּעְתִּי לַאֲבֹתָיו זָבַת חָלָב וּדְבַשׁ וְאָכַל וְשָׂבַע וְדָשֵׁן
וּפָנָה אֶל־אֱלֹהִים אֲחֵרִים וַעֲבָדוּם וְנִאֲצוּנִי וְהֵפֵר אֶת־
בְּרִיתִי: כא וְהָיָה כִּי־תִמְצֶאןָ אֹתוֹ רָעוֹת רַבּוֹת וְצָרוֹת וְעָנְתָה
הַשִּׁירָה הַזֹּאת לְפָנָיו לְעֵד כִּי לֹא תִשָּׁכַח מִפִּי זַרְעוֹ כִּי
יָדַעְתִּי אֶת־יִצְרוֹ אֲשֶׁר הוּא עֹשֶׂה הַיּוֹם בְּטֶרֶם אֲבִיאֶנּוּ
אֶל־הָאָרֶץ אֲשֶׁר נִשְׁבָּעְתִּי: כב וַיִּכְתֹּב מֹשֶׁה אֶת־הַשִּׁירָה
הַזֹּאת בַּיּוֹם הַהוּא וַיְלַמְּדָהּ אֶת־בְּנֵי יִשְׂרָאֵל: כג וַיְצַו
אֶת־יְהוֹשֻׁעַ בִּן־נוּן וַיֹּאמֶר חֲזַק וֶאֱמָץ כִּי אַתָּה תָּבִיא
אֶת־בְּנֵי יִשְׂרָאֵל אֶל־הָאָרֶץ אֲשֶׁר־נִשְׁבַּעְתִּי לָהֶם וְאָנֹכִי
אֶהְיֶה עִמָּךְ: כד וַיְהִי ׀ כְּכַלּוֹת מֹשֶׁה לִכְתֹּב אֶת־דִּבְרֵי

Hashanah 31a), as we find in the prophet *Yechezkel* (9:3): "Then the glory of the God of Israel rose up from atop the Cherub on which it had been to the threshold of the House."

It is known that a prophecy which is accompanied by a demonstration or signs must come to pass. This is why the pillar of cloud left the Tent of Meeting and stood at the entrance of the Tent.

17. וְהָיָה לֶאֱכֹל — *And they will become prey*, [literally "it shall be to eat"]. A person who fulfills God's will has a purpose in life: to serve the Master of the Universe, to learn His Torah in order to know His will, to emulate His attributes, and to earn eternal life. But when a person fulfills his own will, what purpose is there in his vain life? Eating and drinking! He will become what the Torah describes as וְהָיָה לֶאֱכֹל: his הֲוָיָה, his *existence*, is לֶאֱכֹל, *eating* and drinking.

What a pathetic goal people choose for their lives when they stray from God! They live to eat, and they eat to live. It is not for nothing that these people spend their free time at the theaters and the movies, at sports and entertainments, at mindless parties and meaningless celebrations. They want to forget the bitter end that lies ahead, and the emptiness of a life with no other purpose than

but this people will rise up and stray after the gods of the
foreigners of the Land, in whose midst it is coming, and it will
forsake Me and annul My covenant that I have sealed with
it. 17 *My anger will flare against it on that day and I will*
forsake them; and I will conceal My face from them and they
will become prey, and many evils and distresses will
encounter it. It will say on that day, 'Is it not because my God
is not in my midst that these evils have come upon me?' 18 *But*
I will surely have concealed My face on that day because of
all the evil that it did, for it had turned to gods of others. 19 *So*
now, write this song for yourselves, and teach it to the
Children of Israel, place it in their mouth, so that this song
shall be for Me a witness against the Children of Israel.
20 *"For I shall bring them to the Land that I swore to their*
forefathers, which flows with milk and honey, but it will eat,
be sated, and grow fat, and turn to gods of others and serve
them, it will provoke Me and annul My covenant. 21 *It shall*
be that when many evils and distresses come upon it, then
this song shall speak up before it as a witness, for it shall not
be forgotten from the mouth of its offspring, for I know its
inclination, what it does today, before I bring them to the
Land that I have sworn."
22 *Moses wrote this song on that day, and he taught it to the*
Children of Israel. 23 *He commanded Joshua son of Nun, and*
said, "Be strong and courageous, for you shall bring the
Children of Israel to the Land that I have sworn to them, and
I shall be with you."
24 *So it was that when Moses finished writing the words*

---

satisfying one's stomach. They "will become prey," and not necessarily to others who may consume them when God's "face is concealed" from them. They consume themselves — their miserable existence. There are moments when in their heart of hearts they will admit, "is it not because my God is not in my midst that these evils have come upon me?" But it is difficult for them to escape the clutches of the Adversary who holds them in his grip.

22. וַיִּכְתֹּב מֹשֶׁה אֶת־הַשִּׁירָה הַזֹּאת — *Moses wrote this song*. The same expression, "this song," is mentioned in v. 19 above. The *Ramban* explains it as meaning the song of *Haazinu*, whose end (after all the indignation caused by "His sons and daughters," i.e., Israel, and His hiding His face from them) is "O nations, sing the praises of His people, for He will avenge the blood of His servants; He will bring retribution upon His foes, and He will appease His Land and His people" (32:43). The clear indication is that the Covenant will never be broken, until the end of all generations.

לא הַתּוֹרָה־הַזֹּאת עַל־סֵפֶר עַד תֻּמָּם: שביעי כה וַיְצַו מֹשֶׁה
כה־ל אֶת־הַלְוִיִּם נֹשְׂאֵי אֲרוֹן בְּרִית־יהוה לֵאמֹר: כו לָקֹחַ אֵת
סֵפֶר הַתּוֹרָה הַזֶּה וְשַׂמְתֶּם אֹתוֹ מִצַּד אֲרוֹן בְּרִית־יהוה
אֱלֹהֵיכֶם וְהָיָה־שָׁם בְּךָ לְעֵד: כז כִּי אָנֹכִי יָדַעְתִּי אֶת־מֶרְיְךָ
וְאֶת־עָרְפְּךָ הַקָּשֶׁה הֵן בְּעוֹדֶנִּי חַי עִמָּכֶם הַיּוֹם מַמְרִים
הֱיִתֶם עִם־יהוה וְאַף כִּי־אַחֲרֵי מוֹתִי: מפטיר כח הַקְהִילוּ אֵלַי
אֶת־כָּל־זִקְנֵי שִׁבְטֵיכֶם וְשֹׁטְרֵיכֶם וַאֲדַבְּרָה בְאָזְנֵיהֶם אֵת
הַדְּבָרִים הָאֵלֶּה *וְאָעִידָה בָּם אֶת־הַשָּׁמַיִם וְאֶת־הָאָרֶץ:
כט כִּי יָדַעְתִּי אַחֲרֵי מוֹתִי כִּי־הַשְׁחֵת תַּשְׁחִתוּן וְסַרְתֶּם
מִן־הַדֶּרֶךְ אֲשֶׁר צִוִּיתִי אֶתְכֶם וְקָרָאת אֶתְכֶם הָרָעָה
בְּאַחֲרִית הַיָּמִים כִּי־תַעֲשׂוּ אֶת־הָרַע בְּעֵינֵי יהוה לְהַכְעִיסוֹ
בְּמַעֲשֵׂה יְדֵיכֶם: ל וַיְדַבֵּר מֹשֶׁה בְּאָזְנֵי כָּל־קְהַל יִשְׂרָאֵל
אֶת־דִּבְרֵי הַשִּׁירָה הַזֹּאת עַד תֻּמָּם:

---

26. **לָקֹחַ אֵת סֵפֶר הַתּוֹרָה הַזֶּה וְשַׂמְתֶּם אֹתוֹ מִצַּד אֲרוֹן בְּרִית־ה׳ אֱלֹהֵיכֶם וְהָיָה־שָׁם בְּךָ לְעֵד** — *Take this book of the Torah and place it at the side of the Ark of the covenant of Hashem, and it shall be there for you as a witness*. The Torah has already said (v. 19) "so now write this song for yourselves." It is part of *Chazal's* tradition that it is a positive commandment for every Jew to write a Torah scroll, which contains the song of *Haazinu* (*Sefer HaChinuch*, commandment #613). Why, then, did Moses instruct the Levites to put the Torah scroll which he had written "at the side of the Ark of the covenant of Hashem," so that it would "be there for you as a witness"?

We must say that the Torah scroll written by Moses was not placed near the

31
25-30

of this Torah onto a book, until their conclusion: [25] *Moses*
commanded the Levites, the bearers of the Ark of the
covenant of HASHEM*, saying,* [26] *"Take this book of the Torah*
and place it at the side of the Ark of the covenant of HASHEM*,*
and it shall be there for you as a witness. [27] *For I know your*
rebelliousness and your stiff neck; behold! while I am still
alive with you today, you have been rebels against God —
and surely after my death. [28] *Gather to me all the elders of*
your tribes and your officers, and I shall speak these words
into their ears, and call heaven and earth to bear witness
against them. [29] *For I know that after my death you will*
surely act corruptly, and you will stray from the path that I
have commanded you, and evil will befall you at the end of
days, if you do what is evil in the eyes of HASHEM*, to anger*
Him through your handiwork."

[30] *Moses spoke the words of this song into the ears of the*
entire congregation of Israel, until their conclusion.

Ark for the sake of being studied. That would have been impossible, as the Ark was in the Holy of Holies, which no one ever entered, with the one exception of the High Priest on *Yom Kippur*. However, God knew well that in every generation there would be Jews who would falsify the Torah, "progressives" and "reformers" who would attempt to explain God's Torah in keeping with their own petty, small-minded, mistaken and misleading views. This is why God told His devoted servant Moses to preserve the Torah scroll which he personally would write in the securest of places, the Holy of Holies. It was to remain "there for you as a witness" that this is the genuine Torah.

פרשת האזינו
Parashas Haazinu

לב
א־ה

א הַאֲזִינוּ הַשָּׁמַיִם וַאֲדַבֵּרָה וְתִשְׁמַע הָאָרֶץ אִמְרֵי־פִי׃
ב יַעֲרֹף כַּמָּטָר לִקְחִי תִּזַּל כַּטַּל אִמְרָתִי
כִּשְׂעִירִם עֲלֵי־דֶשֶׁא וְכִרְבִיבִים עֲלֵי־עֵשֶׂב׃
ג כִּי שֵׁם יהוה אֶקְרָא הָבוּ גֹדֶל לֵאלֹהֵינוּ׃
ד הַצּוּר תָּמִים פָּעֳלוֹ כִּי כָל־דְּרָכָיו מִשְׁפָּט
אֵל אֱמוּנָה וְאֵין עָוֶל צַדִּיק וְיָשָׁר הוּא׃
ה שִׁחֵת לוֹ לֹא בָּנָיו מוּמָם דּוֹר עִקֵּשׁ וּפְתַלְתֹּל׃

---

1. **הַאֲזִינוּ הַשָּׁמַיִם וַאֲדַבֵּרָה וְתִשְׁמַע הָאָרֶץ אִמְרֵי־פִי** — *Give ear, O heavens, and I will speak; and may the earth hear the words of my mouth*. This phrasing includes a hint that if the prominent people of the community (the "heaven") come to hear rebuke from a Sage, then the common people (the "earth") will pay attention as well.

⁂ **הַאֲזִינוּ הַשָּׁמַיִם וַאֲדַבֵּרָה** — *Give ear, O heavens, and I will speak*. When a person wishes to explain something by way of a parable, he will choose a parable which uses concepts familiar to the listener. To a businessman he will speak about business, to a craftsmen about his trade, and to a thief about robberies. So, too, when Moses called upon heaven and earth to listen to his song, and he wanted to explain to them how worthwhile his words would be, he used examples close to their "interests." When speaking to the heavens he compared his words to rain and dew: "may my teaching drop like the rain, may my utterance flow like the dew." And to the earth he said that his words would be "like storm winds upon vegetation and like raindrops upon blades of grass" — things that grow from the earth, which knows how important and beneficial the winds are to vegetation and the raindrops to blades of grass.

⁂ **הַשָּׁמַיִם וַאֲדַבֵּרָה** — *O heavens, and I will speak*. Relatively speaking, דִּבּוּר connotes harsh words and אֲמָרִים soft ones. When rebuking people of lofty spiritual stature (the "heaven"), even if one speaks to them harshly (אֲדַבֵּרָה) his words will be accepted. But as for addressing the simple people (the "earth"), it would be wonderful if they would accept even soft words! They must be rebuked gently, lest they balk: "may the 'earth' hear the (soft) words of my mouth (אִמְרֵי פִי)."

3. **כִּי שֵׁם ה׳ אֶקְרָא הָבוּ גֹדֶל לֵאלֹהֵינוּ** — *When I call out the Name of Hashem, ascribe greatness to our God*. Why is the obligation to "ascribe greatness to our God" only mentioned now, and not on all the previous occasions when Moses mentioned God's name to the people? *Rashi* appears to take note of this difficulty (*Berachos* 21a, ד"ה כי שם): "When Moses was about to begin the song, he said to the Jews, 'I will bless first, and you answer Amen after me. I will call out the name of Hashem with a blessing, and you ascribe greatness to our God with an Amen.'" The obligation of answering Amen comes up only with holy songs and blessings.

32

1-5

[1] *Give ear, O heavens, and I will speak; and may the earth hear the words of my mouth.*

[2] *May my teaching drop like the rain, may my utterance flow like the dew; like storm winds upon vegetation and like raindrops upon blades of grass.*

[3] *When I call out the Name of* Hashem, *ascribe greatness to our God.*

[4] *The Rock! — perfect is His work, for all His paths are justice; a God of faith without iniquity, righteous and fair is He.*

[5] *Corruption is not His — the blemish is His children's, a perverse and twisted generation.*

However, song had been recited on two previous occasions. Why had Moses not mentioned this obligation to them at that time? We may answer that because the Song of the Sea was said by Moses and the Jewish people together — since the Divine Presence rested on the entire nation at the splitting of the Red Sea — there was no one there to respond Amen. The second song was the Song of the Well (*Bamidbar* 21:17-20), which was said only by the people: "Then Israel sang." Also, because Moses was punished on this occasion he is not mentioned, and so the name of God was not mentioned either out of respect for Moses. There was no need to caution the people to "ascribe greatness to our God," since His name was not mentioned.

This song of *Haazinu* is the only song which was said by Moses alone, through Divine inspiration, while the Jewish people listened. Since God's name is mentioned several times, Moses instructed the people to "ascribe greatness to our God."

4. הַצּוּר תָּמִים פָּעֳלוֹ כִּי כָל־דְּרָכָיו מִשְׁפָּט — *The Rock, perfect is His work, for all His paths are justice*. The Torah teaches the Jewish people that when they experience adversity at the End of Days (which this song testifies to), they should accept and justify the Heavenly decree. They should say, "for all His paths are justice," and not ask, "why did God do this to us?" (as we find among the embittered souls who ask why God empowered the Nazis, of cursed memory, to destroy six million of our Jewish brothers). They must know that He is a "God of faith without iniquity, righteous and fair is He." He is "'righteous' in all that has come upon us, "for He has acted truthfully and we have brought about wickedness." He is "fair" (יָשָׁר) in the sense of "good and upright (טוֹב וְיָשָׁר) is Hashem, therefore He guides sinners on the way" (*Tehillim* 25:8). Through adversity He shows us the way to return to Him.

5. שִׁחֵת לוֹ לֹא בָּנָיו מוּמָם — *Corruption is not His, the blemish is His children's.* "Even when they are full of blemishes, they are called His children" (R' Meir in the *Sifre*).

A son who cuts off his father's arm or leg may find himself expelled from the house and disinherited. But if the son cuts off his own arm or leg, even

לב ו הֲ לַיהוה תִּגְמְלוּ־זֹאת עַם נָבָל וְלֹא חָכָם
ו־ט הֲלוֹא־הוּא אָבִיךָ קָּנֶךָ הוּא עָשְׂךָ וַיְכֹנְנֶךָ׃
ז זְכֹר יְמוֹת עוֹלָם בִּינוּ שְׁנוֹת דֹּר־וָדֹר
שְׁאַל אָבִיךָ וְיַגֵּדְךָ זְקֵנֶיךָ וְיֹאמְרוּ־לָךְ׃
ח בְּהַנְחֵל עֶלְיוֹן גּוֹיִם בְּהַפְרִידוֹ בְּנֵי אָדָם
יַצֵּב גְּבֻלֹת עַמִּים לְמִסְפַּר בְּנֵי יִשְׂרָאֵל׃
ט כִּי חֵלֶק יהוָה עַמּוֹ יַעֲקֹב חֶבֶל נַחֲלָתוֹ׃

---

deliberately, the father would not disinherit him. In fact, after his first spate of anger, he would sympathize with him. This son would continue to remain the equal of any of his brothers.

The same is true of us. If our sins were to cause a blemish, so to speak, in our Father in Heaven, we might think that we would no longer be considered His children. But the "corruption" — the sins with which His sons anger Him — "is not His" — does not affect Him. Rather — "the blemish is His children's" — they brought it upon themselves. This is similar to the idea expressed in *Iyov* (35:6,8): "If you have sinned, how do you affect Him? Though your sins were many, what do you do to Him? . . . your wickedness is towards a man like yourself." Because of this, we remain God's children even if we have committed many sins.

6. הֲ לַה' תִּגְמְלוּ־זֹאת עַם נָבָל וְלֹא חָכָם — *Is it to Hashem that you do this, O vile and unwise people?* Had you received good from a human being and repaid him with evil, the name "vile nation" would be most appropriate. As Abigail told King David, when her husband Naval repaid David's good with bad, "his name is Naval [נָבָל], and vileness [נְבָלָה] accompanies him" (*I Shmuel*, 25:25). But if you acted that way towards the Master of the Universe, then you are not only a "vile" but an "unwise nation." For, aside from all that God has done for you in the past, your entire future lies in His hands! How could you have been so foolish as to behave this way towards God?

הֲלוֹא־הוּא אָבִיךָ — *Is He not your Father?* I am reminded of an incident which took place when I traveled to the Holy Land by boat. Sharing my cabin was an extremely wealthy man who owned factories abroad, as well as gardens and orchards in the Holy Land. His wealth had corrupted him, however, and he had abandoned God, His Torah, and its commandments. During our four days at sea I tried to speak to him about the existence of God, and my words made an impression on him. On the fourth day of our trip, he told me outright that I had bested him, and he now believed in God, but not in the Divine origin of the Torah. Why, for example, should God care if we slaughter an animal from the front of the neck or the back?

By this time our ship was approaching the Jaffa shore, I told him that I was sure that given another four days together, I would convince him also of the Divine origin of Torah. But what could I do now, with so little time left? We dropped the subject and went up to the deck to see the Holy Land from afar. A

32
6-9

[6] *Is it to* HASHEM *that you do this, O vile and unwise people? Is He not your Father, your Master? Has He not created you and firmed you?*

[7] *Remember the days of yore, understand the years of generation after generation. Ask your father and he will relate it to you, and your elders and they will tell you.*

[8] *When the Supreme One gave the nations their inheritance, when He separated the children of man, He set the borders of the peoples according to the number of the Children of Israel.*

[9] *For* HASHEM'*s portion is His people; Jacob is the measure of His inheritance.*

---

while later, I suddenly asked him if he had any children. Yes, he told me, he had a son studying in university, and a daughter still in high school.

"Why burden them with all that studying?" I asked him. "You have a big business and plenty of money, enough to keep them wealthy for the rest of their lives. Neither of them is going to work at the profession they are studying. Why trouble them with all this schooling? Would it not be better simply to allow them to stay home and enjoy themselves? Would that not be more appropriate for the children of a wealthy person like yourself?"

He looked at me with a mixture of amazement and scorn. "They are my children!" he told me. "I have to educate them; otherwise they will be uncivilized boors. It is worth it for them to exert themselves in school, so that afterwards they will be accepted in high society as educated, scientific people. This is as essential to their status as the money I spend on them, and which they stand to inherit."

I was very pleased with his answer. I told him, "Let your ears hear what your mouth has said: It is a father's obligation towards his children not only to provide them with food, clothing, shelter, and even wealth . . . he must also teach them wisdom and understanding. Be consistent. Once you admit that you now believe in God, Creator of man and the world, and that we are His children — accept also that He has to provide not only our physical needs, but also teach us wisdom and understanding, so that we will not be uncivilized boors! If you, a flesh and blood father, understand enough to provide this for your children, then how very much more does the Father of mankind understand! So He gave us the Divine Torah, heavenly wisdom which keeps us on the straight path and teaches us how to be accepted in the high society which we will encounter at the end of our earthly life: the angels in heaven."

My companion saw that his answer had tripped him up. At that moment, the ship docked and it was time to disembark. As he said goodbye, he was left with much to contemplate about God and His Torah.

The Torah reminds us, "is He not your Father?" It is His job to teach us understanding, and He gave us His Torah. How dare we disobey His words and live like wild men, like a vile נָבָל?

לב
י־יז

י יִמְצָאֵהוּ בְּאֶרֶץ מִדְבָּר   וּבְתֹהוּ יְלֵל יְשִׁמֹן
יְסֹבְבֶנְהוּ יְבוֹנְנֵהוּ   יִצְּרֶנְהוּ כְּאִישׁוֹן עֵינוֹ:
יא כְּנֶשֶׁר יָעִיר קִנּוֹ   עַל־גּוֹזָלָיו יְרַחֵף
יִפְרֹשׂ כְּנָפָיו יִקָּחֵהוּ   יִשָּׂאֵהוּ עַל־אֶבְרָתוֹ:
יב יְהוָה בָּדָד יַנְחֶנּוּ   וְאֵין עִמּוֹ אֵל נֵכָר:
בָּמֳתֵי ק׳ שלישי יג יַרְכִּבֵהוּ עַל־°בָּמותי אָרֶץ   וַיֹּאכַל תְּנוּבֹת שָׂדָי
וַיֵּנִקֵהוּ דְבַשׁ מִסֶּלַע   וְשֶׁמֶן מֵחַלְמִישׁ צוּר:
יד חֶמְאַת בָּקָר וַחֲלֵב צֹאן   עִם־חֵלֶב כָּרִים
וְאֵילִים בְּנֵי־בָשָׁן וְעַתּוּדִים   עִם־חֵלֶב כִּלְיוֹת חִטָּה
וְדַם־עֵנָב תִּשְׁתֶּה־חָמֶר: טו וַיִּשְׁמַן יְשֻׁרוּן וַיִּבְעָט
שָׁמַנְתָּ עָבִיתָ כָּשִׂיתָ   וַיִּטֹּשׁ אֱלוֹהַּ עָשָׂהוּ
וַיְנַבֵּל צוּר יְשֻׁעָתוֹ:   טז יַקְנִאֻהוּ בְּזָרִים
בְּתוֹעֵבֹת יַכְעִיסֻהוּ:   יז יִזְבְּחוּ לַשֵּׁדִים לֹא אֱלֹהַּ
אֱלֹהִים לֹא יְדָעוּם   חֲדָשִׁים מִקָּרֹב בָּאוּ

---

10. יִמְצָאֵהוּ בְּאֶרֶץ מִדְבָּר — *He discovered him in a desert land*. Until our ancestors went down to Egypt they were only "Jacob and his sons," a single family. Only in Egypt, when they increased and multiplied greatly, did Pharaoh call them "a nation": "Behold, the people [nation] the Children of Israel . . ." (*Shemos* 1:9).

But at that time they were not called "God's nation," since they worshiped idols in Egypt. When did God "discover" them, then? When they followed Him in the desert: "I remember to your credit the kindness of your youth . . . how you went after Me in the desert, in an unsown land" (*Yirmiyah* 2:2). Then "He encircled him" — with clouds of glory; "He granted him discernment" — through the giving of the Torah; "He preserved him like the pupil of His eye" — the way a man constantly safeguards the pupil of his eye. All this, of course, is to be taken figuratively, as the *Ramban* writes.

13. יַרְכִּבֵהוּ עַל־בָּמֳתֵי אָרֶץ — *He would make him ride on the heights of the Land*. "This refers to the Holy Land, which is higher than all other lands" (*Sifre*).

The Holy Land is like a "stage" (בָּמָה) for all the other countries; everyone watches to see what is happening there. This refers not only to the Jews in the Diaspora, but also to non-Jews: "it is the glory of all the lands" (*Yechezkel* 20:6,15).

In our time, when the right of self-determination has been granted to all nations, dozens of new states have been formed, large and small. But who ever talks about them? The media mention them once a year, if at all. The State of Israel, though it was only established after the Second World War (and after the Nazis murdered more than a third of the Jewish people), is on everyone's lips. There is not a newspaper in the world which doesn't mention Israel literally on

32
10-17

[10] *He discovered him in a desert land, in desolation, a howling wilderness; He encircled him, He granted him discernment, He preserved him like the pupil of His eye.*

[11] *He was like an eagle arousing its nest, hovering over its young, spreading its wings and taking them, carrying them on its pinions.*

[12] *HASHEM alone guided them, and no other power was with them.*

[13] *He would make him ride on the heights of the Land and have him eat the ripe fruits of the fields; He would suckle him with honey from a stone, and oil from a flinty rock;*

[14] *Butter of cattle and milk of sheep with fat of lambs, rams born in Bashan and he-goats, with wheat as fat as kidneys; and you would drink blood of grapes like delicious wine.*

[15] *Jeshurun became fat and kicked. You became fat, you became thick, you became corpulent — and it deserted God its Maker, and was contemptuous of the Rock of its salvation.*

[16] *They would provoke His jealousy with strangers; they would anger Him with abominations.*

[17] *They would slaughter to demons without power, gods whom they knew not, newcomers recently arrived,*

---

a daily basis. The Holy Land is truly a stage, with the whole world as the audience. Perhaps we were granted this dubious privilege because we forgot that God's eyes "are always upon it, [the Land] from the beginning of the year to year's end" (11:12).

15. וַיִּטֹּשׁ אֱלוֹהַ עָשָׂהוּ — *And it deserted God its Maker*. This is a description of how the people will go from bad to worse. At first a person still believes in God in his heart of hearts, but he "deserts" Him, and does not care about His commandments. Afterwards he shows "contempt to the Rock of his salvation." When he needs salvation, he seeks it by sacrificing to the work of the heavens, thus joining the name of idols, or the name of a human being, together with the name of God. There is no greater contempt for God's name than this. Now that this person has "shown contempt to the Rock of his salvation," the next step is "they would provoke His jealousy with strangers" — he denies God entirely.

17. אֱלֹהִים לֹא יְדָעוּם — *Gods whom they knew not*. They refuse to serve God, on the pretext that they have not "seen" Him and do not know Him. But they sacrifice to other gods, even though they never knew them any more than God. It was enough for them to hear from instigators that this idol eats and drinks and that idol does good or bad.

⚜ חֲדָשִׁים מִקָּרֹב בָּאוּ — *Newcomers recently arrived*. There is always a new idol. When the worshipers become convinced that their current idol is both

לב
יח־כב

לֹא שְׂעָרוּם אֲבֹתֵיכֶם׃   יח צוּר יְלָדְךָ תֶּשִׁי
וַתִּשְׁכַּח אֵל מְחֹלְלֶךָ׃   רביעי יט וַיַּרְא יהוה וַיִּנְאָץ
מִכַּעַס בָּנָיו וּבְנֹתָיו׃   כ וַיֹּאמֶר אַסְתִּירָה פָנַי מֵהֶם
אֶרְאֶה מָה אַחֲרִיתָם   כִּי דוֹר תַּהְפֻּכֹת הֵמָּה
בָּנִים לֹא־אֵמֻן בָּם׃   כא הֵם קִנְאוּנִי בְלֹא־*אֵל
כִּעֲסוּנִי בְּהַבְלֵיהֶם   וַאֲנִי אַקְנִיאֵם בְּלֹא־עָם
בְּגוֹי נָבָל אַכְעִיסֵם׃   כב כִּי־אֵשׁ קָדְחָה בְאַפִּי
וַתִּיקַד עַד־שְׁאוֹל תַּחְתִּית   וַתֹּאכַל אֶרֶץ וִיבֻלָהּ

---

worthless and useless, they take up a new one, until they see that that one too is worthless.

This is still true in our times. While we may think that there are no longer any idol worshipers today, this is not so. Any belief that man can improve his lot through his *own* efforts, without God's help, is a form of idol worship. Doctrines of this sort have sprung up like mushrooms in recent times, for example, the Berlin Enlightenment movement, which was supposed to improve the Jew's situation through secular education; democracy; socialism; and communism.

Then came reality and slapped all these modern-day idols in the face. Out of Berlin, cradle of the Enlightenment, came Nazism, whose avowed goal was the destruction of the Jewish people. During those difficult days neither the liberals nor the socialists defended us. They did not exert themselves in the slightest to save the Jews who were being slaughtered and burned.

The latest idol (and may it be the last, so that "His Name alone will be exalted" in our times) has been communism. Despite its motto of freedom, equality and peace, this doctrine was responsible for the vicious persecution of three million Jews trapped behind the Iron Curtain, tormenting them to the point that their lives were no longer worth living. "May God have mercy on them and remove them from distress and relief."

We have witnessed the fall of one specious utopian doctrine after the other. Each new one arises and destroys the one before it. Thus they are "newcomers recently arrived."

לֹא שְׂעָרוּם אֲבֹתֵיכֶם — *Whom your ancestors did not dread*. Parents generally understand, and assume as a fact, that their children will not follow in their footsteps with absolute fidelity. As *Chazal* tell us, "One must always say, 'When will my deeds reach those of my ancestors?" ' (*Tanna Devei Eliyahu Rabbah* ch. 25), indicating that children rarely reach their fathers' level of sanctity.

But in these days of spiritual "revolutions," when idols rise and fall one after the other, the first to serve them are Jewish sons and daughters. Their parents look on and see "their sons and daughters given to another nation" and its culture. They sigh bitterly, and declare that they never dreamed that their children would go so far.

whom your ancestors did not dread.
18 *You ignored the Rock Who gave birth to you, and forgot*
God Who brought you forth.
19 *HASHEM will see and be provoked by the anger of His*
sons and daughters,
20 *and He will say, "I shall hide My face from them and see*
what their end will be — for they are a generation of reversals,
children whose upbringing is not in them.
21 *They provoked Me with a non-god, angered Me with*
their vanities; so shall I provoke them with a non-people,
with a vile nation shall I anger them.
22 *For fire will have been kindled in My nostrils and blaze to*
the lowest depths. It shall consume the earth and its produce,

---

(Elsewhere I applied to these parents the words of the *Tishah B'Av* Dirges: "beloved children are slaughtered (spiritually) while the parents say *Shema*.")

Speaking figuratively, in the past the new generation moved away from the old on foot, or at most on horseback — not so far away, all in all. But today, with the advent of modern technology, the new generation jets thousands of miles away from the old in no time at all.

20. אַסְתִּירָה פָנַי מֵהֶם — *I shall hide My face from them.* "From Sinai descended hatred to the world" (*Shabbos* 89a): hatred of the Jews on the part of the non-Jewish nations, an eternal hatred for the eternal nation. It is only God's mercy and Providence which keeps them from destroying us, God forbid. "If not for God who was on our side when 'a man' rose up against us" (and it takes only one man, one enemy of the Jews, to incite the entire human race against us) "they would then have swallowed us alive" (*Tehillim* 124: 2-3).

We must understand, then, that all it takes is for our Father in Heaven to conceal His face from us, to put us in danger of annihilation, God forbid. But God promised us that He will "see what their end will be." If the gentiles plan to destroy us, then God comes to our rescue, as He promised us: "and also this, even when they are in the land of their enemies, I will neither despise them nor detest them, to destroy them, to breach My covenant with them" (*Vayikra* 26:44).

כִּי דוֹר תַּהְפֻּכֹת הֵמָּה בָּנִים לֹא־אֵמֻן בָּם — *For they are a generation of reversals, children whose upbringing is not in them.* Perhaps after they worship all the other gods and see that they are nothing, they will recognize God and return to Him. After all, there was no idol which Jethro did not worship, yet after seeing all the plagues which God brought upon Egypt, he said, "now I know that God is greater than all the gods" (*Shemos* 18:11). It is certainly possible for this to happen to the Jews, especially after all the blows they will receive in punishment for their sins.

לב וַתְּלַהֵט מוֹסְדֵי הָרִים׃ כג אַסְפֶּה עָלֵימוֹ רָעוֹת
כג־ל חִצַּי אֲכַלֶּה־בָּם׃ כד מְזֵי רָעָב וּלְחֻמֵי רֶשֶׁף
וְקֶטֶב מְרִירִי וְשֶׁן־בְּהֵמֹת אֲשַׁלַּח־בָּם
עִם־חֲמַת זֹחֲלֵי עָפָר׃ כה מִחוּץ תְּשַׁכֶּל־חֶרֶב
וּמֵחֲדָרִים אֵימָה גַּם־בָּחוּר גַּם־בְּתוּלָה
יוֹנֵק עִם־אִישׁ שֵׂיבָה׃ כו אָמַרְתִּי אַפְאֵיהֶם
אַשְׁבִּיתָה מֵאֱנוֹשׁ זִכְרָם׃ כז לוּלֵי כַּעַס אוֹיֵב אָגוּר
פֶּן־יְנַכְּרוּ צָרֵימוֹ פֶּן־יֹאמְרוּ יָדֵנוּ רָמָה
וְלֹא יהוה פָּעַל כָּל־זֹאת׃ כח כִּי־גוֹי אֹבַד עֵצוֹת הֵמָּה
וְאֵין בָּהֶם תְּבוּנָה׃ חמישי כט לוּ חָכְמוּ יַשְׂכִּילוּ זֹאת
יָבִינוּ לְאַחֲרִיתָם׃ ל אֵיכָה יִרְדֹּף אֶחָד אֶלֶף
וּשְׁנַיִם יָנִיסוּ רְבָבָה אִם־לֹא כִּי־צוּרָם מְכָרָם

---

23. **חִצַּי אֲכַלֶּה־בָּם** — *My arrows shall I use up against them.* "My arrows will be used up, and they [My people] will not be used up [destroyed] (*Rashi*)." How can it possibly be that God, so to speak, does not have enough arrows? Only because "they," the Jewish people, will not be destroyed. When they approach a point near destruction, it is as if God has no more arrows left, for He has already told us, "For I am Hashem, I have not changed, and you, the sons of Jacob, have not died out" (*Malachi* 3:6).

29. **לוּ חָכְמוּ** — *Were they wise.* The non-Jewish nations will "comprehend this" and not say "our hand was raised in triumph" (v. 27). "They will understand their end": If Israel receives such punishment, what will be the end of the nations who oppress them?

30. **אֵיכָה יִרְדֹּף אֶחָד אֶלֶף . . . אִם־לֹא כִּי־צוּרָם מְכָרָם וַה׳ הִסְגִּירָם** — *For how could one pursue a thousand... if not that their Rock had sold them out and Hashem had delivered them?* How will they be able to say "it was not Hashem Who accomplished all this" (v. 27)? It is humanly impossible for "two (to) cause a myriad to flee!"

כִּי־צוּרָם מְכָרָם — *That their Rock had sold them out.* Some commentators explain that these words refer to Abraham (the "rock from which they were hewn," i.e., their progenitor), who chose to have his sons be enslaved by the nations rather than be punished in *Gehinnom* (*Bereishis Rabbah* 44:21). Abraham's choice was based on God's advice. We may add that this is why the Torah says "and Hashem delivered them": God's attribute of kindness agreed with this plan, and advised Abraham (at the Covenant Between the Parts), to choose enslavement by the nations; the enslavement would take place in a transitory world, while *Gehinnom* is in an eternal world.

רְבָבָה — *A myriad.* In the blessings in *Parashas Bechukosai* the Torah promised that "five of you will pursue one hundred, and one hundred of you

and set ablaze what is founded on mountains.
23 *I shall accumulate evils against them, My arrows shall I*
use up against them;
24 *bloating of famine, battles of flaming demons, cutting*
down by the noontime demon, and the teeth of beasts shall I
dispatch against them, with the venom of those that creep on
the earth.
25 *On the outside, the sword will bereave, while indoors*
there will be dread — even a young man, even a virgin, a
suckling with the gray-haired man.
26 *I had said, 'I will scatter them, I will cause their memory*
to cease from man' —
27 *were it not that the anger of the enemy was pent up, lest*
the tormenter misinterpret; lest they say, 'Our hand was
raised in triumph, and it was not HASHEM *Who accomplished*
all this!'
28 *For they are a nation bereft of counsel, and there is no*
discernment in them.
29 *Were they wise they would comprehend this, they would*
discern it from their end.
30 *For how could one pursue a thousand, and two cause*
a myriad to flee, if not that their Rock had sold them out,

---

will pursue ten thousand" (*Vayikra* 26:8). *Rashi* asks (ad loc., based on *Sifra*), "Is this the correct calculation? [Proportionally speaking,] it should have said that one hundred will chase two thousand. However, a few people who keep the Torah cannot be compared to many people who keep the Torah; [their merit grows far faster than any numerical proportion]."

We find the same difficulty here. Are the numbers given in this verse the correct calculation? It should have said "and two will chase two thousand." Why, then, does *Rashi* not bring up this question? I found this question in the commentary of R' Eliayahu Mizrahi on *Rashi*. He adds that we cannot say in this case that the few who transgress the Torah cannot be compared to the many who transgress the Torah. We have heard that when the many are righteous, their collective merit is greater than the collective merit of the few, but we have never heard that when the many are wicked, their collective punishment is greater than that of the few. (See R' Mizrahi's commentary for his answer to this question.)

It seems to me that even if the punishment of the many were indeed greater than the punishment of the few, this answer would not apply here. For following this logic, the decisive factor would have to be not the increased number of pursuers, but the increased number of sinners being pursued. This would mean that if one enemy was able to chase a thousand sinners, he should still more be able to chase ten thousand sinners, for their accumulated guilt

לב וַיהוָה הִסְגִּירָם: לא כִּי לֹא כְצוּרֵנוּ צוּרָם
לא־מ וְאֹיְבֵינוּ פְּלִילִים: לב כִּי־מִגֶּפֶן סְדֹם גַּפְנָם
וּמִשַּׁדְמֹת עֲמֹרָה עֲנָבֵמוֹ עִנְּבֵי־רוֹשׁ
אַשְׁכְּלֹת מְרֹרֹת לָמוֹ: לג חֲמַת תַּנִּינִם יֵינָם
וְרֹאשׁ פְּתָנִים אַכְזָר: לד הֲלֹא־הוּא כָּמֻס עִמָּדִי
חָתוּם בְּאוֹצְרֹתָי: לה לִי נָקָם וְשִׁלֵּם
לְעֵת תָּמוּט רַגְלָם כִּי קָרוֹב יוֹם אֵידָם
וְחָשׁ עֲתִדֹת לָמוֹ: לו כִּי־יָדִין יהוה עַמּוֹ
וְעַל־עֲבָדָיו יִתְנֶחָם כִּי יִרְאֶה כִּי־אָזְלַת יָד
וְאֶפֶס עָצוּר וְעָזוּב: לז וְאָמַר אֵי אֱלֹהֵימוֹ
צוּר חָסָיוּ בוֹ: לח אֲשֶׁר חֵלֶב זְבָחֵימוֹ יֹאכֵלוּ
יִשְׁתּוּ יֵין נְסִיכָם יָקוּמוּ וְיַעְזְרֻכֶם
יְהִי עֲלֵיכֶם סִתְרָה: לט רְאוּ ׀ עַתָּה כִּי אֲנִי אֲנִי הוּא
וְאֵין אֱלֹהִים עִמָּדִי אֲנִי אָמִית וַאֲחַיֶּה
מָחַצְתִּי וַאֲנִי אֶרְפָּא וְאֵין מִיָּדִי מַצִּיל:
ששי מ כִּי־אֶשָּׂא אֶל־שָׁמַיִם יָדִי וְאָמַרְתִּי חַי אָנֹכִי לְעֹלָם:

---

and resultant vulnerability would grow increasingly greater the more sinners there are.

Apparently to find a suitable answer we must look carefully at the wording of the verse. In speaking about one, the Torah says he "will pursue [יִרְדֹּף]." But when speaking about two, the Torah says "will cause ... to flee [יָנִיסוּ]." This means that one gentile will see a thousand Jews and pursue them; while ten thousand Jews will fall upon two gentiles, and the gentiles will be able to "cause them all to flee." This verse, then, speaks about two different cases: first about a thousand Jews being pursued by a single gentile, and then about two gentiles who will defend themselves from attack by ten thousand Jews.

34. הֲלֹא־הוּא כָּמֻס עִמָּדִי — *Is it not revealed with Me?* The "wine" (v. 33, "serpent's venom is their wine") which I will give the idol worshipers and enemies of the Jews to drink is "sealed in My treasuries."

36. כִּי־יָדִין ה׳ עַמּוֹ — *When Hashem will have judged His people*. When the Jews are universally called "God's nation," the time for the Redemption will arrive at once, and with it the Day of Judgment: "God will judge [the judgment of] His people" — their claim against their pursuers and oppressors.

39. וְאֵין אֱלֹהִים עִמָּדִי אֲנִי אָמִית — *And no god is with Me. I put to death.* "If there were two Powers, how would people die? Would the two Powers reach an agreement to kill them at the same moment?" (*Sanhedrin* 39a). From the fact that "I put to death" we see that there is "no god with Me" giving life to the world's inhabitants.

and HASHEM had delivered them?

31 *— for not like our Rock is their rock — yet our enemies judge us!*

32 *For their vineyard is from the vineyard of Sodom, and from the fields of Gomorrah; their grapes are grapes of gall, so clusters of bitterness were given them.*

33 *Serpents' venom is their wine, the poison of cruel vipers.*

34 *Is it not revealed with Me, sealed in My treasuries?*

35 *Mine is vengeance and retribution at the time when their foot will falter, for the day of their catastrophe is near, and future events are rushing at them."*

36 *When HASHEM will have judged His people, He shall relent regarding His servants, when He sees that enemy power progresses, and none is saved or assisted.*

37 *He will say, "Where is their god, the rock in whom they sought refuge,*

38 *the fat of whose offerings they would eat, they would drink the wine of their libations? Let them stand and help you! Let them be a shelter for you!*

39 *See, now, that I, I am He — and no god is with Me. I put to death and I bring life, I struck down and I will heal, and there is no rescuer from My hand.*

40 *For I shall raise My hand to heaven and say, 'As I live forever,*

אֲנִי אָמִית וַאֲחַיֶּה — *I put to death and I bring life*. We may ask, have there not been many generations who angered God? Have there not always been enemies of the Jews in every generation who rose up against them to destroy them? Can it be that only the final generation of rebellious sinners and oppressors will be judged and punished? By the same token, will only the Jews alive at that time enjoy the ultimate reward?

It is in answer to these questions that the Torah adds the words "I put to death and I bring life." Says God, I will inflict a violent, eternal death on all those found guilty on the Day of Judgment. I will also revive all the dead: to all the Jews who were persecuted throughout the generations I will grant eternal life, while their oppressors will receive eternal perdition. "Their grave-worms will not die nor their fire go out; it will be loathsome for all flesh" (*Yeshayah* 66:24). As for those alive at the time of Judgment, "I struck down" the wicked and "I will heal" those crippled by the blows of their persecutors and oppressors, "and there is no rescuer from My hand."

40. כִּי־אֶשָּׂא אֶל־שָׁמַיִם יָדִי וְאָמַרְתִּי חַי אָנֹכִי לְעֹלָם — *For I shall raise My hand to heaven and say, "As I live forever."* The commentators explain that this means that an oath was being taken. We find a similar usage in Daniel (12:7):

לב
מא־מו

מא אִם־שַׁנּוֹתִי֙ בְּרַ֣ק חַרְבִּ֔י   וְתֹאחֵ֥ז בְּמִשְׁפָּ֖ט יָדִ֑י
אָשִׁ֤יב נָקָם֙ לְצָרָ֔י   וְלִמְשַׂנְאַ֖י אֲשַׁלֵּֽם׃
מב אַשְׁכִּ֤יר חִצַּי֙ מִדָּ֔ם   וְחַרְבִּ֖י תֹּאכַ֣ל בָּשָׂ֑ר
מִדַּ֤ם חָלָל֙ וְשִׁבְיָ֔ה   מֵרֹ֖אשׁ פַּרְע֥וֹת אוֹיֵֽב׃
מג הַרְנִ֤ינוּ גוֹיִם֙ עַמּ֔וֹ   כִּ֥י דַם־עֲבָדָ֖יו יִקּ֑וֹם
וְנָקָם֙ יָשִׁ֣יב לְצָרָ֔יו   וְכִפֶּ֥ר אַדְמָת֖וֹ עַמּֽוֹ׃
שביעי מד וַיָּבֹ֣א מֹשֶׁ֗ה וַיְדַבֵּ֛ר אֶת־כָּל־דִּבְרֵ֥י הַשִּׁירָֽה־הַזֹּ֖את
בְּאָזְנֵ֣י הָעָ֑ם ה֖וּא וְהוֹשֵׁ֥עַ בִּן־נֽוּן׃ מה וַיְכַ֣ל מֹשֶׁ֗ה לְדַבֵּ֛ר
אֶת־כָּל־הַדְּבָרִ֥ים הָאֵ֖לֶּה אֶל־כָּל־יִשְׂרָאֵֽל׃ מו וַיֹּ֤אמֶר אֲלֵהֶם֙

"He lifted his right hand and his left hand to heaven and swore by the Life of the World" about the time of the Final Redemption. But this refers to an angel who was on earth at the time, and lifted his hand to heaven when he swore. How can it be said (even figuratively) of God, Whose glory fills the universe and Who resides in the heaven above, that He lifted His hand to heaven? I have found that the *Ha'amek Davar* was also aware of this difficulty.

In my opinion it is no question at all. This verse refers to the End of Days, at the time of the War of Gog and Magog before the great Day of Judgment. Of that time the prophet *Zechariah* says, "[God's] feet will stand on the Mount of Olives on the day" (14:4), and then He will lift His hand to the sky and swear by His great Name.

42. אַשְׁכִּיר חִצַּי מִדָּם — *I shall intoxicate My arrows with blood*. Says God, When I struck the Jews, I saved them from extinction: "'I shall use up My arrows on them' — My arrows will be used up, but they will not be used up (i.e., destroyed)" (*Sotah* 9a). But when I extend My hand in judgment against the enemies of the Jews, then I will "intoxicate My arrows with blood."

They will be destroyed, and God's arrows will not be used up. As the prophet *Yeshayah* says, "Have I ever struck [Israel] with the blow that I struck his enemies?" (27:7)

מִדַּם חָלָל וְשִׁבְיָה — *Because of the blood of corpse and captive*. The gentile oppressors deserve this in retribution for the blood of the Jewish dead, and the blood of the wounded Jews whom they took captive.

מֵרֹאשׁ פַּרְעוֹת אוֹיֵב — *With the heads of the riotous enemy* [According to *Ibn Ezra and Targum Yerushalmi*]. I found one commentator who writes that this verse refers to the enemy's monks, who grow the hair on their heads long to cultivate "holiness." In reality, they were the first to instigate riots and pogroms against the Jews in the name of their faith. This song of *Haazinu* is also alluding here to the medieval Crusaders, who gorged themselves on Jewish blood and destroyed many, many Jewish communities. They are also alluded to in *Tehillim* (68:22): "God will cleave only the head of His foes, the hairy skull

41 if I sharpen My flashing sword and My hand grasps
judgment, I shall return vengeance upon My enemies and
upon those that hate Me shall I bring retribution.
42 I shall intoxicate My arrows with blood and My sword
shall devour flesh, because of the blood of corpse and captive,
because of the earliest depredations of the enemy.' "
43 O nations — sing the praises of His people, for He will
avenge the blood of His servants; He will bring retribution
upon His foes, and He will appease His Land and His people.
44 Moses came and spoke all the words of this Song in the
ears of the people, he and Hoshea son of Nun. 45 Moses con-
cluded speaking all these words to all Israel. 46 He said to them,

---

of him who saunters along with his guilt." They too will be punished on the Day of Judgment, even if they acted "for their faith."

43. הַרְנִינוּ גוֹיִם עַמּוֹ — *O nations, sing the praises of His people*. (The word הַרְנִינוּ may also be translated as "gladden.") In this verse, Moses turns to the nations of the world with a request: If the Jews sin and are exiled from their land, try לְהַרְנִין, to bring a bit of song into their lives and make their exile pleasant. If the nations should embitter their resident Jews' lives, they will be punished for it: "for He will avenge the blood of His servants." Even those oppressors of the Jews who only robbed them or abused them economically will be punished: "He will bring retribution upon His foes."

§ **וְכִפֶּר אַדְמָתוֹ עַמּוֹ** — *And He will appease His Land and His people*. "The Land will not be appeased for the blood that was spilled in it, except with the blood of the one who spilled it." (*Bamidbar* 35:33). God will bring all those nations who fought the Jews in the Holy Land and spilled their blood like water around Jerusalem; He will gather them to wage war with them in Jerusalem (*Zechariah* 14:2). With their blood, the Jews will appease His Land.

§ [וְכִפֶּר אַדְמָתוֹ may also be translated as "His Land will atone."] *Midrash Tanchuma* and *Midrash Rabbah* on *Parashas Eikev* explain that the fruits of the Holy Land atone for the Jewish people, through the commandments of first-fruits, tithes, and flour-offerings, which the Jews bring from their produce.

44. וַיָּבֹא מֹשֶׁה — *Moses came*. Where did he come from? The *Sifre* (at the beginning of this *Parashah*) writes that when Moses recited this song he was "close to heaven." This is why he said "Give ear" to the heavens, but since he was "far from the earth," he said "may the earth hear." Now that he came back down from heaven to earth to teach the Jewish people, the Torah says, "Moses came."

§ **הוּא וְהוֹשֵׁעַ בִּן־נוּן** — *He and Hoshea son of Nun*. Moses had previously added the letter י to his original name הוֹשֵׁעַ changing it to יְהוֹשֻׁעַ, and prayed for him, "may God save you from the counsel of the spies." Authority was now

לב שִׂימוּ לְבַבְכֶם לְכָל־הַדְּבָרִים אֲשֶׁר אָנֹכִי מֵעִיד בָּכֶם הַיּוֹם
מז־נ אֲשֶׁר תְּצַוֻּם אֶת־בְּנֵיכֶם לִשְׁמֹר לַעֲשׂוֹת אֶת־כָּל־דִּבְרֵי
הַתּוֹרָה הַזֹּאת׃ מז כִּי לֹא־דָבָר רֵק הוּא מִכֶּם כִּי־הוּא
חַיֵּיכֶם וּבַדָּבָר הַזֶּה תַּאֲרִיכוּ יָמִים עַל־הָאֲדָמָה אֲשֶׁר אַתֶּם
עֹבְרִים אֶת־הַיַּרְדֵּן שָׁמָּה לְרִשְׁתָּהּ׃
מפטיר מח וַיְדַבֵּר יהוה אֶל־מֹשֶׁה בְּעֶצֶם הַיּוֹם הַזֶּה לֵאמֹר׃
מט עֲלֵה אֶל־הַר הָעֲבָרִים הַזֶּה הַר־נְבוֹ אֲשֶׁר בְּאֶרֶץ מוֹאָב
אֲשֶׁר עַל־פְּנֵי יְרֵחוֹ וּרְאֵה אֶת־אֶרֶץ כְּנַעַן אֲשֶׁר אֲנִי נֹתֵן
לִבְנֵי יִשְׂרָאֵל לַאֲחֻזָּה׃ נ וּמֻת בָּהָר אֲשֶׁר אַתָּה עֹלֶה שָׁמָּה

---

being transferred to Joshua, and a few days later he would be sending out spies himself. So the Torah hints that from now on it would be possible to call him Hoshea, the name his father had given him. However, it would only be on this one occasion, to point out the change in his status. Afterwards he would continue to be known by the name his teacher had given him: "Yehoshua."

48. וַיְדַבֵּר ה׳ אֶל־מֹשֶׁה — *Hashem spoke to Moses*. When Moses was informed of this bitter prophecy in *Parashas Pinchas*, the Torah used the word וַיֹּאמֶר, which is used for words spoken softly. Here, in mentioning the same matter, we find וַיְדַבֵּר, used for harsh words, in discussing the very same information. What had happened in the meantime?

We find in the *Malbim's* commentary on *Parashas Pinchas* that at that time Moses was not actually told to ascend the mountain to die there. God even promised him, "you will see it [the Land] and you will be gathered unto your people" (*Bamidbar* 27:13)" — Moses would see the Land a second time before his death. This is why the word וַיֹּאמֶר is used, since the blow was not such a hard one and was softened by a promise.

In the present verse the situation is different. Moses was now being told to ascend the mountain, where he would die that very day. All his entreaties to remain alive as an ordinary person, and the like, were now finally refused. This explains the harsher term וַיְדַבֵּר.

In our commentary on *Parashas Pinchas* we explained at length that Moses's ascent to the mountain on that occasion was so that he would be familiar with the Holy Land (very thoroughly familiar, as we explain there) and would know how much land to give to the tribes of Reuben and Gad in the Trans-Jordan. (These tribes were to receive a share equal in value to that of the other tribes west of the Jordan.) In addition, this view of the Holy Land showed Moses that there was enough territory available to give half of the tribe of Manasseh land in the Trans-Jordan as well.

49. עֲלֵה אֶל־הַר הָעֲבָרִים הַזֶּה — *Ascend to this mount of Abarim* .... From the words "this mount" we understand that Moses was standing next to the mountain in question, and God pointed at it, so to speak. Why, then, was further

32
47-50

"Apply your hearts to all the words that I testify against you
today, with which you are to instruct your children, to be
careful to perform all the words of this Torah, 47 *for it is not*
an empty thing for you, for it is your life, and through this
matter shall you prolong your days on the Land to which you
cross the Jordan, to possess it."
48 *HASHEM spoke to Moses on that very day, saying,*
49 *"Ascend to this mount of Abarim, Mount Nebo, which is*
in the land of Moab, which is before Jericho, and see the
Land of Canaan that I give to the Children of Israel as an in-
heritance, 50 *and die on the mountain where you will ascend,*

---

identification necessary ("Mount Nebo which is in the land of Moab, which is before Jericho")?

We can explain this according to the *Sifre*, which tells us that this mountain had four names: the mount of Abarim, Mount Nebo; Mount Hor; and *Rosh Hapisgah* (3:27). And why was it called "the mount of Abarim" (הַר הָעֲבָרִים)? Because three people were buried there who did not die as a result of sin (עֲבֵרָה): Moses, Aaron and Miriam. (In this case we must say that this mountain was very wide, extending from the border of Edom to before Jericho.) The *Zayis Ra'anan* adds that נְבוֹ, "Nebo," is an abbreviation נָחָשׁ בּוֹ, "a snake involved in it": those buried there died only due to the snake's counsel to Eve.

We may say, then, that the point of all these identifying terms was to appease Moses. His bones would not be buried in the Holy Land. Yet Aaron and Miriam (interred at his feet, near Kadesh,) were also buried on this mountain, Mt. Hor, making it something of a family plot for these three shepherds of Israel. The name Mount Abarim also testified that the three buried there were free of sin. The name Mount Nebo meant that they had only died because of the snake's enticement of Eve, not because of any sins of their own. God also specified that Moses should ascend the "mount of Abarim, Mount Nebo . . . which is before Jericho," so that he could see the Holy Land from this vantage point.

50. וּמֻת בָּהָר — *And die on the mountain*. Can a person choose to die at the moment when he wishes? Do *Chazal* not tell us, "against your will, you die" (*Pirkei Avos* 4:29)?

The *Ibn Ezra* was aware of this difficulty, and added the explanatory words, "he was to prepare himself, for he would bury himself [by closing himself up in a cave]." This is satisfactory according to the opinion that Moses buried himself; but according to the opinion that God buried him, what does "and die" mean?

It seems to me that it means that he must prepare himself to die, the same way as Aaron had — something which Moses wanted very much. He was to lie down on the bier, stretch out his hands and feet, shut his eyes, and close his mouth, as explained in the *Sifre* here and in *Parashas Korach*. This is the meaning of "and die . . . as Aaron your brother died": Moses was to prepare himself for his death just as Aaron had done.

לב וְהֵאָסֵף אֶל־עַמֶּיךָ כַּאֲשֶׁר־מֵת אַהֲרֹן אָחִיךָ בְּהֹר הָהָר
נא־נב וַיֵּאָסֶף אֶל־עַמָּיו: נא עַל אֲשֶׁר מְעַלְתֶּם בִּי בְּתוֹךְ בְּנֵי
יִשְׂרָאֵל בְּמֵי־מְרִיבַת קָדֵשׁ מִדְבַּר־צִן עַל אֲשֶׁר לֹא־
קִדַּשְׁתֶּם אוֹתִי בְּתוֹךְ בְּנֵי יִשְׂרָאֵל: נב כִּי מִנֶּגֶד תִּרְאֶה
אֶת־הָאָרֶץ וְשָׁמָּה לֹא תָבוֹא אֶל־הָאָרֶץ אֲשֶׁר־אֲנִי נֹתֵן
לִבְנֵי יִשְׂרָאֵל:

32 *and be gathered to your people, as Aaron your brother died*
51-52 *on Mount Hor, and was gathered to his people,* [51] *because you*
trespassed against Me among the Children of Israel at the
waters of Meribath-kadesh, in the wilderness of Zin; because
you did not sanctify Me among the Children of Israel. [52] *For*
from a distance shall you see the Land, but you shall not enter
there, into the Land that I give to the Children of Israel."

פרשת וזאת הברכה
Parashas Vezos Haberachah

לג א וְזֹאת הַבְּרָכָה אֲשֶׁר בֵּרַךְ מֹשֶׁה אִישׁ הָאֱלֹהִים אֶת־בְּנֵי
א־ב יִשְׂרָאֵל לִפְנֵי מוֹתוֹ׃ ב וַיֹּאמַר יהוה מִסִּינַי בָּא וְזָרַח מִשֵּׂעִיר
לָמוֹ הוֹפִיעַ מֵהַר פָּארָן וְאָתָה מֵרִבְבֹת קֹדֶשׁ מִימִינוֹ

33.

1. וְזֹאת הַבְּרָכָה אֲשֶׁר בֵּרַךְ מֹשֶׁה אִישׁ הָאֱלֹהִים אֶת־בְּנֵי יִשְׂרָאֵל לִפְנֵי מוֹתוֹ — *And this is the blessing that Moses, the man of God, bestowed upon the Children of Israel before his death*. A blessing is likely to come true if four conditions are fulfilled:

First, that the giver of the blessing loves the recipient and blesses him with all his heart. We find this fulfilled in the words "the blessing that Moses... bestowed." Even heretical sects admitted that Moses loved the Jewish people (*Menachos* 65a).

Second, that the one who bestows the blessing is a righteous person, whose bidding would be done by God. This corresponds to the words "the man of God" in our present verse; the blessing of such a man was indeed a blessing.

Third, that the recipient is capable of receiving the blessing. Here the blessing was bestowed on "the Children of Israel," of whom God Himself had spoken well and said to Balaam, "for he is blessed."

Fourth, that the blessing is given at an opportune time. This is why the Torah says "before his death," when the Divine Presence rested on Moses.

⁂ **הַבְּרָכָה אֲשֶׁר בֵּרַךְ מֹשֶׁה** — *The blessing that Moses... bestowed*. We do not find that Aaron blessed the people before his death. Perhaps this is because for years he had bestowed the Priestly Blessing upon them daily, as part of the service in the Tabernacle.

⁂ **לִפְנֵי מוֹתוֹ** — *Before his death*. We already know that this episode took place before Moses' death. Why does the Torah emphasize it again? Because it wants to let us know how pious Moses was. Even in his very last moments, he did not stop begging God to let him cross the Jordan as just an ordinary person, or at least to allow his bones to be buried in the Holy Land, for which he so longed (as we see in the *Midrashim*). God always answered him, "you shall not come there, you shall not pass there"; neither alive nor dead. And God spelled out the reason for this decree: the sin at the Waters of Strife.

Now, we all know that the Jewish people were responsible for Moses' sin. They quarreled with him at the Waters of Strife, arguing over which stone would be the one from which he produced water. Their interest was not only in water to quench their thirst, but in testing Moses (and God, too); would he be able to bring water out of the stone they showed him? Moses was angered to the point of saying, "Hear, rebellious ones! Shall we bring water for you out of this stone?" (*Bamidbar* 20:10), and so he slipped into error. As Moses told the people, "God was angry with me because of you and did not listen to me."

33
1-2

[1]*And this is the blessing that Moses, the man of God, bestowed upon the Children of Israel before his death.* [2] *He said: HASHEM came from Sinai — having shone forth to them from Seir, having appeared from Mount Paran, and then approached with some of the holy myriads — from His right hand*

At the last minute, God now told Moses again that "because you did not sanctify Me among the Children of Israel . . . there [i.e., to the Land] you will not come" (32:51-52). He commanded him to ascend the mountain and die there, and be buried in the land of Moab.

Another person in his place would certainly have been angry at the Jews, who had brought him to this plight. But the most humble of men, the lover of Israel, even "before his death" in the land of Moab, while his dream crumbled about him, still blessed the Jews wholeheartedly and with open love. For this reason our *parashah* starts "*And* this is the blessing" (וְזֹאת הַבְּרָכָה), linking it to "but you shall not enter there" (32:52), with a connecting letter ו.

☙ Moses had already blessed the people: "May Hashem, the God of your forefathers, add to you a thousand times yourselves, and bless you as He has spoken of you" (1:11). But following this blessing came — the curses of *Ki Savo*.

It was different with the blessing bestowed by Moses before his death. These were the final words of the man of God to the Jewish people. They were also the final testament of a merciful father to his sons, in which he assessed each one's talents and actions. This assessment, which came from the heart of a loving and beloved father, is still preserved in the hearts of his children, to their own benefit and that of their children after them.

2. **וַיֹּאמַר ה׳ מִסִּינַי בָּא וְזָרַח מִשֵּׂעִיר לָמוֹ הוֹפִיעַ מֵהַר פָּארָן** — *He said: Hashem came from Sinai — having shone forth to them from Seir, having appeared from Mount Paran*. *Chazal* learn from this verse that God approached all the nations and asked them if they would accept the Torah. Each nation refused, and so it went until He came to Israel and they accepted the Torah (*Avodah Zarah* 2b). But if God approached every nation of the world, why does the Torah only mention Seir and Paran by name?

We may say that these two nations, the children of Edom and Ishmael, had the opportunity to learn Torah in their father's homes: Ishmael could have learned from Abraham, and Esau from Isaac. (For this reason God first approached Esau, even though Ishmael came first chronologically. Whereas Ishmael spent only a short time in his father's home before being expelled, Esau spent many years in Isaac's home. What is more, he should also have learned from his grandfather Abraham, who was still alive during Esau's lifetime. Instead Esau was responsible for shortening his grandfather's life.)

These two nations had all the prerequisites for accepting the Torah, yet even so, they did not accept it. One could not expect so much of the other nations, since they had neither the family background nor the preparation for fulfilling the commandments of the Torah.

לג °אֵשׁ דָּת ק׳ °אֶשְׁדָּת לָמוֹ: ג אַף חֹבֵב עַמִּים כָּל־קְדֹשָׁיו בְּיָדֶךָ וְהֵם
ג־ו תֻּכּוּ לְרַגְלֶךָ יִשָּׂא מִדַּבְּרֹתֶיךָ: ד תּוֹרָה צִוָּה־לָנוּ מֹשֶׁה
מוֹרָשָׁה קְהִלַּת יַעֲקֹב: ה וַיְהִי בִישֻׁרוּן מֶלֶךְ בְּהִתְאַסֵּף רָאשֵׁי
עָם יַחַד שִׁבְטֵי יִשְׂרָאֵל: ו יְחִי רְאוּבֵן וְאַל־יָמֹת וִיהִי מְתָיו

In the *Yalkut Shimoni* on this *parashah* we find the argument of Esau's descendants why they could not accept the Torah: it says "You shall not murder," but their father Isaac had blessed them with the sword ("you shall live by your sword"). Similarly, the descendants of Ishmael objected to the Torah saying "You shall not steal." Since their father Abraham had banished Ishmael to the desert, where there is no planting or harvesting, they were forced to live by stealing. In other words, they argued that conditions in the desert, and their "upbringing," forced them to live the way they do.

The *Yalkut Shimoni* also records the contention of the descendants of Lot that they, too, could not possibly keep the commandment of "You shall not commit adultery," seeing as their nation came into the world through adultery.

Responses from the other nations are not mentioned at all; apparently they did not even care to ask what it says in the Torah. This is not surprising; the other nations had nothing in their backgrounds to give them an inner motivation to accept the yoke of Torah and its commandments; they were content to live lawlessly. But Esau and Ishmael felt that at the very least they had to excuse themselves for their unwillingness to accept the Torah, seeing as the children of Jacob did accept it.

It was the same with the descendants of Lot, who traveled with Abraham and learned from him many things which are written in the Torah (things which the Jews were later commanded by *Chazal* to observe — our Fathers kept the entire Torah). They also felt the need to justify their refusal. However, the Torah specifically mentions only Esau and Ishmael. They had the merit of ancestry and education, unlike the descendants of Lot, who separated himself entirely from Abraham, and whose progeny are blemished by their incestuous origin.

אֵשׁ דָּת — *The fiery Torah*. Fire illuminates the darkness, shows us the way, warms us when it is cold, and cooks our food. But at the same time, care must be taken not to be burned by its flames or embers; fire consumes all that is in its path, the body and the soul. This is our "fiery Torah."

3. וְהֵם תֻּכּוּ לְרַגְלֶךָ — *They gathered between [planted themselves at] Your feet*.

The Jewish people "gathered between Your feet" and said, "all that God has commanded we will do" — we are willing to be killed for the Torah's sake.

The word תֻּכּוּ is usually understood to be derived from תּוֹךְ, 'midst.' But we could also see it as being a form of לְהַכּוֹת, 'to smite.' In that case, וְהֵם תֻּכּוּ would mean "they are stricken, broken," לְרַגְלֶיךָ, "because of You, for Your sake" [לְרֶגֶל often means 'because of'].

He presented the fiery Torah to them. [3] *Indeed, You loved the*
tribes greatly, all its holy ones were in Your hands; for they
planted themselves at Your feet, bearing [the yoke] of Your
utterances: [4] *"The Torah that Moses commanded us is the*
heritage of the Congregation of Jacob." [5] *He became King*
over Jeshurun when the numbers of the nation gathered —
the tribes of Israel in unity.
[6] *May Reuben live and not die, and may his population be*

The Jewish people set aside their own desires before Your will, to the point of breaking their bodies for Your sake. Just as the *Gemara* tells about Rava, who was so deeply immersed in his study that he was unaware that he had sat on his fingers and they were bleeding. A Sadducee walked by and said, "Reckless people! . . . Why did you say 'we will do' before 'we will hear'? Why did you not first hear how difficult it is [to keep the Torah]?" (*Shabbos* 88a).

יִשָּׂא מִדַּבְּרֹתֶיךָ — *Bearing [the yoke] of Your utterances*. The people said, "Let God speak. Even if His words are difficult, we are ready to fulfill them." These were the people who had said "we will do" before "we will hear."

4. תּוֹרָה צִוָּה־לָנוּ מֹשֶׁה — *The Torah that Moses commanded us*. Even though the Jews only heard two of God's "utterances" (the first two commandments) directly from God Himself, nonetheless the entire Torah is the "heritage of the Congregation of Jacob."

This verse can also be explained in a different way. There was a chance that at the sight of the great fire on Sinai at the Giving of the Torah, the Jews would renege on their resolution to accept it (as we find in the *Tosafos* on *Shabbos* 88a, ד"ה כפה). And in fact, it was necessary to hold the mountain over their heads like a barrel. Yet all the same, they accepted the Torah willingly; and the proof of their willingness is that the Torah became "the heritage of the Congregation of Jacob." Ordinarily, if one accepts an obligation because he was forced into it, then even if he keeps it himself he will not pass it on to his children after him. Since we see that the Torah became "the heritage of the Congregation of Jacob," that shows that it was accepted willingly, with love.

6. יְחִי רְאוּבֵן וְאַל־יָמֹת וִיהִי מְתָיו מִסְפָּר — *May Reuben live and not die, and may his population be included in the count*. Moses prayed for three things for the tribe of Reuben. Since Reuben led the army into war, he prayed that they die neither in battle nor by God's hand, but come home safely. He also asked that their wives and children, whom they left behind across the Jordan, not die during their absence. "May Reuben live" — and not be killed during the war. May he "not die" afterwards at God's hand, during the seven years while the Holy Land was divided among the people. "May his population" — the tribe's families — "be included in the count" — may the men find them all alive when they return from war, the same number of people as when they left them (*Vilna Gaon*).

מִסְפָּר: ז וְזֹאת לִיהוּדָה֒ וַיֹּאמַר֒ שְׁמַ֤ע יהוה֙
ק֣וֹל יְהוּדָ֔ה וְאֶל־עַמּ֖וֹ תְּבִיאֶ֑נּוּ יָדָיו֙ רָ֣ב ל֔וֹ וְעֵ֥זֶר מִצָּרָ֖יו
תִּהְיֶֽה:
שני ח וּלְלֵוִ֣י אָמַ֔ר תֻּמֶּ֥יךָ וְאוּרֶ֖יךָ לְאִ֣ישׁ חֲסִידֶ֑ךָ אֲשֶׁ֤ר נִסִּיתוֹ֙
בְּמַסָּ֔ה תְּרִיבֵ֖הוּ עַל־מֵ֥י מְרִיבָֽה: ט הָאֹמֵ֞ר לְאָבִ֤יו וּלְאִמּוֹ֙
לֹ֣א רְאִיתִ֔יו וְאֶת־אֶחָיו֙ לֹ֣א הִכִּ֔יר וְאֶת־בָּנָ֖ו לֹ֣א יָדָ֑ע כִּ֤י
שָׁמְרוּ֙ אִמְרָתֶ֔ךָ וּבְרִֽיתְךָ֖ יִנְצֹֽרוּ: י יוֹר֤וּ מִשְׁפָּטֶ֙יךָ֙ לְיַעֲקֹ֔ב
וְתוֹרָֽתְךָ֖ לְיִשְׂרָאֵ֑ל יָשִׂ֤ימוּ קְטוֹרָה֙ בְּאַפֶּ֔ךָ וְכָלִ֖יל עַל־מִזְבְּחֶֽךָ:

---

7. וְזֹאת לִיהוּדָה וַיֹּאמַר . . . וְאֶל־עַמּוֹ תְּבִיאֶנּוּ — *And this to Judah, and he said . . . and return him to his people.* *Chazal's* exposition on this verse is explained by *Rashi.* We may explain in a simpler fashion, that Jacob gave the blessing of royalty to Judah ("the scepter shall not depart from Judah"), and, as *Chazal* tell us, Moses began his blessings where Jacob left off.

Moses now had a prophetic vision of the first king from the tribe of Judah: David the son of Jesse, hiding in caves and wandering in the desert, living with Achish, the king of Gath, and expelled from the Holy Land. Moses prayed for him, "return him [safely] to his people," for no one is a king if he has no nation to rule.

He added, "may his hands fight his grievance and may You be a Helper against his enemies." David had many enemies, both within and without, and he fought many wars for the Jewish people. Moses prayed, therefore, that his enemies would fall before him. This prayer was also on behalf of the entire tribe of Judah, whose territory was at the southern border of the Holy Land. He was, of course, obliged to defend his own territory, and thereby defended the entire country as well. (The tribe of Simeon was also included in this prayer, since their portion of the Land fell within that of Judah, so that they fought side by side to conquer their territory [*Shoftim*, ch. 1]. This is hinted at in the words "Hearken [שְׁמַע, suggesting שִׁמְעוֹן], O Hashem, to Judah's voice [prayer.]")

וְזֹאת לִיהוּדָה — *And this to Judah.* Moses put Judah, the younger brother, before Levi, the older brother, following the Torah's rule: "The king comes before the *Kohen Gadol*" (*Horayos* 13a). So first he prayed for King David, and afterwards for the *Kohen Gadol*, "Your devout one."

9. הָאֹמֵר לְאָבִיו וּלְאִמּוֹ לֹא רְאִיתִיו — *The one who said of his father and mother, "I have not favored him."* This verse seems to imply praise not only for Aaron but for all High Priests, who may not come in contact with the remains of even their own parents, siblings, and children. When they pass away, the High Priest must act as if he does not know them and not attend their funerals. This is a very difficult trial to withstand.

In his commentary on *Parashas Emor*, the *Abarbanel* writes that it is very painful for one who has lost a close relative not to be able to be present at the

included in the count.
[7] And this to Judah, and he said: Hearken, O HASHEM, to
Judah's voice, and return him to his people; may his hands
fight his grievance and may You be a Helper against his
enemies.
[8] Of Levi he said: Your Tumim and Your Urim befit Your
devout one, whom You tested at Massah, and whom You
challenged at the waters of Meribah. [9] The one who said of
his father and mother, "I have not favored him"; his brothers
he did not give recognition and his children he did not know;
for they [the Levites] have observed Your word and Your co-
venant they preserved. [10] They shall teach Your ordinances
to Jacob and Your Torah to Israel; they shall place incense
before Your presence, and burnt offerings on Your Altar.

---

burial, nor to be with him in the room when they part forever. Perhaps this is why the Torah permitted an ordinary priest to become defiled for his closest relatives. But the High Priest may not become defiled by contact even with the remains of his own parents. "He shall not leave the Sanctuary": the High Priest may not put aside his own sanctity and attachment to God, no matter what.

According to this, we may easily understand the present verse: "the one who said of his father and mother, 'I have not favored him' [לֹא רְאִיתִיו, literally, 'I have not seen him']." This is exactly what the *Mishnah* (*Sanhedrin* 18a) tells us: "if the High Priest's relative dies, he may not go out after the bier" — he must stay always around the corner, out of sight of the procession, and may turn the corner only when the procession has turned into another street (*Rashi*).

(Although parents are being spoken of, the singular form, 'I have not favored him,'" is logical, since it is rare for both parents to pass away and have their funeral on the same day.)

It is a terribly difficult trial to go through. Everyone wants to see his parents one last time, and escort them on their final journey. Yet the High Priests overcame this compelling personal longing, for "they have observed Your word," not to become defiled, even for their parents, "and Your covenant they preserved," the covenant of priesthood.

10. יוֹרוּ מִשְׁפָּטֶיךָ לְיַעֲקֹב וְתוֹרָתְךָ לְיִשְׂרָאֵל — *They shall teach Your ordinances to Jacob, and Your Torah to Israel.* "Jacob" refers to the masses, who frequently find themselves entangled in quarrels and blows and squabbles over money, and as frequently come to ask the sages questions of Torah law. The priests and Levites judge their cases and teach them Torah law: "they shall teach Your ordinances to Jacob."

"Israel" refers to the elite, the scholars, who do not make such an issue over financial concerns, and willingly waive their claims in monetary disputes. Most of their time is spent on Torah study and spiritual matters. They seek to become

לג יא בָּרֵךְ יהוה חֵילוֹ וּפֹעַל יָדָיו תִּרְצֶה מְחַץ מָתְנַיִם קָמָיו
יא־יז וּמְשַׂנְאָיו מִן־יְקוּמוּן: יב לְבִנְיָמִן אָמַר יְדִיד
יהוה יִשְׁכֹּן לָבֶטַח עָלָיו חֹפֵף עָלָיו כָּל־הַיּוֹם וּבֵין כְּתֵפָיו
שָׁכֵן: שלישי יג וּלְיוֹסֵף אָמַר מְבֹרֶכֶת יהוה
אַרְצוֹ מִמֶּגֶד שָׁמַיִם מִטָּל וּמִתְּהוֹם רֹבֶצֶת תָּחַת: יד וּמִמֶּגֶד
תְּבוּאֹת שָׁמֶשׁ וּמִמֶּגֶד גֶּרֶשׁ יְרָחִים: טו וּמֵרֹאשׁ הַרְרֵי־
קֶדֶם וּמִמֶּגֶד גִּבְעוֹת עוֹלָם: טז וּמִמֶּגֶד אֶרֶץ וּמְלֹאָהּ
וּרְצוֹן שֹׁכְנִי סְנֶה תָּבוֹאתָה לְרֹאשׁ יוֹסֵף וּלְקָדְקֹד נְזִיר
אֶחָיו: יז בְּכוֹר שׁוֹרוֹ הָדָר לוֹ וְקַרְנֵי רְאֵם קַרְנָיו בָּהֶם

---

close to God, and want to learn Torah from the *Kohen*, who is like an angel of God, and who "teaches Your Torah to Israel."

⊌ **יָשִׂימוּ קְטוֹרָה בְּאַפֶּךָ וְכָלִיל עַל־מִזְבְּחֶךָ** — *They shall place incense before Your presence, and burnt offerings on Your Altar*. Why are the words "on Your Altar" not used regarding the incense? This seeming omission is evidently the source for a *halachah* that the *Rambam* mentions (*Hil. Temidim u-Musafim*, ch. 3). If the priest does not find the Golden Altar in the Sanctuary, he rests the incense-bowl on the floor and offers the incense there. This means that the Golden Altar is not an essential part of the incense-offering.

We explained in *Parashas Tetzaveh* that this is why the Torah describes the construction of the Golden Altar last, after detailing all the vessels in the Tabernacle courtyard. Despite the Altar being inside the Tabernacle itself, it is described last because its absence does not stop us from offering the incense (See *Bamidbar* 4:12).

12. לְבִנְיָמִן אָמַר — *Of Benjamin he said*. Moses' blessing to Benjamin follows right after his blessing to Levi, because most of the priestly services were performed in the Holy Temple, which was in Benjamin's territory.

13. וּלְיוֹסֵף אָמַר — *Of Joseph he said*. Benjamin was mentioned between Judah and Joseph, because these two brothers exerted themselves for Benjamin's welfare; Joseph because of his special love for him as his only full brother from both father and mother, and Judah because of his promise to Jacob to bring him home safely.

⊌ **מְבֹרֶכֶת ה׳ אַרְצוֹ** — *Blessed by Hashem is his land*. In all the territory given to the tribes, there was no land so bountiful as Joseph's (*Rashi*). Joseph deserved this bounty because he supported his brothers, as well as the inhabitants of several entire countries. We may also say that while all of the Holy Land was "flowing with milk and honey," Joseph's section was the choicest.

Possession of such blessed terrain brings with it the danger of rebellion against God; the lucky owner simply has it too good. This is why only the descendants

33
11-17

[11] *Bless, O HASHEM, his resources, and favor the work of his hands; smash the loins of his foes and his enemies, that they may not rise.*

[12] *Of Benjamin he said: May HASHEM's beloved dwell securely by Him; He hovers over him all day long; and rests between his shoulders.*

[13] *Of Joseph he said: Blessed by HASHEM is his land — with the heavenly bounty of dew, and with the deep waters crouching below;* [14] *with the bounty of the sun's crops, and with the bounty of the moons' yield;* [15] *with the quick-ripening crops of the early mountains, and with the bounty of eternal hills;* [16] *with the bounty of the land and its fullness, and by the favor of Him Who rested upon the thornbush; may this blessing rest upon Joseph's head, and upon the crown of him who was separated from his brothers.* [17] *A sovereignty is his ox-like one — majesty is his, and his glory will be like the horns of a re'eim; with them*

---

of Joseph, who exerted himself to overcome the most difficult temptations, could be given this land. As the Torah says, "may this blessing rest upon Joseph's head, and upon the crown of him who was separated [נָזִיר] from his brothers." Of all the brothers, Joseph showed remarkable נְזִירוּת, strength to be separate from physical desires, throughout his life.

14. וּמִמֶּגֶד גֶּרֶשׁ יְרָחִים — *And with the bounty of the moons' yield.* "Moons" [יְרָחִים] is in the plural, because the moon disappears and reappears every month; and it is said that each month's moon influences some particular fruit to ripen. (The Jews of the Land of Israel say that each month they have a different fruit over which to say *shehecheyanu.*) But the sun [שֶׁמֶשׁ, the singular form,] runs its course all of a piece the year long, so that all the fruits of a year are ripened by a "single" sun.

15. וּמִמֶּגֶד גִּבְעוֹת עוֹלָם — *And with the bounty of eternal hills.* "Hills that bring forth fruit forever, and never cease producing because of drought" (*Rashi*).

The next verse continues with "and by the favor of Him Who rested upon the thornbush," reflecting *Chazal's* insight: "Why did God appear to Moses in a thornbush? So as to fulfill 'I am with him in distress' (*Tehillim* 91:15)." It is the same here: when the heavens are closed and there is no rain, and Israel are distressed, the Holy One, blessed be He, shows us that He shares our distress, and leaves us a last refuge: the hills that bear fruit without rain. These hills were allotted to the portion of Joseph, who nourished and supported the world during the seven years of famine.

17. בְּכוֹר שׁוֹרוֹ הָדָר לוֹ — *His first-born bull is glorious.* If such riches had been granted to any other tribe, its members might have used the power of their wealth in a bull-like fashion, to 'gore' their brother tribes: to subjugate them and

לג עַמִּים יְנַגַּח יַחְדָּו אַפְסֵי־אָרֶץ וְהֵם רִבְבוֹת אֶפְרַיִם וְהֵם
יח־כג אַלְפֵי מְנַשֶּׁה: רביעי יח וְלִזְבוּלֻן אָמַר שְׂמַח
זְבוּלֻן בְּצֵאתֶךָ וְיִשָּׂשכָר בְּאֹהָלֶיךָ: יט עַמִּים הַר־יִקְרָאוּ שָׁם
יִזְבְּחוּ זִבְחֵי־צֶדֶק כִּי שֶׁפַע יַמִּים יִינָקוּ וּשְׂפֻנֵי טְמוּנֵי
חוֹל: כ וּלְגָד אָמַר בָּרוּךְ מַרְחִיב גָּד כְּלָבִיא
שָׁכֵן וְטָרַף זְרוֹעַ אַף־קָדְקֹד: כא וַיַּרְא רֵאשִׁית לוֹ כִּי־שָׁם
חֶלְקַת מְחֹקֵק סָפוּן וַיֵּתֵא רָאשֵׁי עָם צִדְקַת יהוה עָשָׂה
וּמִשְׁפָּטָיו עִם־יִשְׂרָאֵל: חמישי כב וּלְדָן אָמַר דָּן גּוּר
אַרְיֵה יְזַנֵּק מִן־הַבָּשָׁן: כג וּלְנַפְתָּלִי אָמַר נַפְתָּלִי שְׂבַע רָצוֹן

---

rule over them. But Joseph, the righteous and pious, who paid his brothers back with good in return for the evil they had done him, would never do such a thing. He uses his bull-like power (in the person of Joshua, a scion of the tribe of Ephraim) only to "gore the foreign peoples."

וְהֵם רִבְבוֹת אֶפְרַיִם וְהֵם אַלְפֵי מְנַשֶּׁה — *They are the myriads of Ephraim, and the thousands of Manasseh.* Jacob blessed Ephraim with his right hand and Manasseh with his left hand. Now, the Torah promises us that "a thousand will fall at your [left] side, and a myriad at your right side" (*Tehillim* 91:7), indicating that this is a general relationship between right and left. So Moses gave a blessing of "myriads" to Ephraim, and "thousands" to Manasseh.

19. עַמִּים הַר־יִקְרָאוּ — *The tribes will assemble at the mount. Onkelos* understands this as referring to the Temple Mount, the place where the tribes regularly assemble. This is in line with the typical character of the tribe of Issachar: "And the children of Issachar, who know the deep meaning of the times" (*I Divrei Hayamim*, 12:33) — they were experts in the determination of the New Moon, the intercalation of months, and the calculation of the date of each festival. That is why "assembly" is referred to here with the word יִקְרָאוּ, suggesting the מִקְרָאֵי קֹדֶשׁ, the Holy Festivals which summoned (קָרְאוּ) the tribes to God's Mountain, there to offer their sacrifices.

כִּי שֶׁפַע יַמִּים יִינָקוּ וּשְׂפֻנֵי טְמוּנֵי חוֹל — *For by the riches of the sea they will be nourished, and by the treasures concealed in the sand.* This refers to Zebulun, who has "the riches of the sea" in his portion. These include the sea-snail from which the blue dye (*techeiles*) for *tzitzis* is made, as well as the fish that he catches in his nets; not to mention cheap and ready transportation to anywhere in the world and the successful business that this tribe established by such means.

As for the sandy sea shore, it too hides treasure within its grains: the clear glass that is made from it is a precious item, bringing wealth to its makers.

20. וְטָרַף זְרוֹעַ אַף־קָדְקֹד — *Tearing off arm and even head.* One could always tell which ones they had killed: they would cut off the head together with an arm at one stroke [of the sword]" (*Rashi*).

33 *shall he gore nations together, to the ends of the Land; they*
18-23 *are the myriads of Ephraim, and the thousands of Manasseh.*
[18] *Of Zebulun he said: Rejoice, O Zebulun, in your excur-*
sions, and Issachar in your tents. [19] *The tribes will assemble*
at the mount, there they will slaughter offerings of righteous-
ness, for by the riches of the sea they will be nourished, and
by the treasures concealed in the sand.
[20] *Of Gad he said: Blessed is He Who broadens Gad; he*
dwells like a lion, tearing off arm and even head. [21] *He chose*
the first portion for himself, for that is where the lawgiver's
plot is hidden; he came at the head of the nation, carrying out
HASHEM's justice and His ordinances with Israel.
[22] *Of Dan he said: Dan is a lion cub, leaping forth from the*
Bashan.
[23] *Of Naphtali he said: Naphtali, satiated with favor,*

The *Vilna Gaon*, in *Aderes Eliyahu*, provides the rationale for this: "A person who spoke between putting on the hand-*tefillin* and the head-*tefillin* [and has not yet repented fully] must return home from the war, since there is an element of sin in this. [The present verse] informs us that the children of Gad were perfectly righteous, careful even of this point. Therefore they were granted the ability to cut off the head and arm at one stroke — this was in merit of their heads and arms."

I think that the above will serve to explain the wording of this verse, which is odd in that it puts the arm before the head. A swordsman normally will strike from above downwards, thus taking the head off before the arm. (This is an especially advantageous stroke, since it kills one's opponent at once instead of leaving him the chance to strike back with his other arm.) Why, then, is the order reversed here?

It is as the *Vilna Gaon* explained: the children of Gad were granted this prowess because of their scrupulous observance of the commandments. This extended even to the minutiae of *tefillin*, which are put on first "as a sign upon your hand" and then "as ornaments between your eyes." In order to keep in mind what their true merit was, the Gadites made it their practice to strike from below upwards, in the order that *tefillin* are donned, "tearing off arm and head."

21. צִדְקַת ה׳ עָשָׂה וּמִשְׁפָּטָיו עִם־יִשְׂרָאֵל — *Carrying out Hashem's justice and His ordinances with Israel.* This refers to Moses: just as God chose to carry out His justice and His ordinances all by means of Moses, so too when it will be time for dispensing reward in the World to Come, it is only fitting that this too should be delivered by Moses.

23. נַפְתָּלִי שְׂבַע רָצוֹן וּמָלֵא בִּרְכַּת ה׳ — *Naphtali, satiated with favor, and filled with Hashem's blessing.* This is a double blessing, both wealth and

לג וּמָלֵא בִּרְכַּת יְהוָה יָם וְדָרוֹם יְרָשָׁה: כד וּלְאָשֵׁר
כד־כט אָמַר בָּרוּךְ מִבָּנִים אָשֵׁר יְהִי רְצוּי אֶחָיו וְטֹבֵל בַּשֶּׁמֶן רַגְלוֹ:
כה בַּרְזֶל וּנְחֹשֶׁת מִנְעָלֶיךָ וּכְיָמֶיךָ דָּבְאֶךָ: כו אֵין כָּאֵל יְשֻׁרוּן
רֹכֵב שָׁמַיִם בְּעֶזְרֶךָ וּבְגַאֲוָתוֹ שְׁחָקִים: חתן תורה כז מְעֹנָה
אֱלֹהֵי קֶדֶם וּמִתַּחַת זְרֹעֹת עוֹלָם וַיְגָרֶשׁ מִפָּנֶיךָ אוֹיֵב
וַיֹּאמֶר הַשְׁמֵד: כח וַיִּשְׁכֹּן יִשְׂרָאֵל בֶּטַח בָּדָד עֵין יַעֲקֹב
אֶל־אֶרֶץ דָּגָן וְתִירוֹשׁ אַף־שָׁמָיו יַעַרְפוּ טָל: כט אַשְׁרֶיךָ
יִשְׂרָאֵל מִי כָמוֹךָ עַם נוֹשַׁע בַּיהוָה מָגֵן עֶזְרֶךָ וַאֲשֶׁר־

---

contentment. For it is harder to feel content when one is rich than it is to accept one's lot when he is poor. A popular fable illustrates this:

A king once had an only daughter, who fell ill of depression. The wizards all said that nothing would ever help her unless she were to wear "the tunic of a happy man"; then she would recover. The royal messengers set forth at a frantic gallop to search the king's dominions for a happy man. But they could find no one — until they heard of a little village, far away, where a man lived who considered himself happy. The messengers raced off to bring him before the king. He was indeed a happy, jolly-spirited man. The king told this "happy man" that if he would give his tunic to the princess, the king would make him a rich man, rolling in wealth. At this the man laughed out loud and said, "You've certainly made a hard request of me, Your Majesty. You see, this tunic I'm wearing is my only possession!"

It's just as we say: if a man has a hundred he wants two hundred, if two hundred he wants four hundred. And so the lust for wealth (which makes one dissatisfied for the present) is greater in a rich man than in a poor one. Therefore Moses did not bless Naphtali only with being "filled with Hashem's blessings, possessing the sea and its south shore." He preceded this with the best of all blessings: "Naphtali, satiated with favor."

24. בָּרוּךְ מִבָּנִים אָשֵׁר יְהִי רְצוּי אֶחָיו — *The most blessed of children is Asher; he shall be pleasing to his brothers.* "No other land supports its inhabitants during the Sabbatical year like the land of Asher" (*Sifre*, following the *Vilna Gaon's* reading).

The explanation would seem to be that Asher's land was favorable to olive trees; and in fact I found in the *Zayis Ra'anan* that it was planted all over with olives. As a result there was plentiful fruit available during the Sabbatical year. What is more, everyone would come running to this part of the country during the Sabbatical year to eat the olives, since during that year they were ownerless and free for all to take (whereas the fields were not sown that year, and little grew wild in them). Since everyone benefited from him, Asher was "pleasing to his brothers."

25. בַּרְזֶל וּנְחֹשֶׁת מִנְעָלֶךָ וּכְיָמֶיךָ דָּבְאֶךָ — *May your borders be sealed like iron and copper [literally: may your shoe be iron and copper], and like the days of*

and filled with H*ASHEM's blessing; go possess the sea and its*
south shore.
24 *Of Asher he said: The most blessed of children is Asher;*
he shall be pleasing to his brothers, and dip his feet in oil.
25 *May your borders be sealed like iron and copper, and*
like the days of your prime, so may your old age be. 26 *There*
is none like God, O Jeshurun; He rides across heaven to help
you, and in His majesty through the upper heights.
27 *That is the abode of God immemorial, and below are the*
world's mighty ones; He drove the enemy away from before
you, and He said, "Destroy!" 28 *Thus Israel shall dwell*
secure, solitary, in the likeness of Jacob, in a land of grain and
wine; even his heavens shall drip with dew.
29 *Fortunate are you, O Israel: Who is like you! O people*
delivered by H*ASHEM, the Shield of your help, Who is the*

---

your prime, so may your old age be. If a person wants to retain his physical strength into his old age as it was in the days of his prime, he must keep his spirit and his character restrained in shoes of iron and copper, not allowing his emotions to get out of control (*Sfas Emes*).

27. וַיְגָרֶשׁ מִפָּנֶיךָ אוֹיֵב וַיֹּאמֶר הַשְׁמֵד — *He drove the enemy away from before you, and He said, "Destroy!"* King David told his son Solomon, "God's word was upon me, saying, 'Much blood have you spilled, and great wars have you waged; you shall not build a house for My sake'" (*I Divrei Hayamim*, 22:8). Now, these wars were fought to defend the Jewish people; and for that matter, the Torah never prohibited our waging war against our enemies, for it is impossible for one people to beat its swords into plowshares as long as all the other peoples still make war with each other and with Israel. Sometimes Israel must even make a preemptive strike before their enemy does, as *Chazal* teach: "If someone is coming to kill you, get up earlier and kill him" (*Berachos* 62b). Yet even so, such wars leave "bloodstains" on the souls of all who fight in them.

That was why Moses told Israel that the war against the Seven Peoples, who had sinned so grievously, was neither an optional nor an obligatory war. For God had declared, "You shall leave not a soul alive" of these defiled people. This was a war of destruction, aimed at "removing the evil from your midst." Before it ever began, "He drove the enemy away from before you" with hornets (*Shemos* 23:28), and their exile in Africa atoned for their sins (*Vayikra Rabbah* 17:6). As for the stubborn ones who remained, "God said, 'Destroy!'" You are obligated to destroy them, just as a *Beis Din* is obligated to execute those who have incurred the death penalty, so as to remove the evil from Israel's midst.

The generation that entered the Land was obligated to remove idols and their worshipers from the Land, so that they would not tempt the Jews, or even the gentiles, to sin. Therefore Moses promised that this destruction would leave no stain on the people's souls.

חֶ֣רֶב גַּאֲוָתֶ֑ךָ וְיִכָּחֲשׁ֤וּ אֹיְבֶ֙יךָ֙ לָ֔ךְ וְאַתָּ֖ה עַל־בָּמוֹתֵ֥ימוֹ
תִדְרֹֽךְ׃ א וַיַּ֨עַל מֹשֶׁ֜ה מֵעַֽרְבֹ֤ת מוֹאָב֙ לד
אֶל־הַ֣ר נְב֔וֹ רֹ֚אשׁ הַפִּסְגָּ֔ה אֲשֶׁ֖ר עַל־פְּנֵ֣י יְרֵח֑וֹ וַיַּרְאֵ֨הוּ א־ו
יְהוָ֧ה אֶת־כָּל־הָאָ֛רֶץ אֶת־הַגִּלְעָ֖ד עַד־דָּֽן׃ ב וְאֵת֙ כָּל־
נַפְתָּלִ֔י וְאֶת־אֶ֥רֶץ אֶפְרַ֖יִם וּמְנַשֶּׁ֑ה וְאֵת֙ כָּל־אֶ֣רֶץ יְהוּדָ֔ה
עַ֖ד הַיָּ֥ם הָאַחֲרֽוֹן׃ ג וְאֶת־הַנֶּ֗גֶב וְאֶת־הַכִּכָּ֞ר בִּקְעַ֧ת יְרֵח֛וֹ
עִ֥יר הַתְּמָרִ֖ים עַד־צֹֽעַר׃ ד וַיֹּ֨אמֶר יְהוָ֜ה אֵלָ֗יו זֹ֤את הָאָ֙רֶץ֙
אֲשֶׁ֣ר נִ֠שְׁבַּעְתִּי לְאַבְרָהָ֨ם לְיִצְחָ֤ק וּֽלְיַעֲקֹב֙ לֵאמֹ֔ר לְזַרְעֲךָ֖
אֶתְּנֶ֑נָּה הֶרְאִיתִ֣יךָ בְעֵינֶ֔יךָ וְשָׁ֖מָּה לֹ֥א תַעֲבֹֽר׃ ה וַיָּ֨מָת שָׁ֜ם
מֹשֶׁ֧ה עֶבֶד־יְהוָ֛ה בְּאֶ֥רֶץ מוֹאָ֖ב עַל־פִּ֥י יְהוָֽה׃ ו וַיִּקְבֹּ֨ר אֹת֤וֹ

---

29. וְאַתָּה עַל־בָּמוֹתֵימוֹ תִדְרֹךְ — *But you will tread in their high places.* It is usually difficult to capture the enemy's high places. There he hides between the mountain ridges and among the nooks and crannies, and conducts guerilla warfare against the conquerors. But there, too, you will tread; for "also the hornet-swarm will Hashem, your God, send among them, until the survivors and hidden ones perish before you" (7:20).

34.

1. וַיַּרְאֵהוּ ה׳ אֶת־כָּל־הָאָרֶץ — *Hashem showed him the entire Land.* The human eye cannot see such great distances as "from Dan until Beer Sheba" all from a single vantage point. This, then, was a miracle: "Hashem showed him." All the same, though, Moses was commanded to ascend "to Mt. Nebo, to the summit of the cliff that faces Jericho" — a tall mountain peak in the middle of the Land's longitude — so as to make the minimum possible use of miraculous workings beyond natural law.

5. וַיָּמָת שָׁם מֹשֶׁה עֶבֶד־ה׳ — *So Moses, servant of Hashem, died there.* Why does the Torah suddenly refer to Moses here as the "servant of Hashem"? The answer may lie in *Pirkei D'Rabbi Eliezer* (end of ch. 45), where we learn that after the episode of the Golden Calf Moses excavated a huge subterranean prison cell in the land of the Gadites, and imprisoned the destroying angel called חָרוֹן ("fury") in it. For this angel had spoken against the Children of Israel during the episode of the Calf, and thereafter whenever Israel sinned he would open his mouth to ravage them. While Moses was alive he would pronounce one of God's holy Names and sink this angel back into his prison; now he was to be buried across from that cell, so that whenever the angel rose up in anger he would see Moses' grave and sink back.

Clearly, then, the Faithful Shepherd had a task to perform even after his death. For this reason, at his death scene he is called "servant of Hashem." And perhaps this is also why such an honorable title is juxtaposed to the command

Sword of your grandeur; your foes will try to deceive you, but
you will trample their haughty ones.
34 *1 Moses ascended from the plains of Moab, to Mount Nebo,*
1-6 *to the summit of the cliff that faces Jericho, and HASHEM*
showed him the entire Land: the Gilead as far as Dan; 2 all of
Naphtali, and the land of Ephraim and Manasseh; the entire
land of Judah as far as the western sea; 3 the Negev and the
Plain — the valley of Jericho, city of date palms — as far as
Zoar.
4 And HASHEM said to him, "This is the land which I swore
to Abraham, to Isaac, and to Jacob, saying, 'I will give it to
your offspring.' I have let you see it with your own eyes,
but you shall not cross over to there."
5 So Moses, servant of HASHEM, died there, in the land
of Moab, by the mouth of HASHEM. 6 He buried him

"you shall not cross over to there": to tell us that here, opposite Beth-peor, was Moses' final "guard post."

6. וַיִּקְבֹּר אֹתוֹ — *He buried him.* "R' Yishmael says, 'He buried himself' " (*Rashi*).

In *Yad Moshe* (on *Bereishis Rabbah* ch. 17) I found an explanation of how this might have been: Moses could have entered his grave while still alive, and died there, and this would be called having buried himself. The *Eitz Yosef* (ad loc.) offers the same explanation.

We might ask why Moses needed to die in this way, lying in a grave prepared for him. (It had indeed been ready since the Creation [*Pirkei Avos* 5:8].) The answer might lie in *Chazal's* exposition of why Moses needed to die outside the Land. He brought the people out of Egypt, and then because of their sins that entire generation did not enter the Land, dying instead in the desert. Therefore it was decreed that Moses, too, must die in the desert, so that he would be ready to bring the people into the Land at the time of the Resurrection. For the shepherd must not leave his flock, and he must share their fate.

We can further suggest that since Moses was sharing the fate of the Exodus generation, the manner of his death also had to be the same as theirs. The *Midrash* (quoted in *Tosafos, Bava Basra* 74a, ד"ה פסקי) tells that during those forty years, every *Erev Tishah B'Av* each person would dig a grave for himself, and they would sleep in their graves that whole night. In the morning the announcement would be made, "Let the living separate themselves from the dead," and those who had not died would climb out. (See *Oznayim Bamidbar* 14:29.)

Following the *Yad Moshe,* that whole generation buried themselves. And just such a burial did the Faithful Shepherd choose for himself, sharing his people's fate to the end.

בַּגַּי֩ בְּאֶ֨רֶץ מוֹאָ֜ב מ֣וּל בֵּ֣ית פְּע֑וֹר וְלֹֽא־יָדַ֥ע אִישׁ֙ אֶת־
קְבֻ֣רָת֔וֹ עַ֖ד הַיּ֥וֹם הַזֶּֽה: ז וּמֹשֶׁ֗ה בֶּן־מֵאָ֧ה וְעֶשְׂרִ֛ים שָׁנָ֖ה
בְּמֹת֑וֹ לֹא־כָֽהֲתָ֥ה עֵינ֖וֹ וְלֹא־נָ֥ס לֵחֹֽה: ח וַיִּבְכּ֨וּ בְנֵ֤י
יִשְׂרָאֵל֙ אֶת־מֹשֶׁ֔ה בְּעַֽרְבֹ֥ת מוֹאָ֖ב שְׁלֹשִׁ֣ים י֑וֹם וַיִּתְּמ֔וּ יְמֵ֥י
בְכִ֖י אֵ֥בֶל מֹשֶֽׁה: ט וִיהוֹשֻׁ֣עַ בִּן־נ֗וּן מָלֵא֙ ר֣וּחַ חָכְמָ֔ה כִּֽי־
סָמַ֨ךְ מֹשֶׁ֤ה אֶת־יָדָיו֙ עָלָ֔יו וַיִּשְׁמְע֥וּ אֵלָ֛יו בְּנֵֽי־יִשְׂרָאֵ֖ל
וַיַּֽעֲשׂ֔וּ כַּֽאֲשֶׁ֛ר צִוָּ֥ה יְהוָ֖ה אֶת־מֹשֶֽׁה: י וְלֹא־קָ֨ם נָבִ֥יא
ע֛וֹד בְּיִשְׂרָאֵ֖ל כְּמֹשֶׁ֑ה אֲשֶׁר֙ יְדָע֣וֹ יְהוָ֔ה פָּנִ֖ים אֶל־פָּנִֽים:

מוּל בֵּית פְּעוֹר — *Opposite Beth-peor.* "To atone for the episode of Peor" (*Rashi*).

But who would atone for the golden calves that Jeroboam set up, and which the Children of Israel worshiped all through the days of the kings? And what is special about Baal-peor that Moses should be buried opposite its shrine?

It would seem that Moses, the man of God, through whom God gave the world a Torah of truth and pure faith, needed to be buried opposite the most defiled and disgusting idol in the whole world, whose worship involves the foulest of deeds, and whose worshipers are greatly praised the more they befoul their idol (*Sanhedrin* 64a). Thus the ultimate good would be set against the ultimate evil, to show all men how far one can stray from the straight path and true faith of the Creator. Anyone who leaves the Torah of Moses to run after delusions should know that he is capable of sinking even as low as those who worship Baal-peor. Once this has registered and made an impact, the sinner will surely repent and return to belief in the true God.

10. **וְלֹא־קָם נָבִיא עוֹד בְּיִשְׂרָאֵל כְּמֹשֶׁה** — *Never again has there arisen in Israel a prophet like Moses.* "In Israel none has arisen, but among the nations of the world there has. And who is that? Balaam" (*Bamidbar Rabbah* 14:2).

This is an astonishing thing to say! How can one compare darkness to light, defilement to purity, a miserable ruffian to the man of God? Yet at the same time it is all quite clear:

God searched through all the nations of the world to see if they would accept the Torah, but they would not. Only one nation, the Jewish people, said "we will do" before "we will hear." But the gentiles still had one argument left: God had sent a great prophet to the Children of Israel, and he taught them the way of God, and that was why they had accepted the Torah. As for themselves, if they had had so great a prophet among them, they too would have accepted the Torah.

In order to put an end to this argument, it was necessary to raise up a prophet from among the nations, a prophet as gifted by nature as Moses was. (This much is stated explicitly in *Bamidbar Rabbah* ch. 20 and *Tanchuma Parashas Balak* §1.) But prophetic powers wax and wane, either due to the prophet's own management of his skills or because of the way the people respond to their

34
7-10

in the depression, in the land of Moab, opposite Beth-peor,
and no one knows his burial place to this day. [7] *Moses*
was one hundred and twenty years old when he died; his
eye had not dimmed, and his vigor had not diminished.
[8] *The Children of Israel bewailed Moses in the plains of*
Moab for thirty days; then the days of tearful mourning
for Moses ended.
[9] *Joshua son of Nun was filled with the spirit of wisdom, because Moses had laid his hands upon him, so the Children of Israel obeyed him and did as* H*ASHEM* *had commanded Moses.*
[10] *Never again has there arisen in Israel a prophet*
like Moses, whom H*ASHEM* *had known face to face,*

---

prophet and the purposes they use him for (though God sent him to influence their return to the proper path).

Even regarding Moses we see that when he went up to heaven to receive the Torah, and the Mixed Multitude made the Calf with none rebuking them, God said to Moses "Go, descend, for your people has done corruptly" (*Shemos* 32:7). *Chazal* interpret this as meaning, "Descend from your greatness! Did I ever make you great except for Israel's sake? Now that Israel has sinned; what claim do you have to greatness?" (*Berachos* 32a). Since Moses had not sufficiently influenced the people to the point that even though he was late they would not lose heart and allow the Mixed Multitude to make an idol, he must therefore "descend from his greatness," i.e., lose some of his prophetic power and instead of being the "master of all prophets" become like an ordinary prophet.

Only after he had descended from the mountain, and broken the Tablets, and forcibly burned the Calf and killed its worshipers, and brought Israel back to their Father in Heaven — only then did God give him back his great level of prophecy. He became even greater than before, until his face beamed with glory.

And now let us ask, what did Balaam do with his great prophetic gift? He certainly did not attempt to bring the gentiles back to the good path, even to the extent of keeping the seven Noahide commandments, still less to the point of accepting the Torah. Quite the contrary: when the gentiles heard the awesome Voice of God at the Giving of the Torah, they came to Balaam and asked him whether God was about to bring a Deluge upon the world, and did they need to repent their sins? He answered that God had sworn never to bring a Deluge again, and the thunder and lightning were purely for Israel: "God was giving might" i.e., Torah "to His people, God was blessing His people with peace," but you can go right on doing as you please.

Then what *did* he do with his gift? He used it to curse nations and destroy countries, all for the sake of gold and silver. He also used it to give sordid advice to the elders of Moab: to prostitute their daughters to the young men of Israel and so entrap them in vice and idolatry. No wonder, then, that little by little his

לד יא לְכָל־הָאֹתֹת וְהַמּוֹפְתִים אֲשֶׁר שְׁלָחוֹ יהוה לַעֲשׂוֹת
יא־יב בְּאֶרֶץ מִצְרָיִם לְפַרְעֹה וּלְכָל־עֲבָדָיו וּלְכָל־אַרְצוֹ׃ יב וּלְכֹל
הַיָּד הַחֲזָקָה וּלְכֹל הַמּוֹרָא הַגָּדוֹל אֲשֶׁר עָשָׂה מֹשֶׁה לְעֵינֵי
כָּל־יִשְׂרָאֵל׃

חֲזַק! חֲזַק! וְנִתְחַזֵּק!

---

gift from heaven was taken from him, until he was left blind and lame not only physically but spiritually as well. God would no longer speak to him except at night in a dream, or by day while he was "fallen and with uncovered eyes" (*Bamidbar* 24:4).

Our master Moses continually grew in prophecy, until before his death he was called "the man of God, like whom none has arisen." And this was because he used his closeness to God to bring his people constantly closer to their Father in Heaven. With Balaam it was the opposite: his powers dwindled constantly, because he used them for evil and to gather ill-gotten gain. And as his prophetic gifts, which originally were like those of Moses himself, waned, he turned to sorcery, the very antithesis of heavenly rule, until before his death he was called "Balaam the sorcerer" (*Yehoshua* 13:22).

The prophet who was to be like Moses to the gentiles, became a sorcerer! He became included in the Torah's decree: "You shall not let a witch live"! What a fall from greatness. Nor could the gentiles complain that they should have been given another prophet in the place of Balaam, for they themselves had brought about his downfall into sorcery.

Israel asked their prophet for Torah: "for the people come to me to seek God" (*Shemos* 18:15). When they were commanded about the *Pesach*-offering, those

34 [11] *as evidenced by all the signs and wonders that* HASHEM
11-12 *sent him to perform in the land of Egypt, against Pharaoh*
and all his courtiers and all his land, [12] *and by all the strong*
hand and awesome power that Moses performed before the
eyes of all Israel.

"Chazak! Chazak! Venischazeik!
(Be Strong! Be Strong! And may we be strengthened!)"

---

temporarily defiled cried out, "Why should we be diminished by not offering Hashem's offering?" (*Bamidbar* 9:7). They put doing before hearing, and further told Moses, "You draw near and hear... then we will hear and do."

But the gentiles did the opposite. They used their prophet's gifts for man to kill his fellow, and a nation to destroy its neighbor. Sihon hired Balaam to curse Moab, and Balak was willing to give "the fill of his house in silver and gold" to Balaam if he would curse Israel. The only good they ever got from their "great man" was curses, and all that they ever knew of his greatness was that he could kill the righteous along with the wicked: "for I know that whomever you bless is blessed and whomever you curse is accursed" (*Bamidbar* 22:6). If this is how they made use of their prophet, what good would it do to give them another? They would only drag him, too, down to sin.

11. לְכָל־הָאֹתֹת וְהַמּוֹפְתִים אֲשֶׁר שְׁלָחוֹ ה׳ לַעֲשׂוֹת — *As evidenced by all the signs and wonders that Hashem sent him to perform.* The other prophets also performed signs and wonders; but they prayed to God to do these, because of the need of the times, and God agreed to do the will of those who fear Him. But Moses our Teacher was sent by God expressly to do signs, miracles, and wonders, in order to publicize His name in the world: "that you may relate in the ears of your son and your son's son ..." (*Shemos* 10:2).

ההפטרות ◆

The Haftaros

HAFTARAS DEVARIM

Isaiah 1:1-27

1. [1] The vision of Isaiah son of Amoz, which he saw concerning Judah and Jerusalem, in the days of Uzziah, Jotham, Ahaz and Hezekiah, kings of Judah: [2] Hear, O heavens, and give ear, O earth, for HASHEM has spoken: Children have I raised and exalted, but they have rebelled against Me. [3] An ox knows his owner, and a donkey his master's trough; Israel does not know, My people does not perceive. [4] Woe! O sinful nation, people weighed down by iniquity, offspring of evil, destructive children; they have forsaken HASHEM, they have angered the Holy One of Israel, they have turned away backward. [5] For what would you be smitten, when you still continue waywardly, each head with sickness, each heart in pain? [6] From the foot's sole to the head, nothing in it is whole: sword slash, contusion, and festering wound; they have not medicated, and they have not bandaged, and it was not softened with oil. [7] Your country is desolate, your cities are burned with fire, your land — before you strangers consume it; it is desolate as if overturned by strangers. [8] The daughter of Zion shall be left like a [deserted] watchman's booth in a vineyard, like a shed in a gourd garden, like a city under siege. [9] Had not HASHEM, Master of Legions, left us a trace of a remnant, we would have been like Sodom, we would have resembled Gomorrah.

[10] Hear the word of HASHEM, O chiefs of Sodom; give ear to the Torah of our God, O people of Gomorrah. [11] Why do I need your numerous sacrifices? — says HASHEM — I am satiated with elevation-offerings of rams and the choicest of fattened animals; and the blood of bulls and sheep and he-goats I do not desire. [12] When you come to appear before Me — who sought this from your hand, to trample My courtyards? [13] You shall not continue to bring a worthless meal-offering — incense of abomination is it unto Me; [New] Moon and Sabbath, calling of convocation, I cannot abide mendacity with assemblage. [14] Your [New] Moons and your appointed festivals, My soul hates; they have become a burden upon Me [that] I am weary of bearing. [15] And when you spread your hands [in prayer], I will hide My eyes from you; even if you were to increase prayer, I do not hear; your hands are full of blood. [16] Wash yourselves, purify yourselves, remove the evil of your doings from before My eyes; desist from doing evil. [17] Learn to do good, seek justice, strengthen the victim, do justice for the orphan, take up the cause of the widow.

[18] Go forth, now, let us reason together — says HASHEM — if your sins will be like scarlet, they will whiten like snow, if they have reddened like crimson, they will become as wool. [19] If you will be willing and you will obey, you shall eat the goodness of the land. [20] But if you will refuse and rebel, you shall be devoured by the sword — for the mouth of HASHEM has spoken.

[21] How has she become a harlot! — faithful city that was full of justice, in which righteousness was wont to lodge, but now murderers. [22] Your silver has become dross, your heady wine mixed with water. [23] Your princes are wayward and associates of thieves; the whole of them loves bribery and pursue [illegal] payments; for the orphan they do not do justice, the cause of the widow does not come unto them.

[24] Therefore — the word of the Lord, HASHEM, Master of Legions, Mighty One of Israel — O, how I will ease Myself of My adversaries, and how I will avenge Myself of My enemies. [25] I will return My hand upon you, and refine as with lye your dross, and I will remove all your base metal. [26] Then I will return your judges as in earliest times, and your counselors as at first, after that you shall be called City of Righteousness, Faithful City. [27] Zion shall be redeemed with justice, and her returnees with righteousness.

הפטרת דברים

ישעיה א:א־כז

א א חֲזוֹן יְשַׁעְיָהוּ בֶן־אָמוֹץ אֲשֶׁר חָזָה עַל־יְהוּדָה וִירוּשָׁלָםִ בִּימֵי עֻזִּיָּהוּ יוֹתָם אָחָז יְחִזְקִיָּהוּ מַלְכֵי יְהוּדָה: ב שִׁמְעוּ שָׁמַיִם וְהַאֲזִינִי אֶרֶץ כִּי יהוה דִּבֵּר בָּנִים גִּדַּלְתִּי וְרוֹמַמְתִּי וְהֵם פָּשְׁעוּ בִי: ג יָדַע שׁוֹר קֹנֵהוּ וַחֲמוֹר אֵבוּס בְּעָלָיו יִשְׂרָאֵל לֹא יָדַע עַמִּי לֹא הִתְבּוֹנָן: ד הוֹי ׀ גּוֹי חֹטֵא עַם כֶּבֶד עָוֺן זֶרַע מְרֵעִים בָּנִים מַשְׁחִיתִים עָזְבוּ אֶת־יהוה נִאֲצוּ אֶת־קְדוֹשׁ יִשְׂרָאֵל נָזֹרוּ אָחוֹר: ה עַל מֶה תֻכּוּ עוֹד תּוֹסִיפוּ סָרָה כָּל־רֹאשׁ לָחֳלִי וְכָל־לֵבָב דַּוָּי: ו מִכַּף־רֶגֶל וְעַד־רֹאשׁ אֵין־בּוֹ מְתֹם פֶּצַע וְחַבּוּרָה וּמַכָּה טְרִיָּה לֹא־זֹרוּ וְלֹא חֻבָּשׁוּ וְלֹא רֻכְּכָה בַּשָּׁמֶן: ז אַרְצְכֶם שְׁמָמָה עָרֵיכֶם שְׂרֻפוֹת אֵשׁ אַדְמַתְכֶם לְנֶגְדְּכֶם זָרִים אֹכְלִים אֹתָהּ וּשְׁמָמָה כְּמַהְפֵּכַת זָרִים: ח וְנוֹתְרָה בַת־צִיּוֹן כְּסֻכָּה בְכָרֶם כִּמְלוּנָה בְמִקְשָׁה כְּעִיר נְצוּרָה: ט לוּלֵי יהוה צְבָאוֹת הוֹתִיר לָנוּ שָׂרִיד כִּמְעָט כִּסְדֹם הָיִינוּ לַעֲמֹרָה דָּמִינוּ: י שִׁמְעוּ דְבַר־יהוה קְצִינֵי סְדֹם הַאֲזִינוּ תּוֹרַת אֱלֹהֵינוּ עַם עֲמֹרָה: יא לָמָּה לִּי רֹב־זִבְחֵיכֶם יֹאמַר יהוה שָׂבַעְתִּי עֹלוֹת אֵילִים וְחֵלֶב מְרִיאִים וְדַם פָּרִים וּכְבָשִׂים וְעַתּוּדִים לֹא חָפָצְתִּי: יב כִּי תָבֹאוּ לֵרָאוֹת פָּנָי מִי־בִקֵּשׁ זֹאת מִיֶּדְכֶם רְמֹס חֲצֵרָי: יג לֹא תוֹסִיפוּ הָבִיא מִנְחַת־שָׁוְא קְטֹרֶת תּוֹעֵבָה הִיא לִי חֹדֶשׁ וְשַׁבָּת קְרֹא מִקְרָא לֹא־אוּכַל אָוֶן וַעֲצָרָה: יד חָדְשֵׁיכֶם וּמוֹעֲדֵיכֶם שָׂנְאָה נַפְשִׁי הָיוּ עָלַי לָטֹרַח נִלְאֵיתִי נְשֹׂא: טו וּבְפָרִשְׂכֶם כַּפֵּיכֶם אַעְלִים עֵינַי מִכֶּם גַּם כִּי־תַרְבּוּ תְפִלָּה אֵינֶנִּי שֹׁמֵעַ יְדֵיכֶם דָּמִים מָלֵאוּ: טז רַחֲצוּ הִזַּכּוּ הָסִירוּ רֹעַ מַעַלְלֵיכֶם מִנֶּגֶד עֵינָי חִדְלוּ הָרֵעַ: יז לִמְדוּ הֵיטֵב דִּרְשׁוּ מִשְׁפָּט אַשְּׁרוּ חָמוֹץ שִׁפְטוּ יָתוֹם רִיבוּ אַלְמָנָה: יח לְכוּ־נָא וְנִוָּכְחָה יֹאמַר יהוה אִם־יִהְיוּ חֲטָאֵיכֶם כַּשָּׁנִים כַּשֶּׁלֶג יַלְבִּינוּ אִם־יַאְדִּימוּ כַתּוֹלָע כַּצֶּמֶר יִהְיוּ: יט אִם־תֹּאבוּ וּשְׁמַעְתֶּם טוּב הָאָרֶץ תֹּאכֵלוּ: כ וְאִם־תְּמָאֲנוּ וּמְרִיתֶם חֶרֶב תְּאֻכְּלוּ כִּי פִּי יהוה דִּבֵּר: כא אֵיכָה הָיְתָה לְזוֹנָה קִרְיָה נֶאֱמָנָה מְלֵאֲתִי מִשְׁפָּט צֶדֶק יָלִין בָּהּ וְעַתָּה מְרַצְּחִים: כב כַּסְפֵּךְ הָיָה לְסִיגִים סָבְאֵךְ מָהוּל בַּמָּיִם: כג שָׂרַיִךְ סוֹרְרִים וְחַבְרֵי גַּנָּבִים כֻּלּוֹ אֹהֵב שֹׁחַד וְרֹדֵף שַׁלְמֹנִים יָתוֹם לֹא יִשְׁפֹּטוּ וְרִיב אַלְמָנָה לֹא־יָבוֹא אֲלֵיהֶם: כד לָכֵן נְאֻם הָאָדוֹן יהוה צְבָאוֹת אֲבִיר יִשְׂרָאֵל הוֹי אֶנָּחֵם מִצָּרַי וְאִנָּקְמָה מֵאוֹיְבָי: כה וְאָשִׁיבָה יָדִי עָלַיִךְ וְאֶצְרֹף כַּבֹּר סִיגָיִךְ וְאָסִירָה כָּל־בְּדִילָיִךְ: כו וְאָשִׁיבָה שֹׁפְטַיִךְ כְּבָרִאשֹׁנָה וְיֹעֲצַיִךְ כְּבַתְּחִלָּה אַחֲרֵי־כֵן יִקָּרֵא לָךְ עִיר הַצֶּדֶק קִרְיָה נֶאֱמָנָה: כז צִיּוֹן בְּמִשְׁפָּט תִּפָּדֶה וְשָׁבֶיהָ בִּצְדָקָה:

HAFTARAS VA'ESCHANAN

Isaiah 40:1-26

40. 1 Comfort, comfort My people — says your God.
2 Speak to the heart of Jerusalem and proclaim to
her that her time [of exile] has been fulfilled, that her
iniquity has been conciliated, for she has received from
the hand of HASHEM double for all her sins.
3 A voice calls in the wilderness, "Clear the way of
HASHEM; make a straight road in the plain, a highway for
our God. 4 Every valley shall be raised, and every
mountain and hill shall be made low, the crooked shall
become straight and the rugged a level low land.
5 Revealed shall be the glory of HASHEM, and all flesh as
one shall see that the mouth of HASHEM has spoken."
6 The Voice says, "Proclaim!" and he says, "What shall
I proclaim?" — "All flesh is grass, and all its kindness like
the flower of the field. 7 The grass shall wither, the flower
shall fade, for the breath of HASHEM has blown upon it; in
truth, the people is grass. 8 The grass shall wither, the
flower shall fade, but the word of our God shall stand
forever."
9 Get yourself upon a high mountain, O herald unto
Zion; raise your voice in power, O herald unto Jerusalem,
raise [it], fear not, say to the cities of Judah, "Behold,
your God!" 10 Behold! My Lord, HASHEM/ELOHIM, shall
come with strength, and His arm will rule for Him;
behold! His recompense is with Him, and His wage is
before Him, 11 like a shepherd would graze his flock,
would gather lambs in his arm and carry [them] in his
bosom, would lead the nurslings.
12 Who has measured the waters in His fist, and meted
out the Heavens with the span, and counted in large
volume the dust of the earth, and weighed mountains in
a scale and hills in a balance? 13 Who has meted out the
spirit of HASHEM? Who is His man of counsel that he
might let Him know? 14 With whom did He seek counsel
and give him insight, and teach him in the path of justice,
and teach him knowledge, and the way of understanding
let him know? 15 Behold! the nations are like a bitter drop
from a bucket, and as the dust on the balance are they
considered; behold! the islands are like castaway dust.
16 And the Lebanon is not sufficient kindling; and its
beasts are not sufficient for burnt-offerings.
17 All the nations are as nothing before Him, as
nothingness and emptiness are they considered by Him.
18 To whom can you liken God? And what likeness can you
arrange for Him? 19 The graven image, the artisan's
casting, that the [gold]smith overlaid with gold and the
[silver]smith with silver chains? 20 The pauper sets aside,
he chooses wood that will not rot; he seeks for himself a
wise artisan, to prepare an idol that cannot move. 21 Do
you not know? Have you not heard? Has it not been told
to you from the first? Have you not understood [Who
fashioned] the foundations of the earth? 22 It is He Who
sits on the circumference of the earth, and [Who views]
its inhabitants as locusts; He Who spreads the heavens
like a thin curtain, and stretches them like a tent to dwell
[in]. 23 He Who gives over officers for nought; judges of
land He made like emptiness; 24 even as if they were not
planted, even as if they were not sown, even as if their
stock was not rooted in the ground; and also should He
blow on them, they would dry up, and a stormwind
would carry them away like stubble.
25 And to whom can you liken Me? And [to whom] shall
I be equal? — says the Holy One.
26 Raise your eyes on high and see Who created these:
He brings forth their legions by number; He calls them all
by name; because of His abundant might and powerful
strength, there is not missing even one.

הפטרת ואתחנן

ישעיה מ:א־כו

מ א נַחֲמוּ נַחֲמוּ עַמִּי יֹאמַר אֱלֹהֵיכֶם: ב דַּבְּרוּ
עַל־לֵב יְרוּשָׁלַםִ וְקִרְאוּ אֵלֶיהָ כִּי מָלְאָה צְבָאָהּ כִּי
נִרְצָה עֲוֺנָהּ כִּי לָקְחָה מִיַּד יהוה כִּפְלַיִם בְּכָל־
חַטֹּאתֶיהָ: ג קוֹל קוֹרֵא בַּמִּדְבָּר פַּנּוּ דֶּרֶךְ יהוה
יַשְּׁרוּ בָּעֲרָבָה מְסִלָּה לֵאלֹהֵינוּ: ד כָּל־גֶּיא יִנָּשֵׂא
וְכָל־הַר וְגִבְעָה יִשְׁפָּלוּ וְהָיָה הֶעָקֹב לְמִישׁוֹר
וְהָרְכָסִים לְבִקְעָה: ה וְנִגְלָה כְּבוֹד יהוה וְרָאוּ
כָל־בָּשָׂר יַחְדָּו כִּי פִּי יהוה דִּבֵּר: ו קוֹל אֹמֵר קְרָא
וְאָמַר מָה אֶקְרָא כָּל־הַבָּשָׂר חָצִיר וְכָל־חַסְדּוֹ
כְּצִיץ הַשָּׂדֶה: ז יָבֵשׁ חָצִיר נָבֵל צִיץ כִּי רוּחַ יהוה
נָשְׁבָה בּוֹ אָכֵן חָצִיר הָעָם: ח יָבֵשׁ חָצִיר נָבֵל צִיץ
וּדְבַר אֱלֹהֵינוּ יָקוּם לְעוֹלָם: ט עַל הַר־גָּבֹהַּ עֲלִי־
לָךְ מְבַשֶּׂרֶת צִיּוֹן הָרִימִי בַכֹּחַ קוֹלֵךְ מְבַשֶּׂרֶת
יְרוּשָׁלָםִ הָרִימִי אַל־תִּירָאִי אִמְרִי לְעָרֵי יְהוּדָה
הִנֵּה אֱלֹהֵיכֶם: י הִנֵּה אֲדֹנָי יֱהוִה בְּחָזָק יָבוֹא וּזְרֹעוֹ
מֹשְׁלָה לוֹ הִנֵּה שְׂכָרוֹ אִתּוֹ וּפְעֻלָּתוֹ לְפָנָיו:
יא כְּרֹעֶה עֶדְרוֹ יִרְעֶה בִּזְרֹעוֹ יְקַבֵּץ טְלָאִים וּבְחֵיקוֹ
יִשָּׂא עָלוֹת יְנַהֵל: יב מִי־מָדַד בְּשָׁעֳלוֹ מַיִם וְשָׁמַיִם
בַּזֶּרֶת תִּכֵּן וְכָל בַּשָּׁלִשׁ עֲפַר הָאָרֶץ וְשָׁקַל בַּפֶּלֶס
הָרִים וּגְבָעוֹת בְּמֹאזְנָיִם: יג מִי־תִכֵּן אֶת־רוּחַ יהוה
וְאִישׁ עֲצָתוֹ יוֹדִיעֶנּוּ: יד אֶת־מִי נוֹעָץ וַיְבִינֵהוּ
וַיְלַמְּדֵהוּ בְּאֹרַח מִשְׁפָּט וַיְלַמְּדֵהוּ דַעַת וְדֶרֶךְ
תְּבוּנוֹת יוֹדִיעֶנּוּ: טו הֵן גּוֹיִם כְּמַר מִדְּלִי וּכְשַׁחַק
מֹאזְנַיִם נֶחְשָׁבוּ הֵן אִיִּים כַּדַּק יִטּוֹל: טז וּלְבָנוֹן אֵין
דֵּי בָּעֵר וְחַיָּתוֹ אֵין דֵּי עוֹלָה: יז כָּל־הַגּוֹיִם כְּאַיִן
נֶגְדּוֹ מֵאֶפֶס וָתֹהוּ נֶחְשְׁבוּ־לוֹ: יח וְאֶל־מִי תְּדַמְּיוּן
אֵל וּמַה־דְּמוּת תַּעַרְכוּ־לוֹ: יט הַפֶּסֶל נָסַךְ חָרָשׁ
וְצֹרֵף בַּזָּהָב יְרַקְּעֶנּוּ וּרְתֻקוֹת כֶּסֶף צוֹרֵף: כ הַמְסֻכָּן
תְּרוּמָה עֵץ לֹא־יִרְקַב יִבְחָר חָרָשׁ חָכָם יְבַקֶּשׁ־לוֹ
לְהָכִין פֶּסֶל לֹא יִמּוֹט: כא הֲלוֹא תֵדְעוּ הֲלוֹא
תִשְׁמָעוּ הֲלוֹא הֻגַּד מֵרֹאשׁ לָכֶם הֲלוֹא הֲבִינֹתֶם
מוֹסְדוֹת הָאָרֶץ: כב הַיֹּשֵׁב עַל־חוּג הָאָרֶץ וְיֹשְׁבֶיהָ
כַּחֲגָבִים הַנּוֹטֶה כַדֹּק שָׁמַיִם וַיִּמְתָּחֵם כָּאֹהֶל
לָשָׁבֶת: כג הַנּוֹתֵן רוֹזְנִים לְאָיִן שֹׁפְטֵי אֶרֶץ כַּתֹּהוּ
עָשָׂה: כד אַף בַּל־נִטָּעוּ אַף בַּל־זֹרָעוּ אַף בַּל־שֹׁרֵשׁ
בָּאָרֶץ גִּזְעָם וְגַם נָשַׁף בָּהֶם וַיִּבָשׁוּ וּסְעָרָה כַּקַּשׁ
תִּשָּׂאֵם: כה וְאֶל־מִי תְדַמְּיוּנִי וְאֶשְׁוֶה יֹאמַר קָדוֹשׁ:
כו שְׂאוּ־מָרוֹם עֵינֵיכֶם וּרְאוּ מִי־בָרָא אֵלֶּה
הַמּוֹצִיא בְמִסְפָּר צְבָאָם לְכֻלָּם בְּשֵׁם יִקְרָא מֵרֹב
אוֹנִים וְאַמִּיץ כֹּחַ אִישׁ לֹא נֶעְדָּר:

HAFTARAS EIKEV

Isaiah 49:14 — 51:3

49. 14 And Zion said, "HASHEM has forsaken me; my
Lord has forgotten me." 15 Can a woman forget her
nursling, withdraw from feeling compassion for the child

הפטרת עקב

ישעיה מט:יד — נא:ג

מט יד וַתֹּאמֶר צִיּוֹן עֲזָבַנִי יהוה וַאדֹנָי
שְׁכֵחָנִי: טו הֲתִשְׁכַּח אִשָּׁה עוּלָהּ מֵרַחֵם בֶּן־

of her womb? Even were these to forget, yet I will not forget you. 16 Behold! I have engraved you on [My] palms; your [ruined] walls are before Me continuously. 17 Your children shall hasten [to repent], but your spoilers and your destroyers must depart from you. 18 Raise your eyes about you and see, all of them assemble, they come to you; [I swear] as I live — the word of HASHEM — that you shall clothe yourself with them all as with jewelry, and adorn yourself with them as a bride. 19 For your ruins and your desolations and your spoiled land shall now become cramped with inhabitants, and those who would swallow you up shall be at a far distance. 20 The children of your bereavement shall yet say in your ears, "The place is tight for me; make room for me that I may sit." 21 Then you will say in your heart, "Who has begotten me these? For I have been bereaved of children and alone, exiled and wandering. And who has reared these? Behold! I was left by myself; these, where have they been?"

22 For thus said my Lord, HASHEM/ELOHIM: Behold! I will raise My hand toward the nations, and to the peoples will I hoist my banner, and they shall bring your sons in their arms, and your daughters shall be carried on [their] shoulder. 23 Kings will be your nurturers and their princesses your nurses; with faces to the ground they will prostrate themselves to you; the dust of your feet will they lick; and you shall know that I am HASHEM, that those who hope to Me shall not be ashamed.

24 [You ask,] "Can prey be taken back from a strong one; can the righteous captive escape?" 25 But thus said HASHEM: Even the captive of the strong can be taken back, and the prey of the mighty can escape; I, Myself, will take up your cause, and I, Myself, will save your children. 26 And I will feed your oppressors their own flesh, and as with sweet wine shall they become drunk; then all flesh shall know that I am HASHEM, your Savior and your Redeemer, the Mighty One of Israel.

50. 1 Thus said HASHEM: Where is your mother's divorce document with which I sent her away? Or which of My creditors is it to whom I have sold you? Behold! it is for your iniquities that you have been sold, and for your rebellious transgressions that your mother has been sent away. 2 Why is it that [although] I have come, there is no man? [Why is it] that [although] I have called, there is no answer? Is My hand too very short for redemption? Is there no strength in Me to rescue? Behold! by My rebuke I dry up the sea, I set rivers as a desert, their fish-life putrefies for lack of water, and it dies of thirst. 3 I clothe the heavens in black, and make sackcloth their garment.

4 My Lord, HASHEM/ELOHIM, has given me a tongue for students, to know, to set a time for one thirsty for the word [of HASHEM]; He arouses [me] — every morning — He arouses [my] ear for me to hear like the students. 5 My Lord, HASHEM/ELOHIM, has opened [my] ear for me, and as for me, I did not rebel, I did not turn away backwards. 6 My body I gave to the smiters, and my cheeks to the pluckers; my face I did not hide from humiliations and spit. 7 For my Lord, HASHEM/ELOHIM, helps me, therefore I was not humiliated; therefore I set my face like flint and I knew that I would not be ashamed. 8 My champion is near; whosoever would contend with me, let us stand together; let whosoever is my plaintiff approach me.

9 Behold! my Lord, HASHEM/ELOHIM, shall help me; who will condemn me? Behold! they shall all become worn out like a garment; a moth shall devour them.

10 Who among you fears HASHEM, listening to the voice of His servant? Though he may have walked in darkness with no light for himself, let him trust in the Name of HASHEM, and lean upon his God. 11 Behold! all of you [others] are igniters of fire, girdled with fireworks; go away in the flame of your fire, and in the fireworks you have kindled; from My hand has this come upon you, that you should lie down in sorrow.

51. 1 Listen to me, O pursuers of righteousness, seekers of HASHEM; look to the rock from which you were hewn, and to the hollow of the pit from which you were

בִּטְנָהּ גַּם־אֵלֶּה תִשְׁכַּחְנָה וְאָנֹכִי לֹא אֶשְׁכָּחֵךְ׃
טז הֵן עַל־כַּפַּיִם חַקֹּתִיךְ חוֹמֹתַיִךְ נֶגְדִּי תָּמִיד׃
יז מִהֲרוּ בָּנָיִךְ מְהָרְסַיִךְ וּמַחֲרִבַיִךְ מִמֵּךְ יֵצֵאוּ׃
יח שְׂאִי־סָבִיב עֵינַיִךְ וּרְאִי כֻּלָּם נִקְבְּצוּ בָאוּ־לָךְ
חַי־אָנִי נְאֻם־יהוה כִּי כֻלָּם כַּעֲדִי תִלְבָּשִׁי
וּתְקַשְּׁרִים כַּכַּלָּה׃ יט כִּי חָרְבֹתַיִךְ וְשֹׁמְמֹתַיִךְ וְאֶרֶץ
הֲרִסֻתֵךְ כִּי עַתָּה תֵּצְרִי מִיּוֹשֵׁב וְרָחֲקוּ מְבַלְּעָיִךְ׃
כ עוֹד יֹאמְרוּ בְאָזְנַיִךְ בְּנֵי שִׁכֻּלָיִךְ צַר־לִי הַמָּקוֹם
גְּשָׁה־לִּי וְאֵשֵׁבָה׃ כא וְאָמַרְתְּ בִּלְבָבֵךְ מִי יָלַד־לִי
אֶת־אֵלֶּה וַאֲנִי שְׁכוּלָה וְגַלְמוּדָה גֹּלָה ׀ וְסוּרָה
וְאֵלֶּה מִי גִדֵּל הֵן אֲנִי נִשְׁאַרְתִּי לְבַדִּי אֵלֶּה אֵיפֹה
הֵם׃ כב כֹּה־אָמַר אֲדֹנָי יֱהוִה הִנֵּה אֶשָּׂא אֶל־גּוֹיִם
יָדִי וְאֶל־עַמִּים אָרִים נִסִּי וְהֵבִיאוּ בָנַיִךְ בְּחֹצֶן
וּבְנֹתַיִךְ עַל־כָּתֵף תִּנָּשֶׂאנָה׃ כג וְהָיוּ מְלָכִים אֹמְנַיִךְ
וְשָׂרוֹתֵיהֶם מֵינִיקֹתַיִךְ אַפַּיִם אֶרֶץ יִשְׁתַּחֲווּ־לָךְ
וַעֲפַר רַגְלַיִךְ יְלַחֵכוּ וְיָדַעַתְּ כִּי־אֲנִי יהוה אֲשֶׁר
לֹא־יֵבֹשׁוּ קֹוָי׃ כד הֲיֻקַּח מִגִּבּוֹר מַלְקוֹחַ וְאִם־
שְׁבִי צַדִּיק יִמָּלֵט׃ כה כִּי־כֹה ׀ אָמַר יהוה גַּם־שְׁבִי
גִבּוֹר יֻקָּח וּמַלְקוֹחַ עָרִיץ יִמָּלֵט וְאֶת־יְרִיבֵךְ אָנֹכִי
אָרִיב וְאֶת־בָּנַיִךְ אָנֹכִי אוֹשִׁיעַ׃ כו וְהַאֲכַלְתִּי אֶת־
מוֹנַיִךְ אֶת־בְּשָׂרָם וְכֶעָסִיס דָּמָם יִשְׁכָּרוּן וְיָדְעוּ
כָל־בָּשָׂר כִּי אֲנִי יהוה מוֹשִׁיעֵךְ וְגֹאֲלֵךְ אֲבִיר
יַעֲקֹב׃ **נ** א כֹּה ׀ אָמַר יהוה אֵי זֶה סֵפֶר כְּרִיתוּת
אִמְּכֶם אֲשֶׁר שִׁלַּחְתִּיהָ אוֹ מִי מִנּוֹשַׁי אֲשֶׁר־מָכַרְתִּי
אֶתְכֶם לוֹ הֵן בַּעֲוֺנֹתֵיכֶם נִמְכַּרְתֶּם וּבְפִשְׁעֵיכֶם
שֻׁלְּחָה אִמְּכֶם׃ ב מַדּוּעַ בָּאתִי וְאֵין אִישׁ קָרָאתִי
וְאֵין עוֹנֶה הֲקָצוֹר קָצְרָה יָדִי מִפְּדוּת וְאִם־אֵין־בִּי
כֹחַ לְהַצִּיל הֵן בְּגַעֲרָתִי אַחֲרִיב יָם אָשִׂים נְהָרוֹת
מִדְבָּר תִּבְאַשׁ דְּגָתָם מֵאֵין מַיִם וְתָמֹת בַּצָּמָא׃
ג אַלְבִּישׁ שָׁמַיִם קַדְרוּת וְשַׂק אָשִׂים כְּסוּתָם׃
ד אֲדֹנָי יֱהוִה נָתַן לִי לְשׁוֹן לִמּוּדִים לָדַעַת לָעוּת
אֶת־יָעֵף דָּבָר יָעִיר ׀ בַּבֹּקֶר בַּבֹּקֶר יָעִיר לִי אֹזֶן
לִשְׁמֹעַ כַּלִּמּוּדִים׃ ה אֲדֹנָי יֱהוִה פָּתַח־לִי אֹזֶן
וְאָנֹכִי לֹא מָרִיתִי אָחוֹר לֹא נְסוּגֹתִי׃ ו גֵּוִי נָתַתִּי
לְמַכִּים וּלְחָיַי לְמֹרְטִים פָּנַי לֹא הִסְתַּרְתִּי מִכְּלִמּוֹת
וָרֹק׃ ז וַאדֹנָי יֱהוִה יַעֲזָר־לִי עַל־כֵּן לֹא נִכְלָמְתִּי
עַל־כֵּן שַׂמְתִּי פָנַי כַּחַלָּמִישׁ וָאֵדַע כִּי־לֹא
אֵבוֹשׁ׃ ח קָרוֹב מַצְדִּיקִי מִי־יָרִיב אִתִּי נַעַמְדָה יָּחַד
מִי־בַעַל מִשְׁפָּטִי יִגַּשׁ אֵלָי׃ ט הֵן אֲדֹנָי יֱהוִה
יַעֲזָר־לִי מִי־הוּא יַרְשִׁיעֵנִי הֵן כֻּלָּם כַּבֶּגֶד יִבְלוּ
עָשׁ יֹאכְלֵם׃ י מִי בָכֶם יְרֵא יהוה שֹׁמֵעַ בְּקוֹל
עַבְדּוֹ אֲשֶׁר ׀ הָלַךְ חֲשֵׁכִים וְאֵין נֹגַהּ לוֹ יִבְטַח
בְּשֵׁם יהוה וְיִשָּׁעֵן בֵּאלֹהָיו׃ יא הֵן כֻּלְּכֶם קֹדְחֵי
אֵשׁ מְאַזְּרֵי זִיקוֹת לְכוּ ׀ בְּאוּר אֶשְׁכֶם וּבְזִיקוֹת
בְּעַרְתֶּם מִיָּדִי הָיְתָה־זֹּאת לָכֶם לְמַעֲצֵבָה
תִּשְׁכָּבוּן׃ **נא** א שִׁמְעוּ אֵלַי רֹדְפֵי צֶדֶק מְבַקְשֵׁי
יהוה הַבִּיטוּ אֶל־צוּר חֻצַּבְתֶּם וְאֶל־מַקֶּבֶת בּוֹר

dug. 2 Look to Abraham your forefather and to Sarah who bore you, for when he was yet one alone did I summon him and bless him and make him many. 3 For HASHEM shall comfort Zion, He shall comfort all her ruins, He shall make her wilderness like Eden and her wasteland like a garden of HASHEM; joy and gladness shall be found there, thanksgiving and the sound of music.

נִקַּרְתֶּם׃ ב הַבִּיטוּ אֶל־אַבְרָהָם אֲבִיכֶם וְאֶל־שָׂרָה תְּחוֹלֶלְכֶם כִּי־אֶחָד קְרָאתִיו וַאֲבָרְכֵהוּ וְאַרְבֵּהוּ׃ ג כִּי־נִחַם יהוה צִיּוֹן נִחַם כָּל־חָרְבֹתֶיהָ וַיָּשֶׂם מִדְבָּרָהּ כְּעֵדֶן וְעַרְבָתָהּ כְּגַן־יהוה שָׂשׂוֹן וְשִׂמְחָה יִמָּצֵא בָהּ תּוֹדָה וְקוֹל זִמְרָה׃

HAFTARAS RE'EH

Isaiah 54:11 — 55:5

54. 11 O afflicted, storm-tossed, unconsoled one, behold! I shall lay your floor stones upon pearls and make your foundation of sapphires. 12 I shall make your sun windows of rubies and your gates of garnets, and your entire boundary of precious stones. 13 All your children will be students of HASHEM, and abundant will be your children's peace. 14 Establish yourself through righteousness, distance yourself from oppression for you need not fear it, and from panic for it will not come near you. 15 Behold! One need fear indeed if he has nothing from Me; whoever aggressively opposes you will fall because of you. 16 Behold! I have created the smith who blows on a charcoal flame and withdraws a tool for his labor, and I have created the destroyer to ruin. 17 Any weapon sharpened against you shall not succeed, and any tongue that shall rise against you in judgment you shall condemn; this is the heritage of the servant of HASHEM, and their righteousness is from Me, the words of HASHEM.

55. 1 Ho, everyone who is thirsty, go to the water, even one who has no money; go buy and eat, go and buy without money and without barter, wine and milk. 2 Why do you weigh out money for that which is not bread and [fruit of] your toil for that which does not satisfy? Listen well to Me and eat what is good, and let your soul delight in abundance. 3 Incline your ear and come to Me, listen and your soul will rejuvenate; I shall seal an eternal covenant with you, the enduring kindnesses [promised] David. 4 Behold! I have appointed him a witness to the regimes, a prince and a commander to the regimes. 5 Behold! a nation that you did not know will you call, and a nation that knew you not will run to you, for the sake of HASHEM, your God, the Holy One of Israel, for He has glorified you!

הפטרת ראה

ישעיה נד:יא — נה:ה

נד יא עֲנִיָּה סֹעֲרָה לֹא נֻחָמָה הִנֵּה אָנֹכִי מַרְבִּיץ בַּפּוּךְ אֲבָנַיִךְ וִיסַדְתִּיךְ בַּסַּפִּירִים׃ יב וְשַׂמְתִּי כַּדְכֹד שִׁמְשֹׁתַיִךְ וּשְׁעָרַיִךְ לְאַבְנֵי אֶקְדָּח וְכָל־גְּבוּלֵךְ לְאַבְנֵי־חֵפֶץ׃ יג וְכָל־בָּנַיִךְ לִמּוּדֵי יהוה וְרַב שְׁלוֹם בָּנָיִךְ׃ יד בִּצְדָקָה תִּכּוֹנָנִי רַחֲקִי מֵעֹשֶׁק כִּי־לֹא תִירָאִי וּמִמְּחִתָּה כִּי לֹא־תִקְרַב אֵלָיִךְ׃ טו הֵן גּוֹר יָגוּר אֶפֶס מֵאוֹתִי מִי־גָר אִתָּךְ עָלַיִךְ יִפּוֹל׃ טז הִנֵּה [הן כ׳] אָנֹכִי בָּרָאתִי חָרָשׁ נֹפֵחַ בְּאֵשׁ פֶּחָם וּמוֹצִיא כְלִי לְמַעֲשֵׂהוּ וְאָנֹכִי בָּרָאתִי מַשְׁחִית לְחַבֵּל׃ יז כָּל־כְּלִי יוּצַר עָלַיִךְ לֹא יִצְלָח וְכָל־לָשׁוֹן תָּקוּם־אִתָּךְ לַמִּשְׁפָּט תַּרְשִׁיעִי זֹאת נַחֲלַת עַבְדֵי יהוה וְצִדְקָתָם מֵאִתִּי נְאֻם־יהוה׃ **נה** א הוֹי כָּל־צָמֵא לְכוּ לַמַּיִם וַאֲשֶׁר אֵין־לוֹ כָּסֶף לְכוּ שִׁבְרוּ וֶאֱכֹלוּ וּלְכוּ שִׁבְרוּ בְּלוֹא־כֶסֶף וּבְלוֹא מְחִיר יַיִן וְחָלָב׃ ב לָמָּה תִשְׁקְלוּ־כֶסֶף בְּלוֹא־לֶחֶם וִיגִיעֲכֶם בְּלוֹא לְשָׂבְעָה שִׁמְעוּ שָׁמוֹעַ אֵלַי וְאִכְלוּ־טוֹב וְתִתְעַנַּג בַּדֶּשֶׁן נַפְשְׁכֶם׃ ג הַטּוּ אָזְנְכֶם וּלְכוּ אֵלַי שִׁמְעוּ וּתְחִי נַפְשְׁכֶם וְאֶכְרְתָה לָכֶם בְּרִית עוֹלָם חַסְדֵי דָוִד הַנֶּאֱמָנִים׃ ד הֵן עֵד לְאוּמִּים נְתַתִּיו נָגִיד וּמְצַוֵּה לְאֻמִּים׃ ה הֵן גּוֹי לֹא־תֵדַע תִּקְרָא וְגוֹי לֹא־יְדָעוּךְ אֵלַיִךְ יָרוּצוּ לְמַעַן יהוה אֱלֹהַיִךְ וְלִקְדוֹשׁ יִשְׂרָאֵל כִּי פֵאֲרָךְ׃

HAFTARAS SHOFTIM

Isaiah 51:12 — 52:12

51. 12 It is I, I am He Who comforts you; who are you that you should be afraid of a man who shall die and of the son of man who shall be set as grass? 13 And you have forgotten HASHEM, your Maker, Who spread out the heavens and Who set the base of the earth; yet you are continually in terror, the whole day, of the oppressor's fury as if he were preparing to destroy; where then shall be the oppressor's fury? 14 The wanderer shall be soon released, and shall not die in the pit, nor shall his bread be lacking. 15 And I am HASHEM, your God, Who stirs up the sea and its waves rage — HASHEM, Master of Legions, is His Name. 16 And I have placed My words in your mouth, and with the shade of My hand have I covered you, to implant the heavens and to set a base for the earth and to say unto Zion, "You are My people!"

17 Awaken yourself! Awaken yourself! Arise, O Jerusalem, you who have drunk from the hand of HASHEM the cup of His fury, the phial of the cup of stupefaction have you drunk, have you drained. 18 There is no guide for her among all the children she has borne; there is no one holding her hand among all the children she has reared. 19 Two [are the calamities] that have befallen you; who will bewail you? The plunder and the breakage, the hunger and the sword; with whom shall I comfort you? 20 Your children have fainted, they lie at the head of all streets like a netted wild ox; they are full with HASHEM's fury, with your God's rebuke. 21 Therefore, listen now to this,

הפטרת שופטים

ישעיה נא:יב — נב:יב

נא יב אָנֹכִי אָנֹכִי הוּא מְנַחֶמְכֶם מִי־אַתְּ וַתִּירְאִי מֵאֱנוֹשׁ יָמוּת וּמִבֶּן־אָדָם חָצִיר יִנָּתֵן׃ יג וַתִּשְׁכַּח יהוה עֹשֶׂךָ נוֹטֶה שָׁמַיִם וְיֹסֵד אָרֶץ וַתְּפַחֵד תָּמִיד כָּל־הַיּוֹם מִפְּנֵי חֲמַת הַמֵּצִיק כַּאֲשֶׁר כּוֹנֵן לְהַשְׁחִית וְאַיֵּה חֲמַת הַמֵּצִיק׃ יד מִהַר צֹעֶה לְהִפָּתֵחַ וְלֹא־יָמוּת לַשַּׁחַת וְלֹא יֶחְסַר לַחְמוֹ׃ טו וְאָנֹכִי יהוה אֱלֹהֶיךָ רֹגַע הַיָּם וַיֶּהֱמוּ גַּלָּיו יהוה צְבָאוֹת שְׁמוֹ׃ טז וָאָשִׂם דְּבָרַי בְּפִיךָ וּבְצֵל יָדִי כִּסִּיתִיךָ לִנְטֹעַ שָׁמַיִם וְלִיסֹד אָרֶץ וְלֵאמֹר לְצִיּוֹן עַמִּי־אָתָּה׃ יז הִתְעוֹרְרִי הִתְעוֹרְרִי קוּמִי יְרוּשָׁלַםִ אֲשֶׁר שָׁתִית מִיַּד יהוה אֶת־כּוֹס חֲמָתוֹ אֶת־קֻבַּעַת כּוֹס הַתַּרְעֵלָה שָׁתִית מָצִית׃ יח אֵין־מְנַהֵל לָהּ מִכָּל־בָּנִים יָלָדָה וְאֵין מַחֲזִיק בְּיָדָהּ מִכָּל־בָּנִים גִּדֵּלָה׃ יט שְׁתַּיִם הֵנָּה קֹרְאֹתַיִךְ מִי יָנוּד לָךְ הַשֹּׁד וְהַשֶּׁבֶר וְהָרָעָב וְהַחֶרֶב מִי אֲנַחֲמֵךְ׃ כ בָּנַיִךְ עֻלְּפוּ שָׁכְבוּ בְּרֹאשׁ כָּל־חוּצוֹת כְּתוֹא מִכְמָר הַמְלֵאִים חֲמַת־יהוה גַּעֲרַת אֱלֹהָיִךְ׃ כא לָכֵן שִׁמְעִי־נָא זֹאת

O afflicted one, drunk, but not with wine.
22 Thus said your Lord, HASHEM, and your God Who will
contend for His people: Behold! I have taken from your
hand the cup of stupefaction, the phial of the cup of My
fury; no longer shall you drink from it again. 23 But I will put
it into the hand of your tormentors, who have said to you,
"Prostrate yourself, that we may step over you," who set
your body as the ground and as the street for wayfarers.

52. 1 Wake up! Wake up! Don your strength, O Zion, don
the garments of your splendor, O Jerusalem, the
Holy City, for no longer shall there enter into you any
uncircumcised or contaminated person. 2 Shake the dust
from yourself, arise, enthrone yourself, O Jerusalem;
undo the straps on your neck, O captive daughter of Zion.
3 For thus said HASHEM: Without price were you sold, so
you shall not be redeemed with money.
4 For thus said my Lord, HASHEM/ELOHIM: Egypt! My
people went down at first to sojourn there, and Assyria
oppressed them without cause. 5 And now, what do I
have here — the word of HASHEM — that My people was
purchased without price; those who rule over him praise
themselves — the word of HASHEM — and continuously,
all day, My Name is blasphemed. 6 Therefore, My people
shall know My Name — therefore, on that day — for I am
the One Who speaks, here I am!
7 How beautiful ascending the mountains are the
footsteps of the herald making heard, "Peace!" herald-
ing, "Good!" making heard, "Salvation!" saying unto
Zion, "Your God has reigned!" 8 The voice of your
lookouts, they have raised a voice, together shall they
sing glad song, for every eye shall see when HASHEM
returns to Jerusalem. 9 Burst forth in joy, sing glad song
together, O ruins of Jerusalem, for HASHEM shall comfort
His people; He has redeemed Jerusalem. 10 HASHEM has
bared His holy arm to the eyes of the nations, and all ends
of the earth shall see the salvation of our God.
11 Turn away! Turn away! Go forth from there! A
contaminated person shall you not touch! Go forth from
within it! Cleanse yourselves, O bearers of the vessels of
HASHEM. 12 But it is not in haste that you shall go forth; nor
shall you go in flight; for HASHEM shall go before you, and
the God of Israel shall be your rear guard.

HAFTARAS KI SEITZEI

Isaiah 54:1-10

54. 1 Sing out, O barren one, who has not given birth,
break out into glad song and be jubilant, O one who
had no labor pains, for the children of the desolate
[Jerusalem] outnumber the children of the inhabited
[city] — said HASHEM. 2 Broaden the place of your tent
and stretch out the curtains of your dwellings, stint not;
lengthen your cords and strengthen your pegs. 3 For
southward and northward you shall spread out mightily,
your offspring will inherit nations, and they will settle
desolate cites. 4 Fear not, for you will not be shamed, do
not feel humiliated for you will not be mortified; for you
will forget the shame of your youth, and the mortification
of your widowhood you will remember no more. 5 For
your Master is your Maker — HASHEM, Master of Legions
is His Name; your Redeemer is the Holy One of Israel —
God of all the world shall He be called. 6 For like a wife
who had been forsaken and of melancholy spirit will
HASHEM have called you, and like a wife of one's youth
who had become despised — said your God. 7 For but a
brief moment have I forsaken you, and with abundant
mercy shall I gather you in. 8 With a slight wrath have I
concealed My countenance from you for a moment, but
with eternal kindness shall I show you mercy, said your
Redeemer, HASHEM.
9 For like the waters of Noah shall this be to Me: as I
have sworn never again to pass the waters of Noah over
the earth, so have I sworn not to be wrathful with you or
rebuke you. 10 For the mountains may be moved and the
hills may falter, but My kindness shall not be removed
from you and My covenant of peace shall not falter —
says the One Who shows you mercy, HASHEM.

עֲנִיָּה וּשְׁכֻרַת וְלֹא מִיָּיִן: כב כֹּה־אָמַר אֲדֹנַיִךְ יהוה
וֵאלֹהַיִךְ יָרִיב עַמּוֹ הִנֵּה לָקַחְתִּי מִיָּדֵךְ אֶת־כּוֹס
הַתַּרְעֵלָה אֶת־קֻבַּעַת כּוֹס חֲמָתִי לֹא־תוֹסִיפִי
לִשְׁתּוֹתָהּ עוֹד: כג וְשַׂמְתִּיהָ בְּיַד מוֹגַיִךְ אֲשֶׁר־אָמְרוּ
לְנַפְשֵׁךְ שְׁחִי וְנַעֲבֹרָה וַתָּשִׂימִי כָאָרֶץ גֵּוֵךְ וְכַחוּץ
לַעֹבְרִים: **נב** א עוּרִי עוּרִי לִבְשִׁי עֻזֵּךְ צִיּוֹן לִבְשִׁי ׀
בִּגְדֵי תִפְאַרְתֵּךְ יְרוּשָׁלַםִ עִיר הַקֹּדֶשׁ כִּי לֹא יוֹסִיף
יָבֹא־בָךְ עוֹד עָרֵל וְטָמֵא: ב הִתְנַעֲרִי מֵעָפָר קוּמִי
שְׁבִי יְרוּשָׁלָםִ הִתְפַּתְּחִי [התפתחו כ׳] מוֹסְרֵי
צַוָּארֵךְ שְׁבִיָּה בַּת־צִיּוֹן: ג כִּי־כֹה אָמַר יהוה חִנָּם
נִמְכַּרְתֶּם וְלֹא בְכֶסֶף תִּגָּאֵלוּ: ד כִּי כֹה אָמַר אֲדֹנָי
יֱהוִֹה מִצְרַיִם יָרַד־עַמִּי בָרִאשֹׁנָה לָגוּר שָׁם וְאַשּׁוּר
בְּאֶפֶס עֲשָׁקוֹ: ה וְעַתָּה מַה־לִּי־פֹה נְאֻם־יהוה
כִּי־לֻקַּח עַמִּי חִנָּם מֹשְׁלָו יְהֵילִילוּ נְאֻם־יהוה
וְתָמִיד כָּל־הַיּוֹם שְׁמִי מִנֹּאָץ: ו לָכֵן יֵדַע עַמִּי שְׁמִי
לָכֵן בַּיּוֹם הַהוּא כִּי־אֲנִי־הוּא הַמְדַבֵּר הִנֵּנִי:
ז מַה־נָּאווּ עַל־הֶהָרִים רַגְלֵי מְבַשֵּׂר מַשְׁמִיעַ שָׁלוֹם
מְבַשֵּׂר טוֹב מַשְׁמִיעַ יְשׁוּעָה אֹמֵר לְצִיּוֹן מָלַךְ
אֱלֹהָיִךְ: ח קוֹל צֹפַיִךְ נָשְׂאוּ קוֹל יַחְדָּו יְרַנֵּנוּ כִּי עַיִן
בְּעַיִן יִרְאוּ בְּשׁוּב יהוה צִיּוֹן: ט פִּצְחוּ רַנְּנוּ יַחְדָּו
חָרְבוֹת יְרוּשָׁלָםִ כִּי־נִחַם יהוה עַמּוֹ גָּאַל יְרוּשָׁלָםִ:
י חָשַׂף יהוה אֶת־זְרוֹעַ קָדְשׁוֹ לְעֵינֵי כָּל־הַגּוֹיִם
וְרָאוּ כָּל־אַפְסֵי־אָרֶץ אֵת יְשׁוּעַת אֱלֹהֵינוּ: יא סוּרוּ
סוּרוּ צְאוּ מִשָּׁם טָמֵא אַל־תִּגָּעוּ צְאוּ מִתּוֹכָהּ הִבָּרוּ
נֹשְׂאֵי כְּלֵי יהוה: יב כִּי לֹא בְחִפָּזוֹן תֵּצֵאוּ וּבִמְנוּסָה
לֹא תֵלֵכוּן כִּי־הֹלֵךְ לִפְנֵיכֶם יהוה וּמְאַסִּפְכֶם
אֱלֹהֵי יִשְׂרָאֵל:

הפטרת כי תצא

ישעיה נד:א־י

נד א רָנִּי עֲקָרָה לֹא יָלָדָה פִּצְחִי רִנָּה וְצַהֲלִי
לֹא־חָלָה כִּי־רַבִּים בְּנֵי־שׁוֹמֵמָה מִבְּנֵי בְעוּלָה
אָמַר יהוה: ב הַרְחִיבִי ׀ מְקוֹם אָהֳלֵךְ וִירִיעוֹת
מִשְׁכְּנוֹתַיִךְ יַטּוּ אַל־תַּחְשֹׂכִי הַאֲרִיכִי מֵיתָרַיִךְ
וִיתֵדֹתַיִךְ חַזֵּקִי: ג כִּי־יָמִין וּשְׂמֹאול תִּפְרֹצִי וְזַרְעֵךְ
גּוֹיִם יִירָשׁ וְעָרִים נְשַׁמּוֹת יוֹשִׁיבוּ: ד אַל־תִּירְאִי
כִּי־לֹא תֵבוֹשִׁי וְאַל־תִּכָּלְמִי כִּי־לֹא תַחְפִּירִי כִּי
בֹשֶׁת עֲלוּמַיִךְ תִּשְׁכָּחִי וְחֶרְפַּת אַלְמְנוּתַיִךְ לֹא
תִזְכְּרִי־עוֹד: ה כִּי בֹעֲלַיִךְ עֹשַׂיִךְ יהוה צְבָאוֹת שְׁמוֹ
וְגֹאֲלֵךְ קְדוֹשׁ יִשְׂרָאֵל אֱלֹהֵי כָל־הָאָרֶץ יִקָּרֵא:
ו כִּי־כְאִשָּׁה עֲזוּבָה וַעֲצוּבַת רוּחַ קְרָאָךְ יהוה
וְאֵשֶׁת נְעוּרִים כִּי תִמָּאֵס אָמַר אֱלֹהָיִךְ: ז בְּרֶגַע
קָטֹן עֲזַבְתִּיךְ וּבְרַחֲמִים גְּדֹלִים אֲקַבְּצֵךְ: ח בְּשֶׁצֶף
קֶצֶף הִסְתַּרְתִּי פָנַי רֶגַע מִמֵּךְ וּבְחֶסֶד עוֹלָם
רִחַמְתִּיךְ אָמַר גֹּאֲלֵךְ יהוה: ט כִּי־מֵי נֹחַ זֹאת לִי
אֲשֶׁר נִשְׁבַּעְתִּי מֵעֲבֹר מֵי־נֹחַ עוֹד עַל־הָאָרֶץ כֵּן
נִשְׁבַּעְתִּי מִקְּצֹף עָלַיִךְ וּמִגְּעָר־בָּךְ: י כִּי הֶהָרִים
יָמוּשׁוּ וְהַגְּבָעוֹת תְּמוּטֶינָה וְחַסְדִּי מֵאִתֵּךְ לֹא־
יָמוּשׁ וּבְרִית שְׁלוֹמִי לֹא תָמוּט אָמַר מְרַחֲמֵךְ
יהוה:

HAFTARAS KI SAVO

Isaiah 60:1-22

60. 1 Arise! Shine! For your light has arrived, and the glory of HASHEM has shined upon you. 2 For, behold! Darkness shall cover the earth, and dense cloud the kingdoms; but upon you shall shine HASHEM, and His glory shall be seen upon you. 3 Nations will go by your light, and kings by the brightness of your shine. 4 Lift your eyes about you and see, all of them assemble, they come to you; your sons from afar shall come, and your daughters shall be nurtured alongside [royalty]. 5 Then you shall see and be radiant, anxious and expansive shall be your heart, for the affluence of the west shall be turned over to you, and the wealth of nations shall come to you. 6 An abundance of camels will envelop you, dromedaries of Midian and Ephah; all those of Sheba shall come, gold and frankincense shall they bear, and the praises of HASHEM shall they proclaim. 7 All the flocks of Kedar shall be gathered unto you, the rams of Nebaioth shall minister to you; they shall be brought up with favor upon My Altar, and the House of My glory will I glorify. 8 Who are these? Like a cloud they fly, like pigeons to their cote-windows! 9 For unto Me shall the island-dwellers gather, and the ships of Tarshish [as] in earlier times, to bring your children from afar, their gold and silver with them, for the sake of HASHEM, your God, and for the Holy One of Israel, for He has glorified you. 10 Then the sons of strangers shall build your city-walls and their kings shall minister to you; though I struck you in My indignation, in My favor have I been compassionate to you. 11 And your gates shall be opened continuously, day and night, they shall not be closed, to bring to you the wealth of nations, and their kings under escort. 12 For the nation and the kingdom that will not serve you shall be lost, and the nations utterly destroyed. 13 The glory of the Lebanon [forest] shall come to you — cypress, fir and box tree, together — to glorify the site of My Sanctuary, and the site of My footstool will I honor. 14 They shall go unto you in bent submission, those children of your oppressors; and they shall prostrate themselves at the soles of your feet, all those who slandered you; and they shall call you "the City of HASHEM, Zion, [the City of] the Holy One of Israel." 15 In place of your having been forsaken and hated with no wayfarer, I shall establish you as an eternal pride, a joy for each succeeding generation. 16 You shall nurse from the milk of the nations, from the breast of kings shall you nurse; then you shall know that I, HASHEM, am your Savior and your Redeemer, the Mighty One of Jacob. 17 In place of the copper I will bring gold; and in place of the iron I will bring silver; and in place of the wood, copper; and in place of the stones, iron; I will set your appointed officials for peacefulness and your overlords for righteousness. 18 No longer shall violence be heard in your land, [nor] plunder and breakage in your borders; but you shall call [God's] salvation your [protective] walls, and [His] praise your gateways. 19 You shall no longer have need of the sun for light of day, nor for brightness the moon to illuminate for you; rather HASHEM shall be unto you an eternal light, and your God for your glory. 20 Never again shall your sun set, nor shall your moon be withdrawn; for HASHEM shall be unto you an eternal light, and ended shall be the days of your mourning. 21 And your people, they are all righteous; forever shall they inherit the Land; a branch of My planting, My handiwork, for Me to glory in. 22 The smallest shall increase a thousandfold, and the least into a mighty nation; I am HASHEM, in its time I will hasten it.

הפטרת כי תבוא

ישעיה ס:א־כב

ס א קוּמִי אוֹרִי כִּי־בָא אוֹרֵךְ וּכְבוֹד יהוה עָלַיִךְ
זָרָח: ב כִּי־הִנֵּה הַחֹשֶׁךְ יְכַסֶּה־אֶרֶץ וַעֲרָפֶל
לְאֻמִּים וְעָלַיִךְ יִזְרַח יהוה וּכְבוֹדוֹ עָלַיִךְ יֵרָאֶה:
ג וְהָלְכוּ גוֹיִם לְאוֹרֵךְ וּמְלָכִים לְנֹגַהּ זַרְחֵךְ:
ד שְׂאִי סָבִיב עֵינַיִךְ וּרְאִי כֻּלָּם נִקְבְּצוּ בָאוּ־לָךְ
בָּנַיִךְ מֵרָחוֹק יָבֹאוּ וּבְנֹתַיִךְ עַל־צַד תֵּאָמַנָה:
ה אָז תִּרְאִי וְנָהַרְתְּ וּפָחַד וְרָחַב לְבָבֵךְ כִּי־יֵהָפֵךְ
עָלַיִךְ הֲמוֹן יָם חֵיל גּוֹיִם יָבֹאוּ לָךְ: ו שִׁפְעַת
גְּמַלִּים תְּכַסֵּךְ בִּכְרֵי מִדְיָן וְעֵיפָה כֻּלָּם מִשְּׁבָא
יָבֹאוּ זָהָב וּלְבוֹנָה יִשָּׂאוּ וּתְהִלֹּת יהוה יְבַשֵּׂרוּ:
ז כָּל־צֹאן קֵדָר יִקָּבְצוּ לָךְ אֵילֵי נְבָיוֹת יְשָׁרְתוּנֶךְ
יַעֲלוּ עַל־רָצוֹן מִזְבְּחִי וּבֵית תִּפְאַרְתִּי אֲפָאֵר:
ח מִי־אֵלֶּה כָּעָב תְּעוּפֶינָה וְכַיּוֹנִים אֶל־
אֲרֻבֹּתֵיהֶם: ט כִּי־לִי | אִיִּים יְקַוּוּ וָאֳנִיּוֹת תַּרְשִׁישׁ
בָּרִאשֹׁנָה לְהָבִיא בָנַיִךְ מֵרָחוֹק כַּסְפָּם וּזְהָבָם
אִתָּם לְשֵׁם יהוה אֱלֹהַיִךְ וְלִקְדוֹשׁ יִשְׂרָאֵל כִּי
פֵאֲרָךְ: י וּבָנוּ בְנֵי־נֵכָר חֹמֹתַיִךְ וּמַלְכֵיהֶם
יְשָׁרְתוּנֶךְ כִּי בְקִצְפִּי הִכִּיתִיךְ וּבִרְצוֹנִי רִחַמְתִּיךְ:
יא וּפִתְּחוּ שְׁעָרַיִךְ תָּמִיד יוֹמָם וָלַיְלָה לֹא יִסָּגֵרוּ
לְהָבִיא אֵלַיִךְ חֵיל גּוֹיִם וּמַלְכֵיהֶם נְהוּגִים:
יב כִּי־הַגּוֹי וְהַמַּמְלָכָה אֲשֶׁר לֹא־יַעַבְדוּךְ יֹאבֵדוּ
וְהַגּוֹיִם חָרֹב יֶחֱרָבוּ: יג כְּבוֹד הַלְּבָנוֹן אֵלַיִךְ יָבוֹא
בְּרוֹשׁ תִּדְהָר וּתְאַשּׁוּר יַחְדָּו לְפָאֵר מְקוֹם
מִקְדָּשִׁי וּמְקוֹם רַגְלַי אֲכַבֵּד: יד וְהָלְכוּ אֵלַיִךְ
שְׁחוֹחַ בְּנֵי מְעַנַּיִךְ וְהִשְׁתַּחֲווּ עַל־כַּפּוֹת רַגְלַיִךְ
כָּל־מְנַאֲצָיִךְ וְקָרְאוּ לָךְ עִיר יהוה צִיּוֹן קְדוֹשׁ
יִשְׂרָאֵל: טו תַּחַת הֱיוֹתֵךְ עֲזוּבָה וּשְׂנוּאָה וְאֵין
עוֹבֵר וְשַׂמְתִּיךְ לִגְאוֹן עוֹלָם מְשׂוֹשׂ דּוֹר וָדוֹר:
טז וְיָנַקְתְּ חֲלֵב גּוֹיִם וְשֹׁד מְלָכִים תִּינָקִי וְיָדַעַתְּ
כִּי־אֲנִי יהוה מוֹשִׁיעֵךְ וְגֹאֲלֵךְ אֲבִיר יַעֲקֹב:
יז תַּחַת הַנְּחֹשֶׁת אָבִיא זָהָב וְתַחַת הַבַּרְזֶל
אָבִיא כֶסֶף וְתַחַת הָעֵצִים נְחֹשֶׁת וְתַחַת
הָאֲבָנִים בַּרְזֶל וְשַׂמְתִּי פְקֻדָּתֵךְ שָׁלוֹם וְנֹגְשַׂיִךְ
צְדָקָה: יח לֹא־יִשָּׁמַע עוֹד חָמָס בְּאַרְצֵךְ שֹׁד
וָשֶׁבֶר בִּגְבוּלָיִךְ וְקָרָאת יְשׁוּעָה חוֹמֹתַיִךְ
וּשְׁעָרַיִךְ תְּהִלָּה: יט לֹא־יִהְיֶה־לָּךְ עוֹד הַשֶּׁמֶשׁ
לְאוֹר יוֹמָם וּלְנֹגַהּ הַיָּרֵחַ לֹא־יָאִיר לָךְ וְהָיָה־לָךְ
יהוה לְאוֹר עוֹלָם וֵאלֹהַיִךְ לְתִפְאַרְתֵּךְ: כ לֹא־
יָבוֹא עוֹד שִׁמְשֵׁךְ וִירֵחֵךְ לֹא יֵאָסֵף כִּי יהוה
יִהְיֶה־לָּךְ לְאוֹר עוֹלָם וְשָׁלְמוּ יְמֵי אֶבְלֵךְ:
כא וְעַמֵּךְ כֻּלָּם צַדִּיקִים לְעוֹלָם יִירְשׁוּ אָרֶץ נֵצֶר
מַטָּעַי [מטעו כ׳] מַעֲשֵׂה יָדַי לְהִתְפָּאֵר: כב הַקָּטֹן
יִהְיֶה לָאֶלֶף וְהַצָּעִיר לְגוֹי עָצוּם אֲנִי יהוה בְּעִתָּהּ
אֲחִישֶׁנָּה:

HAFTARAS NITZAVIM

Isaiah 61:10 – 63:9

61. [10] I will rejoice intensely with HASHEM, my soul shall exult with my God, for He has dressed me in the raiment of salvation, in a robe of righteousness has He cloaked me, like a bridegroom who dons priestly glory, like a bride who bedecks herself in her jewelry. [11] For as the earth brings forth her growth, and as a garden causes its sowings to grow, so shall my Lord, HASHEM/ELOHIM, cause righteousness and praise to grow in the face of all the nations.

62. [1] For Zion's sake, I will not be silent, and for Jerusalem's sake, I will not be still, until her righteousness shall go forth like bright light, and her salvation shall flame like a torch. [2] And nations shall perceive your righteousness, and all kings your honor; and you shall be called a new name, which the mouth of HASHEM shall articulate. [3] Then you shall be a crown of splendor in the hand of HASHEM;, and a royal headdress in the palm of your God. It shall no longer be said of you, "Forsaken one," and of your land shall no longer be said, "Desolate place," for you shall be called "My-desire-is-in-her," and your land "Settled," for HASHEM's desire is in you and your land shall be settled. [5] As a young man espouses a maiden, so shall your children settle in you; and like the bridegroom's rejoicing over his bride, so shall your God rejoice over you. [6] Upon your walls, O Jerusalem, have I assigned guardians; all the day and all the night, continuously, they shall never be silent; O reminders of HASHEM, let yourselves not rest. [7] And give not any rest, until He establishes, and until He sets Jerusalem as a praise in the Land. [8] HASHEM swore by His right hand and by His powerful arm: I will not give your grain any longer as food for your enemies; and alien sons shall not drink your wine for which you have exerted yourself. [9] For those who have harvested it shall eat it and praise HASHEM, and those who have gathered it in shall drink it in My holy courtyards.

[10] Go through, go through the gates; clean the people's way; beat down, beat down the highway, clear it of stone; raise a banner over the peoples. [11] Behold! HASHEM has made heard unto the end of the earth: Say unto the daughter Zion, "Behold! Your salvation has come; behold! His recompense is with Him, and His wage is before Him."

[12] And they shall call them, "The holy people, the redeemed of HASHEM"; and you shall be called, "Sought after; city not forsaken."

63. [1] Who is this that comes from Edom, sullied of garment from Bozrah? It is this One Who was majestic in His raiment, Who was girded with His abundant strength? — "It is I Who speaks in righteousness, abundantly able to save." [2] Why the red stain on Your raiment? And Your garments — as one who treads in the wine vat! [3] "A wine press have I trod by Myself, and from the nations not a man was with Me; I trod on them in My anger and trampled them in My wrath, their lifeblood spurted out on My garments, and I soiled My raiment. [4] For the day of vengeance is in My heart and the year of My redemption has come. [5] I looked, but there was no helper; I was astonished, but there was no supporter; so My arm saved Me, and My wrath supported Me. [6] I trampled peoples in My anger, and stupefied them with My wrath, and threw their lifeblood to the ground."

[7] The kindness of HASHEM will I mention, the praises of HASHEM, in accordance with all that HASHEM has bestowed upon us, and the abundant goodness to the House of Israel, which He bestowed upon them in His compassion and in His abundant kindness. [8] For He said, "Yet they are My people, children who will not be false," and He was unto them a Savior. [9] In all their troubles, He was troubled, and an angel from before Him saved them; with His love and with His compassion He redeemed them; He lifted them and bore them all the days of the world.

הפטרת נצבים

ישעיה סא:י — סג:ט

סא י שׂוֹשׂ אָשִׂישׂ בַּיהוָה תָּגֵל נַפְשִׁי בֵּאלֹהַי כִּי
הִלְבִּישַׁנִי בִּגְדֵי־יֶשַׁע מְעִיל צְדָקָה יְעָטָנִי כֶּחָתָן
יְכַהֵן פְּאֵר וְכַכַּלָּה תַּעְדֶּה כֵלֶיהָ: יא כִּי כָאָרֶץ
תּוֹצִיא צִמְחָהּ וּכְגַנָּה זֵרוּעֶיהָ תַצְמִיחַ כֵּן ׀ אֲדֹנָי
יֱהוִֹה יַצְמִיחַ צְדָקָה וּתְהִלָּה נֶגֶד כָּל־הַגּוֹיִם:
סב א לְמַעַן צִיּוֹן לֹא אֶחֱשֶׁה וּלְמַעַן יְרוּשָׁלַ͏ִם
לֹא אֶשְׁקוֹט עַד־יֵצֵא כַנֹּגַהּ צִדְקָהּ וִישׁוּעָתָהּ
כְּלַפִּיד יִבְעָר: ב וְרָאוּ גוֹיִם צִדְקֵךְ וְכָל־מְלָכִים
כְּבוֹדֵךְ וְקֹרָא לָךְ שֵׁם חָדָשׁ אֲשֶׁר פִּי יְהוָה
יִקֳּבֶנּוּ: ג וְהָיִית עֲטֶרֶת תִּפְאֶרֶת בְּיַד־יְהוָה
וּצְנִיף [וצנוף כ׳] מְלוּכָה בְּכַף־אֱלֹהָיִךְ: ד לֹא־
יֵאָמֵר לָךְ עוֹד עֲזוּבָה וּלְאַרְצֵךְ לֹא־יֵאָמֵר עוֹד
שְׁמָמָה כִּי לָךְ יִקָּרֵא חֶפְצִי־בָהּ וּלְאַרְצֵךְ בְּעוּלָה
כִּי־חָפֵץ יהוה בָּךְ וְאַרְצֵךְ תִּבָּעֵל: ה כִּי־יִבְעַל בָּחוּר
בְּתוּלָה יִבְעָלוּךְ בָּנָיִךְ וּמְשׂוֹשׂ חָתָן עַל־כַּלָּה
יָשִׂישׂ עָלַיִךְ אֱלֹהָיִךְ: ו עַל־חוֹמֹתַיִךְ יְרוּשָׁלַ͏ִם
הִפְקַדְתִּי שֹׁמְרִים כָּל־הַיּוֹם וְכָל־הַלַּיְלָה תָּמִיד לֹא
יֶחֱשׁוּ הַמַּזְכִּרִים אֶת־יהוה אַל־דֳּמִי לָכֶם: ז וְאַל־
תִּתְּנוּ דֳמִי לוֹ עַד־יְכוֹנֵן וְעַד־יָשִׂים אֶת־יְרוּשָׁלַ͏ִם
תְּהִלָּה בָּאָרֶץ: ח נִשְׁבַּע יְהוָה בִּימִינוֹ וּבִזְרוֹעַ עֻזּוֹ
אִם־אֶתֵּן אֶת־דְּגָנֵךְ עוֹד מַאֲכָל לְאֹיְבַיִךְ וְאִם־
יִשְׁתּוּ בְנֵי־נֵכָר תִּירוֹשֵׁךְ אֲשֶׁר יָגַעַתְּ בּוֹ: ט כִּי
מְאַסְפָיו יֹאכְלֻהוּ וְהִלְלוּ אֶת־יְהוָה וּמְקַבְּצָיו
יִשְׁתֻּהוּ בְּחַצְרוֹת קָדְשִׁי: י עִבְרוּ עִבְרוּ בַּשְּׁעָרִים
פַּנּוּ דֶּרֶךְ הָעָם סֹלּוּ סֹלּוּ הַמְסִלָּה סַקְּלוּ מֵאֶבֶן
הָרִימוּ נֵס עַל־הָעַמִּים: יא הִנֵּה יהוה הִשְׁמִיעַ
אֶל־קְצֵה הָאָרֶץ אִמְרוּ לְבַת־צִיּוֹן הִנֵּה יִשְׁעֵךְ בָּא
הִנֵּה שְׂכָרוֹ אִתּוֹ וּפְעֻלָּתוֹ לְפָנָיו: יב וְקָרְאוּ לָהֶם
עַם־הַקֹּדֶשׁ גְּאוּלֵי יְהוָה וְלָךְ יִקָּרֵא דְרוּשָׁה עִיר לֹא
נֶעֱזָבָה: **סג** א מִי־זֶה ׀ בָּא מֵאֱדוֹם חֲמוּץ בְּגָדִים
מִבָּצְרָה זֶה הָדוּר בִּלְבוּשׁוֹ צֹעֶה בְּרֹב כֹּחוֹ אֲנִי
מְדַבֵּר בִּצְדָקָה רַב לְהוֹשִׁיעַ: ב מַדּוּעַ אָדֹם לִלְבוּשֶׁךָ
וּבְגָדֶיךָ כְּדֹרֵךְ בְּגַת: ג פּוּרָה ׀ דָּרַכְתִּי לְבַדִּי
וּמֵעַמִּים אֵין־אִישׁ אִתִּי וְאֶדְרְכֵם בְּאַפִּי וְאֶרְמְסֵם
בַּחֲמָתִי וְיֵז נִצְחָם עַל־בְּגָדַי וְכָל־מַלְבּוּשַׁי
אֶגְאָלְתִּי: ד כִּי יוֹם נָקָם בְּלִבִּי וּשְׁנַת גְּאוּלַי בָּאָה:
ה וְאַבִּיט וְאֵין עֹזֵר וְאֶשְׁתּוֹמֵם וְאֵין סוֹמֵךְ וַתּוֹשַׁע לִי
זְרֹעִי וַחֲמָתִי הִיא סְמָכָתְנִי: ו וְאָבוּס עַמִּים בְּאַפִּי
וַאֲשַׁכְּרֵם בַּחֲמָתִי וְאוֹרִיד לָאָרֶץ נִצְחָם: ז חַסְדֵי
יְהוָה ׀ אַזְכִּיר תְּהִלֹּת יהוה כְּעַל כֹּל אֲשֶׁר־גְּמָלָנוּ
יְהוָה וְרַב־טוּב לְבֵית יִשְׂרָאֵל אֲשֶׁר־גְּמָלָם
כְּרַחֲמָיו וּכְרֹב חֲסָדָיו: ח וַיֹּאמֶר אַךְ־עַמִּי הֵמָּה
בָּנִים לֹא יְשַׁקֵּרוּ וַיְהִי לָהֶם לְמוֹשִׁיעַ: ט בְּכָל־
צָרָתָם ׀ לוֹ [לא כ׳] צָר וּמַלְאַךְ פָּנָיו הוֹשִׁיעָם
בְּאַהֲבָתוֹ וּבְחֶמְלָתוֹ הוּא גְאָלָם וַיְנַטְּלֵם וַיְנַשְּׂאֵם
כָּל־יְמֵי עוֹלָם:

HAFTARAS VAYEILECH

The following Haftarah is read on the Sabbath that falls between Rosh Hashanah and Yom Kippur. Some years the *Sidrah* of that week is *Vayeilech,* but most years it is *Haazinu.* When the two *Sidros Nitzavim* and *Vayeilech* are read together, the Haftarah of *Nitzavim* is read, and the following *Haftarah* is read for *Haazinu.* Customs vary regarding how many of the following paragraphs are read and in what order. [Some few congregations omit all of the following and read the *Haftarah* that is read on fast days at *Minchah*.]

Hosea 14:2-10; *Joel* 2:11-27; *Micah* 7:18-20

14. 2 Return, O Israel to HASHEM, your God, for you have
stumbled through your iniquity. 3 Take words with
you and return to HASHEM; say to Him, "May You forgive
every iniquity and accept what is good, and let our lips
substitute for bulls. 4 Assyria shall not save us; we will not
ride the [Egyptian] horse; nor will we ever again call our
handiwork 'our gods'; for only in You will the orphan find
compassion." 5 I will heal their rebelliousness; I will love
them willingly, for My wrath will be withdrawn from
them. 6 I will be like the dew to Israel, it shall blossom
like the rose and strike its roots like the [forest of]
Lebanon. 7 Its tender branches shall spread and its glory
shall be like the olive tree; its aroma shall be like the
Lebanon. 8 They shall return, those who sit in its shade;
they shall refresh themselves like grain; they shall
blossom like the vine, its aroma like wine of Lebanon.
9 Ephraim [shall say]: "What more need have I for
idols?" As for Me, I will respond and look to him; I am
like an ever-fresh cypress; from Me shall your fruit be
found. 10 Whoever is wise will understand these [admo-
nitions], a discerning person will know them; the ways of
HASHEM are just — the righteous shall walk in them, but
sinners will stumble on them.

2. 11 And HASHEM gave forth His voice [in prophetic
warning] before [sending forth] His army, for His
camp is very great, for mighty is He that executes His
word, for great is the day of HASHEM and exceedingly
awesome; who can endure it? 12 Yet even now — the
word of HASHEM — return to Me with all your heart, and
with fasting, and with weeping, and with lament; 13 and
rend your heart and not your clothing, and return to
HASHEM, your God, for He is gracious and compassionate, slow to anger and abundant of kindness, and He
reconsiders regarding the evil. 14 Whoever knows [that
he has strayed] shall return and reconsider [his past],
and it shall leave behind it a blessing, a meal-offering
and a libation to HASHEM, your God.

15 Blow a shofar in Zion: consecrate a fast; call an
assembly; 16 gather the people; ready the congregation;
assemble the elders; gather the infants and the
nurslings; let each bridegroom go forth from his chamber and each bride from her bridal canopy. 17 Between the Hall and the Altar shall the Kohanim, the
ministers of HASHEM, weep, and they shall say, "Have
pity, O HASHEM, upon Your people and do not make Your
heritage into shame for the nations to use as an
example; why should they say among the peoples,
'Where is your God?' " 18 [Then, when you will have
repented,] HASHEM will have been zealous regarding His
land and will have taken pity on His people. 19 Then
HASHEM will have answered and will have said to His
people: Behold! I send you the grain and the wine and
the oil, and you shall be satiated with it; I will not make
you again as a shame among the nations. 20 And [the
plague of] the northerner will I distance from you,
and oust it into a land arid and desolate, its face toward
the eastern sea, and its end toward the western sea; and
its foulness shall ascend, and its stench shall ascend,
for it has done great [evil]. 21 Fear not, O ground, be
happy and be joyous, for HASHEM has done great [good].
22 Fear not, O animals of the field, for the pastures of
the wilderness are cloaked in grass, for each tree bears

הפטרת וילך

The following Haftarah is read on the Sabbath that falls between Rosh Hashanah and Yom Kippur. Some years the *Sidrah* of that week is *Vayeilech,* but most years it is *Haazinu.* When the two *Sidros Nitzavim* and *Vayeilech* are read together, the Haftarah of *Nitzavim* is read, and the following *Haftarah* is read for *Haazinu.* Customs vary regarding how many of the following paragraphs are read and in what order. [Some few congregations omit all of the following and read the *Haftarah* that is read on fast days at *Minchah*.]

הושע יד:ב־י; יואל ב:יא־כז; מיכה ז:יח־כ

יד ב שׁוּבָה יִשְׂרָאֵל עַד יהוה אֱלֹהֶיךָ כִּי כָשַׁלְתָּ
בַּעֲוֺנֶךָ: ג קְחוּ עִמָּכֶם דְּבָרִים וְשׁוּבוּ אֶל־יהוה
אִמְרוּ אֵלָיו כָּל־תִּשָּׂא עָוֺן וְקַח־טוֹב וּנְשַׁלְּמָה
פָרִים שְׂפָתֵינוּ: ד אַשּׁוּר | לֹא יוֹשִׁיעֵנוּ עַל־סוּס
לֹא נִרְכָּב וְלֹא־נֹאמַר עוֹד אֱלֹהֵינוּ לְמַעֲשֵׂה
יָדֵינוּ אֲשֶׁר־בְּךָ יְרֻחַם יָתוֹם: ה אֶרְפָּא מְשׁוּבָתָם
אֹהֲבֵם נְדָבָה כִּי שָׁב אַפִּי מִמֶּנּוּ: ו אֶהְיֶה כַטַּל
לְיִשְׂרָאֵל יִפְרַח כַּשּׁוֹשַׁנָּה וְיַךְ שָׁרָשָׁיו כַּלְּבָנוֹן:
ז יֵלְכוּ יֹנְקוֹתָיו וִיהִי כַזַּיִת הוֹדוֹ וְרֵיחַ לוֹ כַּלְּבָנוֹן:
ח יָשֻׁבוּ יֹשְׁבֵי בְצִלּוֹ יְחַיּוּ דָגָן וְיִפְרְחוּ כַגָּפֶן זִכְרוֹ
כְּיֵין לְבָנוֹן: ט אֶפְרַיִם מַה־לִּי עוֹד לָעֲצַבִּים אֲנִי
עָנִיתִי וַאֲשׁוּרֶנּוּ אֲנִי כִּבְרוֹשׁ רַעֲנָן מִמֶּנִּי פֶּרְיְךָ
נִמְצָא: י מִי חָכָם וְיָבֵן אֵלֶּה נָבוֹן וְיֵדָעֵם כִּי־
יְשָׁרִים דַּרְכֵי יהוה וְצַדִּקִים יֵלְכוּ בָם וּפֹשְׁעִים
יִכָּשְׁלוּ בָם:

ב יא וַיהוה נָתַן קוֹלוֹ לִפְנֵי חֵילוֹ כִּי רַב מְאֹד
מַחֲנֵהוּ כִּי עָצוּם עֹשֵׂה דְבָרוֹ כִּי־גָדוֹל יוֹם־יהוה
וְנוֹרָא מְאֹד וּמִי יְכִילֶנּוּ: יב וְגַם־עַתָּה נְאֻם־יהוה
שֻׁבוּ עָדַי בְּכָל־לְבַבְכֶם וּבְצוֹם וּבִבְכִי וּבְמִסְפֵּד:
יג וְקִרְעוּ לְבַבְכֶם וְאַל־בִּגְדֵיכֶם וְשׁוּבוּ אֶל־יהוה
אֱלֹהֵיכֶם כִּי־חַנּוּן וְרַחוּם הוּא אֶרֶךְ אַפַּיִם
וְרַב־חֶסֶד וְנִחָם עַל־הָרָעָה: יד מִי יוֹדֵעַ יָשׁוּב
וְנִחָם וְהִשְׁאִיר אַחֲרָיו בְּרָכָה מִנְחָה וָנֶסֶךְ לַיהוה
אֱלֹהֵיכֶם: טו תִּקְעוּ שׁוֹפָר בְּצִיּוֹן קַדְּשׁוּ־צוֹם
קִרְאוּ עֲצָרָה: טז אִסְפוּ־עָם קַדְּשׁוּ קָהָל קִבְצוּ
זְקֵנִים אִסְפוּ עוֹלָלִים וְיֹנְקֵי שָׁדָיִם יֵצֵא חָתָן
מֵחֶדְרוֹ וְכַלָּה מֵחֻפָּתָהּ: יז בֵּין הָאוּלָם וְלַמִּזְבֵּחַ
יִבְכּוּ הַכֹּהֲנִים מְשָׁרְתֵי יהוה וְיֹאמְרוּ חוּסָה יהוה
עַל־עַמֶּךָ וְאַל־תִּתֵּן נַחֲלָתְךָ לְחֶרְפָּה לִמְשָׁל־בָּם
גּוֹיִם לָמָּה יֹאמְרוּ בָעַמִּים אַיֵּה אֱלֹהֵיהֶם:
יח וַיְקַנֵּא יהוה לְאַרְצוֹ וַיַּחְמֹל עַל־עַמּוֹ: יט וַיַּעַן
יהוה וַיֹּאמֶר לְעַמּוֹ הִנְנִי שֹׁלֵחַ לָכֶם אֶת־הַדָּגָן
וְהַתִּירוֹשׁ וְהַיִּצְהָר וּשְׂבַעְתֶּם אֹתוֹ וְלֹא־אֶתֵּן
אֶתְכֶם עוֹד חֶרְפָּה בַּגּוֹיִם: כ וְאֶת־הַצְּפוֹנִי
אַרְחִיק מֵעֲלֵיכֶם וְהִדַּחְתִּיו אֶל־אֶרֶץ צִיָּה
וּשְׁמָמָה אֶת־פָּנָיו אֶל־הַיָּם הַקַּדְמֹנִי וְסֹפוֹ אֶל־
הַיָּם הָאַחֲרוֹן וְעָלָה בָאְשׁוֹ וְתַעַל צַחֲנָתוֹ כִּי
הִגְדִּיל לַעֲשׂוֹת: כא אַל־תִּירְאִי אֲדָמָה גִּילִי
וּשְׂמָחִי כִּי־הִגְדִּיל יהוה לַעֲשׂוֹת: כב אַל־תִּירְאוּ
בַּהֲמוֹת שָׂדַי כִּי דָשְׁאוּ נְאוֹת מִדְבָּר כִּי־עֵץ נָשָׂא

its fruit, fig-tree and vine have given forth their assets. 23 O children of Zion, be happy and be joyous with HASHEM, your God, for He has given you a mentor to righteousness; and He has caused the early rains and the late rains to descend for you in the first [month]. 24 The threshing-floors shall be full with grain, and the vats will resound with [the sound of flowing] wine and oil. 25 I will repay you for [the crops of] the years that [the various types of locust —] the arbeh, the yelek, the hasil, and the gazam consumed, My great army that I have sent against you. 26 And you shall eat — eating and being satiated — and you shall praise the Name of HASHEM, your God, Who has done wondrously with you; and My people shall never be put to shame. 27 Then you shall know that I am in the midst of Israel, and that I am HASHEM, your God, and there is no other; and My people shall never be put to shame.

7. 18 Who, O God, is like You, Who pardons iniquity and overlooks transgression for the remnant of His heritage? Who has not retained His wrath eternally, for He desires kindness! 19 He will again be merciful to us; He will suppress our iniquities. And cast into the depths of the sea all their sins. 20 Grant truth to Jacob, kindness to Abraham, as You swore to our fore- fathers from ancient times.

HAFTARAS HAAZINU

When *Haazinu* is read on the Sabbath between Rosh Hashanah and Yom Kippur, the *Haftarah* of *Vayeilech* (*Shabbos Shuvah*) is read. When *Haazinu* is read after Yom Kippur, the following *Haftarah* is read.

II Samuel 22:1-41

22. 1 David spoke to HASHEM the words of this song on the day that HASHEM delivered him from the hand of all his enemies and from the hand of Saul. 2 He said: HASHEM is my Rock, my Fortress, and my Rescuer. 3 God, my Rock, I take refuge in Him; my Shield and the Horn of my Salvation, my Stronghold and my Refuge, my Savior Who saves me from violence. 4 With praises I call unto HASHEM, and I am saved from my enemies. 5 For the pains of death encircled me, and torrents of godless men would frighten me. 6 The pains of the grave surrounded me, the snares of death confronted me. 7 In my distress I would call upon HASHEM, and to my God I would call — from His abode He would hear my voice, my cry in His ears. 8 And the earth quaked and roared, the foundations of the heaven shook; they trembled when His wrath flared. 9 Smoke rose up in His nostrils, a devouring fire from His mouth, flaming coals burst forth from Him. 10 He bent down the heavens and descended, with thick darkness beneath His feet. 11 He mounted a cherub and flew, He swooped on the wings of the wind. 12 He made darkness His shelter all around Him — the darkness of water, the clouds of heaven. 13 From out of the brilliance that is before Him burned fiery coals. 14 And HASHEM thundered in the heavens, the Most High cried out. 15 He sent forth His arrows and scattered them, lightning and He frenzied them. 16 The channels of water became visible, the foundations of the earth were laid bare by the rebuke of HASHEM, by the breath of His nostrils. 17 He sent from on high and took me, He drew me out of deep waters. 18 He saved me from my mighty foe, and from my enemies for they overpowered me. 19 They confronted me on the day of my misfortune, but HASHEM was my support. 20 He brought me out into broad spaces, He released me for He desires me. 21 HASHEM recompensed me according to my righteousness; He repaid me according to the cleanliness of my hands. 22 For I have kept the ways of HASHEM, and I have not departed wickedly from my God. 23 For all His judgments are before me, and I shall not remove myself from His statutes. 24 I was perfectly innocent with Him, and I was vigilant against my sin. 25 HASHEM repaid me according to my righteousness, according to my cleanliness before His eyes.

פִּרְיוֹ תְּאֵנָה וָגֶפֶן נָתְנוּ חֵילָם: כג וּבְנֵי צִיּוֹן גִּילוּ
וְשִׂמְחוּ בַּיהוָה אֱלֹהֵיכֶם כִּי־נָתַן לָכֶם אֶת־הַמּוֹרֶה
לִצְדָקָה וַיּוֹרֶד לָכֶם גֶּשֶׁם מוֹרֶה וּמַלְקוֹשׁ בָּרִאשׁוֹן:
כד וּמָלְאוּ הַגֳּרָנוֹת בָּר וְהֵשִׁיקוּ הַיְקָבִים תִּירוֹשׁ
וְיִצְהָר: כה וְשִׁלַּמְתִּי לָכֶם אֶת־הַשָּׁנִים אֲשֶׁר אָכַל
הָאַרְבֶּה הַיֶּלֶק וְהֶחָסִיל וְהַגָּזָם חֵילִי הַגָּדוֹל אֲשֶׁר
שִׁלַּחְתִּי בָּכֶם: כו וַאֲכַלְתֶּם אָכוֹל וְשָׂבוֹעַ וְהִלַּלְתֶּם
אֶת־שֵׁם יהוה אֱלֹהֵיכֶם אֲשֶׁר־עָשָׂה עִמָּכֶם
לְהַפְלִיא וְלֹא־יֵבֹשׁוּ עַמִּי לְעוֹלָם: כז וִידַעְתֶּם כִּי
בְקֶרֶב יִשְׂרָאֵל אָנִי וַאֲנִי יהוה אֱלֹהֵיכֶם וְאֵין עוֹד
וְלֹא־יֵבֹשׁוּ עַמִּי לְעוֹלָם:

ז יח מִי־אֵל כָּמוֹךָ נֹשֵׂא עָוֹן וְעֹבֵר עַל־פֶּשַׁע
לִשְׁאֵרִית נַחֲלָתוֹ לֹא־הֶחֱזִיק לָעַד אַפּוֹ כִּי־חָפֵץ
חֶסֶד הוּא: יט יָשׁוּב יְרַחֲמֵנוּ יִכְבֹּשׁ עֲוֹנֹתֵינוּ
וְתַשְׁלִיךְ בִּמְצֻלוֹת יָם כָּל־חַטֹּאתָם: כ תִּתֵּן אֱמֶת
לְיַעֲקֹב חֶסֶד לְאַבְרָהָם אֲשֶׁר־נִשְׁבַּעְתָּ לַאֲבֹתֵינוּ
מִימֵי קֶדֶם:

הפטרת האזינו

When *Haazinu* is read on the Sabbath between Rosh Hashanah and Yom Kippur, the *Haftarah* of *Vayeilech* (*Shabbos Shuvah*) is read. When *Haazinu* is read after Yom Kippur, the following *Haftarah* is read.

שמואל ב כב:א־מא

כב א וַיְדַבֵּר דָּוִד לַיהוָה אֶת־דִּבְרֵי הַשִּׁירָה הַזֹּאת
בְּיוֹם הִצִּיל יהוה אֹתוֹ מִכַּף כָּל־אֹיְבָיו וּמִכַּף שָׁאוּל:
ב וַיֹּאמַר יהוה סַלְעִי וּמְצֻדָתִי וּמְפַלְטִי־לִי: ג אֱלֹהֵי
צוּרִי אֶחֱסֶה־בּוֹ מָגִנִּי וְקֶרֶן יִשְׁעִי מִשְׂגַּבִּי וּמְנוּסִי
מֹשִׁעִי מֵחָמָס תֹּשִׁעֵנִי: ד מְהֻלָּל אֶקְרָא יהוה
וּמֵאֹיְבַי אִוָּשֵׁעַ: ה כִּי אֲפָפֻנִי מִשְׁבְּרֵי־מָוֶת נַחֲלֵי
בְלִיַּעַל יְבַעֲתֻנִי: ו חֶבְלֵי שְׁאוֹל סַבֻּנִי קִדְּמֻנִי
מֹקְשֵׁי־מָוֶת: ז בַּצַּר־לִי אֶקְרָא יהוה וְאֶל־אֱלֹהַי
אֶקְרָא וַיִּשְׁמַע מֵהֵיכָלוֹ קוֹלִי וְשַׁוְעָתִי בְּאָזְנָיו:
ח וַיִּתְגָּעַשׁ [ותגעש כ׳] וַתִּרְעַשׁ הָאָרֶץ מוֹסְדוֹת
הַשָּׁמַיִם יִרְגָּזוּ וַיִּתְגָּעֲשׁוּ כִּי־חָרָה לוֹ: ט עָלָה עָשָׁן
בְּאַפּוֹ וְאֵשׁ מִפִּיו תֹּאכֵל גֶּחָלִים בָּעֲרוּ מִמֶּנּוּ: י וַיֵּט
שָׁמַיִם וַיֵּרַד וַעֲרָפֶל תַּחַת רַגְלָיו: יא וַיִּרְכַּב עַל־
כְּרוּב וַיָּעֹף וַיֵּרָא עַל־כַּנְפֵי־רוּחַ: יב וַיָּשֶׁת חֹשֶׁךְ
סְבִיבֹתָיו סֻכּוֹת חַשְׁרַת־מַיִם עָבֵי שְׁחָקִים: יג מִנֹּגַהּ
נֶגְדּוֹ בָּעֲרוּ גַּחֲלֵי־אֵשׁ: יד יַרְעֵם מִן־שָׁמַיִם יהוה
וְעֶלְיוֹן יִתֵּן קוֹלוֹ: טו וַיִּשְׁלַח חִצִּים וַיְפִיצֵם בָּרָק
וַיָּהֹם [ויהמם כ׳]: טז וַיֵּרָאוּ אֲפִקֵי יָם יִגָּלוּ מֹסְדוֹת
תֵּבֵל בְּגַעֲרַת יהוה מִנִּשְׁמַת רוּחַ אַפּוֹ: יז יִשְׁלַח
מִמָּרוֹם יִקָּחֵנִי יַמְשֵׁנִי מִמַּיִם רַבִּים: יח יַצִּילֵנִי
מֵאֹיְבִי עָז מִשֹּׂנְאַי כִּי אָמְצוּ מִמֶּנִּי: יט יְקַדְּמֻנִי בְּיוֹם
אֵידִי וַיְהִי יהוה מִשְׁעָן לִי: כ וַיֹּצֵא לַמֶּרְחָב אֹתִי
יְחַלְּצֵנִי כִּי־חָפֵץ בִּי: כא יִגְמְלֵנִי יהוה כְּצִדְקָתִי כְּבֹר
יָדַי יָשִׁיב לִי: כב כִּי שָׁמַרְתִּי דַּרְכֵי יהוה וְלֹא רָשַׁעְתִּי
מֵאֱלֹהָי: כג כִּי כָל־מִשְׁפָּטָו לְנֶגְדִּי וְחֻקֹּתָיו לֹא־
אָסוּר מִמֶּנָּה: כד וָאֶהְיֶה תָמִים לוֹ וָאֶשְׁתַּמְּרָה
מֵעֲוֹנִי: כה וַיָּשֶׁב יהוה לִי כְּצִדְקָתִי כְּבֹרִי לְנֶגֶד עֵינָיו:

26 With the devout You act devoutly, with the wholehearted strong you act wholeheartedly. 27 With the pure You act purely, with the crooked You act perversely. 28 You save the humble people, and Your eyes are upon the haughty to lower them. 29 For You, HASHEM, are my lamp, and HASHEM will illuminate my darkness. 30 For with You I smash a troop, and with my God I leap a wall. 31 The God! — His way is perfect; the promise of HASHEM is flawless, He is a shield for all who take refuge in Him. 32 For who is God except for HASHEM, and who is a Rock except for our God? 33 The God Who is my strong Fortress, and Who let my way be perfect. 34 Who straightened my feet like the hind, and stood me on my heights. 35 Who trained my hands for battle, so that an iron bow could be bent by my arms. 36 You have given me Your shield of salvation, and Your humility made me great. 37 You have widened my stride beneath me, and my ankles have not faltered. 38 I pursued my foes and overtook them, and returned not until they were destroyed. 39 I destroyed them, struck them down and they did not rise, and they fell beneath my feet. 40 You girded me with strength for battle, You bring my adversaries to their knees beneath me. 41 And my enemies — You gave me [their] back; my antagonists and I cut them down. 42 They turned, but there was no savior; to HASHEM, but He answered them not. 43 I pulverized them like dust of the earth, like the mud of the streets I thinned them and I poured them out. 44 You rescued me from the strife of my people; You preserved me to be head of nations, a people I did not know serves me. 45 Foreigners dissemble to me; when their ear hears of me they are obedient to me. 46 Foreigners are withered, and they are terrified even within their strong enclosures. 47 HASHEM lives, and blessed is my Rock; and exalted is God, Rock of my salvation. 48 The God Who grants me vengeance, and brings peoples down beneath me. 49 You bring me forth from my enemies, and raise me above my adversaries, from a man of violence You rescue me. 50 Therefore, I will thank You, HASHEM, among the nations, and sing to Your Name. 51 He is a tower of salvations to His king, and does kindness to His anointed one, to David and to his descendants forever.

כו עִם־חָסִיד תִּתְחַסָּד עִם־גִּבּוֹר תָּמִים תִּתַּמָּם:
כז עִם־נָבָר תִּתָּבָר וְעִם־עִקֵּשׁ תִּתַּפָּל: כח וְאֶת־עַם
עָנִי תּוֹשִׁיעַ וְעֵינֶיךָ עַל־רָמִים תַּשְׁפִּיל: כט כִּי־אַתָּה
נֵירִי יְהוָה וַיהוָה יַגִּיהַּ חָשְׁכִּי: ל כִּי בְכָה אָרוּץ גְּדוּד
בֵּאלֹהַי אֲדַלֶּג־שׁוּר: לא הָאֵל תָּמִים דַּרְכּוֹ אִמְרַת
יְהוָה צְרוּפָה מָגֵן הוּא לְכֹל הַחֹסִים בּוֹ: לב כִּי
מִי־אֵל מִבַּלְעֲדֵי יְהוָה וּמִי צוּר מִבַּלְעֲדֵי אֱלֹהֵינוּ:
לג הָאֵל מָעוּזִּי חָיִל וַיַּתֵּר תָּמִים דַּרְכִּי [דרכו כ׳]:
לד מְשַׁוֶּה רַגְלַי [רגליו כ׳] כָּאַיָּלוֹת וְעַל־בָּמֹתַי
יַעֲמִידֵנִי: לה מְלַמֵּד יָדַי לַמִּלְחָמָה וְנִחַת קֶשֶׁת־
נְחוּשָׁה זְרֹעֹתָי: לו וַתִּתֶּן־לִי מָגֵן יִשְׁעֶךָ וַעֲנֹתְךָ
תַּרְבֵּנִי: לז תַּרְחִיב צַעֲדִי תַּחְתֵּנִי וְלֹא מָעֲדוּ קַרְסֻלָּי:
לח אֶרְדְּפָה אֹיְבַי וָאַשְׁמִידֵם וְלֹא אָשׁוּב עַד־כַּלּוֹתָם:
לט וָאֲכַלֵּם וָאֶמְחָצֵם וְלֹא יְקוּמוּן וַיִּפְּלוּ תַּחַת רַגְלָי:
מ וַתַּזְרֵנִי חַיִל לַמִּלְחָמָה תַּכְרִיעַ קָמַי תַּחְתֵּנִי:
מא וְאֹיְבַי תַּתָּה לִּי עֹרֶף מְשַׂנְאַי וָאַצְמִיתֵם: מב יִשְׁעוּ
וְאֵין מֹשִׁיעַ אֶל־יְהוָה וְלֹא עָנָם: מג וְאֶשְׁחָקֵם
כַּעֲפַר־אָרֶץ כְּטִיט־חוּצוֹת אֲדִקֵּם אֶרְקָעֵם:
מד וַתְּפַלְּטֵנִי מֵרִיבֵי עַמִּי תִּשְׁמְרֵנִי לְרֹאשׁ גּוֹיִם עַם
לֹא־יָדַעְתִּי יַעַבְדֻנִי: מה בְּנֵי נֵכָר יִתְכַּחֲשׁוּ־לִי
לִשְׁמוֹעַ אֹזֶן יִשָּׁמְעוּ לִי: מו בְּנֵי נֵכָר יִבֹּלוּ וְיַחְגְּרוּ
מִמִּסְגְּרוֹתָם: מז חַי־יְהוָה וּבָרוּךְ צוּרִי וְיָרֻם אֱלֹהֵי
צוּר יִשְׁעִי: מח הָאֵל הַנֹּתֵן נְקָמֹת לִי וּמוֹרִיד עַמִּים
תַּחְתֵּנִי: מט וּמוֹצִיאִי מֵאֹיְבָי וּמִקָּמַי תְּרוֹמְמֵנִי
מֵאִישׁ חֲמָסִים תַּצִּילֵנִי: נ עַל־כֵּן אוֹדְךָ יְהוָה בַּגּוֹיִם
וּלְשִׁמְךָ אֲזַמֵּר: נא מִגְדּוֹל [מגדיל כ׳] יְשׁוּעוֹת מַלְכּוֹ
וְעֹשֶׂה־חֶסֶד לִמְשִׁיחוֹ לְדָוִד וּלְזַרְעוֹ עַד־עוֹלָם:

HAFTARAS SHABBOS EREV ROSH CHODESH

I Samuel 20:18-42

הפטרת שבת ערב ראש חודש

שמואל א כ:יח־מב

20. 18 onathan said to [David], "Tomorrow is the New Moon, and you will be missed because your seat will be empty. 19 For three days you are to go far down and come to the place where you hid on the day of the deed, and remain near the marker stone. 20 I will shoot three arrows in that direction as if I were shooting at a target. 21 Behold! — I will then send the lad, 'Go, find the arrows.' If I call out to the lad, 'Behold! — the arrows are on this side of you!' then you should take them and return, for it is well with you and there is no concern, as HASHEM lives. 22 But if I say this to the boy, 'Behold! — the arrows are beyond you!' then go, for HASHEM will have sent you away. 23 This matter of which we have spoken, I and you, behold! — HASHEM remains [witness] between me and you forever."

24 David concealed himself in the field. It was the New Moon and the king sat at the feast to eat. 25 The king sat on his seat as usual, on the seat by the wall; and Jonathan stood up so that Abner could sit at Saul's side, and David's seat was empty. 26 Saul said nothing on that day, for he thought, "It is a coincidence, he must be impure, for he has not been cleansed."

27 It was the day after the New Moon, the second day, and David's place was empty; Saul said to Jonathan, his son, "Why did the son of Jesse not come to the feast yesterday or today?"

כ יח וַיֹּאמֶר־לוֹ יְהוֹנָתָן מָחָר חֹדֶשׁ וְנִפְקַדְתָּ כִּי
יִפָּקֵד מוֹשָׁבֶךָ: יט וְשִׁלַּשְׁתָּ תֵּרֵד מְאֹד וּבָאתָ
אֶל־הַמָּקוֹם אֲשֶׁר־נִסְתַּרְתָּ שָּׁם בְּיוֹם הַמַּעֲשֶׂה
וְיָשַׁבְתָּ אֵצֶל הָאֶבֶן הָאָזֶל: כ וַאֲנִי שְׁלֹשֶׁת הַחִצִּים
צִדָּה אוֹרֶה לְשַׁלַּח־לִי לְמַטָּרָה: כא וְהִנֵּה אֶשְׁלַח
אֶת־הַנַּעַר לֵךְ מְצָא אֶת־הַחִצִּים אִם־אָמֹר אֹמַר
לַנַּעַר הִנֵּה הַחִצִּים ׀ מִמְּךָ וָהֵנָּה קָחֶנּוּ וָבֹאָה
כִּי־שָׁלוֹם לְךָ וְאֵין דָּבָר חַי־יְהוָה: כב וְאִם־כֹּה אֹמַר
לָעֶלֶם הִנֵּה הַחִצִּים מִמְּךָ וָהָלְאָה לֵךְ כִּי שִׁלַּחֲךָ
יְהוָה: כג וְהַדָּבָר אֲשֶׁר דִּבַּרְנוּ אֲנִי וָאָתָּה הִנֵּה יְהוָה
בֵּינִי וּבֵינְךָ עַד־עוֹלָם: כד וַיִּסָּתֵר דָּוִד בַּשָּׂדֶה וַיְהִי
הַחֹדֶשׁ וַיֵּשֶׁב הַמֶּלֶךְ אֶל־ [על־ כ׳] הַלֶּחֶם לֶאֱכוֹל:
כה וַיֵּשֶׁב הַמֶּלֶךְ עַל־מוֹשָׁבוֹ כְּפַעַם ׀ בְּפַעַם אֶל־
מוֹשַׁב הַקִּיר וַיָּקָם יְהוֹנָתָן וַיֵּשֶׁב אַבְנֵר מִצַּד שָׁאוּל
וַיִּפָּקֵד מְקוֹם דָּוִד: כו וְלֹא־דִבֶּר שָׁאוּל מְאוּמָה בַּיּוֹם
הַהוּא כִּי אָמַר מִקְרֶה הוּא בִּלְתִּי טָהוֹר הוּא כִּי־
לֹא טָהוֹר: כז וַיְהִי מִמָּחֳרַת הַחֹדֶשׁ הַשֵּׁנִי וַיִּפָּקֵד
מְקוֹם דָּוִד וַיֹּאמֶר שָׁאוּל אֶל־יְהוֹנָתָן בְּנוֹ מַדּוּעַ
לֹא־בָא בֶן־יִשַׁי גַּם־תְּמוֹל גַּם־הַיּוֹם אֶל־הַלָּחֶם:

28 Jonathan answered Saul, "David asked me for permission to go to Bethlehem. 29 He said, 'Please send me away, for we have a family feast in the city, and he, my brother, ordered me [to come]; so now, if I have found favor in your eyes, excuse me, please, and let me see my brothers.' Therefore, he has not come to the king's table."

30 Saul's anger flared up at Jonathan, and he said to him, "Son of a pervertedly rebellious woman, do I not know that you prefer the son of Jesse, for your own shame and the shame of your mother's nakedness! 31 For all the days that the son of Jesse is alive on the earth, you and your kingdom will not be secure! And now send and bring him to me, for he is deserving of death."

32 Jonathan answered his father Saul and he said to him, "Why should he die; what has he done?"

33 Saul hurled his spear at him to strike him; so Jonathan realized that it was decided by his father to kill David. 34 Jonathan arose from the table in a burning anger; he did not partake of food on that second day of the month, for he was saddened over David because his father had humiliated him.

35 It happened in the morning that Jonathan went out to the field for the meeting with David, and a young lad was with him. 36 He said to his lad, "Run — please find the arrows that I shoot." The lad ran, and he shot the arrow to make it go further. 37 The lad arrived at the place of the arrow that Jonathan had shot, and Jonathan called out after the lad, and he said, "Is not the arrow beyond you?"

38 And Jonathan called out after the lad, "Quickly, hurry, do not stand still!" The lad gathered the arrows and came to his master. 39 The lad knew nothing, only Jonathan and David understood the matter. 40 Jonathan gave his equipment to his lad and said to him, "Go bring it to the city."

41 The lad went and David stood up from near the south [side of the stone], and he fell on his face to the ground and prostrated himself three times. They kissed one another and they wept with one another, until David [wept] greatly.

42 Jonathan said to David, "Go to peace. What the two of us have sworn in the Name of HASHEM — saying, 'HASHEM shall be between me and you, and between my children and your children — shall be forever!' "

HAFTARAS SHABBOS ROSH CHODESH

Isaiah 66:1-24

66. 1 So said HASHEM, the heaven is My throne and the earth is My footstool; what House could you build for Me, and what could be My resting place? 2 My hand made all these and thus they came into being, the words of HASHEM — but it is to this that I look: to the poor and broken-spirited person who is zealous regarding My Word.

3 He who slaughters an ox is as if he slays a man; he who offers a sheep is as if he breaks a dog's neck; he who brings up a meal-offering is as if he offers a swine's blood; one who brings a frankincense remembrance is as if he brings a gift of extortion; they have even chosen their ways, and their souls have desired their abominations.

4 I, too, will choose to mock them and what they dread I will bring upon them — because I have called, but no one responded; I have spoken, but they did not hear; they did what is evil in My eyes and what I did not desire they chose.

5 Listen to the Word of HASHEM, those who are zealous regarding His Word; your brethren who hate you and distance themselves from you say, "HASHEM is glorified because of my reputation" — but we shall see your

כח וַיַּעַן יְהוֹנָתָן אֶת־שָׁאוּל נִשְׁאֹל נִשְׁאַל דָּוִד
מֵעִמָּדִי עַד־בֵּית לָחֶם: כט וַיֹּאמֶר שַׁלְּחֵנִי נָא כִּי
זֶבַח מִשְׁפָּחָה לָנוּ בָּעִיר וְהוּא צִוָּה־לִי אָחִי וְעַתָּה
אִם־מָצָאתִי חֵן בְּעֵינֶיךָ אִמָּלְטָה נָּא וְאֶרְאֶה אֶת־
אֶחָי עַל־כֵּן לֹא־בָא אֶל־שֻׁלְחַן הַמֶּלֶךְ: ל וַיִּחַר־
אַף שָׁאוּל בִּיהוֹנָתָן וַיֹּאמֶר לוֹ בֶּן־נַעֲוַת הַמַּרְדּוּת
הֲלוֹא יָדַעְתִּי כִּי־בֹחֵר אַתָּה לְבֶן־יִשַׁי לְבָשְׁתְּךָ
וּלְבֹשֶׁת עֶרְוַת אִמֶּךָ: לא כִּי כָל־הַיָּמִים אֲשֶׁר
בֶּן־יִשַׁי חַי עַל־הָאֲדָמָה לֹא תִכּוֹן אַתָּה וּמַלְכוּתֶךָ
וְעַתָּה שְׁלַח וְקַח אֹתוֹ אֵלַי כִּי בֶן־מָוֶת הוּא: לב וַיַּעַן
יְהוֹנָתָן אֶת־שָׁאוּל אָבִיו וַיֹּאמֶר אֵלָיו לָמָּה יוּמַת
מֶה עָשָׂה: לג וַיָּטֶל שָׁאוּל אֶת־הַחֲנִית עָלָיו לְהַכֹּתוֹ
וַיֵּדַע יְהוֹנָתָן כִּי־כָלָה הִיא מֵעִם אָבִיו לְהָמִית
אֶת־דָּוִד: לד וַיָּקָם יְהוֹנָתָן מֵעִם הַשֻּׁלְחָן בָּחֳרִי־אָף
וְלֹא־אָכַל בְּיוֹם־הַחֹדֶשׁ הַשֵּׁנִי לֶחֶם כִּי נֶעְצַב אֶל־
דָּוִד כִּי הִכְלִמוֹ אָבִיו: לה וַיְהִי בַבֹּקֶר וַיֵּצֵא יְהוֹנָתָן
הַשָּׂדֶה לְמוֹעֵד דָּוִד וְנַעַר קָטֹן עִמּוֹ: לו וַיֹּאמֶר
לְנַעֲרוֹ רֻץ מְצָא־נָא אֶת־הַחִצִּים אֲשֶׁר אָנֹכִי מוֹרֶה
הַנַּעַר רָץ וְהוּא־יָרָה הַחֵצִי לְהַעֲבִרוֹ: לז וַיָּבֹא הַנַּעַר
עַד־מְקוֹם הַחֵצִי אֲשֶׁר יָרָה יְהוֹנָתָן וַיִּקְרָא יְהוֹנָתָן
אַחֲרֵי הַנַּעַר וַיֹּאמֶר הֲלוֹא הַחֵצִי מִמְּךָ וָהָלְאָה:
לח וַיִּקְרָא יְהוֹנָתָן אַחֲרֵי הַנַּעַר מְהֵרָה חוּשָׁה אַל־
תַּעֲמֹד וַיְלַקֵּט נַעַר יְהוֹנָתָן אֶת־הַחִצִּים [החצי כ׳]
וַיָּבֹא אֶל־אֲדֹנָיו: לט וְהַנַּעַר לֹא־יָדַע מְאוּמָה אַךְ
יְהוֹנָתָן וְדָוִד יָדְעוּ אֶת־הַדָּבָר: מ וַיִּתֵּן יְהוֹנָתָן
אֶת־כֵּלָיו אֶל־הַנַּעַר אֲשֶׁר־לוֹ וַיֹּאמֶר לוֹ לֵךְ הָבֵיא
הָעִיר: מא הַנַּעַר בָּא וְדָוִד קָם מֵאֵצֶל הַנֶּגֶב וַיִּפֹּל
לְאַפָּיו אַרְצָה וַיִּשְׁתַּחוּ שָׁלֹשׁ פְּעָמִים וַיִּשְּׁקוּ | אִישׁ
אֶת־רֵעֵהוּ וַיִּבְכּוּ אִישׁ אֶת־רֵעֵהוּ עַד־דָּוִד הִגְדִּיל:
מב וַיֹּאמֶר יְהוֹנָתָן לְדָוִד לֵךְ לְשָׁלוֹם אֲשֶׁר נִשְׁבַּעְנוּ
שְׁנֵינוּ אֲנַחְנוּ בְּשֵׁם יהוה לֵאמֹר יהוה יִהְיֶה | בֵּינִי
וּבֵינֶךָ וּבֵין זַרְעִי וּבֵין זַרְעֲךָ עַד־עוֹלָם:

הפטרת ראש חודש

ישעיה סו:א־כד

סו א כֹּה אָמַר יהוה הַשָּׁמַיִם כִּסְאִי וְהָאָרֶץ הֲדֹם
רַגְלָי אֵי־זֶה בַיִת אֲשֶׁר תִּבְנוּ־לִי וְאֵי־זֶה מָקוֹם
מְנוּחָתִי: ב וְאֶת־כָּל־אֵלֶּה יָדִי עָשָׂתָה וַיִּהְיוּ כָל־
אֵלֶּה נְאֻם־יהוה וְאֶל־זֶה אַבִּיט אֶל־עָנִי וּנְכֵה־רוּחַ
וְחָרֵד עַל־דְּבָרִי: ג שׁוֹחֵט הַשּׁוֹר מַכֵּה־אִישׁ זוֹבֵחַ
הַשֶּׂה עֹרֵף כֶּלֶב מַעֲלֵה מִנְחָה דַּם־חֲזִיר מַזְכִּיר
לְבֹנָה מְבָרֵךְ אָוֶן גַּם־הֵמָּה בָּחֲרוּ בְּדַרְכֵיהֶם
וּבְשִׁקּוּצֵיהֶם נַפְשָׁם חָפֵצָה: ד גַּם־אֲנִי אֶבְחַר
בְּתַעֲלֻלֵיהֶם וּמְגוּרֹתָם אָבִיא לָהֶם יַעַן קָרָאתִי
וְאֵין עוֹנֶה דִּבַּרְתִּי וְלֹא שָׁמֵעוּ וַיַּעֲשׂוּ הָרַע
בְּעֵינַי וּבַאֲשֶׁר לֹא־חָפַצְתִּי בָּחָרוּ: ה שִׁמְעוּ
דְּבַר־יהוה הַחֲרֵדִים אֶל־דְּבָרוֹ אָמְרוּ אֲחֵיכֶם
שֹׂנְאֵיכֶם מְנַדֵּיכֶם לְמַעַן שְׁמִי יִכְבַּד יהוה וְנִרְאֶה

gladness and they will be shamed. ⁶ A tumultuous sound comes from the city, a sound from the Sanctuary, the sound of HASHEM dealing retribution to His enemies. ⁷ When she has not yet felt her labor, she will have given birth! When the pain has not yet come to her, she will have delivered a son! ⁸ Who has heard such a thing? Who has seen its like? Has a land gone through its labor in one day? Has a nation been born at one time, as Zion went through labor and gave birth to her children? ⁹ Shall I bring [a woman] to the birthstool and not have her give birth? says HASHEM. Shall I, Who causes birth, hold it back? says your God.

¹⁰ Be glad with Jerusalem and rejoice in her, all who love her; exult with her exultation, all who mourned for her; ¹¹ so that you may nurse and be sated from the breast of her consolations; so that you may suck and delight from the glow of her glory. ¹² For so said HASHEM, Behold! — I shall direct peace to her like a river, and the honor of nations like a surging stream and you shall suckle; you will be carried on a shoulder and dandled on knees. ¹³ Like a man whose mother consoled him, so will I console you, and in Jerusalem will you be consoled. ¹⁴ You shall see and your heart will exult, and your bones will flourish like grass; the hand of HASHEM will be known to His servants, and He will be angry with His enemies. ¹⁵ For behold! — HASHEM will arrive in fire and His chariots like the whirlwind, to requite His anger with wrath, and His rebuke with flaming fire. ¹⁶ For with fire HASHEM will judge, and with His sword against all flesh; many will be those slain by HASHEM.

¹⁷ Those who prepare and purify themselves [to storm] the gardens go one after another to the midst [of the fray]; together will be consumed those who eat the flesh of swine, of abominable creatures and rodents — the words of HASHEM. ¹⁸ I [am aware of] their deeds and their thoughts; [the time] has come to gather in all the nations and tongues; they shall come and see My glory.

¹⁹ I shall put a sign upon them and send some as survivors to the nations: Tarshish, Pul and, Lud, the bow-drawers, Tubal, and Yavan; the distant islands, who have not heard of My fame and not seen My glory, and they will declare My glory among the nations. ²⁰ They will bring all your brethren from all the nations as an offering to HASHEM, on horses, on chariot, on covered wagons, on mules, and with joyful dances upon My holy mountain, Jerusalem, said HASHEM; just as the Children of Israel bring their offering in a pure vessel to the House of HASHEM. ²¹ From them, too, will I take to be Kohanim and Levites, said HASHEM.

²² For just as the new heavens and the new earth that I will make will endure before Me — the words of HASHEM — so will your offspring and your name endure. ²³ And it shall be that, from New Moon to New Moon, and from Sabbath to Sabbath, all flesh shall come to prostrate themselves before Me, said HASHEM.

²⁴ They shall go out and see the corpses of those who rebel against Me, for their worms will not die and their fire will not go out, and they shall be a disgrace for all flesh.

And it shall be that, from New Moon to New Moon, and from Sabbath to Sabbath, all flesh shall come to prostrate themselves before Me, said HASHEM.

בְּשִׂמְחַתְכֶם וְהֵם יֵבֹשׁוּ׃ וּ קוֹל שָׁאוֹן מֵעִיר קוֹל מֵהֵיכָל קוֹל יְהֹוָה מְשַׁלֵּם גְּמוּל לְאֹיְבָיו׃ זּ בְּטֶרֶם תָּחִיל יָלָדָה בְּטֶרֶם יָבוֹא חֵבֶל לָהּ וְהִמְלִיטָה זָכָר׃ ח מִי־שָׁמַע כָּזֹאת מִי רָאָה כָּאֵלֶּה הֲיוּחַל אֶרֶץ בְּיוֹם אֶחָד אִם־יִוָּלֵד גּוֹי פַּעַם אֶחָת כִּי־חָלָה גַּם־יָלְדָה צִיּוֹן אֶת־בָּנֶיהָ׃ טּ הַאֲנִי אַשְׁבִּיר וְלֹא אוֹלִיד יֹאמַר יְהֹוָה אִם־אֲנִי הַמּוֹלִיד וְעָצַרְתִּי אָמַר אֱלֹהָיִךְ׃ יּ שִׂמְחוּ אֶת־יְרוּשָׁלַ͏ִם וְגִילוּ בָהּ כָּל־אֹהֲבֶיהָ שִׂישׂוּ אִתָּהּ מָשׂוֹשׂ כָּל־הַמִּתְאַבְּלִים עָלֶיהָ׃ יא לְמַעַן תִּינְקוּ וּשְׂבַעְתֶּם מִשֹּׁד תַּנְחֻמֶיהָ לְמַעַן תָּמֹצּוּ וְהִתְעַנַּגְתֶּם מִזִּיז כְּבוֹדָהּ׃ יב כִּי־כֹה אָמַר יְהֹוָה הִנְנִי נֹטֶה־אֵלֶיהָ כְּנָהָר שָׁלוֹם וּכְנַחַל שׁוֹטֵף כְּבוֹד גּוֹיִם וִינַקְתֶּם עַל־צַד תִּנָּשֵׂאוּ וְעַל־בִּרְכַּיִם תְּשָׁעֳשָׁעוּ׃ יג כְּאִישׁ אֲשֶׁר אִמּוֹ תְּנַחֲמֶנּוּ כֵּן אָנֹכִי אֲנַחֶמְכֶם וּבִירוּשָׁלַ͏ִם תְּנֻחָמוּ׃ יד וּרְאִיתֶם וְשָׂשׂ לִבְּכֶם וְעַצְמוֹתֵיכֶם כַּדֶּשֶׁא תִפְרַחְנָה וְנוֹדְעָה יַד־יְהֹוָה אֶת־עֲבָדָיו וְזָעַם אֶת־אֹיְבָיו׃ טו כִּי־הִנֵּה יְהֹוָה בָּאֵשׁ יָבוֹא וְכַסּוּפָה מַרְכְּבֹתָיו לְהָשִׁיב בְּחֵמָה אַפּוֹ וְגַעֲרָתוֹ בְּלַהֲבֵי־אֵשׁ׃ טז כִּי בָאֵשׁ יְהֹוָה נִשְׁפָּט וּבְחַרְבּוֹ אֶת־כָּל־בָּשָׂר וְרַבּוּ חַלְלֵי יְהֹוָה׃ יז הַמִּתְקַדְּשִׁים וְהַמִּטַּהֲרִים אֶל־הַגַּנּוֹת אַחַר אַחַת [אַחַד כ] בַּתָּוֶךְ אֹכְלֵי בְּשַׂר הַחֲזִיר וְהַשֶּׁקֶץ וְהָעַכְבָּר יַחְדָּו יָסֻפוּ נְאֻם־יְהֹוָה׃ יח וְאָנֹכִי מַעֲשֵׂיהֶם וּמַחְשְׁבֹתֵיהֶם בָּאָה לְקַבֵּץ אֶת־כָּל־הַגּוֹיִם וְהַלְּשֹׁנוֹת וּבָאוּ וְרָאוּ אֶת־כְּבוֹדִי׃ יט וְשַׂמְתִּי בָהֶם אוֹת וְשִׁלַּחְתִּי מֵהֶם ׀ פְּלֵיטִים אֶל־הַגּוֹיִם תַּרְשִׁישׁ פּוּל וְלוּד מֹשְׁכֵי קֶשֶׁת תֻּבַל וְיָוָן הָאִיִּים הָרְחֹקִים אֲשֶׁר לֹא־שָׁמְעוּ אֶת־שִׁמְעִי וְלֹא־רָאוּ אֶת־כְּבוֹדִי וְהִגִּידוּ אֶת־כְּבוֹדִי בַּגּוֹיִם׃ כ וְהֵבִיאוּ אֶת־כָּל־אֲחֵיכֶם מִכָּל־הַגּוֹיִם ׀ מִנְחָה ׀ לַיהֹוָה בַּסּוּסִים וּבָרֶכֶב וּבַצַּבִּים וּבַפְּרָדִים וּבַכִּרְכָּרוֹת עַל הַר קָדְשִׁי יְרוּשָׁלַ͏ִם אָמַר יְהֹוָה כַּאֲשֶׁר יָבִיאוּ בְנֵי יִשְׂרָאֵל אֶת־הַמִּנְחָה בִּכְלִי טָהוֹר בֵּית יְהֹוָה׃ כא וְגַם־מֵהֶם אֶקַּח לַכֹּהֲנִים לַלְוִיִּם אָמַר יְהֹוָה׃ כב כִּי כַאֲשֶׁר הַשָּׁמַיִם הַחֲדָשִׁים וְהָאָרֶץ הַחֲדָשָׁה אֲשֶׁר אֲנִי עֹשֶׂה עֹמְדִים לְפָנַי נְאֻם־יְהֹוָה כֵּן יַעֲמֹד זַרְעֲכֶם וְשִׁמְכֶם׃ כג וְהָיָה מִדֵּי־חֹדֶשׁ בְּחָדְשׁוֹ וּמִדֵּי שַׁבָּת בְּשַׁבַּתּוֹ יָבוֹא כָל־בָּשָׂר לְהִשְׁתַּחֲוֹת לְפָנַי אָמַר יְהֹוָה׃ כד וְיָצְאוּ וְרָאוּ בְּפִגְרֵי הָאֲנָשִׁים הַפֹּשְׁעִים בִּי כִּי תוֹלַעְתָּם לֹא תָמוּת וְאִשָּׁם לֹא תִכְבֶּה וְהָיוּ דֵרָאוֹן לְכָל־בָּשָׂר׃

וְהָיָה מִדֵּי־חֹדֶשׁ בְּחָדְשׁוֹ וּמִדֵּי שַׁבָּת בְּשַׁבַּתּוֹ יָבוֹא כָל־בָּשָׂר לְהִשְׁתַּחֲוֹת לְפָנַי אָמַר יְהֹוָה׃